AF651768

THE SUPREME WISDOM OF THE UPANIṢADS
An Introduction

THE SUPREME WISDOM OF THE UPANIṢADS

AN INTRODUCTION

Klaus G. Witz

MOTILAL BANARSIDASS PUBLISHERS
PRIVATE LIMITED • DELHI

First Edition: Delhi, 1998

© KLAUS WITZ, 1992, 1993
All Rights Reserved

ISBN: 81-208-1573-4

MOTILAL BANARSIDASS

41 U.A. Bungalow Road, Jawahar Nagar, Delhi 110 007
8 Mahalaxmi Chamber, Warden Road, Mumbai 400 026
120 Royapettah High Road, Mylapore, Chennai 600 004
Sanas Plaza, Subhash Nagar, Pune 411 002
16 St. Mark's Road, Bangalore 560 001
8 Camac Street, Calcutta 700 017
Ashok Rajpath, Patna 800 004
Chowk, Varanasi 221 001

PRINTED IN INDIA

BY JAINENDRA PRAKASH JAIN AT SHRI JAINENDRA PRESS,
A-45 NARAINA INDUSTRIAL AREA, PHASE I, NEW DELHI 110 028
AND PUBLISHED BY NARENDRA PRAKASH JAIN FOR
MOTILAL BANARSIDASS PUBLISHERS PRIVATE LIMITED,
BUNGALOW ROAD, DELHI 110 007

Om Namo Nārāyaṇāya

Om Śrī Bhagavān Satya Sāī Bābāya Namaḥ

Preface

The Upaniṣads (or Upanishads) are the earliest Supreme Wisdom literature of the world. It is not often, however, that they have been presented as a spiritual path or approach in their own right. Even in India, where they have inspired and to some extent shaped a vast civilization, they are studied primarily only in the light of Vedānta, a powerful systematization of the original texts. This book represents an attempt to present the spiritual aspects of the Upaniṣadic teachings on the basis of the texts themselves, and in a way that respects tradition and is defensible in the modern world today. The emphasis is not so much on ideas and issues, as on the meaning which the individual texts have in terms of spiritual life. The Infinite Truths of the Upaniṣads can emerge only when one takes them seriously and makes efforts to live them in one's daily life.

The book was written with the conviction that the Upaniṣads have the capability to uplift mankind today, and that they desperately need to be made available to a wider western-oriented audience. Generally speaking, high level Indian spiritual literature may be divided into three overlapping types: literature focussing on God and God consciousness, such as the medieval bhakti literatures in Hindi, Tamil, etc.; literature detailing yogic and tantric paths; and High Wisdom literature. Of these, the first two are unlikely to find a widespread response in the West. The modern cultural and intellectual climate is not favourable to walking the path of total dedication to love of God. Western Tradition has its own great knowledge-of-God literatures, such as the writings of the Catholic Saints. But these are seldom read and put into practice. There is little appreciation that these works are basically universal documents whose essence can be absorbed and used in one's life without a specifically Christian orientation. Next, the yogic literature undoubtedly has some appeal, and life and practice along such lines may lead to considerable individual uplift and approach to the goal. But without a deep cultural base such as in India, yogic and tantric practice is bound to touch only a few. And even in India the true deeper stages of these paths are almost beyond reach today. High Wisdom literature, by comparison, does not have these kinds of handicaps. Indeed, the general cultural and intellectual climate in the West seems mildly favourable to wisdom paths. Many individuals are seriously pursuing Buddhist practice in Zen or Tibetan traditions, or follow J. Krishnamurty. Western philosophers are turning to Śaṁkara, or Mahāyāna Buddhist philosophy, or to Plotinus, for that matter. And there are many individuals who follow Indian traditions that are permeated by Upaniṣadic teachings. All these trends have vitality, but they are quite small scale. My aim has been to produce an introduction to the Upaniṣads which is based on the original texts and does not hide difficulties of interpretation, but which still enables the reader to get an insight into the Upaniṣadic teachings and at least start thinking about how he/she could bring them into his/her own life. I have tried to write a book which is useful to individuals that are already on an Indian path, as well as one that can speak to persons who are serious about the meaning of life and existence, and who would like to get an introduction to the Upaniṣadic Supreme Wisdom. But the intended audience also includes people who are already somewhat acquainted with Indian philosophy and religion, and who would like to get a deeper understanding in this area.

The core of the book is a small number of *vidyās*, or teachings outlining specific paths involving meditation and leading to highest realization. Modern Indian students of the Upaniṣads and spiritual teachers agree that the *vidyās* are the heart of the Upaniṣads and that any true entrance into the higher Upaniṣadic teachings must be through the *vidyās*. But unfortunately, much of the inner (spiritual, yogic and otherwise esoteric) meaning of the *vidyās* has been lost or is preserved only in small traces. In this book I have tried to recover some of this meaning using first textual analysis, and then consideration of traditional views of the text (*Brahma Sūtra*, Śaṁkara) and modern scholarship. (Textual analysis includes using parallel texts and tracing the use of important terms or phrases of the text elsewhere in the Vedic literature, as well as considering the form of the texts and their literary aspects.) In addition, I have also taken into account comments on a given *vidyā* by great modern spiritual figures such as Sri Ramana Maharshi and Sri Sathya Sai Baba. Obviously the results depend much on my own personal biases and understanding of things; writing the book over the last several years has played a large role in my own spiritual life. But I believe that it is possible in this way to have these Infinite teachings emerge closer to their true form and speak directly to modern spiritual understanding.

Since the main goal is to get a deeper understanding of the Upanisadic teachings themselves, the basic format in the book is one of text and commentary. Typically, an Upaniṣadic text is presented in translation and then discussed by outlining its overall structure, giving necessary background and parallel texts, highlighting or elaborating particular points, and trying to get an idea of its spiritual meaning. I believe that detailed preoccupation with individual texts of this kind is a must. If the Upaniṣadic Wisdom is to take deeper roots in the West, then it must be shown in detail how this Wisdom emerges from the texts. There must be scholarly consideration of innner, deeper aspects of the Upaniṣadic teachings similar to the consideration of biblical passages in Christian or Islamic theology and mysticism. To this end, open discussion of the deeper meaning(s) which one sees in a given text is essential. Whatever general background in Indian tradition is needed is given in chapter 1. Thereafter, specific concepts, historical background, general concepts and issues, and more universal aspects of the Upaniṣadic teachings are all developed gradually and cumulatively in connection with particular passages or texts where they arise. I have met many people who told me that they had tried to read Eastern spiritual literature but found it too difficult to penetrate. I have tried to address this problem by adopting various devices, such as constant translation of Sanskrit terms, references to relevant modern philosophical or scientific developments, attempts to place a particular point in a larger historical context, and attempts to identify some of the more universal validity that a given teaching might have. But with so much modern critical scholarship on top of so many layers of Indian tradition, complexity is unavoidable and there are bound to be many controversial issues.

The book synthesises a large amount of material from many sources while trying to keep the lines of argument clear. The first chapter contains historical and religious-philosophical background; thereafter, scope and spiritual depth increase substantially with every chapter until a highpoint is reached in chapters 5 and 6. Chapter 2 presents great and timeless texts like the Yājñavalkya-Maitreyī Dialogue to give an initial idea of Ātman/Brahman. The next two chapters deal with Puruṣa, the all-encompassing and transcendent "Person", and the "Sense Powers" (Sight, Hearing, Mind, Speech, Breath). They have, however, a very different focus. Chapter 3 discusses four "mythological" and philosophical texts and shows that each of them must be based on some kind of higher realization or "enlightenment". In chapter 4 on the other hand, the interest is on the nature of meditation (which was completely out of the picture in chapter 3). In addition, this chapter is concerned with the problem of how the Upaniṣadic Wisdom arose from out of the Vedic and Brāhmaṇical religions, which are characterized more by Knowledge of Divinity than by Wisdom. To address these questions, the chapter studies three or four texts, including two or three *vidyās*. Only chapters 5 and 6 finally deal with the Supreme Wisdom that one associates with the Upaniṣads, and which forms the substratum of so many later Hindu traditions. They give detailed and comprehensive treatments of three great *vidyās* and cover topics such as *vijñāna* ("higher transcendental awareness," "beginning knowledge of reality"), *ānanda* ("higher bliss"), the "space in the heart," and "merger into Brahman". These are only a few of the universal higher elements in the Upaniṣads' description of the Infinite Reality which is obtained when one pools the dozen or so greatest Upaniṣadic *vidyās*. But these chapters do give a deep introduction to the Upaniṣadic Supreme Wisdom as a whole, and will perhaps be of greatest interest to the reader.

Various individuals and Institutions helped make this book become reality. My greatest debt is to my admired and revered Sanskrit teacher, Prof. Hans Henrich Hock of the University of Illinois Departments of Linguistics and Classics. Prof. Hock not only shepherded me through the basic sequence of Sanskrit courses at the University, but also thereafter unstintingly gave his time in weekly seminars every semester to read texts and answer innumerable questions. It is his influence which is to some extent responsible for the (in retrospect rather strong) reliance on linguistic arguments in the initial approach to the texts. But I was also deeply affected by his selfless dedication to the cause of Sanskrit, and by his uncommon detached objectivity which became a model for me. Profs. G. Ordal, R.S. Hart, and G. Tikku were kind enough to read some early drafts which would be embarrassing if made public now. Prof. J. Koller of Rensselaer was the first scholar to critically read the first draft and gave me generous encouragement, which was invaluable to me. Prof. F.X. Clooney of Boston College and Prof. G. Tikku of the Department of Comparative

Literature here at Illinois read some of the later chapters, and Dr. H. Ladanyi, Prof. R.S. Hart, and my wife Ricki read the entire manuscript and made numerous suggestions for improvements. To all of them I am deeply grateful. Above all, however, I am indebted to an unnamed devotee whose heartfelt comments persuaded me to spend a whole year making the book more readable, and to the editor, Dr. Kanshi Ram, who went several times painstakingly through every word of the text to get the book ready for publication. I cannot thank both of these men enough and their selfless service will be ever in my heart. Special thanks go to the staff of the Word Processing Center of the College of Education at UIUC, including Donna Auble (deceased), Lana Bates, Selena Douglas, Teri Frerichs, Debra Gough, and June Chambliss, Director, who had to struggle for many years with handwritten drafts and endless changes. Among institutions, I gratefully acknowledge the University of Illinois for enabling me to work in the stacks of its excellent library. I also thank the University Research Board for stipends to attend the Eighth and Ninth International Sanskrit Congresses in Vienna and Melbourne, and the University generally for enabling me to attend a number of professional meetings in Vedānta and Asian and Comparative Philosophy. Finally, I would like to express my love and appreciation to my wife Ricki and my family, which have been a haven of happiness through all the years I have been working on this book. Without them, the long-term digestion of the Upaniṣadic teachings presented here might not have been possible.

I bow down to the many scholars, both living and dead, whose work I used, and ask them to forgive me if I did not represent their ideas and intents correctly. I bow down to my teachers, both my teachers in mathematics etc. and my spiritual teachers. May I be worthy of their pure intentions! I bow down to the Infinite Reality, Ātman-Brahman-Bhagavān. May I not have misrepresented It!

Contents

Abbreviations and Conventions

Texts

AitĀr	*Aitareya Āraṇyaka*
AitBr	*Aitareya Brāhmaṇa*
AitUp	*Aitareya Upaniṣad*
BraSū	*Brahma Sūtra*
BraSūBh	*Brahma Sūtra Bhāṣya* of Śaṁkara
BṛhUp(M)	*Bṛhadāraṇyaka Upaniṣad* (Mādhyandina Recension)
BṛhUp(K)	*Bṛhadāraṇyaka Upaniṣad* (Kāṇva Recension)
ChāndUp	*Chāndogya Upaniṣad*
JaimBr	*Jaiminīya Brahmaṇa*
JaimUpBr	*Janiminīya Upaniṣad Brāhmaṇa*
KauṣBr	*Kauṣītaki* (or *Śāṅkhāyana) Brāhmaṇa*
KauṣUp	*Kauṣītaki Upaniṣad*
Māhā-NārUp	*Mahā-Nārāyaṇa Upaniṣad*
MaitrUp	*Maitrāyaṇīya Upaniṣad*
MāṇḍUp	*Māṇḍūkya Upaniṣad*
MuṇḍUp	*Muṇḍaka Upaniṣad*
ŚāṅkhĀr	*Śāṅkhāyana Āraṇyaka*
ŚatBr(M)	*Śatapatha Brāhmaṇa* (Mādhyandina Recension)
ŚatBr(K)	*Śatapatha Brāhmaṇa* (Kāṇva Recension)
ŚvetUp	*Śvetāśvatara Upaniṣad*
TaittĀr	*Taittirīya Āraṇyaka*
TaittBr	*Taittirīya Brāhmaṇa*
TaittSaṁh	*Taittirīya Saṁhitā*
TaittUp	*Taittirīya Upaniṣad*
VājSaṁh	*Vājasaneyī Saṁhitā*
YoSū	*Yoga Sūtra* of Patañjali

Other Abbreviations: ed. = editor, edited by, edition; Jour. = Journal; *n. v.* = *non vidi*; Pub(s). = published, Publisher(s), Publication(s); Skt. = Sanskrit; transl. = translation, translated by, translator; Univ. = University.

Journals and Series

ABORI	Annals of the Bhandarkar Oriental Research Institute
ALB	Brahmavidyā. Adyar Library Bulletin
HIL	A History of Indian Literature (J. Gonda, ed.). Wiesbaden: Otto Harassowitz
HOS	Harvard Oriental Series (G.R. Lanman, ed.). Cambridge: Harvard Univ. Press
IFI	Institute Francaise de 1' Indologie (Pondicherry, South India).
ICO	International Congress of Orientalists
IIJ	Indo-Iranian Journal
JAOS	Journal of the Americal Oriental Society
JIP	Journal of Indian Philosophy
JRAS	Journal of the Royal Asiatic Society
ORT	Orientalia Rheno-Trajectina (J. Gonda and H.W. Obbink, eds)
SBE	Sacred Books of the East (F. Max Müller, ed.). Oxford: Clarendon Press
VKNAWL, NR	Verhandelingen der K. Nederlandse Akademie van Wetenschappen, Afd. Letterkunde, Nieuwe Reeks
WZKSA	Wiener Zeitschrift für die Kunde Süd und Ost Asiens
ZDMG	Zeitschrift der Deutschen Morgenländischen Gesellschaft

Books

Aufrecht, *Rig Veda*
Th. Aufrecht, ed., *Die Hymnen des Rigveda.* 4th ed., 2 vols. Wiesbaden: Otto Harrassowitz, 1968 (reprint of 2nd ed., 1877).

Aurobindo, *Collected Works*
Sri Aurobindo Birth Centenary Edition. Pondicherry: Sri Aurobindo Ashram 1970-72; 24 vols.

Bader, *Meditation*
J. Bader, *Meditation in Śaṅkara's Vedānta*. New Delhi: Aditya Prakasan, 1990.

Bodewitz, *JaimBr* v. 1
H.W. Bodewitz, *Jaiminīya Brāhmaṇa I, 1-65*. Leiden: E.J. Brill, 1973. (ORT, v. 17).

Bodewitz, *JaimBr* v. 2
H.W. Bodewitz, *The Jyotiṣṭoma Ritual. Jaiminīya Brāhmaṇa I, 66-364*. Leiden: E.J. Brill, 1990. (ORT, v. 34).

Böhtlingk, *BṛhUp*
Böhtlingk, O., ed. and transl., *Bṛhadāraṇyakopaniṣad in der Mādhjamdina-Recension*. St. Petersburg: Kaiserliche Akademie der Wissenschaften, 1889.

Böhtlingk, *ChāndUp*
Böhtlingk, Otto v., *Khāndogyopaniṣad*. Leipzig: H. Hässel, 1889 (without Sanskrit).

Coomaraswamy, *Papers*
Lipsey, R., ed., *Coomaraswamy*. v. 2. *Selected Papers: Metaphysics*. Princeton: Princeton Univ. Press, 1977 (Bollingen Series No. 89).

Deussen, *Sixty Ups.*
P. Deussen, transl., *Sixty Upaniṣads of the Veda*. (Transl. from the German by V.M. Bedekar and A.B. Palsule). Delhi: Motilal Banarsidass, 1980 (1st Germ. ed., 1897).

Deussen, *Geschichte*
P. Deussen, *Allgemeine Geschichte der Philosophie mit besonderer Berücksichtigung der Religionen*, in 6 parts, v.1, parts 1 and 2 (*Allgemeine Einleitung und Philosophie der Veda bis auf die Upanishads*, and *Die Philosophie der Upanishads*), 2nd ed. Leipzig: Brockhaus, 1906/7. (First ed. 1884/99).

Deussen, *Phil. Ups.*
P. Deussen, *The Philosophy of the Upanishads*. Transl. by A.S. Geden of part 2 of Deussen, *Geschichte,* above. Edinburgh: Clark, 1906; repr.

Eggeling, *ŚatBr*
J. Eggeling, transl., *The Śatapatha-Brāhmaṇa according to the Text of the Mādhyandina School*. 5 vols. Oxford: Oxford Univ. (1882-99) (SBE, vols. 12, 26, 41, 43, 44) (repr. Delhi: Motilal

Banarsidass, 1963).

Edgerton, *Beginnings*
F. Edgerton, *The Beginnings of Indian Philosophy. Selections from the Rig Veda, Atharva Veda, Upanishads, and Mahābhārata.* London: Allen and Unwin, 1965.

Eliade, *Encyclopedia of Religion*
M. Eliade, ed. in chief, *Encyclopedia of Religion.* New York: Macmillan, 1987.

Falk, *Nāma-Rūpa*
Falk, Maryla, *Nāma-Rūpa and Dharma-Rūpa.* Calcutta: Univ. of Calcutta, 1943.

Gambhīrānanda, *BraSū Commentary*
Swami Gambhīrānanda, transl., *Brahma Sūtra Bhāṣya of Śrī Śaṅkarācārya.* Calcutta: Advaita Ashrama, 1965

Gambhīrānanda, *Eight Ups. Commentary*
Swami Gambhīrānanda, transl., *Eight Upaniṣads with the Commentary of Śaṅkarācārya.* 2 vols. Calcutta: Advaita Ashrama, 2nd ed., 1965.

Geldner, *Rig Veda*
K. Geldner, transl., *Der Rig-Veda aus dem Sanskrit ins Deutsche übersetzt.* 3 vols. Cambridge, Mass: Harvard Univ. Press, 1951 (Harvard Oriental Series, C.A. Lanman, ed., No. 33-35).

Gispert-Sauch, *Bliss*
G. Gispert-Sauch, *Bliss in the Upanishads.* New Delhi: Oriental Publishers and Distributors, 1977 (World's Wisdom Series, No. 2).

Gonda, *Vedic Literature*
J. Gonda, *Vedic Literature* (*Saṁhitās* and *Brāhmaṇas*). Wiesbaden: Otto Harassowitz, 1975 (HIL, v. 1, Fasc. 1).

Gonda, *Studies*
J. Gonda, *Selected Studies.* 4 vols. Leiden: E.J. Brill, 1975.

Grassmann, *Wörterbuch*
Grassmann, H., *Wörterbuch zum Rig-Veda,* 4th ed., Wiesbaden: O. Harassowitz, 1964 (1st ed., 1872).

Griffith, *VājSaṁh*
R.T.H. Griffith, *The Texts of the White Yajur Veda.* 2nd. rev. and enlarged edition. New Delhi: Munshiram Manoharlal, 1987 (1st ed., 1879).

Hacker, *Kleine Schriften*
L. Schmithausen, ed., *Paul Hacker, Kleine Schriften.* Wiesbaden: Franz Steiner, 1978 (Glasenapp-Stiftung, No. 15).

Horner, *Middle-Length Sayings*
I.B. Horner, transl., *The Collection of Middle-Length Sayings* (*Majjhima-Nikāya*). 3 vols. London: Luzac and Co. (Pali Text Society), 1959, 57, 59 resp. (Pali Text Society Translation Series, Nos. 29, 30, 31).

Horsch, *Gāthā Literature*
P. Horsch, *Die Vedische Gāthā und Śloka-Literatur.* Bern: Francke, 1966.

Hume, *Upaniṣads*
R.E. Hume, transl., *The Thirteen Principal Upanishads. Translated from the Sanskrit.* Oxford: Oxford Univ. Press, 2nd ed. 1931 (1st ed., 1921; 2nd ed. repr. Delhi, 1949, paperback, 1983).

Jacob, *Concordance*
Col. G.A. Jacob, *A Concordance to the Principal Upanishads and Bhagavadgītā.* Repr. Delhi: Motilal Banarsidass, 1963 (or. ed., 1891).

Jha, *ChāndUp Commentary*
Ganganatha Jha, ed. and transl., *Chāndogyopaniṣad.* Poona: Oriental Book Agency, 1942.

Keith, *AitĀr*
A.B. Keith, ed. and transl., *The Aitareya Āraṇyaka.* Oxford: Clarendon, 1909 (Anecdota Oxoniensia: Aryan Series, part 9). (Repr. Oxford Univ. Press, 1969).

Keith, *Phil, of Veda*
A.B. Keith, *The Religion and Philosophy of the Veda and Upaniṣads.* 2 vols. Cambridge, Mass: Harvard Univ. Press, 1925 (HOS v. 32).

Keith, *Rig Veda Brs.*
A.B. Keith transl. *Rig Veda Brāhmaṇas. The Aitareya and Kauṣītaki Brāhmaṇas of the Rig Veda.* Cambridge: Harvard Univ. Press, 1920 (HOS v. 25). Repr. Delhi: Motilal Banarsidass, 1971.

Keith, *ŚāṅkhĀr*
A.B. Keith, *The Śāṅkhāyana Āraṇyaka.* New Delhi: Oriental Books Reprint, 1975 (1st ed., London: Royal Asiatic Society, 1908).

Keith, *TaittSaṁh*
A.B. Keith, transl. *The Veda of the Black Yajus School, Taittirīya*

Saṁhitā. 2 vols. Cambridge, Mass: Harvard Univ. Press, 1914 (HOS vols. 18-19). (Repr. Delhi: Motilal Banarsidass, 1967).

Limaye-Vadekar, *Principal Ups.*
Limaye, V.P., and Vadekar, R.D., eds., *Eighteen Principal Upaniṣads.* Poona: Vaidika Saṁśodhana Maṇḍala, 1958.

Mādhavānanda, *BṛhUp Commentary*
Swami Mādhavānanda, transl., *The Bṛhadāraṇyaka Upaniṣad with the Commentary of Śaṅkarācārya.* Calcutta: Advaita Ashrama, 4th ed. 1965 (1st ed., 1934).

Mayrhofer, *Etym. Wörterbuch*
M. Mayrhofer, *Kurzgefasstes Etymologisches Wörterbuch des Alt-Indischen. A Concise Etymological Sanskrit Dictionary* vols. 1- ; Heidelberg: Carl Winter, 1956- .

Mcdonell-Keith, *Index*
A.A. Macdonell and A.B. Keith, *Vedic Index of Names and Subjects,* 2 vols. Repr. Delhi: Motilal Banarsidass, 1958.

MW, *Dictionary*
M. Monnier-Williams, *Sanskrit-English Dictionary.* Oxford: Oxford Univ. Press. 1899 (repr. Delhi: Munshiram Manoharlal, 1976).

Müller, *Upaniṣads*
F.M. Müller, *The Upanishads.* 2 vols. Oxford: Clarendon Press, 1900 (1st ed., 1876; SBE vs. 1, 15).

Mukhopadhyaya, *Studies*
G. Mukhopadhyaya, *Studies in the Upaniṣads.* Calcutta: Sanskrit College, 1960 (Calcutta Sanskrit College Research Series, No. 9).

Nakamura, *History*
H. Nakamura, *A History of Early Vedānta Philosophy.* Part 1. Delhi: Motilal Banarsidass, 1983 (1st Japanese ed., 1950-56).

Oldenberg, *Kleine Schriften*
K.L. Janert, ed., *Herrmann Oldenberg, Kleine Schriften.* 2 vols. Wiesbaden: Franz Steiner, 1967 (Glasenapp-Stiftung, Nos. 1, 1 and 1, 2).

Poona, *Dictionary*
An Encyclopedic Dictionary of the Sanskrit Language on Historical Principles. Vs. 1:1-3:1, ed. A.M. Ghatage; v. 3:3, ed. S.D. Joshi. Poona: Deccan College Postgraduate Research Institute, 1976- .

Potter, *Bibliography*
K.H. Potter, *Encyclopedia of Indian Philosophies. Bibliography.* Princeton: Princeton Univ. Press, 2nd rev. ed., 1983.

Radhakrishnan, *Brahma Sūtra*
S. Radhakrishnan, *The Brahma Sūtra. The Philosophy of Spiritual Life.* New York: Harper, 1960.

Radhakrishnan, *Upaniṣads*
S. Radhakrishnan, ed. and transl., *The Principal Upanishads.* London: Allen and Unwin, 1953.

Raghvachar, *Rāmānuja on Ups.*
S.S. Raghvachar, *Śrī Rāmānuja on the Upanishads.* Triplicane, Madras: Prof. M. Rangacharya Memorial Trust, 1972.

Ramana Maharshi, *Collected Works*
Indian ed.: A. Osborne, ed., *The Collected Works of Ramana Maharshi.* Tiruvannamalai: Sri Ramanasramam. Fifth ed., 1979 (3rd. ed., 1968). British ed.: A. Osborne, *The Collected Works of Ramana Maharshi.* London: Rider and Co., 1959. (The two versions show considerable differences in formulation).

Ramana Maharshi, *Talks*
M.S. Venkataramiah, recorder, *Talks with Sri Ramana Maharshi.* 3 vols. in one. 3rd ed., Tiruvannamalai: Ramanasramam, 1963 (1st ed., 1955 in 3 vols.).

Sarup, *Nirukta*
L. Sarup, ed. and transl., *The Nighaṇṭu and the Nirukta.* 2 vols. in one, 2nd repr., Delhi: Motilal Banarsidass, 1960 (1st eds. 1920 and 1926).

St. Petersburg, *Dictionary*
O. Böhtlingk—R. Roth, *Sanskrit Wörterbuch,* 6 vols. St. Petersburg: 1852-75.

Sathya Sai Baba, *Summer Showers*
Sri Sathya Sai Baba, *Summer Showers in Brindavan.* [Discourses given at Summer Institutes in Indian Spirituality and Culture, various years]: *1972*: 2nd ed., 1981; *1973:* 3rd ed., n.d.; *1974:* Am. ed. 1976; *1976 (= Blue Roses on Summer Mountains):* 1st ed., 1977; *1977:* 1st ed., 1978; *1978:* 1st ed., 1980; *1979:* 2nd ed., 1980. All Prashanti Nilayam: Sri Sathya Sai Education and Publication Foundation.

Sathya Sai Baba, *UpVahini*
Sri Sathya Sai Baba, *Upanishad Vahini.* 2nd ed., Tustin, CA: Sri Sathya Sai Baba Book Center of America, 1970.

Sharma, *Concept of Ātman*
B.R. Sharma, *The Concept of Ātman in the Principal Upaniṣads in the Perspective of the Saṁhitās, the Brāhmaṇas, the Āraṇyakas and Indian Philosophical Systems.* New Delhi: Dinesh Pubs., 1972.

Shastri, *UpBhāṣyam*
S. Subrahmanya Shastri, ed., *Upaniṣadbhāṣyam.* Vol. 1, *Eight Upaniṣads;* vol. 2, *Chāndogyopaniṣad;* vol. 3, *Bṛhadāraṇyakopaniṣad.* Varanasi: Mahesh Research Institute, 1982.

Shastri, *History*
Gaurinath Sastri, *A History of Vedic Literature.* Calcutta: Sanskrit Pustak Bhandar, 1982.

Thibaut, *Rāmānuja BraSū Comm.*
A. Thibaut, transl., *The Vedānta-Sūtras with the Commentary by Rāmānuja.* Oxford: Clarendon, 1904 (Repr. Delhi: Motilal Banarsidass, 1962, 1968) (SBE v. 48).

Thibaut, *Śaṁkara BraSū Comm.*
A. Thibaut, transl., *The Vedānta Sūtras with the Commentary by Śaṅkarācārya.* 2 vols. Oxford: Clarendon, 1904 (Repr. Delhi: Motilal Banarsidass, 1962, 1968) (SBE vols. 34, 38).

van Buitenen, *MaitrUp*
J.A.B. van Buitenen, *The Maitrāyaṇīya Upaniṣad.* 'S-Gravenhage: Mouton, 1962 (Disputationes Rheno-Trajectinae, J. Gonda, ed., No. 6).

van Buitenen, *Studies*
L. Rocher, ed., *Studies in Indian Literature and Philosophy. Collected Articles of J.A.B. van Buitenen.* Delhi: Motilal Banarsidass, 1988.

Vimalānanda, *Mahā-NārUp*
Swami Vimalānanda, Mahānārāyaṇopaniṣad. Mylapore, Madras: Ramakrishna Math, 3rd. impression, 1979.

Vishva Bandhu, *Atharva Veda*
Vishva Bandhu, ed., in collaboration with Bhimdev, Vidyanidhi, and Munishvardev, *Atharva Veda* (Śaunaka) *with the Padapāṭha and Sāyaṇācārya's Commentary.* 4 vols. Hoshiarpur: Vishveshvaranand Vedic Research Institute, 1960—(Vishveshvaranand Indological

Series, Nos. 13-16).

Wackernagel—Debrunner, *Grammatik*

J. Wackernagel and A. Debrunner, *Altindische Grammatik.* In four volumes and an index vol. Göttingen: Vandenhoeck and Ruprecht, v. 1 = part I, 2nd ed. 1957; v. 2 = part II, 1, 1957; v. 3 = part II, 2, 1st ed., 1954; v. 4 = part III, 1930; R. Hauschild, *Register zur Altindischen Grammatik*, 1964.

Weber, *ŚatBr*

A. Weber, ed., *The Śatapatha—Brāhmaṇa in the Mādhyandina—Śākhā.* Varanasi: Chowkhamba Sanskrit Series Office, 1964 (Chowkhamba Sanskrit Series, No. 96; 1st ed. 1849).

Weber, *VājSaṁh*

Weber, A., ed., The *Vājasaneyī Saṁhitā in the Mādhyandina and the Kāṇva-Śākhās, with the Commentary of Mahīdhara.* Varanasi: Chowkhamba Sanskrit Series, Office, 1972 (Chowkhambha Sanskrit Series No. 103).

Whitney, *Atharva Veda*

D.W. Whitney, transl., *Atharva Veda Saṁhitā.* 2 vols. Cambridge: Harvard University, 1905/7 (HOS vols. 7-8).

CHAPTER 1

The Upaniṣads: Background

1. Introduction

Supreme Wisdom Scriptures say that the human being, by proper effort for inner evolution, can attain stages where he or she is unaffected by desire and fear, birth and death, and space and time, where there is complete understanding of the nature of existence and of the arising and passing of the world and the Universe, and where there is Oneness,—"Oneness with the Total of Existence,"— and "being All". In the higher stages or states of evolution toward this goal there may also arise forms of omniscience and of manifestation at cosmic levels. Such teachings are found extensively developed in various scriptural and philosophical literatures in Hinduism, Buddhism, and Jainism. They also occur in individual cases or small movements in Western religions. But historically they first appeared in explicit form in the oldest Upaniṣads, dated by modern-type scholarship 800-600 BCE.

The Upaniṣads in Indian Tradition. The Upaniṣads have had a vast and pervasive influence in Hindu Tradition. Upaniṣadic teachings and Upaniṣadic type realization run through a wide range of Hindu religious literatures as dye through a cloth. For example, some of the great medieval *bhakti* (devotion, and love of God) texts, such as the *Bhāgavata Purāṇa*, the *Guru Granth* (the Scripture of the Sikhs), and more generally the texts of the *Santa* tradition (which includes the *Guru Granth*) are shot through and through with Upaniṣadic concepts and realization. Even for branches of the Hindu Tradition which do not recognize the Vedic Scriptures and the Upaniṣads, such as Āgamic Śaivism and Śāktism, the Upaniṣads provide a basic point of reference and comparison. It is no exaggeration to say that the Upanisads form the backbone of a large portion of the Hindu Tradition, and give it a profound unity and great spiritual height.

Basic Teachings: Ātman and Brahman. The Upaniṣadic teachings crystallize around a number of key terms, the most important of which are Ātman and Brahman. Ātman, "the Self", is at the root of the experience of self, or "I", which is found in every human being. It is the Formless Reality which one is, above Life and Death, and above space and time. Every one is that Reality, although without being aware of it, and It shines in the heart and mind of all living beings. Unlike waking or dream consciousness, it has no finite (empirical) characteristics. If the Ātman is something like Reality approached from the point of view that oneself is the Reality, Brahman, by contrast, is something like the Reality in its aspect of being the basis of everything. "All this"—all this existence, world, experience, whatever—is Brahman. This Brahman is the Invisible, All-pervasive Infinite. All the Upaniṣadic teachings converge to the fact that the individual self is not different from the Ātman, and the latter is not different from Brahman.

The whole Upaniṣadic approach and the types of "realization" or "enlightenment" which are its goal can be described as simultaneously "transcendental" and "integral". The Upaniṣadic teachings are "transcendental" in the sense that they deal with something—experience, being, reality, whatever one may want to call it—that is beyond (or that transcends) mind and matter and consciousness, that is incomparably greater than these and at the same time somehow includes them, and that is the very essence of human existence and the world. At the same time the Being or the Reality that is being taught is something in which all the major modes and categories of human understanding (realism and idealism, mind, matter, and consciousness, self and other, internal and external, individual, society, nature and cosmos, immanence and transcendence, human, divine, and Absolute, etc.), as well as all knowledge and consciousness of the phenomenal world, are all included in an indivisible Integral Aspect, viz. Brahman. The aim of human life and existence is to "realize" that and "become" that Brahman.

Aim of this Chapter. But before taking up the Upaniṣadic texts in more detail, some introduction is desirable, and this is provided in the present chapter. One desideratum is simply a didactic one, viz., to introduce a number of terms, and to set up enough of an outline of the Hindu and Vedic Traditions so as to enable the reader to absorb most of the factual information given in this book without much effort.

But this chapter also aims at making the reader from the very beginning aware of the large range of presuppositions and perspectives from which the Upaniṣads have been and are being approached. A Western reader with serious interest in these texts is likely to be assailed by more and more cognitive dissonance as he picks up different books in the area or talks to different individuals. He will find great differences in world-view, in the commitment to tradition, in degree as well as type of rigour and precision, and in spiritual understanding. Thus some kind of initial orientation in these respects is desirable.

Outline of the Chapter. The first item on the agenda is to give a brief idea of the Hindu Tradition as a whole, and of the role of the Upaniṣads within this Tradition. This is done in sec. 2. Thereafter some more limited contexts are outlined. The Upaniṣads did not arise independently in a vacuum, but in the soil of a remarkable religious tradition, the Vedic religion (3000?-1000? BCE). Vedic religion (or Vedism) involved public ritual sacrifices or *yajñas* performed by priests, the Brahmins (Skt. *brāhmaṇas*). Here Vedic deities were praised with verses called *mantras*, with an almost conscious emphasis on inspired poetic expression of divine experience. As time went on, the original Vedic religion changed into a form called Brāhmaṇical religion or Brāhmaṇism (1500?-600? BCE), characterized by elaborate public as well as simpler household sacrifices. The Upaniṣads as they exist today are part of the literature of Brāhmaṇism, and the Upaniṣadic Wisdom is in many ways the fruit of the Vedic and Brāhmaṇical religions. Accordingly, sec. 3 is devoted to a very brief survey of Vedic literature (which includes the Vedic texts as well as the literature of Brāhmaṇism), and sec. 4 to a discussion of the historical context of the Vedic and Brāhmaṇical religions. Next sec. 5 deals with some of the difficulties in arriving at a deeper understanding of the Upaniṣads. It discusses the bearing which various earlier and later texts and literatures have on understanding the Upaniṣadic teachings, and the fact that these other literatures are often not so well-understood either.

The last section finally briefly tells the story of how the Upaniṣads came to the West, and then asks how the Upaniṣadic teachings fit into the essential philosophical and scientific motivation of the West. The Upaniṣads have a fundamentalness and universality which was already recognized in the 19th century by A. Schopenhauer, C.H.F. Krause, and P. Deussen. These men accepted the Upaniṣads as highest *Erkenntnis* and Truth, and as an attainment of Western philosophy's highest aims. Highest *Erkenntnis* and Truth are also the basic higher motivation operating in modern Science (Physics). This book is written from the conviction that the Upaniṣads (like the High Wisdom literatures in other traditions) do in fact represent highest *Erkenntnis* and Truth in the sense of traditional Western Philosophy and Science. But especially Science would have to purify itself in terms of inner ethical and moral discipline and become much more aware at a human and spiritual level in order to accept this fact.

2. The Upaniṣads and Hindu Tadition, 3000 BCE—Today

Comparison with the Christian Tradition in the West. To get a perspective on the whole Hindu or even the whole Indian religious-philosophical tradition in the space of a few pages is impossible.[1] In what follows we confine ourselves primarily to the essential religious etc. aspects as they are reflected in the Scriptures and high level spiritual literatures in both Sanskrit and the vernacular languages (Hindi, Tamil, etc.). To get an idea of the Hindu Tradition at this level, a comparable summary of the Christian Tadition in the West might be helpful. Here we have first of all the Bible; then (looking only at major groupings of important texts and selected representative figures), the New Testament apocryphal literature (e.g. the *Gospel according to Thomas*); the literature of the Christian Fathers (Origen, *Sayings of the Fathers*, St. Basil, Evagrius Ponticus); the Christian Neo-Platonic Tradition (Dionysius Areopagita, John Scotus Erigena); the literature of the great theologians, monastic founders and Saints of the Catholic Church; and finally a small amount of Protestant literature. The high level literature of the Catholic Church includes the works of some of the Doctors of the Church (e.g., St. Bernhard of Clairvaux, St. Bonaventure); a number of great regional mystical and devotional literatures, often in the vernacular, such as Italian mysticism (Angela of Foligno, Jacopone da Todi), German Bridal mysticism (Mechthild of Magdeburg, Gertrude the Great), classical German mysticism (Meister Eckhart, Henry Suso, the Flemish Jan Van Ruusbroec), English mysticism (the *Cloud of Unknowing*), and Spanish mysticism (St. John of the Cross, St. Theresa of Avila); and a few scattered more recent works.

Several Major Streams of Religion. In a similar summary of the Hindu Tradition, one would have to observe first of all that unlike Christianity, the Hindu Tradition is articulated in several great, constantly intertwining and fusing streams of religion. We already mentioned the Vedic and Brāhmaṇical religions (3000?-1000? BCE and 1500?-600? BCE) as providing India's oldest Scriptures and spiritual literature. Around 600 or 500 BCE two other broad religious currents come into historical view, viz. Vaiṣṇavism and Śaivism. There is general agreement that Vaiṣṇava religion is an amalgamation, fusion, and further elaboration of sub-streams from three different sources: (1) worship of Nārāyaṇa, commonly considered a non-Vedic deity but found already in the literature of Brāhmaṇism; (2) Viṣṇuism, worship of Viṣṇu (English often Vishnu), originally a Vedic deity; and (3) the cult of Kṛṣṇa Vāsudeva (in English often written Krishna), a historical figure. (Viṣṇu-Nārāyaṇa is often shown in human form with four arms holding certain symbolic objects; Kṛṣṇa is typically depicted as a cowherd playing the flute, or as a little boy.) These sub-streams appear unified as a single religion as early as the third century BCE.[2] In Śaivism, the Supreme is Śiva, often represented as a Yogi sitting in lotus posture in meditation, or in a dance pose. Śiva appears to have evolved in a continuous fashion from Rudra, a Vedic deity, with innumerable accretions from local cults, myths etc. Rudra may go still further back in time and have non-Vedic historical origins. In general, then, these two religious movements spread among the people and the ruling class (the *kṣatriyas*). The Vedic Brahmins modified the Vedic sacrifices and kept their highly regulated Brāhmaṇical way of life. But they also adopted the new forms of worship in varying degrees, harmonized them with the Vedic and Brāhmaṇical Scriptures, and served their communities and the kings as Vaiṣṇava or Śaivite priests.[3] By this process they remained the intellectual elite and backbone of Indian culture and learning until modern times. (Brāhmaṇism has continued in various relatively pure forms until today also, however.)

Around 400 to 800 CE, a new religious orientation arose which is described by the terms Tantrism and Śāktism. A broad theme in Tantrism is that the process of ataining Divinity involves intrinsically and in an essential way the use of the body, and Tantrism is generally associated with such practices as intensive repetition of mantras, the laying down of sounds, syllables or deities on parts of the body (*nyāsa*), the use of geometric cosmic symbols (*maṇḍalas*), and *kuṇḍalinī yoga*. Śāktism refers to worship of the All-power which is seen in Creation as a supreme female force or principle, called Śakti. Tantrism and Śāktism affected all forms of Hinduism and even Buddhism, and brought a new religion, worship of Devī, the Universal Mother, in various forms (Kālī, Durgā, etc.). Worship of Devī is called Śāktism also. These broad streams, then, amalgamated with numerous local and regional cults, and spawned numerous subsects, movements, etc.

Major Spiritual Literatures. Now the range of spiritual literatures that leads these religions and sects is so vast as to stagger the comprehension. Already the sheer volume of Scriptures is incredible. A Western reader, used to the Bible and a few volumes of Christian and Jewish Apocrypha and Gnostic texts, is not prepared for collections of Scripture that would run into literally hundreds of volumes in print. The mass of other high level mystical devotional and enlightenment literature by Saints etc. is larger still. An initial idea of the extent of all this may be gathered from J.N. Farquhar's *An Outline of the Religious Literature of India* (1920). Farquhar was intimately acquainted with the condition of religion in the villages, monasteries and sectarian centers and with the *sādhus* (mendicant monks, renunciants) of his time. In addition he covers both Sanskrit literature and literature in the major indigenous languages, and thus provides a unified overall account. But in terms of depth of coverage and historical scholarship his book is now superseded by the series *History of Indian Literature* edited by J. Gonda.[4]

The Epics and Purāṇas. The first literature which should be mentioned is the Epic-Purāṇic literature. Here "Epic" refers to two great Epics, the *Mahābhārata* and the *Rāmāyaṇa*. The *Mahābhārata*[5] in the larger Northern Recension consists of 110,000 verses in 18 books (at 5000 verses per volume, this means 22 volumes of print). Its main story deals with the conflict of two royal families, the Pāṇḍavas (sons of Pāṇḍu) and the Kauravas (sons of Dhṛtarāṣṭra), both descended from a famous king called Bharata. (*Mahābhārata* literally means "the great [epic of the battle] of the Bhāratas," i.e. the descendants of Bharata.) The five Pāṇḍava brothers (princes), led by Dharmarāja (Yudhiṣṭhira) and aided by Kṛṣṇa, are seeking to regain their rightful inheritance, half of the kingdom, from the Kauravas. Eventually most of the peoples and kingdoms of northern India are allied with one side or the other. The conflict culminates in the great battle of Kurukṣetra (northeast of Delhi), which is described in the Epic in books 5-10. The most famous segment in the *Mahābhārata* is the *Bhagavad Gītā* (or simply *Gītā*), consisting of some 700 verses of spiritual instruction given by Kṛṣṇa to Arjuna, one of the five Pāṇḍava brothers, immediately before the battle. The battle of the Bhāratas is already mentioned by Pāṇini, the great grammarian (Western dating, 600-

500 BCE). From a modern historical point of view, the *Mahābhārata* represents more the repository of a whole bardic tradition than a single piece of literature, and the present text is thought to have grown from a much older core by accumulation over a period of several centuries, from 300 BCE to 400 CE. The other Epic, the *Rāmāyaṇa* of Vālmīki,[6] is smaller (24,000 verses), and looks more like a work by a single author. It tells the story of Rāma, prince and finally king of Ayodhyā, and his wife Sītā. Rāma, accompanied by Sītā and his younger brother Lakṣmaṇa, has to live for 14 years in exile in the forest. Sītā is abducted by Rāvaṇa, the ten-headed Demon king of Laṅkā, and is eventually recovered by Rāma and his forces.

The style and content of the Epics continues and is expanded into new mythological and cosmological realms in the Purāṇas.[7] Purāṇas began to appear (perhaps based on older texts or traditions which are now lost) in the 2nd to 4th century CE and were still being produced, added to, etc., in the 13th to 14th century CE. The best known Purāṇa is the *Bhāgavata Purāṇa*, about the size of the Bible and written throughout in a characteristic style of poetry. The *Bhāgavata* is one of the world's great texts of love of God and God consciousness. But also it is pervaded through and through with Upaniṣadic Supreme Wisdom, with a depth that challenges the most profound metaphysical scholars. Incidentally, the *Bhāgavata* is (along with the *Bhagavad Gītā*) the chief Scripture of the Hare Krishna movement, a fact which has helped to introduce it in the West.

Character of the Epics and Purāṇas. At first the *Mahābhārata* and the Purāṇas strike one as unbelievable agglomerations, without parallel in the West. There are semi-historical accounts and stories of the gods, representations of the cyclical history of the world and mankind, long genealogies and dynastic lists, spiritual geography, cosmography, and cosmology, detailed descriptions of systems of worship, temple building, medicine, and more, all worked into one unbelievable fabric of discourse. But this literature also includes documents of Supreme Wisdom and God consciousness, like the *Gītā* and *Bhāgavata Purāṇa*, which have a universal significance. For India, its importance lies in the fact that it contains high and highest level moral and spiritual teaching in a form in which it could be and still is assimilated by the people at large. A.A. Macdonell for example, an influential Indologist of the early part of the century, notes that the Epics "have been a national possession for at least 2000 years, deeply influencing the moral and religious thought of the

Indian population" and calls the *Mahābhārata* "an encyclopedia of moral teaching".[8] In their function of molding the character and consciousness of the people, the most basic factor operating in these texts is the Upaniṣadic element, which can be felt everywhere. Conflicts are posed in terms of the transcendent character of high moral and spiritual values, like *dharma*, "righteousness", and *jñāna*, "knowledge [of the reality]", decisions are made weighing the motivation and forces of the moment against the transience and evanescence of the phenomena and things of the world, and the (moral) consequences of one's actions for oneself in the future (one's *karma*) are always on the horizon:

> The *Rāmāyaṇa* and the *Mahābhārata* are known even to the most illiterate of Hindus as they have come down through the ages by word of mouth. . . . It is because of these books that the most illiterate of our peasants is not ignorant. . . . He carries within him the wisdom of the Upaniṣads which has been conveyed to him by these two major epics in story, ballad or dance form. ...
>
> Through the stories from the *Rāmānayṇa* which are recited to them, the ordinary people learn the difference between right and wrong, develop a high sense of values and understand what ideal behaviour is. The tremendous cultural heritage of the Vedas and Upaniṣads has reached and permeated to the most illiterate of our people through Sage Vālmīki's priceless epic, the *Rāmāyaṇa.* This is why our peasants, even those living in remote villages, know to this day what they can expect from the laws of the land and are not ignorant of their rights nor of what is due to the ruled by the rulers. . . . The illiterate villager is therefore not ignorant as the city-educated think him to be.[9]

The Purāṇic literature has had a similar function. It represents something like a storehouse of the Indian Mind and Subconscious, the "Purāṇic Mind", in which certain deeper spiritual problems are presented and worked out, often in a glaring, or dreamlike quality. There is a constant intermingling of time, space and spiritual realms, of gods, men and personified abstract entities (like virtues), of the actual, the imagined, and the illusory, of highest ideals and stark emotion, and the development is often interrupted by lists, enumerations, and abstract intellectual schemes of all kinds. Perhaps the most important theme in the Epic-Purāṇic literature, which is developed in ever new dimensions, is the notion and phenomenon of *avatāra*, the descent and manifestation of the Supreme Divine in ultimately human form. The theme of *avatāra* is already implicit in Vālmīki's *Rāmāyaṇa* in the figure of Rāma, and is then much more deeply developed in the figure of Kṛṣṇa in the *Mahābhārata* and the *Bhāgavata Purāṇa*. Generally speaking the Epics and Purāṇas represent a powerful unifying element in Hindu culture and Tradition. While showing numerous and often strong sectarian influences, they are basically an interdenominational literature.

Āgamic (or Tantric) Literatures. Hindu Tradition is often described as working with two frameworks, or containing two broad currents of spirituality, the Vedic and the Āgamic. The Epics and Purāṇas belong to the former. They continue the Vedic and Brāhmaṇical heritage by developing or combining it with theistic and new imaginative, etc. forms. Beginning in 400 to 600 CE, however, there arise scriptures called Āgamas which begin to express tantric and Śākta elements. There are several major Āgamic literatures. An important one is that of the *Pañcarātra Saṁhitās*, with about 200 titles and an estimated total of one million verses extant.[10] This literature, whose main purport is "how to serve and propitiate God (*samādhāraṇa*)",[11] is "a bond of union between the older forms of Viṣṇuism known from the *Mahābhārata* and the older Purāṇas . . . and the modern stages of that religion".[12] It sees itself as Vedic (and thus Upaniṣadic). The most famous Pañcarātra works are the three "gems of the Pañcarātra", viz. the *Pauṣkara Saṁhitā, Sātvata Saṁhitā*, and *Jayākhya Saṁhitā*. Another important literature is that of the *Śaiva Āgamas*,[13] a diverse group of texts on which are based three major Śaivite traditions: the Śaiva Siddhānta in the Tamil speaking South, Kashmir Śaivism in the North, and Vīra-Śaivism (or Liṅgāyat religion) in the South-West. The Śaivite Āgamas include a standard list of twenty-eight Āgamas which begins with the *Kāmika Āgama*, and to each of which are attached one or more Upa-Āgamas or ancillary Āgamas.[14] These texts are most commonly used in the Śaiva Siddhānta in the South. Kashmir Śaivism in the North, on the other hand, boasts a famous subtradition, called the Non-Dual Śaivism of Kashmir,[15] which uses mostly another set of Āgamas, such as the *Mālinī-vijaya, Vijñāna- Bhairava*, and *Rudra-Yāmala.*[16] Also associated with this tradition is a galaxy of great Saints, headed by Vasugupta (9th cent. CE) and Abhinavagupta (fl. 1000 CE). And finally the Āgamic literature in a wider sense also contains the Tantric and Śākta literature proper, such as the Northern Śaivite Tantras (e.g., the *Sarvajñānottara* Tantra) and other groups.[17] As said before, there seems to be a strong connection between the Upaniṣadic Wisdom and some of the Pañcarātra texts. But as one moves to the Śaivite and other Āgamic literatures, the connection becomes much weaker.

***Bhakti* Literatures.** Historically the next important development are the many high level medieval *bhakti* (love of and devotion to God) literatures in the vernacular languages[18] mentioned earlier (above, sec. 1). These include the hymns of the Tamil Āḻvārs (Nammāḻvār) and the Śaivite Nāyaṉārs (Appar, Manikarvacakar), the compositions of the great Marathi Saints (Jñāneśvar, Nāmdev, Eknath, Tukārām), the Hindi Sant Tradition (Kabir, the *Guru Granth*, Dādu, Malukadas, Charandas), the Kṛṣṇa and Rāma Bhakti Traditions (Jaideva, Mirabai), the Bengali Caitanya Tradition (which includes the Hare Krishna movement), and others. In virtually everyone of these literatures the Upaniṣadic teachings form an all-pervasive substratum, if not a basis. We have here a state of affairs that has no parallel in the West. Supreme Wisdom, which can be taken as basically nontheistic and as an independent Wisdom Tradition (not dependent on the Vedas), appears fused with highest levels of *bhakti* (devotion to and Love of God), and with highest levels of God realization. It is as if a St. Bernard or St. Francis of Assissi was at the same time also a Buddha or Lao Tsu. In other words, the Upaniṣadic Knowledge was part of the experience of all the great *bhakti* Saints, and the Upaniṣadic Ātman and Brahman form part of the theology, system of stages, etc. of all the schools and sects which they founded.

Vedānta. The most direct continuation of the Upaniṣadic tradition, however, are not the *bhakti* movements or the Epic-Purāṇic Tradition, but Vedānta. Vedānta means literally "the end of the Vedas", *Veda* + *anta*, both in the sense of "the final portion" and "the culmination or goal" of the Vedas. As such it refers to a philosophy based on the Upaniṣads together with spiritual practice.[19] As philosophy, Vedānta operates with ontological, epistemological and metaphysical categories and frameworks, somewhat like Western philosophy. But unlike Western philosophy, it is based on realization. Its basic concepts and frameworks originate from teachers who are Saints or realized or enlightened beings, and are primarily intended to be channels in which true realization can arise and flow. In other words they are subordinate to the goal of attaining realization or union with the Reality, and ultimately do not really have an independent significance of their own. In these respects, therefore, Vedānta philosophy is more comparable to, say, Neo-Platonism, which was also based on and aimed at higher levels of gnosis, than to modern Western philosophy.

In popular usage, the term Vedānta is almost synonymous with Advaita Vedānta, a sub-tradition within Vedānta that has attained such eminence that it tends to overshadow all the rest. Advaita Vedānta as a tradition (with *guru*-disciple succession and texts) was established by Śaṁkara (also called Śaṁkarācārya or Śaṁkarabhagavatpāda, in English sometimes Shankara, ca. 700 CE) and Gauḍapāda (ca. 500 CE), two great Saints and super intellects, and flourished particularly a few centuries following Śaṁkara. It teaches that all is Ātman/Brahman, and that the world and the ordinary self have no fundamental reality (*advaita* is derived from *a + dvi*, "no second" or non-dual, i.e. there is only the formless, distinctionless Reality, Brahman). Important concepts used to explain how it is that we see a world of objects etc. are *adhyāsa*, "superimposition", *māyā*, "(power of) illusion", and *a-vidyā*, "non-knowing, nescience". The world is a superimposition on the Self, just as in the dark, a rope lying on the ground may be perceived as a snake (the snake is superimposed on the rope). The illusory appearance, *avabhāsa*, of the snake, or the world, is due to *māyā*, which is caused by nescience, *a-vidyā*.

Advaita Vedānta is generally regarded as one of the glories in the field of world philosophies.[20] Quite a few of its philosophical texts and manuals have transcendental power because of the force of realization. It is often used as a frame of reference or language by traditional scholars who write from a point of view of *Philosophia Perennis* or Unity of Religions. Fritjof Schuon for instance extols it as "the most direct possible expression of gnosis".[21] Vedānta "appears among explicit doctrines [of the religions of the world] as one of the most direct formulations possible of what makes the very essence of our spiritual reality.[22] "The Vedānta contained in the Upaniṣads, then formulated in the *Brahma Sūtra*, and finally commented and explained by [Śaṁkara], is an invaluable key for discovering the deepest meaning of all the religious doctrines, and for realizing that the *sanātana dharma* [the eternal teaching and true path] secretly penetrates all the forms of traditional spirituality".[23] While Advaita Vedānta thus expresses, as Schuon says, a universal aspect in world religions and philosophies, in India it is also essentially a religious tradition, led by great monastic organizations.[24] It is also sustained by a sizeable body of high-powered Scriptures, including (besides the Upaniṣads) and the *Gītā*) the vast and awesome *Yoga Vāsiṣṭha*, some of the later Upaniṣads (the *Vedānta* and the *Sāmānya Vedānta Upaniṣads*, different from the "classical" Upaniṣads with which we are concerned in this book), and isolated texts like the *Aṣṭāvakra Gītā*.

Vedānta must have existed already two or three centuries BCE as part of an effort by the Brahmin community to systematize and distill the philosophical and spiritual principles implicit in the Upaniṣadic teachings. But it only became a well-defined philosophical-religious system with the appearance of the *Brahma Sūtra of Bādarāyaṇa*[25] (abbreviated *BraSū*), which summarized the existing results in that direction and put them into an overall framework. The *Brahma Sūtra* consists of a sequence of about 450 telegraphic style phrases that serve as mnemonics for the underlying argument (*sūtra* = string). It dates from 200-450 CE, although it incorporates much material that is considerably older. In roughly the same period (200-400 CE), other philosophical systems developed Sūtras which likewise became the source documents for their respective philosophies, and this led in later times to a conception of Indian philosophy as consisting of the six *darśanas*, "views" (cf. Table 1.1). Around 700 CE, Śaṁkara wrote an extraordinary commentary on the *Brahma Sūtra*, called *Śārīrakabhāṣya*,[27] which established Advaita Vedānta as a well-defined, highly visible sub-system within Vedānta. Later there arose other subtraditions within Vedānta, usually basing themselves likewise on new commentaries on the *Brahma Sūtra*. Thus Rāmānuja, the founder of Śrī-Vaiṣṇavism (ca. 1100 CE), established Viśiṣṭādvaita Vedānta with a Commentary called *Śrī-bhāṣya*; Madhva, a great scholar Saint and founder of the Madhva-Sampradāya (Madhva sect) (ca. 1250 CE), established Dvaita (dualistic) Vedānta, writing both a commentary and other works on the *Brahma Sūtra*; and so on.[28]

TABLE 1.1

The Six Darśaṇas, and Dating of Oldest Material in their Sūtras[26]

Vedānta:

Brahma Sūtra of Bādarāyaṇa (500-200 BCE)

Mīmāṁsā:

Mīmāṁsā Sūtra of Jaimini (400-200 BCE)

Sāṁkhya:

(founded by Kapila) *Kārikās* of Īśvarakṛṣṇa (ca. 400 CE)

Yoga-philosophy:

Yoga Sūtra of Patañjali (100 BCE-CE)

Vaiśeṣika:

Vaiśeṣika Sūtra of Kaṇāda (500 BCE)

Nyāya:

Nyāya Sūtra of Gautama (100 CE)

The Upaniṣads and the Indian Mind. So far we have seen that the Upaniṣadic wisdom affected and was embodied in different classes of Hindu spiritual literature in different ways and to different degrees. The Epics depict again and again how an individual with the awareness of the Infinite in him or her acts with righteousness in the world. In the popular *bhakti* literatures, Ātman/Brahman forms the foundational framework of the soul's relationship to God while it is on the path to Him. Here we find all kinds of ways in which the soul commingles with and becomes absorbed in Love and worship, and in Divine Form, Divine Action, and the Formless Infinite. And in Vedānta the Upaniṣadic Infinite is carried into the intellectual sphere, suffusing and controlling keen formulations and arguments to explain how a world bound as mind and matter can exist within or as an all-comprehensive Infinite. All this gives an idea of the depth and pervasiveness of the Upaniṣads in the Hindu Tradition. But the real influence of the Upaniṣads has been on the Indian Mind—on the consciousness and ways of thinking of the common man. In some sense the Upaniṣadic teachings on Self and on Brahman have become part of the way the average person in India views him/herself and the world. They have become part of the Indian consciousness. In a classical study of the Indian Mind, H. Nakamura's *Ways of Thinking of Eastern Peoples* (1956, 1964), almost all the major characteristics of the Indian way of thinking enumerated in the chapter headings, such as "The Concept of the Unity of all Things", "The Static Quality of Universality", "The Primacy of the Universal Self over the Individual Self", and "Subservience to Universals", are already exemplified in strong and clear forms in the Upaniṣads. Since Nakamura's book, the nature of the Indian concept of self and the resulting world view have become an object of study in anthropology,[29] but the conclusion still holds.

Yoga. So far our survey has focussed on classes of texts. But there are in Hindu tradition also other strands which have a special connection with the Upaniṣads. The first of these is Yoga, a term generally denoting certain powerful mental-physical disciplines (a "pan-Indian corpus of spiritual techniques"[30]) leading to supernormal powers, higher inner states, and Union with the Supreme or Realization,

Enlightenment. Yoga has been an independent, extremely powerful element in Indian tradition throughout history.[31] Already highly developed in Harappan civilization (mature phase, 2700-2100 BCE),[32] it has affected all the higher streams of spirituality in India and has a large literature.[33] Two aspects of Yoga must be distinguished: (1) yogic-type phenomena or experience, and (2) Yoga as a systematic path of discipline or practice to attain supernormal power, supernormal states, or higher spiritual levels. References to the former occur already in the Vedas, the Vedic Mantra collections.[34] The early Upaniṣads for the first time hint at Yoga as a path or an essential aid on the path to Ātman/Brahman. But the first explicit texts to this effect appear only in the later *Kaṭha* and *Śvetāśvatara Upaniṣads* and in the *Mahābhārata.*[35] The classical text on Yoga, the *Yoga Sūtra* of Patañjali, is still later, ca. 200-400 CE, although it is thought to incorporate materials going back to 200 BCE.

Generally speaking, high level yogic phenomena play a role in the more advanced stages of many spiritual paths the world over. This is sometimes explicitly mentioned in Scripture and may be verified by studying the lives of various Christian or Islamic Saints. Devotion practiced "twenty-four hours a day" represents a kind of yogic training. *Jñāna*-type practice such as abiding in the Self, or "disregarding things of the world, and not mentally dwelling on any thing", as taught in Vedānta and some forms of Buddhism, is equally a kind of yogic training. A path to the Infinite—God, Liberation, Enlightenment, whatever—will be effective only if one devotes one's whole self, body, mind, and life to it, and in that case, yogic-type inner discipline, concentration and experience are likely to play a role at various stages. It is in this sense that Yoga has a universal significance and plays a role even in the oldest Upaniṣads. One cannot discuss the deeper stages of the Upaniṣadic *vidyās* (higher inner paths) without facing more deeply the whole question of the general significance and role of Yoga. But in this area it is not so easy to maintain a correct overall perspective and also be correct in details.

***Saṁnyāsa*, Renunciation and Hermit Life or Itinerant Mendicancy.** A second strand characteristic of Hindu tradition, comparable in importance to Yoga and likewise intimately connected with the Upaniṣads, is *saṁnyāsa*, i.e. renunciation (turning away from the attractions and fears evoked by the things of the world) and leading the life of a hermit or homeless mendicant. *Saṁnyāsa* has been honored and institutionalized in India throughout history in various forms, making it a basic feature of Indian society.[36] The census of 1901, for example, lists almost 5 million religious mendicants out of a total population of some 250 million. Even today, *sādhus* in orange robes and ascetics of every description may be seen on roads, near temples, in ashrams, etc. though not all of these are necessarily genuine religious aspirants.[37] On the one hand *saṁnyāsa* is connected with the fundamental principle that to the extent to which there is true inner renunciation of the world and its importance, there arises in the self the Infinite. On the other hand, however, the widespread practice of *saṁnyāsa* in India, and its deep-seated acceptance as a basic ingredient of the very fabric of society, must be counted as a major spiritual phenomenon in its own right—a manifestation *sui generis* of the Infinite at the level of history and society. In the West, *saṁnyāsa* is exemplified by Jesus, who also enjoined it on his disciples. But it rarely became a fully accepted social institution. We may recall the difficulties which St. Francis of Assissi had when he tried to practice itinerant mendicancy in Italy. It should be mentioned that *saṁnyāsa* has its own scriptural literature, the small collection of *Saṁnyāsa Upaniṣads*,[38] and isolated works like the *Avadhūta Gītā*, which is perhaps a Nātha Yogi text.

Modern Great Saints and Divine Manifestations. A last important point in this survey of the Upaniṣads and Hindu Tradition is that in the last two centuries or so there have appeared in India some of the very greatest spiritual personalities of modern times, and that all of these have upheld the Upaniṣadic Knowledge and given it a very high place in their own teaching. I am thinking here of figures like Swaminarayan (1780-1832?), Sri Ramakrishna Paramahamsa (1836-1886), Sri Ramana Maharshi (1879-1950), Sree Ananda Mayee Ma (1895-1984), and Sri Sathya Sai Baba (1926-). The lives of these individuals, and the impact which they had on the people around them, have been documented and described in an extensive literature by both devotees and outsiders, and there is no doubt about the Divinity manifested. All of them used the language of the Upaniṣads in their own higher teachings.[39] And beginning with Ramakrishna, all of them taught and embodied in their life the Unity of Religions, and explicitly related essential inner religious practice, such as can be identified in all religions, to Ātman/Brahman and the Upaniṣadic Supreme Wisdom. These facts give the Upaniṣads today a vitality and importance which they have not had for centuries, if not millenia.

Great Tradition vs. Little Tradition. Finally, it should be emphasized that we have been talking in this section about Hinduism only at the level of its higher teachings and spiritual practice. This represents of course only one aspect of the total phenomenon of Hinduism and the Hindu tradition. But it is one which, like a single, large and powerful current, pervades the whole mass of sectarian, regional, and tribal forms of religious practice and experience and the multitude of social-religious forms that one sees in India today. Western anthropology, which has been attempting to get a larger understanding of Hinduism as a whole, has acknowledged such a single Higher Current by its concept of the "Great Tradition". "The Great Tradition, and its 'philosophical-theological themes'. . . —the notions of Brahman, Ātman, Saṁsāra, Karma, and Mokṣa—act as a binding force that hold together the disparate elements" of Hinduism in its multitude of forms.[40] The "Great Tradition" contrasts with the "Little Tradition", essentially regional and local forms of religion, as well as the tribal religions. But "Little Tradition and Great Tradition are bound together in one vast devotional, ethical, ritualistic, artistic, esthetic Body of Tradition."[41] This Body of Tradition in turn is inextricably connected with caste and occupation. There is considerable truth to the statement that "in India, followers of one teacher and, *mutatis mutandis*, of his doctrine, tend to become castes (*jātis*), i.e., endogamous social units".[42] Indian society today may be regarded as made up of several scores or a few hundred recognized "communities", ranging from a few thousand to several million members each, and defined by a combination of caste, range of occupations, religious history and/or sectarian affiliation, and marriage pattern.[43] Hinduism as a religion is in some sense inseparable from this whole social structuring and way of life.

3. Vedic Literature and its Tradition

So far we have been looking at the Upaniṣads in the context of the whole Hindu tradition. But recall that the Upaniṣads are part of the Vedic literature, specifically the literature of Brāhmaṇism. In the present section, we give a brief outline of Vedic literature.[44] The main aim will be to introduce some of the more important extant texts (or classes of texts). The next section will then deal with the historical, social and religious context.

The term "Vedic literature" refers to the sacred literature of Vedic and Brāhmaṇical religion (the Vedic literature proper), plus some ancillary literature called the *Vedāṅga(s)* or "limbs of the Veda(s)",

Veda + *aṅgas*. The Vedic literature proper is considered *śruti*, literally "[what is] heard", i.e., something that arises from beyond human beings and is merely heard by them. It is divided into four parts, namely the *Ṛg* (often written *Rig*), *Sāma, Yajur* and *Atharva Veda,* each considered a "[complete higher] knowledge", Skt. *Veda*. The Vedāṅgas on the other hand are texts dealing with things like phonetics, grammar and astronomy which were considered aids in the study of the Vedas. The Vedāṅgas generally date from post-Brāhmaṇical (post 500 BCE) times, but much of the content goes back to the Brāhmaṇical period.

The Vedas or Veda Saṁhitās. All the four Vedas contain two types of material, *mantras* and *brāhmaṇas*. The *mantras* are metrical stanzas which are chanted, sung, or recited in a special way, while the *brāhmaṇas* are paragraph-sized or longer texts in prose. Most of the mantras are invocations, praises, or prayers to deities, and many either explicitly refer to ritual or imply some use in ritual. By ca. 1000 BCE, the mantras were collected into books called *saṁhitās*. Thus there is the *Ṛg Veda Saṁhitā*, several *Yajur Veda Saṁhitās*, two versions of the *Sāma Veda Saṁhitā*, and two versions of the *Atharva Veda Saṁhitā*. In Western scholarship these Veda Saṁhitās are usually also called Vedas; thus "the Ṛg Veda" means "the *Ṛgveda Saṁhitā*" etc. We follow this usage but sometimes add "Saṁhitā" for clarity.

The oldest, largest, and most important of the Saṁhitās is the *Ṛg Veda*. In its present form it consists of 1027 hymns (*sūktas*) arranged in 10 books (*maṇḍalas*), totalling about 10,500 verses (the *mantras* mentioned earlier). At 10 verses per page, this means 1000 pages of print. Philologically and historically the *Ṛg Veda* represents both the oldest portion of the Vedic literature and the primary initial mantra collection. The other three Saṁhitās show a later stage of language development. While the *Ṛg Veda* still represents the Vedic Religion in its pure form, in the following period of Brāhmaṇism all four of the Veda Saṁhitās served as manuals for different classes of priests involved in the public solemn (*śrauta*) sacrifices. The *Ṛg Vedic mantras* (or *ṛcs* or *ṛks*) were recited (usually in prescribed sets) by the *hotṛ* priests and their associates. The *adhvaryus*, who performed most of the ritual actions, muttered the *Yajur Vedic* mantras or *yajus*. And the *udgātṛs* and other types of *Sāma Vedic* priests chanted the *sāmans*, mostly *ṛcs* set to fixed musical forms also called *sāmans*. The *Atharva Veda* became a generally recognized scripture only at the end or after the Brāhmaṇical period.[45] It was (or became) the domain of the *brahman* priests, the priests who supervised the whole sacrifice and were responsible for expiations in the case of mistakes.

Since the *Sāma Vedic* mantras are almost all taken from the *Ṛg Veda*, only the *Yajur* and *Atharva Veda Saṁhitās* represent independent mantra collections.[46] The best known *Yajur Vedic Saṁhitā* is the *Vājasaneyī Saṁhitā*, which makes up the "white" *(śukla) Yajur Veda*. The other major *Yajur Vedic Saṁhitās* (*Taittirīya*, etc., see table 1.2) are grouped together as black (*kṛṣṇa*) *Yajur Vedic Saṁhitās*. Unlike the *Vājasaneyī* and other Saṁhitās, the "black" *Yajur Veda* hymn collections have interspersed between the metrical (mantra) portions also large chunks of commentarial material which, however, is older than the texts called Brāhmaṇas (see below). Compared with the black *Yajur Vedic Saṁhitās*, therefore, the *Vājasaneyī Saṁhitās* (which probably came later) was *śukla*, white, pure, i.e., it represented a pure *saṁhitā* free from commentarial material, like the *Ṛg* and *Atharva Veda Saṁhitās*.

Vedic Schools and their Literature. The paragraph sized or larger *brāhmaṇas* mentioned earlier are prose passages which explain or give a rationale for specific aspects of ritual, particularly for the mantras that were used. They also provide sacred lore, spiritual insight and mystical and esoteric teaching. Passages of this kind, relating to the mantras and ritual duties of a particular class or priests (*hotṛs* etc.), and hence associated with a particular Saṁhitā, were collected into books called *Brāhmaṇas* (with a capital B). The Brāhmaṇas and the Saṁhitās to which they are attached were cultivated and passed on from one generation to the next in so-called Vedic schools or *śākhās*.[47] These schools had originally a local character[48] and membership in them was hereditary in Brahmin families. But in the course of time they increased in numbers, formed sub-schools, etc., and spread over all of India. Extant Saṁhitās and Brāhmaṇas may therefore be available in different recensions or greatly differing versions depending on the school in which they were cultivated (cf. table 1.2). For example, the *Vājasaneyī Saṁhitā* comes in two recensions which differ only very slightly from each other, that of the *Mādhyandina Śākhā* and that of the *Kāṇva Śākhā*. The *Śatapatha Brāhmaṇa*, or Brāhmaṇa of a hundred (*śata*) paths (*patha*), is the Brāhmaṇa of the *Vājasaneyī Saṁhitā*. Like the latter it also comes in a *Mādhyandina* and a *Kāṇva* recension. But only 90% or so of the material in each recension is found also in the other (usually in the same order). The *Vājasaneyī Saṁhitā* is named after the school (*śākhā*) of the Vājasaneyins, themselves named after a famous teacher, Yājñavalkya, whose patronymic was *Vājasaneyī*, "descendant of Vājasani". The Kāṇvas and Mādhyandinas were off-shoots of the Vājasaneyins:

TABLE 1.2
Summary of Śruti Literature[49]

	Schools	Saṁhitā	Brāhmaṇa	Āraṇyaka	Upaniṣad
Ṛg Veda	*Śākala*	*Ṛg*	*Aitareya*	*Aitareya*	*Aitareya*
	Bāṣkala		*Śāṅkhāyana*	*Śāṅkhāyana*	*Kauṣītaki*
Yajur Veda	*Kṛṣṇa* (Black):				
	Taittirīya	*Taittirīya*	*Taittirīya*	*Taittirīya*	*Taittirīya*
	Kāṭhaka	*Kāṭhaka*	*Kaṭha*	*Kaṭha*	*Kaṭha*
	Maitrāyaṇī	*Maitrāyaṇī*			*Maitrāyaṇī*
	Śukla (White):				
	Mādhyandina	*Vājasaneyī*	*Śatapatha*		*Bṛhadāraṇyaka*
	Kāṇva	*Vājasaneyī*			and *Īśa*
Sāma Veda	*Kauthuma*		*Pañcaviṁśa*		*Chāndogya*
	Rāṇāyanīya		*Ṣaḍviṁśa*		
		Sāma			
	Jaiminīya or *Talavakāra*		*Jaiminīya*	*Jaiminīya UpBr*	*Kena* or *Talavakāra*
Atharva Veda	*Śaunaka*	*Atharva*	*Gopatha*		*Muṇḍaka*,
	Paippalāda				*Māṇḍūkya*, etc.

At the end of or immediately following the Brāhmaṇical period individual schools also compiled so-called *Sūtras* which dealt in detail with the whens and hows of the rituals. These Sūtras complement and greatly extend the information on the rituals in the Brāhmaṇas and are classed as one of the six major Vedāṅgas, called (*kalpa-*) *Sūtra*.

Vedic Study. In the growth and development of the Vedic literature, and more generally in the shaping of the Brahmin culture to the point where it could be the backbone of Indian civilization for millennia, the nature of instruction in the Vedas played an essential role. As portrayed in the Sūtras immediately following the Brāhmaṇical period, Vedic study[50] was compulsory for sons of Brahmins, and normally began at ages seven or eight years. Acceptance by a teacher, beginning and end of a semester, holidays and other interruptions, and the end of Vedic study were all marked by suitable rituals, and even simple verbal exchanges, mode of sitting, etc. during instruction were regulated. Students (*brahmacārins*) lived with the teacher in his house, had to remain chaste, and were obligated every day to get wood for the fire, beg their meals in the village, sleep on the ground, and obey the teacher. Instruction was entirely oral, and was ultimately based on memorization of texts, mantras and incisive sentences such as one finds highlighted in the Brāhmaṇas and Sūtras. (The whole Vedic literature was only assembled into books for purposes of such instruction.) As regards mantras, the teacher would say and the student would repeat the mantra word for word, and aids were used such as a word-for-word analysis (*pada-pāṭha*) in which individual words appeared in unmodified form. There are indications that the learning of mantras was not only verbal, but involved the whole body, i.e. had a kinesthetic or action component. If so, this would mean that the Vedic corpus was incorporated into the mind-body complex much more deeply than it would be with mere memorization of words. One line of evidence on this point relates to the tones of the Vedic tonal system. In modern *Ṛg Veda* instruction among the Nambudiri Ṛg Vedins in Kerala, for example, the teacher tilts the student's head sharply 90° sideways when the word he is uttering has a "mixed tone" or *svarita*. Other "head points" are used for the other two tones.[51] This practice is said to be "intended for teaching purposes only".[52] But W.S. Allen notes that in the ancient Vedic texts on phonetics (the *prātiśākhyas*), the Vedic tones are described in terms that at the same time also describe the hand movements that accompany the recitation of the Vedic texts.[53] In other words, the present-day practice of headpoints, the gestures[54] mentioned by the *Ṛk* and *Vājasaneyī Prātiśākhyas,* and the analytical descriptions of tones used by these *Prātiśākhyas* all three depend on the same acoustic-kinesthethic mind-body system.[55] Since the Prātiśākhyas are quite old (one estimate is 250-200 BCE),[56] this tonal-kinesthetic complex may have conceivably already been employed for some kind of whole body or action learning and recitation in the Brāhmaṇical period. Obviously, learning and ritual behaviour that has such a whole body or action component is likely to give to an individual and the tradition much greater stability than learning and performance based only on purely verbal (and visual) modes. It is also likely to provide a more profound basis for deeper meanings to arise.[57]

Brāhmaṇas, Āraṇyakas, Upaniṣads. In English the Brāhmaṇas might add up to 25 or 30 volumes of print, but only about two-third of the available material has been translated. At any rate, the Brāhmaṇas make up the bulk of what is generally called the "Brāhmaṇa literature". The small remainder consists of the *Āraṇyakas* and the *Upaniṣads*. Texts of both of these types are often found attached to the end of Brāhmaṇas, but may also be handed down as separate works. The Āraṇyakas are similar to Brāhmaṇas in style, diction, etc. But they tend to deal more with recondite, inner or esoteric aspects of rituals. They also discuss only a very limited range of Vedic mantras and sacrifices.[58] Only a handful of Āraṇyakas are extant, all of them except *Taittirīya Āraṇyaka* available in English translation. The Upaniṣads contain some Āraṇyaka-like material. But they go beyond the Āraṇyakas in various ways and bring Supreme Wisdom teachings in universal formulations. It should be noted that in Indian tradition about 250 or 300 texts carry the title Upaniṣads.[59] But only a dozen or so of these are part of the Vedic literature. The rest were composed in later times. Of the Vedic Upaniṣads, again, about half are parts of Brāhmaṇas or Āraṇyakas. The others are somewhat younger, but are traditionally attributed to certain Vedic schools.

Forest Study. *Araṇya* means "forest," and "the Āraṇyakas . . . were to be imparted to and studied by advanced students in the solitude of the forest because their contents were too 'sacred,' too secret and esoteric, too uncanny and dangerous to be communicated and learnt in the villages"[60] (J. Gonda). Such special "forest study" was different from normal Vedic study.[61] According to the *Śāṅkhāyana Gṛhya Sūtra* for example, before any "forest study" could be undertaken, the student had to keep a special vow or observance (*vrata*) for one year (either a *śākvara* or a *vrātika* or an *aupaniṣada* ["Upaniṣadic"] *vrata*, depending on the type of material to be covered).[62] Before beginning the study, the teacher first asked whether the student had kept the observance.[63] Then he wrapped a fresh garment around the student's head (three times from left to right) and instructed him to fast for three days in a holy place without performing his normal daily duties (getting and putting wood on the fire etc.). When the student left the village to meet the teacher outside, he had to avoid certain disturbing sights. The place of instruction[64] in the forest had to be clean and pure and was marked off by pouring water in a semicircle that screened it against the village and was open toward the forest. Instruction began at sunrise with various prescribed mantras. At the end there were again mantras and water oblations. Other Sūtras give a similar picture. Some even speak of an in-between initiation, or *antara-dīkṣā*, for forest study which annulled for a time the initiation into the status of a Vedic Student (*upanāyana*).[65] The distinction between normal Vedic study and forest-study was also emphasized by laying down that days that immediately followed Veda study should not be used for forest study.[66] At any rate, with this general conception of "forest study", the import of Gonda's characterization of Āraṇyakas above is clear: Āraṇyakas are what is studied in "forest study". This perspective was first set forth by H. Oldenberg in some remarkable papers in 1915/16.[67]

Oldenberg's thesis needs to be carefully considered, because in the Sūtras, texts called *upaniṣads* are treated as subjects of "forest study" on a par with other Āraṇyaka-type texts. The *Śāṅkhāyana Gṛhya Sūtra* for example, when specifying the mantras to be said at the beginning of instruction at sunrise, names the *mahāvratam* (*ŚaṅkhĀr* I-II), the *Śakvari* mantras (not found in *Śāṅkhāyana Āraṇyaka* but in the closely related *Aitareya Āraṇyaka)*, the *upaniṣads* (*ŚāṅkhĀr* III-VI, together known as *Kauṣītaki Upaniṣad*), the *saṁhitās* (mystical teachings of a certain type, *ŚāṅkhĀr* VII-VIII) and the *mantha* rite (*ŚāṅkhĀr* XI).[68] The general term for all these types of texts is *rahasya*, "secret teaching".[69] So at the time of the *Śāṅkhāyana Gṛhya Sūtra*, which is later than the Āraṇyakas and the old Upaniṣads, the bulk of *Śāṅkhāyana Āraṇyaka* (including *Kauṣītaki Upaniṣad*) was the subject of "forest study". A similar picture emerges from *Āśvalāyana Gṛhya Sūtra* in regard to *Aitareya Āraṇyaka* and the Upaniṣad in that Āraṇyaka, viz. Aitareya Upaniṣad.[70]

But it seems doubtful that most of the material in what are now called "Āraṇyakas" and "Upaniṣads" was the subject of "forest study".[71] It is not clear that the Sūtras specifically implicate the majority of the Āraṇyaka and old Upaniṣadic material (incl. *Jaiminīya Upaniṣad Brāhmaṇa* and *Bṛhadāraṇyaka* and *Chāndogya Upaniṣads*) for this purpose. Even if this was the case, there would still remain the fact that quite a bit of that material has precursors or more or less close parallels in the Brāhmaṇas which would be part of normal Vedic study. If the Brāhmaṇa material was part of normal Vedic study, why should the relatively similar Āraṇyaka or Upaniṣadic material be singled out for instruction in the forest? Oldenberg motivated the assignment to forest study in a number of specific cases by the "terrifying", "magical", "occult", or recondite and otherwise secret character of the material. But his examples are not typical of the majority of the Āraṇyakas and old Upaniṣads, whose contents are often described as "speculative".

It seems therefore at present to be more prudent not to treat being subject to 'forest study'" as a clear-cut "emic" concept that can be uniformly and categorically applied to groups of texts as we know them. It seems quite possible that the same text was taught as part of normal Vedic study by some teachers and in forest study by others. And it seems quite possible that as a result of the practice of specific individual teachers or a local tradition of teachers, different texts were grouped into larger complexes in different ways, some to be taught in "forest study" and some to be covered in normal Vedic study.

The Chronology Brāhmaṇa-Āraṇyaka-Upaniṣad. Looking over the traditional progression of Brāhmaṇa-Āraṇyaka-Upanisad, however, some general statements may be made. In Āraṇyaka-type texts, specific bodies of mantras or aspects of ritual or sacred lore began to become a stimulus to contemplate or somehow become more aware of the spiritual essence or higher meaning which they embodied—the reality which they gave rise to and became in the "inner I". Such preoccupation with mantras, etc. seems to acquire the same or even greater importance than using them in ritual, etc. In the Āraṇyakas therefore, thought and inner spiritual awareness started to separate subtler, deeper aspects from the context of ritual performance and myth with which they had been united up to then. This process was then carried further and brought to completion in the Upaniṣads. "There can . . . be no doubt that in the course of time the tendency was for the explanation contained in definitive portions of the Brāhmaṇas to develop into expositions of meta-ritualism, and then to grow independent of the ritual until the stage was reached where the name Āraṇyaka [as a type of teaching] was no longer applicable because the subject-matter has passed into that of an upaniṣad. At that stage the growth of speculation, as leading to the highest goal, had gradually resulted in the suppression of ritualism."[72] We would say: At that stage, i.e. in certain Upaniṣadic texts, inner awareness which had come to rest in the Highest Goal began to produce formulations which dealt with the Highest Goal directly, independent of ritual and sacred lore. The knowledge and attainment of the Highest Goal had been there from Vedic times. But in the Upaniṣads inner awareness, aided by major intellectual breakthroughs, arrived at a language in which the Highest Goal could be dealt with directly, independent of ritual and sacred lore.

Chronology Based on Linguistic Criteria. This completes our survey of Vedic texts. The traditional way of conceptualizing the chronology of the Vedic corpus is Saṁhitās—Brāhmaṇas —Āraṇyakas—Upaniṣads—Sūtras. But a more reliable indicator is the language of the texts—grammatical forms, etc. Following Witzel,[73] one can distinguish five "linguistically attested" levels:

1. *Ṛg Veda*;
2. Mantra texts (*Atharva Veda, Sāma Veda*, mantra portions of *Yajur Veda Saṁhitā, Ṛg Veda Khilas*);
3. Prose portions of *Yajur Veda Saṁhitās (Maitrāyaṇī Saṁhitā, Kāṭhaka Saṁhitā, Taittirīya Saṁhitā);*
4. Brāhmaṇas *(Aitareya Brāhmaṇa* etc., including the Āraṇyakas and the older Upaniṣads such as *Bṛhad-āraṇyaka* and *Chāndogya,* and the oldest Sūtras such as *Baudhāyana Śrauta Sūtra*); and
5. Sūtras.

We will follow this scheme when necessary.

4. Historical Context

As we have seen, the Vedic literature comprises a considerable body of texts. But the historical background of these documents, including their absolute chronology, is even in major outlines still rather problematic. Different sections of scholarship which have not been communicating much with one another paint different pictures.

According to the standard historical account in the early part of this century,[74] the *Ṛg Veda Saṁhitā* represents the religion of the Aryan tribes soon after they had entered the Indus and Ganges valleys from the East, beginning ca. 1500 BCE. This Vedic or Aryan Religion was a religion of foreigners on Indian soil, imported from their Aryan homeland. The Ṛg *Vedic* hymns are thought to have been composed over a period of several centuries, the Vedic Period, ca. 1500-1000 BCE, the conquests of cities mentioned in them being interpreted as references to remnants of post-Harappan civilization. By the end of the Vedic period the system of four castes was established, and the subequent Post-Vedic Period (1000-600 BCE) saw the rise of the Brāhmaṇa literature and the elaboration of the original Vedic ritual into *Classic Vedic* (i.e. Brāhmaṇical) ritual.[75]

Linguistic Picture. The preceding account is part of a larger picture developed by Indo-European and Indo-Iranian scholarship.[76]

According to this, the Vedic religion is actually a development of a still earlier Indo-Iranian religion that prevailed among the Indo-Iranian tribes long before their migrations in the second millenium BCE. The language of the *Ṛg Veda Saṁhitā* is Vedic or Vedic Sanskrit, which later (ca. 500 BCE) developed into classical Sanskrit. Vedic Sanskrit is closely related to Avestan (or Avestic), the language of the Iranian *Avesta*. The *Avesta* is the scripture of Zoroastrianism, one of the great religions of the West, founded by Zarathustra. The linguistically most archaic portion of the *Avesta*, a set of hymns called the *Gāthās* of Zarathustra, are linguistically so close to the language in the *Ṛg Veda* that "it is quite possible to find verses in . . . [the *Gāthās*], which simply by phonetic substitutions according to established laws can be turned into intelligible [Vedic] Sanskrit".[77] Both Vedic and Avestic are hieratic forms of language derived almost directly from (Proto-) Indo-European (= Proto-Aryan or Indo-Germanic). This is the reconstructed root language of the Indo-European family of languages, which includes Hittite, Sanskrit, Greek, Latin, Old Gothic, as well as modern French, German, and English. (Proto-) Indo-European is thought to have been spoken by the Aryan tribes in their original homeland in the steppes of what is today Soviet Central Asia. At that time these tribes still formed a single group, with a common religion, the Indo-Iranian religion (basically a hypothetical construction consisting of a number of characteristic features which the *Avesta* and the *Ṛg Veda* have in common).[78] "At some point in the third millennium BC, there occurred a split in the group that resulted in the division between Indo-Aryans and Iranians. Around 1500 BC both groups began to move down out of the steppes into various areas of ancient civilizations . . . The Indo-Aryans finally settled both in the northwestern part of India (the Punjab) and in Anatolia; the Iranians settled in Iran, that is . . . modern Iran, Afghanistan, and parts of Soviet Central Asia."[79] The Vedic religion is thus the religion of those Indo-Aryans that settled in Northern India. The religion of the other migratory branch, the Iranians, is called Old Iranian Religion. It too has been reconstructed, mostly on the basis of the *Avesta*, and forms the matrix within which arose the original religion of Zarathustra, probably in the second millennium BCE.[80]

Archaeology. In the last decade or so some consensus seems to be emerging as far as the archaeological identification of the Proto-Indo-European community is concerned.[81] But in spite of intensive efforts, it has so far not proved possible to correlate the culture described in the *Ṛg Veda* unambiguously with archaeological data.[82] Among Indologists, the most extensive and detailed attempts to interpret archaeological data have been made by A. Parpola and M. Witzel.[83]

Indian Perspectives. Traditional Indian scholarship and learning, of course, has a quite different orientation. Orthodox Hinduism for example holds that the Vedas are eternal, not man-made, and that they are the foundation of the world. Such views (and analogous ideas in Western traditions) have their own validity and do not always or necessarily have to be in conflict with scientific-historical reconstructions. (It is perfectly consistent to have a deep understanding of St. John's Logos or the Vedic *Vāc*, "Speech", like Bhartṛhari or Coomaraswamy, and have no quarrel with scientific accounts of the origins of the world or historical accounts of the origin of a sacred text). On the other hand, there have also been two thrusts by traditional Indian scholarship to use Western type historical reasoning to argue for a greater antiquity of the *Ṛg Veda* than recognized by Western philological scholarship.

The first is based on certain passages in the Vedic literature which contain astronomical information, and was developed independently by H. Jacobi, one of the great figures in Indology around the turn of the century, and B.R. Tilak, an Indian savant. One of Jacobi's arguments, for example,[84] is based on the fact that in the ancient Hindu wedding ritual, as described in the *Śāṅkhāyana* and *Āśvalāyana Gṛhya Sūtras* (dated ca. 400 BCE), the pole star symbolizes firmness in marriage and is called *dhruva*, "immovable" or "standing fixed".[85] Jacobi argues that this implies that already centuries before that time there was a star of considerable magnitude near the north pole that was so close to the pole that it was considered standing fixed (while all other stars revolved around it during the night). From astronomical calculations, however, it is known that around 400 BCE no such star existed. The only stars of any magnitude at that time were $4\frac{1}{2}^\circ$ and 6° respectively from the pole. Since in India the north pole is only a few degrees over the horizon, the nightly revolution of such a star around the pole would be very obvious (remember the diameter of the moon is about $\frac{1}{2}^\circ$), and the star would not be called *dhruva*. It turns out that the only times since 5000 BCE when there existed a star of some magnitude close enough to the north pole to be considered fixed were ca. 2780 BCE and today. Hence this feature of the wedding ritual of the *Gṛhya Sūtras* should go back to 2780 BCE. Jacobi's and Tilak's arguments provoked heated discussion. The Vedic passages on which the arguments depend are not entirely unambiguous. But there seems to be no satisfactory resolution of the issues from a combined modern philological-historical-astronomical point of view.[86]

A second interesting line of research has been to attempt to estimate the age of the Vedas on the basis of statements and information in the Epics and Purāṇas. Results, however, depend greatly on how one handles the mass of conflicting information (what one considers more reliable than what). One factor is how one evaluates the Epics and Purāṇas in regard to the possibility of containing historically usable information (to what extent they may be embodying older traditions, and whether they may be getting valid information by supernatural experience). Western positions on these issues usually take a rather hard line, but without much substantive empirical basis. There is little hard research on what happens when information is handed down over many generations, and Western scholars have little experience with supernatural transmission of information in *bona fide* spiritual contexts (as opposed to transmission by paranormal, i.e. yogic, psychic, or occult means). An important figure in the area of historical interpretation of the Epics and Purāṇas was F.E. Pargiter, a great scholar in the early part of the century who had an astonishing ability to see order in the mass of Purāṇic data. Reading him is something of a shock—the incredible Purāṇic Mind assumes a certain specific form![87] Pargiter argues that the Aryans came to India ca. 2050 BCE. As recently as 1988 an independent Western observer, K. Klostermaier, judged his case to be "quite strong".[88] Again, in the last few decades much effort has been expended to determine the date of the great Mahābhārata war on the basis of dynastic lists and astronomical statements.[89] Most of the dates arrived at this way fall around 3100 BCE, 1400 BCE, and 900 BCE. The first two would tend to push the age of the early Ṛg Vedic hymns back further than 1500 BCE. Orthodox Hindu tradition relates the war to the beginning of the *Kali-yuga*, the fourth epoch (*yuga*) of the world cycle (*kalpa*) in which we are currently living. The traditional date for the begin of the Kaliyuga, 3101 BCE, is given in the Indian astronomical tradition, where it is first found in Āryabhaṭṭa (ca. 450 CE). But some evidence for the antiquity of the 3100 BCE timeframe is information by the Greek historian Megasthenes (300 BCE) to the effect that at that time (300 BCE) the Indians believed that 138 generations of kings had passed since the time of Kṛṣṇa.[90] Counting an average of 20 years per reign, this gives a date of 2760 + 300 = 3060 BCE for Lord Kṛṣṇa.

5. The Problem of a Deeper Understanding of the Vedic Literature

In trying to get an understanding of the Upaniṣadic texts, two aspects must be distinguished: understanding their spiritual import, and understanding them accurately as expressions within the framework and experience of Vedic and Brāhmaṇical religion. As presented in sec. 3, the Wisdom of the Upaniṣads developed out of some of the heart and soul of the Vedic and Brāhmaṇical Religion. The same Knowledge as in the Upaniṣads is already implicit in the Saṁhitās and Brāhmaṇas. But there it is fused with the particular religious forms of the times to a degree which makes it very difficult to pinpoint. In the Upaniṣads, however, it is given a distinctly modern form, in which it is much more generally accessible.

Even so, to get an accurate deeper understanding of the Upaniṣads is difficult. In the form in which we have them today, the Upaniṣads are basically made up of a mass of semi-independent pieces of text, unified in terms of content, and varying in length from a few sentences to 10 pages or so in translation.[91] Further, this mass of fragments is obviously the result of centuries of accumulation and development, and shows signs of phenomena like addition of glosses or comments to older texts, reformulation of well-known older texts by later teachers, and editing and rearrangement of smaller units. Because of its brevity, the detailed spiritual intent of a given piece can often only be determined with any degree of assurance by locating that piece in some larger context of Vedic and Brāhmaṇa Tradition. This in turn depends on a deeper spiritual understanding of the Vedas and Brāhmaṇas. This means that the two aspects mentioned at the beginning (the spiritual and the correct understanding of the Upaniṣadic texts in their Vedic and Brāhmaṇical context) are mutually interdependent and are both to some extent dependent on a deeper understanding of Vedic and Brāhmaṇa Religion and spiritual experience.

Apart from the Vedic literature, the other main source relevant for developing a deeper understanding of the Upaniṣads is the interpretation of the Upaniṣads in subsequent Tradition, primarily in Vedānta. Of course the different types of Vedānta all have their own sets of glasses with which they look at the Upaniṣads. But here there arises another difficulty. Vedānta has been studied in the West primarily as a philosophy in the Western sense of the term. But as a spiritual enterprise it is much less well-understood. This means that there are difficulties in correctly interpreting Vedāntic statements and evaluating their scope also. With this general background, we now survey various relevant classes of Vedic and Vedāntic literature with a view to the difficulties that arise when one tries to use them to get a deeper understanding of the Upaniṣads. We begin with the *Ṛg Veda*.

Understanding the *Ṛg Veda*. In many ways the Upaniṣads merely unfold something the foundations of which are already laid in the *Ṛg* and *Atharva Vedas*. But serious questions may be raised regarding whether a fully satisfactory deeper understanding of these texts is available or has been attained. The *Ṛg Veda* has been intensively studied by western philological scholarship since the middle of the 19th century. The text has exerted a fascination over generations of scholars, and many of the great Western Sanskritists[92] have labored to elucidate it. Problems like unusual forms, unknown words, unclear syntax and difficulty in interpreting referents and allusions arise in one out of every two verses, although in this century enormous progress has been made and innumerable details have been clarified. The only complete modern translation available is that of F.K. Geldner, in German[93] (there are only selections in English).[94] When it comes to a deeper, larger understanding of the text, however, there are problems. "Fortunately the material [of the Saṁhitās] is abundant but seldom viewed with a unifying vision."[95] A straightforward translation like Geldner's makes a peculiar impression. The constant invocations and praises of the many gods, the endless praises of their attributes and deeds read like some kind of code.[96] One stands in awe at the relationship these seer-poets must have had with the Divine, but one cannot get a clear handle on the exact experience or consciousness involved. Much of western scholarly discussion of the *Ṛg Veda* is still in terms of "mythology",[97] which automatically works against getting a deeper understanding as inner experience. In spite of considerable intellectual and literary effort and sophistication, sometimes even brilliance, one keenly feels a fundamental non-penetration at a spiritual level, a kind of uniform wall.

This is not to say that there have been no efforts to deal with the problem. The late J. Gonda for example, one of the two or three most influential Western Vedic scholars of the last several decades, in his *The Vision of the Vedic Poets*,[98] made an important start. Gonda concentrated on the ubiquitous Ṛg-Vedic *dhī*, "vision, intuition", where "'vision' is the exceptional and supranormal faculty, proper to 'seers', of 'seeing', in the mind, things, causes, connections as they really are, the faculty of acquiring a sudden knowledge of the truth, of the functions of and influence of the divine powers, of man's relations to them etc. etc. It is this 'vision' which they attempt to give shape, to put into words, to develop into intelligible speech . . . ."[99] Discussing scores of occurrences of *dhī* and related terms as well as passages speaking of inner light, *jyotiḥ*, and of the heart, *hṛt*, the author makes many insightful points, but his work has not been taken further. A promising direction has recently been opened up by G. Elizarenkova, based on Russian work in pragmatic linguistics.[100] Elizarenkova argues convincingly that the phrase "worshipping the gods with a new song", which occurs often in the hymns, refers not so much to creation of new poetic content but to "engaging in an act of communication with the deity". The latter has connotations of a circular exchange, and involves a sense of a cyclic flow of time. While the poet-seer is addressing the deity always with a "new song", his song is at the same time identified with the "old song" in the idea that the deity should bless him now as it did before when it was praised with the old song. By this identification the old song (old blessing) in the past is made to anticipate the future or the future is treated as a repetition of the past. Elizarenkova goes on to show by examples how the hymns employ many literary devices typical of direct "acts of communication." The idea that the hymns represent "acts of communication" between the worshipper and the deity, backed as it is by modern type linguistic (or literary) analysis, has the potential to serve as a common ground between modern critical scholarship and traditional Hindu piety, which sees the *Ṛg Veda* as sacred, timeless revelation.

History of Views and Interpretation of the *Ṛg Veda*. In Indian tradition, some knowledge of the inner experience that accompanied the Ṛg Vedic Hymns can still be felt in the Brāhmaṇas, but seems then to have been largely lost by the time of the Nirukta,[101] commonly dated 600 BCE. In the Brāhmaṇas, e.g. in the *Śatapatha Brāhmaṇa,* all kinds of explanation of Vedic mantras may be given—"etymological, sacerdotal, historical or legendary, and metaphysical as well as physical"—but the tone is such that "the differences in such explanations were neither of principles nor of a vital nature. There was an essential unity behind them".[102] In other words, there was still somehow a shared silent understanding, a continuity with the original Vedic consciousness. But the Brāhmaṇas are not centered in that consciousness, and they are not focussed on maintaining it. Instead they are engaged in developing a different mode of living the Divine (different from the original Vedic consciousness), namely, living the Divine ritually. There is still some continuity with the original state, which is not commented on. But the creative energy is directed elsewhere. The *Nirukta*, attributed to the sage Yāska, is the only surviving examples of "etymology", *Nirukta*, one of the six Vedāṅgas. It is basically an effort to explain an ancient list of groups of Ṛg Vedic terms, the *Nighaṇṭu*, by interpreting Ṛg Vedic Mantras in which these terms occur. The *Nighaṇṭu* strikes one as rather enigmatic and seems to have served as a tool in interpreting the Ṛg Vedic texts.[103] In Yāska's time, this tool had become not understood, and the question of the meaning of the Mantras was a severe problem that was threatening the Brāhmaṇical tradition.[104] Later a tradition of commentaries on the Vedas arose, with Skandasvāmin (ca. 600 CE) and Sāyaṇa (14th cent. CE) as best known exponents.[105] But while providing a mass of detail on ritual aspects associated with individual hymns and on the etymology of words, this literature does not seem to be tapping any major new sources of spiritual insight. In modern times, finally, fresh, fundamental attempts to get at the original meaning and consciousness in the Ṛg Vedic hymns were made by Svāmī Dayānanda (1824-1883),[106] Sri Aurobindo (1872-1950),[107] and V.S. Agrawala (1904-1972).[108] The state of the Hindu tradition with respect to the Vedas is somewhat reminiscent of that of Judaism with respect to the revelation on Sinai. There is a memory or idea of Divine Events, of an encounter with the Divine of unfathomable proportions, which reverberates in the collective Jewish consciousness or soul for millennia. And a living understanding of these Events or whatever is forever enshrined in *Exodus*. But the subsequent Tradition cannot sustain the original understanding or state. Similarly with the Vedas. There is a memory or idea of a Divine State, of priesthood so in harmony with the Divine as to exceed comprehension. And remnants of the state of the Vedic Seers, the Ṛṣis, is ever present to the subsequent tradition as a body of sound-formation, a body of hymns. But the subsequent tradition does not or cannot maintain this state.[109]

The *Atharva Veda*. The *Ṛg Veda* is something like a large ocean of light which stands behind the entire remaining Vedic literature. But the *Atharva Veda* is more difficult to characterize. It has a reputation for magic and sorcery, and there is a Purāṇic statement that in its hymns there is both darkness and light.[110] But the *Atharva Veda* is also known as the *Brahma Veda*, the Veda that reveals and speaks the Brahman. Thus the Śaunaka recension (the recension mostly studied and translated by philological scholarship) contains about a score of awesome, high level mystical hymns expressing Brahman. And in the still uncharted portions of the Paippalāda recension, the amount of high level material is said to be still larger and more developed.[111] The *Atharva Veda* does seem to have a unity in terms of overall spirit and spiritual life, but no deeper sympathetic attempts to penetrate the text are available. The Veda is important for Upaniṣadic studies because it anticipates in its mystical hymns some of the most characteristic Upaniṣadic teachings (cf. below).

Understanding the Brāhmaṇas and Āraṇyakas. The Brāhmaṇas represent the immediate environment in which the Upaniṣads arose. Though deeply steeped in ritual (recall that their basic purpose is to explain the ritual and the mantras used in it), they are shot through and through with metaphysical, mystical, and esoteric passages and are everywhere breathing spiritual wisdom. There is no question that they are one of the most important early spiritual literatures extant. This is partly due to their volume, but also to the fact that they represent a culture and a world-view that are metaphysically completely integrated and permeated by the Universal Divine.

Apart from good translations, western-type scholarship has produced detailed descriptions of the major types of Vedic rituals. There are also influential studies on general issues such as the pre-scientific (rational) nature of Brāhmaṇa thought, the nature of the Vedic sacrifice, the role of the mantras in the sacrifice, the phenomenon of caste and hierarchy, etc.[112] But in-depth, sympathetic and empathic exposition of the essence and unity of Brāhmaṇa religious life and higher religious experience is lacking.[113]

The *Brahma Sūtra*. The first post-Upaniṣadic text that has a bearing on the interpretation of the Upaniṣads is the *Brahma Sūtra*[114] (cf. sec. 2 above). Many of the Sūtra's aphorisms argue that the import of various Upaniṣadic teachings is Brahman (e.g. *BraSū* I.2.13, "The [person] within [the eye, mentioned in several Upaniṣadic teachings, is Brahman,] because of appropriateness"). Others deal more generally with various principles relating to a rational philosophy and practice of the Upaniṣadic Ātman/Brahman, how the Upaniṣads should be read etc. So overall, the *Sūtra* is elaborating a unified philosophy of, and a philosophy of spiritual life aiming at, Ātman/Brahman.[115] It is sometimes held that the *Sūtra* is primarily a scholastic work, a product of intellectual scholarship without much of a deeper spiritual element. This is surely a mistake. Its singleness of focus on Brahman, its deep view of *upāsanā* (meditation), its basic outlook of regarding individual existence/experience as consisting only of self and limitations (senses, incl. mind, vital breaths, body and Karma—later called *upādhis*, "limiting adjuncts")[116]—all these are things that have a power and a sweep which can only be due to spiritual knowledge. At the same time the *Brahma Sūtra* has a keen intellectual spirit which helped it gain also the attention of philosophers outside of Vedānta.

According to modern scholarship the *Brahma Sūtra* in its present form dates from somewhere between 200 and 450 CE.[117] Like the Sūtras of the other philosophies (*darśanas*), it is the culmination of and expresses the conclusions of a whole tradition which must almost have reached back to the Upaniṣads themselves.[118] Even so, it might not have attained the stature it has today if Śaṁkara had not written his commentary on it several centuries later.[119] Śaṁkara's commentary in turn inspired numerous later commentaries as well as subcommentaries, glosses, etc. Thus when using the *Brahma Sūtra* as an aid in interpreting the Upaniṣads, one has to distinguish:

(1) the intent of the text as it presents itself (the intent of the final redactor[120]—the philosophy and practice of Ātman/Brahman mentioned above);
(2) the way the *Sūtra* is interpreted by the great later Vedāntic commentators, particularly Śaṁkara; and
(3) earlier material and views which the Sūtra incorporated into its composition.[121]

Since the individual aphorisms are not really intelligible by themselves, the *Sūtra* is usually always studied together with a commentary like Śaṁkara's. Similarly its philosophy and earlier positions which it incorporates are inferred or reconstructed using the commentaries and a historical approach. In using the *Sūtra* as an aid to interpret the Upaniṣads, (3) is most directly relevant. According to Nakamura, "the sections of the *Sūtra* which deal directly with verses of the Upaniṣads, e.g., I.1-3, III.3, etc., can be taken, for the most part, to have been compiled prior to the Christian era".[122]

Śaṁkara. The fact that the spiritual content of the Upaniṣads is today accessible at all is largely due to the influence of Śaṁkara, the great exponent of Advaita Vedānta. In addition to his commentary on the *Brahma Sūtra,* Śaṁkara also wrote commentaries (*bhāṣyas*) on the *Gītā* and on ten Upaniṣads,[123] and an independent work, the *Upadeśasāhasrī*, or "Thousand Teachings".[124] The commentaries on the Upaniṣads are of great importance as the first extensive, in-depth discussion of the Upaniṣadic texts in Hindu Tradition extant and also the first to reach a large audience. In these works, Śaṁkara assimilated the enormous mystical and esoteric range and profundity of the Upaniṣads to a single, rather clear-cut conceptual system. Regardless of how one relates to that system, however, there is no doubt that he explicated the Upaniṣads from a very high level of spiritual understanding. For that reason alone, his writings have remained an invaluable aid for the interpretation of the Upaniṣads ever since.

For a Western student, however, there is a problem how to read Śaṁkara. For Śaṁkara can be regarded in different ways, and one's idea of what he is or represents has a strong effect on how one interprets what he says. In Indology perhaps his most common role has been as historical testimony—how something he says or how some attitude he has has a bearing on certain historical questions or states of affairs.[125] But since Deussen, his works have been studied by Western philosophers for their independent philosophical interest and their relevance to philosophy today.[126] There has also been a growing recognition that Śaṁkara is not so much setting forth a philosophy as carrying the banner for a whole spiritual tradition and a spiritual path. This is really his significance today. One can meet many educated Indians (academics, scientists, engineers) who have a deeper understanding of Ātman/Brahman developed primarily by studying Śaṁkara's commentaries. In other words, far from being a mere product of scholasticism or the like, these works have even today the power to engender higher spiritual knowledge and a correct orientation to life that eventually leads to leading a strict spiritual life and progress toward the goal.

Śaṁkara's commentaries suggest an image of the historical Śaṁkara as a great saint and intellect, a Brahmin steeped in the Vedānta and Brāhmaṇical tradition of his time, familiar with Vaiṣṇavism and aware of other philosophies like Sāṁkhya and Buddhist Mādhyamika, but mostly shaping a comprehensive, strictly Advaitic philosophy in close contact with the *śruti* texts. This is the traditional image espoused by modern scholarship. But Indian tradition presents also another image of Śaṁkara, namely that of a great religious leader, with enormous popular impact, who as a *saṁnyāsin* traveled the length and breadth of India to establish Advaita Vedānta and unify it with the then existing forms of religion. Thus he is said to have founded four (or according to some sources, five) great seats of learning or *maṭhas* in different parts of India to become Advaitic centers and havens for *saṁnyāsins.*[127] Today the heads of these *maṭhas* carry the title *Śaṅkarācārya* (*ācārya* = "teacher") and are leaders of strong living religious traditions.[128] Another set of traditions presents Śaṁkara as unifying on his travels six forms of religion (the *ṣaṇ-matas,* viz. worship of Gaṇapati, Śiva, Viṣṇu, Śakti, Sūrya or the Sun, and Kumāra or Subrahmaṇya) by showing how they could be regarded as alternative modes with the same common Advaitic basis.[129] Modern critical scholarship tends to discount the authenticity of all these traditions.[130] It also does not consider the many devotional hymns and Vedāntic tracts ascribed to Śaṁkara to be genuine.[131] However, here one has to be careful. Śaṁkara commonly calls Brahman *Īśvara*, "Supreme Lord", a fact that does not harmonize with the exclusively "extreme Advaita" image of Śaṁkara in modern Western scholarship.[132] In view of the great spiritual power that is lodged in Śaṁkara's writings, there may well be more to Śaṁkara's whole spiritual configuration than the pure Advaita that comes out in the classical commentaries. The lives and personalities of Saints do not usually fit common patterns, which is, after all, all that is invoked by modern scholarship.

Vedāntic Commentarial Literature. After Śaṁkara, the Vedāntic commentarial literature focusses largely on the *Brahma Sūtra*, very little on the Upaniṣads themselves. Ānandagiri, Vācaspati Miśra, and others wrote commentaries on Śaṁkara's commentaries and "rightly claimed that their works were the 'flourishing' and 'radiance' of his texts".[133] This literature is untranslated and virtually unexplored. Other ācāryas like Rāmānuja (cf. sec. 2 above), wrote commentaries modifying many of Śaṁkara's concepts and interpretations. Only a handful of these are translated.[134] Here one can often find alternative readings and new interpretations of Upaniṣadic passages, especially in theistic terms. But these are not necessarily of use in trying to estimate the original spiritual intent of the passage.

6. The Upaniṣads and the West

Why has there been so Little Interaction Between the Upaniṣads and Western Thought? We close this background chapter with a brief account of the relation between the Upaniṣads and the West. If the Upaniṣads are really so important as stated in sec. 1, if they are really Universal Supreme Wisdom, why are they so little-known in the West today? Why has there been so little fundamental interaction with "Upaniṣadic thought," why has Upaniṣadic thought been brought so little into relationship with the basis of Western thought, the basis of Science, the Western approach to the Universe and the nature of man? Is it that the Upaniṣads simply don't share the fundamental motivation of Science and Philosophy in the West?

Of course these questions are not specific to the Upaniṣads. They can be asked equally about the other great Supreme Wisdom literatures of the world, e.g. the Buddhist *Prajñā-Pāramitā Sūtras* or the Cin-mātra literature. And, of course, there are many answers. One is that Western society and civilization have become so secularized that there is little fertile ground for such an interaction. People who hold this kind of view feel that the mainstream of Western thought, so inextricably tied up with science and technology, and so extremely focussed at the level of sensory manifestation, is unaware of the importance of inner discipline and ethics in true wisdom and of its own fallen ethical condition. They feel that Western thought cannot even grasp the nature of these literatures and does not recognize its own inability to deal with them in an adequate way. Another answer is that Judaism and Christianity, which have some equivalent teachings and realization in their own traditions and should be able to treat the Eastern traditions as allies and kin, are so weak and have walled themselves doctrinally in to such an extent that they are unable to do so. People who have this kind of a view may feel that part of the problem is that the great spiritual literatures of Christianity, for example (cf. sec. 2 above), constant preoccupation with which seems essential for a true, living religious tradition, are mostly unread within Christianity at large.

Yet a third answer is that the Upaniṣads (as also the Buddhist literatures mentioned) have been and are in fact recognized as the Supreme Wisdom that they are, but that this recognition is often only by subtle implication, or with a shrug of resignation, and not emphasized. For actually there was a meeting of the Upaniṣads and Western thought, albeit limited. Schopenhauer acknowledged them as perfectly relevant to philosophy as normally understood in the West, and praised them as the core of "the first of the highest human *Erkenntnis* and Wisdom". *Erkenntnis* in Germany and the West has forever been the goal of philosophy! And Deussen, a Kantian who followed Schopenhauer, gave the West a concrete vision of the Upaniṣads and

Vedānta taking their place beside, and on an equal footing with, Greek and modern Western philosophy, as part of a general human philosophy enterprise. Both of these thinkers saw the Upaniṣads as achieving the goal of the central metaphysical and scientific motivation of the West. But their vision found no response. It was never really rejected, but ignored. In what follows we first give a brief account of this story, relying largely on the books by Schwab and Halbfass.[135] Then we briefly come back to the general question of how the Upaniṣads fit in with the essential metaphysical and scientific motivation of the West.

The *Oupnek'hat*. The first important event in the Upaniṣads' journey into the West was the appearance of *Oupnek'hat*, a Latin translation of 60 Upaniṣads by A.H. Antequil Duperron, a French scholar, philosopher and India traveler, in 1801-1802.[136] Antequil was a remarkable man. Although always remaining a Christian, the main theme of his life and work was the oneness of the major religions and *philosophia perennis.* "A leaf glued into . . . the rough drafts [of the *Oupnek'hat*] declared, after quotations from Saint-Cyrian, Le Maitre, Arnaud, and Saint Augustine: 'The *Zend* books [i.e. the Zend Avesta which he had translated earlier] and the *Oupnek'hat* present the same truths as the works of the Platonic philosophers, and perhaps these philosophers received them from the Oriental philosophers.'"[137] In the preface to *Oupnek'hat* Vol. 1, Antequil says that there is *unicum principium spirituale, in antiquis nationum libris traditum*, "one single spiritual principle which is handed down in the ancient books of the peoples".[138] And in a following lengthy "dissertation", he then sets Upaniṣadic concepts side by side quotations from Jewish, Greek, early Christian, and Catholic authors, emphasizing their common direction or intent. "The copious notes to the *Oupnek'hat* (his solitary table-talk) . . . decisively linked the concerns of Western philosophy with those of Hindu learning,"[139] and he "asks the philosophers of many countries, . . . particularly 'the followers or opponents of the profound Kant', . . . to regard the teachings of the Upaniṣads not only as a testimony of Indian antiquity, but to take them seriously as a philosophical challenge".[140] His deep immersion in the Upaniṣadic wisdom may be seen from the fact that the second volume of the *Oupnek'hat* is dedicated to the Sages of India (*Indiae Sapientibus*), and that Antequil asks them "not to look with disdain on the work of one of their disciples".[141]

Antequil did not translate from the original Sanskrit but from a translation of the Upaniṣads into Persian that had been completed in 1657 in Delhi by Brahmin scholars under the leadership of Prince Dārā Shikōh, a brother of the Muslim emperor, Aurangzeb. His own translation was apparently relatively faithful to the spirit of the text. But "it must have taken a special sixth sense to recognize in Antequil's Latin, which follows word for word, haltingly and stumblingly, the Persian text, the original sense of many passages, concepts, and expressions."[142] In the German philosophical world of the time, only two major figures, Arthur Schopenhauer, and Karl Christian Friedrich Krause, were deeply affected.[143]

Schopenhauer saw the work for the first time in 1814 and immediately responded. Already that year he drafted a remarkable fragment[144] in which he formulated in his own way a spiritual insight that is at the heart of the Upaniṣads and forms a cornerstone of virtually every high wisdom (*jñāna*, enlightenment, etc.) literature since. This is that desire (or "wanting something") is at the root of all suffering, and that liberation from desire is attained by Insight (lit. "recognizing something to be the case", *Erkenntnis, jñāna*). In support Schopenhauer quoted from Antequil's translation of *Ātmā* Upaniṣad: *"tempore quo cognitio simul advenit, amor e medio supersurrexit"*—"at the same time when knowledge (*cognitio*) arrived, desire (*amor,* love) left from the premises". And he explained that *amor*, "love", here meant Skt. *māyā*, "illusion", the illusory and deluding power of attraction of the things of the world. In 1818 Schopenhauer made this same quote the motto for part IV of *The World as Will and Idea*, his chief philosophical work. Now he mentions the Vedas as "the fruit of the highest human knowledge (*Erkenntnis*) and Wisdom, whose core has finally come to us, as the greatest present of this century, in the Upaniṣads",[145] and then cites the "great utterance", *"tat tvam asi"*, "You are That (Absolute)", from *Chāndogya Upaniṣad.*

Antequil's translation became for Schopenhauer the principal spiritual resource in his life and a chief inspiration for his whole philosophical work. According to W. Gwinner, his first biographer, "before he went to bed, he would not infrequently open up his Bible, the *Oupnek'hat*, in order to perform in this way (lit.: in that) his devotion".[146] "In the whole world," said Schopenhauer himself, "there is no study, except that of the originals, so beneficial and so elevating as that of the *Oupnek'hat*. It has been the solace of my life, it will be the solace of my death"![147] Schopenhauer was also the first major Western thinker to place the Upaniṣads explicitly higher than Western philosophy, as for example parenthetically in the following passage from a small work, *Sketch of a History of the Doctrine of the Ideal and the Real:*

> Indeed, one might wonder why pantheism was not able to carry off a complete victory over "theism" already in the 17th century, since the most original, most beautiful, and most thorough presentations of the former (yet compared with the Upaniṣads of the Veda, all that is of course nothing!) all came to light in this period: namely through *Bruno, Malebranche, Spinoza,* and *Scotus Erigena,* which latter . . . was for the first time printed [only] in 1681, that is to say, four years after Spinoza's death . . .[148]

The important thing with Schopenhauer was not just simply a *philosophia perennis* orientation to philosophy and religion, with a true perception of the Upaniṣadic teachings as Supreme Wisdom. Rather, this orientation and perception were the expression of a genuine, irreducible spiritual element. Schopenhauer's possible influence in the 19th century, however, was effectively annulled by Hegel who, working from his own conceptions and premises, came to mostly negative conclusions about Indian Wisdom. "Hegel's [negative] judgement guided the official academic world (Karl Marx included), drove Schopenhauer into isolation, and killed the hopes for a new Renaissance based on the writings of the classical Indians"[149] which Schopenhauer and many others at that time were having.

K.C.F. Krause. While Schopenhauer has always been well-known, the second great systematic thinker in whom Antequil's Upaniṣads found a deep resonance, K.C.F. Krause (1781-1832), had only little impact in his lifetime. However, Krause's stature has been steadily rising. The 1923 edition of the *Überweg*, for example (a standard reference on the history of philosophy in German), devotes to him a whole separate number, sandwiched in between Hegel and Schleiermacher.[150] This is the more significant because Krause's kinship with Vedic and Upaniṣadic thinking seems to be fairly close, comparable to that of, say, Plotinus. Starting from a pre-existing base of Upaniṣadic type insight or knowledge, and working within the dimensions and concepts brought to Western philosophy by Kant, Fichte, Hegel, and Schelling, Krause developed a systematic framework and language within which he then dealt powerfully with topics like human society, law, art, and history.[151] There is hope that as the only major systematic philosophical effort of this type after Kant,

Krause's work will be studied more intensively in the future. His neglect in the past is partly due to the spiritual dimension of his thought, and a strange-looking (technical or mystical, depending on the point of view) vocabulary in which most of his works are written. Alone among his peers, Krause "engaged in systematic contemplative exercises (even assuming specific body postures), and encouraged his students to attain . . . oneness with the One Substance (*Wesenseinigung*)".[152] His philosophical writing is dominated by the One Infinite Substance which is everything and in which everything is (called by him *Wesen*, "essence", with connotations of "being"). The harmony of Krause's intellectual activity with the sense of this One Substance, and the level of true realization involved may be seen from a letter to his father. "If philosophical etc. knowledge (*Wissenschaft*) is developed within this Principle (= the Infinite Substance, *Wesen*), then. . . it takes such a pure heart (lit. *Sinn*, "psyche"), such a kindness of the heart, to be competent in its doctrines that it is not advisable to teach it to others unless they have been prepared by prolonged education. . . The more I enter into the Sanctum of Truth, the quieter it becomes in my psyche (*Gemüt*), the more light [it becomes] in my soul, the warmer [it becomes] in my heart . . . Philosophical and other knowledge (*Wissenschaft*) and being-in-God-ness (*Gottesinnigkeit*, also "feeling God in my heart") have become one in me to such an extent that I could not separate them, and I would already consider myself as possessing beatitude in life if I was able to live strictly according to and completely pure for this Oneness of Everything".[153]

Krause's relationship to the Upaniṣads has not been carefully studied. It is known that he read the *Oupnek'hat* several times from 1805 on. In his letters he calls it a work which "in profundity at least does not stand behind any of our most profound rigorous-philosophical (*wissenschaftlich*) works, even though it does not appear in strictly scientific (*wissenschaftlich*) form".[154] Of course Krause's basic spiritual understanding and the key dimensions of his overall framework developed independently. Nevertheless one may perhaps see the fact that he explicitly identifies one of the three or four key syllables of his vocabulary, om, with the Upaniṣadic *om*,[155] a mystic embodiment of Brahman, as a direct response of his to Upaniṣadic thought.

F. Max Müller. After Antequil's translation, an important milestone in the history of the Upaniṣads in the West was the appearance, in 1879, of the first part of F. Max Müller's (1823-1900) English translation of twelve classical Upaniṣads as volume 1 of the *Sacred Books of the East*.[156] This made for the first time a high quality translation of the Upaniṣads available to a large Western audience. In the introduction Müller, intimating Schopenhauer's high estimate of the text, urged a more considerate reception of it than in the past. Besides exemplifying first rank Sanskrit scholarship, Müller also took pains to arrive at an accurate rendering of the "original thoughts" in the text. He was not satisfied with literal translations that resulted in sequences of words "with which we cannot connect any definite thoughts", and he equally eschewed facile assimilation to familiar Western philosophical terms. Illustrating his points with an important passage from *Chāndogya Upaniṣad* (VI.8 ff.), he writes:

> No doubt this translation sounds strange to English ears, but as the thoughts contained in the Upaniṣads are strange, it would be wrong to smooth down their strangeness by clothing them in language familiar to us, which, because it is familiar, will fail to startle us, and because it fails to startle us, will fail also to set us thinking.[157]

Müller's struggles with translation represent an early effort to penetrate the original spiritual content of the text from a general scholarly point of view.

Paul Deussen. The man who did the most to put the Upaniṣads on the intellectual map of the West, however, was not Schopenhauer or Müller but Paul Deussen (1845-1919). Deussen was "'the recognized head, one may perhaps say, the hierophant of the German Schopenhauer community',. . . [and] the only holder of a chair for philosophy in Germany (since 1889 in Kiel) who was simultaneously an outstanding Sanskritist and who devoted his time and energy primarily to Indian philosophy".[158] He was a philosopher who, in Nietzsche's words, "had the faith", i.e., "the operating out of Schopenhauer-Kantian presuppositions."[159] He also produced translations and presentations of the Upaniṣads and of Vedānta which were "pioneer achievements of Indology of the first rank".[160] But in terms of a new vision that includes both the Upaniṣads and Vedānta in the aspirations of the West, his most important work was his *Allgemeine Geschichte der Philosophie mit besonderer Berücksichtigung der Religionen*, "General History of Philosophy, with a special taking into account of the Religions," in 6 parts.[161] The work presents the Indian philosophical tradition, with its religious-metaphysical roots, as on a par with the Western philosophical tradition, with its Greek and Judaeo-Christian roots, and as sharing the same basic motivation. Already a look at its overall organization is revealing. Part 1: The Veda Saṁhitās and Brāhmaṇas; Part 2: The Upaniṣads; Part 3: The Later Six Classical Systems of Indian Philosophy, with a Section on Chinese Philosophy; Part 4: Greek Philosophy, up to Philo and Plotinus; Part 5: The Development and Working-itself-out of the Christian Influence (in two sub-parts: (a) the development of Judaism, and Jesus, Paul, and the 4th Gospel; and (b), the patristic and scholastic periods, including Arabic and Jewish scholasticism, Eckhart's mysticism, etc.); and Part 6: Modern Western Philosophy, from Descartes to Schopenhauer. Even in its Western portions this was not just a standard re-telling of a familiar story, but an intellectual and spiritual working through by one of the active, vital philosophical minds of time. Indeed, appearing over a 23-year period (1894-1917), the work bears very much the stamp of Deussen's whole own philosophical-spiritual development.

"[The *General History*] presents the image of a peculiar, pronounced, also in philosophical respects exemplary unity and intensity".[162] This unity (lit. *Geschlossenheit*, ordered completeness), etc. was essentially the manifestation of a spiritual vision, a spiritual path. For example, Deussen's principle was "to follow all ideas to their source, to the point at which they have sprung from the Nature of things *which lies also open* (present) *to us*"[163] (italics added). This really meant that he followed each idea to its ground *in himself, in us*, and that he took the attitude that in every individual, in every age, the same problem-ground evokes in the soul both philosophical and religious responses. ("The Nature of things", which evokes them, "is also present to us", i.e. is present in everybody and in everybody equally). It is obvious that such an attitude, pursued honestly, is spiritual in origin and that it is bound to overcome distinctions such as epistemology vs. metaphysics, facts vs. values, and religion vs. philosophy. And it is also evident that such an attitude will bring one to a much more accurate understanding of the fundamental metaphysical impulses in human history. Deussen had the courage to develop and uphold this kind of attitude to his fellow philosophers at the time, and subordinate his entire learning and scholarship to it.

It is not clear to me how the *General History* was received. Halbfass remarks several times on its exceptional stature within the genre of histories of philosophy in the 19th and beginning 20th century.

"[Deussen's] 'ideal concept' of Philosophy, which does not separate Religion and Philosophy, which allows him to include the metaphysical efforts of all peoples and all ages, is not shared by the academic historians of philosophy".[164] One reason for this is that this "ideal concept" of Philosophy represented a return to a state in which ethical-spiritual vision informs the whole of an author's philosophizing—a state found in Western philosophy e.g. in Plato but relatively less often from Descartes on. Another reason for the isolated position of the *General History* may have been the fact that like Schopenhauer, Deussen identified the Upaniṣadic Brahman with the Kantian noumenon or *Ding-an-sich*, which is perceived as the objects in the world. This is a testimony to his sincerity and spiritual groundedness, but it was presumably an embarrassment to Kantianism as usually understood.

The Upaniṣads and the Ideal of *Erkenntnis* and Truth in Science. The fact that Schopenhauer, Deussen, and Krause regarded the Upaniṣads as essentially expressing highest *Erkenntnis* and Truth *in the sense of Western philosophy* is significant. For these men, *Erkenntnis* and Truth formed a single Ideal, and this Ideal was at the same time also felt to be the essential motivation in Western Philosophy and Science. In addition, this Ideal was basically a metaphysical one, in the sense that it involved metaphysical experience and striving driven by a metaphysical awareness. In this century, however, *Erkenntnis* and Truth have ceased to be the primary quest of Western philosophy, although they are (in my opinion) still a fundamental motivation in modern Physics. (This fact might not be acknowledged by many physicists, or recognized by modern philosophy of science—modern philosophy in general has not addressed Physics as having an *Erkenntnis* and Truth Ideal and as an *Erkenntnis* and Truth enterprise.) So the example of Krause, Schopenhauer and Deussen is important because in these men, *Erkenntnis* and Truth is still a single motivation which comprehends the whole of philosophical, ethical and scientific striving.

The Upaniṣads and the other Supreme Wisdom literatures of the world (*Prajñāpāramitā*, etc.) have the potential to awaken such a unified motivation again today,—motivation, that is, toward *highest Erkenntnis* and Truth, to walk toward and become Reality. Under their guidance, the metaphysical vision can deepen naturally into divine experience and into knowledge and realization of the Universal Divine, and along with this there can be the dawning of the Reality that is declared in all the Supreme Wisdom literatures—Ātman/

Brahman, Suchness, the Pure Mind, etc. In this way, Science, which plays such a prominent role in the Western world-view, could be unified with highest spiritual aspirations and values and become a supportive element in the uplift of Western society. For an individual to attain such higher goals, however, depends on purity of heart and can happen only when he/she lives according to high and highest moral-ethical standards. If Science is to lead the society with the Ideal of highest *Erkenntnis* and Truth as one single, unified motivation, there needs to be moral-ethical purification of the whole mentality of Science and of doing and using Science. Only then can Science truly contribute to the uplift of society and to individual fulfilment.

NOTES

1. An excellent introduction to Hinduism is K. Klostermaier, *A Survey of Hinduism*. Albany: SUNY Press, 1988. The standard scholarly treatment is J. Gonda, *Religionen Indiens* (see Abbreviations and Conventions).
2. In the oldest layer of the Mahābhārata, and in some inscriptions.
3. For historical perspective on the Vedic and the rival Āgamic streams, see V. Sh. Pathak, *Smārta Religious Tradition*. Meerut: Kusumanjali Prakashan, 1987, chrs. 1-2 (pp. 1-37).
4. Farquhar, J.N., *An Outline of the Religious Literature of India*. Oxford: Oxford University Press, 1920; repr. Delhi: Motilal Banarsidass, 1967; J. Gonda ed., *A History of Indian Literature*. Wiesbaden: Otto Harassowitz, 1973—present, abbreviated below as *HIL*. The *HIL* was planned in 10 volumes, with several fascicles to a volume; some 25 fascicles have appeared.
5. P. Lal, *The Mahābhārata*. Lake Gardens, Calcutta: Writers Workshop, 1968? is a very successful verse by verse "transcreation", in free verse and prose. J.A.B. van Buitenen started on a modern translation for a general Western audience but died before he could finish the project. J.A.B. van Buitenen, *The Mahābhārata*. Chicago: University of Chicago Press. V. 1, 1974; v. 2 (books 2 & 3), 1976; v. 3 (books 4 & 5), 1978. (Also in paperback).
6. The standard English translation for both general reader and specialist promises to be R.P. Goldman (ed.), *The Rāmāyaṇa of Vālmīki: An Epic of Ancient India*. V. 1, R.P. Goldman, transl., *Bālakāṇḍa* (i.e., book 1 of seven books); v. 2, S.I. Pollock, transl., *Ayodhyākāṇḍa*; v. 3, S.I. Pollock, transl., *Araṇyakāṇḍa*; v. 4, R. Lefeber, transl., *Kiṣkindhākāṇḍa*. All Princeton, NJ: Princeton University Press, 1985, 1986, 1991, and 1994, resp.
7. Scholarly English translations of many of the important Purāṇas are now available in the series *Ancient Indian Mythology and tradition* (J.L. Shastri, ed.), Delhi: Motilal Banarsidass, 1970. As of 1995, almost 60 volumes have appeared.
8. A.A. Macdonell, in the *Encyclopedia of Religion and Ethics* (ed. J. Hastings), v. 10. New York: Scribners, 1919, p. 574.

9. Jagannathan, S., *Hinduism: An Introduction*. Bombay: Vakils, Feffer and Simons, 1984, pp. 12 and 16. This important point appears to have been little studied by modern scholars.
10. At 10 verses per page and 500 pages per volume, this would make 200 volumes of print. The literature is described in J. Gonda, *Medieval Religious Literature in Sanskrit*. Wiesbaden: Otto Harassowitz, 1977 (*HIL* II.1), pp. 39-139 (the one million figure is mentioned p. 40).
11. Gonda, *ibid*., pp. 40-41
12. *Ibid*., p. 39.
13. Gonda, *op. cit.*, pp. 163-215.
14. Gonda, *ibid*., p. 181; on the Upa-Āgamas, *ibid*., p. 182.
15. For a summary of modern scholarship on Kashmir Śaivism and Non-Dual Kashmir Śaivism, see P.E. Muller-Ortega, *The Triadic Heart of Śiva. Kaula Tantricism of Abhinavagupta in the Non-Dual Śaivism of Kashmir*. Albany: SUNY Press, 1989, pp. 18-24, 42-47, 55-63.
16. Gonda, *op. cit.*, pp. 202 ff.
17. Described in T. Goudriaan and S. Gupta, *Hindu Tantric and Śākta Literature*. Wiesbaden: Otto Harassowitz, 1981 (*HIL* II.2), chapter II.
18. There is really no good comprehensive introduction to this vast and incredible field for the general Western reader. E. Zelliot's survey, The Medieval Bhakti Movement in History. An Essay on the Literature in English. In Smith, Bardwell L. (ed.) *Hinduism New Essays in the History of Religions*. Leiden: E.J. Brill, 1976, pp. 143-168, is now dated.
19. The articles in part II of H. Bhattacharya (ed.), *The Cultural Heritage of India*, v. 3, *The Philosophies*. 2nd ed., Calcutta: Ramakrishna Mission Institute of Culture, 1953, give a survey of the various subtraditions of Vedānta from a combined Indian and Western point of view. While "not forgetting the interest of the scholar and student", the book is written for "men and women who are seekers of the spiritual truth . . . without the highly technical equipment of a philosopher".
20. Leading western scholars on Śaṁkara's Advaita Vedānta include P. Deussen (discussed in sec. 6 below), Paul Hacker, and Tilman Vetter. Outstanding traditional treatments, alive as well as reliable from a scholarly point of view, may be found in the books of T.M.P. Mahadevan, e.g., *Superimposition in Advaita Vedānta*. New Delhi: Sterling Pubs., 1985.
21. F. Schuon, *Gnosis, Divine Wisdom*. London: John Murray, 1959 (or. French ed., *Sentiers de Gnose*, 1957), p. 77, note 2.
22. F. Schuon, *Language of the Self*. Madras: Ganesh & Co., 1959, p. 15. (The book is made up of articles that appeared earlier elsewhere. Only Chapter 2 is on Vedānta.)
23. F. Schuon, One of the Great Lights of the World. In T.M.P. Mahadevan, ed., *Spiritual Perspectives. Essays in Mysticism and Metaphysics*. New Delhi: Arnold Heineman, 1975, p. 91.
24. Including the institutions associated with the five *Vidyāpīṭhas*, lit. "seats of learning", monasteries originally founded by Śaṁkara and headed by the *Śaṁkarācāryas* (cf. sec. 5 below), and the Ramakrishna Organization, founded by disciples of Sri Ramakrishna Paramahamsa. The latter is the main representative of Vedānta in the West. See A.M. Williams, The Ramakrishna Movement: A study in Religious Change, in R.D. Baird, ed., *Religion in Modern India*. 2nd rev. ed., New Delhi: Manohar, 1989.

25. Transl. Radhakrishnan, *Brahma Sūtra* (see Abbreviations and Conventions).
26. Datings after Klostermaier, *op. cit.*
27. Transl. Thibaut, *Vedānta Sūtras Commentary*, and Svāmī Gambhīrānanda, *Brahma Sūtra Commentary* (see Abbreviations and Conventions). Thibaut's version has a useful index.
28. See the articles in *The Cultural Heritage of India, op. cit.*, note 19 above.
29. E.g. A. Bharati, The Hindu Self in Action. In Marsella, A.J., DeVos, G., and Hsu, F.L.K., *Culture and Self. Asian and Western Perspectives.* New York: Tavistock, 1985, pp. 185-230. Bharati comments on some of the existing literature in this area.
30. Mircea Eliade, Yoga: *Immortality and Freedom.* Princeton: Princeton University Press (Bollingen series v. 56), 2nd ed. 1969 (orig. Fr. ed., 1954), p. 359.
31. Cf. "Yoga constitutes a characteristic dimension of the Indian Mind, to such a point that wherever Indian religion and culture have made their way, we also find a more or less pure form of yoga . . . Indian religious experience finds the yogic methods of 'meditation' and 'concentration' a necessity" (Eliade, *ibid.*, p. 359).
32. For the dating see K.S. Ramachandran, Dating the Indus Civilization, in Lal, B.B., & Gupta, S.P., eds., *Frontiers of the Indus Civilization (Sir Mortimer Wheeler Commemoration Volume).* New Delhi: Books & Books (for Ind. Archeol Soc.) and Ind. Hist. & Cult. Soc., 1984, pp. 538-539. Yoga in Harappan civilization is suggested by three famous seals from Mohenjo-daro, Mackay Nos. 420, 222 and 235, which show a male deity in the form of an ascetic with a large mask-like face and seated in a yogic pose. Nos. 420 and 222 are particularly realistic and show features typically seen in modern Indian *sādhus*, such as the elongated form of the thighs and their "squat on the floor" aspect. See E.J.H. MacKay *et al.*, *Further Excavations at Mohenjo-Daro.* v. 2 (Plates). New Delhi: Government of India Press, 1937, Plates C and LXXXVII. Seal No. 420 has been analyzed in detail by D. Srinivasan, The so-called Proto-Śiva Seal from Mohenjo-Daro: An Iconological Assessment, *Archives of Asian Art*, v. 29 (1975-76) pp. 47-58. A general continuity of Harappan Religion with Vedic Religion is taken for granted by scholars such as S.R. Rao, *Lothal and the Indus Civilization.* New York: Asia Publishing House, 1973 (cf. the chapter on Religion). But the identification of Seal No. 420 as a prototype of Śiva is being abandoned. Cf. D. Srinivasan, Vedic Rudra-Śiva, *JAOS*, v. 103 (1983), pp. 543-56.
33. See G. Feuerstein, *Encyclopedic Dictionary of Yoga.* New York: Paragon House, 1990; and Ram Kumar Rai, *Encyclopedia of Yoga.* Varanasi: Prachya Prakashan, 1975 (Chowkamba Indological Reference Series) (mostly made up of excerpts from about 100 Yoga scriptures). The first systematic survey of the whole literature is likely to be G. Larson's forthcoming volume in K. Potter's *Encyclopedia of Indian Philosophies.*
34. Discussion of individual texts, but not generally accepted by other scholars: J.W. Hauer, *Die Anfänge der Yogapraxis im alten Indien.* Berlin: Kohlhammer, 1922 (based entirely on *Ṛg* and *Atharva Veda*).
35. Cf. E.W. Hopkins, Yoga-technique in the Great Epic. *JAOS*, v. 22 (1901), pp. 333-79; pp. 333-339; V.M. Bedekar, Yoga in the Mokṣadharmaparvan

of the Mahābhārata. *WZKSA*, v. 12-13 (1968-69), pp. 43-52.

36. Cf. P. Olivelle's entry Saṁnyāsa in Eliade, *Encyclopedia of Religion*; P.V. Kane's treatment in his *History of Dharma Śāstra*, v. 2, pt. 2. Poona: Bhandarkar Oriental Research Institute, 1941, pp. 930-975; and J.F. Sprockhoff, *Saṁnyāsa. Quellenstudien zur Askese im Hinduismus*. I. *Untersuchungen über die Saṁnyāsa-Upaniṣads*. Wiesbaden: Franz Steiner, 1976 (Abhandlungen für die Kunde des Morgenlandes, E. Wagner, ed., No. 42, 1).
37. For an example of current conditions, see D.M. Miller and D.C. Werz, *Hindu Monastic Life: The Monks and Monasteries of Bhubaneswar*. Montreal: McGill-Queen's University Press, 1976.
38. P. Olivelle, transl., *Saṁnyāsa Upaniṣads*. New York: Oxford Univ. Press, 1992.
39. Representative high level spiritual texts: H.T. Dave (transl.), *Vachanamritam*. Bombay: Bharatiya Vidya Bhavan, 1977 (Discourses by Swaminarayan). Gupta, M. (recorder), *The Gospel of Sri Ramakrishna* (transl. Swami Nikhilananda). New York: Ramakrishna-Vivekananda Center, 1977 (orig. Bengali ed., 1887-1932). Shree Shree Ananda Mayee Ma, *Sad Vani* (recorder, Bhaiji; transl., Atmananda), 2nd ed. 1975 (1st Bengali & Engl. ed., 1935); *Matri Vani*, vol. 1 (compiler, Gurupreya; transl., Atmananda), 4th ed. 1977 (1st ed., 1959); *Matri Vani*, vol. 2 (compiler, Sister Uma; transl., Atmananda), 2nd ed., 1982 (first ed., 1977); all Calcutta: Shree Shree Anandamayee Charitable Society. For Sri Ramana Maharshi and Sri Sathya Sai Baba, see Abbreviations and Conventions.
40. Holland, B., *Popular Hinduism and Hindu Mythology: An Annotated Bibliography*. Westport, Conn.: Greenwood Press, 1979, p. xxii. The phrase 'philosophical-theological themes' is quoted from P. Ashby.
41. Holland, *ibid.*, p. xxii.
42. A. Bharati, *op. cit.*, p. 188.
43. Chopra, Pran Nath, *Religions and Communities of India*. Atlantic Hinghlands, NJ: Humanities Press, 1982.
44. A balanced survey is R.N. Dandekar, The Literature of Brāhmaṇism in Sanskrit, in Dandekar, R.N., *Select Writings II: Insights into Hinduism*. Delhi: Ajanta Publications, 1979, written both from the point of view of Indian learning and Western-type scholarship. The standard modern reference is J. Gonda, *Vedic Literature*, and the same author, *The Ritual Sūtras*, 1977, resp. (*HIL* vols. I.1 and I.2). More traditional: Shastri, *History*. J.A. Santucci, *An Outline of Vedic Literature*. Missoula, Montana: Scholars Press, 1976 (American Academy of Religion Aids to the Study of Religion Series, No. 5) is a helpful annoted bibliography of editions and translations of the primary sources.
45. The Bhagavad Gītā and the Pāli Canon (the earliest Buddhist scripture) still speak of "the three Vedas".
46. Of the 1875 stanzas of the *Sāma Veda Saṁhitā*, all but 75 are variants of material in the *Ṛg Veda*. Even of the *White Yajur Veda Saṁhitā*, about half of the 1975 verses have analogues in the *Ṛg Veda*.
47. Cf. Gonda, *Vedic Literature*, pp. 29-32.
48. M. Witzel, The Formation of the Vedic Canon and the Development of the Vedic Schools. Abstract of a paper given at the International Vedic Workshop, Harvard University, June 1989, p. 2. Regarding the localiza-

tion of different schools, M. Witzel gives a summary in his Tracing the Vedic Dialects. In C. Caillat (ed.), *Dialects dans les Litteratures Indo-Aryennes* (Proceedings of an International Colloquium, Sept. 1986). Paris: Institut de Civilization Indienne, 1989, pp. 110-117, esp. the maps pp. 113 & 114.

49. Adapted from Staal, F., with C. V. Somayajipad and M. Itti Rasi Nambudiri, *Agni. The Vedic Ritual of the Fire-altar*, v. 1. Berkeley: Asian Humanities Press, 1983, p. 36. A more detailed table of the same kind may be found in Witzel, Tracing the Vedic Dialects, *op. cit.*, pp. 122-123.

50. On Vedic study see A. Hillebrandt, *Ritual-Literatur. Vedische Opfer und Zauber*. Strassburg: Karl Trübner, 1897 (Grundriss der Indo-Arischen Philologie und Altertumskunde, G. Bühler, ed., III.2), §§ 24-35 (pp. 50-63); K. Glaser, Der indische Student, *ZDMG*, v. 66 (1912), pp. 1-37.

51. Cf. J.F. Staal, *Nambudiri Veda Recitation*. 'S-Gravenhage: Mouton & Co., 1961 (Disputationes Rheno-Trajcetinae, J. Gonda, ed., No. 5), pp. 40-41 and particularly Fig. 3, facing p. 41. Similar headpoints may be seen in a brief scene in the movie *Agnicayana*.

52. Staal, *Nambudiri Veda Recitation, op, cit.*, p. 41.

53. J. Sidney Allen, *Phonetics in Ancient India*. London: Oxford Univ. Press, 1953 (repr. 1961, 65) (London Oriental Series No. 1), p. 91. I am grateful to Prof. H.H. Hock for referring me to this book. On the *prātiśākhyas* see H. Scharfe, *Grammatical Literature*. Wiesbaden: Otto Harassowitz, 1977 (*HIL* fasc. V. 2), pp. 127-134.

54. For example, "The verb *praṇihaṇyate*, 'is made to fall', likewise used in the phonetic description of the *svarita*, again appears in the description of the gesture accompanying it. Uvaṭa commenting on the *Ṛk Prātiśākhya's* phonetic use of '*ākṣepa*' had equated it with '*tiryag-gamana*', 'a moving across', and this term also appears in the gestural section of the *Vājasaneyī Prātiśākhya*, where Kaṇva is quoted as teaching that for one type of *svarita* the hand is to be moved 'across and downwards', i.e., diagonally downwards. It thus appears probable that some of the tonal terminology is really based on gestural movements, which are of course related in turn to the kinesthetic and acoustic phenomena." (Allen, *op. cit.*, p. 91). The "tilting of the head sharply 90 degrees sideways" in the present-day practice is at some level kinesthetically equivalent to a *pra-ṇi-haṇyate*, i.e. to a "is made to fall" (the head behaves like a lifeless limb), as well as to a *tiryag-gamana*, i.e. to a "moving across".

55. The *udātta* and *anudātta*; Allen, *ibid.*, p. 91.

56. See Scharfe, *op. cit.*, p. 129. *The Vājasaneyī Prātiśākhya* is post-Pāṇini.

57. It represents a deeper, more holistic type of learning which occupies a larger portion of the functioning of the organism and is much more resistant to change than purely verbal memory.

58. E.g. the *mahāvrata* and *pravargya*, very specialized inserts into the *agnicayana*, and others.

59. Virtually all the Upaniṣads have been edited by the Adyar Library (in seven volumes, with six of these translated).

60. Gonda, *Vedic Literature*, p. 423.

61. Cf. H. Oldenberg, Zür Religion und Mythologie des Veda. 9. Āraṇyaka. *Nachrichten v.d. Königlichen Gesellschaft der Wissenschaften zu Göttingen*. Phil.-Hist. Klasse, 1915, pp. 382-401 (repr. Herrmann Oldenberg, *Kleine*

Schriften, pp. 419-438); p. 383 (resp. 420); J.F. Sprockhoff, Āraṇyaka und Vānaprastha in der Vedischen Literatur. Zweiter Hauptteil. *WZKSA*, v. 28 (1984), pp. 5-43; pp. 11-15.

62. *ŚāṅkhGṛSū* II.12.2. Transl. H. Oldenberg, *The Gṛhya-Sūtras*. Part 1. Oxford: Clarendon Press, 1886 (repr. 1967) (*SBE* v. 29), pp. 12-158; p. 79. The *vratas* are mentioned earlier in *ŚāṅkhGṛSū* II.11; Oldenberg, *op. cit.*, pp,. 76 ff. See also Hillebrandt, *Ritual-literatur, op. cit.*, § 29.
63. For this and the following details, cf. *ŚāṅkhGṛSū* II.12.2 ff.; Oldenberg, *ibid.*, p. 79 ff.
64. *ŚāṅkhGṛSū* VI.2 ff.; Oldenberg, *ibid.*, p. 142 ff.
65. Sprockhoff,. *op. cit.* (note 60), p. 14 and note 23.
66. *ŚāṅkhGṛSū* VI.1.8; Oldenberg, *ibid.*, p. 142. This contrast becomes sharper in the later *dharma* literature, cf. Sprockhoff, *ibid.*, p. 16.
67. In the paper cited in note 61 above, and *ibid.*, 8. Die Mahānāmnī-verses, pp. 412-418.
68. *ŚāṅkhGṛSū* VI.4; see also Oldenberg, "Āraṇyaka," *op. cit.* (note 61 above), p. 420.
69. *ŚāṅkhGṛSū* II.11.13.
70. Oldenberg, *op. cit.* (note 61), p. 420.
71. I am grateful to Prof. H.H. Hock for conversations on the following points.
72. Gonda, *Vedic Literature*, p. 423.
73. M. Witzel, Tracing the Vedic Dialects, *op. cit.* (note 47 above), pp. 121-127.
74. Cf. T. Burrow, *The Sanskrit Language*. 3rd. ed., London: Faber & Faber, 1973, Chr. 1 and Appendix 3, pp. 390-392; Malandra, W.W., *An Introduction to Ancient Iranian Religion. Readings from the Avesta and Achaemenid Inscriptions*. Univ. of Minnesota Press: Minneapolis, 1983; pp. 3-16.
75. Cf. F. Staal, *op. cit.*, p. 32. Staal summarizes the current understanding of the ritual implicit in the various Vedas by modern western scholarship on pp. 32 ff.
76. Cf. Malandra, *op. cit.*; K. Werner, The Indo-Europeans and the Indo-Aryans: The Philological, Archaeological, and Historical Context. *ABORI*, v. 66 (1988), pp. 491-523.
77. Burrow, *op. cit.* p. 4.
78. Cf. the articles under Indo-European Religions in the *Encyclopedia of Religion*.
79. Malandra, *ibid.*, p. 6.
80. Old Iranian religion is discussed in Malandra, *op. cit.*, pp. 4-16. Zarathustra's original religion is represented virtually only by the Gāthās; cf. S. Insler, *The Gāthās of Zarathustra*. Leiden: E.J. Brill, 1975 (Acta Iranica 8; Third Series: Textes et Memoires, v. 1). The sixth century BCE dating of Zarathustra which was sometimes advocated earlier is now being abandoned. Cf. e.g. P. Kingsley, The Greek Origin of the Sixth Century Dating of Zoroaster. *Bulletin of the School of Oriental and African Studies, Univ. of London*, v. 53 (1990), pp. 245-265.
81. See the review by D.W. Anthony, The Archaeology of Indo-European Origins. *The Journal of Indo-European Studies*, v. 19 (1991), pp. 205-222, and the publications by J. Mallory and M. Gimbutas cited there.

82. An initial strategy was to try to identify the Aryans with one of the archaeologcal cultures that flourished in the Indus and Ganges valleys between 1500 and 500 BCE, but this did not lead to conclusive results (R. Thapar, The Archaeological Background to the Agnicayana Ritual. In Staal, F. & MacFarland, *op. cit.*, pp. 3-40). In the last two or three decades the outlines of the Harappan (or Indus valley) civilization have begun to become clearer, and the question of the *Ṛg Vedic* Aryans has been approached in terms of trying to identify traces of interaction between the Aryans and the last vestiges of Harappan civilization. Such traces are expected if a supposedly racially distinct, pastoral and tribal people (the Aryans) invade areas with larger urban settlements. But physical anthropology has been unable to establish any systematic differences in skeletal remains (*e.g.* K.A.R. Kennedy, A Reassessment of the Theories of Racial Origin of the People of the Indus Valley Civilization from Recent Anthropological Data. In K.A.R. Kennedy and G.R. Possehl, eds., *Studies in the Archaeology and Paleoanthropology of South Asia.* New Delhi: Oxford & IBH Publishing Co., 1984. Kennedy calls the Aryans a "linguistic phenomenon": "Archaeological evidence of Aryan speaking peoples is questionable and the skeletal evidence is nil" (p. 104). Archaeological evidence for practices or elements reminiscent of descriptions in the *Ṛg Veda* or the Brāhmaṇas is often dated earlier than 1500 BCE and involves a spectrum of cultures or sites which are related to Harappan civilization in many different ways (R.H. Dyson, Paradigm Changes in the Study of the Indus Civilization. In G.L. Possehl, *Harappan Civilization, A Contemporary Perspective.* New Delhi: Oxford and IBH Publishing Co.,1982, pp. 417-427, particularly the summary on p. 423, col. 1 and middle of col. 2).

83. By Parpola see The Coming of the Aryans to Iran and India and the Cultural and Ethnic Identity of the Dāsas. *Studia Orientalia*, v. 64 (1988), pp. 192-302, especially the maps pp. 300-302. H. Falk in his review in *IIJ*, v. 34 (1991), pp. 57-60 briefly mentions some competing positions by well-known archaeologists (*ibid.*, p. 58). Witzel discusses his correlations in his Tracing the Vedic Dialects, *op. cit.* (note 47 above), pp. 241-251.

84. H. Jacobi, Über das Alter des *Rig-Veda. Festgruss an Rudolf von Roth*, 1893, p. 68-74; English transl., On the date of the *Ṛg-Veda. Indian Antiquary*, v. 23 (1894), p. 154-159; Der Vedische Kalender und das Alter des Veda. *ZDMG*, v. 49. (1885), p. 218-30; Nochmals das Alter des Veda. *Ibid.*, v. 50 (1896) pp. 69-83. The German papers are reprinted in B. Kolver, ed., *Herrmann Jacobi, Kleine Schriften*, v. 1, Wiesbaden: Franz Steiner, 1970, pp. 258-292.

85. See *ŚāṅkhGṛSū* I.17.2-4, *ĀśvalGṛSū* I.7.22; transl. H. Oldenberg, *op. cit.*, pp. 11 and 170 resp. This is still so in the ceremonies used today.

86. In India the controversy is still alive. Cf. N.N. Law, *Age of the Ṛg Veda*. Calcutta: Mukhopadhyay, 1965; K.C. Varma, The Kaliyuga Era and the Ignored Glimpses of Indian Antiquity, *ABORI*, v. 58-59 (1977-78, Diamond Jubilee Volume), pp. 1025-1047.

87. Pargiter used to publish in *JRAS*, where he had exchanges with Keith.

88. K. Klostermaier, *op. cit.* (note 1 above), p. 29.

89. Pusalker, A.D., *Studies in the Epics and Purāṇas*. Bombay: Bharatiya Vidya Bhavan, 1955, pp. 105-109, summarizes earlier literature in this

area. In 1975, D.C. Sircar, "an eminent epigraphist and a former Chief Epigraphist to the Government of India, declared unequivocally that the Mahābhārata war was a myth" (Gupta and Ramachandran, p. 4, cf. below). This produced a spate of controversy in which archeology began to figure prominently. See Gupta, S.P., and Ramachandran, K.S. (eds.), *Mahābhārata: Myth and Reality. Differing Views.* Delhi: Agam Prakashan, 1976.

90. Megasthenes was Greek ambassador at the court of Chandragupta. Arrian, *Indica* IX, says (based on Megasthenes) that the Indians counted 153 kings and 6042 years from Dionysos to Sandrokottos (= Chandragupta), and that Dionysos preceded Herakles (= Kṛṣṇa) by 15 generations. (Cf. the translation in J.W. McCrindle, *Ancient India as described by Megasthenes and Arrian*. Calcutta: Chuckerverty, Chatterjee & Co.,1926; repr. from *Indian Antiquary,* 1876-77). This leaves 138 kings between Kṛṣṇa and Chandragupta. But the first two figures would suggest an average reign of almost 40 years per king. Cf. C.V. Vaidya, *The Mahābhārata: A Criticism.* Delhi: Mehar Chand Lachhman Das, 1966 (orig. ed. earlier), pp. 57-59.

91. This perspective is fundamental to a modern approach. For then standard historical etc. methodology applies and requires that these content-units first be analyzed individually (philologically and as literature) and compared to other similar units. See P. Hacker, Zur Methode der geschichtlichen Erforschung der anonymen Sanskrit Literatur des Hinduismus. *ZDMG,* v. 111 (1961), pp. 483-492; *Kleine Schriften,* pp. 8-17; p. 486 (resp. p. 11).

92. J. Gonda reviews the history of Western Vedic Studies in *Vedic Literature*, pp. 56-63. For a different view, see J. Miller and G. Feuerstein, Some Notes on Ṛgvedic Interpretation, in Feuerstein, G., and Miller, J., *Yoga and Beyond: Essays in Indian Philosophy*. New York: Schocken Books, 1973 (orig. ed., *A Reappraisal of Yoga*, 1971), pp. 48-63.

93. Geldner, *Rig-Veda* (see Abbreviations and Conventions). Geldner, also known for his 1896 edition of the *Avesta*, died in 1929; the translation was published 30 years later. Since Geldner's work, the most important and massive effort in translation has been L. Renou's, published in *Etudes Vediques et Panineenes*, 17 vols., Paris: Editions E. de Boccard, 1955-69 (Publications de 1' Institut de Civilization Indienne). Renou's work was left unfinished when he died in 1966.

94. E.g. Velankar, H.D., *Ṛgveda Maṇḍala* VIII [7th book of the *Ṛg Veda*]. Bombay: Bharatiya Vidya Bhavan, 1963.

95. V.S. Agrawala, *Vedic Lectures*. (see note 108 below), p. ii.

96. Elizarenkova, in the paper discussed in note 100 below, cites as characteristics of the *Ṛg Vedic* hymns their monotony, their small number of mythological motives which are typically only alluded to and often repeated, frequent lists of gods, etc.

97. See the bibliography in J.C. Heesterman's entry on Vedism and Brāhmaṇism in Eliade, *Encyclopedia of Religion*, under Vedic Mythology.

98. J. Gonda, *The Vision of the Vedic Poets*, The Hague: Mouton, 1963.

99. Gonda, *The Vision of the Vedic Poets, op. cit.*, pp. 68-69.

100. A. Elizarenkova, paper given at the VIII. World Sanskrit Conference in Vienna, Sept., 1990. The following remarks are based on my notes of her talk (no abstract was available), and should be compared with her forth-

coming book.

101. Cf. Lakshman Sarup, *The Nighaṇṭu and the Nirukta*. Text and Translation. Delhi: Motilal Banarsidass, 1960 (first eds., 1920 and 1926).

102. S.K. Gupta, Ancient Schools of Vedic Interpretation. *Journal of the Ganganatha Jha Research Institute*, v. 16 (1958/9), pp. 143-153; p. 144.

103. C. Vogel, *Indian Lexicography*. Wiesbaden: Otto Harassowitz, 1979, (*HIL*, V. 4), pp. 1-2, argues that the *Nighaṇṭu* "did not . . . constitute the prototype of the dictionaries (*kośas*) of later times" (*ibid.* p. 1), and must therefore have had a different purpose. For linguistic perspectives on the *Nirukta* see H. Scharfe, *Grammatical Literature*. Wiesbaden: Otto Harassowitz, 1977 (*HIL*, V. 2), pp. 117-123.

104. Cf. Sarup's introduction to the *Nirukta*, *op. cit.*, pp. 71 ff.

105. Cf. R. Gopal, *The History and Principles of Vedic Interpretation*. New Delhi: Concept Publ., 1983, pp. 95-140.

106. For his approach, see the first two of a planned twelve volume English translation of his translation and commentary on the *Ṛg Veda*: Dharma Deva Vidya Martananda (transl.), *The Ṛg Veda with Maharishi Dayānanda Sarasvatī's Commentary*. New Delhi: Sarvadeshik Arya Pratinidhi Sabha (International Aryan League), Vol. 1 (*Ṛg Veda* I.1-61), 1974; vol. 2 (*Ṛg Veda* I.62-136), 1978. Dayānanda's thought and spiritual understanding are not easy to penetrate, and I found Parmanand (transl.), *Svāmī Dayānanda Sarasvatī's Ṛg-Vedādi Bhāṣya Bhūmikā*. New Delhi: Meharchand Lachhmandas, 1984, very helpful.

107. Sri Aurobindo Ghose, *Hymns to the Mystic Fire*. Pondicherry: Sri Aurobindo Ashram, 2nd. ed. 1952 (first ed., 1946). *On the Vedas*, Pondicherry: Sri Aurobindo Ashram, 1956 (repr. Sri Aurobindo, *Collected Works*, vols. 11 and 10). See also the additional manuscript material published in *Sri Aurobindo Archives and Research*, a quarterly journal published from the Ashram since 1977.

108. V.S. Agrawala, *Vedic Lectures*. Proceedings of the Summer School of Vedic Studies [at Benares Hindu University], May-June, 1960. Varanasi: School of Vedic Studies, BHU, 1963; same author, *Sparks from the Vedic Fire*. Varanasi: 1962 (*n.v.*); same author, *The Thousand Syllabled Speech*. I. *Vision in Long Darkness* [*Ṛg Veda* I.164.1-52]. Varanasi: pub. by author, 1963.

109. The vision of the Vedas as embodying an extraordinary state of integration with the Divine is based on my own impression of the *Ṛg Vedic* hymns, as well as on the numerous substantive comments on the Vedas by Sri Sathya Sai Baba. Sai Baba's extraordinary expositions (e.g. in *Summer Showers*, 1974) are having an effect on traditional scholarship, but have yet to be discussed in their own right in the West.

110. *Mārkaṇḍeya Purāṇa* 102.7. This view is largely shared by modern scholarship, which regards the *Atharva Veda* as serving mostly magical ends. Shastri, *History*, pp. 90 ff., argues against this.

111. Cf. Durgamohan Bhattacharyya, The *Brahma Veda* and the *Brahma Sūtra*, *PICO* 26, 1964, v. 3, Pt. 1. Poona Bhandarkar Oriental Institute, 1969, pp. 28-32. E.g. "In the unscrutinized part of . . . [the] Paippalāda text, the concept of the spiritual oneness of the world is taught in an abundantly greater degree as also in an appreciably developed form [compared to the

Ṛg Veda Saṁhitā]" (*ibid.*, p. 28). On the Paippalāda recension of the *Atharva Veda*, see D. Bhattacharyya, On the New Material in the *Atharva Veda Paippalāda. IIJ*, v. 27 (1984), pp. 173-188.

112. See the bibliographies in J.C. Heesterman's entry Vedism and Brāhmaṇism in Eliade, *Encyclopedia of Religion*, v. 17, pp. 241, col. 2, and 242, col. 2.
113. The long expected exposition by J.C. Heesterman, *The Broken World of Sacrifice*. Chicago: Univ. of Chicago Press, 1993, does not deal with spiritual aspects *per se*.
114. There seems to be no comprehensive discussion of the methodological problems that one faces when one tries to use the Sūtra to elucidate the original intent of the Upaniṣadic texts, however.
115. Radhakrishnan in his translation, *BraSū* (see abbreviations and conventions), draws on twelve commentaries, including Śaṁkara's, and also points out more general philosophical issues which the aphorisms may be raising. A detailed analysis of the Sūtra from a historical point of view may be found in Nakamura, *History*, v. 1, pp. 369-532.
116. Nakamura, *op. cit.*, pp. 500-511. Hence its traditional name of *śārīraka*, "that which has a body", "[the self] within the body". Cf. Nakamura, *ibid.*, p. 426.
117. Nakamura, *ibid.*, pp. 435-436 and note 7, p. 437.
118. Nakamura discusses the sages referred to in the Sūtra (*ibid.*, pp. 369-408, all of them are from BCE) and gives a rough outline of its probable development (*ibid.*, p. 433). "The original of the *Brahma Sūtra* is . . . very ancient, and its inception can be traced bank to the period of the formation of the *Kalpa Sūtra*" [i.e., the *Śrauta & Gṛhya Sūtras* in the period immediately following the old Upaniṣads] (*ibid.*, p. 433).
119. Translations: see note 27 above. For more detailed study, Belvalkar's translation and leisurely notes are still of interest: Belvalkar, S.K., *The Brahma-Sūtras of Bādarāyaṇa with the Comment of Śaṅkarāchārya*, Chapter II, Quarters I & II. 3rd ed. Ponna: Bilvakunja Pub. House, 1938, as well as the *Word Index to the Brahma Sūtra Bhāṣya of Śaṅkara*, 2 vs., Madras: Centre of Advanced Study in Philosophy, 1971-73.
120. Nakamura in addition distinguished the philodophy of the last redactor of the Sūtra (ca. 400-450 CE) from that of Bādarāyaṇa (dated variously between 300 & 0 BCE), although that redactor mostly follows Bādarāyaṇa. Cf. Nakamura, *ibid.*, pp. 406, 423.
121. Both the thoughts of sages that are explicitly quoted as such, and generally accepted principles or aphorisms.
122. Nakamura, *ibid.*, p. 436.
123. Translations: Swami Mādhavānanda, *BṛhUp Comm.*; Jha, *ChāndUp Comm.*; and Svāmī Gambhīrānanda, *Eight Ups. Commentary*.
124. Transl. S. Mayeda, *A Thousand Teachings*. Tokyo: Univ. of Tokyo Press, 1979.
125. In early twentieth century Indology he is usually only "the commentator" or "the scholiast".
126. The biennial International Congress of Vedānta at Miami University, Oxford, Ohio, usually attracts about 200 participants, many of them teaching philosophy at U.S. Colleges and Universities. In addition to philosophical there is also considerable theological interest in Vedānta,

particularly in Rāmānuja.

127. At Badari (in the Himalayas), Dvaraka (in Gujurat), Puri (in Orissa), Sringeri (in Karnataka), and (disputed by some) Kanchipuram near Madras.

128. On the history of these *maṭhas*, and on the Śaṅkarācāryas and the institutions connected with them today, see W. Cenkner, *A Tradition of Teachers: Śaṁkara and the Jagadgurus Today*. Delhi. Motilal Banarsidass, 1983 (chr. 5, The Śaṅkarācāryas and the Seats of Learning, pp. 109-134). Cenkner says that "[the 68th Śaṅkarācārya at Kañchi, Sri Candraśekharendra Sarasvatī, who served from 1919 to 1970 and then went into seclusion] and Sri Ramana Maharshi and Sri Aurobindo Ghose have dominated South India as religious personalities in modern times, but the Śaṅkarācārya had the broadest appeal and effectiveness among the people" (Cenkner, *ibid*., p. 123). Certainly with the Śaṅkarācāryas, "Advaita Vedānta . . . [is] a living religion relying on revealed scripture as ultimate authority, prescribing a specific lifestyle, aiming at transcendence, possessing a religious tradition of its own, with its own forms of piety and its own religious institutions," K. Klostermaier, Advaita Vedānta as a Living Religion. *Abstracts of Papers, International Congress of Vedānta*, Miami University, Oxford, Ohio, 1990, p. 20.

129. He is *ṣaṇ-matasthāpana-ācārya*, the teacher (*ācārya*) who brought the six forms of learning (*ṣaṇ-mata*) to a "standing up" (*sthāpana*). This type of unification is still a function of the Śaṅkarācāryas today. For example, at Kañchi, Śaṁkara's itinerant, bridgebuilding life serves as an inspiration to the present Śaṅkarācārya, with the result that "the temple, monastery, and ācārya himself create a circulatory mechanism which integrates social strata, ritual diversity and the world of the gods". W. Cenkner, "The Śaṅkarācārya of Kañchi and the Kāmākṣī Temple as Ritual Center." *Abstracts of Papers, International Congress of Vedānta*, Miami Univ., Oxford, Ohio, April 1990, p. 7.

130. Cf. P. Hacker's review of J. Gonda, *Religionen Indiens*, v. 2, in *Orientalistische Literaturzeitung*, v. 59 (1964), pp. 231-245; pp. 235-239 (repr. Hacker, *Kleine Schriften*, pp. 476-483; pp. 478-480).

131. At first on the basis of fairly strict manuscript criteria proposed by P. Hacker, Śaṅkarācārya and Śaṅkarabhagavatpāda, *New Indian Antiquary*, v. 9, 1950 Nos. 4-6, pp. 1-12; repr. with revisions in Hacker, *Kleine Schriften*, pp. 41-58 (Hacker lists and classifies some 50 odd writings attributed to Śaṁkara on pp. 48-50). More recently R.E. Gussner, A Stylometric Study of the Authorship of Seventeen Sanskrit Hymns Attributed to Śaṁkara, *JAOS*, 96 (1976), pp. 259-267, has used statistical methods comparing the frequency of key words in the text with their frequency in the *Upadeśa-sāhasrī*.

132. Cf. P. Hacker, Eigentümlichkeiten der Lehre und Terminologie Śaṁkaras: Avidyā, Nāmarūpa, Māyā, Īśvara. *ZDMG*, v. 100 (1950), pp. 246-286, repr. Hacker, *Kleine Schriften*, pp. 69-109; pp. 276 ff. (99 ff.). Hacker concludes from his survey that "the words (*param*) *brahma or paramātman* are throughout exchangeable with *īśvara*; that *īśvara* can be replaced in the great majority of cases by (*param*) *brahma* or *paramātman*, and that finally there where the subject of discussion is *upāsanā* [=contemplation, meditation, cf. chr. 4], *aparam brahma* can stand in place of *īśvara* just as well as *param brahma* or also *paramātman*" (*ibid*., pp. 284-285, resp.

107-108). The author then tries to explain this "peculiar mixed-up-ness" (*merkwürdige Verworrenheit*) (*ibid.*, pp. 285-286, resp. 108-109).

133. F.X. Clooney, The Splendour of Śaṁkara: Reading Śaṁkara through the Later Commentators, *Abstacts of Papers, International Congress of Vedānta*, Miami Univ., Oxford, Ohio, 1990.
134. Including those of Bhāskara, Madhva, Nimbārka and Śrīkaṇṭha. For an orientation, see Radhakrishnan, *Brahma Sūtras*, pp. 25-102.
135. R. Schwab, *The Oriental Renaissance. Europe's Rediscovery of India and the East*, 1680-1880. New York: Columbia University Press, 1984 (or. French ed., 1950); W. Halbfass, *Indien und Europa: Perspektiven ihrer geistigen Begegnigung*. Basel and Stuttgart: Schwabe Verlag, 1981; Engl. rev. ed., *India and Europe: An Essay in Understanding*. Albany, NY: SUNY Press, 1988 (with four new articles added on pp. 378-402).
136. Antequil Duperron, A.H., *Oupnek'hat, id est, Secretum Tegendum*. Paris: Levrault, 1801-2 (2 volumes).
137. Schwab, *op. cit.*, p. 159. Schwab also wrote a life of Antequil which was unfortunately not accessible to me (*Vie d'Antequil Duperron*, Paris: E. Leroux, 1934, *n. v.*).
138. Antequil Duperron, *op. cit.*, v. 1, p. 1 of index.
139. Schwab, *op. cit.*, p. 162.
140. Halbfass, *op. cit.*, p. 83, quoting Antequil Duperron, *op. cit.*, p. 722.
141. Schwab, *op. cit.*, p. 161, whence Schwab dubs him "disciple of Indian Sages" (*ibid.* p. 158).
142. Hübscher, A., Schopenhauer und die Religionen Asiens. In *60. Schopenhauer Jahrbuch für das Jahr 1979*. Frankfurt a. M.: Verlag Waldemar Kramer, 1979, pp. 1-16; p. 5.
143. Apart from Schopenhauer and Krause, Antequil's work also influenced Johann Joseph Görres and Thaddaeus Anselm Rixner. Görres, a major personality of the German Romantic movement and later historian of Christian mysticism, reacted in a general way. To him "the ancient Indian secret teaching was producing a sound 'like a giant Harp stretched over the resonating depth of Nature, in a full, solemn, peculiarly strange sounding tone; from the dawn of ages, there seemed to be here speaking a people which had let the gifts of contemplation go forward to the ultimate depth of knowledge" (Hübscher, *ibid.*, p. 5, citing Görres' review of the *Oupnek'hat* in the *Heidelberger Jahrbücher der Literatur*). Rixner is little known. He first served as Dominican priest and then became professor of philosophy at the Lyceum (girls school) at Amberg. Antequil's translation inspired him to a tract *Versuch einer neuen Darstellung der ur-alten indischen All-Eins-Lehre*, Nuremberg: 1808 (*n.v.*). But later in his lecture notes on the history of philosophy, he only lists Antequil's book and gives a couple reference on the dates of the Upaniṣads under the heading "the ancient, mythic and phantastic All-One-doctrine, of the still immature understanding (*unmündiger Verstand*) which had not yet matured to reason (*Vernunft*) and still less to Science". T.A. Rixner, *Handbuch der Geschichte der Philosophie* (3 vols.) v. 1. 2nd rev. ed. Sulzbach: Seidelsche Buchhandlung, 1829 (1st ed., 1822), p. 21.
144. Schopenhauer, A., *Der Handschriftliche Nachlass*, ed. A. Hübscher, v. 1. Frankfurt A.M.: Verlag Waldemar Kramer, 1966, p. 120. On Schopenhauer and the Upaniṣads, see the article by Hübscher in note 142, and H. von

Glasenapp, Schopenhauer and India, *Schopenhauer Jahrbuch* 35, 1955. Reprinted in H. von Glasenapp, *Ausgewählte Kleine Schriften* (H. Bechert and V. Möller, eds.). Wiesbaden: Franz Steiner, 1980, pp. 504-509.

145. Schopenhauer, A., *Die Welt als Wille und Vorstellung*, v. 1, p. 419; in Schopenhauer, A., *Sämtliche Werke*, ed. A. Hübscher, v. 2. Wiesbaden: F.A. Brockhaus, 3rd ed. 1972; transl. E.F.J. Payne, *The World as Will and Representation*. Indian Hills, Col.: Falcon's Wing Press, 1958, p. 355
146. Gwinner, W., *Arthur Schopenhauer aus persönlichem Umgang dargestellt*. Leipzig: F.A. Brockhaus, 1862, p. 215.
147. *Parerga und Paralipomena* II. In *Sämtliche Werke* (see note 145), v. 6, p. 422; transl. E.F.J. Payne, *Parerga and Paralipomena*. Oxford: Clarendon Press, 1974, p. 397.
148. *Parerga und Paralipomena* I, p. 6. *Sämtliche Werke* (see note 145), v. 5, p. 6; transl. E.F.J. Payne, *op. cit.*, pp. 5-6.
149. P. Gaefke, in a book review in the *JAOS*, v. 102 (1982), p. 550.
150. *Fr. Überwegs Grundriss der Geschichte der Philosophie. 4. Teil. Die Deutsche Philosophie des 19. Jahrhunderts und der Gegenwart.* 12th ed., completely revised by T.C. Österreich. Berlin: E.S. Mittler & Sohn, 1923, pp. 102-112. In English, Arnulf Zweig gives a sympathetic account in the *Encyclopedia of Philosophy*.
151. These are areas in which Krause had some impact. According to Österreich, *op. cit.*, p. 108, his most significant achievement was his philosophy of law, and his social philosophy became influential outside Germany, particularly in Spain, where "Krausism" was a major movement up to the 20th century. Krause was an extraordinarily prolific author most of whose work was published only gradually in the course of the 19th century. There is no scholarly edition of his collected works. Besides philosophy he also wrote on metaphysical subjects in the occult sense of the term, including music and metaphysical mathematics. Cf. the entries in the GV (*Gesamtverzeichnis des deutsch-sprachigen Schriftums*) 1700-1910 and 1911-1973.
152. H. v. Glasenapp, Indien in der Gedankenwelt des Philosophen Karl Christian Friedrich Krause. In H.O. Günther (ed.), *Indien und Deutschland. Ein Sammelband*. Frankfurt a. M.: Europäische Verlagsanstalt, 1956, pp. 16-22. Reprinted in H. v. Glasenapp, *Ausgewählte kleine Schriften, op. cit.*, pp. 504-507.
153. P. Hohlfeld & A. Wünsche, eds., *Briefwechsel K.C.F. Krauses*, v. 1. Leipzig: Dieterich, p. 362 (*n.v.*), cited in v. Glasenapp, *op. cit.*, p. 506.
154. *Briefwechsel*, p. 441, cited in v. Glasenapp, *op. cit.*, p. 507.
155. K.C.F. Krause, *Vorlesungen über das System der Philosophie*. Göttingen: Dieterich, 1828, p. 416. Cited in v. Glasenapp, *op. cit.*, p. 509.
156. Ed. Müller. Oxford: Clarendon Press, 1879-1910 (50 volumes).
157. Preface to the SBE. In M. Müller, ed., *SBE*, v. 1, p. xxxvi.
158. Halbfass, *op. cit.*, pp. 145-146, quoting H. Scholz, Paul Deussen +. *Kantstudien* 24 (1920), pp. 316 ff.
159. Halbfass, *op. cit.*, p. 147, quoting a letter by Nietzsche to P. Gast dated 8.9.1887.
160. Halbfass, *ibid.*, p. 147.
161. See Abbreviations and Conventions.
162. Halbfass, *op. cit.*, p. 151.
163. Deussen, *Geschichte*, pt. I.1, p. 32.
164. Halbfass, *op. cit.*, p. 165.

CHAPTER 2

The Great Teachings

1. The Five Oldest Upaniṣads: General Approach in this Book

Although the Upaniṣads are testimonies from the distant past, they often speak directly to a modern reader and one feels an extraordinary higher knowledge. This is illustrated by the two texts from *Bṛhadāraṇyaka Upaniṣad* which, after a brief orientation, form the focus of the present chapter. Our approach will be basically to highlight and respond maximally to the high-level "transcendental element" in these texts, without going more deeply into historical and religious questions, or questions of interpretation, inner experience and practice. While this procedure has its dangers, it will give us an opportunity to get an initial idea of Ātman/Brahman by seeing how the Upaniṣads talk about Ātman and Brahman. The texts chosen also illustrate the role and importance of "rising above and transcending desire (and fear etc.)" in the Upaniṣadic approach. Beginning with chapter 3 we will then try to understand other texts more specifically in their proper context and in more detail.

The Principal Upaniṣads. The fourteen or so so-called "principal" (or "Vedic") Upaniṣads may be roughly grouped chronologically as shown in Table 2.1.[1] Only the texts in the first and third group are similar to each other in terms of content and style and are likely to come from the same historical context. The others are grouped together for convenience. The two largest and most substantial works are *Bṛhadāraṇyaka* and *Chāndogya Upaniṣads*, accounting for more than half of the total volume of the fourteen. They are closely related to each other and together with *Aitareya, Kauṣītaki*, and *Taittirīya Upaniṣads* form the group of five "oldest Upaniṣads". These texts represent the original Upaniṣadic Tradition. *Īśā* (or *Īśāvāsya*) and *Kena Upaniṣads*, the next two in Table 2.1, are small works. They are part of older texts (*Īśā* is the last chapter of the *Vājasaneyī Saṁhitā* and *Kena* occurs in *Jaiminīya Upaniṣad Brāhmaṇa*), but they may have been added to these later and their historical position is uncertain. *Kaṭha, Muṇḍaka*, and *Śvetāśvatara Upaniṣads* form the "middle group" Upaniṣads. They are almost entirely in verse, with on the order of a hundred stanzas each, and are clearly later than the Upaniṣads of the oldest group (cf. below). Next, *Mahā-Nārāyaṇa* and *Maitrāyaṇīya Upaniṣads* are aggregates of diverse material. Both consist of small

TABLE 2.1
The Principal (or Vedic) Upaniṣads

Name	Abbreviation	Dating
Bṛhadāraṇyaka Upaniṣad	*BṛhUp*	
Chāndogya Upaniṣad	*ChāndUp*	
Aitareya Upaniṣad	*AitUp*	800-600
Kauṣītaki Upaniṣad	*KauṣUp*	BCE
Taittirīya Upaniṣad	*TaittUp*	
Kena Upaniṣad	*KenaUp*	unclear
Īśā Upaniṣad	*ĪśāUp*	
Kaṭha (or *Kāṭhaka*) *Upaniṣad*	*KaṭhaUp*	
Muṇḍaka Upaniṣad	*MuṇḍUp*	600-200
Śvetāśvatara Upaniṣad	*ŚvetUp*	BCE
Mahā-Nārāyaṇa Upaniṣad	*Mahā-NarUp*	mixed
Maitrāyaṇīya Upaniṣad	*MaitrUp*	
Praśna Upaniṣad	*PraśUp*	after
Māṇḍūkya Upaniṣad	*MāṇḍUp*	200 BCE

cores of older (Āraṇyaka-type) material and extensive additions made over the course of many centuries. *Praśna* and *Māṇḍūkya Upaniṣads* finally are unified compositions that are later than groups one through three. They are "late" Vedic Upaniṣads.

The Five Oldest Upaniṣads. In this book we are concerned primarily with the five oldest Upaniṣads, *Bṛhadāraṇyaka Upaniṣad* etc. Various facts suggest that these are definitely older than the texts in the middle group (*Kaṭha Upaniṣad* etc.). Many sections and passages in them have parallels in the Brāhmaṇas and Āraṇyakas, or consist of mystical or esoteric commentary on particular features of Vedic ritual (such as the *agnihotra*, the daily offering of milk into the fire, or *sāman* chanting, a special type of chanting by special types of priests in the *soma* sacrifices). In the middle group Upaniṣads, material of this type is much less common.[2] The ostensibly oldest works are also largely written in the same style as the Brāhmaṇas and Āraṇyakas.[3] At the sentence level, a prominent pattern is one of explanation or association or elaboration, "an x is (i.e. has the connotations of, means, signifies, has the same nature as) a y", where x is what is intended to be elaborated etc. and y is the new aspect to which attention is being drawn. Content extending over several paragraphs is often developed using schemas familiar from the Brāhmaṇas. Thus the text may elaborate on a standard series of deities, or on the four directions, or the three sacred fires, or the five breaths, etc., or it may set up a system of correspondences or (stratified) analogies involving such series. Longer developments are also often given with a frame story (a wisdom contest among Brahmins, a teacher teaching someone who approached him for teaching, a contest for superiority among gods and demons, etc.). Also common are appeals to what look like wordplays or "folk-etymologies" (based on alliteration, syllable counts, etc.) to support inner or esoteric meanings of words and teachings. All these devices are often met with in the Brāhmaṇas. One idea behind them is a didactic one—to lay something out in reasoned form.

The Middle Group Upaniṣads are compositions that represent great spiritual statements in the form of inspired poetry. They make a completely different impression. They are meant to inspire, or to exalt or celebrate; there is little attempt to lay things out in reasoned form. The five oldest Upaniṣads are part of the normal corpus of sacred literature (Brāhmaṇas or Āraṇyakas) of particular Vedic schools. They represent the deepest understanding of these schools, the culmination of their revealed literature, which is taught to the Brahmin student in the later stages of his training and which he would try to live in his own experience and priestly practice throughout his later life. The middle group Upaniṣads on the other hand are relatively sophisticated literary compositions, structured and unified at various levels from literary points of view. As such they may have been studied in a slightly different spirit, by groups of students and teachers in which the spiritual enterprise was combined with a poetic interest.

The Status of the Five Oldest Upaniṣads as Highest Wisdom. Simply setting the Upaniṣads up as a well-defined group of texts as in Table

2.1 tends to suggest that they were acknowledged as a special class of literature from the very beginning. But here we have to careful. The conception of the class of texts which we are calling "the Upaniṣads" varies depending on the historical period and even varies within a period.[4] In particular, the appreciation of the Upaniṣads as we have them today as a particular set of works dealing with highest Wisdom may only go back to about the beginning of the Christian era. It is not even certain when the oldest Upaniṣads at least were first acknowledged to form a literature dealing directly with higher knowledge and different from the Āraṇyakas. No doubt the term *upaniṣad* (and the adjective *aupaniṣada*, "taught in or by an *upaniṣad*") used in the oldest Upaniṣads has a specific set of meanings which must be closely connected with the earliest idea of the nature of these texts. In some places *upaniṣad* refers to brief, two or three word formulas that encapsulate entire higher spiritual or esoteric teachings;[5] in others it may refer to a more extensive exposition of such teachings.[6] The term also occurs several times in a standard enumeration of types of texts and of types of knowledge,[7] next to *ślokas* and *sūtras*, "verses (in a certain meter)" and "aphorisms", two well-defined genres. The most important piece of evidence, however, is *BṛhUp* III.9.28 (K), where the sage Yājñavalkya challenges the Brahmin Śākalya with ". . . I ask you about that Upaniṣadic person" (*aupaniṣadam puruṣam*, "Person or Entity taught in the *Upaniṣads*"). Here the implication is that the *upaniṣads*—may be the brief formulas—are all teaching the same "Person" or "Entity". Indeed almost immediately before this, Yājñavalkya described this Entity by "This Self is *'not', 'not'*. It is not graspable [by hands or mind] because it is not grasped" etc. (cf. below). Hence the implication is that all these *upaniṣads* teach the Self, Ātman. According to Oldenberg, the old Upaniṣads originally were only collections of such two or three word *upaniṣads* (and similar sayings) and expostion of them.[8] However, texts of this kind account only for a portion of the total volume of the material in the oldest Upaniṣads. There must have occurred some extension of the concept to get from texts of this type to the entire corpus of the (oldest?) Upaniṣads.[9]

In this connection, Western scholars have tried to determine the basic meaning of the term *upaniṣad* and related terms from their etymology and a study of their occurrences. *Upaniṣad* is derived from *ni-sad*, to sit down (on something), and *upa-*, a prefix which adds the meaning "up close to", with a connotation of "looking up from below". A traditional Indian interpretation, supported by Deussen, takes this to mean "drawing close to the teacher" and interprets *upaniṣad* as a "secret teaching" (a secret formula or way of approaching Brahman) which the teacher communicates to his students while they are sitting close around him.[10] Oldenberg argued that this should be modified to "a reverential sitting down in which the pious and wise concentrate their thoughts on the highest object of all ponderings, viz. the Ātman or Brahman", so that an *upaniṣad* is "(a mode of) adoraton (of Ātman/Brahman)".[11] Recently H. Falk has emphasized the meaning of "power to bring about a desired effect" which the term also has in the Brāhmaṇas and Vedas.[12] All these meanings are illuminating and each fits well in some cases and is less applicable in others. All of them are more or less compatible with Yājñavalkya's "person (or entity) taught in the *upaniṣads*". Perhaps Yājñavalkya's idea is connected with the fact that in the five oldest Upaniṣads, one often feels a tacit understanding that a given teaching belongs to a common tradition or enterprise, viz. the knowledge and elaboration of Ātman/Brahman to which most of the old Upaniṣadic teachings contribute, and which is represented by them as a whole.[13] But it is not clear how much of this reflects the understanding of the sages who originally expounded these teachings, and how much represents the effects of later redactors and compilers.

Moving up in time, the middle period Upaniṣads no doubt presuppose the original Upaniṣadic tradition. But they refer to the oldest Upaniṣads surprisingly little while constantly citing each other.[14] Indirect evidence that the oldest Upaniṣads were regarded as a unified universal Supreme Wisdom literature are the beginnings of the philosophical preoccupation with the Upaniṣadic texts that eventually resulted in the *Brahma Sūtra*. This might have taken place in the second century BCE or earlier.[15] The earliest explicit recognition of most of the Principal Upaniṣads as a separate class of texts (a la Table 2.1) is only found in texts from the first few centuries CE.[16]

General Approach to the Meaning of the Upaniṣadic Teachings in this Book. In trying to enter more deeply into the Upaniṣadic teachings, particularly into their spiritual substance, the question arises as to what approach should be adopted. To follow the thought of *Bṛhadāraṇyaka Upaniṣad* or *Chāndogya Upaniṣad* sequentially, from section to section, is not feasible in an introductory treatment. As noted earlier, these works are compilations of dozens of texts ranging from two or three word phrases such as *satyam Brahma*, "Brahman is the True (or Real)," to mystical teachings a few paragraphs in length, to elaborate expositions extending over several pages. While there may be immediately apparent connections between some of these units, larger themes and the exact specific role and teaching of a given unit often become apparent only when there is considerable familiarity with the corpus as a whole. On the other hand, to give a systematic exposition of "old Upaniṣadic teaching" and merely quote selected passages to illustrate a particular point is also problematic. It would severely distort the nature of these works and destroy much of the power which they have in their traditional format. And the basic parameters of the over all picture would arise mostly unnoticeably from the author's own philosophical and spiritual categories, rather than evolve in full view of the reader out of an interaction with the texts. As a compromise, therefore, we work with individual sections or other sizeable portions of text which are to some extent self-contained and can be approached as independent units. This approach also allows the use of parallel texts to get a better understanding of a given text, a basic strategy of modern philological-historical and literary textual analysis.[17] However, this strategy has its own very great dangers. I fully agree with Coomaraswamy that "it is far safer to distrust our own powers of understanding than to pick and choose what seems to us plausible or implausible in its context. We have no right to denature our sources".[18]

Bibliographical Note.[19] There are perhaps a score of English translations of the major Upaniṣads as a whole. The best known ones are the one volume editions by R.E. Hume and S. Radhakrishnan (see under Abbreviations and Conventions). Hume gives straightforward, rather literal translations of 13 Upaniṣads. The literalness is an advantage when one studies the texts more deeply. Also, metrical form is indicated typographically (by printing the translation of a verse so that it looks like a verse to the eye), and larger patterns that extend over several paragraphs are likewise conveyed by typographical means. Radhakrishnan covers 18 Upaniṣads, complete with the original Sanskrit (in transliteration), English translation, and extensive notes. His renderings are usually more readable than Hume's. His book is invaluable because he gives the Sanskrit text and often comments more generally on the teaching, citing traditional commentaries as well as related passages in Christian, Islamic, Buddhist and other Traditions.

Apart from these and other single-author translations of the principal Upaniṣads as a group,[20] several series of publications provide in-depth treatment of individual Upaniṣads by different authors. Thus *Les Upanishad* is a French series of editions and translations under the editorship of the late L. Renou which exemplifies high modern philological-historical scholarship.[21] In India the Ramakrishna Math, the educational and publishing arm of the Ramakrishna Order, has published and is continually reprinting their *Upaniṣad Series*, with traditional interpretations based mostly on Śaṁkara's commentaries[22]. The same organization has also made Śaṁkara's commentaries widely available[23] (always with the Upaniṣadic text included). The translations in the *Sacred Books of the Hindus*[24] are based on and include the commentary of Madhva (12th cent. CE), the founder of Dvaita (dualistic) Vedānta, who approaches the Upaniṣads in terms of theistic experience.

2. *Bṛhadāraṇyaka Upaniṣad. BṛhUp* IV. 4.16-31 (M): Text

Bṛhadāraṇyaka Upaniṣad has been called "the crowning achievement of Vedic literature".[25] It "seems to incorporate in itself the central teachings of all the principal Upaniṣads", . . . "whether . . . by way of recapitulation or anticipation".[26] Indian tradition and some modern Indian scholars hold that it "exhibits an overwhelming unity of thought",[27] and this will be confirmed by our study in this book. But modern historical and philological scholarship has emphasized its character as a composite work.[28] The Upaniṣad is part of the *Śatapatha Brāhmaṇa*, or "Brāhmaṇa of a Hundred (*śata*) paths (*patha*)". This is the largest of all Brāhmaṇas (Eggeling's English translation in the Sacred Books of the East runs to five volumes)[29] and is a great spiritual text in its own right. It deals with the ritual actions and accompanying mantras of the *adhvaryu* priests, constantly explaining their rationale and inner meaning. If one takes the Vedic ritual seriously and regards it as a fundamental spiritual mode and discipline that pervades a person's mind and life at many levels, then the Brāhmaṇa becomes intensely vital. There are constantly all kinds of spiritual comments and mysticism, and especially in the sustained developments it attains a level of mystical intensity and concentration which is extraordinary and completely absorbing.

The *Śatapatha Brāhmaṇa* is the Brāhmaṇa of the *Vājasaneyī Saṁhitā*, the Saṁhitā of the *Śukla Yajur Veda*, because it discusses the rituals and mantras in the *Vājasaneyī Saṁhitā* mostly in the order in which they occur there. Like the Saṁhitā, this Brāhmaṇa exists in two recensions, the Mādhyandina and the Kāṇva (named after two Vedic schools), in 14 and 16 (or 17) books respectively.[30] In both of them, *Bṛhadāraṇyaka Upaniṣad* occurs at the very end, in the last book. The two versions of the Upaniṣad are substantially the same. But sometimes there are significant differences in phrasing, and now and then a group of verses may be rearranged, or individual phrases or whole verses may be missing.[31]

The Upaniṣad[32] consists of 6 chapters (*adhyāyas*, "lessons") which are further subdivided into sections called *brāhmaṇas* (cf. chr. 1.3). A good starting point are chapters III and IV, in which the sage Yājñavalkya is the teacher and which make up the *Yājñavalkyakāṇḍa*, or "section (*kāṇḍa*) of Yājñavalkya".[33] Yājñavalkya is generally considered to be a historical personality.[34] He is traditionally the author of *ŚatBr* I-V and XI-XIV, and according to *BṛhUp* VI.5.3 he also revealed and taught the mantras of the *Yajur Veda*.[35] The *Yājñavalkyakāṇḍa* consists of four major units:

III.1-9	A great "wisdom-contest", organized by King Janaka of Videha, in which Yājñavalkya replies one after another to the questions of eight Brahmins, including one woman (the Videhas lived northeast of modern Patna, in northern Bihar);
IV.1-2	A dialogue between Yājñavalkya and Janaka of Videha;
IV.3-4	Yājñavalkya's great instruction to Janaka of Videha;
IV.5	(almost the same as *BṛhUp* II.4): Yājñavalkya teaches his wife Maitreyī;
(IV.6	Succession of teachers for III-IV).

". . . These philosophical discussions. . . [form] a brilliant formulation of the major thesis of the Upaniṣad in philosophical terms . . . It is a great pleasure to follow these enquiries . . ."[36] The tone is amazingly modern: expository, objective, cumulative over longer stretches, with systematic use of sequences of metaphors and shifts in point of view —an awesome, incredible intelligence speaking to the modern mind from the deep past.

***BṛhUp* IV.4.16-32 (M).** Our first text is *BṛhUp* IV.4.16-32 (M), the end of the great instruction *BṛhUp* IV.3-4, where Yājñavalkya begins to deal explicitly and at some length with the Self, Ātman. The translation is by Franklin Edgerton, with a few changes indicated in the notes.[37] It follows the Mādhyandina recension, which is less often translated, but gives Kāṇva variants in parentheses.

16. If a man should well-understand the Ātman[a], saying 'I am It'—seeking after what, for desire of what, should he pursue (Kāṇva: crave after, be troubled about) the body?
17. He who has found and awakened his Self, that is entered into this thicket of a bodily mold (impenetrable bodily complex), he is the All-creator; for he is the Maker of everything;
    Heaven is his; nay rather, he *is* Heaven outright!
18. When one looks upon[b] this, the Self, directly as God,
    the Lord of past and future, then he shall not falter.
19. That in which the five orders of five[c] and the ether have their foundation,
    even that I hold to be the Self; knowing [I hold it to be] Brahman; immortal, [I hold it to be] the Immortal.[d]
20. On this side of whom (or: Before which) the year revolves with the days,
    that the gods worship as the light of lights—yes, as life, as immortality.
21. The life (-power) of life (-power), the eye of the eye likewise, and the ear of the ear, the food of food,[e] the mind of mind—those who know his, they have understood the Brahman, the ancient, the primal.
    By the mind alone must it be perceived that there is nothing manifold in this world.
22. Death after death attains he who thinks he sees manifoldness in this world.
    That imperishable, constant one must be perceived only with the mind;
23. (It is) the unborn, great, constant Self, free from impurity, higher than the ether.
    A man of insight, a brāhmaṇa having understood this (Self), should make knowledge for himself.
    Let him not muse on many words; for that is only wearing out the voice.
24. Now it is this Self that is the controller of all, the lord of all, the sovereign of all; it governs all this universe, whatever is at all. It becomes not greater by good deed, nor less

by evil deed. It is overlord of creatures; it is the lord of the world(s); it is the guardian of the world(s); it is the dike that holds apart these worlds, lest they should crash together (i.e. it keeps the world order from falling into chaos).

25. This it is which they seek to know through repetition of the Vedas, through celibate life, through asceticism, through faith, through sacrifice, and through fasting. When one knows this he becomes a Muni (silent sage). This it is which wandering ascetics seek as their heavenly world when they wander forth as ascetics.

26. Therefore those brāhmaṇas of old, learned and wise, desired no offspring, thinking: What shall we do with offspring, we who possess this Self, this (equivalent of the) Heavenly World (which is the traditional object of begetting sons)?—Abandoning both the desire for sons and the desire for possessions and the desire for heaven, they wandered forth a-begging. For the desire for sons is the same as the desire for possessions, and the desire for possessions is the same as the desire for heaven; for both are nothing but desires.

27. This Self is (simply described as) 'Not, not'. It is ungraspable, for it is not grasped. It is indestructible, for it is not destroyed. It has no attachment, and is unfastened [to anything]; it is not attached, and (yet) is not unsteady. For it, immortal, passes beyond both these two stages (in which one thinks) 'For this reason I have done evil', 'For this reason I have done good'. It is not disturbed by good or evil things that are done or left undone; its heaven is not lost by any deed.

28. This is meant by this *Ṛg Vedic* verse:[f]
This is the constant greatness of the *brāhmaṇa* (knower of Brahman);
It increases not nor becomes less by deed.
This (greatness) it is, the basis of which one should seek to find. Having found it, one is not stained by evil deed. Therefore, one who knows this, becoming pacified, controlled, at peace, full of faith (Kāṇva: in concentration), should see the Self in the Self alone. He looks upon everyone as it. Everyone comes to be his Self; he becomes the Self of everyone. He passes over all evil; evil does not

pass over him. He subdues all evils; evil does not subdue him. He is free from evil, free from age (Kāṇva: from impurity), free from hunger (Kāṇva: from doubt), free from thirst (Kāṇva omits), a *brāhmaṇa*, whoso has this knowledge.

29. This verily is that great unborn Self, the eater of (sacrificial) food, the giver of wealth (i.e., who has the functions of the Vedic gods). Whosoever knows thus this great unborn Self, the eater of food, the giver of wealth, he finds Wealth.

30. This is that great unborn Self, ageless, deathless, fearless immortal—the Brahman. You have attained fearlessness, O Janaka! Thus spoke Yājñavalkya.—I now give unto your reverence the Videhas, and myself too along with them, in servitude.

31. This is that great unborn Self, ageless, deathless, fearless, immortal, the Brahman. The Brahman, in sooth, is fearlessness; fearlessness surely he becomes, he becomes Brahman, who has such knowledge.[37]

Clearly, this is an extraordinary text. There is something very great here. In the authority and sureness one senses a consciousness, an intelligence that has somehow risen above the problems of human life and the univese, of multiplicity, appearance and existence, that has gone beyond the limitations of aspirations, and that has come to a state of changeless Knowledge. At the same time incomprehensible things are being said: "He is the All-Creator . . . He is Heaven outright . . . He is the Self of everyone . . . ." Let us step back and get some bearings.

3. Ātman/Brahman

"The Self", Ātman. The text talks about "The Self", Ātman. It says that in every human being there is a level at which, or "being at which", he or she is somehow all: "He is the All Creator," He "governs this universe, whatever is at all"; "he becomes the Self of everyone", etc. At the same time, there is at this level "nothing manifold", there is no multiplicity (*nānā*). Instead this level, or "being at this level", is "fixed," *dhruva*. Another term often used later in this connection is "non-dual", *a-dvaita*.[38] For example v. 27 implies that "at this level" (of consciousness? of being? of existence? whatever! no term really fits exactly), or when "there obtains" this One, this Oneness, then the realm of action has been somehow completely transcended. There is at that point no more question of this action versus that, or this reason versus that, or good versus evil. In other words, there is then no more duality, no two-ness, or opposition of two conflicting things. Thus this "state", the Self, is nondual and constant. Finally the Self is what is really at the basis of the "feeling of 'I' " or the "sense of 'I'," *asmitā*, which every human being has. In other words, "being at the level" of the Self is "experientially akin" to and connected with the root of the "feeling of 'I'." The latter may also be described as the "feeling of being the seer", or "the feeling of being of the nature of the seer", *dṛg-bhāvanā*. (These terms are from the later Yoga and Vedānta Traditions.[39]) In short, the Self is the reality underlying "I", myself as a conscious subject, or "the Reality which I am", but at a level where the manifoldness of objects and of action has been transcended (and therefore "conscious subject" must have a different meaning). Sanskrit *Ātman* is a noun (masculine) which is found already in the *Ṛg Veda* with the meaning "breath, life-breath, life-principle".[40] Beginning in the *Atharva Veda* and the *Yajur Veda Saṁhitās* it then also takes on the meaning "[my-, he-, her-] self", functioning much like "self" in English.[41] Its basic meaning in the Upaniṣads is clearly "the self" (as a noun). It is sometimes translated as "Spirit", as in "God is Spirit", or "Worship God in Spirit and in Truth". This is often also correct, together with "Self". But it is very important to keep the term "Self".

As portrayed in the text, the Self resists all normal categorizations and conceptualizations. Most astonishing, *there is only one Self*. Although there are many human beings in the world each of whom feels his or her own self to be different from all the others, in reality there is only one Self which "shines" in all the individual selves (and in all minds, in all individual consciousnesses).[42] At first this sounds incredible or even contradictory. In Western culture the usual idea is that one is somehow carrying ones's own self (including one's own mind and consciousness) around with oneself, within one's own body (in the head, between the eyes, whatever).[43] The problem is much reduced if we think of the Self as "the reality which one is", because it is quite reasonable to think that all are the same Reality. At any rate, to distinguish the One Self or Ātman from the individual self, we will write it with a capital S. So the One Self shines in every individual, in his or her individual self. But one does not have two selves, one with a lower case s and the other with a capital S.

Besides the fact that one Self abides in all beings, there are also other difficulties. For example, the Self is sometimes talked about as if it was a state of consciousness, so that it should come under the heading of "subjective experience" or "awareness". But it is also often described the same way one would normally describe a physical object, i.e., it is treated as if it was an externally existing entity. In fact, these two ways and the connotations they carry alternate and mingle so freely that one gets the feeling that the Self, or "having realized the Self", may possibly have somewhat the quality of each, but that really it is somehow beyond these categories. Evidently we must simply accept the text as it stands, with all its apparently contradictory connotations and implications, and let it settle in us as it may, having faith that somehow, over time, some truer understanding will arise.

The Text: Nature of the Self. With these preliminaries, let us consider the text in more detail. Recall that the Self, the Ātman, can be "found", "awakened in oneself", "perceived" and "known",[44] *while one is alive*. We will say that there are various types, levels, or degrees of "knowledge" or of "realization of the Self". Knowledge of the Self, or *Ātma-jñāna* (from *jñā*, "know") suggests a permanent or timeless aspect in one's self or consciousness which is not affected by death. High-level realization of the Self is called *Ātma-sākṣātkāra*.[45] Knowledge or realization of the Self is obviously not something that consists in understanding certain ideas. Nor is it memory of experiences in meditation which can be written off as transient or illusory, as purely subjective, psychological effects. "He who has found and awakened his Self, . . . , he is the Maker of Everything" (v. 17); ". . . he becomes the Self of everyone . . . he passes over all evil . . he subdues all evils . . . He is free from evil, free from age, free from hunger, free from thirst" (v. 28);. . . . "he finds Wealth" (v. 29). Obviously the scripture is talking about something permanent, something that transcends one's body, one's life, as well as space and time. And equally obviously, these things must at the same time also be in some sense "experiential", they must be somehow "literally true". In fact they must be even somehow reflected in externally observable, objective effects that an outsider could see in the person. The elevated nature of the writing makes this clear. The text is pointing to something that is beyond comprehension. We might say that realization of the Self overcomes the entire physical and mental world manifold that we see. (This "overcoming" the world must be of a completely different order from the overcoming the world that is involved in sleeping or using drugs.) The Self is somehow ineffably greater than all this physical and mental manifold. It is not limited by it and in actuality governs every aspect of it, "whatever is at all" (v. 24). In fact king Janaka, attaining realization, gives Yājñavalkya his whole kingdom and himself (body and mind) in servitude (vs. 30). The entire world, including his status and consciousness as a king, have become insignificant to him. *This* is an observable aspect of "he is free from evil . . . free from hunger, free from thirst" here.

So Ātman and Brahman are not concepts, and statements about Ātman and Brahman are not "facts" or "theories". The Upaniṣads, being Scriptures, do not expound doctrines about the nature of the world or of human existence in the way in which Science, for example, expounds facts and concepts and theories. In the Upaniṣads the Infinite is speaking, and as such they utter only the Infinite, teach only the Infinite. In Christian terms, Spirit utters only Spirit, Spirit (Christ) teaches only Spirit. The words in the text before one are all Spirit. What arises in the heart or mind when one reads them is Spirit. The words are not understood unless there is Spirit. So the Upaniṣads, and indeed Scriptures generally, always only *point* to something—the Goal of Life, the Supreme Good, the One God, Brahman, Emptiness, whatever. We will say that they "teach" what they point to. The Upaniṣads teach Ātman and Brahman just like Jesus in the Gospels teaches the Kingdom of God, or God, or just like some of the Catholic Saints teach Union with God and Eternal Beatitude while living. Further, that what is being taught, that what is being pointed to, is not really comprehensible by mind. It is of a different order, a different register—different from the order, the register of the world and the mind which we know. And finally, in such reaching or pointing to the concepts that are being used, and the statements that are made, are all basically only instruments or aids to make the pointing effective. They are aids in awakening one's soul, one's self, or aids in enabling one to walk the path to that Incomprehensible. This is the spirit in which we have to understand the text—the text here, and any text that speaks the Infinite.

Knowledge of the Self. Continuing, we see that the Scripture pictures the process of attaining knowledge of the Self as proceeding gradually, by degrees, over a whole lifetime. Various disciplines serve this end and all may and should be practiced (v. 25): memorization of the Vedas, celibate life, austerity (*tapas*), a life of faith, etc. In addition, there are also some beautiful examples of being at intermediate stages. One is v. 23, "A man of insight, . . . , by understanding this, should make knowledge for himself. Let him not muse on many words. . ." In other words: when something of this has dawned in a person, when it *has* become a true knowledge in his or her heart and being, so that there *has* been realization of some degree, even if faint, then "(that person) should make [more] knowledge for himself". That person should promote or increase the dawning, following what his/her innermost soul which is bent toward this tells him/her. Another phase is mentioned in v. 28: "Therefore, one who knows this, becoming pacified, at peace, patient, full of faith, should see the Self in the Self alone. . ." etc. When a true sense of "the greatness that knows no increase or decrease" dawns in one's mind or heart (see the beginning of the verse), then this is signalled by the fact that one becomes pacified, controlled, at peace in one's life. A person at this stage "should see the Self in the self alone," i.e., he/she should then live ever inward—directed, abiding in the Self, he should not look outside, he should not lose his self-center. Still another phase is mentioned in v. 25: "When one knows this (i.e., the Self, cf. v. 24), then one becomes a silent sage." That is, when a certain level of true knowledge of the Self has been reached, when there has been a true vision of the Self, then the desires fall off and one becomes a silent sage.

Another point is that one should develop understanding or insight amounting in its clarity virtually to perception, and one should make this understanding part of living one's life. Most important is v. 21: "By the mind alone must it be understood that there is nothing manifold in this world." This enjoins mental discipline, mental endeavor —contemplation, meditation, going into the depths of one's consciousness and of being, existence. "The life of life, the eye of the eye," and so forth: the one foundation of all these principles or phenomena must be discriminated, found, by the mind. This is confirmed in v. 22: "That imperishable, constant one must be perceived (Skt. root *dṛś*, "see") only by the mind." Again this means a whole lifetime endeavor so that such perception might arise in one and become permanent. But the Scripture also endorses faith and worship as an approach to the Reality which it declares. V. 18 teaches to look at the Self directly as the one God that one worships, and v. 20 says that even the gods to which one relates by worship and sacrifice, even they worship the Supreme Reality as light of lights etc. In fact, vs. 28-29 are themselves worshipful formulas.

Brahman. Finally the Scripture also exalts Brahman, and this brings up the questions of the meaning of Brahman, of the difference between Ātman and Brahman, and of their relationship to each other. Brahman is defined in the old Upaniṣads in two kinds of ways: (1) as the basis of Universe or of all manifestation; and (2) as the ground of all experiences, of cognition, consciousness, as well as self. "[That], verily, from which these beings [here] are born, [that] by which, having been born, they live, [that] which, when departing, they enter, that seek to know. That is Brahman" (*TaittUp* III.1.1). This is also the starting point of the *Brahma Sūtra*. "[Brahman is that] from which [comes] the origin etc. (i.e., origin, maintenance and dissolution) of this [world here]" (*BraSū* I.1.2). So on the one hand, Brahman is the basis (*pratiṣṭhā*)[46] of all things, all phenomena. It is the *Sat* (Being, Reality) which is all things. It is that of which all things consist, that what they fundamentally are, as well as the impulse and Supreme Intelligence that "brought them into existence". In later Vedānta it is characterized as the material and efficient cause of the world.[47] At the same time Brahman is *jñāna*, "knowledge", "the enlightened condition", and as such *ananta*, endless, infinite (*TaittUp* II.1.2). Again it is *ānanda*, "bliss" (*BṛhUp* III.9.28 (K)), and *prajñāna*, "the arising of illumination" or "full illumination" (*AitUp* III.2). So Brahman is at the same time both the transcendent-immanent ground of the Universe (the external world) and of consciousness (awareness, experience), indicating a fundamental oneness of the two.[48]

This essential comprehensiveness of Brahman is already foreshadowed in the meaning which the term has in the *Ṛg Veda*. There *brahman* occurs in two forms: one, neuter and accented on the first syllable (*bráhman*), which later becomes the Upaniṣadic Brahman; and the other masculine and accented on the second syllable (*brahmán*).[49] The first occurs 247 times and often refers to the *Ṛg Vedic* mantras or hymns or the making of mantras or hymns. Adapting somewhat Thieme and others,[50] it means something like the "giving form or shape [to the Divine experienced within] in the form of a mantra, hymn, song, or thought".[51] "Like all action nouns, especially those formed with *-man*, brahman can denote either the activity itself or its result,"[52] i.e., either the process of mantra making or the mantra etc. itself. The poet's act of giving verbal form to the Divine that he experiences, the mantra or hymn that results from this (which is Divine Word), and the act of uttering the mantra in the ritual with knowledge and with feeling of its meaning, all in one way or another embody Divine power.

Thus *bráhman* also has a connotation of "(Divine) power" (Gonda).[53] Finally such *bráhman* or "giving (verbal) form to the Divine and Supreme Divine in oneself" has as highest expression the enigmatic correspondences and other mystical statements about the cosmos called "cosmological *bráhmans*".[54] Through these the *Ṛg Vedic bráhman* is clearly connected with the characteristic of the Upaniṣadic Brahman to encompass both cosmos and consciousness[55] (althought other aspects are involved also)[56]. Thus there is considerable continuity between the *Ṛg Vedic* feeling for Universal Divinity as it is expressed in the concept of *bráhman* and Brahman in the Old Upaniṣads.[57] In later Vedānta Brahman is then characterized as *sat-cit-ānanda*: Sat = the (one and only) Existent, Being; *cit* = "(pure) consciousness"; and *ānanda* = "bliss", it being understood that it is a single Reality that manifests as these three apparently different aspects.[58]

Ātman and Brahman. But where does this leave the Ātman? Ātman and Brahman represent two different comprehensive forms of understanding/experiencing/being the same Infinite Reality. But in general, "Ātman" always includes a connotation of "that aspect in oneself that knows, sees, experiences". In this sense the Ātman is always something that one is actually already directly familiar with (although one may not know so). Brahman on the other hand is something that is known by knowing Ātman. It is something to be pointed out in the Ātman, when there is knowledge of Ātman. Knowledge of Ātman is one way of getting knowledge of Brahman. But knowledge of Brahman can also come in other ways, e.g., through (or in the form of) knowledge of the Sacred Syllable *Om*, or through knowledge of *Vāc*, "Speech", i.e., the Logos. This difference is illustrated in the present text also. V. 19 says that the "five orders of five" —all things in the world—and the ether which encompasses the whole Universe have their foundation in the Self—in the foundation of "I". (This is consistent with v. 24 and also with v. 17.) That foundation of "I" beyond the mind *should be considered* the Brahman, the immanent-transcendent Infinite. V. 21 says that the one Self, which is the Life (-power) of all individual life, the one Seer that sees through every eye, the one Intelligence that works in every individual mind—this Self *is actually* also the Infinite Brahman. The immediately following transition to "seeing nothing manifold" is typical in descriptions of Brahman: becoming Brahman *is* becoming this Oneness; the invisible Brahman *is* the One that comprises everything. In the same way vs. 30 and 31 glorify the Self, and indicate Brahman as an aspect seen in and become through the Self.

4. Rising Above Desire, *BṛhUp* IV.4.6-15 (M)

In the preceding two sections we tried to get an initial idea of Ātman and Brahman. Now there is a fundamental ingredient which characterizes the Upaniṣadic approach to Ātman and Brahman, namely, gradually rising above and transcending desire. This is brought out in the verses that immediately precede the excerpt in secs. 2 and 3. Here Yājñavalkya talks about how the way in which a man lives his life determines what he attains in life and at death.

BṛhUp IV.4.6-15 (M). Text

6. Now this Self (*ātman*), verily, is Brahman. It is composed of intelligence, thought, speech, life (vital power of breath), sight, hearing, ether, wind, heat (fire), water, earth, anger and non-anger, joy and non-joy, right and non-right; it is composed of everything. Now whenever it is composed of this thing or of that thing,—however it acts, however it operates, so it becomes (in the next life). Acting well it becomes good; acting ill it becomes evil. As a result of right action it becomes what is good; as a result of evil action it becomes what is evil.
7. Now in this connection they say: This person (individual, *puruṣa*)[a] consists simply of desire. As is his desire, so is his resolve; as is his resolve, so is the deed he does; as is the deed he does, so is that which he attains unto.
8. So there is this verse:

   That upon which his characteristic mark (tag, namely) his thought, is intent—being just that,[b] man goes unto that along with deeds.
   Having come to the end of (the effects of) that action, of all whatsoever he does in this world,
   he returns again from that world (beyond) unto this world, unto action.

   So far one who is desirous. Now one who no longer desires. He who is desireless, who is without desire, who desires (only) the Self, who has attained his desires—from him the vital powers (of the body) do not mount upward [at death]; they are collected together right in him. Being just the Brahman, unto the Brahman he arrives.
9. Now on this there is this verse:

When all desires are expelled, which lurk within his heart, then a mortal becomes immortal; he attains the Brahman here (in this world).

10. Just as the slough of a snake lies dead, thrown down upon an ant-hill, even so this body lies (dead). Then this boneless, bodiless, intelligent Self (*ātman*) *is* just the Brahman—*is* just Heaven, O king. Thus said Yājñavalkya.—I now give your reverence a thousand (cows). Thus said Janaka of Videha.

11. Now in this connection there are these verses *(ślokas):*

    Narrow is the way—penetrating (Kāṇva: 'extended'), ancient; it has reached unto me, by me likewise has it been discovered;

    by this way the wise knowers of the Brahman, rising upward, arrive at the heavenly world, released from this world.

12. Therein, they say, is white and blue, yellow, green, and red (fluid);

    this way was discovered, verily, by the Brahman; on it travels the Brahman-knower, the radiant, and the doer of right.

13. Into blind darkness enter they who are devoted to not-coming-into-being;

    into what seems even greater darkness than that, those who take delight in coming-into-being (who crave rebirth, further existence).

14. Those worlds are called the demons' worlds; they are enveloped in blind darkness.

    Ignorant, foolish folk enter into them after death.

15. Being just that, even that we become (Kāṇva: being in this [world], we yet know this; or possibly: we have yet, somehow, realized it); dire disaster comes to him who knows it not.

    Those who know it become immortal; on the other hand the others attain naught but suffering.[59]

Vs. 6-10. Transcendence of Desire. In what follows we will concentrate only on vs. 6-10, because these verses establish a distinction which, as time went on, was realized to be fundamental for the entire Upaniṣadic teaching. They set up in the strongest possible terms a contrast between "one who is desirous", i.e. who has desires, aversions, etc., and "one who no longer desires"—"who is desireless, who is without desires, who desires (only) the Self, who has attained his desires" (2nd half of v. 8). Everything that was said up to this point about death, about taking on another body to live another life (vs. 4-5, not given above), and about how the nature of the desires of one's heart determine one's later fate (vs. 6, 7, 8a) and are responsible for taking this new body,—all this describes only the person who is desirous, who thinks and acts on the basis of desire. However, if a person has risen above desire, things are completely different. Such a person's self, on death, goes to Brahman, the One Infinite Existent. Indeed, he attains Brahman even before death: "When all desires are expelled which lurk within his heart, then the mortal becomes immortal, he attains Brahman here (in this world)" (v. 9); "He *is* just the Brahman, *is* just Heaven" (v. 10). In other words, totally having put away desire (and aversion, etc.) means immortality, or eternal beatitude, while still living. This is the "ancient way" to the Infinite which has "reached unto" Yājñavalkya and which was discovered by him (v. 11).

If one is on the path to God, to Reality, then as one gradually rises above desire (and aversion, etc.), there dawns slowly premonition, an *Ahnung*, of the Infinte, the Reality, Brahman. And conversely, when there is some kind of dawning of the Infinite in the mind or the heart, then desires, interests, and activities all begin to pale and there is growing non-attachment to the outcomes in the world. There is an intrinsic inner connection between rising above attachment to and inner involvement with worldly things and outcomes, on the one hand, and some kind of awareness of the Infinite or of Reality, on the other. Not only that. In the rising above desire and fear, accompanied by growing across-the-board non-attachment and dispassion, there is a certain taste or flavor, combined with a certain sense of absoluteness. One knows that one is "tasting" something definite beyond mind, beyond quality-permeated consciousness. This is a taste in the direction of *jñāna*, "knowledge" (of the Infinite, of Ātman or Brahman), the taste of the direction of Reality. In general, the inner connection between "rising above Desire" and knowledge of Reality is at the basis of all the wisdom paths in the world's religions and philosophies.[60] However, v. 9 shows it in a special, extreme form which is characteristic of the High Wisdom literatures. "When all desires are expelled which lurk within his heart," i.e., when the whole dimension of self-referenced desire has been completely left behind, "then the mortal becomes immortal", then one attains the One Reality, "here", i.e., while still living in this world. This is an Infinite principle, embodying the actual power of Spirit, of the Ātman. And this principle is not limited to the Upaniṣads. It is the fundamental point of all the High Wisdom literatures of the world, in fact it can be taken as their defining characteristic.[61]

In our text the juxtapostion of 6b-8a versus 8b-10 in effect raises transcendence of desire to a Supreme Principle, virtually equivalent to Brahman. V. 7 says "This spirit (man, *puruṣa*) consists simply of desire." What looks at first so important—a person's talents and personality, his life-enterprise, and to a large extent even his human spirit—all that consists simply of desire. And vs. 7 and 8a go on to say that as is a person's desire, so he acts, i.e., so will be the way in which he lives his life, and that in turn determines what he becomes after death in his next life. But regardless of whether his action was good or not good, as long as there is desire, he is bound to return to go through another life. *He will not truly attain the Infinite, he will not merge into Brahman.* For the nature of desire (and fear, etc.) is that the mind-substance or consciousness has a "characteristic mark (or tag)," *liṅgam*, namely precisely the attachment to the object of desire (precisely the longing, the wanting to, the lust, the fear, the anger, and so on). This "characteristic mark" is traditionally thought of as a kind of semi-permanent modification of the mind-substance embedded in the mind-substance or ordinary consciousness. When there are no such semi-permanent modifications, the mind-substance or consciousness "shines" as the inexpressible Brahman. But when there are such semi-permanent modifications, the mind-substance or consciousness is tainted. This taintedness, in the waking state, consists of the seeing and relating to the world as one normally does, i.e., it is identical with the common state of mankind. Thus, having gone completely beyond desire is close to being Brahman.

Karma and Reincarnation. Vs. 6-8a together form an early statement of the later almost universal Indian doctrine of "karma and reincarnation".[62] Karma and reincarnation are often considered the cardinal principle of the Indian religions. But it is significant that here they appear primarily in the role of highlighting transcendence of desire as *the* Supreme Principle. For this is precisely the whole point of the juxtaposition of vs. 6-8a against 8b-10. Transcendence of desire lifts the self out of the constant returning to this world, out of the whole inner working of desire: of desire prompting acting, of being bound by desire, of desire leading to good or evil action, of good and evil action having effects on oneself, and eventual return to another life. And transcendence of desire results in becoming Brahman. It is only transcendence of desire (as described in 8b) that can liberate the self from the vast inner working of the principle of desire and lay bare the true Immortality, the Supreme Divinity which is the self's true nature.

The word *karma* in vs. 6 ff. means an action or deed to done, in particular a ritual action.[63] But because of the effects which *karma* has beyond death (vs. 7 & 8a), there arises the idea that there is "an autonomous potency or force with its own inherent lawfulness"[64] that comes into play in any particular act, and that makes that act later have consequences. This "autonomous potency" is then the "karma" associated with the action in the sense of later Hindu tradition and in the popular conception of "karma" in the West.[65] In this context vs. 6-8 make several fundamental statements. The first basic insight is v. 6b: "Now whenever it (= the self or Self) is composed of this or that—however it (or he, the person) acts, however it (he) conducts itself (himself), so it (he) becomes. Acting well (i.e., good, like a good person, *sādhu*), he (or it) becomes good (*sādhu*), acting ill (evil, *pāpa*), he (it) becomes evil (*pāpa*). As a result of right action (literally, by means of what is right or meritorious, *puṇyena*) he becomes what is good (*puṇya*), as a result of evil action (by means of what is evil, *pāpena*) he becomes what is evil (*pāpa*)." (The last statement occurs also in *BṛhUp* III.10.13.) This is the general principle that the moral and ethical character of how one lives one's day to day life affects one's future life and one's fate after death. In every sphere—in the sphere of intelligence (*vijñāna*), or in what one speaks, sees, or hears, in anger or joy, in everything there obtains the principle of "as one does, as one conducts oneself, so one becomes (in life as well as after death)".[66] "As a man soweth, so he reapeth" says the Bible, and Radhakrishnan quotes Plato (*Laws* 904C): "Such as are the trend of our desires and the nature of our souls, just such each of us becomes." The text then reformulates this basic insight more sharply in terms of desire, *kāma* ("this person here is of desire-consisting indeed", v. 7) and finally even more pointedly in terms of the "intent" or "aim" of the desire (v. 8a). The crucial element that determines what happens after death is "being intent on" something—being attached to it and pursuing it for that reason. This attachment and the corresponding action will have "corresponding" effects after death ("being just that, man goes unto that along with deeds"). Eventually, when the effect of one's activity (and of the mentality that stood behind it) are "exhausted", one returns again to this world, for another life. The element of "being intent on" etc. is expressed by *liṅgam*, "aim, goal, characteristic". (In later Vedānta *liṅgam* comes to mean the "subtle body" which contains in some form the "traces" of these intents, wants.) This expresses a universal principle, viz. that it is precisely the attachment and self-interest that is involved in the desire, that has consequences later. "He who *wants to* save his life will lose it" says Jesus. But taken as a whole, v. 8 has a another message which is specifically Upaniṣadic. Action based on desire (attachment, greed, self-interest, etc.), it says, results in return to another life, but does not lead to Brahman. The only way Brahman can be attained and the constant return can be stopped is by rising above and transcending desire. This makes transcendence of desire a Supreme Principle, radically different from other principles relating to attaining the Infinite, such as good deeds, good thoughts, a devoted ritual life, etc. All these things, though perhaps helpful or even in a particular religious or cultural context necessary on the path, do not by their nature lead to Brahman or the Self. Rather, the path to Brahman involves Transcendence of Desire, and Brahman has the experiential color of Desirelessness. To realize that "as is one's desire, good or evil, so one becomes", and to realize that *that* is what keeps one in the perennial cycle of desire-bound life—to realize these things is an important step. "Those who know it (this fact) become immortal; on the other hand the others attain nothing but suffering" (v. 15).

Transcendence of Desire in *BṛhUp* IV.4. 16-32. With hindsight it appears that the whole theme of transcendence of desire continues through the remainder of the section (*BṛhUp* IV.4.16-32, our first excerpt). IV.4.16 says that when there is realization of the Self to the point where one knows "I am the Self," there will be complete cessation of desire. For since then everything is "self (= Self)" (cf. v. 28) and there is no manifoldness, what motive could one possibly have to seek something, to try to obtain or attain something, and what could one possibly seek? For what oneself is is never sought, because one is it already. V. 25 says that when one knows the Self, one becomes a silent sage. All one's "wanting something" ceases, there is unshakeable, permanent contentment, and the need or tendency to talk completely drops away from one. Next, v. 26 brings out the fact that it is the very nature of desire (of wanting something, longing for something, being anxious about something, etc.) to be incompatible with the Infinite State. All desires are the same—they are "nothing but desires"—and lead in a direction 180 degrees opposite to the Infinite, the One Reality ("therefore", the Brahmins of old "abandoned" all desires and "wandered forth abegging"). When finally the Self is attained, transcendence of desire is absolute, for the state of being the Self is utterly beyond, and untouched by, desire: "For It passes beyond these two states (in which one thinks): 'For this reason I have done good.'... It is not disturbed by good or evil things that are done or left undone" (v. 27). The knower of Brahman who has realized the Self "increases not nor becomes less by deed", like an ordinary human being (v. 28). He is not in doubt or disturbed over his own action and experience or about what he should be or will be or has been doing or experiencing. For when one is disturbed like this, there is still desire operating—desire to gain an advantage, to avoid something, to improve oneself, whatever. When the Self and Brahman have been attained, the transcendence of desire is also absolute ethically, "karmically": "one is not stained by evil deed". And finally v. 28 turns into a veritable hymn to desirelessness. When a human being has realized the Self, "he/she is free from evil", because the evil in the heart (self-interest, ill-will, etc.) is indissolubly bound up with desire; when one is expelled, so is the other. "He/she is free from hunger, free from thirst"—free from any kind of hungering after something, free from any kind of thirsting after something, because these are desire. The Kāṇva version has here "He is free from doubt," because doubt comes from desire. So really all these verses elaborate the same Great Truth.

To summarize, therefore, in vs. 6-10 the Upaniṣad draws an extremely powerful distinction between two ways of being, two ways of living in this world, and correlates them with two kinds of goals in life, as well as with two kinds of destiny after death. On the one hand there is "being desirous". In this case one lives one's life in order to get satisfaction in the things of the world, or one leads an upright life devoted to ritual, in order to obtain Heaven after death (cf. v. 13). And in this case one will return to this world for another life, for continued action. On the other hand, there is also "being without desire", or we will say "having risen above desire". In this case the goal of life is or must be only Brahman (this is implied but not explicitly stated), and one will merge after death into Brahman, or even be Brahman while living. With transcendence of desire one does not overcome life—its sorrows etc.—in order to get a heavenly or other reward. Rather, with transcendence of desire one overcomes life and death and life after death and Heaven (mental or divine states)—one goes beyond *all* of them to the Infinite, Supreme Divinity. Having gone beyond desire one will be Brahman: the state beyond desire, the state in which ego and self-interest are expelled, is Brahman. The present text is one of the earliest (if not the earliest) to clearly formulate Transcendence of Desire as a Supreme Principle.

There are other important elements in the text besides transcendence of desire, such as the characterizaion of the Self in v. 6. But this and other points will be discussed in connection with other texts. At this point we turn to the second major text of this chapter, the very next section of *Bṛhadāraṇyaka Upaniṣad*, called the "Yājñavalkya-Maitreyī Dialogue."

5. Yājñavalkya-Maitreyī Dialogue

The Yājñavalkya-Maitreyī Dialogue (*BṛhUp* IV.5) is one of the most famous passages in the old Upaniṣads.[68] It has a deep inner unity and strikes some deep chords in the soul that make her long for (or that reawaken her memory of) the Infinite. Even from a purely philosophical point of view, it makes a stunning statement. The same text occurs with very little change also at the end of chapter II, as section II.5, where it forms a kind of high-powered capstone on the whole instruction represented by chapters I & II.[69] Its repetition here as the final teaching in the *Yājñavalkyakāṇḍa* suggest its importance—no other larger text is repeated in the Upaniṣads in its entirety like this. As usual, there is a frame-story. Yājñavalkya is about to leave home to become a hermit. One of his two wives, Maitreyī, asks him for instruction on what would give her immortality, and the great sage teaches her what he knows.

Yājñavalkya-Maitreyī Dialogue (*BṛhUp* IV.5). Text

1. Now Yājñavalkya had two wives, Maitreyī and Kātyāyanī. Of these two Maitreyī was fond of theological discussion, but Kātyāyanī was, as one might say (Kāṇva: 'was only') of feminine intelligence. He, being about to change his mode of life—
2. Said Yājñavalkya: Maitreyī, behold, I am going to depart

from this place as a wandering ascetic. Look, I will make a division between you and Kātyāynī here.

3. Said Maitreyī: Pray, Sir, if all this world filled with riches were mine, should I by that be immortal, or not?—No, said Yājñavalkya; just as is the life of people of means even so would be your life; but there is no hope for immortality through riches.
4. Said Maitreyī: What should I then do with that by which I could not become immortal? Tell me rather, Sir, all that you know.
5. Said Yājñavalkya: Of course you are dear to me, madam, and you have acted in a manner dear to me (Kāṇva: 'you have added to what is dear or pleasing [to me in you]'). Well then, madam, I will explain and expound this to you. But do you weigh my words carefully while I am expounding it.—Speak, Sir.
6. Said Yājñavalkya: Behold, not for the love of husband is husband dear to one, but for the love of the Ātman is husband dear. Behold, not for the love of wife is wife dear to one, but for the love of the Ātman is wife dear . . . [And so on: with 'sons', 'possessions', 'the Brahmin caste', 'the warrior caste', 'worlds', 'gods', 'Vedas', 'sacrifices', 'creatures', 'everything'.] . . . Behold, the Ātman is that which is to be seen, heard, thought, and meditated upon, Maitreyī. Behold, in seeing, hearing, thinking, and understanding the Ātman, everything is known.
7. The Brahmin caste renounces him who thinks the Brahmin caste anything other than the Ātman. The warrior caste renounces him who thinks the warrior caste anything other than the Ātman . . . [And so on: with 'the worlds', 'the gods', 'the Vedas', 'the sacrifices', 'the creatures', 'everything'.] This is the Brahmin caste, this is the warrior caste, this is the worlds, this is the gods, this is the Vedas, this is the sacrifices, this is the creatures, this is everything—namely the Ātman.
8. It is just as one could not grasp the sounds of a drum that is struck when they have left it; but by grasping the drum, or the one who beats it, the sound is grapsed.
9. It is just as one could not grasp the sound of a lute that is played when they have left it; but by grasping the lute, or its player, the sound is grasped.

10. It is just as one could not grasp the sounds of a horn that is blown when they have left it; but by grasping the horn, or its blower, the sound is grasped.
11. It is just as when a fire has been laid with wet kindling wood, its clouds of smoke go forth severally in different directions; behold, just so [all] this is the exhalation of that Great Being; namely the *Ṛg Veda,* the *Yajur Veda*, the *Sāma Veda*, the Atharvans-and-aṅgīrases (*Atharva Veda*), the Itihāsa and Purāṇas (legends and tales), the sciences, the Upaniṣads, the verses, the Sūtras, the explanations and commentaries; —(sacrificial) gifts, oblations food, drink, both this world and the world beyond, and all creatures, all these are exclusively Its exhalations.
12. It is just as the sea is the sole locality of all water; thus the skin is the sole locality of all touchings, thus the nostrils are the sole locality of all smells, thus the tongue is the sole locality of all tastes, thus the eye is the sole locality of all forms (sights), thus the ear is the sole locality of all sounds, thus the thought-organ is the sole locality of all resolves, thus the heart is the sole locality of all sciences, thus the hands are the sole locality of all deeds, thus the feet are the sole locality of all journeys, thus the genital organ is the sole locality of all delights, thus the anus is the sole locality of all evacuations, thus speech is the sole locality of all Vedas[a].
13. It is just as a lump of salt, which has no interior and no exterior, but is as a whole just a mass of flavour; even so this Great Being has no boundaries, no limits [lit: even so this Great Element, or Being (*bhūta*) (Kāṇva: this Self, Ātman) is endless (*ananta*), limitless (*apara*)] (Kāṇva adds: this Self, (Ātman) is without interior and exterior), but as a whole is just a mass of intelligence (*prajñānaghana*). Arising out of these elements [in the form of the individual mind], it disappears (dissolves) into the same. After death there is no [sense-based] consciousness (*saṁjñā*), lo, I say! said Yājñavalkya.
14. Then said Maitreyī: Just here you have brought me into a state of confusion, revered Sir; I do not understand this, when you say that having gone on there is no consciousness.

15. Then said Yājñavalkya: I say nothing confusing; this Ātman is imperishable, its nature is indestructible; but it has association with matter (up to release, after which this and all duality ceases).
(Vs. 16-23, which repeat *BṛhUp* IV.3.23-30 (M), are missing in the Kāṇva version and in *BṛhUp* II.4 and are omitted here.)
24. If there were, as one might say, something else (than the One [Self]) (Kāṇva: a duality), then one would see something else (Kāṇva: someone else), one would smell something else, one would taste something else, one would think on something else, one would touch something else, one would know something else.
25. But when all of this (or, of him) has become just the Ātman, then by what means should It see—whom? By what means should It smell—whom? By what means should It taste—whom? By what means should It address—whom? By what means should It hear—whom? By what means should It think on—whom? By what means should It touch—whom? By that means should It know—whom? By what means could one know that by which all this (Universe) knows? (Kāṇva at this point adds: This Self, Ātman, is [characterized by] 'not, not', *sa eṣa neti, netyātmā*. It is ungraspable, for it is not grasped. It is indestructible, for it is not destroyed. It has no attachment, and it is unfastened; it is not attached and (yet) is not unsteady). By what means, I say, could one know the Knower? Now the lesson has been declared to you, Maitreyī. This, I say, is all there is on the subject of immortality.—Having spoken thus Yājñavalkya entered upon the life of a wandering ascetic.[70]

Another extraordinary document, rather different from *BṛhUp* IV.4. The text is incredibly alive, one senses an incredible intelligence moving in it. Yājñavalkya is constantly taking different approaches while all the time trying to explain the same thing.

Verse 6 is very famous. At the simplest level it challenges one to get to the root of all the loving something, holding something dear, enjoying, etc. that one has been doing and is doing all the time in one's life. Raghavachar explains that "the desiring agent, the subject that desires, is the point under discussion".[71] He notes that all the classical commentaries take "for the love of the Ātman" as "desire on the part of [the Ātman]",[72] while Tagore takes it as "desire for [the Ātman]".[73] However, the two are closely connected. All loving and holding something dear, both as far as being one who loves and as seeing the object as dear is concerned, is really a manifestation of (the power of) the Self. The Self is Love. "Analysis [of our experience] will show that all joy is in us, for us, and from us. The moon that shines in the waters of a million lakes is one; the shine in the lake is due to the reflections; look up and know the truth."[74] When one knows oneself as the one single Existent, this becomes the experience. Thus the Ātman is the central element of meaning and meaningfulness in life and existence (giving meaning and desirability to everything external—to being a Brahmin, to the worlds, etc.). Therefore It is the thing that is to be known, sought and attained above all, —It is the Supreme Good. Hence "The Ātman alone has to be loved; all of the things are loved for the sake of the Ātman. When the Ātman is understood, everything else is understood. All effects are subsumed under the cause. . . ."[75] From this it is only a small step to the reading of Tagore and some other modern traditional commentators.[76] The Self is the only thing that is dear; all cases of holding something dear are really holding the Self dear.

The Self, the source of all love and meaningfulness and the one thing to be sought and attained, is "that [one thing] which is to be seen, heard, thought, and meditated upon" (v. 6). The process of coming to understand the Self is a total life endeavor, involving the total of one's faculties—seeing It, hearing It, thinking about It, and meditating on It [cf. above, *BṛhUp* IV.4.25 (M)]. Only when all forces of the individual's body, mind, and self are bent toward knowing It, does the Self come to be known. And when the Self is known, It is known with the senses and the mind and the understanding, i.e. in what is then the individual's normal state (he/she does not have to be in some special mystical state to have this knowledge).

But that is not all. "Behold, in seeing, hearing, thinking and understanding the Self, everything is known." When walking in the world with the Knowledge of the Self, "everything is known." The text leaves no doubt about the incalculable, incomprehensible change that comes with attaining knowledge of the Self. Before knowledge of the Self, it is "just as [if] one could not grasp the sound of a drum that is struck" (v. 8) —one's understanding of the world is similar to that of a man who tries to grasp the sound made by a drum with his bare hands. Such a man gets nowhere. He has no grasp whatever of the phenomenon that his sense of hearing is showing him. He has no grasp whatsoever of the world which his senses are showing him. But when there is knowledge of the Self, the world is suddenly understood, just "as by graping the drum, or the one who beats it, the sound is grasped". What before could not be grasped, is now grasped totally in a completely different way, viz., by grasping the cause of the sound, the movement of the membrane or the drummer. The world which before could not be understood is now grasped totally in a completely new way. The old way was by matter and mind (the Upaniṣad would say: by name and form). The new way is ineffable. The weight and importance of this point is emphasized by giving essentially the same simile in three forms (vs. 8-10).

In "[the Self is] that which is to be seen, heard, thought, and meditated upon", the words used for "to be seen . . ." are *draṣṭavya* (from *dṛś*, see), *śrotavya* (from *śru*, hear), *mantavya* (from *man*, think), and *nididhyāsitavya* (literally, "to be thought, reflected on, remembered, perceived (root *dhyai*) down (*ni*)" i.e., deep down, in, or into, *ni,* oneself). These terms inspired Vedānta to conceptualize the path to Brahman as involving three means or processes or stages, *śravaṇa, manana*, and *nididhyāsana.*[77] *Śravaṇa* is "hearing" (the higher truth or instruction, which has a transcendental impact on one), *manana,* "thinking about, occupying oneself in one's mind with" (the teaching) (this includes reasoning), and *nididhyāsana* "realizing by meditation and meditative living; realization". Different Vedāntic teachers use these terms in different ways, with different conceptions as to what the crucial element in each is, how they are related, etc.[78] In the Upaniṣad, however, all four terms *draṣṭavya*, etc. function together as a single characterization in the way explained. All one's processes, one's senses, mind, and inmost (*ni-*) self, should be united in the endeavor,[79] and when the Self realized, all these will be part of the Self-realized state.

Verse 7. Vs. 6 and 7 form a pair (we saw already that v. 7 is implicit in v. 6), but compared with v. 6, v. 7 takes an external, objective rather than a subjective point of view. It describes how things will react against one if one considers them to be other than self. Unless one treats a given realm or level in society or in the world as (part of one-) self, that realm or level is bound to ultimately reject one. For example, if one sees one's own caste—let us say one's occupation or whole occupational realm and function—as something different from one's self, there is bound to arise at some point one's own will, or view, or one's own desire or self-interest against it. There is bound to be an uprising of self-will and self-assertion against it. This will then be internal conflict which is bound to lead to external conflict with the occupational realm and occupational function in general. But one's occupational realm and function, as a social object, is a greater entity than one's own self-interest. It is an entity of a higher order. Hence conflict with that realm is almost certainly conflict with the larger order of the Universe and will lead to rejection of oneself—of one's own interest—by that realm or function. And the same holds for all the other realms or functions enumerated. Seeing any of these things—indeed, seeing anything in the world—as different from self leads ultimately to conflict and suffering. This is summed up by "this Brahman caste, this warrior caste, etc., . . . everything here is what this Self is". Clearly Yājñavalkya is speaking here directly from a state or level of direct realization. Everywhere and in everything he sees "only the Self". In this state or at this level, there is complete transcendence of desire. When "everything here is what Self is", there can be no uprising of self-will, no insistence on one's own view or interest as opposed to that of an other. Then one has gone beyond desire, and then evil will not touch one (then "he passes over all evils; evil does not pass over him", *BṛhUp* IV.4.28 (M) above).

From a larger perspective, the problem addressed is that of the human condition. In secs. 2 and 3 above, the root of the human condition was seen to be desire, or wanting something, and it was taught that the human condition could be transcended by transcendence of desire. But the fact of desire was not further analysed. Essentially this is also the situation, for example, in *Genesis*. The rise of self-will, the assertion of self-interest in Adam and Eve which lead to the fall (or which in fact *are* the "fall") are not further analyzed. They are essentially givens, the givens of the human condition, and we all have them in varying degrees. These givens or original sin, can be overcome, or completely transcended, with God's grace, by Love of God, by complete surrender of self-will etc. to Him, etc. (which likewise lead to some form of transcendence of desire). Here in the present text, the problem of the human condition is identified as one of seeing things as other than Self, and it is taught that the human condition is transcended by seeing all as Self, or equivalently, by not maintaining a boundary between an (ultimately not true or real) self with a small s and the world.

Verses 11-13. Summarizing, then, vs. 6 and 7 say that the Self is the Highest Good and realization of the Self is All-encompassing, and vs. 8-10 amplify this. Next vs. 11-13 continue the description and give furthier glimmers of Oneness that arises with Knowledge of the Self. V. 11 is in a worshipful attitude, a verse of praise or adoration: Just as the one smoke that rises from a single fire divides and breaks up into many pieces, so all the great things and activities in the world—from the holy utterances and actions to the creatures and the world itself—are the one exhalation of the Great Being (*Mahad Bhūta*).[80] V. 12 is similar to v. 6. But instead of using the idea of "being dear", it uses the idea of "one locality", *ekāyana*. Just as one grasps the sea as the one locality, the merging place of all water, the eye as the one locality, the one process in all seeings, etc., in the same way should one know the Self as the one locality of all things that exist.[81] Just as in v. 6, this means that ultimately the Self should be experienced as the *ekāyana* of everything—in the world, in one's mind, in one's being. Continuing, the beginning of v. 13 powerfully transcends the distinction between internal and external, the experience of limits and boundaries, and draws a picture of the Self as something infinite, without boundaries, of *prajñāna-ghana*, "a mass of illumined intelligence-consciousness". It arises in the form of normal individual consciousness in conjunction with the body (moulded by "I", "my", the senses, etc.), and eventually disappears in this form upon death, or when there is realization. (The exact sense here is not clear; the text is ambiguous.)[82] At this point Maitreyī gets confused and stops her husband, but Yājñavalkya is unperturbed. He knows what he is saying. The Self, although shining in the ordinary consciousness formed by the self, is different from this ordinary consciousness-cum-self. It is imperishable, indestructible, etc. It is only ordinary individual consciousness which ceases.

The statements at the end of v. 13, finally, are the climax of the whole movement of vs. 11-13. While vs. 11-12 and the beginning of 13 are in terms of metaphors taken from the external world and experience of the world, this final summation is in terms of the language of the self or soul. Śaṁkara paraphrases (Swami Mādhavānanda's inspired translation):

> Like this illustration, O Maitreyī, is this great Reality called the Supreme Self, from which you have been cut off by ignorance as a separate entity, through your connection with the

> limiting adjuncts of the body and organs, and have become mortal, subject to birth and death, hunger and thirst, and other such relative attributes, and identified with name, form and action, and think you are born of such and such a family. That separate existence of yours, which has sprung from the delusion engendered by contact with the limiting adjuncts of the body and organs, enters its cause, the great Reality, the Supreme Self, which stands for the ocean, which is undecaying, immortal, beyond fear, pure and homogeneous like a lump of salt, and which is Pure Intelligence, infinite, boundless, without a break and devoid of differences caused by the delusion brought on by ignorance. When that separate existence [the state in which you are now] has entered and been merged in its cause, in other words, when the differences created by ignorance are gone, the universe becomes one without a second, "the great Reality", *Mahad Bhūta*. Great (*Mahat*), because It is greater than everything else and is the cause of the ether etc.; Reality (*Bhūta*)—always a fact, for It never deviates from Its nature.[83]

6. The One Seer

We have seen how Yājñavalkya, using ever new angles of approach, tried to give Maitreyī a glimpse of the Ātman, and how this precipitated the dramatic high point in vs. 14-15. Maitreyī becomes confused, but the sage remains unperturbed. At first he merely says that he has said nothing wrong (v. 15).[84] But then he takes another approach. The general trend of this new response is the same in both recensions of the text. But the Kāṇva version continues with what in the Mādhyandina is vs. 24-25 (M), while the Mādhyandina has an additional sequene [vs. 16-23 (M)] which logically fits with vs. 24-25. "When he then doesn't see, verily, seeing he doesn't see [i.e., while he doesn't see objects, he is still seeing in some sense] . . ." and similarly with "seeing" replaced by smelling, tasting, speaking, hearing, thinking, knowing (*vi-jñā*). The basic point is that it is really the Ātman that sees, smells etc., thinks and knows, not the individual self (vs. 24-25). The Ātman is the real Seer, Knower, Experiencer. In addition, this Ātman is "'not,' 'not'", *neti, neti*; "It is ungraspable because It is not grasped (by the mind)" etc. (Kāṇva).

The fact that it is really the Ātman that sees and knows forms a kind of undercurrent throughout Yājñavalkya's arguments in the great wisdom contest *BṛhUp* III. At *BṛhUp* III.7.31, for example, he says: "The Unseen Seer, the Unheard Hearer, the Unthought Thinker, the Unknown Knower. There is no other Seer, there is no other Hearer, there is no other Thinker, there is no other Knower. This is your Self, the immortal Inner Controller." Or at *BṛhUp* III.4.2 (K) he exclaims regarding "the Self which is in all things": "You cannot see the Seer of (or in) Sight. You cannot hear the Hearer of (or in) Hearing. You cannot think (of) the thinker of (or in) thought. You cannot understand the understander of (or who is in) understanding. It is the Ātman which is within everything!" In later Vedānta, the theme of the one Seer is then extensively further developed under the heading of the "Witness" or the one "witnessing Consciousness", *sākṣin*.[85]

Ātman/Brahman can not be an Object of Knowledge. The One Seer, being the One Subject that really sees, cannot be seen, thought or understood by Sight, Mind and Understanding, for that would require another seer. In other words, Ātman/Brahman should not be treated the way one normally treats any object of knowledge, as something that can be seen or grasped as something external to one's self. It is *neti, neti*. By giving it a name and discussing it, we have unfortunately already made it into a separate entity or phenomenon—we have made it an It. But Ātman/Brahman is not an it. It cannot be known in this way. We can only somehow *be* It. So, far from trying to make a logical point, or merely formulating an interesting paradox, Yājñavalkya is making a major positive statement about the state of highest Knowledge and the path to it. Immediately after *BṛhUp* III.4.2 (K), in *BṛhUp* III.5.1 (K), he gives a touching description which illustrates the nature of the process of becoming the Seer which is not an object of sight, mind, and knowledge.

> . . . [That] which is the desire for sons, that is the desire for wealth (position in life), (and that) which is the desire for wealth, that is the desire for [the various] worlds [before and after death], for both these are [nothing but] desires. Therefore let a Brahmin, when he has done away with scriptural learning, desire to live like a child. Having done away with scriptural learning and childlike-ness, then [he becomes] a silent meditator (*muni*). Having done away with both non-meditativeness and meditativeness, he then becomes [really] a Brahmin (*brāhmaṇa*, a Brahmin and also a knower of Brahman—a word play). "Being a knower of Brahman, how does he behave?" "However he behaves, by that he is such . . ."

This describes precisely the responses of a person who has realized that the Ātman is not an object of knowledge in the usual sense but must somehow be him, or the existence which he is, whatever, and who is trying to proceed on that basis. Such a person will be one who is (to a certain extent) done with Scriptures, for he already has a glimmer of the Infinite that he somehow is. He knows what needs to happen with his mind and heart, he knows the direction he needs to go. But the difficulty is of actually going and getting there, and the Scriptures can help him with that only indirectly. So this person conceives that he wants to live like a child, without any further clever designs in the spiritual or indeed any arena of his life, only simply devoting himself to this Infinite. After some years, he comes to be in a state where he is beyond trying to live and living childlike, where he is done with that, where this dimension has dropped completely from his horizon. Then, he will be one who lives silently and meditatively. Then, after some further years, he will be one who is done with living meditatively and living non-meditatively, according to some standard etc.; both of these, or this whole dimesion, will have dropped from his horizon, he will have no such thoughts and conflicts any more. Then he has become a real Brāhmaṇa (Brahmin), viz. a knower of Brahman. Actually this is equally well an elaboration of rising above and transcending desire and shows a sequence of stages which is alluded to also in *BṛhUp* IV.4. 23 (M) (secs. 2 and 3 above). Indeed these stages foreshadow the stages of the standard path of knowledge in later Vedāntic tradition.[86]

Neti, Neti. The fact that Knowledge of the Ātman is somehow a matter of being or existence (being the Ātman) is intimately connected with the practice and state of "'not', 'not' (*neti, neti*)" (mentioned in the Kāṇva verse corresponding to *BṛhUp* IV.5. 25, as well as in *BṛhUp* IV.4.27 (M), sec. 2 above). *Neti, neti* is literally *na iti, na iti,* "'not', thus; 'not', thus". *Iti*, "thus", is the standard way of quoting something that has been said. So *neti*, "'not', thus", recalls and epitomizes the state of saying "not", or "no", *na*. And therefore, *neti, neti* suggests the attitude in which everything perceived or conceived is being said "not" to or "no" to, i.e. is mentally said "[this is] not [my self]", "[this is] not [part of me]" to. When one lives and meditates like this, then gradually there comes growing intuition of the true direction of the Self. Indeed the text goes on "(This Self) is ungraspable for it is not grasped. It is indestructible for it is not destroyed," in other words the attitude of *neti, neti* should be adopted in part because of the very nature of the Self itself. The Self is ungraspable *because* it is not an object of grasping. "Capable of being grasped" is a category that simply does not apply to it. Similarly "being destructible" is not applicable to It. Not that It is indestructible in the sense that it is a substantial something that is untouched by all efforts to destroy it. Rather, "destructibility" is not applicable to It. It is beyond destructibility (and indestructibility). This "being beyond destructibility" has, however, an "experiential" color to it.

The Nature of the One Seer or Witness. Summarizing, therefore, "that everlasting Principle which receives, which possesses and which enjoys the objects is eulogized as Ātman".[87] To a modern mind this Principle of the One Seer may look like a rather "marginal" phenomenon—a completely colorless common denominator of all "seeing" without any deeper aspect, unrelated to what is "seen". But just the opposite is true. The One Seer is Complete Fullness. "The *sākṣin* is the inner core of everything, the 'Immanent', the embodiment of *Sat, Cit* and *Ānanda.* There is nothing beyond it or outside it. To say that such fullness is I is a meaningless expression. It is wrong also to call it the Vision or the *Sākṣātkāra.* . . ."[88] (Recall that *BṛhUp* III.4.2 (K) says that this One Seer is in everything, cf. above.) It is very important not to try to imagine what different levels of realization of the Ātman might be like, and at least periodically free oneself from conceptions and images of them.

NOTES

1. Adapted from H. Nakamura, *Religions and Philosophies of India. A Survey with Bibliographical Notes.* Chapters I and II (Brāhmaṇism), Tokyo, Hokuseido Press, 1973, p. 77. Upaniṣads: pp. 77-94 (Chapters III and IV, Hinduism, and The Orthodox Philosophical Systems, 1974, are available separately in mimeographed form from the same publisher). For more detailed discussion, cf. Nakamura, *History,* v. 1, pp. 9-43, and the summary on p. 42. Nakamura's dating of *Kaṭha Upaniṣad* and of the middle group Upaniṣads generally is questioned by A. Sharma, *Philosophy East and West,* pp. 325-331; pp. 325-326.
2. This could presumably be shown by suitable tabulations.
3. For a formal attempt to describe Brāhmaṇa style, see S. Einoo, Analysis of Brāhmaṇa Style. Summary of a paper given at the International Vedic Workshop, Harvard University, June, 1989.
4. Thus the edition by Limaye and Vadekar, *Principal Ups.,* which represents traditional learning as well as mordern scholarship, reflects a modern trend by including *Jaiminīya Upaniṣad Brāhmaṇa,* usually classed as an Āraṇyaka, as an Upaniṣad. It also includes four smaller Upaniṣads, *Bāṣkala-mantra, Chāgaleya, Ārṣeya,* and *Śaunaka,* which were previously known from the *Oupnek'hat,* but the Sanskrit originals of which

were discovered only in this century (C.K. Raja, supervising ed., *Unpublished Upanishads*. Adyar, Madras: Adyar Library and Research Centre, 1933). These works seem to be all from the beginning of the CE, however. On the other hand, Limaye and Vadekar omit three small texts from *Vājasaneyī Saṁhitā* (the *Uttaranārāyaṇa, Tad-eva,* and *Śiva-saṁkalpa*) which were considered to be Upaniṣads by the pundits responsible for the *Oupnek'hat*. Śaṁkara wrote commentaries on 10 of the 14 Upaniṣads given in Table 2.1 (all except *KauṣUp, ŚvetUp, MaitrUp,* and *Mahā-NārUp*), which probably contributed to establishing the conception of a dozen or so "Vedic" Upaniṣads as in this Table.

5. At *BṛhUp* II.1.20 (K) and *MaitrUp* VI.32 it refers to the phrase *satyasya satyam*, "the True of the True", and at *BṛhUp* V.5.3 and 4 to the words *ahar*, "day", and *aham*, "I", as Names of Brahman.
6. In *ChāndUp* III.11.3 it refers to the entire preceding teaching, the *Madhu Vidyā* (*ChāndUp* III.1-11) or its high point (*ChāndUp* III.10-11); in *TaittUp* II.9 to the whole *Five Sheaths Vidyā* (*TaittUp* II); and in *TaittUp* III.10.6 either to *TaittUp* III.10 or III.7-10 or *TaittUp* III. (Similarly also at *ŚvetUp* I.16.) In a somewhat different sense, *TaittUp* I.11 speaks of a "Veda Upaniṣad," *TaittUp* I.3.1 of an "Upaniṣad [on the theme] of saṁhitā, 'conjunction' " (*saṁhitasya upaniṣad*), and *ChāndUp* I.13.4 of an "Upaniṣad of the Sāman chants" (*sāmnām upaniṣad*). In the remaining passages (*BṛhUp* IV.2.1, *KenaUp* IV.7, *ŚvetUp* V.6) the reference is to mystical or esoteric teachings generally.
7. ". . . the *Ṛg Veda*, the *Yajur Veda*, the *Sāma Veda*, Atharva-Āṅgirasa, historical stories (*itihāsa*), ancient lore (*purāṇa*), sciences (*vidyās*), *upaniṣads, ślokas, sūtras*, . . .," *BṛhUp* II.4.10 (K), IV.1.2 (K), IV.5.11 (K). *Upaniṣads* are also named as one of five classes of sacred texts in the Madhu Vidyā, *ChāndUp* III.1-11.
8. "The oldest Upaniṣads (also called *ādeśa, nāmadheya*) consisted in brief instructions as to in what form or under what definite name the pious had to conceive of the Brahman. Round this nucleus those further prose and metrical elements which followed the diction used in the Brahman texts gathered themselves that we find combined in such texts as the *Bṛhad-āraṇyaka* or in the *Chāndogya Upniṣad*." *Trübner's Record*, 247 (1889), p. 148, repr. Oldenberg, *Kleine Schriften*, p. 1320.
9. Some of the oldest Upaniṣads have been handed down in manuscripts in two ways, viz. as part of the Brāhmaṇa or Āraṇyaka of which they form a part, and separately as an Upaniṣad. This suggests that they were regarded as a separate type of literature. I don't know, however, how far back this separate transmission goes.
10. Deussen, *Phil. Ups*., pp. 12-13.
11. H. Oldenberg, Vedische Untersuchungen 6. Upaniṣad, *ZDMG*, v. 50 (1886), pp. 457-462; p. 460; repr. Oldenberg; *Kleine Schriften*, p. 38.
12. H. Falk, Vedisch *upaniṣad*, *ZDMG*, v. 136 (1982), pp. 80-97, nos. 3-7 (pp. 82-94). Perhaps the strongest evidence is that in a supplementary hymn of the *Ṛg Veda, Ṛg Veda Khila* I.3.7, the Aśvins (two deities) are addressed as *upaniṣads*. This usage is also found in the *Gṛhya Sūtras*.
13. E.g. sometimes "Ātman" does not appear until the end of a teaching, as climax, "this [what has just been described] is the Ātman," with a suggestion that the student is already familiar with the term and with the fact that

attaining the Ātman is the Goal of Life. Again either Ātman or Brahman may be used in the very beginning of a teaching, e.g. " 'Brahman is Mind'—[thus] should one meditate" (*ChāndUp* III.18) or "In the beginning, verily, all this [Universe] was the Ātman, one only," *AitUp* I.1.1, which likewise presupposes some familiarity with the terms. A comparative study of ways which Ātman and Brahman are introduced in the discourse would be helpful.

14. Cf. the concordance by C.O. Hass in Hume, *Principal Ups*. While recent scholarship suggests that *Kaṭha* and *Śvetāśvatara Upaniṣads* have strong connections with the pre-Upaniṣadic *agnicayana*, I do not have a clear sense of how these Upaniṣads see themselves in relation to the old Upaniṣadic tradition, which they are undoubtedly carrying on.
15. The *Brahma Sūtra* treats the Upaniṣads *de facto* as a unified literature, viz. that which deals with the *Brahma-vidyās*. For background discussion and the dating, see Nakamura, *History*, pp. 432-436.
16. One example of such recognition may be *MaitrUp* II.3, "Now indeed, this is the knowledge of Brahman (*brahma-vidyā*), the knowledge of all the Upanishads (*sarvopaniṣad-vidyā*), oh King. . . . I will tell it to you. . ."
17. Cf. P. Hacker, Zur Methode der geschichtlichen Erforschung der anonymen Sanskritliteratur des Hinduismus. *ZDMG*, v. III (1961), pp. 483-492; repr. Hacker, *Kleine Schriften*, pp. 8-17. Hacker calls the approach in question the "method of comparison of multiple text versions", *die Methode des Vergleichs von Mehrfachüberlieferungen* (*ibid*, p. 489, resp. p. 14).
18. A.K. Coomaraswamy, Rebirth and Omniscience in Pāli Buddhism. *Indian Culture*, v. 3 (1936/37), pp. 19-33; p. 22.
19. See P. Lienhard, Historical Bibliography of Upaniṣads in Translation. *JIP*, v. 23 (1995), pp. 223-246. The most comprehensive general bibliographic reference on editions, translations and numerous other topics is R.M. Dandekar, *Vedic Bibliography*. V. 1; 1930-1946, Bombay: Karnatak, 1946; v. 2, 1946-1960, Poona: Univ. of Poona, 1961; v. 3, 1961-1972, Poona: Bhandarkar Oriental Research Institute, 1973; v. 4, 1972-1983, Poona: Bhandarkar Oriental Research Institute, 1985.
20. Deussen's translations of the sixty Upaniṣads of the *Oupnek'hat* in *Sixty Ups*. (see Abbreviations and Conventions) are still important, in part for their broad attempt to identify content units that might correspond to original units of teaching, later additions, etc. Also of note: P. Thieme, *Upanishaden: Ausgewählte Stücke*. Stuttgart: Reclam, 1977 (Reclam's Universalbibliothek No. 8723) (Thieme is a well-known Indo-european linguist); and Shree Purohit Swami and W.B. Yeats, *The Ten Principal Upanishads*. New York: Macmillan, 1937. In the preface the great poet looks askance at the "latinized", "hyphenated words", and the "polyglot phrases, sedentary distortion of unnatural English" (*ibid*., p. 7) which characterize most translations, including ours in this book.
21. 20 vols., all Paris: Adrien-Maisonneuve, 1943-74.
22. All Mylapore, Madras: Ramakrishna Math.
23. Viz. the translations by Swami Gambhīrānanda and Swami Mādhavānanda (see under Abbreviations and Conventions).
24. All Allahabad: Pāṇini Office. The SBH have been reprinted New York: AMS Press, 1974.

25. J.A. Santucci, *An Outline of Vedic Literature*. Missoula: Scholars Press, 1976, p. 37.
26. Raghavachar, *Rāmānuja on Ups*. (see Abbreviations and Conventions), pp. 64, 65.
27. Mukhopadhyaya, *Studies*, p. 9. S.S. Raghavachar argues explicitly that all the classical Upaniṣads embody a single doctrine of which all the central elements are found in *Bṛhadāraṇyaka Upaniṣad*. (*Rāmānuja on Ups.*, pp. 64-66.)
28. E.g., Rau, W., Zur Textkritik der Bṛhadāraṇyakopaniṣad. *ZDMG,* v. 105(2), 1955, p. 58*. Basing himself only on comparisons of printed editions, Rau says that there is evidence that both recensions of the Upaniṣad go back to common *written* original.
29. Eggeling, *ŚatBr* (see Abbreviations and Conventions).
30. Basically the Kāṇva divides three books of the Mādhyandina into 2 parts each. The most thorough comparison of the two versions, with a discussion of the implications of the results for the hisoty of the text, is W. Caland, *The Śatapatha Brāhmaṇa in the Kāṇvīya Recension*. Delhi: Motilal Banarsidass, 1983 (single vol. repr. of 3 vols.; 1st ed., Lahore, 1926, Panjab Sanskrit Series No. 10), Introduction, chrs. 4 and 5, pp. 85-120.
31. For a convenient comparison of the two versions in tabular form, see Belvalkar, S.K., and Ranade, R.D., *History of Indian Phiosophy. The Creative Period*. New Delhi: Oriental Books Reprint Corp., 1974 (repr. of 1927 ed.), pp. 110-111. Both Hume and Radhakrishnan translate the Kāṇva version, which is also the one commented on by Śaṁkara. The Mādhyandina version is available in German (Böhtlingk, *BṛhUp*, see Abbreviations and Conventions).
32. The only complete modern translations accessible to me were Böhtlingk, *BṛhUp*, who gives an accented Sanskrit text of the Mādhyandina recension and a German translation, and E. Roer, *The Brihad A'ranyaka Upanishad and the Commentary of Sankara A'cha'rya on its First Chapter*. Calcutta: Society for Resuscitation of Indian Literature, 1908. Details of Böhtlingk's translation are discussed by W.D. Whitney, Böhtlingk's Upanishads, *American Journal of Philology*, v. 11 (1890), pp. 407-439; and by Böhtlingk himself, in *Berichte über die Verhandlungen der königlich sächsischen Gesellschaft der Wissenschaften zu Leipzig, philologisch-historische Classe*. Zu den von mir bearbeiteten Upanishaden, v. 43 (1891), pp. 70-95; Bemerkungen zu einigen Upanishaden, v. 49 (1897), pp. 78-100; pp. 93-96; Kritische Beiträge, *ibid.*, pp. 127-138; pp. 129-130. There is still no critical edition of the Upaniṣads based on manuscript research (cf. M. Witzel's comments in his review of a critical edition of *BṛhUp* I (K) in a dissertation by D. Maue, *ZDMG,* v. 130 (1980), pp. 613-616); recent scholarship has been using the edition of Limaye-Vadekar, *Principal Ups.*, for this purpose. The most important traditional commentary (*bhāṣya*) is Śaṁkara's *Bṛhadāraṇyakopaniṣad-bhāṣya* (cf. chrs. 1.2 and 1.5), which is further elaborated in a voluminous subcommentary by Sureśvara, a disciple of Śaṁkara's. This provides the deepest but also the least accessible discussion of the text. Commentaries by contemporary Indian spiritual teachers include Swami Krishnananda, *The Bṛhadāraṇyaka Upanishad*. An Interpretive Exposition. Shivanandanagar: Divine Life Society, 1984; and Swami Shivananda, *The Brihadaranyaka Upanishad*. Shivanadanagar: Divine

Life Society, 1985.

33. Already E. Frauwallner acknowledged that these texts formed a unity and called them "Yājñavalkya doctrine". (Untersuchungen zu den älteren Upaniṣaden. *Zeitschrift für Indo-Iranistik.*, v. 4 (1926), pp. 1-45; repr. in G. Oberhammer and E. Steinkellner, eds., *Erich Frauwallner, Kleine Schriften.* Wiesbaden: Franz Steiner, 1982, pp. 95-139.) In his later *History of Indian Philosophy*, the author then analyzed them as a development of the "Agni-Doctrine".

34. He is often mentioned in the *Śatapatha Brāhmaṇa*, in books I-V and XI-XIII. Two quotes of his views in *Śāṅkhāyana Āraṇyaka* and some stories in *Jaiminīya Brāhmaṇa* appear to be taken from there. His sayings in *Śatapatha Brāhmaṇa* and other relevant passages are collected in I. Fišer, Yājñavalkya in the Śruti Traditions of the Veda. *Acta Orientalia* 45 (1984), pp. 55-87. Fišer divides the material into three major categories: (1) isolated quotes of Yājñavalkya's views on subtle points of ritual, mostly in *ŚatBr* I-IV; (2) *ŚatBr* XI.3 and 6, in which Yājñavalkya is presented in contests "compet[ing] for the recognition of superiority in the knowledge of the ritual and its esoteric meaning" (*ibid.*, p. 57); and (3) *BṛhUp* III-IV, modelled on (2) but with quite different contents. Fišer considers these as representing different images of Yājñavalkya prevalent at different periods of time. Some sayings of Yājñavalkya's are also given in an early Jain text, the Isibhāsiyāiṃ, which is independent of the Brāhmaṇical tradition. Cf. H. Nakamura, Yājñavalkya and the Upaniṣadic thinkers in a Jain tradition, *ALB*, v. 31-32 (1967-68), pp. 214-28; *History*, v. 1, pp. 274-277.

35. This is elaborated in *Mahābhārata* XII.318.6 and thereafter in the Purāṇas, e.g. *Brahmāṇḍa Purāṇa* I.2.34.5 ff. For Purāṇic references to Yājñavalkya, see S.A. Dange, *Encyclopedia of Purāṇic Beliefs and Practices*, 5 vols. New Delhi: Navrang 1986-; v. 4, pp. 1249-51.

36. Raghavachar, *Rāmānuja on Ups.*, p. 87.

37. *BṛhUp* IV.4.16-32(M), transl. Edgerton, *Beginnings*, pp. 163-166. For a philological discussion of vs. 23 ff. (= Kāṇva IV.4.22.25), see E. Hanefeld, *Philosophische Haupttexte der Älteren Upaniṣaden.* Wiesbaden: Otto Harassowitz, 1976 (U. Schneider, ed., Freiburger Beiträge zur Indologie, v. 9), pp. 38-41. Vs. 16-23 are *ślokas* and are discussed in detail by Horsch, *Gāthā Literature*, pp. 166-173. (a) or himself. (b) or sees, realizes. (c) Edgerton has "five types of creatures". (d) Edgerton has "even that I, intelligent and immortal hold for the immortal, Brahman". The translation given follows Horsch, *op. cit.*, p. 170. (e) "food of food" omitted in Kāṇva. (f) The verse is not found in the extant *Ṛg Veda*, and is a *śloka*. (g) Edgerton has "he".

38. Used already in *BṛhUp* IV.3.32 (K), then in *MāṇḍUp* 7, both times in connection with Ātman/Brahman.

39. *Asmitā* or "the sense of 'I'" is discussed in Patañjali's *Yoga Sūtra*. E.g. *YoSū* I.17 together with Vyāsa's commentary says that "complete concentration on *asmitā*", or *sa-asmitā samāpatti*, leads to a "pure sense of 'I'," or *asmitā-mātra*, a form of *saṁprajñāta samādhi*, which may ultimately become a permanent condition (cf. Swami Hariharananda, *Yoga Sūtra*, p. 49). *Dṛg-bhāvanā*, or "the feeling of being of the nature of the Seer (*dṛk*)", occurs e.g. in Śaṁkara's *Upadeśasāhasrī* or "Thousand Teach-

ings", in the *pari-saṁkhyāna* meditation in the prose part.

40. Grassman, *Wörterbuch*, col. 175. The normal nominative form of *ātman* is *ātmā*; in compounds, the form is *ātma-*.

41. Cf. Wackernagel-Debrunner, *Grammatik*, part III, 240 (b) and (c) (pp. 489-491). For a general discussion of the word, see Sharma, *Concept of Ātman*, pp. 11-15.

42. This includes the aspect of *cetanaścetanānām*, "[the] one consciousness in [the many] consciousnesses" (*ŚvetUp* V.13), which Sri Aurobindo regarded as one of the "four grand truths which form the foundation of Upanishadic teaching". "Based on these four grand truths. *nityo' nityānām, cetanaścetanānām, so'ham, aham brahmāsmi*, as upon four mighty pillars, the lofty philosophy of the Upaniṣads raised its front among the distant stars." Sri Aurobindo, Philosophy of the Upanishads (from his Baroda period), *Collected Works*, v. 12, p. 7.

43. This way of talking appears to be free from self-contradiction and not inconsistent with any empirical facts. For example, two different individual selves (individual minds, or consciousnesses) may be thought to in large part overlap, so that the bulk of one's self (mind or consciousness) is shared. Conceptualizing individual minds or consciousnesses as "overlapping" has been largely ignored in the West. The author recalls that long ago he wrote a paper on this subject: K. Witz, Groupmind. Committee on Culture and Cognition, University of Illinois, Technical Report No. 3 (1979).

44. *anu-vittaḥ and prati-buddhaḥ* (v. 17), *viduḥ* (v. 21), *anu-draṣṭavyaḥ* (v. 22), *vijñā-* (v. 23).

45. From *sākṣāt*, "with one's own eyes". "The realization that you are the Ātman and that there is nothing except the Ātman anywhere at anytime—this is Self-realization, it is the *Ātma-sākṣātkāra* . . . This is also called *Bhūmā*, the Vast Limitless, the Changeless, the Unaffected—by Time and Space. . . ." Sri Sathya Sai Baba, *Sathya Sai Speaks* v. 7, p. 334.

46. *Pratiṣṭhā* occurs numerous times in the Upaniṣads, although Brahman is called a basis or *pratiṣṭhā* for everything only later. *Sat* and *Satyam* here as in the *Sad* and *Satya Brahman* Vidyās, *ChāndUp* VI and *BṛhUp* V.4-5.

47. E.g., in Prakāśātman (middle of 10th cent. CE), in his *Pañca-pādikā-vivaraṇa*, a commentary on Padmapāda's *Pañca-pādikā*, itself a commentary on a portion of Śaṁkara's Commentary on the *Brahma Sūtra*. Cf. K. Cammann, *Das System des Advaita nach der Lehre Prakāśātmans*. Wiesbaden: Otto Harassowitz, 1965, § 35 (pp. 119-122) (cf. also the immediately preceding § 34).

48. Deussen, *PhilUps*, pp. 126 ff., explains Brahman under the headings "Brahman as Being and Not-Being (*sat* and *a-sat*), Reality and Not-Reality", "Brahman as Consciousness, Thought (*cit*)", and "Brahman as Bliss (*ānanda*)".

49. Cf. M.H. Mishra, Brahman: A Semantic Discussion. *Charu Deva Shastri Felicitation Volume*, v. 1. Delhi: CDF Felicitation Committee, 1974, pp. 112-114; p. 112.

50. The problem of the meaning of *brahman* in the *Ṛg Veda* has engaged some of the best Western scholars in this century and seems to have been to some extent resolved by the joint efforts of H. Oldenberg, L. Renou, J. Gonda and P. Thieme. See the remarkable paper by Thieme, Brahman.

ZDMG, v. 102 (1952), pp. 91-129; repr. in P. Thieme, *Kleine Schriften*. Wiesbaden: Franz Steiner, 2nd ed., 1984. (Glasenapp Stiftung, No. 5), pp. 100-138 and the references in notes 53 and 54 below.

51. Thieme takes it as "*Formulierung, Gestaltung, Formung*, "[verbal] formulation, giving shape, giving form" (*ibid.*, p. 102) and seems to understand by this something involving creative poetic intuition. But clearly what is referred to must be something like "bringing something into verbal form under the influence of divine experience or in a state of divine inspiration".

52. Thieme, *ibid.*, p. 103 (resp. p. 112); similarly Renou.

53. This aspect has been developed by J. Gonda, *Notes on Brahman*. Utrecht: 1950.

54. Such as *Ṛg Veda* X.61 and I.152 which are "explicitly and emphatically called *bráhman*". (Thieme, *op. cit.*, p. 102). *Bráhmans* of this type were emphasized by Renou (in collaboration with L. Silburn), Sur la notion de 'bráhman', *Journal Asiatique*, v. 237 (1949), pp. 1-46, and led him to conclude that "*bráhman* [in the *Ṛg Veda*] is nothing else but this type of thinking in riddles (*enigmè*)" (*ibid.*, p. 13). Renou's paper inspired W. Johnson to investigate "enigmatic *bráhmans*" and in particular "Sanskrit world view *bráhmans*" from the point of view of poetry, "speculative vision" and "visionary consciousness", "archetypical images", and their role in the "special oratorical contests" called *brahmodyas*. Cf. W. Johnson, *Poetry and Speculation of the Ṛg Veda*. Berkeley: Univ. of California Press, 1980 esp. pp. 1-41, 69-125.

55. Thieme notes that the mystical/enigmatic *bráhmans* in note 54, as well as others elsewhere in the Vedic literature (*Atharva Veda* I.32, *TaittBr* II.2.1.4), are explicitly characterized as a special kind of *bráhman* ("a *bráhman* given by Rudra", "an incomprehensible *bráhman*", "great *bráhman*", "secret *bráhman*"). This suggests that the Vedic Seers themselves felt *bráhmans* of this type to be the highest form of *bráhman* (Thieme, *ibid.*, p. 102).

56. E.g., the aspect of *akṣara*, syllable, in *Ṛg Veda* I.164, or the Logos idea represented by *Vāc*, Speech, which in later tradition became *Śabda-Brahman*, the "Word-Brahman".

57. Cf. Sri Sathya Sai Baba: "The word Brahman which occurs in the Vedas is also used to give the same meaning in the Upaniṣads." *Summershowers* 1974, p.33.

58. Deussen thought (*Phil Ups.* p. 127) that *sat-cit-ānanda* appears first in *Uttarā-Nṛsiṁha-tāpanīya Upaniṣad* IV.67 f. and in *Pūrvā-Rāma-tāpanīya Upaniṣad* 92 and *Uttarā-Rāma-tāpanīya Upaniṣad* 2, 4 and 5; for translations see Deussen, *Sixty Ups.*, v. 2. But these works are hard to date. It also occurs in *Paiṅgala Upaniṣad*. L. Burridge (*Proceedings 28th ICO, 1971*, Wiesbaden: Otto Harassowitz, 1976, pp. 135-136) notes that the term occurs in the *Ahirbudhnya Saṁhitā*, a well-known *Pāñcarātra* text from the 6th century CE, but with a different meaning. Burridge feels that its meaning there accounts for much of the history of the term in later Vedānta. At any rate *sat-cit-ānanda* is used in many of the smaller words traditionally attributed to Śaṁkara, but whose authenticity is doubted by modern scholarship, such as the *Ātmabodha* (vs. 21, 25-25, 64), *Ātma-anātma-viveka* (v. 21), *Vākya-vṛtti* (v. 12), and *Dṛg-dṛśya-viveka* (v. 22).

It also occurs in the *Mānasollāsa*, a commentary (traditionally attributed to Sureśvara) on the *Dakṣinā-mūrti Hymn* often attributed to Śaṁkara. (For editions and translations, see Potter's *Bibliography*.)

59. *BṛhUp* IV.4.7-15. Transl. Edgerton, *Beginnings*, pp. 161-163. Vs. 8, 9, 11-15 are *ślokas* and are discussed in detail by Horsch, *Gāthā Literature*, pp. 162-168. (a) Edgerton has "spirit". (b) or "that is the real (*sat*), to that he goes along with his deeds". (c) The following verses are not being quoted by Yājñavalkya and may be an addition. V. 12 alludes to Yogic knowledge, cf. chr. 6. Vs.13-14 occur also in *ĪśāUp* 9 and 3. Horsch argues that the versions here are older. V. 15 overlaps with *KenaUp* 13 (2, 4). The intended meaning of vs. 13-15 is uncertain; Edgerton's reading is reasonable.

60. With "wisdom" or *Weisheit* is usually associated some level of detachment and control of the senses and self, as well as some kind of awareness of a larger order operating in the world and living according to and completely in harmony with this order. The great majority of the world's major religious and philosophical traditions have sapiental components and subtraditions in which these qualities are cultivated and considered essential for higher knowledge. Obvious examples are Pythagoreanism, Platonism, Stoicism, Neoplatonism and Neo-pythagoreanism; I would also add certain forms of the mystery religions and gnosticism. But more careful exploration of this point in the classical ancient Near Eastern wisdom traditions (Israelite, Egyptian, Mesopotamian, and Iranian) would be desirable.

61. After the Upaniṣads, it is found in the Pāli canon, e.g. in the *Majjhima Nikāya* (which must be counted as a Supreme Wisdom Scripture), in the first Discourse, or in the great chain of origination (*paticca-samuppada*) (see Horner, *Middle Length Sayings*, v. 1, pp. 3-8 and pp. 316-320); then of course also in the *Prajñā-pāramitā* and *Cin-mātra* literatures, which are Supreme Wisdom literatures par excellence, and in Lao Tsu's *Tao Te-Ching*. Supreme Wisdom literatures may be considered pinnacle formulations of what H. Nasr calls the Eternal Wisdom, the *sophia perennis* or *philosophia perennis universalis* (Coomaraswamy) of the West or the *sanātana dharma* of Hinduism or *al-ḥikmat al-khālidah* of Islam. Cf. Nasr, S.H., *Knowledge and the Sacred*, Gifford Lectures, 1981. New York: Crossroad, 1981, pp. 68-72.

62. Gonda (*Religionen Indiens*, p. 207; *BṛhUp* IV.4.5 (K) = IV.4.7 (M)) calls it "the oldest text which treats of the doctrine of transmigration". Other early statements: *BṛhUp* III.2.10-13 (K), *BṛhUp* VI.2, and *ChāndUp* V.3-10. Recent scholarship in the area: H.W. Tull, *The Vedic Origins of Karma*. Albany: SUNY Press, 1988.

63. In the *Ṛg Veda* it is used mostly to refer to the deeds of the gods. Cf. Grassman's *Wörterbuch*.

64. Gonda, *ibid.*, pp. 207-208.

65. Cf. the summaries of the doctrines of *karma* in Patañjali's *Yoga Sūtra* and in Śaṁkara's Vedānta by K.H. Potter, Karma-theory in some Indian Philosophical Systems, in W.D. O'Flaherty, ed., *Karma* and *Rebirth in Classical Indian Traditions*. Berkeley: Univ. of California Press, 1980, pp. 241-267 (pp. 243-248 and 249-259 resp.).

66. H.W. Tull, *op. cit.* (note 62 above), pp. 28 ff., reads this passage as well as the related *BṛhUp* III.2.10-13 differently. In connection with the latter he argues that ". . . it is not entirely certain that the expression 'one becomes good by good action [*karman*], bad by bad' refers to a broad spectrum of conduct. The context in which this phrase occurs and certain aspects of the phrase itself, suggest that it refers only to the activity of the sacrifice. The context . . . clearly recalls the symbolism of the Brāhmaṇic ritual . . ." (*ibid.*, p. 30). Regarding the present passage [*BṛhUp* IV.6 (M) ff.] he notes that the preceding verses [*BṛhUp* IV.4-5 (M), not given here], which describe the self (or Self) taking on "another newer and more beautiful form", enumerates seven such forms of beings [man, fathers, gandharvas (celestials), gods, Prajāpati, Brahmā, and other beings] which may have been made to fit the seven spheres of the Brāhmaṇical cosmos, and which later the sacrificer attains as a result of merit accumulated through a lifetime of sacrifice (*ibid.*, p. 32, and note 112, p. 135). Tull also feels that if the Upaniṣadic text really had intended a moral criterion for taking the different forms, it would have depicted "a *loka* (a realm) that is exclusively associated with evil-doers [i.e., a hell];" failure to depict such a *loka* "is in accord with the Brāhmaṇical notion that the poorly done (*duṣ-kṛta*) sacrifice results in the diminution or destruction of the sacrificer's world of merit (*su-kṛta loka*), rather than the attainment of a lower form of life or of a hell" (*ibid.*, p. 135).
67. Cf. the discussion of the verse in Horsch, *Gāthā Literature*, p. 137.
68. This text is one of the 32 traditional *vidyās* or teachings leading to Brahman, cf. Table 4.1 below. Detailed modern-type discussion: E. Hanefeld, *Philosophische Haupttexte der älteren Upaniṣaden.* Wiesbaden: Otto Harassowitz, 1976 (*Freiburger Beiträge zur Indologie* v. 9), pp. 71-115. Classical commentaries include Śaṁkara's (transl. Swami Mādhavānanda, *BṛhUp Comm.*, pp. 348-376), and Rāmānuja's commentary on *BraSū* I.4.19.
69. Hanefeld (*op. cit.*, pp. 72-82) gives IV.5 (K) and II.4 (K) in parallel, with facing German translations, and Mādhyandina variants in footnotes. His comparison shows (pp. 84-88) that IV.5 contains seven passages that are expanded compared to II.4, as well as a few significant changes which appear "systematic and follow a definite tendency" (*ibid.*, p. 88). He concludes that IV.5 is a later version, with II.4 representing a more original version (*ibid.*, p. 88).
70. *BṛhUp* IV.5, transl. Edgerton, *Beginnings*, pp. 166-167. (a) This follows the Kāṇva; the Mādhyandina has "the mind as the sole locality of all the sciences" and "the heart as the sole locality of the Vedas".
71. Raghavachar, *Rāmānuja on Ups.*, p. 76.
72. *Ibid.*, p. 76.
73. *Ibid.*, p. 76.
74. Sri Sathya Sai Baba, *Voice of the Avatar* [Selections]. Prasanthi Nilayam: Sri Sathya Sai Books and Publications, Am. ed., 1980. vol. 1, p. 143.
75. Sri Sathya Sai Baba, *UpVahini*, p. 42; American ed., p. 39.
76. E.g., Swami Shivananda: "[the text shows that] in truth, our love for the Self is the basis for our love of all other objects". Swami Shivananda, *The Brihadaranyaka Upanishad*. Shivanandanagar: Divine Life Society, 1985, p. 199.

77. Beginning, apparently, with Śaṁkara. Commenting on the same passage *BṛhUp* II.4.5 (K), he says: "[The Self] *should* first *be heard* of from a teacher and from the Scriptures, then *reflected on* through reasoning, and then *steadfastly meditated* upon." In the introduction to his commentary on *BṛhUp* II.5 he calls this "the way to this realization". (Transl. Swami Mādhavānanda, *BṛhUp Comm.*, pp. 357, 377 resp.)
78. Cf. the survey by K. Pratap, *Śravaṇa, Manana, Nididhyāsana as Triple Means to Mokṣa*. Tirupati: pub. by author, 1983.
79. Śaṁkara takes "the Self is to be seen, *draṣṭavya*", as "the Self is to be realized", "is worthy of realization", *darśanārhaḥ*, or "should be made the object of realization", *darśanaviṣayatām āpayitavyaḥ* (cf. Swami Mādhavānanda, *BṛhUp Comm.*, p. 357; Shastri, *UpBhāṣyam* v. 3, p. 193), and interprets the other three terms as describing the path.
80. In the parallel version *BṛhUp* II.4.1-14 [=*ŚatBr* XIV.5.4.1-16 (K) etc.], the portion from "(sacrificial) gifts" to "creatures" is missing. This has led some modern scholars to think that this portion represents an addition, and that the original version referred only to the various texts and different kinds of human knowledge as the "exhalation of Great Being" (cf. Hanefeld, *op. cit.*, pp. 94-95). But Śaṁkara in his commentary on *BṛhUp* IV.5.11(K) (transl. Mādhavānanda, *op. cit.*, p. 779) sees little difference between the two: since all words are the exhalations of the Great Being, "by implication" so are also the objects denoted by them. This is consistent with the Vedic and Upaniṣadic view of *Vāc*, the (Divine) Word or Speech.
81. For Śaṁkara, "the examples are illustrative of dissolution" i.e., the dissolution of the Universe in the future (commentay on *BṛhUp*. II.4.11(K) = our verse 12, transl. Swami Mādhavānanda, *BṛhUp Comm.*, p. 364). In our exposition they are illustrative of the resolution of all manifoldness into the One Self (similar, but more specific: Deussen, *Sixty Ups.*). Hanefeld, who discusses the verse extensively (*op. cit.* pp. 95-100), notes that the touchings (*sparśāḥ*), smells (*gandhāḥ*), tastes (*rasāḥ*), forms (*rūpāṇi*) and sounds (*sabdāḥ*) anticipate the five subtle elements (*tanmātras*) of later classical Sāṁkhya.
82. Literally the sentence says "arising out of (from, but alternatively also: for) these *bhūtas*, into them it again disappears". The "it" must refer to the "great Being", i.e. Ātman. But what arises must be the Ātman as ordinary consciousness, as we know it. Hanefeld has "After it (= Ātman) arose for these beings, it dissolves with them (resp. into them) [at death]" (Hanefeld, *op. cit.*, p. 79). Y.K. Wadhwani, New Light on *Bṛhadāraṇyaka Upaniṣad* 2.4.12 = 4.5.13, *Bulletin of the Deccan College Research Institute*, v. 34 (1974), pp. 211-216, translates "The psychic activity arises (=manifests itself) on account of these 'beings' (*i.e.* the bodies and their organs) and vanishes after their destruction."
83. Commentary on *BṛhUp* II.4.12 (K), transl. Swami Mādhavānanda, *op. cit.*, pp. 368-369.
84. In the simplest version of the text, *BṛhUp* II.4.13 (K), he merely says "I say nothing confusing. This is enough for knowledge (*vijñāna*)" (no "this Ātman is imperishable. . . .").
85. See e.g. A.O. Fort, The Concept of Sākṣin in Advaita. *JIP*, v. 12 (1984), pp. 277-290.

86. It follows the description of the third and fourth *bhūmikās* (stages) of the seven stage path of knowledge given in *Yoga Vāsiṣṭha* and *Akṣi Upaniṣad.*
87. *Liṅga Purāṇa* I.70.96, and similarly Śaṁkara, Comm. on *KaṭhaUp* II.1.1; cited by Sharma, *Concept of Ātman*, p. 13, note 3.
88. Sri Sathya Sai Baba, *Jñāna Vahini*, p. 58.

CHAPTER 3

The Infinite Behind Mythology

1. Three Levels of Approach to Ātman/Brahman

The teachings on Ātman/Brahman in chr. 2 are extraordinary statements that stand on their own, largely independent of time, culture, and historical background. One resonates to them and is affected by them. But in order for there to arise Knowledge of the Reality which they teach, much more is needed. In this chapter, accordingly, we begin to enter more deeply into the Upaniṣads and into the world of Vedic and Brāhmaṇical thought and religion which stands behind them. As a start, we look at some texts in which Knowledge of the Self and Brahman is expressed in a mythological fashion. But first, we have to get a general idea of different roles which the Upaniṣadic teachings can play in developing such Higher Knowledge.

More detailed study shows quickly that the Upaniṣads (particularly the old Upaniṣads) resonate to the whole of Vedic and Brāhmaṇa thought and experience, and present an image of extraordinary diversity and richness. Being essentially compilations of dozens of smaller and larger pieces ("teachings"), their language is now archaic, now modern, their diction now poetic, now didactic, and now philosophical, and their thought now concrete and now abstract-intellectual. They speak symbolically, and their thought is undifferentiated, "magical". But they also have a predilection for abstract patterns, and have been called "prescientific". These kinds of aspects have been studied extensively, and they do of course have to be taken into account in translation and interpretation. But they are not intrinsically related to the awareness of Divinity and the Knowledge of Reality which these texts are expressing. Accordingly, we will not focus specifically on them. Instead, we proceed in a manner so that this Divinity, this Knowledge of Reality or Level of Being, whatever, emerges more clearly and directly.

Three Levels of Approach to Ātman/Brahman. Judging from the Upaniṣadic texts themselves, there are, broadly speaking, three ways in which, or three levels at which, knowledge of and merger in Ātman/Brahman may be promoted and pursued in one's living:

(1) by what we may call "walking the path of Agni (the Sacrificial Fire)", i.e., leading a dedicated conventional religious life in the framework of Brāhmaṇism and Brāhmaṇical ideas;

(2) by internalizing certain conceptions or values or "ways of thinking" related to Ātman/Brahman, which pervade the Vedic literature (Vedas, Brāhmaṇas, Āraṇyakas, and Upaniṣads), and which are so fundamental that they might be almost regarded as "ways of existentially being"; and

(3) by inner effort (or inner discipline, control etc.) and spiritual life, including meditation and meditative life.

(1) Living a Religious Life in the Context of Brāhmaṇical Religion. The Upaniṣads presuppose that the student is living his life fully in the framework of Brāhmaṇa ritual and ideals. The role which this played in the pursuit of Brahman in Upaniṣadic times can at this point only be guessed, but it can hardly be overestimated. It is clear that deeper and deeper realization of Ātman/Brahman as we see it in the different Upaniṣadic teachings was not only firmly rooted in "walking the path of Agni". It was also made possible by the moral purity and inner discipline inherent in that path and by the opportunities which that path afforded for a deeper, more universal vision that was not riveted on one's own fortunes.[1] But a full treatment of these matters is at present not possible, and we have to limit ourselves to points arising in connection with specific texts and in specific contexts.

(2) Higher Understanding Conveyed Through Words. Next, level (2) is the level of "emic" concepts, of specific religious (cosmological etc.) conceptions, myths and cultural forms. This is typically the level of anthropological and hermeneutic analysis. Here we have things like the institution and inner reality of the Vedic sacrifice (*yajña*); the conception and reality of *Agni* (Fire) and *Āditya* (Sun), two Vedic deities; and the intuition and reality of *Vāc*, "Speech" or "the Word", somewhat similar to "the Word" or "the Logos" in Western Tradition. Here we find also the Idea of the *Puruṣa*, the primeval-transcendental "Person" (Skt. *puruṣa*), from whom arose, and who in some sense constitutes, everything. These conceptions and cultural forms go back to the *Ṛg Veda*, and are part of *Ṛg Vedic* cosmology. (Much of the deepest knowledge of Divinity and of the Supreme in the *Ṛg Veda* is expressed in terms of cosmology).[2] In the Brāhmaṇas, the *Ṛg Vedic* conceptions are further developed and we find additional things like the notion of *prāṇa*, "breath, life-force", and numerical patterns, becoming prominent.[3] Now all these notions and cultural elements are used in the Upaniṣads in various ways to help the student approach Ātman/Brahman. So immersing oneself in them and absorbing them is one way in which one can develop some understanding of Ātman/Brahman. This represents approaching Ātman/Brahman at level (2).

But here we must be very careful. The concepts, schemata, and myths of level (2) are no doubt used to point to and symbolically refer to Ātman/Brahman, and to show a direction of approach. But we must distinguish the concepts and myths used to indicate a metaphysical, Divine or Transcendental entity clearly from actual knowledge/experience of that entity. The concepts and myths are part of Vedic and Brāhmaṇical culture. In anthropological terms, they represent ways of thinking-and-feeling (or in other words, intangible structure) which any competent member of the culture (any Brahmin) lives in his daily life. But they are at the same time more than that. They represent ways in which a person's living, his or her thought and feeling can be channelled so that knowledge/experience of God, of Reality, may arise. In a spiritually mature member of the culture, they will in fact embody such knowledge and experience, and they will also be the language that this person uses to communicate this knowledge and experience to someone else. But actual knowledge of the Divine or of the Reality is quite different from the public meanings of the concepts and myths in question (although in a well-functioning society, the two would not be completely disjoint—there would be a general awareness, shared by all, that behind the myths there was something like the Divine and the Reality). Just as a river presents two aspects, the water that flows and the river bed in which it flows, so any higher (metaphysical, divine, transcendental) knowledge or realization in a person has two aspects: the actual higher element in the person's consciousness or being (the water), and the beliefs and concepts and cultural forms within which that element shines and flows and in which it manifests itself (the river bed). The outer beliefs, etc. (the river bed) are cultural. The higher, purer stages of the inner consciousness, the realized Divine, the Infinite or the Reality (in Christian terms, Spirit, or God) are not. And it is just a combination of outer content and inner realization that presents itself to a modern student as a particular Divine Form, as a particular Saint, as a type of Mysticism, or as a level of Realization.

(3) Meditation and Inner Spiritual Life. To get to these "higher, purer stages of the inner consciousness", to get to higher realization, knowledge of Spirit, God, Ātman/Brahman, whatever, simply understanding and living the great religious-cultural concepts, myths, etc. in one's daily life, such as would in most cultures be exemplified by any "competent member of the culture", is not enough. For that reason, we must acknowledge a third level, beyond concepts, schemata, great cultural and trans-cultural myths and specific cultural forms. This is level (3) above, for convenience labelled "meditation and (inner) spiritual life". This level is the most important. We take it broadly to include any kind of inner effort and discipline toward the Supreme, including "spiritual practices" like meditation, and constant inner moral and ethical discipline. (These will normally be integrated with outward activity such as performance of rituals, right conduct in the performance of one's societal duties, or *yoga*). But "meditation and spiritual life" also includes the inner life of the soul, the inner spiritual life of the student or aspirant or devotee, "continual meditation" in a higher sense. It is in such meditation and inner spiritual life that concepts like Puruṣa, Vāc, Prāṇa, Veda, etc. flower into higher knowledge. In the Upaniṣads this aspect is usually always implied, but specifics are scarce.

2. Puruṣa and the "(Sense-) Powers". Outline of the Chapter

The Themes of Puruṣa and the "(Sense-) Powers". Among the conceptions, schemata, and myths in the Vedic literature, a rather prominent one is the theme of the "Powers of Intelligence", i.e., Sight, Hearing, Mind, Speech, as well as *Prāṇa*, "Breath, Life-force." These "Powers" (often also called *prāṇas*, in the plural, "sense powers", or "intelligent life-forces") are usually thought to be presided over by certain Deities or Divines: Sight by Āditya, the Sun-Divine; Hearing by the Directions, Diśas; Mind by the Moon; Speech by Agni, the Fire-Divine; and *Prāṇa* by Vāyu, the Wind-Divine. The theme of these "Powers" and Deities is in part traceable to a great *Ṛg Vedic* hymn, the *Hymn of Puruṣa, Ṛg Veda* X.90, where the Deities in question are described as being formed from the Eyes, Ears, Mind, Mouth and Breath of the primeval Puruṣa. The Puruṣa is a "person", *puruṣa* (masculine), "with a thousand heads, a thousand eyes, a thousand feet", which encompasses the whole Universe and extends beyond it. It (or He) is all that exists, ever existed, and will exist, the Creation as well as the Indivisible Divine, the Transcendental. In the following Āraṇyakas and Upaniṣads there are then many descriptions to the effect that the (Sense-) Powers are all inhabited by, or function as manifestations of, a single Intelligence-Entity, viz. (ultimately) the Great Puruṣa or Ātman, and ultimately this theme is used as a device to teach Ātman/Brahman. This theme, then, represents a particular approach to Ātman/Brahman *at level (2).*

The "Powers" of Sight, Mind, *Prāṇa* and so on emerge first as a recurring motif in the Brāhmaṇas. They are typically set in correspondence with various elements of the ritual, and are thought of both as powers existing in an individual and as generics or Universals.[4] It is therefore not surprising that in the Upaniṣads the entity that is seen as their indwelling intelligence or Seer is both the individual self and the Ātman (Yājñavalkya's One Seer, cf. chr. 2.5). Further, because the Powers represent a complete realm (viz. the realm of human life, consciousness and cognition, actually implicit in the term *prāṇas*, "sensory, etc. Powers"), the corresponding Deities also have a tendency to represent a complete realm, viz. the realm of the orderly operation of the external world. In the Upaniṣads this process comes to completion with the teaching that one and the same Aspect underlies both realms, viz. Ātman = Brahman. So historically, the preoccupation with the "(Sense-) Powers" and their Deities in the Brāhmaṇas represents the beginning of a drive toward the realization of Ātman/Brahman. The subsequent evolution of this drive in the Āraṇyakas and the Upaniṣads suggests further that the preoccupation was one with human experience and knowledge processes, and that it thus represents a kind of "epistemological" interest (in the Western sense of the term). This aspect is one of the greatnesses of the Brāhmaṇical Tradition, comparable to or on the same order as the "objective spirit" of classical Greece, and is one element that makes the Upaniṣads have an affinity with Western Philosophy and Science (see chr. 1.6). The importance of the theme of the "(Sense-) Powers" in the Brāhmaṇical Tradition is illustrated by its frequent "mythological treatment". It is unusual that such (to us) relatively abstract entities as these (Sense-) Powers should be so deeply mythologized. Contests of the Powers among themselves to determine which is superior, for example, are almost an Āraṇyaka and Upaniṣadic stock in trade. Stories utilizing the connection between the Powers and their corresponding Deities are likewise fairly common. These remarks are sufficient to suggest that there may be a lot more depth in the Vedic literature than meets the eye to contain this set of themes and to culminate in the conceptions/experience of Ātman/Brahman.

Mythology, Philosophy, and *Vidyā* all in the Service of Realization. In this chapter we first discuss the Puruṣa Hymn and then three texts illustrating the theme of the Sense Powers. Of these four texts, two (the Puruṣa Hymn and *AitUp* I) are "mythological", one (*BṛhUp* I.4) uses mythological images but does this too consciously and loosely to be really mythology, and the last one (*KauṣUp* III) is "philosophical". All four operate largely at what we called level (2) above. In each case, we will try to clarify the conceptions and ideas involved. But in addition we will argue that although these texts are "mythological" or "philosophical", there must be underlying each one of them some kind of realization, some kind of higher or highest illumination or "enlightenment". (The exact nature of this realization can only be vaguely sensed and not made more immediately apprehensible.) This suggests that corresponding embryonic or emergent levels of realization were already implicit in the Brāhmaṇas, when the themes of the Sense Powers and of Puruṣa were being developed. But that is not all. We will also see that the Upaniṣadic seers had acquired an extraordinary freedom to express their realization.) They not only used the old mythological patterns creatively. (*AitUp* I represents a rather traditional tratment, while *BṛhUp* I.4 may be described as consciously using mythological images for a new purpose.) They also developed new genres, such as the philosophical approach in *KauṣUp* III. The most important innovations, however, will only become apparent in the next chapter, where we will discuss texts which teach to meditate on the Powers as being Brahman, for example. Explicit injunctions toward inner spiritual effort such as "worshipful meditation", *upāsanā*, and walking a "path of illuminating knowledge", a *vidyā*, appear only in the Āraṇyakas and Upaniṣads. So mythological treatment, philosophical argument, and *upāsanā* and *vidyā* are all put in the service of pointing the student toward realization of Ātman/Brahman.

Argument of the Chapter. The general theme of this chapter is illustrated by *BṛhUp* I.4.7, to the effect that "all these [Powers of Speech, Sight, Hearing, Mind] are merely His (Brahman's, Puruṣa's) action-names":

> When breathing, He (Āman/Brahman) becomes Breath (*Prāṇa*) by name; when speaking, Speech, *Vāc*; when seeing, Sight, *Cakṣus;* when hearing, Hearing, *Śrotra*; when thinking, Mind, *Manas*: these are merely the names of His acts (*karma-nāmāni*, lit. His "action-names", his names according to His activities).

The intent is clear. All the actions, perceptions, thoughts, which one normally thinks of as elements of one's individual existence, experience, etc., are the activities of a One, viz. the Puruṣa. And further, one should live according to this teaching, one should see oneself and all things in this way, one should first practice and eventually experience this, realise this. In particular this teaching is meant as a general world-view for living one's life, and to some extent Upaniṣadic teachings of this kind have in fact become part of the Neo-Hindu subconscious. Now this text, and the whole section of which it is a part (*BṛhUp* I.4), are basically an elaboration of the Puruṣa Hymn. For an aspirant on the path to the Infinite, it leads to a cosmic-cosmological existential stance, which expresses itself for instance in a tendency toward *aham-graha*-type meditation (i.e., meditation in which one meditates that "I am the Universal Divine, the Brahman"). It also engenders a powerful tendency to reach the Ātman, which is "before Creation", by rising above Creation by renunciation.

After the Puruṣa Hymn (sec. 3) and *BṛhUp* I.4 (secs. 4 and 5), our third text is *AitUp* I (sec. 6), like *BṛhUp* I.4 another elaboration of the Puruṣa Idea. It begins with "In the beginning all this was the Self, one only," and then, like a straightforward creation account, goes on to describe how the world was evolved from that one Self. The whole looks very much like a systematization and expansion of the creation story of the Puruṣa Hymn. But it turns out that it represents a rather advanced inner teaching on Ātman/Brahman, and is comparable in power to some of the *vidyās* discussed later.

The last text finally, *KauṣUp* III (secs. 9-10), is in some ways similar to *BṛhUp* I.4 but has a different spirit. It teaches that the Sense Powers are animated by *Prāṇa*, life-energy and vital force, and *Prajñā-ātman*, the intelligence-self (or consciousness-self). These two are considered to be the same thing which only appears divided in different individuals. As in *BṛhUp* I.4, Speech, Sight, Hearing etc. are treated partly as localized and experienced in the individual and partly as universal entities (presided over by deities). And as in that text all these powers are ensouled, pervaded or animated by a higher aspect. But there is one major difference. In *BṛhUp* I.4, this indwelling higher aspect is Ātman or Self, both cosmological/cosmic and manifesting as the individual self. From this Ātman sprang all the features of human experience—man and woman, speech, sight, hearing, etc., the classes of society, *dharma* etc. All are names according to His actions (*karma-nāmāni*). So a student who tries to live this text takes in his or her spiritual life a cosmic-cosmological stance, "Self is all there is," which is never lost sight of. In *AitUp* I, the situation is basically the same. But in *KauṣUp* III, the orientation is strictly in terms of individual experience. Although the various powers are also understood as supra-individual or universal entities, an explicit cosmological and cosmos-embracing stance is absent. Indeed the text reads almost like a philosophical argument, showing that behind powers like speech and seeing familiar from one's individual experience, there must be a unitary and ultimately supra-individual entity that "mounts" them, or takes a hold of them, viz. *Prāṇa* = *Prajñā-ātman*. No wonder Keith and others[5] have presented it as a valuable piece of philosophy in the Western sense. While *BṛhUp* I.4 provides practical ways of thinking that are part of the mainstream of the old Upaniṣadic thought and eventually developed into the Puruṣa conception of early (pre-Śaṁkara) Vedānta, *KauṣUp* III lies more on the line of later Sāṁkhya philosophy.[6] Vedānta and Sāṁkhya are the two main philosophies built directly on the Vedic literature, and these two texts illustrate *in nuce* their difference in philosophical temperament.

As can be seen, the overall plan of the chapter is to discuss first major Puruṣa-type texts, which together define a Puruṣa approach to Āman/Brahman, and then bring in the *Prajñā-ātman* as a similar but alternative development. In all of these texts, the theme of the Sense-Powers is utilized to make the intuition of the Puruṣa flower into that of Ātman/Brahman. This alone suggests a historical development Puruṣa—Ātman/Brahman. Sec. 7 therefore takes time out to present two important texts from *Vājasaneyī Saṁhitā*, the *Uttara Nārāyaṇa* and the *Tad-eva*, which might be intermediate links in such an historical evolution, while sec. 8 outlines the further development of the Puruṣa Idea to the point where it merges into what is now a general Indian conception of the Supreme Divine, *īśvara*. (The *Uttara Nārāyaṇa* actually anticipates this development by essentially praising the Puruṣa as *īśvara*). Finally, the chapter closes with a section which reflects on a larger issue. This is the assumption, in our treatment of the three Upaniṣadic texts, that behind the myth and philosophy of the texts there stood a core of higher (metaphysical, Divine, Ātmic/Brahmic) Knowledge or Realization, and that our task was to bring that Higher Realization more clearly into focus. This assumption is part of a more general view to the effect that many of the world's high spiritual literatures involve a common "fabric" or "substance" or "level" of Higher Knowledge/Experience/Being. The Upaniṣadic Seers were the first to try to express this level purely in its own terms, and the mythical and philosophical texts represent their first semi-independent fruits in that direction.

3. The Puruṣa Hymn

The *puruṣa sūkta*, or "hymn (*sūkta*) of the person (*puruṣa*)", *Ṛg Veda* X.90,[7] has played a profound role in Indian Tradition and we will come back to it again and agin. It is in 16 verses and divides naturally into two parts: vs. 1-5 give a vision of the Puruṣa, "the One Person", while vs. 6-16 describe the origin of the world in terms of Sacrifice with the Puruṣa itself as the sacrificial offering.

Puruṣa Hymn, *Ṛg Veda* X.90

1. The Puruṣa has a thousand heads, a thousand eyes, and a thousand feet. He, encompassing the world on all sides, stood out ten fingers' length beyond [it].
2. The Puruṣa alone is all this universe, what has been, and what is to be. He rules likewise over (the world of) immortality (viz. the gods), which he grows beyond, by (sacrificial?) food.
3. Such is the extent of his greatness; and the Puruṣa is still greater than this. A quarter of him is all beings, three quarters are (the world of) the immortal in heaven.
4. In his three-quarters the Puruṣa arose to the upper regions; a quarter of him, on the other hand, came to be here below. From this (quarter) he expanded manifoldly into the things that eat and those that do not eat (animate and inanimate beings).
5. From him the Shining One (*Virāj*) was born, from the Shining One (was born likewise) the Puruṣa. Being born (from the Shining One), he extended beyond the world, behind and also before.

6. When the gods, with the Puruṣa as oblation, extended (performed) the (cosmic) sacrifice, Spring became the butter for it, Summer the firewood, Autumn the oblation.
7. They consecrated on the sacred grasss this sacrifice, (namely) the Puruṣa, born in the beginning. With him the gods sacrificed, the Sādhyas, and the Seers.
8. From this sacrifice, offered as whole-offering, the ghee-mixture (the juice that flowed off) was collected; it made these animals—those of the air, of the jungle, and of the village.
9. From this sacrifice, offered as whole-offering, the stanzas of praise (the *Ṛg Veda*) and the melodies (*Sāma Veda*) were produced; the meters were produced therefrom, the sacrificial formulas (*Yajur Veda*) were produced therefrom.
10. Therefrom were produced horses, and whatever animals have (cutting-) teeth on both jaws. Cattle were produced therefrom, therefrom were born goats and sheep.
11. When they divided the Puruṣa (as the victim at the cosmic sacrifice), into how many parts did they separate him? What did his mouth become? What his two arms? What are declared to be his two thighs, his two feet?
12. The Brahman (priestly caste) was his mouth, his two arms became the Rājanya (warrior caste); his two thighs are the Vaiśya (artisan caste), from his two feet the Śūdra (serf caste) was produced.
13. The Moon sprang from his thought-organ, the Sun was produced from his eye; from his mouth Indra (war-god and soma-drinker) and Agni (the Fire-god), from his breath Vāyu (the Wind-god) was produced.
14. From his navel arose the atmosphere, from his head the heaven evolved; from his two feet the earth, from his ear the directions. Thus they fashioned the worlds.
15. Seven were his surrounding sticks (at the burnt offering), thrice seven were made the pieces of kindling wood when the gods, extending (performing) the (cosmic) sacrifice, bound the Puruṣa as the victim.
16. With offering the gods offered the offering; these were the first (holy) institutions. Verily these Powers have followed up to heaven, where are the Sādhya-gods of old.[8]

The Puruṣa is a transcendental One. He "has a thousand heads" etc. and "stood out ten fingers length beyond" the world-total, *i.e.*, He is a transcendental Entity that cannot be limited by the dimensions of matter and mind.[9] The past tense "stood out" suggests not only a past state of affairs, but also the seer's memory of a deep realization. "He rules over" both the mortal world and the world of immortality, i.e., He is the One that is above these aspects, but at the same time He determines them: they reflect Him in detail, in every object and event. He is immanent in all beings— "He has a thousand heads, a thousand eyes, and a thousand feet." He is the One Intelligence in the minds and intellects of all people, of all beings. He is the One Seer that sees through all the eyes of all beings, and He is the One that moves in all bodies. "He is this All." Besides being the one and only existent, creation of the Universe is represented as His unfoldment, or in terms of change in Him (vs. 4-5) and of sacrifice of Him (vs. 7 and 8). "He is the explanation both of the unity as well as [of] the origin of the Universe; the same being, or principle, is the Universe and its origin."[10] Although logically already implicit in vs. 1-2, this is elaborated in different sets of images in vs. 3-4 and 5 ("He expanded manifoldly into" animate and inanimate things, and "he extended beyond the world, behind and also before"). Vs. 3-4 continue vs. 1 and 2 with the same kind of language and in the same kind of metaphysical framework. But with v. 5 things become somewhat unclear. Geldner glosses *Virāj* in a general way as "the female creation principle".[11] It must be an experiential aspect that was felt to be an essential ingredient or phase in the bringing about of the manifold world.[12] In *Atharva Veda* VIII.8 and 9 the Virāj is described in mystical terms similar to the Puruṣa Himself. The meaning of the Virāj being born from Puruṣa and Puruṣa from Virāj is also not completely clear. There are several Vedic and Epic-Purāṇic parallels, but they do not give a single meaning.[13] Indian tradition and modern scholarship interpret the Puruṣa born from Virāj in v. 5 as a second Puruṣa, different from the *Ādipuruṣa* or "original Puruṣa" of vs. 1-4. This second Puruṣa (or sometimes Virāj) is the "First Born". It is conceivable, however, that the text does not intend this kind of a distinction. In later Epic and Purāṇic tradition, the first born is Nārāyaṇa.[14] The Mudgala Upaniṣad, an early Viṣṇuite (non-Vedic) Upaniṣad, identifies the Ādi-Puruṣa with Viṣṇu = Hari, and Puruṣa divided into four quarters in v. 3, which it calls *Pāda-Nārāyaṇa*, with Aniruddha, an aspect of Viṣṇu.[15] It also says that the birth of Virāj and Puruṣa from each other in v. 5 points to the origin of *prakṛti* and *puruṣa,* the Sāṁkhya principles of Matter and Spirit.[16]

The "Great Thought" of Puruṣa and its Significance for Later Tradition. Clearly vs. 1-5 evoke in a few lines an extraordinary higher conception/realization, a single Great Thought. This Thought, coming from the Infinite, has lodged in it great Power. The Puruṣa that is described represents a very specific conception/experience of the One, and of the relationship between One and the Many, between the one Reality and the manifoldness of the world and one's experience. N. Brown has shown[17] that the basic descriptors in vs. 2 and 4 ("immortality", "rising beyond", "food arose", and "expanding manifoldly" —*amṛtatvá, áti-ruh,, ánna ud+ī,* and *vi+kram*) are in the *Ṛg Veda* predominantly associated with Agni (Fire), Sūrya (the Sun), and Viṣṇu. Hence the Puruṣa incorporates "a combination of characteristics derived from" "(a) Agni, as the typical male, . . . essence of plants, waters, all that moves and stands and the sacrifice, . . . lord of immortality; (2) Sūrya, as rising above the worlds to the place of immortality; [and] (3) Viṣṇu, as the encompasser of earth, air, and sky".[18] In other words, it is a conception that is formed entirely with ingredients present elsewhere in the *Ṛg Veda*. Yet this conception foreshadows the Upaniṣadic Ātman/Brahman. As that from which all things arise and which is all this Universe, the Puruṣa is Brahman. At the same time, by the very choice of the term *puruṣa*, "person, man", the hymn also brings in the aspect of self, Ātman. When the person or self is stripped of all that is finite, then it becomes clear that it is above the entire creation of Time and Space and Experience, and that it somehow contains and is all that. This is the fundamental Knowledge poetically suggested in the hymn. "You appear as separate individual bodies because the eye that sees them, seeks only the outer bodies. When you clarify your vision and look at them through the Ātmic eye, then you will see others as Waves of the Ocean of the Absolute, as the thousand heads, the thousand eyes and the thousand feet of the Puruṣa sung in the *Ṛg Veda*. . ."[19] As a prefiguration of Ātman/Brahman, the Puruṣa shows some of the same features that struck us as almost contradictory attributes of the Ātman in chr. 2.2.

Historically, the "Great Thought" of the Puruṣa is not only prominent in the Upaniṣads, but it has also had a vast influence in Indian Tradition. Here we only note that the teaching and experience that God Himself has become and is all this world, but that He is at the same time also the Transcendent Infinite, is not foreign to Western

Tradition.[20] But in Hindu Tradition, beginning with the Brāhmaṇas, it is almost general world-view. (In the Brāhmaṇas, it is not a single doctrine, but rather implied or stated in innumerable different ways. The one element of continuity through the weave of teachings is always the Puruṣa Hymn.) Already in the *Vājasaneyī Saṁhitā* (in the *Tad-eva*) the Puruṣa is the Ātman. The Self, the core of oneself, is All. Later *BṛhUP* I.4.1 says "In the beginning this world was Ātman alone"; thereafter Ātman created all this world.

G. Mukhopadhyaya has tried to put his finger on the element which the Puruṣa Hymn contributed to Indian Tradition by saying that in Indian Tradition from the very beginning the understanding of transcendence and immanence has been quite different than in the West. In Indian Tradition, "transcendence never signifies an aloofness or an exclusiveness because *the Brahman of the Upaniṣads is not a unitary principle which is opposite to the multiplicity of Creation*"[21] (italics added). "From [that] which beings [are born, from that they are] not different"[22] says *Mahā-Nārāyaṇa Upaniṣad*, referring to Prajāpati, i.e. (in this case) Brahman as Puruṣa. An awareness to the effect that somehow one is not different from the Supreme Divine may have been part of one's life from childhood on, or it may come to one naturally and gradually, like a kind of maturity, or it may develop in the course of spiritual life. But in any case, it is characteristic of much of Hindu spirituality. Again, "immanence [as in "God's immanence in the world"] does not mean merely a pervasiveness through all space and time. Rather it signifies the principle of sustenance which makes things exist and appear. It is that aspect of Reality which is in Identification with existence".[23] But however one tries to characterize the principle at the bottom of this hymn, the fact remains that it expresses a Great Thought, a Thought of incalculable Power and Greatness. One broad and very general traditional way of trying to get knowledge of Brahman in Brāhmaṇical and Upaniṣadic times was to approach Brahman intuitively through this Great Thought of the Puruṣa Hymn.

4. *BṛhUp* I.4 (*Puruṣa-vidha Brāhmaṇa*)

As mentioned in sec. 1, *BṛhUp* I.4, the *Puruṣa-vidha Brāhmaṇa* or "section on 'in the form of (*vidha*) a person (*puruṣa*)'," [24] unfolds the Great Thought of Puruṣa in the Puruṣa Hymn in various ways. The text is of central importance in the thought of *Bṛhadāraṇyaka Upaniṣad* as a whole. Chapters I and II of the Upaniṣad form the *madhu kāṇḍa*, the "division (*kāṇḍa*) on honey (*madhu*)", so called after *BṛhUp* II.5, the "honey teaching" of the Seer Dadhyaṅc Atharvan. This division is traditionally considered to be "instruction", *upadeśa*,[25] and as such the most fundamental for the serious student. (By comparison the great Yājñavalkya chapters III and IV are only "exposition" or "demonstration", *upapatti*). But even within chapters I and II, I.4 stands out as central. Thus Swami Krishnananda of the Divine Life Society, who has made a deep study of the whole train of thought of *Bṛhadāraṇyaka Upaniṣad*, considers chapter I to be the most important chapter of the whole Upaniṣad and the *Puruṣavidha Brāhmaṇa* to be the most important section of chapter I.[26] Deussen too felt that the text was fundamental.[27]

BṛhUp I.4. Text

1. In the beginning this [world] was indeed only the Self (Ātman), in the form of a Person. He (the Person), looking around, saw nothing other than himself. He uttered first: "This is I (*so' ham asmi*)."[a] From this came to be the name I (*aham*)[b]. Therefore also today, when one is addressed, having first said 'This is I,' one then announces whatever is one's name. Since He previous to (*pūrva*) this world burned up (root *uṣ*) all evils, therefore He is a person (*puruṣa*). He who knows this, he verily burns up him who desires to be ahead of him.
2. He (or It, the Ātman) was afraid. Therefore one who is alone is afraid. He then, this one, thought to himself: 'Since there is nothing else than me, of what then am I afraid?' Thereupon, indeed, His fear departed, for of what should He have been afraid? Verily fear arises from a second [only].
3. He, verily, had no delight (root *ram*). Therefore one alone has no delight. He desired a second. He was, indeed, as large as a woman and man closely embraced. He caused that self (or body, *ātman*) indeed to fall (root *pat*) into two pieces. Therefrom arose a husband (*pati*) and a wife (*patnī*). Therefore this— "One's own (*sva*) [person] is like a half-pea (i.e. an incomplete half),"—[this] verily, Yājñavalkya used to say. Therefore this space is filled by a wife. He became united with her.[c] Therefrom human beings were produced.

4. She, then, this one, thought to herself: 'How now does He (i.e., how can He) unite with me having produced me just from Himself? Oh, let me disappear.' She became a cow. He became a bull. He did indeed unite with her. Then cattle were born. She became a mare, He a stallion. She became a female ass, He a male ass; He did indeed unite with her. Then were born solid-hoofed animals. She became a she-goat, He a he-goat; She a ewe, He a ram; He did indeed unite with her. Then goats and sheep were born. Thus, indeed, He created all, whatever there exists in pairs, even down to the ants.
5. He knew, "I, indeed, am the creation, for I created all this." Then (or thus) there arose Creation.[d] Verily, he who knows thus comes to be in that Creation of His. . . .

7. Verily, at that time this [world] was undifferentiated. It became differentiated just by name and form, [in the manner of]: "He has such a name, such a form." Even today this world is differentiated just by name and form, [in the manner of]: "He has such a name, such a form."

   He (Ātman, cf. v. 8 below) entered in here, even to the fingernail-tip, as a razor might be placed into a razor-case, or fire in a fireholder. Him they see not, for [as usually seen] He is incomplete (*akṛtsna*). Breathing, He becomes Breath (*Prāṇa*) by name; speaking, he becomes Speech (*Vāc*); seeing, he becomes Sight (*Cakṣus*); hearing, he becomes Hearing (*Śrotra*); thinking, he becomes the Mind (*Manas*): These are merely of Him these action-names. Whoever meditates on (worships, regards, *upās*-) one or another of these—he knows not; for He is incomplete [if regarded] in the manner of one or another of these.[e] One should worship [Him] [in the manner of] "[He is my-] self (*ātman*)." For there [in self] all these become one. What this Self is, that is that which enables the tracking, step by step, of this All, for by it (i.e. by the self) one knows this All. Just as, verily, one might find [something] by a footprint (*pada*), in the same way he finds fame and praise who knows this.
8. That very Self is dearer than a son, is dearer than wealth, is dearer than all else, being innermost.[f]

If of one who speaks of anything else than the Self as dear, one should say, 'He will lose what he holds dear,' he would indeed be likely to do so. One should meditate on (regard, etc., *upās-)* the Self alone as dear. He who regards (*upās-*) the Self alone as dear—what he holds dear, verily, is not perishable.....

10. Verily, in the beginning this world was Brahman. That knew itself (*ātmānam*): "I am Brahman" (*aham brahma asmi*). Therefore It became the All. Now whoever of the gods became awakened to this, he indeed became It; likewise in the case of seers, likewise in the case of men. Seeing this, indeed, the seer Vāmadeva began:

'I was Manu and the Sun (*Sūrya*)'! . . .

This is so now also. Whoever knows thus, 'I am Brahman!', becomes this All; even the gods do not control the non-being of it (=can't prevent it), for he becomes their self (*ātman*).

So whoever worships another divinity (*devatā*), thinking 'It is one and I another,' he knows not. He is like a sacrificial animal for the gods. Verily, indeed, as many animals would be of service to a man, even so each single person is of service to the gods. If even one animal is taken away, there is unpleasant [effect]. What, then, if many? Therefore, it is not pleasing to those [gods] that men should know this.

11. Verily, in the beginning this world was Brahman, one only. That being one, was not differentiated. It created beyond itself a superior form, rulership (*kṣatra*), even those who are rulers among the gods: Indra, Varuṇa, Soma, Rudra, Parjañya (Rain), Yama, Mṛtyu (Death), Īśāna. Therefore there is nothing higher than rulership. Therefore at the *rāja-sūya* ("Anointing of the King") ceremony, the Brahmin sits below the ruler (*kṣatra*). Upon rulership alone does he confer this honor. [Nevertheless,] Brahminhood (*brahma*) is the source of rulership. Therefore, even if the king attains supremacy, he rests finally upon Brahminhood as his own source. So one who injures him [i.e. a Brahmin], he hits his own source. He becomes worse off in proportion as he injures one who is better.

12. He was not yet differentiated. He created the *Viś* (the "commonality"), those kinds of gods that are mentioned in numbers: the Vasus, the Rudras, the Ādityas, the Viśvedevas, the Maruts.
13. He was not yet developed. He created the Śūdra (the serf), Pūṣan. Verily, this [earth] is Pūṣan, for she nourishes (root *puṣ*) everything that is.
14. He was not yet differentiated. He created still further a better form, *dharma*, "right conduct, righteousness". This is the power (*kṣatra*) of the (noblemen and) ruler class (i.e. of the Kṣatriyas), viz. *dharma*. Therefore there is nothing higher than *dharma*. So a weak man controls a strong man by *dharma*, just as if by a king. Verily, that which is *dharma* is Truth. Therefore they say of a man who speaks the truth, 'he speaks the *dharma*', or of a man who speaks the *dharma*, 'he speaks the truth'. Verily, both these are the same thing.

15[a]. So that Brahman [appeared as] *Kṣatra, Viś*, and *Śūdra*. So among the gods Brahman appeared by means of Agni, among men as a Brahmin; [It appeared] as a Kṣatriya by means of the [divine] Kṣatriya, as a Vaiśya by means of the [divine] Vaiśya, as a Śūdra by means of the [divine] Śūdra. Therefore people desire a place among the gods in Agni, among men in a Brahmin, for by these two forms [pre-eminently] Brahman appeared.

[b] Now whoever departs from this world without having seen the world [as] his own, to him it is of no service, because it is unknown, as the unrecited Vedas or any other undone deed [do not help him].

Verily, even if one performs a great and holy work—without knowing this, that work of his merely perishes in the end. One should worship (regard, meditate on, *upās-*) the world as [his/her] Self. The work of him who worships the world as the Self does not perish, for out of that very Self he creates whatsoever he desires.

16. Now this Self, verily, is the world (*loka*) of all created things. In so far as a man makes offerings and sacrifices, he becomes the world of the gods. In so far as he learns [the Vedas], he becomes the world of the seers (*ṛṣi*). In so far as he offers libations to the fathers and desires off-

spring, he becomes the world of the fathers. In so far as he gives lodging and food to men, he becomes the world of men. In so far as he finds grass and water for animals, he becomes the world of animals. In so far as beasts and birds, even to the ants, find a living in his houses, he becomes their world. Verily, as one would desire security for his own world, so all creatures wish security for him who has this knowledge. This fact, verily, is known when it is thought out.

17. In the beginning this world was just the Ātman, one only. He wished: "Would that I had a wife; then I would procreate. Would that I had a wealth; then I would offer sacrifice." So great, indeed, is desire. Not even if one desired, would one get more than that. Therefore even today, when one is lonely, one wishes: "Would that I had a wife, then I would procreate. Would that I had wealth, then I would offer sacrifice." So far as he does not obtain anyone of these, he thinks that he is, assuredly, incomplete. Now his completeness is as follows: his mind, truly, is his self (*ātman*); his speech is his wife; his breath is his offspring; his sight is his worldly wealth, for with his sight he finds; his hearing is his heavenly [wealth], for with his hearing he hears it; his body (central part, *ātman*), indeed, is his work, for with his body he performs work.

The sacrifice is fivefold. The sacrificial animal is fivefold. A person is fivefold. This whole world, whatever there is, is fivefold. He obtains this whole world who knows this.[28]

Structure of the Text. There are several semi-independent content units ("a series of loosely lined up images of creation"—Deussen)[29], viz. vs. 1-5, with 6 added; v. 7, with v. 8 as added comment; v. 10, parallel to 7, and introduced by v. 9; vs. 11-15a; vs. 15b-16; and v. 17. Let us take them in order.

Verses 1-6. Vs. 1-6 deal with how all is generated from Self. Beginning with "being self only," or simply "being" (v. 1), they describe the genesis of the principle of husband-wife and of male-female pairing, as well as the generation of human beings and animals (vs. 3-4), all out of Self. V. 5 sums up the gist of the teaching: "I, indeed, am this creation, for I emitted it all from myself." It is the real concluding statement of this unit, for v. 6 only adds as an additional comment that worship, which centers around the domestic fire, and all the gods are generated from the self in the same way. They are not independent higher principles as one might think.

"Being Self alone" ("not seeing anything other than oneself") in v. 1 is the basic way of being. It comes before everything else, before this entire world (including perceptions, thoughts, etc.). This "Self alone," says the text, which is before and in this sense different from any thought and world, is still present as a knowledge, or as a transcendental element when one says "I". It is due to that transcendental element that when called "who is there?", one spontaneously responds "It is I (me)" and only then says one's name. That spontaneous response is really an echo from the Reality which one is, an echo from That which one was before Creation[30] (cf. Jesus' "before Abraham was, I am") and which one is now. This Reality which one is, is above Evil, and hence, in a wordplay that has deeper significance, It is called *puruṣa*—It is "before" (*pūrva*) [Creation] and "burns up" (*uṣ-*) Evil. So the Self before Creation is "in the form of a person", *puruṣa-vidha*, or as Gonda suggests, "in the shape of *the* Puruṣa [of the Puruṣa Hymn]."[31] Even though it is before Creation, before any form or structure or name, it is "in the form of a person". This apparently self-contradictory element is already present in the Puruṣa Hymn. It is this element, combined with the fact that the Puruṣa or Self comprises the total of existence, that makes the Thought of Puruṣa so transcendental-powerful.

V. 2 teaches that vision of multiplicity is connected with fear.[32] "To be Self only" is to be entirely free from fear. For fear exists only when there is the thought that there is something else that is different from oneself. Fear and Thought-of-Other form one inseparable principle. When one "is Self only", fear cannot arise because there is no thought of something or someone other. Knowledge that there is only Self or that all is Self makes fear impossible. In a similar way vs. 3-4 teach the nature and origin of male-female relationship. Husband and wife, male and female, form a single principle. The normal tendency when one is alone is "to have no delight", and to yearn to have delight. When there is yearning for delight, something comes that completes that yearning,—viz., the wife. That wife is actually self, she is one's yearning and one's fulfilment-of-yearning. But when one takes her as other (in order to have delight—to see her, have her love, etc.), one's self is split and has fallen down in two pieces. Hence

Yājñavalkya's simile for a husband: he is only a half-fragment. But the principle of male-female fulfilment is also a more universal principle that is instantiated in the animal orders. Every act of uniting is His (Ātman's) act of uniting. Every state of yearning for delight and of male-female happiness is His (Ātman's) state of yearning for delight and of male-female happiness. Every act or state of fear is His act or state of fear. So all these states, says the text, are not really facts or realities at the level of the individual, we are not dealing with a multiplicity of acts and situations. Rather we are dealing with a single phenomenon, a single Reality, viz. "Self-in-everything." This Aspect of "Self-in-everything" is Divine, is bliss and non-structure (structure is an empirical word), and is endless. The falling apart of the One into two pieces, husband and wife, and the reappearing of the same pair in different species show the non-multiplicity of the One in the different phenomena in an exemplary and graphical or analogue form. "Thus indeed He (actually It, viz. the Self) created all, whatever pairs there are, even down to the ants". He created all, in respect to whatever principles they exemplify, down to the most insignificant looking details. Finally v. 5 summarizes the Divine State: "He *knew*: I indeed am this creation, for I emitted it all from myself." To have this knowledge clearer than direct perception is a Divine state and is the goal.

Verses 7-8. V. 7 brings a new image. He—Brahman, the One Self—"entered in here, even up to the fingernail tips, as a razor would be hidden in a razor-case". In Upaniṣadic creation accounts, the Ātman typically first creates the world and then enters it as its Self (as the self of everything).[33] This is often taken as merely a metaphor, or as required by the logic of the exposition. But it may also reflect an "experiential" feature of the state of realization that stands behind the text; for example, one thinks of Sri Ramakrishna:

> Do you know how I see? Trees, plants, men, animals, grass—these and all other things I see as different coverings like pillow cases, some made of fine cotton and others of coarser stuff, some round in shape and others square. But within all these pillow cases there is one and the same substance, cotton. In the same way all the objects of the world are stuffed with the unconditioned *Saccidānanda* [=Brahman].[34]

Next, one's powers of Breath, Speech, Sight, etc., as well as these Powers as universal entities, "are merely His action-names". They have no independent status. If one takes them as independent realities in one's daily life, in one's philosophy and worship, one does not see Him, and one is not a Knower. Rather, the way to meditate on Him (worship Him, regard Him, *upās-*) is as one's self. For "there (in oneself) all these [Powers, things experienced, etc.] become one". The unity of one's self and one's experience across all realms of experience has been a focus in Western philosopohy and psychology since Descartes.[35] The Upaniṣad gives it as a chief clue to the Fact of the One Self. Again, one's self "is the *padanīyam* of this All", it is that which deals with (*-anīya*) tracking everything in the Universe step by step (*pad*). "For by it [i.e., by one's self] one knows this All." This is another fundamental point, related to the preceding one. Instead of asking "Why is it that one's experience is *unified* across all experience," the question becomes "how is it that one can think of and know *everything* in the Universe?"—an epistemic or epistemological angle, rather than a phenomenological one. In Western philosophy this issue has played a role in certain forms of metaphysical and epistemological idealism.[36] Here it serves as another hint that one's finite self is not disjoint from the One Self. For one has no doubt that in principle one can understand everything, anything that there may be. This conviction is a clue to the fact that one somehow knows and is everything to begin with.

V. 8 is a complement to, or a further stage of, v. 7. In v. 7 the focus was on the cognitive element. But now the subject is *priya*, being "dear", in other words love, or bliss, *ānanda*, manifesting as love felt for something, or the dearness of something. The movement from the cognitive aspect that is dominent in vs. 1-5 and 7 to bliss in v. 8 is paralleled in the *Five Seaths Vidyā* (chr. 5) and has deep significance. Both the cognitive element and bliss are major modes of manifestation of Brahman, but bliss, which is close to "being Self only", is the more fundamental (cf. chr. 5). V. 7 says that the All, this Universe and existence which we are experiencing, may seem important, but it is really the Self that is all this. But from a still higher point of view, the whole cognitive aspect as it appears in science, philosophy, and ordinary knowledge is transitory whereas the aspect of *priya*, "dear", is more fundamental. V. 8 then says that this aspect of *priya* points to the Self also. One's (true) self is "nearer" to one than every other thing, and hence is "dearest". One's self is the only thing that cannot be lost. "He who worships the self alone as dear, what he holds dear, verily, is not perishable".

Verses 9-10. V. 10 is parallel and complementary to v. 7. "[The Infinite, Brahman] knew itself indeed [only] [as] "I am Brahman," *aham Brahmāsmi.* Therefore (or "from that", *tasmāt*) it became all that [that is], *tat sarvam*". Knowing "I am Brahman" leads to becoming All; indeed, that is part of its nature. This point is emphasized by the immediately following examples of the gods and men and the summary: "This [following statement here is] also [true] today: Who knows thus, [in the manner of] 'I am Brahman,' he becomes all this [world here]." And then come some extraordinary hints why this is so. If a person knows "I am Brahman", "even the gods do not have the power (or the command, root *īś*) to prevent his becoming All, "*for he becomes* (or *is*) *their self*". When there is only the thought and knowledge "I am Brahman" and no other, then there are no boundaries or limits. Then one isn't really facing physical or mental powers and forces, then the self is so "subtle" that one is their self, their soul. So in general, by sublimating by means of the thought "I am Brahman," and by transcending by means of the gradually developing knowledge "I am Brahman," all other thought and knowledge, one ultimately becomes the Soul of the total world process, the Self of the total world entity, which produced/is that world entity anyway. "Whoever worships (*upās-*) another Divinity—*devatā*, i.e., another Deity, or another Divine Aspect—[in the manner] 'that [Divinity] is one thing, I am another', he does not [really] know." For when one takes for granted that the Divine aspect in question is not one's self—it is out there somewhere to be adored or the like—then one remains bound, a bundle of reactions to one's impulses and to forces that one imagines impinge on one from the outside. "One remains a service-animal to the gods."

Overall, then, v. 10 is devoted to the Knowledge "I am Brahman." "I am Brahman" is the Truth of the individual, and as such is the attitude he or she should take in worship and meditation (*upāsanā*). It might be noted that in later Vedānta, *aham Brahmāsmi* becomes one of the four "Great Sayings," or *mahā-vākyas*, which are considered to express the quintessence of Upaniṣadic teaching.[37] And in medieval esoteric tradition it appears as a powerful mantra, mental repetition of which (with meaning) is a mighty stimulus to liberation. Here, this formula is not so much enjoined as spiritual practice as it is simply a powerful expression of a state of Higher or Highest Knowledge, *jñāna*. Anyone—human beings, *Ṛṣis* (seers), and gods—can be "awakened to" the knowledge or state of "I am Brahman", and the text gives the example of Vāmadeva, a famous Vedic *Ṛṣi*.[38] Finally v. 10 operates also at another level and has a message there. It begins as a creation account ("In the beginning this [world] was Brahman . . . therfore it became all that," similar to v. 7), but then assimilates the "becoming all" of Brahman to the "becoming all" of any one who knows "I am Brahman." The usual idea of Creation is thus superseded by a higher, spiritual category, viz. the "becoming All", which accompanies the knowledge "I am Brahman." So v. 10 as a whole is an incredible statement about the One. "In the beginning all this [world] was Brahman [only]." But it is so also now: the before-creation is somehow the same as now after-the-creation, for "It *became* the All". There is only a One, the same One before and after; the difference arises only because of our idea of how the world is now.

Verses 11-15a. Just as v. 3 teaches the Divinity of male-female fulfilment (they are both from Self), so vs. 11-15a, which make up the next unit, teach the Divinity of the society, the social organism, up to and including *Dharma*, "righteousness", or "the inner truth awareness of which leads to right conduct". The account—the vision—is more complex, illustrating the extraordinary richness of the Vedic world of thought. As in vs. 2 and 3, the story begins with the One feeling an incompleteness. "That, being One, was not differentiated. It created beyond itself a superior form, *Kṣatra*, "power-of-rulership", namely those who are *kṣatras*, rulers among gods: Indra, etc." Hume glosses *kṣatra* as "power and dominion; temporal power; the military and princely class", in other words the temporal power in a society which is used to maintain its stability and welfare and which was embodied in the king and the nobility. Now this power and its embodiments or carriers are a Divine Principle. Just as the senses and the mind are considered independent elements (Powers) which are really His (Brahman's, the Self's) forms, so also the *Kṣatra* is an independent element which is really His form. But while the senses (and loneliness and male-female) are principles that are instantiated at the level of individuals, *Kṣatra* is instantiated at the level of the collective. Its creation is thus at a correspondingly higher level. Brahman creates (=becomes, cf. v. 15) the great ruler gods, Indra, Varuṇa, etc., which embody the *Kṣatra* at the cosmic level. The human *kṣatriya* class (warriors, kings and noblemen) is then a reflection of the *Kṣatra* principle among the gods. Brahman has become that too (cf. v. 15).

Vs. 12 and 13 summarily indicate the corresponding picture for the two other non-Brahmin castes: *Viś*, "the Commonality", is the

Divine principle represented in the citizens whose daily activities make up the bulk of the activities of the society (the merchants and artisans, *vaiśyas*). Like *Kṣatra*, it is first embodied among the gods, namely in those that come in groups, like the Ādityas, and thereafter finds a reflection among men. The nourishment and support function (*Śūdra*) which characterizes the manual labor class (*śūdra*) appears first in the form of Pūṣan, "nourisher, protector" (root *puṣ*), a Vedic solar deity. The whole picture of the Divine Societal Functions is completed by Brahman, the highest principle, appearing first in the cosmic-divine sphere as Vedic Agni, Fire and Sacrificial Fire, and then as the Brahmin caste (the Brahmins ministrate the Sacrificial Fire). Evidently this whole teaching elaborates the origin of the four castes in Puruṣa Hymn v. 12: The Brahmin caste arose from the Puruṣa's mouth, the warrior caste from His arms, etc.

V. 14 finally expands the teaching on the *Kṣatra, Viś*, and *Puṣ*-principles in vs. 11-13 in a new direction by introducing a principle higher than them, namely *Dharma*. This is the principle of duty and right conduct which applies to everybody in the society, which controls even the king, and of which the Law is an institutionalized, materialized manifestation. *Dharma* is the inner truth that dictates that duty and conduct. As such, it is even superior to the *Kṣatra* or temporal power principle which is the function of the Kṣatriya class. It is the *Kṣatra* of the *Kṣatra*, the inner power of temporal power. The inner soul of *Dharma* is *Satya*, Tṛuth, the Unchanging.

Evidently, what is taught in vs. 11-15a is an awareness and perception that the social organism is Divine. In a harmoniously functioning society in which beauty of character and high moral principles flourish, and in which the citizens are happy and fulfilled, the temporal power (*Kṣatra*) which maintains harmony and order is Divine. Its vast, pervasive sway, the ways in which it is lodged in the mind of the group and is taken for granted by every citizen—all these are such incredible things that the whole phenomenon must be Divine. The *Vidyā* of the Sixteen Parts of Brahman (cf. chr. 4 below) teaches that the Earth, Intermediate Space, Heaven and Ocean-Expanse are one foot of Brahman, called the Endless. This means a Divine Aspect can be seen in them, by meditation, for example. The temporal power which maintains the society, as a total phenomenon lodged in the mind of both ruler and ruled, can similarly be seen to be a Divine Aspect. The powers of labor, production, service and the large scale coordination found in the society—all these are likewise awesome, incredible things, and are likewise Divinity. In the West, one sometimes feels that such processes can be explained by suitable models and simulations, and that they are therefore not divine. But such an attitude is grievously deluded. If the model or simulation reduces the phenomenon in one's eyes to an arbitrarily controllable thing, and if as a result one respects it less and feels one has it mastered, etc., then this is due to the qualities of one's mind, and one should investigate these qualities and correct oneself appropriately. In addition, one must be aware of what one is doing when one is creating such a model or theory or simulation. For then one will know *exactly* how much the model does for one. Then the model will be like a chair: something that has been created (i.e. put together with available materials) for very specific uses. To identify the model with the thing modelled and relate to it personally on that basis is perilous and is on the road to delusion.[39]

Verses 15b-16. All the teachings which we have been discussing so far may be said to be of the form "such and such is one of His action-names." Brahman created all these principles by appearing as the corresponding phenomenon; thus they are all "His actions (or action-names)." By being (or appearing) happy as husband-and-wife, He creates and is husband-and-wife. By being (or appearing as) the *Kṣatra* gods and the *kṣatriyas* (noble warriors) on earth, He becomes, He is *Kṣatra*. "Creation in time" is assimilated to the present, to "being now". Time, past and future as well as change all become "(names of) His modes of manifestation". Beginning with the husband-and-wife principle, they are all "His forms". Ātman became all this—all this is my Self. This is precisely the thrust of the great summation in v. 15b. "The world must be as one's own"—all is my Self. When the world is seen and known like this, then one's action will be holy, it will correspond to the One True Will. It will live, it will fulfil its meaning and existence, it will be part of a fullness of perfection. Otherwise, even if it is great and holy in the eyes of the world, it will not really be right. It will still be tainted by things like desire or making distinctions. Hence one should "meditate on and worship (*upās*) the world as one's Self". Then there will be no self-interest; instead there will be oneness, perfection.

So "this self" —one's own self—"is [really] the world of all beings". The Skt. *loka*, "world", can also mean "object of enjoyment", and for this reason the passage is sometimes taken to describe how the ordinary self, the ego, becomes the object of enjoyment of gods, seers, fathers and the other types of beings enumerated (because of attachment and desire).[40] In this reading, "he becomes the world of the gods" means that by his participation in the sacrifices to the gods, he comes to constitute this world and be part of it. And similarly for the other worlds. So "this self (one's limited self, ego) is the world of all beings" in the sense that it is the world which one lets (by one's attachments with respect to beings and one's interactions with them) claim him. But the passage can also be read as expressing the all-comprehensive universality of the Self. "This self is the world of all beings" means that all spheres of experience are in oneself, are in the Self. By being devoted to Vedic ritual, one becomes the world of the gods—one brings out the experience in that world. By learning the Vedas from memory, one becomes the world of the Ṛṣis, the Vedic Seers, one becomes part of the experience and enjoyment in that world. And so on, for every world. This is because one's self is actually the One Self. The One Self plays all these roles, it is all this.

5. The New Focus on Ātman

The Shift from Puruṣa to Ātman. The Puruṣa unfolds Itself as the Universe, as both the manifest (what has been and will be) and the higher, the immortal and Divine, and from His parts and powers (and from the sacrificial events at his sacrifice) arise the major aspects of Nature and the principles of Society. At the same time the Puruṣa is the Unfathomable Infinite Ground of all this. This is the Great Thought of the Puruṣa Hymn. *BṛhUp* I.4 takes this Thought and infuses it with a new element: an emphasis on self and Self, Ātman. "In the beginning this [world] was indeed only the Self, in the form of a person" (v. 1); "He knew 'I, indeed, am this creation, for I emitted it all from myself'" (v. 5); one should worship [Him] [in the manner of] "[He is my] self (*ātman*)" (v. 7); "'I was Manu and the Sun'" (v. 10). And this is then further recast in the language of Ātman/Brahman [cf. "Verily, in the beginning this world was Brahman . . ." (v. 10); "In the beginning this world was Brahman, one only . . ." (v. 11)] So in passing from the Puruṣa Hymn to *BṛhUp* I.4, there is an enormous shift in focus and inner approach. The *Ṛg Vedic* hymn describes the Puruṣa from an external point of view as the Unfathomable, Incalculable, Infinite Entity. It describes it as the Sole Existent, the One Infinite Glory. It works at least partly in the manner of myth by engaging the reciter fully with his whole mental and emotional powers in the Super

Archetype, the Great Thought which it presents. The Upaniṣad reshapes this fundamentally by focussing entirely on a universal "ground-of-self", the Ātman. The Puruṣa of the Puruṣa Hymn, it says, is really this ground-of-self.

***BṛhUp* I.4 as Instruction for the Inner Attitude One should have when Living One's Life.** But equally important, the Upaniṣad doesn't stop here. By its partly mythical, partly explaining, partly instructing tone it also articulates a new vision and attitude which a person should take in his daily life. All things are His action-names, His actions; the world should be seen as one's very own; one should meditate on (worship, regard) the world as Self. For the most striking thing about the text is its whole tenor and form. It is a series of loosely arrayed images of creation which are hard to place in a definite, concrete context. They are not really "creation accounts", nor are they myths like the tribal and creation myths of primitive peoples. The narrative moves peculiarly without any reference points, as if in some kind of space or limbo. It is true that all the different units deal basically with the same thing—how to understand one's experience of life and the Universe, how to relate to the total of one's consciousness and existence. For that reason, the text has a profound thrust, with definite effects in terms of world-view. But this is not achieved by any kind of structure and content such as we find typically in myth (like in the *Vṛtra* myth of the *Ṛg Veda*). From the loose way in which the different units are strung together, one gets the impression that they are not really that seriously intended as creation accounts or foundational myths to begin with. Something quite different is going on. The text is expressing a consciousness that has in stillness become aware of its own basis—its timeless being, existence, its basis apart from, and thus "before," any form or creation. More than that: the author must have a distinct awareness of the arising of the world from this basic state in himself. For several units try to communicate such an arising in different ways, taking different topics as examples. It is this that gives the impression of several floating vignettes all trying to express the same thing. So the text fulfils a double function. On the one hand, in its cumulative impact it demonstrates a world-view for living, adapting the Vedic and Brāhmaṇa world-view to a new focus, Ātman. But at the same time, by so doing, the text gives the student who is committed to actually go to Ātman/Brahman some deeper directions and tools.

Cosmic-Cosmological Stance. First, the student is shown to have the attitude, from the very beginning and throughout his *sādhanā* (inner effort toward merger into Brahman), that the Self which is at the basis of his individual self is at the same time the whole cosmos, is all beings as well as the immortal in heaven in short, is ultimately the source of All and is All. In other words, the text shows an approach to spiritual life where one takes a mental and existential "self-stance" that is cosmic-cosmological: "I indeed am this creation, for I emitted it all from myself" (*BṛhUp* I.4.5 above). Note that such a stance favors meditation which is *aham-graha*, i.e., of the form "I am such and such" (where "such and such" names the all-immanent and all-transcendent Divine). This is illustrated by the present text: "One should worship (or regard, *upās-*) [Him in the manner of] '[He is my-] self, *ātman*,'" (I.4.7); "This (*sa*, He) I am, *so 'ham*,'" (I.4.1); "[Brahman] knew only Itself: '*I am* Brahman'" (I.4.10) (italics added). These are all standard forms of *aham-graha* meditation that are widely used today. In fact most of the meditative paths (*vidyās*) in the Upaniṣads are *aham-graha*, and several of them involve a cosmic-cosmolgical stance of the self.

Being Self Only and Rising above Creation. But while there is a cosmic-cosmological stance, the text at the same time evokes in the student a mighty current to drop all the detailed perception of and involvement with the aspects of the world (cosmos, society, his bodily self) and become that Ātman which was/is "before creation"—which is not subject to form but which has become/is all that is formed. This Self is to be approached by "being Self only". "In the beginning, this [world] was just the Self, One only" (I.4.17 above). I, the Self, am now as well as before creation (and also after creation dissolves again). "I" (pointing to the One Self that I am) "am" as much now as before creation (and as much as when creation is no more). And "I" "before creation" is (or am) "Self only," indeed "Self, one only" (I.4.17 above). Overall we can say that the Upaniṣad is teaching an attitude of at the same time *accepting all things as being Self,* i.e. as not being separate from oneself, *and* of one's true Self being the Self before Creation, utterly independent of Creation, and to be realized by *rising above Creation*. It is this combined attitude that is pointed out as a right path.

We note that rising above Creation also implies rising above any *concept* of Creation and any "creation account". Although the text is "a series of loosely arrayed images of creation" (Deussen, above), in the awareness to which it leads, the concept of creation and the necessity of "giving an account" of creation—the very thing the images are doing—are transcended. Usually "creation" means "creation at, or before, the beginning of time". But generally speaking, by giving one's mind to such a temporal aspect, the soul is kept locked in at a level of mind and matter. In both *BṛhUp* I.4 and the Puruṣa Hymn, however, the element of going back in time to an origin and original state is merged or resolved into inner states that lead to rising above all the temporal phenomena of the created world. In the Puruṣa Hymn, this is accomplished by becoming the ever praising, mantra-making servant of the Ineffably Great Entity. By this the level of form is distanced and higher, more formless levels emerge and become the center of life, existence. In *BṛhUp* I.4, the path is one of both accepting the world totally as part of self (Self), of dropping one's focus on the things of the world by realizing That Formless of which Creation is only an emanation or reflection or whatever. This process leads to factual transcendence in the form of dispassion, tranquillity, etc.

If the Puruṣa Hymn represents a direct cosmic-cosmological approach, *BṛhUp* I.4 represents a peculiarly modified one. But in this it is not an isolated case. In general, in the Upaniṣads, reflection and meditation on the origin on the world—why is there anything all? What was there before the world arose? Why is there I?—form a major avenue to Ātman/Brahman. In fact, the Upaniṣadic *sādhanā* (inner effort toward realization of Ātman/Brahman) is often presented as one of retracing the cosmic evolution, the arising of the world manifold, to its source. This general "cosmological" approach[41] is developed in innumerable ways already in the Brāhmaṇas and finds profound expression in several Upaniṣadic *vidyās*. One strand of it is represented by the Puruṣa Idea [*BṛhUp* I.4, *AitUp* I, cf. secs. 6, 7, and 8 (1)-(4) below]. Another strand derives from another *Ṛg Vedic* Super Hymn, the *Nāsadīya Sūkta, Ṛg Veda* X.129. This hymn is associated in the Upaniṣads with teachings on *Sat* ("the Real, the Existent"), *Satyam* (the True), and *Satya* Brahman and with what v. Buitenen has called "the *sat-tya* speculations" (cf. chrs. 5 and 6). But the cosmological approach also takes other forms where it is more difficult to pinpoint.[42]

All Meanings and Values Lodged Directly in Puruṣa = Ātman/ Brahman. Finally the Puruṣa Hymn and its major expositions like *BṛhUp* I.4 also have a philosophical implication which is never specifically elaborated in the Vedic literature, but which should already be mentioned at this stage. This is that all meanings (the meaning evoked by objects and events, and the "semantic" meaning of words and sentences) as well as all values (moral, ethical, and aesthetic values, life-importance etc.) is irreducibly and somehow directly lodged in Ātman/Brahman, in the Puruṣa. Because one and the same Puruṣa thus manifests in and as the variety of beings and objects in the world, this gives all the meanings and values in the human mind and in human experience an epistemologically and ontologically privileged status. In the Puruṣa Hymn, for example, a Puruṣa or Ātmic basis of all things is suggested by the Puruṣa having body parts and faculties (mind), from which arise the major features of the universe and society. The Puruṣa has a thousand heads, a thousand eyes; He is the thinker of all the thoughts in all the heads, the seer (and understander) of all the forms seen by all eyes. He is the one who thinks and feels all the meanings that arise in the human mind. This can only be if all the thoughts, forms, feelings are in some sense directly He, directly (expressions of) the Divine or the Reality. In *BṛhUp* I.4, this point is developed further. To call the One Reality behind everything *puruṣavidha*, to feel that "these [Powers—Prāṇa, Speech, Sight, etc.] are merely names of His acts (or His acts)", and the expositions in vs. 15 and 16 all presuppose in various ways that Ātman is the direct source of all human perceptions, of all names = meanings (which ultimately = objects and actions), and of all values. The stories of the arising of the male-female principle and of the societal classes and powers express this also. The principle of husband-wife and male-female springs directly from Ātman, the powers and functions in society spring directly from Ātman, *Dharma* springs directly from Ātman, and so on.

In general, an Ātmic basis for all the meanings and values that ever moved and will move the heart of man no doubt implies that these meanings and values occupy an epistemologically and ontologically privileged position. Such a view is found in Plato, for example.[43] But today, when meanings of words or visual scenes or ideas (if not the consciousness that accompanies them) are routinely given explicit representations in artificial intelligence, and when neural modelling is one of the most active areas of research, reductionism, which denies any Divine basis to the details of human thought and understanding, is the rule.[44] The assumption is that meaning and values (with or without the consciousness that goes with them) may be explained by suitable models, and that the very existence of a good model precludes any such privileged status. Similarly, there are many efforts to explain moral-ethical, aesthetic, and other types of values in terms of survival value or maximization of some observable quantity, in other words in terms of principles completely within the ambit of scientific concepts operating on a physical-observational base.[45] This is not the place to consider these issues. Suffice it to say that in the Vedic literature, the view that human meanings, perceptions, feelings and ideals occupy a "privileged position" is supported by deep and awesome *vidyās* (higher teachings), involving direct knowledge and often forms of omniscience (e.g. the *Dahara Vidyā*), and by the doctrine of *Vāc*, Speech (similar to "the Word" or Logos in Christian tradition).[46] More generally we are dealing here with a "traditional" position in the sense of Coomaraswamy and Nasr.[47] There is agreement across many higher spiritual traditions and philosophies that the entire human experience and the world as we know it are a unitary and a Divine or otherwise Higher Entity, and that prototypical divine meanings, feelings, forms etc. may be known by direct apperception at the level of this entity.[48] This will become clearer in the following chapters.

But ultimately, *BṛhUp* I.4 does not intend to provide an account of the world in terms of a Logos, and its aim is not to teach apperception at the level of such a Logos. It is true that "I am Brahman, for I created all this" implies to some extent an epistemologically priviledged origin of all meanings (and thus of the structure world) in the self. But this great saying is not so much a philosophical account of "all this" as an instruction to drop all presuppositions and hold the mind and one's striving—without depending on any meaning—in the self so that a true understanding of the Self may arise. Depending on the aspirant, this may or may not include intuition in the direction of *Vāc*.

6. *AitUp* I.1-3

If *BṛhUp* I.4 is a profound recasting of the Great Thought of the Puruṣa Hymn, moving it from a form of "praise of the Supreme Entity" to one of "self-awareness and Self-awareness", the text to be considered next, *AitUp* I.1-3, looks at first only like a systematization of it. *Aitareya Upaniṣad* (= *AitUp*)[49] is a small work of a few pages. It is the culmination of the sacred literature of the Aitareyins, a *śākhā* or school of the *Ṛg Veda,* and was therefore cultivated by Ṛg Vedins, viz. the hotṛ priests, who recite the *Ṛg Vedic* mantras, and their associates. The work is part of the *Aitareya Āraṇyaka*[50] and consists of six sections (*adhyāyas*) grouped into three chapters, I.1-3, II.1.2 and III. I is a creation account; II teaches that a man has three births, one in his mother's womb, one in his son, and one in his next life; and III is a high level text culminating in the "great saying" *Prajñānam Brahma* or "Brahman is Prajñāna". *AitUp* I[51] may be regarded as a more specialized example of the path of (*Ādi-*) Puruṣa = "the Self before any Creation."

AitUp I.1-3. Text

I.1.1. The Self (Ātman), verily, was all this [Universe], [a single] One indeed in the beginning. Nothing else whatsoever blinked. He thought: "Let me now ceate (*sṛj*) the worlds (*lokas*)."

2. He created these worlds: the Water (*ambha*), the Lights (*marīci*, plural), the Mortal (*mara*), [and] the Waters (*ap*). This Water (*ambha*) is above the heaven (*dyauḥ*), and heaven supports it. The Lights are the intermediate space (*antarikṣa*). The Mortal is the Earth (*pṛthivī*). What is underneath, that is the Waters (*āpaḥ*).

3. He thought: These here are now the worlds. Let me now create the world-protectors (*loka-pālas*). He, having pulled up the Puruṣa from the very waters (*āpaḥ*), shaped [the Puruṣa].

4. He (Ātman) willed over Him (the Puruṣa) (*abhi+tap-*)[a]. Of Him (i.e., the Puruṣa) [who was thus] willed over, the mouth burst open as [when] an egg [opens]. From the mouth [arose] Speech (Vāc), from Speech, Agni. The nostrils burst open. Fom the nostrils [arose] Breath (Prāṇa), from Breath, Wind (Vāyu). . .[52]

Other Powers and Deities are similarly generated as shown in the first two columns of Table 3.1:

TABLE 3.1
Scheme of *AitUp* I.1.4

1. Mouth, *Mukha*	*Vāc*, Speech,	Agni (Fire)
2. Nostrils, *Nāsikā*	*Prāṇa*, Breath	Vāyu (Wind, Air)
3. Eyes, *Akṣiṇī*	*Cakṣus*, Sight	Āditya (Sun)
4. Ears, *Karṇau*	*Śrotra*, Hearing	Diś (Direction)
5. Skin, *Tvak*	Hair	Plants
6. Heart, *Hṛdaya*	*Manas*, Mind	Candramas (Moon)
7. Navel, *Nābhi*	*Apāna*, Vital Air	Mṛtyu, Death
8. Generative Organ	*Retas*, Semen	Ap, Waters

I.2.1-4 continues the creation account by detailing how the universal cosmic powers or deities (Agni, Vāyu, Āditya . . .) become the individual's power of speech, breath, sight. . . . The deities (*devatā*) fall into the ocean of the world (*mahārṇava*) and the Self subjects the latter to hunger and thirst. Thereupon the deities ask Him "find us an abode, *āyatana*, established in which we may eat food". The Self brings them a cow and a horse, both of which they reject, and then a man, *puruṣa,* whom they accept with "well-done (*sukṛta*), truly". (I.2.3). Then

> I.2.4. Agni, having become Speech, entered (*pra+viś-*) the mouth.
> Vāyu, having become *prāṇa*, entered the nostrils. . .

and so on, as in the right-hand side of Table 3.1.

So far the account provides a conceptual analysis and systematization of what in the Puruṣa Hymn is virtually a single Idea. It separates as distinct elements and systematizes several of the aspects of the Puruṣa Idea, and presents them in graphic form. To begin with, the creation "of the worlds" the universal or Divine world-Frame or prototype (*ambha*, etc., v. 2), is simply conceptually separated from the creation of the detailed objects, deities, and powers that populate it and that constitute its detailed contents (i.e., the creation of the Puruṣa, v. 3 ff.). What is called Puruṣa in I.1.3 is really an undifferentiated complex out of which arise the major universal aspects of the world, viz. the universal powers (Speech, Smell, Sight) and deities (Agni, Vāyu, Āditya etc.). In this, too, the creative Impulse and Intelligence behind Creation are in effect separated from the process and final product of Creation, which are visualized on and as this Puruṣa.[53] Ātman shaped the Puruṣa, its limbs and organs, and then willed the powers and deities to develop from It and associated with It. The process is strictly systematized into the pattern: body parts (organ-forms, i.e. mouth, nostrils, eyes etc.), universal powers (Speech, Breath through the nose, Sight, . . .) and deities (Agni, Vāyu, Āditya, . . .). For comparison, the schema in the Puruṣa Hymn (vs. 13-14) is shown in Table 3.2. Here the eight aspects of Puruṣa on the left give rise to ("give birth to", "become", etc.) the corresponding deities on the right. The latter are all cosmic or universal. It is not clear to me whether some of the aspects on the left are functional powers or body parts. In any case Table 3.1 represents a systematization of Table 3.2.

TABLE 3.2
Scheme in Puruṣa Hymn (vs. 13-14)

1.	Mind, *Manas*	Moon, Candramas
2.	Sight, *Cakṣus*	Sun, Sūrya
3.	Mouth, *Mukha*	Indra (or Agni)
4.	Breath, *Prāṇa*	Wind, Vāyu
5.	Navel, *Nābhi*	Midregion, Antarikṣa
6.	Head, *Śirṣa*	Sky, Dyauḥ
7.	Feet, *Pādau*	Earth, Bhūmi
8.	Hearing, *Śrotra*	Quarters, Diśaḥ

Finally in I.2.1-4, an individual man, *puruṣa*, a new principle which is *su-kṛta,* well-made, is motivated and introduced. In I.2.4 the universal deities enter into this man, thus demonstrating graphically their concrete participation in the individual and their own individualization.

The next two units, I.2.5 and I.3.1-10, introduce Hunger, Thirst and Food as universal principles operative in Creation:

I.2.5. To Him (=Ātman), Hunger and Thirst said: Find [an abode] for us (too). He said to them: I assign to you [a place] in (locative) these deities (*devatā*). I make you (both) sharers in (locative) them. Therefore, to whatever deity an offering is made, in that [deity], indeed, Hunger and Thirst become (two) sharers.

I.3.1. He (Ātman) thought "These here then are the worlds and the world protectors. Let me create (*sṛj-*) food (*anna*) for them."

2. He willed over the waters (*ap*). From them, [so] willed over, form (*mūrti*) was born. Verily, what is produced as that form, that verily is food.

3. That created [entity, viz. food], being pressed[a], wanted to run away. That (food) he (the person) sought to seize with Speech. That (food) he was unable to seize with Speech. If he had seized it with Speech, [then] having [merely] uttered [something], he would have had the satisfaction of food.

The episode in v. 3 is repeated verbatim (apart from the first sentence) with Speech replaced by Prāṇa (Breath), Sight, Hearing, Skin, Mind, the Generative Organ, and the *Apāna* vital air (vs. 4-10). Only with the latter did the person (Puruṣa and the individual) succeed:

10. That (food) he sought to seize with the *Apāna* vital air[b]. He obtained (*āvayat*) it. He is that grasper of food what is Vāyu (a wordplay). This one, living on food (*annāyu*), verily, [is] what Vāyu is (another wordplay).[54]

The fact that Hunger and thirst afflicted the Puruṣa and the gods that arose from it shows that a basic fact of life—desire wanting fulfilment—affects the whole of Creation from the gods on down. This is first of all given its proper place in the world order, the sacrificial scheme of things (I.2.5). By satisfying the gods with the sacrificial offering, Hunger and Thirst are also satisfied. Thus man by sacrificial offerings keeps up the world order (Hunger and Thirst will not afflict the gods) as well as promotes his own welfare (Hunger and Thirst will not afflict him). Then I.3.1-10 gives a deeper analysis of the principle of food.[55] I.3.11-14 finally describes how the Ātman enters the man (*puruṣa*).

11. He thought: "Well, how can this[a] be without me?" He thought: "Through what [way] shall I enter (*pra+pad-*)[b]?" He thought: "If through Speech there is [what is] uttered, if through Prāṇa there is [what is] breathed, if through Sight there is the seen, if through Hearing there is the heard, if through Skin there is the touched, if through mind there is [what is] thought over, if through breathing out there is [what is] breathed out, if through the generative organ there is [what is] emitted, then who am I? (i.e., what is my role in all this?)."
12. He, having opened the top-edge (*sīman*) [of the skull], entered (*pra+pad-*) by that door. This is the door called *vidṛti* ("the tearing asunder"). This is that blissful [aspect] (*nāndana*). Of that there are three dwelling places [*āvasatha*], three (kinds of) dreams (*svapna*, "dream-like states", see chr. 5): this dwelling place; this dwelling place; this dwelling place.
13. He, being born, looked at (or perceived) all beings. "What else here would one desire to speak?" (or: "What other [Self, principle] would one wish to proclaim?") He saw indeed this Puruṣa, the most widely extended Brahman (or: completely pervaded by Brahman). "I have seen this (*idam adarśam*)" [he said].

14. Therefore his name is *Idam-dra* ("seeing this"). Yes, *Idandra* is the name. Him who is *Idandra* they speak of as "Indra" indirectly. For the gods seem to like the indirect.[56]

High-level Realization Underlying the Text: Verse I.3.13. For a deeper understanding of the whole text, Śaṁkara's overall estimate gives a clue. At the beginning of his commentary on *AitĀr* III, Śaṁkara writes that "there are three classes of men who want to acquire knowledge. The highest consists of those who have turned away from the world, whose minds are fixed on one subject, and who yearn to be free at once. For these a knowledge of Brahman is intended, as taught in *AitĀr* II.4-6 (which = *AitUp* I-III). The middle class consists of these who wish to become free gradually by attaining to the world of Hiraṇyagarbha [=cosmic God]. . . . The lowest class consists of those . . . who desire nothing but offspring, cattle, etc."[57] If *AitUp* I.1-3 is really only a myth or elaboration of the creation account of the Puruṣa Hymn, why should it be intended only for aspirants of the highest caliber, who are already turned away from the world, and who therefore might be expected to have the least use for creation accounts? Sathya Sai Baba's comments are similar. The Upaniṣad, he says, "shines bejewelled by six chapters (*adhyāyas*) which describe the Absolute Ātmic Principle,"[58] and he recalls its traditional designation *ātma-ṣaṭka*, "the Ātmic Six". "The Vision of the Ātmā which results from the destruction of Illusion and Ignorance is made possible for the aspirant by this Upaniṣad."[59] How is it possible that this "creation myth" describes the "absolute Ātmic principle" and can result in "the destruction of Illusion and Ignorance (*māyā* and *avidyā*)", as Sai Baba implies?

The answer is that the text shows a high level of realization, and is actually an expression of enlightened vision. This is most obvious in *AitUp* I.3.13. Ātman, being born in the individual human being (the *puruṣa* or person which He introduces in v. I.2.3 and enters into in v. I.3.12), looks at or views all beings and sees all as (Him-) Self. "What else here would one desire to speak,"[60] He says, in view of the fact that He, Ātman, is all beings. Alternatively the exclamation may be translated "What other [Self] would one desire to proclaim?" (since He has entered all beings).[61] "I have seen this," He goes on, *adarśam idam*, and this makes Him *Idandra*, or Indra, the Vedic Divinity that often represents the individual self. (*Idam*, "this", also carries connotations of "this world here", and so *adarśam idam* may be interpreted

"I have seen this [world as it really is])." In any case, v. 13 unmistakably expresses a state of knowledge or realization. Thus it plays a double role: It is the climax of the account I.1-3, and it expresses a particular state of realization. As climax of the creation account, it summarizes the whole point, it freezes the logic of the whole account into a single graphic image. Having entered all beings in v. 12, all that Ātman sees is Himself, the One Self, there is nothing else to say or no other entity to proclaim, because He created/animates All. (He also sees "the most widely extended Brahman.") But at the same time, seeing only oneself in all beings, and seeing all as Brahman, is high-level Realization. The text seems to be saying: If one assimilates this narrative to the depth of one's being, in the right way, then one will arrive at this realization.

Verse I.3.12. The same two levels of meaning may also be distinguished in v. 12. On the hand v. 12 is just a description of how the Ātman, having finished the work of Creation (Universe plus the human condition—individual vs. universal, and Hunger, Thirst and Food), enters into the individual. On the other hand it makes various possibly yogic, but at any rate experiential allusions. Ātman enters by cleaving, *vi-dṛ*, the top edge, *sīman*, of the skull. This is the gate, *dvāra*, and this is the bliss-bringing one, *nāndana*. *Sīman*, "a separation or parting of the hair like a furrow",[63] is used in a famous mystical stanza in the *Atharva Veda* (IV.1.1) where it is associated with direct vision of Brahman:[64]

> The *brahman* that was first born of old [lit. "afore"]
> Vena has unclosed from the well-shining (*su-rucas*) edge (*sīman*)[a].
> He unclosed the fundamental nearest shapes (*viṣṭha*) of it,
> the womb of the existent and the nonexistent.[65]

The earliest commentary on the verse, *ŚatBr* VII.4.1.14, takes both *brahman* and Vena to be the Sun, and interprets the first two lines as saying "Brahman (the Sun), first born afore (i.e. in the East), [the same as] Vena, [rises and] uncloses from the summit (i.e. the noon position) the shining [worlds]."[66] This is grammatically possible, and rather different from the translation given above. As an interpretation however, it seems to be somewhat forced, in part perhaps to fit the use of the mantra at *VājSaṁh* IXXX.3 in the ritual which the Brāhmaṇa is explaining.[67] Now the first two lines say that Vena, a gandharva or semi-divine being, has unclosed, or opened up for mankind, "the Brahman which was first born of old", in other words has unclosed the (second) Puruṣa which was the first aspect (the Consciousness, Being, whatever) to appear at the beginning of Creation.[68] On this second reading, therefore, the verse must be referring to a Realization or Vision of the Puruṣa. The latter would thus involve experience of light (*surucas*, "highly shining") at the top of the head (at the *Scheitel* or parting of the hair, *sīman*).[69] Ātman's entry into the person which he had formed by the top edge (*sīman*) of the skull in *AitUp* I.3.12 might therefore allude to similar experience. Following this line of interpretation, the remainder of *Atharva Veda* IV.1.1 would then simply continue to describe what Vena "unclosed". This would be a vision of Brahman just as in *AitUp* I.3.13. In this case the "deepest-level shapes fashioned close to Brahman"[70] would refer to "primal shapes" of "Will", "Form", whatever, that are "at the beginning of Creation"; "perception" of these "primal shapes" would exemplify some "form of limited omniscience" as discussed in chr. 6.14.[71]

Another text which suggests that the Ātman's entry into man in *AitUp* I.3.12 has overtones of high level spiritual experience is *TaittUp* I.6, undoubtedly a yogic text.[72] "That which hangs down at the palate like a nipple (the uvula), that is the womb of Indra. Where the hair goes into different directions (*vivartate*), splitting (*vyapohya*) the skull bone, [and thinking:] "*bhūr*", he (the sage) rests in Agni; [thinking:] "*bhuvaḥ*", [he rests] in Vāyu (the Wind-Divine); [thinking] "*suvaḥ*", [he rests] in Āditya (the Sun-Divine); [thinking] "*Mahaḥ*" ("the Great"), he rests in Brahman. He obtains self-rule. He attains to the Lord of Mind. . ." (*Bhūr, bhuvaḥ, suvaḥ* is a mystical formula, part of the Gāyatrī mantra of the *Ṛg Veda*). This text does not use the word *sīman*, but it refers to the place on the head where the hair forms a whorl. Note also the similar connotations of "splitting", *vyapohya*, the skull bone in *Taittirīya Upaniṣad*, and "tearing asunder", *vidṛ-*, in *Aitareya Upaniṣad,* and the fact that while in *Taittirīya Upaniṣad* the splitting through the skull is the beginning of different higher planes (*bhūr*-Agni, etc.), *Aitareya Upaniṣad* speaks of the *sīman* as a "door" or "gate".[73] Of course *Atharva Veda* IV.1.1 and *TaittUp* I.6 may refer to different kinds of yoga, and only one of them might be alluded to in *AitUp* I.3.12. But together they make it probable that *sīman, vidṛ*, and the door in the *Aitareya* text make a reference to higher spiritual (perhaps yogic) experience.

Nāndana, the last term in *AitUp* I.3.12 to be considered, has a different circle of connotations. It is derived from *nand*, which is often used in the *Ṛg Veda* to refer to the joys of heaven.[74] A *Ṛg Vedic khila* (supplementary) stanza (which is also found in the *Sāma Veda*) says: "The purificatory (verses) [in the Soma ritual] are auspicious, with them a man goes to heaven (*nandanam*). . . ."[75] If the Aitareya passage were taken as a creation account, *nāndana* as a designation of the place of entry of the Ātman into the body would be unintelligible. But from a point of view of spiritual experience it is completely natural. Knowledge/realization at the level of *TaittUp* I.6 or *Atharva Veda* IV.1.1 would be accompanied by bliss.

Finally, having entered the individual, the Ātman has (in general, in all individuals) three dwelling places, *āvasathas*, corresponding to three "dreamlike states", *svapnas*. Śaṁkara suggests that these are the right eye (the eyeball), corresponding to the waking state; the "mind inside", corresponding to dream; and the space within the heart, corresponding to deep sleep.[76] This assimilates the text to the later teaching on the three states of consciousness found in *Māṇḍūkya Upaniṣad*. Sai Baba ties the dwelling places to phenomena that arise when one gets close to realization of Brahman.[77] This agrees with our view here, that the Upaniṣad is in this verse alluding to stages of a process of realization.

***AitUp* I as a Whole, and Realization**. Summarizing our discussion, therefore, it apears that both the entering through the top and having three dwelling places in v. 12 can be read not only as an account of the creation of the individual but also as referring to stages or experience on the path to realization. Similarly v. 13 not only concludes the whole creation picture but also portrays a state of realization. Now these facts in turn suggest that more generally the whole of *AitUp* I.1-3 represents and aims to teach direct *Brahma-jñāna*, knowledge of Reality, and that it uses the form of a creation account largely as an outward garb. Indeed, the whole text seems to be mostly a description of how the world into which one finds oneself born appears to a realized being. It enumerates some of its general characteristics as they were thought of in Upaniṣadic times and shows how they should be considered. The state of realization or enlightenment that underlies the text comes through not only in the conceptual schema that is thereby set up, but also in the detached clarity with which the whole is presented. Thus *AitUp* I.1, by describing creation of the Divine Framework or Prototype for the world and of the Universal Powers and Deities, simply acknowledges these entities as fundamental Elements and Universals. I.2.1-4 (the Deities become the individual Powers of Speech, etc., and enter individual man) then says that apart from these Fundamentals, there is also the principle of Individuation, which functions with man as its highest expression.

(The horse and cow are rejected but man has the capacity to realize the Ātman, and is therefore accepted.) Next I.2.5—I.3.10 teaches some "basic facts of life" for walking the spiritual path. I.2.5 says that Hunger and Thirst, representing the principle of Desire, affect all levels of creation from the Universal Deities on down. And I.3.1-10 teaches a metaphysical understanding of Food and of satisfaction of Hunger and Thirst which are helpful in overcoming being subject to them. In vs. I.3.11-13 finally, the Ātman enters the individual and sees from within the individual the nature of everything. In effect, the text is saying: "Look, here is the Divine World Framework, here is the principle of individuation, here are these basic facts of life, and this (vs. 12-13) is the paradigm for becoming seeing and aware of the whole construction. You, having entered in this construction (of yours), see this now as it really is." A similar approach is also found in the *Sad Vidyā, ChāndUp* VI, and in some of Buddha's discourses in the *Majjhima Nikāya*: A released consciousness enumerates the fundamental constituents of the world, and this is all that there is besides Itself. But here there are some additional aspects. The fact that in all four phases (Divine World Framework, Individualization, etc.) Ātman creates and directs everything means that all these creations and processes are of a lower order compared to the Ātman itself. They are mere effects, forms; the basic reality is Ātman. In the dispassionate enumeration of different creatings, and by constantly repeating "Ātman created such and such," "Ātman did, supervised such and such," "Ātman caused such and such to happen," the text conveys a single Transcendental Power. This Power, the Ātman, is the only Reality. It is what one really is; and all the major ingredients of the world are insignificant effects of It.

Here the use of the term Ātman, Self, is crucial. The text clearly teaches that Ātman, the Universal Self, is not different from one's own self. But obviously, realization of this is not attained by an ordinary understanding of the creation account given, or by any by semantic understanding of any semantic content, for that matter. The Ātman is approached when in one's inmost one is turned away from all aspects of the world—Deities, Powers, Perception; as Sai Baba says, "the stages of wakefulness, dream and deep sleep are unrelated to the Ātman",[78] and Divine World Frame, Deities, Powers, desire, all belong to wakefulness and dream. So the text doesn't teach the Ātman by the specific creation account which it gives, or even by being a creation account, period, for that matter. Rather it teaches It by appealing to the living one, the *jīva*, to reflect on creation, and to take to heart how he/she is before or without any creation, or apart from the mere phases wakefulness, dream, and sleep.

7. *Uttara Nārāyaṇa* and *Tad-eva*

BṛhUp I.4 and *AitUp* I represent two rather different developments of the Puruṣa Idea. The first provides a more general reorientation at the level of daily living. The images of the creation of male-female and the social orders and powers, as well as the whole tenor of "He is all this" and "I am all this", offer a person who lives in the world, and to whom family and society are the main arena of life, an inner understanding of the world and his self which can develop in a natural way into a spiritual life toward Ātman/Brahman. The text is "instruction" for developing the foundations of a correct world-view, so that eventually a deep approach to Ātman/Brahman becomes possible. But it also speaks as a consciousness that has in a very fundamental way become aware of Reality. We are not dealing here with philosophical meanderings or contemplative images. On the contrary, statements like "I am Brahman," or "in the beginning this was only the Self, in the form of the Puruṣa" are aids to the inner consciousness that enable it to throw off some of the bonds that have kept it in unspeakable darkness since time immemorial. *Ait Up* I is only one of several elaborations of the Puruṣa Idea in *Aitareya Āraṇyaka*.[79] But it also shows a striking tenor of detachment, and an unusually radical and fundamental distinction between the Created or Seen, and the Ātman from which all Created arises and which is that which Sees. These aspects suggest a similar "consciousness risen above the world and become aware of its basis". This basis is here the Reality that was before Creation and is equally now.

But while *BṛhUp* I.4 and *AitUp* I are both developments of the Puruṣa Idea, our discussions suggest that in view of the literary devices used, they are also rather sophisticated products. This, together with the rather extraordinary new language of Ātman, in turn suggests that it must have taken considerable development to get from the Puruṣa Hymn to these texts. One text which historically seems to stand intermediate between the Puruṣa Hymn and *BṛhUp* I.4 is the *Tad-eva*, a hymn from *Vājasaneyī Saṁhitā* (= *VājSaṁh* XXXII.1-12, with variations = *TaittĀr* X.1.2-4).[80]. The *Tad-eva* calls the Highest "That," and treats It as the one God or Supreme Divine which is all the other major gods. In addition it describes It also as the Puruṣa and identifies It as the Self, Ātman. The *Tad-eva* is usually discussed together with the *Uttara Nārāyaṇa* (*VājSaṁh* XXXI.17-22) which immediately precedes it. The *Uttara Nārāyaṇa* is presented in the *Vājasaneyī Saṁhitā* as a continuation of the Puruṣa Hymn and exalts the Puruṣa as the Universal Divine. Both the *Tad-eva* and *Uttara Nārāyaṇa* are basically testimonies of realization of the Supreme Divine, and in both of them, the Puruṣa of the Puruṣa Hymn is used as a framework to express this realization. In addition, in the *Tad-eva*, the core of the realization is explicitly "becoming" Ātman/Brahman. Both hymns must have been familiar to the author(s) of *BṛhUp* I.4. Note, however, that *BṛhUp* I.4 does not teach a Supreme Divine. Instead, it emphasizes the Aspects of Ātman and of Ātman being Brahman, which represents primarily a *jñāna* orientation.

Vājasaneyī Saṁhitā. As mentioned in chr. 1.3, the *Vājasaneyī Saṁhitā* is the youngest of the *Yajur Vedic Saṁhitās*.[81] It consists of 40 chapters, of which the first 18 probably form an older nucleus. They are explained mantra by mantra in *ŚatBr* I-IX (which is thus probably also the original nucleus of the *Śatapatha Brāhmaṇa*), and also have close parallels in all the Saṁhitās of the *Black Yajur Veda*. Parallels to *VājSaṁh* XIX-XL, on the other hand, are found mostly only in *Taittirīya Brāhmaṇa* and *Taittirīya Āraṇyaka*.[82] The sections of *Vājasaneyī Saṁhitā* and *Śatapatha Brāhmaṇa* which contain the *Uttara Nārāyaṇa* and *Tad-eva* were probably added not long before the earliest Upaniṣads.

***Uttara Nārāyaṇa* (*VājSaṁh* XXXI.17-22)**[83]

17. Created from the [primeval] Waters (*ap*) and the sap of Earth (*pṛthivī*),
He arose in the beginning from Viśvakarman ("All-maker").
Tvaṣṭṛ keeps arranging his form.
Thus the mortal's origin in the beginning [is what is] Divineness (*devatvam*).
18. I know that Puruṣa, the great one,[a]
of the color of the Sun (*Āditya*), beyond darkness (*tamas*).
Him indeed having known, one goes beyond death.
There is no other path found for going [beyond death].
19. Prajāpati goes around within the womb.
Unborn, He births himself[b] diversely in many places.
His origin (*yoni*) see only the sages.

But in Him (*tasmin*) exist all created things.
20. [He] who radiates heat to the gods,
Who is placed ahead of the gods[c],
[Who is] born before the gods,
obeisance to the shining one, the Brahman-like (masc.).[d]
21. The gods, bringing about the Shining Brahman-like One,[e]
said this in the beginning:
That Brahmin who would know you indeed,
the gods will be at his wish.
22. Śrī and Lakṣmī (Beauty and Fortune) are your wives . . .[84]

According to Uvaṭa, the oldest (600 CE) commentator, Tvaṣṭṛ (lit. "fashioner", a Vedic deity) in v. 17 is Prajāpati and Brahman. So perhaps, "Tvaṣṭṛ keeps fashioning His Form" involves the same kind of conceptual separation as that between the Puruṣa and the Ātman which shapes the Puruṣa etc., in *AitUp* I.1. At any rate, v. 17 refers to the second Puruṣa. The Seer knows that very Puruṣa, He (or It) is essentially the One Universal Divine which is felt as Light—"of the color of the Sun-Divine, Āditya". This Knowledge is an Infinite Knowledge: it dispels the darkness in which one has been enveloped as far as one can remember, and one knows oneself as beyond death. The same One Universal Godhead is then further praised and worshipped in the concluding v. 20 (note "obeisance to the shining one", *ruc*-).

This Divine is also worshipped as Prajāpati, the Lord of Creatures (Offspring) or the Divine manifesting Itself in the creatures and the workings of the world (a central conception-experience of Brāhmaṇa theology). Though Unborn, He "births Himself" in all the different creatures, i.e., he becomes manifold, like the *Ṛg Vedic* Puruṣa. Indeed, "*In* Him [Prajāpati-Puruṣa] exist all-created things." The "in" here is rather unexpected. The *Dahara Vidyā* and other texts teach that the Self is in the Heart and contains all things in the Universe (cf. chr. 6). Similarly *Taittirīya Brāhmaṇa* says that all things are contained in Brahman "like in a boat" (cf. chr. 6.3). Since such teachings also have a long tradition in the *Atharva Veda*, we take the line to allude to Ātman/Brahman in one's heart or in one's self. So the Great Divine, "of the color of the Sun" (actually "of the color of the Sun-Divine, Āditya [seen in concentrated devotion and meditation]") and "beyond darkness", which is in the last verse worshipped as "higher than the gods", includes what plainly seems to be an ingredient of one of the basic forms of realization of Ātman/Brahman taught in the old Upaniṣads. (Perhaps for this reason it is in v. 20 called "Brahman-like".) Finally, Prajāpati's origin, i.e. the origin of the workings of the Great Divine in the creatures and the world, or in other words the mystery of creation, is hidden. It is only seen by the sages (*dhīras*, "steady ones"), explained as "the yogis who have put away everything by the abandoning of all [objects of desire and fear]".[85]

***Tad-eva* (*VajSaṁh* XXXII.1-12)**

1. That indeed (*tad-eva*) [is] Agni, that [is] Āditya (Sun),
that [is] Vāyu (Wind) and Candramas (Full Moon).
That indeed is the pure (*śukram*), that [is] Brahman,
the (primeval) Waters, He is Prajāpati.
2. All time-spans came into existence,
all lightnings, from the Puruṣa.
Not in height, not in breadth, not in the middle
would one comprehend[a] that one.
3. There exists no counterpart (*pratimā*) of Him
Whose name is "Great Glory".[b]
(continues by giving references to *Ṛg Veda* X.121.1-4, 9)
4. He is the God in regard to all dominions[c],
Yes, born before, he is within the womb.
He indeed, already born, will be born,
He stands in beings, facing in all directions.
5. Before whom nothing whatsoever was born,
who came about as all beings (or worlds),
Prajāpati, rejoicing on account of his offspring,
maintains the three Lights, He of Sixteen Parts.
6. (*Ṛg Veda* X.121.5.)
7. (References to *Ṛg Veda* X.121.6-8.)
8. Vena is seeing the Highest (lit. "That," *Tat*), [which is] placed in secret,
Where all becomes a single (resting) place[d] (i.e. unified into one).
"In that all this [world] goes together (=unites) and [from it like a source it separates] apart.[e]"
Distributed[f], he is woven one way and another in creatures.
9. Let the knowing Gandharva (Vena) declare the immortal, the [supreme] abode (*dhāman*);
Having become manifold, [it is] placed in secret.

Three quarters of that (supreme abode) are placed in secret.
Who knows them would be the father's father.

10. He, our kin-father, the creator,
he knows the abodes, [he knows] the beings all,
[there] where the gods, obtaining immortality,
have risen,[g] in the third abode (the third heaven).

11. Having gone around[h] the beings, having gone around the worlds,
having gone around all regions and cardinal points,
Having waited on (worshipped) the firstborn (fem.) of Ṛta (the World Order),[i]
he enters with [his] self the Self.[j]

12. Having altogether gone around heaven and earth,
and also the worlds and also the cardinal points and heaven,
having untied the stretched out weft of Ṛta,
he saw That (Absolute), became That, was That.[k][86]

Vs. 1-7 are a great paean to the One Supreme Divine. The tone is that of a Sage extolling what he is aware of or sees in direct vision. The mantras quoted in vs. 3 and 6-7 cover almost the whole of *Ṛg Veda* X.121, which likewise glorifies the One God. (In all these verses this One is never named; only in the last verse of *Ṛg Veda* X.121—v. 10, not quoted here—it is called Prajāpati). Vs. 8-12 then bring certain supreme utterances on Ātman/Brahman mentioned by Deussen. This portion of the hymn is almost an independent composition. Its five verses are formed from the five verses of an *Atharva Vedic* hymn (II.1), using bits and pieces and even whole lines from the latter and keeping a similar overall plan but making some profound new statements.[87] Vena in vs. 8-9 stands for the Sage who has reached the Highest. V. 8 describes him attaining a Highest Oneness out of which all things come and into which all things merge (in both cases the Skt. root is *i*, go). The language is pure direct knowledge, awareness, vision. V. 9 switches to a more traditional format, praising this One in a manner familiar from the *Ṛg Veda* and with numerous allusions to the Puruṣa and other mystical *Ṛg Vedic* passages. Then (v. 10) the tone becomes that of a worshipper, expressing feelings of being taken care of and being in the all-knowing providence of that Divine, of that Creator. And finally vs. 11-12 identify the One or the Oneness of v. 8 as the Ātman and describe the merger of the (finite) self into

Ātman/Brahman. The limited self *enters into* the Ātman (Skt. root *viś*, v. 11) and *becomes* That, *is* That (v. 12). The language is both that of Enlightenment (full-realization and merger into the Self), and of complete God-realization (oneness with the Supreme Divine). As Deussen says, we have here "[the thought] which Antequil Duperron rightly set as motto at the head of his translation of the Upaniṣads: *Quisquis Deum intelligit, Deus fit* ["Whoever sees God, becomes God"]. The Sage, when he sees God, becomes God, because in truth he always was God (*tad apaśyat, tad abhavat, tad āsīt* ["he saw That (=the Highest), he became That, he was That," *Tad-eva* v. 12])."

As noted at the beginning of this section, apart from being extraordinary high-level spiritual documents in their own right, these hymns have enormous implications. On the one hand they show that in some of the earliest passages in which Ātman/Brahman is clearly visioned, It appears as Aspect of Highest God Realization or Merger into the Highest Universal Divine. Transcendence of Desire or Renunciation is not explicitly mentioned: Vena is represented as attaining the Highest after maximum exertions to reach the Truth ("going around ..." etc.—he goes to the ends of the world for the Highest)—and after always worshipping the "First-born of Ṛta." This is quite in the compass of the religious life of a Brāhmaṇical sage. The only distinguishing feature is absolute dedication to a goal of Highest Knowledge and Divinity. So these extraordinary hymns confirm the impression one gets from the *Atharva Veda*, that the initial formulations/experience of Ātman/Brahman arose in the context of, and were inseparable from, Knowledge of merger into Universal, All-encompassing Highest Divinity. Only later, in the mature old Upaniṣads, was Ātman/Brahman beginning to be treated as something distinct from Divinity. The *Tad-eva* at least, standing at the very beginning of a clear vision and expression of Ātman, is thus the clearest testimony of the fact that the Ātman is the very heart and core of Highest Divinity, and Knowledge of the Merger into Ātman/Brahman is the core of Knowledge of and Merger into All-encompassing Highest Divinity.

Sacrificial Contexts of *Uttara Nārāyaṇa* and *Tad-eva*. Finally, any discussion of the *Uttar Nārāyaṇa* and *Tad-eva* would be incomplete without mentioning that these hymns are found in rather strange sacrificial contexts. The *Uttara Nārāyaṇa* is part of the *puruṣa-medha,* "sacrifice *(medha)* of man,"[88] and the *Tad-eva*, part of the *Sarva-medha*, "sacrifice of all (everything) (*sarva*)".[89] As presented in *Śatapatha Brāhmaṇa*,[90] these are something like symbolic and contemplative enactments which illustrate how a sacrifice in which the sacrificer wants to achieve certain supreme goals should proceed.[91] In the *puruṣa-medha* the goal is to "overpass all beings" and "become everything here", and a certain Puruṣa Nārāyaṇa (perhaps the non-Vedic Supreme Deity Nārāyaṇa, identified with the Puruṣa to form what looks like a version of Prajāpati) is said to have attained these goals by performing the *puruṣa-medha.*[92] In the *sarva-medha*, the sacrificer offers all conceivable "sacrificial essences" to "offer up his own self in the creatures and the creatures in his own self". By doing so, he "compass[es] all beings, and supremacy, sovereignty and lordship", just as Brahman *Svayambhū*, the self-created Brahman, did *in divinis.*[93] At another level, however, these sacrifices (or images of sacrifices) represent certain higher knowledge or realization. It is sufficient to *know* them rather than to perform them, to attain the same goals.[94] By knowing them one becomes their inner fruit, i.e. one becomes the highest state. The exact nature of the *puruṣa-* and *sarva-medha* sacrifices is somewhat controversial, but a detailed treatment is beyond our scope here.

8. The Puruṣa Idea in Vedic and Hindu Tradition

In sec. 2 we described the Puruṣa Hymn as expressing a "Great Thought" of incalculable power. In the following sections, it turned out that this "Great Thought" became a kind of framework for extraordinary expressions of combined Knowledge of Ātman/Brahman and God-realization, as well as for fundamental texts like *BṛhUp* I.4 and *AitUp* I. But this represents only a minute fraction of its total unfoldment, which as a phenomenon staggers the imagination. The repercussions of the Puruṣa Idea in Brāhmaṇism and Hinduism are of a magnitude which has few parallels in the History of Religion. They go far beyond what one would expect if this Idea was simply a divine archetype.[95] Much of the higher knowledge/experience in Vedic Hinduism is colored by and fused with the Puruṣa Idea. To understand this phenomenon, a new category of how the Divine acts in the History of Thought and Religion seems to be called for. In what follows, we try to indicate the general outlines of the whole phenomenon to sensitize the reader to some of the issues involved. To this end, we group Puruṣa-related developments under several headings and briefly comment on each.

(1) In the Brāhmaṇas, the sacrifice of the Puruṣa in the Puruṣa Hymn (vs. 6-13) is taken as the true meaning of the Vedic

> sacrifice, except that the Puruṣa is replaced by Prajāpati, who in the Brāhmaṇas functions as God the Creator.[96] Every Vedic sacrifice repeats and participates in the sacrifice of the Puruṣa, thereby re-figure-ing (confirming) it and actively participating in the creation and maintenance of the world. The Brāhmaṇas, however, take the idea very much further by identifying Prajāpati, who is being sacrificed, with the sacrificer (the patron of the sacrifice) and with the sacrificer's self. For the sacrificer makes the offering "in lieu of his own self".[97] In the *Śatapatha Brāhmaṇa*, this identification is developed to its most elaborate and deepest ritual-mystical form in the *agni-cayana*, the great Vedic sacrifice of the piling up of the fire place (*agni*, identified with the Vedic deity Agni).[98]

That the meaning of the Vedic sacrifice was understood to be a sacrifice of Prajāpati along the lines of the sacrifice of Puruṣa in the Puruṣa Hymn is remarkable enough. Apparently the sacrificial act and the conception and awareness of it were fused with the awareness of a pervasive Divine and of cosmic order in a special way which has yet to be sympathetically and empathically portrayed by scholarship. This kind of integrated consciousness may be assumed to be ingrained even in the average Brahmin, if for no other reason than the fact that in the Brāhmaṇas these ideas are constantly being repeated.[99] At any rate, it is clear that "the figures of Puruṣa and Prajāpati came to fuse".[100] This brings up an important point. In the Vedas and Brāhmaṇas Prajāpati functions to some extent as a great Deity, worshipped and related to as a personal god. Puruṣa, being essentially a specific high level of realization expressed in a hymn of praise, does not. But in the Brāhmaṇa period, Prajāpati "came, to a certain extent, to be fused with Brahman, Brahmā [both the masc. form of Brahman and the God Brahmā of later tradition] and other deities and divine concepts so as to lose his [original] individuality [as a deity] almost completely".[101] Sometimes he is even "the unlimited and undefined Supreme God who is more than the thirty-three gods whom he encompasses and who is identified with the vital breath, the year, the sacrifice, King Soma, the Puruṣa, Brahman".[102] The fact that the Puruṣa Idea, with its connotation of "self is all this", was absorbed into the conception of such a (partly personal and partly impersonal) Deity that is more or less a universal Divinity is significant. It foreshadows the fact that the Puruṣa Idea became incorporated into most of the conceptions of God in later Hinduism [cf. (4)-(5) below].

(2) The description in Puruṣa Hymn vs. 13-14 of the parts and powers of the Puruṣa giving rise to the Deities Sun, Moon, Agni, Vāyu, etc. and to the Powers Sight, Hearing, Mind etc. (Table 3.2) leads in the Brāhmaṇas and Upaniṣads to preoccupation with and meditation on these Powers and Deities to attain deeper realization. In teachings of this type, the Powers and Deities are often paired in more or less standard ways and occur in sets of three, four, or five.

This is a large topic, because teachings of this type, mostly involving Powers and Deities drawn from the same pool of Powers and Deities, are very common in the later Brāhmaṇa and early Upaniṣadic literature.[103] But the principle or reason by which a specific set of meditations leads to a deeper level of knowledge appears to be different in different cases and does not seem to depend that much on the specific sets of Deities and Powers involved. The exact connection with Puruṣa-type thought also varies from case to case (cf. the examples in the next chapter). So even though the theme of the Powers and Deities seems to have been stimulated by the Puruṣa Idea, it is unusual that it should be so widespread and pervasive:[104]

(3) In the late portions of the Brāhmaṇas and in the old Upaniṣads, a few important *vidyās* (higher teachings) involving meditation on the Powers and Deities actually aim at the realization of the Vedic Puruṣa as Ātman/Brahman. The Puruṣa Idea may also be connected with one of the most central and widely elaborated Upaniṣadic teachings, viz. that the Self and the whole Universe are contained in the Heart, and that the Heart is Prajāpati and is the whole Universe.

The emphasis here is on the fact that the meanings implicit in the Puruṣa Idea form the matrix and guiding ideals for many paths to Highest Realization, Enlightenment. The *Śatapatha Brāhmaṇa* version of the *Vaiśvānara Vidyā*, for example, says explicitly that the *Vaiśvānara* aspect of Agni which it is teaching is the Puruṣa. In the Upaniṣadic version, Puruṣa is not mentioned, but the essence of the teaching is still the same. In the mystical *Gāyatrī Vidyā*, the Puruṣa is a central element, and this is even more true for the *Parama Puruṣa Vidyā* in *PraśnaUp* V, one of the later Vedic Upaniṣads. All these *vidyās* represent very different ways of walking the path of the incalculable Puruṣa Thought.

Regarding the second point, that the Puruṣa Hymn is connected with the teaching that the Self is in the Heart, etc., we have seen that already the *Uttara Nārāyaṇa* says of Puruṣa—Prajāpati that "In Him are all created things," and that the Upaniṣads teach this to be part of the Knowledge of Ātman/Brahman in the Heart.[105] Since the *Uttara Nārāyaṇa* is a direct continuation and expansion of the Puruṣa Hymn in later language, it may be argued that already in the original Puruṣa Hymn, the Puruṣa must have been connected with the Infinite in the Heart. But it is not clear to what extent the relevant Upaniṣadic *vidyās* are stimulated by the Puruṣa Hymn.

(4) In the *Mahābhārata* (and thus rather early throughout a sizeable part of India, say 300 BCE), the univeral God of Vaiṣṇavism is described as Nārāyaṇa.[106] This universal Divinity seems to be alluded to by the *Puruṣa Nārāyaṇa* in the *puruṣa medha* section of *Śatapatha Brāhmaṇa* and in *ŚatBr* XI.3.4.[107] In both of these texts, *Puruṣa Nārāyaṇa* is said to "be all" or "have become all", and in both of them there is an implication that the sacrificer/devotee can unite with the godhead (now also Puruṣa-Nārāyaṇa) and thereby become all. Thus in these texts, which contain perhaps the earliest mention of Nārāyaṇa, "becoming all" (which is always clearly derived from the Puruṣa of the Puruṣa Hymn) is associated specifically with Nārāyaṇa. If (as seems likely) Nārāyaṇa was already then worshipped as Highest and Universal God,[108] these passages would be the earliest expression of the standard teaching in later tradition that by worshipping and attaining the Supreme Lord (Nārāyaṇa-Viṣṇu, Śiva) one becomes All.

From the point of view of Christian or Islamic tradition, the idea that highest knowledge or union with God implies "becoming all" may appear striking. Individual Christian or Muslim Saints may have talked in these terms,[109] but no such teaching is found in the Scriptures. In Hindu tradition, "becoming all" is initially part of the stream of Knowledge/Experience of the Puruṣa Hymn. In the two *Śatapatha Brāhmaṇa* texts mentioned, "[The self] becoming all" is likewise tied to the *Ṛg Vedic* Puruṣa. But in addition, it is also associated with Nārāyaṇa, and in *ŚatBr* XIII.7.1, with Brahman Svayambhū (here regarded as the Supreme Deity).[110] In other words, it is associated with a Supreme Divine which one relates to as God. So these two texts can be seen as showing how an idea or experience that was initially part of the Thought or realization of the Puruṣa becomes associated with the thought or experience of the Universal Supreme Divine.

(5) Later, the Idea of Puruṣa is found incorporated into the conceptions of Narāyāṇa-Viṣṇu and Śiva to form an essential aspect of the Universal Supreme Divine. As a result, many of the deeper aspects implicit in the Puruṣa Idea (the cosmic stance of self and the principle of *ahamgraha* meditation, Puruṣa = Self, Puruṣa = Brahman, and "becoming all") entered and became part of the theology, spiritual practice and Experience of the two major streams of (monotheistic) religion in India, leaving an imprint which is still a dominant feature today.

This is an even larger topic than (2)-(3).[111] "The Puruṣa-Hymn is a core element of Nārāyaṇa worship;"[112] it is "so to say, . . the foundation stone of Viṣṇuite philosophy".[113] In Viṣṇuism, major texts along this line are *Mahā-NārUp* XII-XIII (dated 3rd century BCE), parts of the *Nārāyaṇīya* section in the *Mahābhārata* (XII.321-339), and the *Bhagavad Gītā*, especially chrs. 8, 10 and 11. In *Mahā-NārUp* XIII.1-5,[114] Nārāyaṇa is invoked as "the Divine (*deva*) having a thousand heads", "the All-god", "the *puruṣa* that animates this whole universe" (vs. 1 and 2), all clear references to the Puruṣa Idea. In the climax, v. 5, he is adored as the Supreme Light, the Ātman, the Supreme, and the Brahman-*tattva* (fundamental substance). Not surprisingly, the same Upaniṣad opens with a hymn to Prajāpati in which the latter is glorified as Nārāyaṇa and Śiva. The *Gītā*, in which Kṛṣṇa speaks as Nārāyaṇa although Nārāyaṇa is never mentioned,[115] brings various additional elements. For example, it specifically ties obtaining the Puruṣa to unswerving *bhakti* (Love and Devotion of God):[116]

> This is the supreme Spirit (*puruṣaḥ sa paraḥ*), son of Pṛthā (=Arjuna),
> to be won (*labhya*), however, by unswerving devotion,
> within which all beings are fixed,
> by which this Universe is pervaded (*Gītā* VIII.22).[117]

The great dramatic high point of the *Gītā*, where Kṛṣṇa (=Nārāyaṇa) shows Arjuna His universal form, likewise shows the Vedic Puruṣa concept.[118] Gonda has given other examples of Viṣṇu being regarded as the Vedic Puruṣa.[119]

As far as Śaivism is concerned, it is becoming more accepted that worship of Śiva as the Supreme Divine developed in part in the Vedic ritual tradition in a continuous process from the worship of Vedic Rudra,[120] but incorporating traces of many non-Vedic and popular influences.[121] In the *Ṛg Veda* Rudra is a significant but not particularly prominent deity, associated with terrifying natural phenomena and invoked with fear to stay his wrath, but also possessed of healing powers. In the later Saṁhitās, however, several major texts show him already "unmistakably on his way to becoming an All-God".[122] Finally in *Śvetāśvatara Upaniṣad* he is the Supreme Lord, identified with Brahman and the Puruṣa. Of the intermediate texts, the most important is the *Śatarudrīya*, "that which pertains (*-iya*) to the one-hundred (*śata*) Rudras", *VājSaṁh* XVI.[123] Consisting of 66 stanzas and 425 accompanying oblations, it invokes Rudra with one-hundred names. The text shows a perception of Rudra as absolutely universal Divinity which is, however, quite different from the line of thought represented by the Puruṣa Hymn.

In general, therefore, the Vedic and Upaniṣadic Puruṣa was absorbed in the last centuries BCE naturally and more or less completely into the theology and meditation of Viṣṇu-Nārāyaṇa and of Śiva. This in turn helps understand why:

> (6) In the early centuries CE, when Vedānta acquired the status of a distinct philosophical school that could be compared with Buddhist and other philosophies, it was seen by outsiders as a philosophy with Puruṣa as one of its three or four most fundamental concepts.

For most of the Brahmins in the early centuries CE who were developing what was to become Vedānta Philosophy, were very likely also worshipping Śiva or Viṣṇu-Nārāyaṇa and serving as priests in Śaivite and Vaiṣṇava communities. To outsiders like the Buddhists, as well as to the Brahmins' own communities, a central doctrine like Puruṣa = God = Ātman = Brahman served as an ideal means to identify and characterize their nascent philosophy. H. Nakamura, in his path-breaking *History of Early Vedānta Philosophy*, discusses several major accounts of early pre-Śaṁkara Vedānta by Buddhist philosophers all of which feature doctrines of this kind.[124] An example is the treatment by Bhavya (490-570 CE), founder of the Svātantrika branch of Madhyamaka Buddhist philosophy, in his *Madhyamaka-hṛdaya-kārikā* (stanzas, *kārikās,* on the essence, *hṛdaya*, of Madhyamaka philosophy).[125] This work is the first to name the classical "six systems of

Indian philosophy" (the six *darśanas*), along with five Buddhist systems. Chr. 8 deals with Vedānta and consists of 96 verses, of which the first sixteen outline the Vedāntic position (using quotes or close paraphrases of Vedic and Upaniṣadic passages).[126] The first eight of these all deal with Puruṣa, e.g.:

4. Whatever is past, present or future, it is all regarded as the Puruṣa,
   He is within and without, far and near, and is the Doer.
5. From him are born all things in the Universe like threads coming out of a spider.
   Wise men who have merged themselves within him, do not get a second birth.
6. .... it does not stand to reason that immortality could be attained without there being an awakening into (the state of) that person (Puruṣa).
7. As there is nothing higher [than Him], as there is not found any thing superior
   or even subtler [than Him], by Him alone is this all [= this diversity of the world] held together.
8. For the seer, all beings are in Him, He becomes indeed the ātman,
   And ignorant and learned, outcasts and Brahmins, etc. are equal.[127]

Nakamura feels that in this text, "the Absolute is called Brahman, Ātman, Puruṣa, *Īśvara*, and Maheśvara, all of which are held to be names of the same fundamental principle".[128] He argues that Bhavya must be presenting a conception of Puruṣa which has been merged with Śiva, and more generally that he is describing the Vedānta of a particular Śaivite sect.[129]

Another classical Buddhist critique of the Vedānta school is chrs. 6 and 7 of *Tattva-saṁgraha* by Śāntarakṣita (680-740 CE), with a commentary by Kamalaśīla (ca 700-750 CE), a disciple of his.[130] The chapters are entitled "Examination of Puruṣa" and "Examination of Ātman," resp., again illustrating the importance of the Puruṣa concept in Vedānta in the eyes of outsiders like the Buddhists. Śāntarakṣita characterizes the doctrine of the Veda-vādins in only two stanzas. They ". . . assume that Puruṣa with qualities the same as those of the Lord (*īśa*) is the cause of the world. It is said that He possessed a power of knowledge which is not annihilated even at the time of dissolution of everything, and [He] is the cause of all living beings, just as the spider is [the cause] of (its) thread [which it extrudes]."[131] This summarizes in a nutshell the whole development in (4)-(6) above. The Puruṣa has become indistinguishable from the Lord or an aspect of the Lord. To Śāntarakṣita it mostly looks as if the Veda-vādins are people who believe in a single God with unusually comprehensive metaphysical qualities. The spider-thread simile occurs in *BṛhUp* II.1.20, where it is used to describe how the world came out of the Ātman.

The preceding six points articulate some of the major developments involving the Puruṣa Idea. But there are others which are currently topics of research. Thus in the *Jayākhya Saṁhitā*, one of the "three gems of the Pañcarātra" literature (see chr. 1.2), the basic superstructure for the ranges of higher inner experience intimated in that text may be ultimately traceable back to the Puruṣa Idea.[132] There are also suspicions that Puruṣa-Ātman texts or traditions may have inspired the nondual Śaivism of Kashmir.[133] In the Purāṇas, however, the Puruṣa idea is mostly used to reconnect the Vaiṣṇava and Śaivite traditions with their earlier Vedic and Vedic-Epic forms.

9. *KauṣUp* III: The Highest as *Prāṇa*

The Upaniṣads speak in many voices, but in an extraodinary harmony! Partly to illustrate this and partly to introduce a new circle of teachings—centering on *Prāṇa* as the Highest—we complete our excursion into "Powers and Deities" texts with a relatively lengthy text from *Kauṣītaki Upaniṣad. KauṣUp* III describes and argues graphically how the various Powers Speech, Sight, Hearing, Mind must all be underlain and controlled by a single intelligent principle. In *BṛhUp* I.4 the same Powers were the action-names of the Ātman, the Puruṣa. But in the *Kauṣītaki* text the cosmic-cosmological stance implicit in *BṛhUp* I.4 is missing. The Powers are "mounted" by a Universal "Intelligence-Self" or "Consciousness-Self", *Prajñā-ātman*, which is indissociable from *Prāṇa*, "Universal Life", but there is no cosmic Puruṣa which is/becomes all there is. So *BṛhUp* I.4 and *KauṣUp* III have a common denominator in that they both deal with Speech, Sight, Ear and Mind, and in that they treat them both as individually experienced or manifested, and as curiously detached, Universal Aspects or elements. But they take these elements and incorporate them into two very different overall conceptual frameworks, with correspondingly different inner mental stances or attitudes assumed in thought and reflection. In *BṛhUp* I.4 this is a framework of Ātman = the Cosmic Puruṣa. In *KauṣUp* III, it is a framework of Ātman = *Prajñā-ātman* and Brahman = *Prāṇa*.

Kauṣītaki Upaniṣad. *Kauṣītaki Upaniṣad*[134] is named after Kauṣītaki, a teacher or series of teachers whose followers are called Kauṣītakins. Just as *Aitareya Upaniṣad* is a section of *Aitareya Āraṇyaka*, which in turn is basically a continuation of the *Aitareya Brāhmaṇa*, so *Kauṣītaki Upaniṣad* is a part of *Śāṅkhāyana* (or *Kauṣītaki*) *Āraṇyaka*, which itself is essentially a continuation of the *Kauṣītaki* (or *Śāṅkhāyana*) *Brāhmaṇa*.[135] The term *Śāṅkhāyana* here refers to another teacher, next is line after Kahola Kauṣītaki, who is held to have been the author of the Āraṇyaka.[136] *Kauṣītaki Upaniṣad* is most famous for its first chapter, which describes a journey through various heavens, with various unusual stations on the way, and ending at Ultimate Reality. But *KauṣUp* III and IV are also well-known. The latter is one version of the *Ajātaśatru-Bālāki Dialogue*, another version of which occurs at *BṛhUp* II.1.

In *KauṣUp* III, the Aspect which is taught, the *Prajñā-ātman*, is considered to be same as *Prāṇa*, "(Universal) Life." Much of *Aitareya Āraṇyaka* and *Śāṅkhāyana Āraṇyaka* are concerned with elaborating *Prāṇa* as the Supreme. *KauṣUp* III is an effort, within this class of texts, to approach this *Prāṇa* via an analysis of the cognitive functions in the individual self. Before looking at the text in detail, however, we need to get an idea of what is intended when the Supreme is said to be *Prāṇa*. To this end we briefly consider *AitĀr* II.2.3 and *KauṣUp* II.1, both of which deal with *Prāṇa*.

***AitĀr* II.2.3.** In *AitĀr* II.2.3,[137] Indra, the chief of gods in the *Ṛg Veda*, teaches Viśvāmitra, a famous *Ṛg Vedic* seer:

3.1. Indra sat down beside Viśvāmitra who was about to recite the hymns of this day. He, saying "This is food," recited the thousand *bṛhatīs* [*Ṛg Vedic* stanzas in the *bṛhatī* meter]. Thus he went to Indra's dear home.

3.2. Indra said to him, "Seer, thou hast come to my dear home. Do thou, seer, repeat a second hymn." He, saying, "This is food," recited the thousand *bṛhatī* verses. Thus he went to Indra's dear home.

3.3. Indra said to him, "Seer, thou hast come to my dear home. Do thou, seer, repeat a third hymn." He, saying, "This is food," recited the thousand *bṛhatī* verses. Thus he went to Indra's dear home.

3.4. Indra said to him, "Seer thou hast come to my dear home. I give thee a boon." He said, 'Let me know thee.'[a] Indra

> said, 'I am *Prāṇa*, thou, seer, art *Prāṇa*, all creatures are *Prāṇa*, he that shines (i.e., the Sun) is *Prāṇa*. In this form, I pervade all the quarters[b]. This my food is my friend, my support. This is the food of Viśvāmitra. I am he that shines." Thus said he.[138]

When Viśvāmitra begins to recite the thousand *bṛhatī* verses, he feels Indra's presence beside him and has a deep spiritual experience. He is transported to Indra's heavenly abode, where he has a vision of Indra and where eventually Indra reveals to him his (Indra's) nature. This text is particularly closely related to *KauṣUp* III because of the similarity in the two frame stories. In both accounts, Indra grants a boon. In *Aitareya Āraṇyaka* Viśvāmitra asks him "let me know thee", while in *Kauṣītaki Upaniṣad*, where the hero-king Pratardana wants Indra to choose the boon for him, Indra eventually tells him "understand me, Myself". And then both teachings begin with Indra saying: "I am *Prāṇa*, . . ."

Now here in *Aitareya Āraṇyaka, Prāṇa* cannot possibly refer merely to life and energy as they manifest throughout the Universe. For *Prāṇa* is treated as something to be realized, it is treated as the highest knowledge, the Highest State. It is the State of Indra. Indra's teaching, "I am *Prāṇa*, you, seer, are *Prāṇa*, all creatures are *Prāṇa*, He that shines (the Sun) is *Prāṇa* . . ." shows an astonishing Universality which is quite different from the universality that is tied to a set of instantiations and with which we are so familiar in Western logic and science. It is a Universality which is itself almost an entity (or state). One feels that Indra is uttering something that is almost independent of himself, and that is not dependent on any of the specific manifestation of *Prāṇa*, gross or subtle, subjective or objective, which the term refers to. The most important hint, however, that what Indra is calling *Prāṇa* is a Transcendental and Universal Divine comes in the references to the Sun: "He that shines is *Prāṇa*. I am he that shines." This not only places the realization of *Prāṇa* in the path of worship of and meditation (*upāsanā*) on the Sun. It also means "My being, my State is that what you reach when you meditate on the Sun as the transcendental entity that, in the form of *Prāṇa*, pervades and vivifies all life and consciousness in the world."

***KauṣUp* II.1-2.** A second important *Prāṇa* text is *KauṣUp* II.1-2,[139] which says that Brahman is *Prāṇa:*

> II.1. "Brahman is *Prāṇa*"—thus indeed Kauṣītaki used to say.

> Now of this same *Prāṇa*, [i.e.] Brahman, verily, the messenger is the Mind; the guardian[a] is Sight; the announcer[b] is Hearing; the handmaid is Speech. He who, verily, knows Mind as the messenger of the *Prāṇa*, [i.e.] of Brahman, becomes one having a messenger; he who knows Sight as a guardian, becomes one having a watchman; he who knows Hearing as the announcer, becomes one having an announcer; he who knows Speech as the handmaid, becomes one having a handmaid.
>
> To this same *Prāṇa*, the Brahman, verily, all these divinities without His (= *Prāṇa's*) begging bring offering. Likewise, indeed, to this same *Prāṇa* all beings, without His begging, bring offering.
>
> Of him who knows this, the secret rule (*upaniṣad*) is: "One should not beg." . . .[140]

"Brahman is *Prāṇa.*" *Prāṇa* is treated as a single level, in some sense "experiential" and higher than the functions/deities of Mind, Sight, etc. It appears combined with them, but is greater than them. The text teaches to realize the *Prāṇa* in inner experience, and to realize that It is Brahman. The Powers of Mind, Sight, Hearing and Speech are all intelligential, and are fundamental forms of human consciousness. For a person who knows them as substantively connected with and subservient to this *Prāṇa* = Brahman, they will become amplified and become larger blessings. So *Prāṇa* = Brahman appears here as something that, being higher than the Powers, includes their intelligence and consciousness aspects *in a higher form.* This tends to make the equation *Prāṇa* = *Prajñā-ātman* in *KauṣUp* III plausible.

But we can go a little further. The references to the Sun in *AitĀr* II.2.3 suggest that we also look at the description of the three daily prayers to the Sun of Sarvajit Kauṣītaki described later in the Upaniṣad.

***KauṣUp* II.7**

> Now next come the three [daily] meditations (*upāsanās*, see chr. 4.1) of Sarvajit Kauṣītaki. Sarvajit ("all conquering") Kauṣītaki stood before (*upa-sthā-*) the rising Sun. Having put on (ritually) the sacred thread, bathed with and poured three times into a water vessel, [he said] 'You are a lifter (deliverer), lift from me my evil (*pāpman*).' In the same way [he worshipped] the noon Sun: 'You are up-lifter, lift up [from me] my evil.' In the same

way [he worshipped] the setting Sun: 'You are the full (or away-) lifter. Lift fully (away) my evil . . .'[141]

A man who lives like this, and who is called all-conquering and regarded as a great teacher, may be expected to have an understanding of pervasive Divinity, and to be in harmony with the forces and processes of life and in the Universe. One may expect in him total acceptance of *Prāṇa* "in Universality" as part of his being. If sacred tradition now records that such a man "used to say" that "Brahman is *Prāṇa*,"[142] etc., how would we interpret this? We would assume that he was describing his highest wisdom, the fruit of his life experience, the highest state he had come to. We would think that he was expressing the One Reality which he saw as ever underlying his state and the Universe. But at the same time we would not necessarily assume that his realization was realization of Brahman as taught in the highest Upaniṣadic *vidyās*. The conclusion is the same if his realization of *Prāṇa* as the Supreme is assumed to have been attained with meditation on the Sun (as in *KauṣUp* II.7). Meditation on the Sun as a spiritual path may lead the aspirant-devotee to various stages, including knowledge of all pervasive Divinity as well as realization of Ātman/Brahman. On the other hand, however, "This *Prāṇa* indeed is the *Prajñā*-Self, bliss, ageless, immortal" (*KauṣUp* III.8, below in our main text) does imply that in this text, *Prāṇa* = Ātman/Brahman.[143]

***KauṣUp* III.** The preceding sets the stage for our main text, *KauṣUp* III.[144] The first section, *KauṣUp* III.1, introduces the whole chapter as the teaching of Indra, the Lord of Gods, to Pratardana Daivodāsi, a king, after his death in battle.[145] Pratardana arrives at Indra's abode where Indra tells him to choose a boon. In reply the King asks him to choose what would be most beneficial for a human being. Indra at first refuses, but eventually he tells him that he should "understand Me, Myself. This indeed I deem most beneficial for a human being, namely that he should understand Me." Then comes the body of the teaching, *KauṣUp* III. 2-8. We give the text in two parts, III.2.1-III.4.1 and III.4.2-III.8. For ease of reference, the traditional subdivisions III.2 etc. have been subdivided further; thus III.2.1, III.2.2, and so on.

***KauṣUp* III.2.1-4.1**

III.2.1. Then he [Indra] said: I am *Prāṇa*, the *Prajñā*-Self (*Prajñā-ātman*).[a] As such (*tam*), worship (*upās-*) me as "Life (*āyus*)," as "the Immortal (*amṛta*)". *Prāṇa* is Life; Life, verily, is

Prāṇa. Prāṇa, indeed, is the Immortal.[b] For, as long as *Prāṇa* dwells in this body, so long is there life. For indeed, with *Prāṇa* one obtains immortality in this world; [for] with higher spiritual consciousness/wisdom (*Prajñā*),[c] [one obtains] true conception (*saṁkalpa*).

So he who worships (regards, *upās-*) me as "Life," as "the Immortal", reaches a full life in this world; he obtains immortality, indestructibility (*akṣiti*) in the heavenly world (*svargā-loka*).

2.2. Now as to this, some say: "The *prāṇas* (Powers), verily, go into a unity.[e]" For [otherwise] no one would be able to make a [nameable] thing conscious-known[f] by means of Speech, a form by means of Sight, a sound by means of Hearing, a thought by means of Mind. Having verily become a unity, they [= the Powers] each one make conscious-known all these [things] here.

2.3. All the Powers speak along with Speech when it speaks[g]:
When Sight sees, all the Powers see along [with it].[h]
When hearing hears, all the Powers hear along [with it].
When Mind thinks, all the Powers think along [with it].
When Breath breathes, all the *prāṇas* breathe along [with it].

2.4. "That is indeed so," said Indra. "There is, however a superior excellence among the Powers."

3.1. One lives with Speech gone,[i] for we see the dumb;
one lives with Sight gone, for we see the blind;
one lives with Hearing gone, for we see the deaf;
one lives with Mind gone, for we see the childish;
one lives with arms cut off, one lives with legs cut off, for thus we see.

3.2. Now then, *Prāṇa*, indeed the *Prajñā*-Self (*prajñā-ātman*), having seized [*pari-gṛhya*] this body, makes it stand up (*ut-thā-*). Therefore "one should worship (*regard, upās-*) it as the *Uktha*" (a recitation of Rig Vedic mantras sung at the *ekāha* or one day Soma sacrifices). This is the All-obtaining (*sarvāpti*) in the *Prāṇa*. What *Prāṇa* [is]—verily, that is the *Prajñā*-Self (*Prajñā-ātman*). What the *Prajñā*-Self is—verily, that is *Prāṇa.*

3.3. This is the seeing (*dṛṣṭi*) of it, this is the knowledge (*vijñāna*) of it:

When that person who is asleep (*puruṣaḥ suptaḥ*) sees no dream whatever, then in this *Prāṇa* they [= the Powers] become one.[j] Then

Speech together with all names [=objects] goes into (*apyeti*) it;

Sight together with all forms goes into It;

Hearing together with all sounds goes into It;

Mind together with all thoughts goes into It.

When he wakes up, —just as from a blazing fire sparks fly off in all directions, so indeed from this *Ātman* the Powers fly off according to their [respective] stations (*āyatanas*), from the Powers the gods, from the gods the worlds. This *Prāṇa* indeed, the *Prajñā-ātman,* grasps this body [around from all sides, *pari-gṛh-*]. Therefore "one should worship it (contemplate it, etc., *upās-*) as the *Uktha*". This is the All-obtaining in the *Prāṇa*. What verily the *Prāṇa* is, that is *Prajñā,* and what verily *Prajñā* is, that is *Prāṇa.*

3.4. This is the proof (accomplishment, *siddhi*) of it, this the understanding [of it]:

When a sick person, about to die, having become weak, goes into a stupor, then they say: 'His thought (*citta*) has departed. (Or: 'Has it [=the *Prāṇa*] [(perhaps already)] departed?') Then he hears not. He sees not. He speaks not with Speech. He thinks not. Then [the Powers] become one in the [one] *Prāṇa*. Then

Speech together with all names goes to it (*apyeti*);

Sight together with all forms goes to it;

Hearing together with all sounds goes to it;

Mind together with all thoughts goes to it.

When It [=the *Prāṇa*] departs from this body, It departs together with all these [Powers].

4.1. Speech releases[k] from that one (*tasmāt*—from *Prāṇa*, or, with Frenz: from the body) all names (i.e., [concepts of] objects); [for] with Speech one obtains all names ([concepts of] objects).

Breath *(Prāṇa)* releases from that one all odours; [for] with Breath one obtains all odours.

Sight releases from that one all forms; [for] with Sight one obtains all forms.

> Hearing releases from that one all sounds; [for] with Hearing one obtains all sounds.
>
> Mind releases from that one all thoughts; [for] with Mind one obtains all thoughts.
>
> This is the All-Obtaining in the *Prāṇa*. What, verily, the *Prāṇa* is, that is *Prajñā*, and what, verily, *Prajñā* is, that is *Prāṇa*.[146]

Life, Awareness is Consciousness-endowed-with-Intelligence. I move and operate in many arenas of life—on the street, at home in the circle of family, at work; sometimes in a scientific frame of mind, sometimes relaxing, enjoying, etc. In all of them I move with intelligent consciousness: with perception and attention, with understanding, sensitivity and judgment, ultimately with decisions regarding action. Today we tend to look at "intelligence" often in terms of modes of its external manifestation, e.g. visual pattern recognition, logical inference, mechanical ability, algorithmic ability, spatial imagination, "social skills," and so on. But actually, all this intelligence, all these kinds of intelligence, are simply oneself, are simply "self" living, being. I, (my-) self, assume consciousness-endowed-with-intelligence in all situations, in all moments of life; for ordinary consciousness is never completely devoid of every trace of what one normally calls, or has to call, intelligence. All the diverse forms of intelligence that I exhibit when looked at from the outside—all the forms of intelligence that I am—all that I am, all that is myself.

Now "as to this point", the Upaniṣad cites a wonderful holistic understanding of the untiy of the various Powers or *prāṇas* (III.2.2-4). "The Powers, verily go into (*gacchanti*) a unity (*ekībhūya*, into a 'becoming one')"; "all Powers speak along (*anu-vadanti*) with Speech speaking (i.e. when Speech is speaking)" and so on, even though each has its own specific function. Thus, the analysis of the intelligent-conscious process or phenomenon into separate Powers cannot be the whole story. But Indra at once goes a step further. "That (i.e. the fact that Powers go into a unity) is indeed so. There is, however, a superior excellence, *niḥśreyasa*, among the Powers" (III.2.4). In other words, Indra is saying, logically the oneness in the functioning of the Powers is not enough to imply a higher order entity or level. In addition to the oneness in their functioning, there is a "superior excellence" which belongs to them (III.2.4). None of the Powers by itself is necessary for Life (*āyus*) (III.3.1), for "one [still] lives with Speech gone away, for we see the mute [person living]," etc. The real reason for that is that then the "superior excellence" is still always present.

The fact that the "superior excellence" really refers to a deeper level of realization, and that Indra by this statement is really pointing out a higher spiritual state, is suggested by *KauṣUp* II.14 (Hume, = II.13 Frenz). This text begins "Now next [regarding] the attainment of the Superior Excellence," *niḥśreyasādāna*, and tells a story of a dispute of the Powers (Speech, etc.). "The deities (*devatāḥ*, i.e. the Powers), disputing as to I—excellence, *aham-śreyasa*, [all] rose up from this body," leaving the latter lifeless. Then they entered it one by one. So the body first lay speaking, then speaking and seeing, then speaking, seeing, and hearing. But it never got up. When *Prāṇa* entered it, however, it arose all at once. Thereupon

> all these deities, having known the superior excellence in the *Prāṇa,* having become one (*abhisam-bhūya*) with *Prāṇa*, indeed the *Prajñā- ātman*, all of these together indeed rose up[a] from this body. They, having entered (*pra-viś-*) Vāyu (Wind or Air), having the body (or nature) of space[b], went to Heaven (*svaḥ*). In the same way indeed does one who knows thus, having known the superior excellence in the *Prāṇa*, having become one (*abhisam-bhūya*) with *Prāṇa*, indeed with the *Prajñā-ātman*, arise together with all of these from this body. He, having entered into Vāyu, having the body (or the nature) of space, goes to Heaven. He then goes to where the gods (*devas*) are. Having reached that, [he] who knows this becomes immortal since the gods are immortal.[147]

The text makes a distinction between *Prāṇa* which, in general, makes the body move, and the "superior I excellence" of the *Prāṇa* which makes the body move *and lets it become again the individual person* which it was before. The body not only begins to move, but it moves as an individual person who says "I", *aham* (hence "superior *I* excellence"). It is the knowledge of this superior excellence which makes the gods go to Heaven and men become immortal. In III.3.2 the idea is the same. In fact, the "standing up" in III.3.2 may well refer to the "rising up at once" in II.14. So that what ensouls a person and makes him move, talk, see and so on as a whole person, that is a higher *Prāṇa,* viz. the superior excellence in *Prāṇa* mentioned in III.3.2 and III.2.1. This is the *Prajñā-ātman*.

10. *Prajñā* and *Prajñā-Ātman*

***Prajñā*, "Higher-Order Knowing or Consciousness."** This brings us to the *Prajñā-ātman* or *Prajñā-Self*. To begin with, what is *prajñā?* The usual meaning of *prajñā* is "consciousness" or "intelligence, understanding".[148] Already Frauwallner observed that in the oldest Upaniṣads, the term *prajñā* and its derivatives are found almost only in *Kauṣītaki Upaniṣad, AitUp* III, and *BṛhUp* IV, and that it seems to be similar to and replace *vijñāna*.[149] *Vijñāna* ordinarily means "knowledge", and "a type of consciousness that emobdies and de facto represents knowledge" (such as "the consciousness, *vijñāna*, of the senses", *BṛhUp* II.1.116). But in the Old Upaniṣads, it then also means "emerging or more developed knowledge of Ātman", or "Ātman-consciousness" (considered as a form of higher consciousness or as a spiritual state) (see chr. 5). So a reasonable conjecture is that the meaning of *prajñā* in "*Prajñā-ātman* is something like "consciousness which constitutes or represents higher (spiritual) knowledge."[150] There is however a difference between (higher) *prajñā* and (higher) *vijñāna*. In the case of *vijñāna* (except in its highest forms), the higher *vijñāna* consciousness in question is assumed to include an element of "I", or a "seen by an individual". With higher *prajñā*, there is no presupposition of this kind. So (higher) *prajñā* suggests higher knowledge or intelligence, or consciousness constituting higher knowledge or intelligence, which is not limited by a direction of "seen by an individual". In the compound *Prajñā-ātman*, the self is therefore suggested to be *prajñā* and thus free from such a direction.

The fact that *prajñā* indicates "higher-order spiritual knowledge or consciousness" is illustrated by other passages in the Upaniṣads. One of these is *BṛhUp* IV.4.21 (K) = IV.4.28 (M) discussed in chr. 2.2, "Let the steady Brahmin, after knowing (*vijñāna*) that one [= the Great Self of the preceding verse], make high wisdom (*prajñā*) for himself. Let him not reflect on many words . . ." More definitive, however, is a reference to *prajñā* in *KauṣUp* I.5. Recall that *KauṣUp* I[151] tells the story of how the sage destined for immortality after Death eventually enters the path that serves the gods and comes to the world of Brahmā (masc.), a deity representing Brahman. There he comes to a throne called *vicakṣaṇa*, "looking far, seeing clearly" and a couch or bedstead called *amitaujas*, "of immeasurable strength", on which Brahmā is seated (*KauṣUp* I.5). *Vicakṣaṇa* (from *cakṣus*, "sight", and *vi*, "distinct"), says the text, "is *Prajñā*, for by *prajñā* one sees clearly".[152] Similarly *amitaujas* is *Prāṇa*. Now before arriving at the throne, the sage comes to the river *vijarā*, "Ageless", and crosses over it with the mind. "By that he shakes off [his] good and evil deed[s]. . . As one driving with a wagon would look down on the (constantly turning) wheels of the wagon, in that way he looks down on day and night, on good and evil deed and on all pairs of opposites."[153] In other words, by crossing over the river "Ageless" he has transcended good and evil, and he sees everything *sub specie aeternitatis*, in the way that is characterisitic of seeing when there is transcendence of desire. Thereafter, successively the fragrance, smell, taste, *tejas* (brilliance, power), and splendour of Brahman enter into him, and only then does he come to the throne and couch. From the whole description, as well as from the questions and answers in I.2-3 and I.5-6, it is obvious that although the text has the form of an account of a king's path after death, it is also a description of progress in spiritual knowledge (or inner realization) with a view of guiding the aspirant. In other words, crossing the river "Ageless", getting the fragrance etc. of Brahman, having Indra and Prajāpati flee from the person, and coming to the throne and couch are all allusions to definite spiritual events, symptoms, states, whatever. Hence the statement that the throne *vicakṣaṇa*, "distinct-seeing", is *Prajñā* because "by *prajñā* (intelligence, consciousness) one sees distinctly" means that *vicakṣaṇa* refers to a state of higher *prajñā*, a state of being characterized by higher seeing and spiritual consciousness and wisdom. So in this explanation, *Prajñā* is a higher *prajñā* which comes after spiritual stages such as "crossing the river Ageless" and so on.

Universal, Cosmic or Cosmos-embracing Aspect of *Prajñā*. But Indra equates the *Prajñā*-Self with *Prāṇa*, and hence *Prajñā* should also have a universal, cosmic or cosmos-embracing aspect. Is there precedent for this elsewhere in the Vedic literature also? The only clear example I am aware of occurs in Yāska's *Nirukta*, soon after the time of the old Upaniṣads (the *Nirukta* is often dated 600-500 BCE). Explaining *Ṛg Veda* III.55.19, a mantra exalting Tvaṣṭṛ as the fashioner of the manifold manifestation of this world (cf. above, sec. 7), Yāska glosses the divine power exalted in the refrain "great is the Asura (Lordly) power of the gods"[154] as "the state of being endowed with wisdom, *prajñā-vat-tva*, or [the state of being endowed with] the bread of life, *ana-vat-tva*"[155] (*ana* =*prāṇa*). Since the Asura power of the gods is primarily of a universal and cosmic dimension, the same must in some sense hold also for the higher aspects (*prajñā* and *ana*

= *prāṇa*) of which it is an outward expression.

The *Nirukta* passage may perhaps in turn be connected with the later use of the term *prajñā* in *YoSū* III.5.[156] (The *Yoga Sūtra* is often dated to the 5th cent. CE, but this material is likely to go back much further.) *YoSū* III.5 is part of a lengthy teatment of *saṁyama* meditation, a type of meditation for which the Sūtra is famous[157] and which also leads to the supernormal powers described in the remainder of *YoSū* III. Aphorisms III.1-3 define three stages of meditation, *dhāraṇā, dhyāna,* and *samādhi*, defined as "binding the mind to a particular region" (like the heart, or the place between the eyebrows), "meditative absorption [there]", and finally, arising from that, "a state where only the object of meditation shines, nothing else", resp. (these are short paraphrases only). Next III.4 defines *saṁyama* as what emerges when there is "integrated performance" of *dhāraṇā, dhyāna,* and *samādhi* on the same object of meditation.[158] And finally *YoSū* III.5 says that "through mastery in that [practice of *saṁyama*] comes 'the realm of *Prajñā*', *Prajñā-loka*". Since numerous higher powers mentioned in aphorisms III.16 ff. all results from *saṁyama* on certain things, it is reasonable to interpret the *Prajñā* in III.5 in a very broad way as something like "higher seeing, knowing", "a state of higher consciousness equivalent to higher knowledge". This *Prajñā* would include supernatural knowledge of things in the world as well as higher spiritual knowledge, and it would denote this knowledge as well as as the type of consciousness in which this knowledge was contained.[159] All this is completely consistent with the uses of *prajñā* in *BṛhUp* IV.4.21 (K) and *Nirukta* I.34 above.

It is noteworthy that this general meaning of *prajñā* is still found in use today. For example there is a story that Ramana Maharshi once criticized the administration of his Ashram for writing to a devotee to send country oranges for pickling because he (Maharshi) had expressed a desire for them the day before. At the climax of the discussion, a railway contractor entered the hall with two sealed parcels for which no papers had been received, one with sweet oranges for eating and the other with sour ones for pickling. When asked whether this coincidence should be considered a miracle, Maharshi "quoted a verse from *Yoga Vāsiṣṭha* which says: 'This *prajñā*, which is treasured up in the heart of the wise, is *cintāmaṇi* (the mystic precious stone). Like *kalpalatā* (the celestial creeper [vine]), it fulfils instantly whatever is thought of.' He also cited . . . [the] definition of *prajñā* in *Vivekacūḍāmaṇi* as 'thought that is pure consciousness devoid of *vāsanās* (fluctuating tendencies).'"[160] Sathya Sai Baba's explanations of *prajñā* are also consistent with this traditional meaning.[161]

***Prajñā* in *KauṣUp* III.** In view of this meaning of *prajñā*, therfore, the fact that Indra in *KauṣUp* III.2.1 expands his teaching to Viśvāmitra, "I am *Prāṇa*," to "I am *Prāṇa*, the *Prajñā*-Self," and then insists that *Prāṇa* is the same as the *Prajñā*-Self, has considerable implications. For both *Prāṇa* and *Prajñā* have universal and cosmic-level dimensions. But *Prāṇa* has no connotation of "subjective experience, cognition". The realization of *Prāṇa* as the Highest, as represented in *AitĀr* II.2.3 or *KauṣUp* II.14, is not in terms of any principle of consciousness or knowing. The *Prajñā*-Self on the other hand must of course be something like "a universal Self which is *Prajñā*, Higher Seeing, Higher Knowing". And in passing from one's ordinary condition to a knowledge of and state of the *Prajñā*-Self, no doubt "self" and "cognition"are implied to be a common factor. Hence by "qualifying" the Supreme, i.e. *Prāṇa*, to be also a *Prajñā*-Self, a Supreme-Knowledge Self, Indra is essentially saying: I am indeed the One *Prāṇa* that you worshipped and glimpsed before, but more: "I am that what the individual seeing and knowing self comes to when it infinitizes itself completely and becomes truly universal, cosmic, unlimited, the Universal. You can attain my state, which is the same as being me, by this Infinitization." Note that with this addition of the *Prajñā*-Self, Indra is now finally able to say directly that He indeed is the Reality as a whole. In *Aitareya Āraṇyaka* he was not really able to do so: "I am *Prāṇa*, you, seer, are *Prāṇa*, the Sun is *Prāṇa*, . . . , I am the Sun." But now he says: "I am—" (where—stands for the Whole Reality, known as a single, but expressed as a juxtaposition, *Prāṇa-Prajñā-ātman*).

Practice (*Upāsanā*) for Attaining the *Prajñā*-Self. Let us continue with the text. Having stated that there is indeed a higher thing (state, level of being, whatever) (2.5-3.1) of which the unity of the cognitive act is only one effect (2.3-4), Indra next teaches how this state is to be obtained. It is, he says, intimately connected with the *Uktha*, and can be obtained by worship of and meditation (*upāsana*) on the *Uktha* as the *Prajñā*-Self (III.3.2). The *Uktha* is the recitation of a certain set of *Ṛg Vedic* mantras in the one-day Soma-sacrifices. Being one of the high points and most important moments in the sacrifice, it is one of the most important functions of the *Ṛg Vedic* priests, the *hotṛs*, to which the Upaniṣad is addressed. So Indra is saying: "Worship the *Uktha*, this great praise of the gods which is your supreme function in the sacrifice, as the essence of the *Prāṇa* = *prajñā*-Self which I am teaching. Contemplate it (see the discussion of *upās*- in chr. 4), no: live it, experience it as the *Prāṇa*, the *Prajñā-ātman*. This practice is really the 'Obtaining All in the *Prāṇa*'—it will become and result in a true 'Obtaining All'."

"As Small Sparks Fly Off a Fire . . ." The *upāsanā* of the *Uktha* is therefore the foundational practice by which the *Prāṇa* = *Prajñā*-Self is to be approached. But then come two further statements, III.3.3 and III.3.4-III.4, which detail the nature of the realization that is being taught. III.3.3 deals with deep sleep and the III.3.4-4.1 with death, and in both cases the Powers are said to "go into" the universal Prāṇa: Since the same formulas "Speech together with all names goes into it," etc. are used both times (in both 3.3 and 3.4), these formulas represent a felicitous formulation that can be used effectively in both contexts (of deep sleep and death) rather than, say, an accurate description of a process (of going to sleep or dying). Let us consider 3.3. The image of sparks flying off a fire is clearly intended to describe the arising of the worlds (Earth, Air, the Heavens) from the *Prajñā-ātman* or Ātman: "As (*yathā*) small sparks fly off," and so on, "*just so* (*evam*) the Powers fly off from this *ātman*". The following "from the Powers the gods, from the gods the worlds" has cosmological overtones reminiscent of the production of the world in the Puruṣa Hymn and in *AitUp* I. But from the very beginning, this whole description is set in a context of waking up from sleep: "When he wakes up—as small sparks fly off . . ." What is the text really trying to convey by juxtaposing the arising of the worlds, etc. from the Ātman and waking up from sleep this way?

To begin with, "When he wakes up—as small sparks fly off . . ." makes a specific, substantive point. Immediately before this the topic is the nature of deep sleep. In deep sleep, all the powers become one. Conversely, the text continues, when one wakes up, they all fly off from this Ātman to their respective stations. Indeed, this is how (in the waking up process) the *Prāṇa* = *Prajñā*-Self grasps the body all around (*pari-gṛh*-). This suggests that "When he wakes up—as sparks fly off . . ." is intended as a substantive analogy between waking up and the creation/arising of the world from (*Prajñā*-) Ātman: just as, when one wakes up, all one's (sense-) powers fly off to their stations, so from the Ātman arise the Universal (Sense-) Powers. The arising of the Prāṇas, gods, and worlds from the Ātman, which is like sparks flying off from a fire, is just like one's "coming to" when one wakes up—it is just like these faculties "coming in" at the moment of waking up. When one sees the arising of the world in this way, then this is the real seeing, the true knowing (*vijñāna*), of *Prāṇa* = *Prajñā*-Self.[162] At the same time the *Prāṇa* = *Prajñā*-Self grasping the body when waking up alludes to the *Prāṇa* seizing the body and making it stand up which is mentioned at the begin of III.3.2 (and which probably refers back to II.14, cf. above). For that reason, III.3.3 continues with the Uktha just like III.3.2.

***KauşUp* III.4.2-III.8.** The remainder of *KauṣUp* III is less concerned with the *Prajñā*-Self as with describing a general "model" which is consistent with III.4.1. It is possbile that III.1-III.4.1 represents an original nucleus and that this remaining portion (itself completely unified) was added by another hand.[163]

4.2. Now then, we will explain how all beings (*bhūta*) become one with this *Prajñā*.

5. Of that [*Prajñā*], Speech indeed is a unified prominent limb;[a] the objective element (*bhūta-mātrā*) corresponding to it (lit: set externally near it[b]) is the (named) object (*nāma*).[c]

Of that [*Prajñā*], *ghrāṇa* (=*prāṇa*) is a unified prominent limb; the objective element externally corresponding to it is odour (*gandha*).

Of that [*Prajñā*], Sight is a unified prominent limb; the objective element externally corresponding to it is form (*rūpa*) . . .

Similarly for seven additional pairs:

Hearing —sound;
Taste —taste-object;
two hands —work (*karman*);
body —pleasure and pain;
generative organ —bliss, delight, procreation;
two feet —goings;
mind (*manas*) —thoughts;
[an alternative reading for the
last one is intelligence (*prajñā*) —thought (*dhī*)]

6. *Prajñā* having mounted on Speech, with Speech one obtains all objects.

Prajñā having mounted on Breath (*prāṇa*), with Breath one obtains all odours.

Prajñā having mounted on Sight, with Sight one obtains all forms.

(Similarly for the remaining seven pairs.)

7. For truly, with *Prajñā* gone away, Speech would not make cognizant (*pra* + *jñā*) of any (named) thing whatsoever. 'My mind was elsewhere,' one says: 'I did not cognize that thing.'

For truly, with *Prajñā* gone away, Breath would not make cognizant of any odour whatsoever. 'My mind was elsewhere,' one says: 'I did not cognize that odour.'

For truly, with *Prajñā* gone away, Sight would not make cognizant of any form whatsoever. 'My mind was elsewhere,' one says: 'I did not cognize that form.'

(Similarly for the other seven pairs.)

8.1. Speech is not what one should desire to understand. One should know the Speaker.

Smell is not what one should desire to understand. One should know the Smeller.

Form is not what one should desire to understand. One should know the Seer.

(Similarly for the other seven pairs.)

8.2. These ten objective elements (*bhūta-mātrāḥ*), verily, are with reference to Intelligent Consciousness (*adhi-prajñam*). the ten elements of Intelligent Consciousness (*prajñā-mātrāḥ*) are with reference to Existence (*adhi-bhūtam*). For truly, if there were no elements of existence (*bhūta-mātrāḥ*), there would be no elements of intelligent consciousness (*prajñā-mātrāḥ*). Verily, if there were no elements of intelligent consciousness, there would be no elements of existence. For truly, from either alone no appearance (*rūpa*) whatsoever would be effected.

And this [world here] is not a diversity.[d] But as the felly of a chariot is fixed on the spokes and the spokes are fixed on the hub, even so these elements of Existence are fixed on the elements of Intelligent Consciousness, and the elements of Intelligent Consciousness are fixed on the *Prāṇa*.

This same *Prāṇa*, in truth, is the *Prajñā*-Self (*Prajñā-ātman*). [It is] bliss (*ānanda*), ageless (*ajara*), immortal (*amṛta*). It does not become greater through good action, nor indeed lesser with bad action.

This one, truly, indeed, causes him whom It wishes to lead up from these worlds, to perform good action. This one, also, indeed, causes him whom It wishes to lead downward, to perform bad action.

It is the world-protector (*loka-pāla*). It is the world-sovereign (*loka-adhi-pati*). It is the lord of all.

'It is my self (*ātman*)'—this one should know. 'It is my self'—this one should know.[164]

The main theme is the systematically carried through mutual reference and complementarity of "elements of Intelligent Consciousness", *prajñā-mātrāḥ*, and elements of Existence, *bhūta-mātrāḥ*. But this complementarity is obviously completely in the service of the enlightened state, the state of realization of *Prāṇa* = *Prajñā-ātman* that is being taught. This is clear from the transition to "this is not a diversity", *no etan nānā*. The categories *Bhūta* and *Prajñā*, the ten pairs of elements of Existence and Intelligent Consciousness, and their relationships do not have any fundamental reality of their own. Only the experienced unity, the state of realization does. *Prāṇa-Prajñā-ātman* is the Reality. It is bliss; It is outside time. It has no structure; there is in It no duality.

11. Postscript on Methodology

While our course through the mythological and philosophical texts in this chapter has come to an end, the reader may be left with a feeling of incompleteness. Compared to the extraordinary teachings in chr. 2, the three main texts in this chapter do not seem to come to a common conclusion. They seem to be so many partial illuminations—the fact that they are really all motivated by the same Truth and that this Truth is the same as that of the teachings in chr. 2 is not very obvious. Such feelings are natural and are likely to persist until chrs. 5 and 6, where the teachings on Ātman/Brahman discussed in chr. 2 are unfolded for the first time in their real depth. For the time being we can only point to the testimony of the texts themselves, all of whom say that they are teaching the Ātman. In addition, there is the consensus of orthodox tradition. "Whether we talk of the Veda or we use the term Brahman or the word Puruṣa, these are only different names given to the same idea that is contained in all these words. The words are different but they describe one and the same idea."[165] (To these terms one could easily add Ātman and a few others.) Because this is plainly presupposed in the texts, this must be the ideal for one's own interpretation and approach, and the criterion for one's own knowledge/experience. Apparent enormous differences between different teachings may be expected because we are at this point still operating largely only at a level of the verbal content of the text. Once meditation and other disciplines are taken into account, it is much easier to see similar knowledge operating in different teachings than when the criterion is only verbal content. Also, one's understanding of the essence of a given teaching, and of how two teachings are related, depends very much on one's spiritual state. Certainly my own understanding has often changed completely over the years.

So a discussion of whether the three main texts in this chpater all teach Ātman/Brahman as that was understood in chr. 2 is still somewhat premature. However, we will briefly consider another issue which concerns our treatment of these texts. For our method was always to show that the text in question must have involved some kind of higher knowledge or realization (metaphysical, divine, transcendental, whatever), and then to try to get an idea or glimpse of this knowledge. In the following chapters, where we proceed the same way, this approach is completely justified. For the texts there—most of them "*vidyās*"—more or less explicitly teach such higher knowledges and realizations or are generally held to embody such. But here in this chapter we are dealing with "mythology", or "theological speculation" (the Puruṣa Hymn, *BṛhUp* I.4, *AitUp* I), or "philosophy" (*KauṣUp* III). To focus in such texts so strongly on a core of metaphysical, Divine, or Transcendental knowledge/experience assumes that this "higher core" with its "experiential" overtones and base is in fact their most important constituent. It assumes that this core is the central aspect that is operative in the text and thereby gives this core an overwhelmingly privileged position. This is a strong assumption for texts that would ordinarily be called "mythic", "speculative", or "philosophical", and deserves some comment.

To begin with, it is significant that in the case of the three major Upaniṣadic texts (*BṛhUp* I.4, *AitUp* I, and *KauṣUp* III), this approach was relatively successful. In each case we found that there was in fact an underlying higher realization, a higher knowledge, that informed the text, and which was reflected in it in various ways. Indeed, utterances like "in the beginning this world was the Self only. . ." or "I am

Brahman," which lead the supposed "mythology" or "speculation," are generally recognized to have a "transcendental power" which goes beyond the usual levels of the inner appeal that myth makes. And the texts as a whole breathe the same spirit and realization as other great *vidyās* (recall Śaṁkara's estimate of *AitUp* I). Their wisdom is continuous with, or of the same stock as, the Supreme Wisdom of the great *vidyās*. To explicate these things an approach of trying to identify in more detail the kind of realization that is working in the text is very useful. At the same time, however, this appraoch did not work so well for the Puruṣa Hymn. There we could still talk of the seer's vision and "realization", but judging only from the text, the specific nature of this "realization" remained elusive. The more detailed categories which will be used in the following chapters did not really seem to apply, and we settled instead on the phrase "a Great Thought" as possibly pointing to a new category.

The assumption that even many "non-mystical", mythological or philosophical Upaniṣadic passages embody and represent various levels of higher realization,—metaphysical, divine, transcendental, whatever,—is closely connected with the acknowledgement, in sec. 1, of "meditation and (inner) spiritual life" that represents a third level of engagement with Ātman/Brahman over and beyond the levels of conventional regulated religious life and of foundational concepts and myths which are part of the general culture. For what else is inner spirtual life in this context than trying to "hear" these higher dimensions in oneself and "become" them? What else is it than trying to conduct (and actually conducting) one's life in such a way that these dimensions arise in oneself and that one finds that one becomes them more and more purely and fully? The old Upaniṣads, at least, cannot be read and assimilated without the enlargement of the inner man and the transformation of self that comes with such "meditation and inner spiritual life". The latter is essential, if you will, for their adequate "hermeneutics". Of the three levels distinguised in sec. 1 at which a person can promote knowledge of Ātman/Brahman in his/her life, we cannot today cultivate (1). But we can enter into (2) and (3), —most deeply of course into (3).

The higher core of a given teaching is generally only experienced and realized clearly in the course of what we have called "meditation and (inner) spiritual life". If one operates primarily at a level of conceptual understanding, feeling and reflection [i.e., level (2)], it is realized only to a small extent and with much distortion. By pointing to the metaphysical, divine, transcendental and so on core of a given text, there is an implication that the text should be approached in terms of meditation and spiritual life, or level (3), not only in terms of conceptual understanding, feeling and reflection, or level (2). In fact the very notion of realization of a metaphysical or other higher aspect, or of knowledge and stages at the level of such aspects, as something *sui generis* that is somehow more true, more permanent, or more real than ordinary knowledge or consciousness, is bound up with "meditation and spiritual life". It is only through the latter that, with the Grace of the Infinite, such knowledge arises and becomes steady in one and one can continue to the highest goal.

In other spiritual traditions the situation is similar. Embodied in each major text of a great tradition (the early Christian Fathers, the medieval Catholic Saints, the Sufi Saints, early Buddhism, Mahāyāna, Buddhism, or later Hindu traditions), there are various metaphysical, etc. aspects which are almost palpable in their presence, which are half consciously or consciously felt by all the followers of that tradition, and which can be felt even by outsiders. (This state of affairs is sometimes described by saying that "mysticism is the core of all the world's religions".) And in each tradition, these higher aspects are realized, and one merges into them with one's self and being, by "meditation and spiritual life". Thus, ranging through all these traditions, there is a common substance or continuum of knowledge, experience, and being—sometimes called the "Perennial Philosophy" or Universal religion—the deeper levels of which depend on "meditation and spiritual life". The terms "metaphysical", "divine", "Universal Divine", "transcendental", "rising above desire", and "Reality", which are used in this book to describe the various qualitatively different aspects and phases of the Upaniṣadic Realization, may also be used to circumscribe this whole Knowledge, Experience and Being of Perennial Philosophy. But one must be careful in making general statements. Higher Reality may express itself in individual experience and in culture in ever new ways and forms.

NOTES

1. There seems to be no detailed modern treatment of these matters.
2. A. Scharbau, *Die Idee der Schöpfung in der Vedischen Literatur*, Stuttgart: Kohlhammer, 1932, p. 168, note 166, says that "the depth and greatness

of the theological insight (*Erkenntnis*) of the *Ṛg Veda* lags by no means behind that of Vedānta". The overwhelming centrality of cosmology in the *Ṛg Veda* is well-known. "The *Ṛg Veda* is . . . a document of *sṛṣṭividyā* [knowledge of creation]. All Vedic scholars will admit that the problem of the *Ṛg Veda* is the problem of cosmology." V.S. Agrawala, The Traditional Approach to Vedic Interpretation. *Proc. 26th ICO* (1964), v. 3, pt. 1, Poona: Bhandarkar Oriental Research Institute, 1969, pp. 1-13; p. 1.

3. The basic Western scholarly discussion of the evolution of high level spiritual and mystical concepts in the Brāhmaṇas is still Deussen's *Geschichte*, v. 1, pt. 1, 1884. Deussen discusses Prajāpati (pp. 181-209), Brahman (including Brahmaṇaspati, *Brahma prathamajam*, and *Brahma svayambhū*) (pp. 240-264), Ātman, Puruṣa, and Prāṇa (p. 282-294), and a number of the mystical conceptions in the *Atharva Vedic* hymns (pp. 209-239, 264-282, 305-324). Scharbau (cf. preceding note) is suggestive but his interpretations tend to be coloured by theistic conceptions/experience.

4. There is apparently no detailed study of the theme of the "(Sense-) Powers" in the literature.

5. Keith, *ŚāṅkĀr*, p. xiii. E. Frauwallner, *History of Indian Philosophy*, v. 1. Delhi: Motilal Banarsidass, 1972 (1st Germ. ed., 1953), p. 68, says that *KauṣUp* III "can be counted on account of its large compass, and the boldness of its thought, among the most remarkable creations of the Vedic Period".

6. Keith, A.B., *Phil. of Veda*, v. 2, p. 537. Bakker, H., On the Origin of Sāṁkhya Psychology, *WZKSA*, v. 26 (1982), pp. 117-148; p. 144 ties the text to a set of *ślokas* in the *Mokṣadharma* in the *Mahābhārata* which is thought to contain an early formulation of Sāṁkhya principles.

7. The hymn occurs wholly or partially with or without variations in several other Vedic Saṁhitās and is referred to almost a dozen times in the Vedic post-Saṁhitā literature. For a survey, see N.J. Shende, The *Puruṣa-Sūkta* (*ṚV* 10.90) in the Vedic Literature. *Journal of the Univ. of Poona, Humanities Section*, v. 23 (1966), pp. 45-51. Substantive Western treatments include Geldner's notes on the hymn, in K. Geldner, *Der Ṛg Veda in Auswahl*, part 2, *Kommentar*. Stuttgart: Kohlhammer, 1909, pp. 187-189; W.N. Brown, The sources and nature of *puruṣa* in the *puruṣasūkta* (*Ṛg Veda* 10.91), *JAOS*, v. 51 (1931) pp. 108-118; A.K. Coomaraswamy, *A New Approach to the Vedas*. London: Luzac, 1933, pp. 69-75; M. Falk, *Nāma-Rūpa*, pp. 2-4; J. Gonda, Vedic Cosmogony and Viṣṇuite Bhakti, *ABORI*, 1974, pp. 85-111; pp. 93 ff.; V.S. Agrawala, *Vedic Lectures*. Varanasi: School of Vedic Studies, Banaras Hindu University (1963), pp. 164-189; the same author, *Puruṣa-Sūkta*, in G.T. Deshpande *et al.*, ed., *Dr. Mirashi Felicitation Volume*. Nagpur: Vidarbha Samshodhan Mandal, 1965, pp. 7-23. Traditional Indian commentaries are those of Sāyaṇa, Ranganatha Muni, and Sri Raghavendra Swami.

8. Transl. Edgerton, *Beginnings*, pp. 67-68. For explanations of individual phrases according to the traditional commentaries, see Geldner, *Ṛg Veda*, v. 3, pp. 286 ff.

9. Coomaraswamy, *op. cit.* (note 8), pp. 71-72, defends a traditional Indian interpretation according to which "ten fingers wide", *daśāṅgula*, refers to the heart (which in *Mahā-Nārāyaṇa Upaniṣad* is ten fingers breadth below the adam's apple). Cf. Geldner, *Ṛg Veda*, v. 3, pp. 286-387, note

1d, for references.

10. Gonda, *op. cit.* (note 8), p. 95.

11. Geldner, *Ṛg Veda*, v. 3, p. 287, notes. Agrawala calls her "the [unmanifest] Mother principle or universal infinite nature, also called *Mahat* and *Yoni*, the womb which receives the seed of creation from *Svayambhū* or the Self-existent Brahman [=the Ādi-Puruṣa]" (V.S. Agrawala, *op. cit.*, p. 169). J. Gonda, *Aspects of Early Viṣṇuism*. Delhi: Motilal Banarsidass, 1969 (repr. of 1st ed., 1954), pp. 67-68 and elsewhere in the book cites over a dozen passages on Virāj in the Vedic literature to illustrate "how much the ancient thinkers wrestled with the problem of defining this idea and giving it its place in a cosmological and philosophical system" (*ibid.*, p. 67). But in "Vedic Cosmogony . . ." (see note 8) he describes her as "the universe conceived of as a developing, expanding and creative whole . . . [Her] name literally means 'the One who expands mightly'" (*op cit.*, p. 96). The literal meaning of *virāj* in the *Ṛg Veda* is "ruling far and wide" (*vi* + root *rāj*, rule) (Grassmann, *Wörterbuch*; Gonda, *Aspects of Early Viṣṇuism*, p. 67).

12. So Panikkar: "This uncreated being [i.e., Virāj], whose ontological function is mediatorial in character, ascends and descends into every being and every activity. . ." (*Vedic Experience*, p. 74). More generally, Panikkar thinks that "the theology of *Virāj* might offer a fruitful point of encounter between the different notions of the first uncreated emanations . . . found in more than one religious tradition: *Śakti*, Logos, Wisdom, preexistent Christ, etc." (*ibid.*, p. 77, note 5).

13. "That Puruṣa is both the son and the progenitor of *Virāj* is not necessarily surprising: as the essence and source of all, Puruṣa must even be that out of which he rises in concrete form." W.N. Brown, *op. cit.*, p. 116, note 1. But I am not so sure that this is the explanation. The closest parallel in the *Ṛg Veda* cited by Brown is *Ṛg Veda* X.72.3-4."3. In the first age of the gods, *a-sat* ('Non-Being') was born from *sat* ('Being'). Thereafter the spaces (*āśā*) were born; from the *uttānápād* (literally "[the being] with soles turned up") again the *sat*. 4. Earth was born from the *uttānápād*. From Earth were born the spaces. Aditi was born from Dakṣa (and) from Dakṣa Aditi." (Aditi here is a female, Dakṣa a male creation principle.) (Translated after H. Falk, Die Kosmogonie von *ṚV* X.72. *WZKSA*, v. 38 (1994), pp. 1-22, pp. 6-13). A different example is *Ṛg Veda* I.95.4, on Agni: "Who of you has known this hidden one? The calf generated the mothers by its own judgement . . ."

14. In Epic-Purāṇic literature, v. 5 is continued in two lines of tradition: one in which Nārāyaṇa was born from Dharma, which in turn was born from (Ādi-) Nārāyaṇa (= Ādi-Puruṣa), and another called *Nara-Nāra-Nārāyaṇa*. In the first, "the first [= Ādi-Puruṣa] is the Father, [Virāj] is the mother, and [*Vairāja* Puruṣa, or the Puruṣa born from Virāj] is the son". According to the second tradition, "the father principle [= Ādi-Puruṣa] is called *Nara* ["man"], the mother principle Virāj is called *Nāra* which is the same as *Āpaḥ*, the [primeval] Waters, or Soma-Parameṣṭhī. The offspring produced by the union of these two universal parents is called Nārāyaṇa, who is the same as Sūrya [Sun], Hiraṇyagarbha [the golden germ], Manu, Agni, Indra, Prāṇa etc." (V.S. Agrawala, *Vedic Lectures*, *op. cit.*, pp. 170-171). The second line of development is represented first in the *Laws of*

Manu, e.g. I.10: "The waters are called *nārāḥ*, (for) the waters are indeed the offspring of Nara [= Ādi-Puruṣa]; as they were his first residence (*ayana*), he thence is named Nārāyaṇa" [Bühler, A., *The Laws of Manu*. Oxford: Clarendon Press, 1886 (*SBE*, v. 25); p. 5].

15. *Mudgala Upaniṣad* I.2-5. Cf. J. Gonda, Mudgalopaniṣad, *WZKSA*, v. (1978) (E. Frauwallner Commemoration volume), pp. 102-113, p. 107. Gonda cites parallels to the identifications with Aniruddha in the Mahābhārata and in the *Ahirbudhnya Saṁhitā*, a Pañcarātra work (*ibid.*, p. 110, note 1.4). See also J. Gonda, On Viṣṇu's Name Aniruddha, *Studies*, v. 4, pp. 42-50; pp. 42-43.
16. Gonda, Mudgalopaniṣad, *op. cit.*, p. 107.
17. W.N. Brown, *op. cit.*, pp. 110-112.
18. *Ibid.*, pp. 113-114.
19. Sri Sathya Sai Baba, quoted by E.B. Fanibunda, *Vision of the Divine*. Prashanthi Nilayam: Sri Sathya Sai Books and Publications Trust, 1984 (1st ed., 1976), p. 29.
20. It is found in various forms and in varying degrees of directness in Neoplatonism, in the Kabbalah and Hasidism, and even in Medieval Christian Philosophy.
21. Mukhopadhyaya, *Studies*, p. 51.
22. *Yasmājjātā na parā, Mahā-NārUp* XII.6A, a much abbreviated version of *TaittBr* III.7.9. See Swami Vimalānanda, *Mahā-NārUp*, p. 133.
23. Mukhopadhyaya, *Studies*, p. 72.
24. Modern treatments: v. Buitenen, Studies in Sāṁkhya (II), *JAOS*, v. 77 (1950), pp. 15-25; pp. 17-21; repr. *Studies*, pp. 53-73. I. Kesarcodi-Watson, *Studies in Hindu Wisdom*. New Delhi: Allied Publishers, 1981, pp. 76-79 defends *BṛhUp* I.4.1-5 against the view of B. Kumarappa that the "crude anthropomorphism where the Prime Being is conceived of on the analogy of animal reproduction stamps the theory [in vs. 1-5] as one of the oldest [and thus most primitve] preserved for us in the Upaniṣads" (*ibid.*, p. 78). For a traditional Indian treatment, see Swami Maheshananda Giri, Introduction, in Shastri, *UpBhāṣyam*, v. 3, pp. 8-14.
25. Śaṁkara, Commentary on *Bṛhadāraṇyaka Upaniṣad*, Introduction to the *Yājñavalkyakāṇḍa*.
26. Swami Krishnananda, *The Bṛhadāraṇyaka Upaniṣad. An Interpretive Exposition*. Shivanandanagar (Rishikesh): Divine Life Society, 1984, p. 143.
27. The section is "of deep significance" (*Sixty Ups.*, p. 409); it contains "the most original and significant creation myth of the Upaniṣads . . .," *Phil. Ups*, p. 188.
28. (a) Böhtlingk (*BṛhUp*, p. 9) and v. Buitenen (*op. cit.* p. 17) translate "I am here," Hume simply "I am." (b) Alternatively: "Thereupon It (the Self) obtained the name of I" (so Böhtlingk). (c) *tām samabhavat*. (d) *tataḥ sṛṣṭir abhavat*; so also Hume. Alternatively: "Then (or therefore) He (or It, the Ātman) became the creation" (so both Böhtlingk and Radhakrishnan). (e) lit. *ekaikena*, so "via, through, by the device of one or the other". (f) *antaratara*, "more interior, closer".
29. Deussen, *Geschichte*, v. 1.2, p. 170 (*Phil. Ups*, p. 158).
30. Van Buitenen interprets the Self's first utterance as "creative" "crying out", and "self-formulation". This is a "condition of creation", and he

goes on to discuss "creation-by-naming" (*op. cit.*, p. 17-18). The treatment here is instead in terms of the transcendental aspect. Connotations of *Vāc*, "Speech" (similar to the Logos), and of "creation by naming" may well be intended.

31. Gonda, *op. cit.* (note 7), p. 100; also J. Gonda, *Prajāpati's Relations with Brahman, Bṛhaspati and Brahmā.* Amsterdam: North Holland, 1989 (*VKNAWL, NR*, No. 138), p. 63.

32. Śaṁkara takes the incompleteness ("fear" and "yearning") in vs. 2 and 3 as indicating that the "state" envisaged in vs. 1-5 is that of Prajāpati, the Creative Divinity, since it is still to some extent bound ("with a worldly tendency") and not the Ātman. Further, because these things happen to Prajāpati, who is the material cause of the Universe, they happen also to his effects, viz. the living creatures today.

33. Cf. *BṛhUp* I.3.7, *ChāndUp* VI.3.2, *TaittUp* II.6, and *AitUp* I.3.12. This feature is found already in some of the Brāhmaṇa creation accounts and in *Ṛg Veda* X.121. Deussen feels that the present text shows that it is "merely a metaphor designed to render intelligible the assumed identity of the soul [=*ātman*] with the first principle of the universe" (*Phil. Ups*, p. 171).

34. *Sayings of Sri Ramakrishna.* Mylapore, Madras: Sri Ramakrishna Math, 10th ed., 1965, p. 315.

35. It is generally taken as the chief defining characteristic of consciousness. "Consciousness (*Bewusstsein*) is the uniform connectivity (*Zusammenhang*) of psychic events in an individual (individual consciousness, *Individualbewusstsein*) or in a social community (collective consciousness, *Kollektivbewusstsein*, or general consciousness, *Gesamtbewusstsein*) . . . 'A consciousness'is the continuous proceeding (*Ablauf*) of experiences centered around an I." Eisler, R., *Wörterbuch der philosophischen Begriffe*, 4th ed., v. 1. Berlin: E.S. Mittler and Sohn, 1927, pp. 207 and 208. In this connection it is significant that Eisler in the same paragraph defines "knowledge of something" (*Gewusstsein, Wissen von etwas*) as "consciousness in the narrowest sense of the term". (The other two senses are consciousness as "experience with attention" (*aufmerksames Erlebnis*), and "consciousness in the most general sense of the term", as that is commonly understood). Since Eliser is trying to summarize the understanding of "consciousness" in Western Tradition, this suggests that the more "timeless" elements of conscious experience, which are essential ingredients in the Indian *jñāna* or wisdom, are not foreign to Western Tradition either.

36. From the point of view of chr. 6.14 below, an intuitive feeling that one can in principle understand all things that are in any way meaningful in the Universe is an expression of the soul's embryonic awareness that she is omniscient.

37. The concept of the "great sayings" is found in Sureśvara, a disciple of Śaṁkara's, in his subcommentary on Śaṁkara's commentary on *Bṛhadāraṇyaka Upaniṣad*. Sureśvara discusses whether hearing the *mahāvākyas* is necessary for and can bring about direct knowledge of Brahman (under *BṛhUp* IV.4.21-22 and *BṛhUp* I.4.7).

38. The reference is to *Ṛg Veda* IV.26.1:
   I was Manu and the Sun (Sūrya),

I am Kakṣīvat, the inspired Seer,
I forced Kutsa, the Son of Arjuna,
I am the Poet-sage Uśanā. Look at me!

According to the *Anukramaṇi*, the seer of the hymn is Vāmadeva, and in vs. 1-3 either Vāmadeva identifies himself with Indra, or Indra is presented as praising himself. In either case (more so in the first) the mantra is based on some kind of knowledge and realization of Vāmadeva's. *Ṛg Veda* IV.26 is closely connected with or continued in *Ṛg Veda* IV.27, which contains a second powerful memory/realization of Vāmadeva's. The fact that the Upaniṣad cites Vāmadeva as an example suggests that it regards itself as carrying on a tradition of realization among Brahmins that goes back to Vedic times. This in turn justifies regarding the text as teaching realization.

39. The whole idea that empirical things are to be understood in terms of "models" whose elements may be completely unrelated in meaning to the thing modelled but which nevertheless have their own appeal as cognitive tools is inspired by and historically first exemplified in physics. There a model is first a representation and analysis of a concrete phenomenon (like planetary motion) in terms of appropriate quantities and conceptions (trajectory, force, energy, potential and so on). In the 19th century this then led to things like the heat equation and electromagnetic fields (Maxwell's equations) being "models", and the now universal practice of modelling complex physical situations by simplified "models" involving simplified geometry and physical assumptions.

40. So in Swami Nikhilananda, *The Upaniṣads*, v. 3, *Aitareya and Bṛhadāraṇyaka*. New York: Harper and Brother, 1956, pp. 130-131.

41. E.g. M. Falk calls it "the habit of representing the soterical process as an inversion of the cosmogonic evolution" (M. Falk, *Nāma-rūpa*, p. 36).

42. Cf. for example the teachings on the three *vyāhṛtis* or "hidden utterances", *bhūr, bhuvaḥ, svāḥ*, or the cosmic roles played by the Vedic meters in the Brāhmaṇa literature. Another kind of example is the theme in *Aitareya Āraṇyaka* that the *Uktha* (a set of *Ṛg Vedic* stanzas recited at soma sacrifices) is the Universal Prāṇa.

43. E.g. in the "theory of Forms" and in the conception of *anamnesis* (cf. chr. 6.14). The Platonic Forms or *ideas* are often divine prototypes, or aspects or principles which may be directly apprehended in inner experience when one becomes truly devoted to them. See P. Friedlander, *Plato*, v. 1. New York: Pantheon (Bollingen Series, v. 59.1), 1958; pp. 15 ff., and particularly the "digression" pp. 20-21.

44. It is also common in modern philosophy. For example most of the approaches to the mind-body problem in analytic philosophy since the 1950s surveyed by T. Metzinger, Kriterien für eine Theorie zur Lösung des Leib-Seele-Problems. *Erkenntnis*, v. 32 (1990), pp. 127-145 are reductionist.

45. M. Stöckler in his entry *Reduktionismus* in J. Ritter and K. Gründer (eds.), *Historisches Wörterbuch der Philosophie*, v. 8, Basel: Schwabe, 1992 distinguishes reduction of values to imperatives, and to social and similar factors. It is of interest that reductionism in this sense and in the sense of the preceding note is a new concept that only came into general use in the middle of this century (Stöckler, *op. cit.*, p. 378).

46. *Vāc*, "Speech," like the Word in St. John's prologue, generates the world.
47. I.e., referring to both form and content of a metaphysical or divine or transcendental orientation which is presupposed in the great civilizations other than the modern West (including the religions and philosophies which shaped them, their arts, etc.). The term is a rallying point for a group of modern scholars [Rene Guénon (1886-1951), Ananda K. Coomaraswamy (1877-1947), Fritjof Schuon (1907-)] who have been trying to revive universal traditional wisdom (*sophia perennis, sanātana dharma, al-hikmat al khalidah*) and doctrines in the West. "Tradition . . .means truths or principles of origin, . . . , along with all the ramifications and applications of these principles in different realms, including law and social structure, art symbolism, the sciences, and embracing of course [also] Supreme Knowledge along with means for its attainment." S.H. Nasr, *Knowledge and the Sacred*. New York: Crossroad, 1981 (The Gifford Lectures, 1981), pp. 67-78. Nasr discusses the term on pp. 65-72 and ff.
48. Cf. Coormaraswamy, *Papers*, pp. 192-197, and 236-240. At a more general level, cf. Nasr in the context of *scientia sacra*, the traditional version of what in a secular context is called knowledge: "The Logos or *buddhi* or *aq'l*, as the Intellect is called in various traditions, is the luminous center which is the generating agent of the world—for it was by the Word that all things were made—of man, and of religion. It is God's knowledge of Himself and [is] the first in his Creation." (Nasr, *op. cit.*, p. 147).
49. Transl. and philological discussion: O. Böhtlingk, Drei kritisch gesichtete und übersetzte Upanishad mit erklärenden Anmerkungen. *Berichte über die Verhandlungen der könglich sächsischen Gesellschaft der Wissenschaften Leipzig*, v. 42, pp. 127-197; Keith, *AitĀr*, pp. 226-267; text, pp. 118-124; in French: L. Silburn, ed. & transl., *Aitareya Upaniṣad*. Paris: Adrien-Maisonneuve, 1950 (Les Upanishad No. 10), *n.v.* Modern scholarship: U. Schneider, Die Komposition der *Aitareya-Upaniṣad. IIJ*, v. 7 (963), pp. 58-69. Classical commentaries include Śaṁkara's *bhāṣya* (transl. Gambhīrānanda, *Eight Ups.*, v. 2. pp. 1-75), Ānandagiri's (ca. 1200 CE) subcommentary (*ṭīkā*) thereon, Sāyaṇa's (ca. 1350 CE) commentary, part of his commentary on the whole of *Aitareya Āraṇyaka*, and Ṣaḍguruśiṣya's commentary (ca 1100 CE).
50. *AitUp* I-III = *AitĀr* II.4-6.
51. Modern treatment: J. Brereton, The Upaniṣads, in W.T. de Bary and I. Bloom, eds., *Approaches to the Asian Classics*. New York: Columbia Univ. Press, 1990, pp. 115-135; pp. 120-122.
52. (a) The root *tap-* means "glow, heat up". Keith, following Müller, translates "He brooded over Him".
53. Deussen (*Sixty Ups.*, p. 14) see this as very different from the Puruṣa Hymn, because "in the Upaniṣad, the *Ur*-man (primeval man) is a being dependent on the Ātman, which the Ātman brings forth out of the primeval (*Ur-*) waters created by it, forms, and hatches." Our treatment minimizes the difference.
54. (a) *abhisṛṣṭam*, "being attacked". Cf. Schneider, *op. cit.*, p. 59, note 1. (b) Ewing, The Hindu Conception of the Functions of Breath, *JAOS*, v. 22 (1901), pp. 249-308; p. 276 suggests that the *apāna* vital air here refers

to the vital air involved in digestion and evacuation.

55. The analysis is as much an analysis of what it is to obtain something as it is one of food. It is also not clear to me whether the point which the text wants to make is about digestion or about *apāna* or an esoteric point about Vāyu to be understood by yoga. Vāyu is the deity presiding over the vital airs.

56 (a) *idam*, the entire creation described, or the way of obtaining food by digestion. (b) lit., "drop down".

57. Transl. F. Max Müller, *The Upanishads*, v. 1. Oxford: Clarendon, 1900 (*SBE*, v 1), p. 200.

58. *UpVahini*, p. 60.

59. *Ibid.*, p. 65.

60. So Radhakrishnan, *Principal Ups.*, p. 520. Keith discusses this passage in a long note (*AitĀr*, p. 231, note 11).

61. So Müller, Deussen, and Keith (*ibid.*, p. 231, note 11).

62. Commentary on *AitUp* I.3.12; transl. Swami Gambhīrānanda, *Eight Ups.*, pp. 41-42.

63. MW Dictionary.

64. The verse occurs about a dozen times in the Vedic literature, see Whitney, *Atharva Veda*, v. 2, p. 143. Modern treatments of the whole (7 verse) hymn: A. Weber, *Indische Studien*, v. 18, pp. 2 ff., *n.v.*; Deussen, *Geschichte*, v. I.1, pp. 225-226.

65. Transl. Whitney, *ibid.*, p. 143. The problematic *sīmatás*, here analysed as *sīma* + *tas*, is discussed in detail by M.A. Mehendale, *Nirukta Notes*, Series I. Poona: Postgraduate Research Institute, 1965 (Deccan College Building Centenary and Silver Jubilee Series no. 24), pp. 47-49.

66. "'The Brahman first born in front;' the Brahman doubtless is yonder Sun, and he is born day by day in front (in the east);—'from he summit he, the longing [one], overspread the shining'; the summit doubtless is the middle, the shining ones are these worlds and the longing [one] is yonder Sun...." Transl. Eggeling, *ŚatBr*, v. 3, p. 366.

67. According to *Śatapatha Brāhmaṇa*, the mantra is used at the very beginning of the building of the fire altar (*agnicayana*). The sacrificer lays down a lotus leaf where the centre of the altar will be built (*ŚatBr* VII.4.7), symbolic of a womb for the Agni (the fire altar, regarded as the deity) that is to be born there, and then places on it a golden plate representing the Sun. The mantra is uttered while putting down the plate (VII.4.14). At *TaittSaṁh* IV.2.8.2 and *Sāma Veda* I.4.3.9, however, the *Śatapatha Brāhmaṇa* reading fits less well.

68. This "experiential line" of interpretation is already found in Deussen, *Geschichte*, v. 1.1, p. 255, who talks about a direct revelation to the Seer, and argues explicitly that several expressions in the later verses all refer to the Sage.

69. M. Falk, Il mito psicologico nell'India antica. *Atti della R. Accademia Nazionale dei Lincei*, Mem. della Cl. Science morali, storiche e filologiche, Ser. VI, vol. 8 (1938-39), pp. 289-738; pp. 337-338, interprets *Atharva Veda* IV.1.1-2 specifically as experience involving the *sahasrāra cakra* and the *brahma-randhra*.

70. *budhnyāḥ* = "relating to the bottom", *budhna*, so "deepest, deepest level [things]"; *upamāḥ*, from *mā*, to measure out, fashion, so "fashioned close

to", "nearest"; and *viṣṭhāḥ*, = "[things, aspects] standing (root. *sthā*) apart or distinct (*vi*)", so "shapes, forms".

71. Such perception is alluded to by Sri Sathya Sai Baba.
72. I am not familiar with a modern treatment of this text or a reliable discussion of the yoga which it describes.
73. Deussen (*Sixty Ups.*, v. 1, pp. 225-226) regards the text as a counterpart to the description in *AitUp* I.3.12, historically in a "middle or transitional position" between *ChāndUp* VIII.6.6 and *MaitrUp* VI.21.
74. See J. Gonda, The meaning of Skt. *nānd-*, *Acta Orientalia* (Leiden), v. 21, 1953, pp. 81-90 (repr. in Gonda, *Studies*, v. 2, pp. 312-321); and Gispert-Sauch, *Bliss*, pp. 147-158.
75. Gispert-Sauch translates the Sāma Vedic version, *Sāma Veda* (*Kauthuma*) 2.5.2.86 in *Bliss*, pp. 156-157.
76. Śaṁkara, Commentary of *AitUp* I.2.12.
77. "The Paramātmā [= Supreme Self], who is limited as *jīva-ātmā* [= the self of the living being], has three areas of recreation: The eye, the throat and the heart. The eyes shine with a special splendour when the realization of Brahman is achieved or even attempted. This is an evident fact." Sri Sathya Sai Baba, *UpVahini*, Indian ed., p. 69.
78. Sri Sathya Sai Baba, *ibid.*, p. 69.
79. Another is *AitĀr* II.1.7, discussed in chr. 4 below.
80. Translations and discussions: Griffith, *VājSaṁh*, pp. 290-292; Deussen, *Geschichte*, v.1 (= part I, 1), pp. 291-294; *Sixty Ups.*, pp. 897-900.
81. Transl. Griffith, *VājSaṁh*. The classical commentaries are by Uvaṭa (dated before Skandasvāmin, who fl. 600 CE) and by Mahīdhara (ca 1550 CE), with Uvaṭa giving much simpler explanations. The edition I used is Jagdishlal Shastri, ed., *Vājasaneyī Mādhyandhina Śukla-Yajur Veda-Saṁhitā, with mantra-bhāṣya of Uvaṭa and Vedadīpa-bhāṣya of Mahīdhara*. Delhi: Motilal Banarsidass, 1971.
82. Gonda, *Vedic Literature*, p. 328.
83. Translations and discussions: Griffith, *VājSaṁh*, pp. 288-289; Deussen, *Geschichte*, v. 1 (=part I, 1), pp. 288-291; *Sixty Ups.*, pp. 895-896. The *Taittirīya Āraṇyaka* version is given by Swami Vimalānanda in *Mahā-NārUp*, pp. 16-20. See also A. Weber, Analyse der in Antequil du Perron's Übersetzung enthaltenen Upanishaden (Fortsetzung), *Indische Studien* v. 2. Berlin: F. Dummler, 1853, pp. 81-84.
84. (a) *mahāntam*, literally "the great limit". (b) *vijayate*, both "is born" and as a quasi-stative reflexive, "generates himself". (c) the literal meaning of *purohita* (so Uvaṭa); usually it means a king's personal priest. (d) *brāhmaye*, an unclear form, explained by Uvaṭa as "descendant of the Brahman Puruṣa". (e) *rucam brāhmaṁ janayanto devāś*; perhaps also a reference to the Sun (Griffith).
85. *Sarva tyāgena pariharanti* (Uvaṭa on v. 19).
86. (a) *pari+grabh-*. (b) *mahad-yaśa*. (c) *pradiś*. (d) *eka-nīḍa*. (e) *saṁ ca vi ca*. This half line is quoted with *iti*—a kind of *upaniṣad*. (f) *vi-bhū*. (g) *airayanta*, caused themselves to rise. (h) *parītya*, having gone (walked, *itya*) around (*pari*). (i) *prathamajāmṛtasya*. (j) *ātmanātmānam abhi saṁviveśa*. (k) *tad apaśyat, tad abruvat, tad āsit*.
87. Cf. Deussen, *Geschichte*, part I, 1, p. 255. Deussen treats *Atharva Veda* II.1, *ibid.*, pp. 253-255.
88. *VājSaṁh* XXX-XXXI, *ŚatBr* XIII.6.

89. *VājSaṁh* XXXII, *ŚatBr* XIII.7.1.

90. In the *puruṣa-medha*, a large number of representative victims (158 + 26) are "seized", bound to stakes, and then released (see Eggeling, *ŚatBr*, v. 5, pp. 407-408). E.g. "For the priesthood he seizes a Brahmin, for the Brahmin is the priesthood; he thus joins priesthood to priesthood" and so on down a long list of mostly "personifications of activity, positions in life, or mental traits and dispositions" with which the representative victim is characteristically endowed (*ŚatBr* XIII.6.2.10, transl. Enggeling, *op. cit.*, p. 409, and A. Weber, Über Menschenopfer bei den Indern der vedischen Zeit, *Indische Streifen*, v. 1, Osnabrück: Biblio Verlag, 1983 (1st ed., 1868), pp. 54-89; p. 75). The Brahman priest supervising the sacrifice then recites the sixteen verse Puruṣa Hymn over the assembled victims—"thus (he does) for the obtainment and securing of everything, for everything here [in this world] consists of sixteen parts, and the *puruṣa-medha* is everything" (*ŚatBr* XIII.6.12, transl. Eggeling, *ibid.*, p. 410). If the sacrifice is performed by a Brahmin, "he should bestow all his property. . . And having taken up the two fires within himself [ritually, by breathing their smoke], and worshipped the Sun with the *Uttara Nārāyaṇa*, let him betake himself to the forest without looking around" and live there as a hermit (*ŚatBr* XIII.6.2.19-20, Eggeling, *ibid.*, p. 412). But he may continue to live in the village if he wishes (*ibid.*). The *sarva-medha* seems even more fantastic.

91. There is agreement that no actual human sacrifice took place in the Brāhmaṇa period (see Eggeling, *op. cit.*, pp. xxiii-xlv), and that "it is impossible to recognize the Puruṣa-medha as a genuine member of the sacrificial system" *(ibid.*, p. xlv). That does not prevent anthropologists and others from thinking that the Brāhmaṇa *puruṣa-medha* preserves memories of an actual archaic practice. It may be assumed that great hymns like the *Uttara Nārāyaṇa* and *Tad-eva* came first and set very high level religious goals. The presentations of the *puruṣa-medha* and *sarva-medha* in the Brāhmaṇas may then be understood as visualizations or tentative sketches of what the new goal and the path to it might mean in terms of the world-view of a deep ritualist. This can be supported textually, because in places the Brāhmaṇa reads like a meditation.

92. *ŚatBr* XIII.6.1.1; transl. Eggeling, *ibid.*, p. 407.

93. *ŚatBr* XIII.7.1.1; transl. Eggeling, *ibid.*, pp. 417-418.

94. E.g. *ŚatBr* XIII.7.1.14, "he who, knowing this, performs the *sarvamedha*, or who even knows this, overpasses all beings here" (transl. Eggeling, *ibid.*, p. 421).

95. It would be difficult to name a phenomenon of comparable magnitude and depth in another religion.

96. On this sacrificial theory, see Eggeling, *ŚatBr*, v. 4, pp. xvi ff. In the Puruṣa Hymn, the three seasons spring, summer, and autumn are the parts of the Puruṣa which form the ghee, the offering-fuel, and the oblation resp. In the Brāhmaṇas, "Prajāpati is the year," and it is He that is offered in the sacrifice.

97. *Ibid.*, pp. xvi-xvii. He does so "either in the sense that the oblation is sent up to the gods to prepare the way for the Sacrificer,. . . or . . . that along with the burnt-offering the human body of the Sacrificer is mystically consumed, and a new, divine body prepared to serve him in the celestial

abodes. Intimately connected with this notion we find another, introduced rather vaguely, which makes the sacrifice a mystic union in which the Sacrificer generates from out of the *vedi*, cr altarground, his future divine self". Eggeling, *ibid.*, p. xvii.

98. For a 3 page summary of the *agnicayana* see Gispert Sauch, *Bliss*, pp. 33 ff.

99. Here a survey would be helpful.

100. Gonda, J., *Prajāpati's Relations with Brahman, Bṛhaspati and Brahmā, VKNAWL, NR*, no. 138, p. 62.

101. *Ibid.*, pp. 65-66. These "deities and divine concepts" also include Viśvakarman and Vāyu, Svayambhū, Bṛhaspati and the Brahman priest, all discussed by Gonda in relation to Prājapati in the monograph.

102. J. Gonda, *Prajāpati's Rise to Higher Rank.* Leiden: E.J. Brill, 1986, pp. 1-2.

103. Some of this is dealt with in modern scholarship under the heading "correlations", "correspondences", and "triads", tetrads", "pentads" etc. But there seems to be little systematic investigation of sets of Deities, sets of Powers, and sets of pairings of Powers and Deities across the Vedic literature.

104. One explanation might be Coomaraswamy's general thesis that from the *Ṛg Veda* onward, the Vedic literature is imbued by a "traditional psychology" to the effect that "our human self is an association (*sambhūtiḥ*) of breaths or spirations (*prāṇāḥ*)", including what we have been calling "Powers" (Coomaraswamy, On the Indian or Traditional Psychology, or rather Pneumatology, *Papers*, v. 2, pp. 333-378; p. 336). These "Intelligences which are the constituents of our psychic personality . . . are called by many other names; we shall consider them accordingly as 'Breaths' (*prāṇāḥ*), 'Glories' (*śriyaḥ*), 'Fires' (*agnayaḥ*), Faculties (*indriyāṇi*), Seers or Prophets (*ṛṣayaḥ*), 'Storms' or 'Gales' (*marutaḥ*), and as Gods or Angels (*devāḥ, devatāḥ*)" (*ibid.*, pp. 344 ff.). All these Intelligences are as in *BṛhUp* I.4 and *AitUp* I, etc. animated by a single "inner person", equivalent to the Upaniṣadic Ātman.

105. Cf. Ramana Maharshi: "The *Puruṣa Sūkta* says that the Self is in the heart." (A. Osborne, ed., *The Teachings of Sri Ramana Maharshi in his Own Words*. London: Rider, 1962, p. 154.)

106. Cf. S. Jaiswal, *The Origins and Development of Vaiṣṇavism from 200 BC to AD 500*. New Delhi: Munshiram Manoharlal, 2nd ed., 1981, p. 32. For example Lord Kṛṣṇa in the *Gītā* speaks as Nārāyaṇa (*Gītā* XI), and the invocations at the beginning of every book of the Mahābhārata invoke Nara-Nārāyaṇa. See also R.C. Bhandarkar, *Vaiṣṇavism, Śaivism, and Minor Religious Systems*. Varanasi: Indological Book House, 1965 (1st ed., Encyclopedia of Indo-Aryan Research, A. Bühler, ed., v. 3, fasc. 6, 1913), chrs. III and VII, who argues only on the basis of standard sources and is still worth reading.

107. This is virtually universally assumed (e.g. Bhandarkar, *op. cit.*, p. 31; Jaiswal, *op. cit.*, pp. 30-31, 37). But *Puruṣa Nārāyaṇa* may simply mean "*puruṣa* son of man (*nara*)" (Prof. Hock).

108. For a survey of modern theories on the origins and development of Nārāyaṇa worship, see Jaiswal, *op. cit.*, pp. 32-52.

109. E.g. Stephen Bar Sudaili, and Abul Hasan al Kirkhani.

110. Cf. H. Krick: ". . .The old concept of the cosmic Puruṣa/Prajāpati . . . was integrated into the new theistic systems of Śaivism and Viṣṇuism and in general has remained fundamental in Hinduism." H. Krick, Nārāyaṇabali und Opfertod, *WZKSA*, v. 21 (1977), pp. 71-142; p. 92.
111. Cf. J. Gonda, The Mudgalopaniṣad (*op. cit.* note 15 above), pp. 102-104; Vedic Cosmogony . . .(*op. cit.* note 7 above), pp. 101 ff.; H. Krick, *op. cit.*, pp. 91 ff.; S. Jaiswal, *op. cit.*, pp. 36 ff.
112. Cf. Krick, *op. cit.*, p. 91; Gonda, The Mugdalopaniṣad, *op. cit.*, pp. 101 ff.
113. Gonda, Vedic Cosmogony . . ., *op. cit.*, p. 96, and elsewhere.
114. Transl. Swami Vimalānanda, *Mahā-NārUp*, pp. 155-160.
115. Cf. *Gītā* XI.
116. Noted by Gonda, *op. cit.*, pp. 106 ff.
117. Transl. F. Edgerton, *The Bhagavad Gītā*, v. 1, Cambridge, Mass: Harvard Univ. Press, 1944 (*HOS*, no. 38), p. 85.
118. D.D. Kosambi, The Avatāra Syncretism and Possible Sources for the Bhagavad Gītā, *Journal of the Bombay Branch of the Royal Asiatic Society*, vols. 24-25 (1948-49), pp. 121-134, suggests that Arjuna's vision in *Bhagavad Gītā* XI echoes *Mahābhārata* III.186-187, Mārkaṇḍeya's vision of Nārāyaṇa, The verses in which Nārāyaṇa describes Himself (*Mahābhārata* III.187.1-34 *et passim*), one of the important self-descriptions of Nārāyaṇa in the epic, have as one of their sources the Puruṣa Hymn (Kosambi, *ibid.*, p. 125). E.g., *Mahābhārata* III.187.13 rephrases *Puruṣa Sūkta* 11-12, etc.
119. Gonda, *op. cit.*, pp. 108, 110 mentions the Viṣṇu *bali* ritual of *Vaikhānasa Smārta Sūtra* X.9-10 (4th century CE), Mudgala Upaniṣad, the Mandasore inscription (404 CE), and others.
120. D.M. Srinivasan, Vedic Rudra-Śiva. *JAOS*, v. 103 (1983), pp. 543-556. For a larger picture see M. Chakravarti, *The Concept of Rudra-Śiva through the Ages*. Delhi: Motilal Banarsidass, 1986, Chr. I.
121. On Rudra in the *Ṛg Veda*, see Chakravarti, *op. cit.*, pp. 1-6.
122. Gonda, The *Śatarudriya*. In M. Nagatomi, B.K. Matilal, J.M. Masson, and E. Dimock (eds.), *Sanskrit and Indian Studies*. Essays in Honor of Daniel H.H. Ingalls. Dordrecht, Holland: D. Reidel, 1980, pp. 75-91; p. 82.
123. Transl. Griffith, *VājSaṁh*, pp. 154-161; Eggeling, *ŚatBr*, v. 4, pp. 150-155.
124. H. Nakamura, *History*, v. 1, chapters IV and V (pp. 129-294). A case might be made that the Vedāntic teaching that first attracted the Buddhists' attention was the "*Īśvara*-doctrine," or the doctrine that the universe and all human experiences is directly derived from *Īśvara*, God. E.g. chrs. 6 and 7 of the *Yogācāra-bhūmi-śāstra*, attributed to Maitreyanātha (270-350 CE), deals with the *īśvara-ādikāraṇa-vādins* or "those who regard God, etc., as the world-cause" (Nakamura, *History*, v. 1, p. 180). Nakamura interprets the passage as criticizing "the theory which asserts that everything in the world is produced by 'Īśvara' (= presiding deity) or puruṣa" (*ibid.*, p. 180). But it is not clear to what extent the text implies a reference to the Vedic-Upaniṣadic idea of Puruṣa.
125. Nakamura, *op. cit.*, pp. 182-217.
126. The *Mādhyamaka-hṛdaya-kārikā* comes with a gloss (*vṛtti*), also by Bhavya, called *Tarkajvālā*, which is available only in Tibetan translations. For the

first 16 verses of the *Kārikā* (which give the Vedāntic position), along with Bhavya's gloss, see V.V. Gokhale, The Vedānta-Philosophy described by Bhavya in his *Mādhyamakahṛdaya, IIJ,* v. 2 (1958), pp. 165-180. The remainder of the 96 Kārikās (which contain Bhavya's rebuttal) (Skt. plus Tibetan transl.) is edited in Nakamura, *op. cit.*, pp. 186-206.

127. Vs. 4-6 as in Gokhale, *op. cit.* above.
128. *History*, p. 206.
129. *Ibid.*, pp. 208 ff.
130. Nakamura, *History*, v. 1, pp. 221-257.
131. *Tattvasaṁgraha* 15304; transl. Nakamura, *ibid.*, p. 230. Kamalaśīla in his commentary cites *Puruṣa Sūkta* 2 and notes that among various schools of Veda-vādins, the Puruṣa-vādins think that there are no other causes and that Puruṣa is the cause of everything in every sense.
132. Based on conversations with G.D. Flood in connection with his paper Ritual, Cosmos and the Divine Body in the *Jayākhyasaṁhitā,* presented at the VIIIth World Sanskrit Conference, Vienna, 1990 (see *Abstracts* [of Papers], Vienna: Institut für Indologie, 1990).
133. Based on discussions with G.D. Flood and B. Bäumer.
134. Translations: Keith, *ŚāṅkhĀr*, pp. 16-41, with useful notes; Frenz, A., *Kauṣītaki Upaniṣad. IIJ,* v. 11 (1968-69), pp. 79-129 (a new critical edition, with German translation).
135. *KauṣUp* I-IV = *ŚāṅkhĀr* III-VI. The Brāhmaṇa has been translated by Keith, *Ṛg Veda Brs.*, pp. 345-530.
136. Cf. A.B. Keith, The *Śāṅkhāyana Āraṇyaka. JRAS,* 1908, pp. 363-88; p. 384.
137. Translations: Müller, *Upanishads*, v. 1, pp. 218-219; Keith, *AitĀr*, p. 214.
138. Transl. Keith, *AitĀr*, p. 214. (a) *tvām eva jānīyām.* (b) *etena rūpeṇa sarvā diśo viṣṭho'smi*
139. Transl. Keith, *ŚāṅkhĀr.*, p. 21. The text is discussed by H. Bakker, *op. cit.* (note 6 above), pp. 117-148; pp. 121-122.
140. (a) *goptṛ*, something that "preserves or protects or defends or cherishes," MW Dictionary; (c) *saṁ-śrāvayitṛ*, something that causes (*-ay-*) hearing (*saṁ-śru*).
141. I don't know of any modern discussion of this text.
142. It is not clear whether *KauṣUp* II.1 is ascribed to Sarvajit Kauṣītaki, or to Kahola Kauṣītaki, but the general point is still valid. The saying is the life-wisdom of a man who lives a life wholly dedicated to Brāhmaṇical values and ritual.
143. A point make by Sri Sathya Sai Baba, *Sutra Vahini*, Prasanthi Nilayam: Sri Sathya Sai Books and Publications Trust (1981?), p. 64.
144. Modern discussions or comments: E. Frauwallner, *History of Indian Philosophy, op. cit.*, pp. 62-68; H. Zimmermann, Vor-sāṁkhyistisches and proto-sāṁkhyistisches in alten Upaniṣaden. *Asiatische Studien* v. 35(2) (1981), pp. 201-219; p. 211; H. Bakker, *op. cit.* (note 6 above), pp. 117-148; pp. 128-136. Zimmerman discusses *KauṣUp* III.7 as an example of a "pre-Sāṁkhya" "philosophical schema" foreshadowing but in details still "far away" from the system of 24 + 1 classical Sāṁkhya categories. Bakker sees in it a "psychology", a "theory of the psychic complex" in which "a principle of thought (*prajñātman*) underlies all psychic phe-

nomena and outward appearances related to these" and "is the transcendental subject of all acts of consciousness (*prajñā*)" (Bakker, *op. cit.*, pp. 128, 135-136). The standard traditional treatment is *BraSū* I.28-31.

145. Pratardana is mentioned several times in the Vedic literature. Cf. Macdonell-Keith, *Index*, v. 2, pp. 29-30.

146. (a) Read throughout as "the self of higher knowledge and consciousness"; (b) Following the text of the Ānandāśrama Series; (c) which by III.2.1 is indissociable from Prāṇa. (d) *amṛtatva*, in contrast with *amṛta* earlier; (e) *ekabhūyam gacchanti* (f) *prājñāpayitum*, literally "to cause to know", i.e., "to cause [that he would know what is named by] a name by means of Speech", etc.; Frenz: "let a [nameable] thing get to consciousness"; (g) literally "all *prāṇas* speak after (or along with) Speech [when it is] speaking". (h) lit. "[With] Sight seeing, all *prāṇas* see after (or along with) [lit]," etc. (i) literally "as one with speech gone away", etc. (j) *ekadhā bhavanti* (k) *abhi-vi-sṛjate*.

147. (a) *uccakramus*; (b) *ākāśa-ātman*.

148. E.g. in *KauṣUp* II.3, 4 and 15 (in the last two the supplicant says "my *prajñā*"), and in *AitĀr* II.3.2.

149. E. Frauwallner, Untersuchungen zu den älteren Upaniṣaden. *Zeitschrift für Indien und Iran*, v. 4, 1926, pp. 1-45; repr. in G. Oberhammer and E. Steinkellner, eds., *Erich Frauwallner, Kleine Schriften*. Wiesbaden: Franz Steiner, 1982 (Glasenapp-Stiftung, v. 22), pp. 4-5 (resp. pp. 98-99). Frauwallner uses the distribution of these terms to argue for a "Kauṣītaki-Doctrine," affecting and ultimately being absorbed by the "Yājñavalkya Doctrine," *BṛhUp* II.1 and III-IV.

150. Frenz translates "*Bewusstsein*" throughout, Hume, "intelligence", and Frauwallner, "*Erkenntnis*" (*ibid.*, pp. 3-4, resp. 97-98). Deussen has both.

151. Modern philological treatment: P. Thieme, Der Weg durch den Himmel nach der Kaushitaki-Upanishad. *Wissenschaftliche Zeitschrift der Martin-Luther-Universität Halle-Wittenberg*, v. 1, 1951/2, pp. 21-36 (Gesellschafts— und Sprachwissenschaftliche Reihe, No.1), repr. Paul Thieme, *Kleine Schriften*. Wiesbaden: Franz Steiner, 1984 (1st ed., 1970), pp. 82-99. On *KauṣUp* I.1-2 see Bodewitz, *JaimBr* v. 1, pp. 52 ff.

152. *sā prajñā, prajñayā hi vipaśyati*. Thieme considers this to be a later addition. Even if it was, this would only weaken, not necessarily invalidate its value as an aid to deeper understanding of both *vicakṣaṇa* and *prajñā*.

153. The sequence transcendence of desire (crossing the river 'Ageless') ⟶ higher wisdom, *prajñā*, is echoed in Sai Baba's gloss of *prajñāna*, which is very similar to *prajñā*, as "the higher learning, the art of controlling the inner feelings and the many layers of consciousnes". *Sathya Sai Speaks*, v. 7. 2nd ed., Prasanthi Nilayam: Sri Sathya Sai Books and Publications, 1982, p. 230 (discourse "The most profitable job").

154. *mahaddevānām asuratvam ekam.*

155. *mahaccāsmai devānām asuratvam ekam/prajñāvattvaṁ vā/anavattvaṁ vā /*, "And for him is [i.e., to Tvaṣṭṛ belongs] 'the one great divinity [=Asura-power] of the gods', i.e., the state of being endowed with wisdom, or [the state of being endowed with] the bread of life," *Nirukta* 10.34; transl. Sarup, *Nirukta*, p. 165. *ana-vat-tva* lit. means the condition (*-tva*) of being endowed with (*-vat*) life breath (*ana*); Sarup's rendering

as "bread of life" is justified because the term glosses "the great unique Asura power of the gods". Yāska goes on to support his gloss by saying that *asu* means *prajñāna*; may be he is defending his own spiritual understanding.

156. Vedekar and Limaye, *Principal Ups*, p. 316, cite this Nirukta passage as relevant to *Kauṣītaki Upaniṣad's prajñā=prāṇa*.

157. G. Oberhammer, *Strukturen yogischer Meditation*. Österreichische Akademie der Wissenschaften, Phil.-Hist. Klasse, No. 322 (1977), pp. 134-230, using a combined textual-conceptual-phenomenological approach, distinguishes four "types of meditation" in the *Yoga Sūtra*: *YoSū* I.2 and 12-12, dealing with stilling the mind; I.23-28, a theistic form of the preceding; I.41-50, "meditation of the *samāpatti* type"; and II.54-III.7, "*saṁyama* meditation" (*ibid.*, pp. 134-135). Other Western efforts to analyse the composition of the *Yoga Sūtra* agree that *saṁyama* meditation is a unitary constituent of the Sūtra.

158. *Saṁyama* is literally "constraint" or "overall constraint", and *Yoga Sūtra* III.4 defines it simply as "The three (*dhāraṇā* etc.) in one [is] *saṁyama*." But Oberhammer seems to take it as an experiential aspect that pervades at least *dhāraṇa* and *dhyāna* and gives the whole complex of *dhāraṇā*, *dhyāna*, and *samādhi* a unity.

159. For textual discussion see F. Tola and C. Dragonetti, *The Yoga Sūtras of Patañjali on Concentration of Mind*, Delhi: Motilal Banarsidass, 1987 (1st. Span. ed., Barcelona: Barral Editores, 1972), pp. 172-180.

160. G.V. Subbaramayya, *Sri Ramana Reminiscences*. 2nd ed., Tiruvannamalai: Sri Ramanasramam, 1979 (1st ed., 1967), pp. 13-14.

161. "We should recognize that by wisdom, one gets two kinds of *prajñā*. One relates to the world and the other relates to the spirit. One that relates to the world enables you to understand what you see around you and how the material world goes on. We should take this to mean that even before we understand the form and the meaning of the external things, they are already contained within us. This [is] knowledge which relates to the Ātmā with which you have already seen and known [something][a] in some form within you and which is now being seen as an external thing. I am now looking at this peice of cloth but the form of this piece of cloth has already been imprinted in my mind even before I see the cloth. Thus, that which establishes the true form of what already exists as inner knowledge is the first kind of *prajñā*. The second type of *prajñā* is that which enables you to see aspect of *ātmā* in all living beings as one and the same. This has been proclaimed by the rishis by saying '*prajñānam brahma*'. This aspect of *prajñāna* which is identical with Brahman is present in every individual . . ." Sri Sathya Sai Baba, *Summer Showers*, 1974, p. 233.

162. Frenz translates as if the simile of the sparks is merely a description of waking up: "*Wenn er wieder erwacht, stieben, wie aus einem brennenden Feuer die Funken nach allen Richtungen auseinanderstieben, so auch aus diesem Ātman die Prāṇas je nach [ihrem] Standort auseinander, . . .*" (Frenz, *op. cit.*, p. 117). The interpretation given here is supported by the fact that in the parallel text *BṛhUp* II.1.16-20, the same simile of the sparks occurs in the last verse, but waking up is never mentioned (cf. chr. 5 below). Thus, the teaching is plainly that one should realize that the worlds emerge from the Ātman like sparks emerge from a fire. Here in

Kauṣītaki Upaniṣad the teaching is exactly the same.

163. Bakker, *op. cit.*, p. 132, note 58 cites the fact that in III.4.2-III.8 the powers, *prāṇāḥ*, "as such are no longer referred to" and that "for the first time a complete standard list of nine 'senses' is given without variance. The nine are the same as those listed afterwards among the ten *indriyāṇi* ["senses and organs of action"] (*pāyu* is missing)". The change from the few *prāṇas* in III.1-4.1 to the nine factors in III.4.2-III.8 seems indeed unusual.
164. (a) *aṅgam udūḷham.* (b) *parastāt prati-vi-hitā*, "arranged near [to them] from the outside"; (c) lit. "name", i.e. the object in so far it is conceived of as an object by having a name. (d) *siddhyen no etan nānā.*
165. Sri Sathya Sai Baba, *Summer Showers*, 1974, p. 22. The *Brahma Sūtra* has the same attitude.

CHAPTER 4

Teachings with Meditation on Sense-Powers and Deities

1. Introduction and Outline

The creation texts discussed in chr. 3, and to some extent also the more phiiosophical *KauṣUp* III, promote a metaphysical outlook and provide a framework that is helpful for approaching the great truths in chr. 2. But by and large, they operate only at a verbal level. A modern reader, although sensing the metaphysical intensity, has little other choice than consider *BṛhUp* I.4 as mytho-poieic, or inspired, or *KauṣUp* III as philosophical. In a world where traditional teachings are the basis of all of the individual's deeper orientation to life and society and existence, these texts may play a fundamental role. But today, such primarily verbal-discursive presentations have little real force. In a single anthropology course a student may have a score of descriptions of world-views on his reading list, and every couple decades scholarship paints a new picture of the foundations of a given tradition. But we do not take any of these presentations serious in terms of living. They are only of passing interest. And we are often not able to separate the true higher metaphysical, Divine etc. elements from the many cultural aspects.

So metaphysical language, powerful myth, or exalted poetry are not enough. In addition, a teaching must be lived or put into practice so that its truth is experienced and the higher aspect which it teaches is realized. An essential part of this is some kind of inner spiritual discipline or spiritual practice, like meditation, repeating a mantra or a name of God, or a *jñāna* practice like *neti neti*, or Buddha's "this is not mine, this am I not, this is not myself".[1] For it is through such practice or discipline that knowledge of Divinity, levels of formless knowledge, non-attachment, and bliss are able to arise in the individual over the long term, and true inner transformation can take place.

In the old Upaniṣads, the standard term for a specific type of practice is *upāsanā*. (The later term for "meditation", *dhyāna*, occurs also, but rarely, and sometimes only in the sense of "thinking".[2]) Exactly what *upāsanā* means in terms of inner practice and living and experience, however, is somewhat problematic. We will see that it has some of the connotations of meditation, viz., (reverential) fixation of heart and mind on something, leading to absorption and immersion in the higher aspect meditated on, without much body awareness. In this respect *upāsanā* includes aspects of worship, and may lead to higher states, higher experience and knowledge. But it also has pronounced cognitive connotations, viz. regarding something as something, holding it to be Brahman, for example.

A second important term is *vidyā. Vidyā* in general means "knowledge", but in connection with the Upaniṣadic teachings it has the sense of "a path for attaining Brahman", "a direction of inner knowledge which, if pursued and practiced, leads to becoming Brahman". By extension, it also means a particular text that expounds such a path or direction. By lumping together or pooling two or more texts that seem to teach the same approach to and knowledge of Ātman/Brahman, the mass of Upaniṣadic texts can be reduced to a smaller number of "paths" which are relatively independent of each other in terms of practice and lead to some kind of knowledge of Brahman. This idea is already found in the *Brahma Sūtra*, and Śaṁkara calls such paths *vidyās*. Exactly what it is that makes a *vidyā* a *vidyā*, however, is again moot. For this tends to touch on the question what is the highest (or the highest form of) Brahman, and what in inner life and practice will lead to that as opposed to other forms of the Divine, the Transcendent, etc. Nevertheless some concept like that of a *vidyā* is needed to organize the Upaniṣadic teachings into a manageable number of salient units or complexes.

But a detailed understanding of *upāsanās* and *vidyās* is not only needed to enable the modern aspirant/devotee to enter the Upaniṣadic Wisdom more deeply, it is also required if one wants to understand how the Upaniṣads arose as the first exemplar of Enlightenment Literature in the world. No doubt the Upaniṣads stand in the soil of the

Vedic and Brāhmaṇical religion. But their significance and importance for humanity today consists in their universal message the authority for which is ultimately their own realization. They speak Supreme Wisdom without any other support—they are the very embodiment of the Infinite, the Ātman/Brahman that they teach. How did this come about? The earlier literatures were not like this. The Vedas are harmony of thought, word and deed with the Divine. One feels a completely natural absorption into a Divine life. The Brāhmaṇas present a picture of total immersion in and religious unfoldment through ritual. Where then did the self-aware authority of Enlightenment come from? How did the detached Consciousness arise that sounds so rational and that speaks the same universal language in all the Supreme Wisdom literatures of the world since? It is a fact that the Upaniṣads express themselves primarily in terms of *upāsanās* and *vidyās*. For that reason alone, any account of their specific nature as a Supreme Wisdom literature, or of their rise as the first such literature, is likely to involve an account of the nature of *upāsanās* and *vidyās* in the corpus of Brāhmaṇa literature.

Overall Structure of the Chapter. The present chapter consists of several semi-independent parts. First, the nature of *upāsanās* and *vidyās* is discussed in a general way (secs. 2 and 3). Then the remainder of the chapter is devoted to three specific teachings, one *upāsanā*, *ChāndUp* III.18 (secs. 4-7) and two *vidyās*, the Sixteen Parts *Vidyā* (secs. 9-11) and the *Vaiśvānara Vidyā* (secs. 13-19). Since the *Vaiśvānara Vidyā* comes in a Brāhmaṇa version and an Upaniṣadic version, one can also count the number of texts as four. These texts were chosen for several reasons. All of them are still steeped in Brāhmaṇa and Āraṇyaka type thought. But they each illustrate the emergence of the Upaniṣads as an independent voice, more "modern" in spirit and thought, more universal than the earlier literatures, and ultimately, in the great *vidyās*, independent of them. In addition, at least the *vidyās* can still be meaningfully practiced today. They are perhaps not specified in sufficient detail to lead unambiguously to the highest levels of realization. But they undoubtedly lead to various stages of knowledge of the Divine and Transcendental, and form a broad type of approach to Brahman. Thus this chapter is to some extent introductory to the great *vidyās* that follow (chrs. 5 ff.). Its main aims are to get an idea of (1) how the Upaniṣadic teachings and the Upaniṣadic "style of instruction in enlightenment" arose out of the Brāhmaṇa and Vedic literature, and (2) how, by practicing such teachings and trying to live according to them, one can indeed draw closer to Ātman/Brahman. A reader who is more interested in the great *vidyās* in the later chapters may wish to read in this chapter only sec. 2 and one of the *vidyās* to get some background for what follows.

Finally, the texts in this chapter, together with the mythological Puruṣa type texts in the last chapter, represent one of the four or five major approaches to Ātman/Brahman in the old Upaniṣads. All of them deal with the (Sense-) Powers and Deities already met with in chr. 3, Speech, Prāṇa, Sight, Hearing, Mind; and Agni, Vāyu (Wind), Āditya (Sun), Diśas (Directions), and Candramas (Moon) or Ākāśa (Space). Like the texts in chr. 3, they all have a cosmic aspect, and were indeed basically understood as *upāsanās* and *vidyās* for deeper realization of Ātman/Brahman=Puruṣa. But the three Upaniṣadic texts differ from the texts in chr. 3 in the fact that they explicitly use "meditation", *upāsanā.* In other words, in terms of chr. 3.1, they are primarily operating at level (3), "meditation and spiritual life".

Outline of the Chapter. A brief outline of the chapter is as follows. Sec. 2 discusses the nature of *upāsanā* and *vidyā* in the old Upaniṣads as this can be gleaned from the extant texts and tradition. Sec. 3 is an appendix which briefly describes the *Brahma Sūtra's* view of *upāsanā* and Śaṁkara's attitudes. This material is useful for reading Śaṁkara or for a more rigorous historical reconstruction of the Upaniṣadic *vidyās*, but is not absolutely essential for understanding the *upāśanās* and *vidyās* in the remainder of the book. The next four sections deal with *ChāndUp* III.18. The text begins "'Mind is Brahman'—thus should one meditate (*upās-*). . . '*Ākāṣa* ("Space, Ether") is Brahman' [—thus should one meditate]," and thereafter Mind and Ākāśa are further epitomized into Speech, Prāṇa, Sight, and Hearing and into Agni, Vāyu (Wind), Āditya (Sun), and Diśas (Quarters), respectively. Sec. 4 first introduces *Chāndogya Upaniṣad* as a whole, and then gives the text of *ChāndUp* III.18 and discusses its overall structure. The next section brings in a parallel text, the so-called *prahitām saṁyoga, AitĀr* II.6.2-4, although this turns out to be not as closely related as it first appeared. The real direction of *ChāndUp* III.18 is finally determined in secs. 6 and 7, by using the mature Vedāntic characterization of Brahman as *asti, bhāti, priya*, "it is, it shines [it is] dear", which is term for term equivalent to *sat-cit-ānanda.* The argument is that when the *Chāndogya* text says "Speech is a foot of Brahman. It shines with Agni as light," etc., it uses "shines", *bhāti*, like the *bhāti* in *asti, bhāti, prīya.* The *upāsaṅā* also assumes a similar "existential position" as "*asti, bhāti, priya*". Both the *prahitām saṁyoga* and *ChāndUp* III.18 and many other Brāhmaṇa and Upaniṣadic teachings raise the question to what extent the correspondences Speech-Agni, Prāṇa-Vāyu etc. which they involve may be said to have any "objective content", and how this in turn affects the validity of the knowledge attained by pursuing these teachings. This is an important issue if these teachings are to be practiced today, and is briefly discussed in sec. 8.

Next comes our first real *vidyā*, the *Ṣoḍasá-kala Vidyā* or *Sixteen Parts Vidyā*, which is related to *ChāndUp* III.18. It is a deep truth that man and nature are made "in the image of God". The approach in the *Sixteen Parts Vidyā* is to meditate that "the Directions (Quarters) (of space) are God," "the Sun is God," etc. By meditating in this way on the Images of God, there develops after some stages knowledge of God. This *vidyā* is important because it may be pursued to a considerable extent without entering very deeply into the Brāhmaṇa and Vedic world of thought and is thus accessible to everyone irrespective of culture and education. As usual we first try to understand the text itself (secs. 9-11), and then add some comments of a historical and general philosophical nature (sec. 12).

The third and last major teaching is the *Vaiśvānara Vidyā* (secs. 13-19). This is not only important as a path in its own right, but also as a stepping stone to the *vidyā* of *Māṇḍūkya Upaniṣad*, one of the most profound teachings of Vedānta. In the frame story, six prominent Brahmins approach king Aśvapati of Benares for instruction. One of them had meditated on Heaven as the Self, the second on the Sun as the Self, and so on. They are all guided in their quest by an idea of a "Universal Self," or *Vaiśvānara Ātman*, but they can not agree on the nature of that Ātman. The king tells them that the "Brightly Shining" (the Heaven-Self which the first one of them had realized) was the head of the Universal Self; the "Manifold" (the Sun-Self which the second one had attained) was the eye of the Universal Self and so on. Thus all the Selves which the Brahmins had realized by their meditations were really only parts of the Universal (or *Vaiśvānara*) Ātman.

It turns out that idea of *Vaiśvānara*, which led the six Brahmins to their conception of *Vaiśvānara Ātman*, is derived from the Vedic and Brāhmaṇa *Agni Vaiśvānara*, an aspect of Agni. This is clear from the parallel version of the text in *ŚatBr* X.6.3, where almost the same six Brahmins with almost the same objects of meditation are seeking to realize [Agni] Vaiśvānara. We first focus on this *Śatapatha Brāhmaṇa* version (secs. 12-17), because here the Vedic and Brāhmaṇa parallels and background provide a much richer base for reconstructing or intuiting the original intent than is available for the Upaniṣadic version. The latter is then approached by contrasting it with the *Śatapatha Brāhmaṇa* version (secs. 18-19). Accordingly, sec. 13 gives the *Śatapatha Brāhmaṇa* text and notes some preliminary problems; sec. 14 analyses a key Brāhmaṇa parallel passage, *ŚatBr* X.3.3.2-6; and secs. 16-17 deal with the *Śatapatha Brāhmaṇa vidyā* itself. *ŚatBr* X.3.3.2-6 suggests that *Vaiśvānara* must have meant to the six Brahmins something like "the One in the Many", or "the One ensouling, animating, whatever, all the objects and deities of the World", and also explains why the six Brahmins meditated on, and knew, the *Vaiśvānara* as Heaven, Sun, etc. Sec. 15 is an appendix which gives a more detailed treatment of Vedic and Brāhmaṇa Agni Vaiśvānara to complement the analysis in sec. 14. In the Brāhmaṇa passages discussed, the concept of *Vaiśvānara* begins to look very similar to the crucial element of the Idea of Puruṣa, and it is thus not so surprising that in the *Śatapatha Brāhmaṇa* version, the king explicitly identifies Agni Vaiśvānara with the Puruṣa. The Upaniṣadic teaching is closely related (secs. 18-19), but there are various new elements, and the *vidyā* sets up a new emphasis which is only fully realized in later *vidyās*.

The chapter closes with some reflections on what distinguishes the Upaniṣadic texts in this chapter from their parallels and forerunners in the Brāhmaṇas and Āraṇyakas (sec. 20). The general picture that emerges is that these texts indeed represent intermediate stages in the transition from the highly specialized and relatively inaccessible forms of Brāhmaṇa wisdom to the great *vidyās* to be discussed in the following chapters. Although they introduce relatively modern forms of thought and increasingly sophisticated expression of inner knowledge and realization, in comparison to the *Five Sheaths* and *Dahara Vidyās* for example, they are still largely silent on the higher and highest stages of Knowledge. On the other hand, they represent a rich spectrum of knowledge of the Divine, virtually all of it distilled from or further elaborating the vast Brāhmaṇa heritage.

2. *Upāsanā* and *Brahma Vidyā*

***Upāsanā*. Meaning of the Term *Upāsanā*.** The term *upāsanā* is the noun-form derived from the verb *upa-ās*, literally "to sit close to someone (looking up to him, waiting on him)", which is used already in theVedas in the sense of "to honor, serve, worship, be devoted to", "to regard something as".[3] In western-type scholarship the nature of Upaniṣadic *upāsanā* has been discussed since the turn of the century, and the topic still generates interest today.[4] The most basic initial characterization was given by H. Oldenberg. He took *upās-* to mean *verehren*, "to worship, adore, give reverence to",[5] and emphasized that in the Upaniṣads this *Verehrung* is directed to formless things (*geistigen Wesenheiten*) like "the absolute I and the absolute Holy", i.e. Ātman and Brahman. Before the Upaniṣads, "the pious man approached the gods with sacrificial offerings. But the more *geistige* [spiritual] powers to which faith turned in the new [Upaniṣadic] age required a different *Verehrung* [adoration]: ... pious meditation was the only thing that one could consecrate to [the Ātman]".[6] Then Oldenberg went on to discuss *upāsanā* as meditation. "For [the purpose of] such meditation, now, one transmitted to each other certain [verbal] formulas: Names which served to bring the Mysterious closer to understanding. These formulas we find now called *ādeśa*, "instruction" (*Anweisung*), now *nāmadheya*, "signification" (*Benennung*); then again they are called *upaniṣad*, "[specific] form of worship" (*Verehrungsform*)."[7] A quarter century later S. Schayer published a paper arguing that the important element in *upās-* was not *verehren* but *umwerben, bedrängen*, "to court [the Ātman etc.], press on [it with wishes]".[8] According to Schayer, this courting or pressing on a metaphysical principle or "substance" typically took the form of courting it as "magically" "equivalent" to another substance; e.g. "one must court or press on Mind as Brahman [*ChāndUp* III.18.1]".[9] Hence "*upāsanā* is without doubt the psychic act by which man wins for himself an essence-aspect (*Wesenheit*) as equivalent to this or that substance (*Substanz*). In addition, *upāsanā* is also the procedure, the method, which is supposed to lead to attainment of magical rulership (*Herrschaft*)".[10] It is somewhat surprising that Schayer's paper was so influential, because none of his many examples contains concrete specific evidence that would point specifically to his interpretation. They are all of the form "[one should etc.] *umwerben* (*upās-*) X as Y," i.e. present merely the phrase to be elucidated, without any additional evidence why it should be read in this particular way. Indeed Schayer simply supplied an interpretation that was predetermined by his general conception of the nature of Brāhmaṇa ritual in general: "[In the Brāhmaṇas and Upaniṣads] the theologian of the sacrifice steps up to the magical substances [Ātman/Brahman, Deities, Sense-

Powers] not in order to adore them, but to master them and to be lord over them. We are moving throughout in the sphere of magical techniques and practices."[11] At any rate, Schayer's idea that *upāsanā* dealt principally with "equivalences" was developed further by first rank scholars like Renou and Thieme.[12]

***Upāsanā* as Meditation.** In Vedānta, there is a large tradition on the nature of *upāsanā*. But the question is whether the traditional views reflect the original meanings which *upāsanā* had in late Brāhmaṇ and Upaniṣadic times. At the most general level, an *upāsanā* is "a form of approach to the Ideal"—the Ideal being Brahman, or the Infinite Lord.[13] In Vedānta, Śaṁkara's definitions are authoritative.[14] "Meditation [*upāsanā*] consists in a current of uniform concepts [*tulya-pratyaya-saṁtatiḥ*, literally a continuous succession, *saṁtatiḥ*, of comparable, *tulya*, basic conceptions, beliefs, *pratyaya*, not interspersed with dissimilar ones, which proceeds according to the scriptures and relates to an object enjoined in the scriptures."[15] Commenting on *BṛhUp* I.3.9, "This deity (*devatā*) is called *Dūr*, for Death is far away (*dūra*) from it. Death comes to be far away from one who knows thus," he in effect equates one "who knows thus", *ya evam veda*, with one "who has realized by *upāsanā*", and says:

> Meditation (*upāsanā*) is mentally approaching the form of the deity or the like as it is presented by the eulogistic portions of the Vedas relating to the objects of meditation, and concentrating on it, excluding conventional notions, till one is as completely identified with it as with one's body, conventionally regarded as one's self. Compare such *śruti* [=scriptural] passages as, 'Being a god, he attains the gods' (*BṛhUp* IV.1.2), and 'What deity are you identified with in the east?' (*BṛhUp* III.9.20).[16]

These statements suggest that *upāsanā* for Śaṁkara is similar to *dhyāna* or meditation in the general sense in that it involves absorption or immersion into essentially a single thought.[17] This is consistent with the general understanding of *upāsanā* and *vidyā* in the *Brahma Sūtra* as "knowledge" and may therefore reflect the meaning of *upāsanā* in the Upaniṣads.[18]

***Upāsanā* as Inner Practice During the Day.** But *upāsanā* does not only refer to meditation. The fact that Śaṁkara cites "Being a god, he attains the gods" does not only illustrate the strength of the "identification" that is to be aimed for in *upāsanā*, it also suggests that this identification should manifest in one's daily life: one must '*be* a god'. The same thing is found in *BṛhUp* IV.1.2. Yājñavalkya implies that when one meditates on (verb *upās-*) Speech as Brahman, then one becomes a god, and "having become a god, *devo bhūtvā*, one attains the gods [after death]". So by *upāsanā* in the sense of meditation one may get knowledge of Divinity, but this must also be lived in daily life, for otherwise one does not "become a god". Hence an *upāsanā* like "Speech is Brahman" is a larger enterprise than simply meditation. It includes meditation, but in addition it includes living the basic formulation ("Speech is Brahman") in daily life, letting it be a principle that guides the attitudes one takes and one's behavior and indeed one's inner intelligence. For only then is it possible that there occur some of the results which the Upaniṣads regard as the fruits of an *upāsanā*[19]—like here "becoming a god".

In Vedāntic tradition there is also the view that *upāsanā* comes under the general heading of "constant remembrance", or "constant meditation", i.e., remembrance or meditation all the time when one is moving about in the world. This teaching was championed by Rāmānuja (ca. 1100 CE), both a great Vedāntin and devotee of God (Nārāyaṇa). But it is already taught by Brahmānandin (or Ṭaṅka), an Advaitin dated 500-550 CE, whom Rāmānuja cites as authority.[20] Brahmānandin's views on the matter may be inferred from his remark that "*upāsanā* would be knowledge (*vedana*), on account of the scriptures [= Upaniṣads] on this topic. *Upāsanā* would then be firm-continuous-remembrance also, *dhruvā-anu-smṛti*, on account of seeing".[21] Here the term *dhruvā-anu-smṛti* (*dhruvā*=firm, steady, *smṛti* =remembrance, *anu*=an intensive, so "repeated, constant") is presumably inspired by *ChāndUp* VII.26.2: "[When] nourishment [is] pure, nature [is] pure. [When nature [is] pure, memory [is] firm (*dhruvā smṛti*). [When] memory is firm, there is release of all knots [of the heart] . . ." This passage describes the stages of the spiritual path and the nature of the process of merging into the Supreme in very general terms. It is a kind of epilogue to the whole of *ChāndUp* VII, which outlines a lifetime wisdom process and includes a graded series of 15 *upāsanās* to attain knowledge of Prāṇa as Brahman (and then goes further). Thus it does not refer only to something that happens only when one sits in meditation. Rather, it refers to stages one reaches in spiritual development, or general conditions of the inner consciousness. "When memory is firm"—at that stage, it says—"all knots [of the heart] are loosened." So when Brahmānandin says that "*upāsanā* should be firm-constant-remembrance", *dhruvā-anu-smṛti,* he is not likely to be only referring to concentration when one sits in meditation. He must be talking about what *upāsanā* at an advanced stage should be like in general and what the student should aim for. And he is saying that *upāsanā* should become a condition of *dhruvā-anū-smṛti,* i e., remembrance or memory throughout all levels of the inner consciousness that is *dhruva*, unmoving, firm, regardless of what one is doing at the moment. Such an understanding of *upāsanā* may be assumed to be shared also by Śaṁkara, who respected Brahmānandin greatly, and may therefore represent the general Vedāntic (*Brahma Sūtra* based) view at the time.

The preceding suggests, therefore, that *upāsanā* is not merely contemplation or meditation as in "sitting in meditation", but also fixing one's inner consciousness on the Self, Brahman, whatever, *in everyday life as best as one is able.* "Sitting in meditation" may be an important element, to be sure. Already *BraSū* IV.1.7 declares sitting to be necessary if the goal is to be reached. But ultimately, "meditation" has to be carried into every aspect and moment of one's living. This is consistent with fundamental texts like "The Ātman, Oh Maitreyī, should be seen, heard (of), revolved in the mind, and fully contemplated on" [*BṛhUp* II.4.5 (K) = IV.5.6 (M), chr. 2.3 above]. Indeed for that very reason, Yājñavalkya's last three terms, "hearing, revolving in the mind, and completely internalizing", *śravaṇa, manana*, and *nididhyāsana*, became the Vedāntic catchword for the process of spiritual evolution.[23] Only if life is ever more fully dedicated to the Supreme, to Ātman/Brahman, can realization of Ātman/Brahman and other higher fruits of *upāsanā* be obtained. If we take the Upaniṣadic texts seriously and assume that the *upāsanās* enjoined actually have the fruits described, then *upāsanā* can not be merely once a day worship or meditation, or developing specific beliefs or identifications. *Upāsanā* is in fact completely comparable to deeper modes of practice in many other religious traditions, which also tend to involve some kind of constant remembrance or meditation.[24] Rāmānuja, for example, develops a powerful conception of *upāsanā* as meditation, *dhyāna*, which has the form of continuous remembrance, and springs from and is an expression of highest *bhakti*, love for and devotion to God.[25]

Vidyās. *Vidyā* generally means "knowledge". The term *Brahmavidyā* occurs already in the Upaniṣads and means "knowledge of Brahman"[26] (including sometimes also only verbal knowledge). In this book, however, we will use *vidyā* and *brahma-vidyā* to denote "a line of wisdom, including a method of meditation, expounded in a particular Upaniṣadic text, which leads to Brahman". For this is a common meaning of *vidyā* in Śaṁkara's commentary on the *Brahma Sūtra*. The aphorisms in *BraSū* I.1 argue that in spite of the fact that certain Upaniṣadic teachings use different terms such as *puruṣa*, the object is in each case always Brahman. Another entire section of the Sūtra, *BraSū* III.3, deals with the fact that certain teachings (*vidyās*) in different Upaniṣads which look similar are essentially the same (in our terms: they are the same *vidyā*), while others, though described in very similar terms, are not (they are not the same *vidyā*).[27] In both these sections, therefore, the Sūtra implies in various ways that particular Upaniṣadic passages teach particular meditative paths, and Śaṁkara calls these paths *vidyās*.[28] The Sūtra alludes fairly specifically to perhaps two dozen *vidyās*, but it does not have a term for them and it does not give a list. It also does not specifically distinguish *vidyās* from *upāsanās*. [Both Śaṁkara and Rāmānuja note as apparently well-known that in the (early) Upaniṣads, the roots *vid*, "know", and *upās*, "worship", are used without distinction.][29] In the 19th century, however, theologians of Rāmānuja's school developed a list of thirty-two *vidyās* found in the Upaniṣads.[30] These are now the traditionally accepted *Brahma-vidyās* of the Upaniṣads. Adding a few texts suggested more recently, the total may be brought to thirty-five which are shown in Table 4.1.[31] *Vidyās* in our sense of "lines of wisdom, often including one or more *upāsanās*, which, when cultivated throughout life, lead to Brahman" are usually based on one or a combination of several of these thirty-five. Further, for us a *vidyā* is a relatively extensive text that is built around or leads up to a central, basic formula or key formulation.[32] E.g., *Dahara Vidyā* for us refers to *ChāndUp* VIII.1-3.2 or VIII.1-6, not only to *ChāndUp* VIII.1.1 (which contains the term *dahara*, "small, subtle"). The references in Table 4.1 are to the verses that contain these keywords:

TABLE 4.1
Traditional *Brahma Vidyās*[31]

	Name	Source
1.	*Īśā Up. Vidyā*	*ĪśāUp* 15-16
2.	*Parama Puruṣa Vidyā*	*PraśnUp* V.5
3.	*Sad Vidyā*	*ChāndUp* VI.2.1
4.	*Vaiśvānara Vidyā*	*ChāndUp* V.18.1

	Name	Source
5.	*Ānandamaya Vidyā*	*TaittUp* II.1.1
6.	*Prāṇa Vidyā*	*ChāndUp* V.1.1
7.	*Śāṇḍilya Vidyā*	*ChāndUp* III.14.1
8.	*Saṁvarga Vidyā*	*ChāndUp* IV.3.1
9.	*Upakosala Vidyā*	*ChāndUp* IV.10.5
10.	*Uddālaka Antaryāmī Vidyā*	*BṛhUp* III.7.1
11.	*Bhūma Vidyā*	*ChāndUp* VII.23.1
12.	*Dahara Vidyā*	*ChāndUp* VIII.1.1
13.	*Gargyakṣara Vidyā*	*BṛhUp* III.8.8
14.	*Madhu Vidyā*	*ChāndUp* III.1.1
15.	*Bālāki Vidyā*	*KauṣUp* IV.18
16.	*Maitreyī Vidyā*	*BṛhUp* IV.5.6
17.	*Pañcāgni Vidyā*	*ChāndUp* V.10
18.	*Ādityamaṇḍalastha Satyabrahma Vidyā*	*ChāndUp* IV.15.1, *BṛhUp* V.5.2
19.	*Akṣiṇi Satyabrahma Vidyā*	*ChāndUp* IV.15.1, *BṛhUp* V.5.2
20.	*Śrīman Nyāsa Vidyā*	*TaittNārāyaṇīyaUp* 79
21.	*Parajyotir* or *Raukṣeya jyotir Vidyā*	*ChāndUp* III.13.7
22.	*Nāciketa Vidyā*	*KaṭhaUp* III.2
23.	*Akṣaraparā Vidyā*	*MuṇḍUp* I.1.5
24.	*Ṣatyakāma Vidyā*	*ChāndUp* VIII.7.1
25.	*Aṅguṣṭha-mātra Vidyā*	*Kaṭha Up* IV.12, *ŚvetUp* V.8
26.	*Jyotiṣām Jyotir Vidyā*	*BṛhUp* IV.4.16
27.	*Uṣasta Kahola Vidyā*	*BṛhUp* IV.4.2
28.	*Ākāśa Vidyā*	*ChāndUp* VIII.14.1
29.	*Antarāditya Vidyā*	*ChāndUp* I.6.6
30.	*Pratardana Vidyā*	*KauṣUp* I
31.	*Paryaṅka Vidyā*	*KauṣUp* I.3
32.	*Gāyatrī Vidyā*	*ChāndUp* III.12.1
33.	*Ṣoḍaśakala Vidyā*	*ChāndUp* IV.5-9
34.	*Satya Brahma Vidyā*	*BṛhUp* V.4
35.	*Udgītha Vidyā*	*ChāndUp* I.3-9, *BṛhUp* I.3

The Central "Formulas" and "Key Formulations" in *Vidyās*. There is some general agreement that the central "formulas" and "basic formulations" are the heart of the *vidyās*. These "formulas" include both the one or two word phrases (*upaniṣads*, and *ādeśas*) discussed earlier as one meaning of the term *Upaniṣad*, and somewhat larger statements (cf. Table 4.3 below). It is, however, not completely clear what role these formulations play in the *vidyās*. To focus matters, we quote from a recent discussion by the editor in *Prabuddha Bhārata*,[33] apparently Swami Ananyananda. (*Prabuddha Bhārata* or

"Awakened India" is a monthly published by the Ramakrishna Order.)

> . . . So the great sages of the Upaniṣads used various familiar objects of the phenomenal universe like the sun, *ākāśa, vāyu* (air), water, *prāṇa, manas* (mind), words, etc. to represent Brahman. However what the sages attempted was not mere concentration of mind on one of these symbols. . . What they actually did was to connect each symbol to a certain framework of meaning—a spiritual formula. *Upāsanā* in the Upaniṣads are meditations on these spiritual formulas. These formulas are devices to guide the mind from the symbol to Reality. When a mind which is sufficiently purified meditates on such a formula, its true meaning—the ultimated Reality—will be revealed to it. These meditation formulas were called *vidyās*.[34]

The description of *upāsanās* as involving symbols is already found in Deussen,[35] whom the author quotes. But here there is a new emphasis, viz. that the "spiritual formula" which gives the symbol amounts to a "framework of meaning" by which the mind is guided "from the symbol to reality". Meditation on the formula (or *śravaṇa, manana, nididhyāsana* of the formula) brings about the spiritual effect by an unfolding of inner meaning ("true meaning—the ultimate reality"). Swami Ananyananda's characterization applies to what we are calling *upāsanās* as well as *vidyās*. Examples of *upāsanās* (for convenience defined here by the explicit use of the verb *upās-*) are shown in Table 4.2. The specification of the *upāsana* includes a key phrase or

TABLE 4.2
Some Prominent *Upāsanās*

Upāsanā	Text
BṛhUp I.4.7	One should meditate [on the powers] [as] "self".
BṛhUp I.4.8	One should meditate on (regard) what is dear as [being one's] self.
BṛhUp I.4.15	One should meditate on (regard) the world as (being one's) self.
BṛhUp II.1.2	"Him (the person in the Sun) indeed I meditate on (regard) as Brahman". . . "Verily I worship (meditate on, regard) that one as 'the head that stands out among all beings, the King'."
BṛhUp II.1.3	"Him (the person in the moon) indeed I meditate on as Brahman". . . "Verily I worship (meditate

Upāsanā	Text
	on, regard) that one as 'great white robed King Soma'..."
BṛhUp IV.1.2	One should meditate on that one (viz., Speech, *Vāc*) as "Intelligence" ("*prajñā*"). . . One should meditate on that one (viz. *Prāṇa*, Life-Breath) as "The Dear" ("*priyam*"). . . (This pattern repeated in *BṛhUp* IV.1.3-7).
ChāndUp I.1.1	One should meditate on the udgītha as "Om", that syllable . . .
ChāndUp I.3.1	He who glows yonder (the Sun), Him one should meditate on as the *udgītha* (?; perhaps the other way around). (Similarly not clear to me: I.3.3, I.3.6, and so on).
ChāndUp III.18	"'Brahman is Mind,' (thus) one should meditate". . . "Brahman is Space," [(thus) one should meditate].
ChāndUp VII.1.3, 4	Meditate on Name. . . He who meditates "Brahman is Name," .
ChāndUp VII.2.1, 2	Meditate on Speech. . . He who meditates "Brahman is Speech,". . . (This pattern repeated in VII.3-14).
TaittUp II.2.1	Those who worship food as Brahman . . .
TaittUp II.3.2	Those who worship *Prāṇa* as Brahman . . .
TaittUp II.5.2	[they] worship *vijñāna* as the eldest Brahman . . .
KauṣUp II 6	Let him meditate "That [Uktha] is the *Ṛg* mantra,". . .let him meditate "That [Uktha] is the *Yajur* mantra,". . .let him meditate "That [Uktha] is Prosperity," . . .
KauṣUp III.2	as such (viz. as *prāna* = *prajñā-ātman*), meditate on me as "life, immortality".

"formula", often but not always specially highlighted by *iti* ("unquote", or "thus", shown in the table by quotation marks). Even without *iti*, the basic formulation certainly sets up a whole "framework of meaning" and intent in the student. For *vidyās* the situation is more complex, and the range of diversity is much greater (Table 4.3). The key formulations again set up a whole framework of meaning, indeed they evoke whole new levels of sensitivity and inner meanings. But whether these formulations are the same as Swami Anayananda's "spiritual formulas" is not clear.

Swami Ananayananada says that the spiritual formulas were called *vidyās* and he seems to regard them as mantras repeated in meditation.

TABLE 4.3
Key Formulations in Some Well-known *Vidyās*
(Hume's translation)

Vidyā	Key Formulation Giving "Paradigm"
Gāyatrī V., *ChāndUp* III.13.1 *ChāndUp* I.6.6	Verily, the Gayatrī [meter] is all that has come to be . . . What that Gāyatrī is, is, verily, what this Earth is . . . Verily, what is called Brahman, that is what the space outside a person is . . . that is what the space here within the heart is . . .
Antar-āditya V.,	Now the white light of the Sun is *sā* and the blue, exceeding darkness, is *ama*. That makes *sāman*. Now that golden person who is seen within the Sun has a golden beard and golden hair . . .
Madhu V., *ChāndUp* III.1-10	Verily yonder Sun is the honey of the gods. Of this the sky is the crossbeam, the atmosphere is the honey-comb, the particles of light are the brood. The eastern rays of that Sun are its eastern honey cells. The *Ṛg* verses are the producers of honey... After having risen in the zenith, he (the Sun) will no more rise nor set. . .
Śāṇḍilya V., *ChāndUp* III.14	"Verily, this whole world is Brahman, *taj-ja-lān*." Tranquil, one should meditate on it. . . He who consists of mind, whose body is *prāṇa*, whose form is light, . . . containing all works, containing all desires, containing all odours, . . this is myself within the heart, smaller than a grain of rice, . . . greater than the earth . . .
Dahara V., *ChāndUp* VIII.1-6	Now, here in this city of Brahman (the body) is an abode, a subtle lotus flower (the heart). Within it is a subtle space . . . Within [the space within the heart] indeed are contained both heaven and earth, both fire and air, . . .

V. Raghavan, one of the great Indian Sanskrit scholars of this century, held that one time there used to be texts which provided *Sūtras* provide detailed rules for the execution of the Vedic rituals.[36] He even argued that "it is clear from some of the authorities now available that each *upāsanā* included a mantra to be repeated in *japa* (mental repetition); in fact, the term *vidyās* is used for such mantras."[37] So may be Swami Anayananda's "spiritual formulas" are these mantras. But according to Raghavan, these mantras are almost all lost and survive only in a very few cases.[38] Swami Anayananda's "spiritual formulas" are closely tied to the "framework of meaning", the "paradigm" set up by the *vidyā*, which is contained in the extant text This would suggest that they are identical with the "key formulations" in Table 4.3.

> *Vidyās* are paradigms of Brahman. In ancient India each teacher developed his own concept model of Brahman and taught it as a meditation technique to his disciples. . . The *vidyās* really hold the key to the Upaniṣads, and no man can properly understand the Upaniṣads without understanding the *vidyās*.
>
> The *vidyās* are said to be thirty-two in number, but many more must have been known to the ancient sages. Among these *gāyatrī-vidyā, antar-āditya-vidyā, madhu-vidyā, śāṇḍilya-vidyā* and *dahara-vidyā* are well-known . . . They are to be learnt directly from competent teachers who have attained illumination through them. But long before the beginning of the Christian era the lineage of Vedic *ṛṣis* [=seers] had ended. And in the absence of a living tradition, the *vidyās* ceased to be practised and their true inner meaning was soon forgotten.[39]

The *vidyās* are not only "paradigms" or "models" for Brahman. They open up planes of spiritual sensitivity, modes of inner illumination, by which the student, meditatively and prompted by the higher forces in him, can walk the path to highest realization. The key formulations in a *vidyā* continually act anew in the inner consciousness to guide him and unclose to him new levels. In such an enlarged conception of a *vidyā*, it is not necessary to assume that the *vidyā* must include a mantra to be repeated in *japa*, and that this mantra is, or is not a part of what we have been calling the central or key formulations in the *vidyā*. The fact that the latter sets up a "framework of meaning" which "guides" the inner consciousness at higher and inner planes ("from the symbol to Reality") is the main thing and is enough. Apart from the Supreme Divine in the self of the aspirant, another key element operating is the Power of the Divine Word or Logos,[40] an expression of the Higher Divinity inherent in the formulation. In addition, there is also the repetition of the usual ("secular") semantic meaning of the formulation. It is of course possible that a given *vidyā* originally involved a mantra to be used in *upāsanā* which represented an additional element, not contained in the *vidyā's* extant text. This mantra may have been transmitted orally as part of a living tradition, and may have been connected with the teaching in subtle, esoteric ways. (This seems to be Raghavan's view). But even though almost all mantras of this type together with the living traditions may be lost, the *vidyās* as they are available today (via the key formulation which they contain) have a transcendental power and can serve as true guides for some of the further stages of spiritual path.

***Vidyās* Distinguished from *Upāsanās*.** Finally we also want to distinguish *vidyās* from *upāsanās*, to the extent this is possible without violating traditional usage. The basic difference between the two suggested is by Sai Baba: "Purity of consciousness is the essential prerequisite for *upāsanā*. Single-minded concentration is essential for Knowledge of Brahman. These can be got by *karma* [action] and *upāsanā*; thus is *Brahma-jñāna* won."[41] This echoes Śaṁkara on *AitĀr* II.1.2: "Afterwards [after the performance of sacrifices, i.e., when one has led a regulated religious life] arises a desire for knowledge [of Brahman, *jñāna*], which cannot be satisfied until a man has first attained complete concentration of thought [= one-pointedness, *ekāgratā*]. In order to acquire that concentration, the performance of certain *upāsanās* and meditations is enjoined . . . [such as those on Puruṣa and Prāṇa in *AitĀr* II.1-3]."[42] The suggestion is that *upāsanā* serves as a more or less necessary preparation for *Brahma-jñāna*, knowledge of Brahman, but that something more is needed for attaining knowledge of Brahman than *upāsanā*. This view is not really found in the *Brahma Sūtra*, but is widely shared in Advaita Vedānta.[43] But the additional element that is required beyond *upāsanā* is not so easy to pinpoint and may take various forms. Generally speaking it is "[knowledge of and proficiency in] the manner of acquisition of true knowledge".[44] This prevents the inner intelligence from stopping at other goals that may have been reached. In any case, in the Upaniṣads such additional elements would be somewhat different for different *vidyās* and would have to be determined separately in each case.

Summarizing, therefore, *upāsanās* will be something like meditations which have to somehow pervade one's life and living; *vidyās* will be paths to Ātman/Brahman often involving various *upāsanās* but containing as crucial elements certain "knowledge formulations". Both *upāsanās* and *vidyās* involve elements of "knowledge", and both involve key formulas or formulations which figure in the meditations and guide progress on the path generally. But they seem to do so in different ways. There are large differences between one *upāsanā* and another, and between one *vidyā* and another.

3. Appendix: *Upāsanā* in Vedānta

In this Appendix we sketch briefly the understanding of *upāsanā* in the *Brahma Sūtra* as well as Śaṁkara's approach to Upaniṣadic *sādhanā*. As noted in sec. 1, this material is not absolutely needed for the remainder of this book. But it is of independent interest because it gives a significant insight into modern Advaita Vedāntic practice. Śaṁkara's Vedānta, as it is carried on by the Śaṁkarācāryas and the Ramakrishna organization, is the living tradition that is most directly and exclusively based on the Upaniṣadic teachings. One cannot try to intuitively understand the Upaniṣadic paths and ignore this tradition. In addition, being aware of the conceptions of *upāsanā* and *vidyā* in the *Brahma Sūtra* and Śaṁkara also helps make one sensitive to certain dimensions and issues that are not explicit but may play a role in some of the Upaniṣadic texts.

In the *Brahma Sūtra*, and in Śaṁkara, we are facing some highly reflected on and digested concepts of *upāsanā*. This stands in stark constrast to the Upaniṣads, where one finds scores of calls for specific *upāsanās* (typically using the verb *upās-* with 2nd and 3rd person imperatives), or of descriptions of specific *upāsanās* and of fruits of them, but virtually no statements on *upāsanā* in general or as such. Jacob's Concordance shows over 200 occurrences of the verb *upās-* and two occurrences of *upāsanā* as a neuter noun; the feminine form *upāsanā* which we have been using is documented and becomes standard only later. More than 90% of the occurrences of *upās-* are found in the old Upaniṣads.[45] There we find everywhere practice toward Ātman/Brahman in the form of specific ways of *upās-*, "worshipping, regarding, meditating", but no thought of systematizing the kinds of approach used, and no reflection about *upāsanā* in general. Approaching Ātman/Brahman generally seems to have been a relatively wide open field. But already in the verse Upaniṣads, the spirit changes completely and *upāsanās* do not seem to have been pursued in the way they were before. In the *Brahma Sūtra, upāsanā* is carefully elaborated as a general type of practice.

***Upāsanā/Vidyā* in the *Brahma Sūtra*.** The *Brahma Sūtra* has an amazingly deep, unified conception of *upāsanā/Vidyā* which goes far beyond what is found in the Upaniṣads themselves.[46] The Sūtra can almost be described as the distilled wisdom of how to practice the Upaniṣadic teachings and live them. This wisdom was not so much based on continuous traditions handed down in individual families, by guru-disciple relationship. (As Swami Ananyananda says, above, "long before the Christian era, the lineage of Vedic *ṛṣis* [= seers] had ended.") Rather it represents something like the collective insight, pooled and accumulated over centuries, of teachers who learned the texts, wrestled with their interpretation and practiced them in their own way. From the point of view of *this* tradition, then, *upāsanā* appears as a kind of generic activity, the same everywhere, and the *Sūtra* is deeply concerned with setting up some general principles regarding how this activity is to be carried out.

The conception of *upāsanā* as a generic activity is illustrated by *BraSū* III.3.11-13, a section or *adhikaraṇa* of three aphorisms which deals with how to think of Brahman when one meditates on something as Brahman. The section begins with "Bliss and the other [qualities—plural] of the chief entity (Brahman or Ātman) [are to be assumed in all texts dealing with Brahman and thus should be included in all meditations]" (*BraSū* III.3.11).[47] Śaṁkara explains that the reference is to qualities (*guṇas*) like "being of the form of bliss", "being knowledge itself", "being omnipresent", "being the Self of All", and others.[48] Brahman should always be understood to be of such a nature as is described by these general qualities. In particular, when one meditates that something is Brahman, then these meanings should be present in one's mind as part of what one thinks of as Brahman. "On the other hand (*tu*), [qualities or descriptions like] 'having joy for its head' (*TaittUp* II.5) do not obtain everywhere, for (*hi*) variability[a] [is found] in difference (*bheda*)," continues the Sūtra (*BraSū* III.3.12). That is, attributes or descriptions that admit variability—either in the attribute itself or in the fact that it is applicable in a specific context only[49]—should not be regarded as implicit whenever Brahman is mentioned, and should be used in meditation only in the *vidyās* in which they are specifically mentioned. And lastly, "essential and unalterable qualities like bliss and knowledge"[50] should be used whenever one meditates on Brahman "because of sameness of import (or meaning)," *arthasāmānyāt* (*BraSū* III.3.13). In other words, these qualities all really refer to the same thing. They look as if they are describing different aspects, but these differences arise because of our minds, they have no analogue in Brahman.

Now this "generic" conception of *upāsanā* reflects a much more general attitude of the *Sūtra* which is summarized in *BraSū* I.1.2-4: "[Brahman is] the origin and so forth (i.e., origin, subsistence, and dissolution) of this [world]" (aphorism 2); "[this knowledge of Brahman arises] from Scripture as origin" (aphorism 3), "but that [is known] from the 'going together after the same thing' (*samanvaya*) (i.e., the harmony of the different scriptural teachings)" (aphorism 4).[51] Much has been written about these statements, but this much is clear: They exalt Brahman as something that in the most total manner imaginable encompasses everything in Creation. And they connect the knowledge of this Brahman, which is beyond the actions of the mind, with the Scriptures, principally the Upaniṣads, which are seen as all "going together in harmony, according to, or following after the same thing", namely Brahman (*samanvaya*, from *sam*, "together", *anu*, "following after, in accordance with, repeated", and root *i*, "go"). In other words, for the *Sūtra*, Brahman is such a large, all-dominant (immanent and transcendent) entity, that "the meaning of all Scriptural passages is Brahman";[52] all the Upaniṣadic teachings are "going together after the same thing". As a result of this, the *upāsanās* have all basically the same character, viz., they are all generic "*upāsanā* aiming at Brahman". The teachers of the *Sūtra* feel the same pull of the Infinite Brahman in every Upaniṣadic text and see every text as enjoining a similar activity and effort to go to that Infinite. Whatever it may be in detail, *upāsanā* is for the *Sūtra* nothing but the striving, in meditation and corresponding living, to attain that Infinite completely. This complete dominance of Brahman in the vision of the *Sūtra* expresses itself in many ways, and the *Sūtra's* uniform view of *upāsanā* is only one of these.

The principle that in *upāsanā*, the thought of Brahman should always include "essential and unalterable qualities" such as "being of the form of bliss", or "being knowledge itself", is not the only thing that gives the conception of *upāsanā* in the *Sūtra* such a generic, uniform quality. Another contributing factor is the *Sūtra's* general philosophy of combining or pooling, within a particular *vidyā* or line of wisdom, the various attributes of Brahman or Ātman that are mentioned to the maximum extent possible.[53] The principle of always including the "essential and unalterable qualities" in meditation on Brahman may itself be regarded as one reason for, or as one type of, combining and pooling qualities. (It says that such essential and unalterable qualities should be combined because they are ultimately only different ways of describing the same Aspect of Entity; the differences exist only in our mind.) Other groups of aphorisms (*adhikaraṇas*)[54] in *BraSū* III.3 elaborate other reasons for, or types of, combining or pooling. These include:

adhikaraṇa 1 (= *BraSū* III.3.1-4), to the effect that "[apparently different meditations] described in all the Vedānta [texts] [are not different, and thus may be combined into one meditation, when there is] nondifference of injunction and so on" (*BraSū* III.3.1);
adhikaraṇa 2 (= *BraSū* III.3.5), to the effect that different attributes or qualities of Ātman/Brahman which are mentioned in different versions of a given *upāsanā* or *vidyā* should be combined and merged into that total state or flow. "[There should be] combination (i.e., unification into a combined total, *upa-saṁ-hāra*) [of several attributes] on account of nondifference of [their basic] import, [just as] in the common and subsidiary instructions [in different manuals regarding a given sacrifice]" (*BraSū* III.3.5);
adhikaraṇa 6 = *BraSū* III.3.11-13 discussed above; and
adhikaraṇa 10 (= *BraSū* III.3.19), to the effect that "in [meditations of different texts belonging to] the same [Vedic school], it is so also (i.e. the meditations should also be combined), on account of nondifference [of the specific object of meditation described in the two texts]".

BraSū III.3.5 may be regarded as virtually implying a view of *upāsanā* as a state in which there is a "continuous succession of comparable fundamental conceptions" (*tulya-pratyaya-saṁtatiḥ*) a la Śaṁkara. All the principles in these *adhikaraṇas* go far beyond the Upaniṣads. There, the *vidyās* are handled much more freely and broadly. Much greater variability seems to be countenanced, one easily accepts allusions to other known teachings as helpful for or in the same direction as the knowledge to be taught. Above all the emphasis is much more on attainment of the fruit (attainment of the knowledge), not on the fact that certain particulars or certain rules are followed.

Finally within the general outlook and framework just sketched, the *Brahma Sūtra* accepts also another fundamental principle, viz. that Brahman should ultimately be realized as the Self. "[The Scriptures] acknowledge and make [the student] grasp [Brahman] [as, or in the manner of] 'self, *ātman*' " (*BraSū* IV.1.3).[55] Other types of *upāsanā* are also accepted, but, the *Sūtra* insists, ultimately the understanding of Brahman must be as one's self. In *upāsanā* in which a symbol (*pratīka*) is used for meditation on Brahman (like "Brahman is the

Sun", "Brahman is Mind"), the Sūtra continues, "[The student is] no [to see the Self] in the symbol, because he is not that" (*BraSū* IV.1.4).[56] Instead "[there should be] a regarding [of the symbol] as Brahman because of uplift" (*BraSū* IV.1.5).[57] We see that in IV.1.4, the *Sūtra* is not interested in making the point that in meditating "Brahman is the Sun" one will not realize Brahman because the Self is not explicitly involved—a point which would be natural immediately after IV.1.3 if the latter was meant to exclude *pratīka upāsanās*.[58] Instead it only wants to prevent that the preceding IV.1.3 is wrongly applied. The meditation "Brahman is the Sun" means that the Sun should be seen (*dṛś-*) as Brahman, or the idea of Brahman should be imposed on the Sun; this results in "uplift" (of the Sun and the self), which is useful. So here we have a very broad minded attitude that although ultimately meditation/knowledge must lead to knowledge of Brahman as the Self, all kinds of meditation besides *ahaṁgraha* ones ("I am Brahman") are accepted. This attitude represents another effect of the dominance of Brahman in the *Sūtra's* vision of things.

Śaṁkara in his Commentary on the *Brahma Sūtra*. In his Commentary on the *Brahma Sūtra*, Śaṁkara basically accepts the whole attitude of the *Sūtra* on *upāsanā* (all the aspects we have discussed).[59] But he re-positions it and re-evaluates it in a fundamental way by distinguishing sharply between (realization of) the highest Brahman, which is without attributes (*nir-guṇa*) and without any dualit (*a-dvaita*), and other forms of (realization of) the Universal Divine and Supreme, often called *sa-guṇa* Brahman. To establish that the difference is really fundamental and we are not dealing with comparable, mutually compatible types of realization, the great Teacher uses several additional distinctive principles and concepts. These include the principle that "the transcendent is conveyed indirectly by [first] attributing empirical characteristics to it that are subsequently denied";[60] the teaching that there is a fundamental distinction between action (*kriyā*) and Knowledge (*jñāna*);[61] and concepts like *a-vidyā*, "non-knowledge, nescience", *adhyāsa*, "super-imposition", and *māyā*, "(power of) illusion".[62] The result is that *upāsanā* is for Śaṁkara basically an activity which is helpful or possibly even necessary in beginning and intermediate stages, but which can *in principle* not lead to realization of the Highest Brahman. Realization of the Highest Brahman is something which is *sui generis* and can only arise from the Reality itself. We illustrate the basic argument with two excerpts.

> [A] But is not knowledge in fact mental action? Not so, for its essential characteristics are different. Mental action (*kriyā*) is something enjoined. It is not (like knowledge) determined by the nature of what already exists, but results from the free working of the human mind. . . Meditation is mentally dwelling on something. Though it is mental, it is to be noted that it depends on human will, and can either be done or not done or done in this or that alternative way. Knowledge, on the other hand, is what arises from the application of one of the means of knowledge (*pramāṇa*), and a means of knowledge bears on the true (and fixed) nature of an already existent object. Knowledge, therefore, is not anything that can be done or not done or done in this or that alternative way. It is conditioned neither by a command nor by human will but by the nature of an already existent reality. Thus, although knowledge is mental, there is a very great difference between it and a mental action such as meditation.[63]

This distinguishes between action, including *upāsanā* as mental effort, and Knowledge of Brahman. *Upāsanā* or meditation is still mental action, and the resulting knowledge of Divinity of the Supreme is still connected with that action is some way. "For we have such Vedic texts as 'under whatever form one meditates on him, that one's self becomes'; 'What a man wills in this world, that he becomes after death' . . ."[64] In other words, the resulting Knowledge of Divinity and Reality is still not absolute, it still involves *guṇas*, attributes, divinized or entered into Supreme Divinity through the *upāsanā*. But Knowledge, i.e., knowledge of the highest Brahman or liberation, is something different. It comes about only from "application of a means of knowledge (*pramāṇa*)" (recall Sai Baba's "manner of acquisition of true knowledge"above, sec. 1). This application is effective because the means of knowledge are intrinsically connected with an already existing object, viz. Brahman (the only object that really exists, in Śaṁkara's system):

> [B] And in this section [i.e., in *ChāndUp* I-V] devoted to knowledge within the sphere of duality, some meditations leading to a higher worldly station are taught. The ones included here, however, lead on ultimately to high results,

> approximate to liberation. They have for their subject-matter the Absolute in a form only mildly distorted from its true non-dual nature, as in such texts as "Made up of mind, with the Vital Energy as its body . . ." [the *Śāṇḍilya Vidyā*]. . . All the various Vedic meditations (*upāsanās*) have this one point in common with knowledge of non-duality, namely that they consist in a mere manipulation of the mind. What, then, is the difference between knowledge of non-duality and these meditations? The answer is that knowledge of non-duality puts an end once and for all to that notion of a distinction between agent, action, factors of action and results of action which we have the natural tendency erroneously to superimpose onto the actionless Self. It is like the dissolution of the superimposed snake or the like which occurs through right knowledge of the true nature of the rope. Meditation, however, is different. Here one takes some conception laid down by the Vedic texts and makes the stream of ideas in one's mind conform to it continuously over a period, without admitting the intrusion of ideas of anything different. Such meditations contribute to the final understanding of the metaphysical truth by purifying the mind, and are in this sense auxiliaries to knowledge of non-duality: and because they offer a definite conception for the mind to hold on to they are easy to practise, and are hence placed here at the beginning of the Upaniṣad, before the transition to the metaphysical teaching proper.[65]

The argument is clear. Meditation, *upāsanā*, involves "making the stream of ideas in one's mind conform" to a "conception laid down in the Vedic texts" "continuously over a period". This leads to something that still depends to some extent on the conceptions in question. It leads to forms of perception/knowledge of the Universal Divine, or of Brahman, which are still to some extent colored by the conception, the symbol or the paradigm laid down in the key formulations of the text. But the Highest Brahman does not involve any duality; it *is* non-duality. Perception/Knowledge of *that* "puts an end *once and for all* to that notion of a distinction between agent, action, factors of action [such as time and location] and results of action. . ." This is an extraordinarily powerful criterion, and almost certainly reflects Śaṁkara's own realization. He knew Brahman as *a-lakṣaṇa*, "without distinguishing marks", and as "immediately available" and "[actually already] ever attained by everybody".[66] As such, it cannot be known by any of the ordinary means of knowledge, like perception and inference, or any other mental activity, including *upāsanā*. Although the early Upaniṣads do not specially distinguish between *saguṇa* and *nirguṇa* Brahman (see below), Śaṁkara's emphasis on *nirguṇa* Brahman paradoxically does bring him closer to the Upaniṣads which, in their *vidyās*, emphasize the emergence of Knowledge in one's self and also regard worship-meditation as a preparatory, in practice possibly necessary, but in principle only ancillary means.

Śaṁkara's Personal Teaching. If *upāsanā*, being a mental manipulation, does not lead directly to knowledge of (*nirguṇa*) Brahman, how then can Brahman be attained? Śaṁkara's answer is that ultimately it can only be attained or known through *śabda-pramāṇa*, the means of knowledge (*pramāṇa*) represented by the word (*śabda*), specifically the word of Scripture (i. e. the Vedas, Brāhmaṇas, Āraṇyakas and Upaniṣads).[67] There is an intrinsic element in the word of *śruti* which enables it to impart knowledge of Brahman, and therewith liberation, *mokṣa*. More specifically, in the *Upadeśasāhasrī*, his main noncommentarial work, Śaṁkara teaches that one should focus on the great sayings or *mahā-vākyas*, particularly "You are That," *tat tvam asi*, in certain ways or using certain *jñāna*-methods. Apparently, according to him, this qualifies as the "means of [acquisition of] Knowledge" (sec. 2 above). At the same time he also endorses in his commentaries on the Upaniṣads the traditional *jñāna* paths of *adhyātmayoga* and *asparśayoga*.

Śaṁkara's *jñāna*-methods include *anvaya-vyatireka*, "agreement and difference", and various forms of *abhyāsa*, "practice, repetition". *Anvaya-vyatireka* is used to understand the meaning of "you", *tvam*, in the great saying *tat tvam asi*, "You are That". "That", *tat*, refers to Brahman, and *asi*, "[you] are" indicates that that what is referred to by "you" (which is something the person addressed is completely familiar with) is identical with Brahman.[68] *Anvaya-vyatireka* is the process of searching, with complete concentration, which aspects of "you" (i.e., "I", the meditator, the person addressed by the great saying) agree with "That", and which ones are different.[69] By this process, the correct meaning of "you" (i.e., of "I") is attained. As soon as that happens, the real meaning of the sentence, viz. "I am ever free", "becomes manifest".[70] The only aspect of "you" (i.e., "me") which is compatible with "That" or Brahman is feeling or awareness of one's "inner self", the *pratyag-ātman*. For only that is painless, like the "That," or Brahman.[71] *Abhyāsa* refers to repetition of fundamental truths such as the fact that one's true self is unrelated to anything.[72] Both *anvaya-vyatireka* and *abhyāsa* involve holding one's concentration to the point of loss of awareness of body and surroundings. But that concentration and more generally these methods are not *upāsanā*; they may be *nididhyāsana*.[73] Both *anvaya-vyatireka* and *abhyāsa*, for example, involve a degree of *yukti*, "reasoning", or better, "inner discrimination supported by reasoning couched in verbal form". They also rely on the power of the Transcendental Word.[74]

Adhyātmayoga and *asparśayoga* are ancient *jñāna* disciplines. Generally speaking, *adhyātmayoga* means for Śaṁkara the withdrawal of the mind from the sense objects and its concentration on the Self".[75] But more specifically it refers to the inner path outlined in *KaṭhaUp* I.3.13:

> The wise should merge Speech in the Mind,
> that [mind] he should merge in the knowledge self (*jñāna-ātman*).
> The knowledge self he should merge in the Great [Self] (*mahat*),
> that [Great Self in turn] he should merge in the Tranquil Self (*śānta ātman*).[76]

Asparśayoga or the *yoga* of noncontact (*a-sparśa*, non-touch, nonrelationship, of the mind or consciousness with external things through the senses) is held up as an already familiar type of spiritual discipline (or as a familiar path) by Gauḍapāda in his *Māṇḍūkya Kārikās*. Most probably Gauḍapāda means by it the disciplines and path enjoined in *Kārikās* III.40-46,[77] which are expounded in the context of a larger segment on the nature of Brahman/Ātman as "birthless, formless, ever effulgent, everything, and a knower" (*Kārikās* III.36), "supremely tranquil, . . ., immutable and fearless." The term *asparśa* in this context presumably refers to consciousness in which there is absence of normal mentation, and knowledge that there is only consciousness, no objects with which consciousness has contact.[78]

4. *Chāndogya Upaniṣad: Upāsana* on Mind and *Ākāśa* (*ChāndUp* III.18)

Chāndogya Upaniṣad. Since the *upāsanās* and *vidyās* in this chapter are all from *Chāndogya Upaniṣad,* we start with a few introductory comments on this text.[79] The word *Chāndogya* is derived from *chandas* + *gā*, "metre-singing", a term used to denote *sāman* chanting. While *Bṛhadāraṇyaka Upaniṣad* belongs to the *Yajur Veda*, the Veda of the *adhvaryu* priests who perform most of the ritual actions in the sacrifice, *Chāndogya Upaniṣad* belongs to the *Sāma Veda*, the Veda of the *udgātṛ* priests and their associates who chant the *sāmans*. It is part of the sacred literature of the *Kauthuma* school (*śākhā*) of the *Sāma Veda*, which has preserved the most detailed body of ancient writings on *Sāma Vedic* practice and is still found in India today.[80] The Upaniṣad consists of eight chapters (*prapāṭhakas*, "lectures") and is appended to the *Mantra Brāhmaṇa*, a text in two chapters which mostly give Vedic Mantras which should be used in rites such as for birth and marriage.[81] The combined text of ten chapters is called *Upaniṣad Brāhmaṇa* and is one of the eight canonical Brāhmaṇas of the Kauthumas. The fact that the Upaniṣad was combined with the *Mantra Brāhmaṇa* into a single text is significant. Just as everyone in society is blessed and made part of the overall divine societal, social and world order by the household rites in the *Mantra Brāhmaṇa*, so everyone can direct his life toward the Infinite Reality by the numerous *upāsanās* and *vidyās* of *Chāndogya Upaniṣad.*

As a wisdom text, *Chāndogya Upaniṣad* is closely related to *Jaiminīya Upaniṣad Brāhmaṇa*,[82] the only major Āraṇyaka-like text of the *Sāma Veda* (see chr. 1.3). The *Jaiminīya Upaniṣad Brāhmaṇa* belongs to the sacred literature of the *Jaiminīyas*,[83] the other main branch (*śākhā*) of the *Sāma Veda* besides the Kauthumas. *Chāndogya Upaniṣad* is also closely related to the *Śatapatha Brāhmaṇa*, however, which belongs to the *Yajur Veda*. The connections are complex. Several of the more important teachers of *Śatapatha Brāhmaṇa* (Śāṇḍilya, Uddālaka Āruṇi, Śvetaketu Āruṇeya) also figure prominently as teachers in *Chāndogya Upaniṣad*. *ŚatBr* X, the *Agnirahasya* or mystical teaching (*rahasya*) of Agni, the Fireplace in the *agni-cayana* ritual, contains close parallels of several important *vidyās* in *Chāndogya Upaniṣad*.[84] And there are numerous textual parallels with *Chāndogya Upaniṣad* in *Bṛhadāraṇyaka Upaniṣad*, which is the concluding portion of *Śatapatha Brāhmaṇa*.[85] It is not clear how all this fits together with the history of formation of the two texts.[86] Finally, there seems to be also a special relationship between *Chāndogya Upaniṣad* and the *Brahma Sūtra*. For an unusually large portion of the allusions of the

Sūtra to the Upaniṣads (particularly direct quotes) refer to *Chāndogya Upaniṣad*.[87]

The Upaniṣad may be divided naturally into 3 parts: chapters I-II, III-V, and VI-VIII, respectively. Chapters III-V are a collection of more than 20 *upāsanās* and *vidyās* of diverse kinds, and the three main texts of the present chapter are all from this part. The opulence of these chapters is difficult to communicate: the most diverse aspects of universe, life, mind, and experience are developed into inner paths. The following summary may give an idea:

III.1-11	*Madhu Vidyā* (meditations on Divine aspects of the Sun, and Brahman as the Sun);
12-13	*Gāyatrī Vidyā* (starts with the *Gāyatrī* meter common in the *Ṛg Veda* as the Logos that creates the world);
14	*Śāṇḍilya Vidyā* (meditation of the Self in the heart);
15	(a section showing modes of worship);
16-17	*Upāsanās* of life and activities as sacrifice (*yajña*);
18	*Upāsana* on Mind and *Ākāśa*, "Space", being Brahman;
19	*Upāsanā* of the Sun as Brahman, and the rising Sun as Creation;
IV.1-3	*Saṁvarga* ("All-Absorber" or "All-Devourer") *Vidyā;*
4-9	*Sixteen Parts Vidyā;*
10-14	*Upakosala Vidyā* (teachings of the Four Fires to Upakosala Kāmalāyana);
15	*Devapatha Vidyā* (the northen path of light to Brahman);
V.1-2	*Prāṇa Vidyā;*
3-10	*Pañcāgni Vidyā* (taching of the Five Fires);
11-18	*Vaiśvānara Vidyā* (*Vidyā* of the "One-in-the-Many");
19-24	Mental offering of food to the *prāṇas* (an adjunct to *Vaiśvānara Vidyā*).

Chapters VI-VIII consist of three or four major *vidyās* of great depth and profundity:

VI.	*Sad Vidyā* (*Sat* is "Being," "The Existent", "the one Reality");
VII.	*Bhūma Vidyā* (*Bhūman* is "the Infinite", "the Vast");
VIII.1-6	*Dahara Vidyā* (on the subtle (*dahara*) space that is within the heart);

VIII.7-15 The teaching of Prajāpati to Indra on Ātman, an adjunct to the *Dahara Vidyā*.

These *vidyās* are comparable to some of the great sections in *Bṛhadāraṇyaka Upaniṣad* in exaltedness of what is taught and clarity of formulation. The two remaining chapters of the Upaniṣad are more difficult to characterize. *ChāndUp* I is "Āraṇyaka-like".[88] It is basically a ramified *vidyā* that consists of several loosely connected sub-*vidyās*. *ChāndUp* II, finally, shows a sophisticated and unified literary treatment which makes it difficult to judge as spiritual teaching.

***ChāndUp* III.18: Text.** Our first text from the Upaniṣad is *ChāndUp* III.18, sometimes called "[higher] knowledge of mind" (*mano-vijñāna*).[89] It begins "The mind is Brahman," and expounds *upāsanas* on Mind and *ākāśa*, "Space", "Ether", as Brahman. But in our terms it has more the character of a brief *vidyā* than of an *upāsanā*. In the remainder of this section we give the text and briefly discuss its basic format. This gives a general outline of what is intended. Then in the next two sections, we bring in some parallel texts to try to get at its deeper meaning.

***ChāndUp* III.18**

1. "'Brahman is Mind (*manas*),' [thus] one should meditate (*upās-*)."[a] Thus [goes the teaching] with regard to the body (or oneself, *ātman*). Next, [the teaching] with regard to the gods: " 'Brahman is *ākāśa* ("space", "ether"),' [thus one should meditate]." The instruction is twofold, with regard to the body (or oneself) and with regard to the gods.
2. "This same Brahman has four feet: One foot is Speech (*Vāc*), one foot is *Prāṇa* (Life-Breath), one foot is Sight (*Cakṣus*), and one foot is Hearing (*Śrotra*)." Thus [the instruction] with reference to the body. Next, with reference to the gods: "One foot is Agni (Fire), one foot is Vāyu (Wind), one foot is Āditya (Sun), and one foot are the Quarters (Diśaḥ)." The instruction is twofold, with reference to the body (or oneself and with reference to the gods.
3. Speech is a foot, a one-fourth, of Brahman. It shines (*bhāti*) and glows (*tapati*) with Agni as light (*jyotiḥ*). [Since Vedic

times Agni is associated with Speech]. He who knows thus, shines and glows with fame and celebrity and with Brahman-effulgence.

4. Life-Breath is a foot, a one-fourth, of Brahman. It shines and glows with Vāyu as light. He who knows thus, shines and glows with fame and celebrity and with Brahman-effulgence.
5. Sight is a foot, a one-fourth, of Brahman. It shines and glows with Āditya as light. He who knows thus, shines and glows with fame and celebrity and with Brahman-effulgence.
6. Hearing is one of the four feet of Brahman. It shines and glows with the Quarters (Diśaḥ) as light. He who knows thus, shines and glows with fame and celebrity and with Brahman-effulgence—yea, he who knows thus.[90]

Structure of the Text. "'Brahman is Mind'—[thus] should meditate." By itself, this means that I should feel, meditate, comprehend that "my mind is Brahman"—"all my thinking, speaking, smelling is Brahman, my every experience, my every moment of consciousness is Brahman". When I am speaking (v. 2), my mind as it is involved in the speaking is Brahman, and whenever I am speaking, there should be the thought or awareness or knowledge that my speaking is Brahman. Similarly "me seeing things around me" is Brahman, "me hearing" is Brahman, and so on. This is the most literal and direct interpretation.[91] The instruction is to realize deeply, in meditation, and to have the knowledge or awareness in one's daily activities. If there is deep experience in meditation, that will persist in oneself and in one's daily activities. The aim is to develop an awareness and knowledge that abides naturally in one's conscious states of mind.

But to meditate "the mind is Brahman" is only one aspect of the teaching. It is the part that "pertains to the body", to an individual's experience in the framework of his own mind and body. The real teaching consists of two parallel instructions (*ādiṣṭas*), viz. "'Brahman is Mind' —thus one should meditate," *and* " 'Brahman is *ākāśa*, Space or Ground of Existence'—thus should one meditate." (*Ākāśa* sometimes means "space", but more commonly "space as a primal generative principle or matrix for the whole manifestation of the physical world.") "Meditate" here is *upās-*, so we are dealing with a teaching that involves (in terrms of Table 4.2) two *upāsanās*, both involving "formulas" which are marked with *iti*. These two *upāsanās* are first cited or displayed as instructions (*ādiṣṭas*), and then coordinated into a double instruction in terms of the familiar schema of "[one is] with regard to the body, or self, *adhyātmam*, [the other is] with regard to the deities, *adhidaivatam*". Next, this double instruction is amplified in v. 2 by statements which expand Mind and *Ākāśa* into four sub-aspects each, all divine principles or deities. The remaining verses 3-6 then constitute an exposition of what the teaching means and how it is to be practiced. That is, they elaborate on the *upāsanās* taught (they may or may not be themselves *upāsanās*). The sub-aspects are grouped in pairs, with each body (or self or subjective) aspect forming a unity with a divine aspect of the external world. So the real teaching is: "Brahman is four-footed, *catuś-pād*," with the feet corresponding to the four pairs, Speech—Agni, Prāṇa—Wind Divine (Vāyu), Sight—Sun Divine (Āditya), and Hearing—the Four Directions (Diśaḥ). Note that while as far as the body or the self is concerned, we have "Mind is Brahman," the four aspects of Mind, namely Speech and so on, are each only "a foot of Brahman". Thus although Mind may not be exactly superordinate to Speech, Prāṇa, etc, in the way it is for us,[92] it is in effect treated as a higher category that comprehends the other four. By v. 2, the same thing holds for *Ākāśa* and its sub-aspects, as well as for the pair Mind—*Ākāśa* and the subordinated pairs, the "feet" Speech—Agni, and so on. The fact that Speech is called a foot of Brahman but Agni is not (and similarly in the case of the other pairs) may be interpreted as indicating that the subjective or self-aspect is treated as primary. But one cannot really draw any further conclusions from this.

Clearly this whole text is remarkable. There is an extraordinary, epistemological-looking focus on the Sense-Powers, and an equally stunning and surprising declaration of oneness. The teaching embodies the highest philosophical (metaphysical and epistemological) ideals. At the same time it operates and attains its aim with the simplest, most basic tools—the experience of one's own senses and mind, and the Divinity that can be felt in the basic features of the world around one (Sun, the Quarters, etc.). And finally, it uses these tools with utmost parsimony. There is no appeal to a priviledged experience, revelation, or the like. There is only direct, authoritative statement such as comes from Knowledge. There is no question that the text speaks from Brahman and teaches Brahman. We will see that the other two major texts in this chapter have the same character.

There is no more mythic language. Instead, Realization speaks in the language of Knowledge, of highest philosophical *Erkenntnis* (Knowledge, Insight).

To enter more deeply into the text we have to consider vs. 3-6 and get some feeling for what these might involve in terms of inner experience, spiritual life, whatever. To this end we first look at a similar text which contains almost the same pairs and in which the nature of the experiential aspect is much clearer.

5. The Union of the External Deities with, or in, the Self

AitĀr II.1.5.2-4, the so-called *prahitām saṁyoga*, describes a realization of oneness of Speech, Sight, Mind and Hearing with the corresponding deities Agni, Sun, Moon, and Quarters. While it uses some of the same powers and correspondences with deities as *ChāndUp* III.18, it involves rather different meditations and as far as it is presented may not necessarily lead to realization of Brahman. But it will help clarify the overall intent of the *Chāndogya* text.

Aitareya Āraṇyaka. The *Aitareya Āraṇyaka (AitĀr)* is an esoteric mystical text of great importance for Upaniṣadic studies.[93] It is part of the *Aitareya Brāhmaṇa*, and contains the *Aitareya Upaniṣad* (which = *AitĀr* II.4-6). The passage of interest here occurs in a set of mystical teachings on Prāṇa and Puruṣa, *AitĀr* II.1-3. This whole segment of *Aitareya Āraṇyaka* "forms a unity" and Keith considers it to be also an Upaniṣad, "the oldest long Upaniṣad extant" (coming before the Yājñavalkya teachings).[94] It consists of a network of knowledges and realizations which historically were the immediate precursors of some of the Upaniṣadic teachings, including of the three main texts of the present chapter. Most of the longer texts are meditations or myths are connected with the *Uktha*, a recitation of *Ṛg Vedic* mantras performed by the *hotṛ* priest at the midday session of the *Mahāvrata* ritual (a Soma ritual). Typically, the *Uktha* is identified with Prāṇa (here understood as a type of realization of Brahman) and the Puruṣa, and it is in this overall framework that the divine knowledges and realizations are presented.

Prahitām Saṁyoga:[95] Text

2. "Agni is Speech, this Sun (Āditya) is Sight, Mind is the Moon, Hearing is the Quarters. This is the *prahitām saṁyoga* (the union, *saṁ-yoga*, of the [deities] impelled forward,

pra + root *hi*).[a] These deities here (Agni, etc.) are bodily (*adhyātmam*), but manifest before the eyes yonder (*āvis*) they are deity-wise (*adhidaivatam*)." Exactly this has been said.

3. And also Hiraṇyadant Vaida, having realized (*vidvān*) this, used to say: "He does not dispose over [that] what he would not give to me."[b] The *prahitām saṁyoga*, verily, I know, body-wise established.[c] That is that.
4. To him who knows this, all creatures bring offering without being commanded.[96]

Structure of the Text. The initial identifications are meant as identities: *Vāg agniḥ*, "Agni is Speech," etc. And knowledge/experience of these identities, as a unitary state or as a level of spiritual development, is the *prahitām saṁyoga. Saṁyoga* means "union with, absorption in". *Prahitām* should probably be read as a past passive principle from *pra* + root *hi*, "to create (impel) forwards"[97] (so Ṣadguruśiṣya, the deep and oldest (11th century CE) traditional commentator on the *Aitareya Āraṇyaka* and *Aitareya Brāhmaṇa*.[98]) So the phrase means something like "absorption in the [deities Agni, Sun, . . . that were] created (or impelled) forwards", out of Self, the Puruṣa, in the creation of the world (in the typical Brāhmaṇa creation account, or in an account of the creation of the world from Self). Alternative readings are "union with, or absorption of the impellers" (referring to the deities Agni etc. as impellers) (Keith)[99] and "union with the [deities] placed forward" (Sāyaṇa).[100] "These deities here (*imā devatāḥ*) [are] bodily, *adhyātmam*," i.e., in this state or at this level of *prahitām saṁyoga* the deities Agni, etc. are experienced as part of the body or the physical self. But "before the eyes, yonder" (as opposed to "here") "they are deity-wise, *adhidaivatam*", i.e., they are experienced the way Agni, the Sun-Divine, etc. are usually experienced in the world. "Exactly this has been said:" The text just given has been quoted exactly, in keeping with its status as a high level, mystical-esoteric teaching. There is no *iti* ("unquote" or stop) after the four identities. This suggests that these identities are not being cited as a teaching and then explained. Rather, the whole statement is cited as a single inspired statement of someone to whom it was reality (note *imā devatāḥ*, "these deities here [present now]").

The teaching so far was the teaching proper. Next the Brāhmaṇa cites Hiraṇyadant Vaida as one who was a knower, *vidvān*, of this "union" or *saṁyoga* (v. 3). He was a knower because he "used to say 'what [persons] do not give to me, he (*sic*) himself is not lord over (roots *īś*).'" The Sanskrit is problematic, see the notes, but perhaps we can read: a person would give him (Hiraṇyadant) anything he needed—the only things a person wouldn't give him were things which he (the person) did not own (was not lord over) to begin with. This suggests a higher state of oneness with things, a state which would affect the people around him and make them share freely with him what they had (there was no difference between them and him). This is an effect which saints are sometimes said to have on people. In v. 4, finally, the Brāhmaṇa says that in general, something like Hiraṇyadant's experience is always a fruit of the *prahitām saṁyoga*.

Interpretation. What, then, is the meaning of the text as a whole? Our general approach must be to take it as expressing spiritual experience, or a spiritual state, and as spiritual instruction. The chief clues regarding the spiritual state taught are the individual statements or formulas, "Agni is Speech", "this Sun is Sight", and so on. These are rather unusual and we must look at them closely. Take for example "this Sun is Sight", *cakṣur-asav-āditya. Āditya* indicates the Sun seen as a Divinity, as something Divine. So *asav āditya* means "this Sun-Divine which I worship, this Divine which I see or perceive when I meditate on the Sun, or when I am in touch with the Divine during the day". Hence the basic teaching might be rendered "This Sun-Divine, which I know and perceive when I meditate on the Sun or when I am in touch with the Divine, is the same as Sight, *Cakṣus*, is the same as my seeing, or seeing-consciousness." That such a direct meaning of "this Sun is Sight" is in fact intended is underlined by the immediately following "these deities [here] are *adhyātmam*, 'body-wise, self-wise.'" Strictly speaking *adhyātmam* is an adverb meaning "at the level of the body; at the level of one's experience as a physical person". It is usually contrasted with *adhidaivatam,* "deity-wise, at the level of the deities that are ruling in the world", like here. So by saying "these deities [here] are body-wise," the text is expressing in the strongest possible terms that what is usually a correspondence, is in the state of *prahitām saṁyoga* an identity, or experienced as a oneness. The same Divine, Āditya, exists body-wise or self-wise, as (my) seeing, *and* at the same time yonder as the Sun. The other formulas, "Agni is Speech" etc., must be understood similarly. "My speaking is really the Divine which I know as (or which is) Agni. Agni exists *adhyātmam*, 'body-wise,' as my bodily speaking as a physical individual, while at the same time I experience him as the metaphysical or divine principle yonder in the fire." The emphasis on the bodily here is justified because the text makes a contrast of "here" (*imā*, these here) versus "before the eyes over there", *āvis*.

So the text is teaching a oneness, *saṁ-yoga*, of the great "Divines" which one sees in the world with one's perception, mind, and life-forces. Neither aspect is favored: Agni is Speech, Āditya is Sight, but Mind is Moon (not the other way around) and Hearing is the Quarters. The same Divines exist self- or body-wise as well as deity-wise. Further, the text hints at a union or oneness of *all* deities, or of every Divine, with or in oneself, not just of specifically the four mentioned. This is not explicitly stated. But it is suggested by the fact that the state cited by Hiraṇyadant as exemplifying this oneness is not intrinsically connected to any particular one of them. This higher state, in which people around one share with one what they have if there is need, has nothing specifically to do with Agni, Āditya, Moon, and the Directions. So the *prahitām saṁyoga*, beyond the four identities "Agni is Speech" etc., is also meaning to teach a single state that is deeper than the four identities and transcends them. Indeed the individual statement "Agni is Speech," if taken as *upāsanā*, have an additional inner dimension. If one meditates "Agni is Speech" and so on, at least after some time one does not only think only of Agni and Agni being Speech. Rather there emerges also an unquestioning taking for granted that a single Divine is to be felt in and constitutes all one's knowledge processes, and that Agni being Speech is only one of an arbitrary number of its "surface manifestations". This one-pointed commitment and trust in a single One that absolutely transcends all "articulations" or "surface manifestations" of "objective" and "subjective" is implied in all four of the *upāsanās*, not only in "Agni is Speech." It is a pure emanation of the heart (an unchanging thing, not a process) and represents the most important element of the *prahitām saṁyoga*. Indeed it is this whole aspect of a single One "shining" as both the external deities and knowledge objects and as the subjective knowing processes that makes this teaching relevant to *ChāndUp* III.18.

Comparison with *ChāndUp* III.18. On the one hand, the knowledge/perception in the *prahitām saṁyoga* that the Deities out there exist at the same time "bodily" or "self-wise" as "Sense-Powers" gives us some confidence to interpret *ChāndUp* III.18.3-6 literally also. "Sight is one foot of Brahman. It glows and shines with Āditya as light" does not simply mean that Sight depends on the Sun. Rather it means that a single Divine or Transcendental, the same (foot of) Brahman, is manifesting ("shining" and "glowing") as both (my) Sight and Āditya, the Sun-Divine. Similarly, a single One, Brahman, is shining and glowing as both the external Deities and knowledge objects and as the Powers of subjective experience. Indeed, while in the *prahitām saṁyoga* this single highest aspect is only implicit in the devotional attitude, in *Chāndogya Upaniṣad* it is abundantly explicit. It is explicitly named as Brahman. It is explicitly said to be shining in the objective, external world and in the subjective, internal world: both "Mind is Brahman" and "*Ākāśa* is Brahman." And the fact that the thought of this One, and trust in this One must be present throughout is clear from the fact that the phrases "is a foot of Brahman", and "shines" and "glows" "by the light of . . .," *bhāti* and *tapati jyotiṣā,* all occur in the common refrain in all four of the verses explaining the four feet.

In terms of inner attitude and practice in the beginning stages, the two texts have therefore some affinities. But there are also significant differences. Above all they appear to describe and lead to different higher states and goals. Sāyaṇa says that *AitĀr* II.1.5, of which the *prahitām saṁyoga* forms the main part, deals with *Prāṇa*. Śaṁkara and Advaita Vedānta generally identify knowledge of *Prāṇa* with realization of Hiraṇyagarbha, stereotypic for a level of union with the Divine but not necessarily realization of Brahman. Since Sāyaṇa often tends to follow Śaṁkara, this suggests that the *prahitām saṁyoga* represents a level of realization of Universal Divinity but not full-realization of Brahman. In support one might cite the *Bhūma Vidyā, ChāndUp*, VIII where knowledge of Prāṇa is the fifteenth of a series of twenty-three steps and so not the highest knowledge. The latter is knowledge of *Bhūman*, "the Vast", Brahman. But it may be argued that it is not really clear what the *Bhūma Vidyā* has in mind with "knowledge of Prāṇa".

In the *prahitām saṁyoga*, the stark formulations *vāg agniḥ*, "Agni is Speech," and so on, and the fact that "these Deities exist body-wise, *adhyātmam"*, suggest a rather specific, still mixed-with-body quality of experience of the Divine. This would likewise argue against the *prahitām saṁyoga* indicating a state that was close to knowledge of Brahman. But this argument is based on the ordinary meaning of the words and may not correspond to the actual state. The upshot is that while the *prahitām saṁyoga* obviously represents more than a beginning level of knowledge of (Universal) Divinity, it is not clear how close it is to knowledge of Brahman. *ChāndUp* III.18 on the other hand undoubtedly aims at knowledge of Brahman as understood by the highest Upaniṣadic *vidyās* and by Advaita Vedānta (see below).

6. *Asti, Bhāti, Priyam; Tapati*

So far we have seen that the teaching in *ChāndUp* III.18 of a unitary single Aspect which shines and glows both inside and outside should be taken seriously. But we still don't really have an idea of the kind of inner experience or state at which the teaching is aiming. In this section we consider two hints that direction. These are contained in the phrase "it shines, *bhāti*, and glows-heats, *tapati*, with—as light (*jyotiḥ*)", which forms the common refrain and the heart of the instruction in III.18.3-6. For *bhāti* "it shines" points to the *bhāti* of what in mature Vedānta is called *asti, bhāti, priyam*, "it is, it shines, [it is] dear", a characterization of Brahman term for term similar to *sat-cit-ānanda*. In other words, *bhāti* indicates inner experience in the direction of *cit*, "pure knowing, awareness". *Tapati* on the other hand indicates higher experience of the Universal Creative aspect and of universal Prāṇa.

Asti, Bhāti, Priyam. Of the terms *bhāti, tapati* and *jyoti* in the Upaniṣad, *bhāti* gives the deepest clue. In Vedic leterature, *bhā-*, "to shine, be bright or luminous, . . . [to] shine forth, appear, show oneself",[101] is found already in the Brāhmaṇas in mystical contexts related to the Sun.[102] This alone is enough to suggest that meditation to the effect that "Speech shines, *bhāti*, with Agni as light" leads to some knowledge of Divinity. But the meanings "to shine forth, appear (as), to show itself (as)", found even in the *Ṛg Veda* and also the Brāhmaṇas,[103] suggest a reference specifically to Brahman. For in the Upaniṣads, *bhāti* is most often used for the shining of the one Ātman/ Brahman,[104] and in later Vedānta it then describes how Brahman appears as objects and phenomena, i.e. knowledge-objects.[105] The most developed form of this is the characterization of Brahman as *asti, bhāti, priya*, "[it] is, [it] shines, [it is] dear" given in the *Dṛg-Dṛśya-Viveka*.[106] The *Dṛg-Dṛśya-Viveka* is a small but high-level document of 46 stanzas (*ślokas*) most commonly ascribed to Bhāratī Tīrtha (ca. 1350 CE).[107] It also contains some other well-known formulations besides *asti, bhāti, priyam*:[108]

20. *Asti*, "[it] is", *bhāti*, "[it] shines", *priyam*, "[it is] dear," *nāma*, "name," *rūpam*, "form,"—[that is] the fivefold [which is a] sharing-in[a] (i.e., that is the constellation of five aspects in which all things share, or of which they all consist). [Of this] the first triad is characteristic of Brahman,[b] the next two are characteristic of the world.[c]
21. In ether (*kha* = *ākāśa*), air, fire, water and earth, in gods, animals and men, the [aspects] *sat-cit-ānanda* are undivided (or common, *abhinna*). Form-and-name vary.[109]

These stanzas give a completely fresh, "experiential" description. The first one says that all there is *asti, bhāti, priyam*, name and form, and that all things share in that, or are an indissociable part of that. But *asti, bhāti, priyam* is an indivisible aspect which all things share uniformly (v. 21), while names and forms (or things the way they normally look) vary. Verse 21 also suggests that *asti, bhāti, priyam* corresponds term for term to *sat-cit-ānanda* (Being, Consciousness, and Bliss) in the usual description of Brahman as *sat-cit-ānanda*. *Asti, bhāti, priyam* is an important way of talking about Brahman because of the point of view or the "mental stance" which it implies. Verse 21 literally says "'*asti-bhāti-priya*-name-form'—[that is] the fivefold forming-a-portion," i.e., "that is the 'everything [is] having a fivefold portion [in it].'" In other words, *asti, bhāti, priyam, nāma, rūpa* is represented as a single homogeneous entity or state ("one homogeneous *vastu*"—Sai Baba). Of this single entity, however, the first trio of qualities, i.e., *asti, bhāti, priyam*, "is of the form of Brahman", the last pair "is of the form of the world". This unusual way of speaking keeps Brahman and the world in a common famework—it provides a way of talking about both at the same time. In addition, it avoids the usual "stances" of "I am Brahman" (Brahman as the Self) and "Brahman is . . ." (e.g., "is the origin etc. of everything", or "is *sat-cit-ānanda*"). By taking the attention off from the usual I, the seer, and from what is seen, and not requiring participation in either of them, it enables something else, something more subtle, new to emerge. (*Sat-cit-ānanda*, by comparison, simply combines "subjective" and "objective" terms.) *ChāndUp* III.18 is very similar. Neither an approach of "I [am Brahman etc.]" nor an approach of "Brahman is . . ." is dominant. Instead, the limited self with its self-interests and so on is enabled to quietly step aside and allow something larger to dawn.

Sai Baba often uses *asti, bhāti, priyam* in his discourses:[110]

> [A]...The Vedas have also taught us the following aspects in this context: 'Being', 'Awareness' and 'Delight' (*asti, bhāti, priyam*). These are Divine attributes and can be found in everything. Here is a tumbler. Whether you see it or not, the tumbler exists (*asti*) and it is (*asti*) here. The fact that it exists is 'being' (*Sat*). The light that falls on it is reflected to you, making its presence felt and it makes the tumbler shine (*bhā*). This light is 'awareness' (*Cit*). The moment we set our sight on the tumbler we are filled with a sense of joy (*ānanda*, because the tumbler is dear, *priya*). So being means that which exists, awareness makes it glow, and delight is the experience of joy derived on perceiving it. All that you see around you is a conglomeration of material objects. In these material entities you have being-awareness-delight together. But then, these three aspects are permanent, or beyond change of any kind. However the tumbler itself could undergo some change.[111]

The basic statements are that *asti, bhāti, priyam* are Divine Attributes, that they form a unity, and that this Divine unitary aspect *is beyond change of any kind*. We should see this *asti, bhāti, priyam* in all that we see around us, at all times. Sai Baba introduced *asti-bhati-priya* in [A] in the context of explaining the famous stanza "That is full; this is full . . ." (*pūrṇam adaḥ, pūrṇam idam, . . .*) from the *Heart* and *Satya Brahma Vidyā*. In a more recent discourse, he relates it to the Ātman and to the "quality" of the Ātman called *caitanya*, "pure (or universal) consciousness".

> [B] . . . There is nothing in the world separate from you. All the diverse objects are images of the One. For all worldly things there is a *kartā* (creator [doer]), *karma* (causal action) and *kriyā* (the end product). In the sphere of the spiritual, however, there is only the Creator (*Kartā*). There is no *Kriyā*. He is the Doer. He is also the one who gets things done. He is the Outcome of what is done. The Ātmic principle, which represents the unity of all these three, is the One that pervades the entire Cosmos. It is the Universal Consciousness (*Caitanya*). It is impossible for it to be present in some and not in others.

> It is this Cosmic Consciousness that has been presented to the common people as *Sat-Cit-Ānanda* so that they can comprehend its nature. The Vedāntins looked upon these three as reflections of each other. These three have also been called "*Asti*", "*Bhāti*" and "*Priya*" in Vedāntic parlance. In fact, all three are one and the same. When one says, "Here is a tumbler," the *Is-ness* is *Asti*. This is *Sat*. We are seeing it. The quality of being perceivable is *Bhāti*. This is *Cit* (cognisability). "I am enjoying it." This is *Priyam* or *Ānanda*. *Sat, Cit* and *Ānanda* are one. It is one and the same thing which *is*, which *shines* and which gives *Ānanda*. Though there is only One, because of our mental processes, we are seeing It in many forms and names.[112]

The main point is that *asti, bhāti, priyam* are a single Aspect. It is this Aspect, this One, which is seen as *sat, cit*, and *ānanda*, and as so many individual objects.

7. Meaning of *ChāndUp* III.18

The preceding helps to get a much clearer idea of the teaching of *ChāndUp* III.18. to begin with, the use of *tapati* and to some extent also of *bhāti* before the Upaniṣads suggests that the phrases "Speech shines and glows with Agni as light" and so on all refer to knowledges of Divinity which exist already in the aspirant in some form. For example, Speech includes the power to conceptualize, to put in words, to name and evoke, so that something becomes meaningful, becomes a goal, an object one relates to, a presence. This power has in it, and is "presided over" by, a divine element, namely Agni, the Fire-Divine, and the student is likely to have come to know this already earlier in his spiritual life. Sight is much more than visual perception of objects. "The Eye is the truth deposited among men," says *Aitareya Brāhmaṇa*. It should be worshipped (*upās-*) as truth (*satya*), Yājñavalkya tells Janaka (*BṛhUp* IV.1.5). Sight is "being truth"—its quality of being truth (*satyatā*) is shown by the fact that "when they say to one who sees 'have you seen,' [and] he says 'I have seen'—that is truth." Sight is having a complete and holistic understanding of a situation. Sight is complete clarity. Again, Sight leads to illumination. And so on. Sight has in it, and is blessed by, Āditya, the Sun-Divine. The Sun gives the daylight where the truth is seen—the daylight of truth. As

Sight sees all, so Sun shines on all. As Sight is truth and illumination for the self, so Sun, which illumines, is Brahman. And so on. As diamonds and precious stones are seen sparkling and luminous in the dark earth, so divine elements may be perceived in Speech, Sight, Hearing, and Prāṇa. This kind of perception and understanding may be expected to have come to the student naturally already earlier in the course of a sincere and devoted religious life. So the statements "Speech shines and glows with Agni as light" and so on recall not only other similar Brāhmaṇa teachings (such as Dhīra Śātaparṇeya's teaching, or the *prahitām saṁyoga*), but also appeal to the student's already existing inner knowledge of Agni, the Fire-Divine, or of Āditya, the Sun Divine.

But while it alludes to and appeals to this knowledge, the text uses it for a very different purpose. "Brahman is Mind," "Brahman is the Space-Time Matrix,"—Brahman is really whatever there is, inside oneself and outside. "The divine aspect that you know as Agni working in Speech—that is in reality Brahman, that is in reality the shining and glowing of Brahman. The divine aspect that you know as Āditya working in Sight—that likewise is Brahman shining and glowing. And so on. Don't be content with your present understandings of Agni, etc.,—there is only one Aspect shining, glowing, illumining (*jyotiḥ*) in all your sensory awareness, namely Brahman." So the injunction is really to give up the knowledge of Agni shining as Speech, and instead meditate, worship, regard, love, whatever!, that only Brahman shines and glows as all the Powers. It is significant that injuction for *upāsanā* is found only in v. 1. Vs. 3-6 do not contain *upās-*. They merely recall past teaching and knowledge and show how it is to be modified in the light of v. 1.

As a result, the perception/knowledge of Brahman that ultimately arises from this is perhaps somewhat similar to the perception/knowledge of *asti-bhāti-priyam* as that is described in the *Dṛg-Dṛśya-Viveka* and by Sri Sathya Sai Baba. The reiteration in vs. 3-6, that the various Sense-Powers are all feet of Brahman and shining with the light of their respective deities, simply describes the *asti-bhāti-priyam* that is "shared in" by everything, with an emphasis on the *bhāti* (and perhaps also, but to a much lesser extent, on the *priya*). This would explain why all four verses end with the same "He who knows (*vid-*) this, . . ." There is only one *asti-bhāti-priyam*-name-and-form everywhere, the same thing is described in every verse, and so knowing that has always the same fruit. The "intermediate stance" in *ChāndUp*

III.18 of neither taking a strictly subjective point of view nor presenting an objective description also fits with intuition and realization of *asti-bhāti-priyam*, because the latter presupposes a similar intermediate stance. In *ChāndUp* III.18, the "intermediate stance" is suggested in the fact that the text gives itself out as a double instruction, pertaining to the self" and "pertaining to the deities" (the external world) (v. 1). In addition it is reflected in the switch in the "causative subject" in vs. 3-6, i.e. the switch from "Speech (being a foot of Brahman)" to "(shining with) the light of Agni", from "Sight (being a foot of Brahman)" to "(shining with) the light of Āditya," and so on. For when one thinks these sentences, because of this switch one does not have to, and in fact must not, identify with Speech or Agni as the subject and thereby take a uniformly subjective or objective position in regard to the sentence as a whole. A similar "non-identification effect" is forced by the strict parallelism between the self and deity aspects in vs. 1 and 2. These features, accordingly, tend to free the meditator and allow a much more fundamental intuition to arise. *This*, the text says, is an intuition in the direction of Brahman.

At the same time the knowledge/realization that is taught cannot be simply equated with knowledge/perception of *asti-bhāti-priyam*-name-form, or of *asti-bhāti-priyam*. This is suggested by the *tapati*, "it glows, heats". For this term points to Brahman in a very different way from *asti-bhāti-priya*. In the *Ṛg Veda*, *tapas* (noun from the verb root *tap*, "heat, glow, make effort") is the primary cosmogonic force at the beginning of the creation of anything.[113] In the Brāhmaṇas, in many creation accounts, the standard pattern is that first *sa tapo 'tapyata*, "He [Prajāpati, the Creative] heated (*tap-*) his *tapas*,"[114] and that He then typically created such and such. So "Speech glows, *tapati*, by Agni as light" suggests the name-and-form-creating power of Agni-Prajāpati (and thus, Brahman). In the *Atharva Veda* and the Brāhmaṇas, *tapati* is mostly used of the Sun (which is "He who glows, *tapati*,"[115]), particularly when it is identified with Indra[116] or Prāṇa.[117] Of particular importance here is *ĀitAr* II.2.3.4, where Indra teaches Viśvāmitra about the Sun: "I am Prāṇa, you, seer, are Prāṇa, all creatures are Prāṇa, he that shines (*tapati*) (i.e. the Sun) is Prāṇa . . . I am He that shines" (above, chr. 3.9). And this teaching is further elaborated in the following section (*AitĀr* II.2.4), with the teacher saying: ". . . what I am, He [i.e. the Sun] is; what He is, I am. A Ṛṣi (seer) says (*Ṛg Veda* I.115.1): 'The Sun is the self of all that goes and stands [all things moving and stationary].' Let one consider this."[118] The identity of the self with the Sun is one of the earliest forms of knowledge of Ātman.[119] Thus *tapati* has connotations of the glowing of universal Prāṇa, of Indra as Prāṇa, and of the Ātman also. Summarizing, therefore, the use of *tapati* in *ChāndUp* III.18.3-6 suggests that here one's whole sense-level experience is seen as the glowing (*tap*) of universal creative power (Prajāpati), of a Universal Prāṇa which is All. As already said, this aspect is not really found in the knowledge/perception of *asti-bhāti-priyam.*

Looking at the teaching as a whole, the critical step is indeed to give up the specific divine knowledges of Agni shining in Speech, etc. which the student may already have, and to see instead the Formless Reality shining and glowing-creating in all one's Sense- and Mental Powers. This is an extraordinary step which forces the student to rise to extraordinary levels of formlessness and non-attachment. Compared to a perception of Agni, the Fire-Divine, as being inherent in Speech, or of Āditya, the Sun-Divine, as being inherent in Sight, realization of a single Supreme Aspect shining and glowing-creating in all the knowledge organs with the light of all the Divines is of a different order. Perceptions of Agni as a Divine aspect in Speech (and thus perception of Speech as metaphysical and Divine), for example, are qualitatively still affected by and cannot really be separated from the qualities of Speech and Fire, or other perceptions of Speech and Agni. But the knowledge/perception of Brahman taught by the text as a whole is not bound to qualities or lower level perceptions of Divinity. This Brahman is not connected with specific divinized qualities.

8. Appendix: The "Correspondences" Speech-Agni, Prāṇa-Vāyu, etc.

We have identified the inner direction in which *ChānUp* III.18 takes the student, and the specific realization at which it is aiming, and this essentially completes our discussion of the text. The reader may have some questions, however, regarding the "correspondences" Speech-Agni, Prāṇa-Vāyu etc., which are used in the text and which often occur in other teachings involving the Sense-Powers. Do these "correspondences" have any scientific or otherwise "objective basis"? If they don't, doesn't this affect the validity of the realization that arises from *upāsanās* carried out in this framework? If one is seriously interested in following these teachings today, should the details of the *upāsanā* which are involved in the correspondences be ignored? These kinds of issues, it is true, are more pressing for teachings in the Brāhmaṇas and Āraṇyakas than in the Upaniṣads. But they may be important to the reader and are thus briefly discussed here. We first lay out the problem in more detail, and then discuss some of the deeper issues using Prāṇa-Vāyu as an example.

What is the Basis for "Correspondences" Like Speech-Agni and Prāṇa-Vāyu? Pairings like Speech-Agni and Prāṇa-Vāyu have been discussed by Western scholars under general headings like "magical equivalences" (with *upāsana* on them as "the procedure, the method which will [or is supposed to] lead to the attainment of "magical control" or *magischer Herrschaft*, Schayer),[120] "connections" (Renou[121]), or "substitutions, replacements, identifications" (Thieme[122]). More specifically they have been conceived of as "micro- macro-cosmic equivalences," or "identifications" of aspects of the self or body (the powers) with aspects of the cosmos (the deities). The role of these equivalences and the inner truth behind them, however, has been evaluated very differently by different authors. Keith regarded them as merely a habitual device for organizing the different categories involved (providing a "basis for identification").[123] Deussen and others treat them as a kind of spiritual development,[124] while Coomaraswamy takes them as an intrinsic (objective) mystical relationship between the self (or man) and the Divine.[125] They may also be considered as occult connections.[126] In our own discussions we assumed that they involved genuine spiritual insights, and that they represented lower level realizations or partial knowledges of Divinity, which served as background for or stepping stones to the higher knowledge that was being taught.

Some pairings like Sight-Āditya, Prāṇa-Vāyu, and Hearing—the Quarters (Diśaḥ) can be traced back to the Puruṣa Hymn, and could thus be regarded as basically elaborations of the mythological (or archetypical) theme there. The fact they are also found in passages where they do not play a cosmogonic role but still give a cosmic dimension to human action may then be regarded as an extension of this pattern. On the other hand, micro- macro-cosmic correspondences often occur in standard sets of three, four, five or six, and this gives them metaphysical overtones. For example, the fact that in *ChāndUp* III.18.2 Brahman is "four-footed", *catuśpād*, is reminiscent of the fact that the Puruṣa has four feet (*Puruṣa Hymn* 3), and evokes the sense of completeness and fullness associated with the number four.

This in turn tends to strengthen a "universal theology" view like Coomaraswamy's, which sees in the *adhyātmam—adhidaivatam* parallelism a general contrast between "within man" and *in divinis*, or between "literal" and "spiritual," without perhaps worrying much about the how and why of the pairings.[127]

But to a Western mind, the question of "the basis" for the pairings is of great interest. Of course one would expect specific correspondences to be developed mythologically and in the ritual. But do not these correspondences themselves, by relating Speech to Fire, Life-Breath to Wind, and so on, imply certain intuitive knowledge about the "objective world" (fire, wind), which knowledge would therefore (according to our own Western cultural understanding) necessarily have an "objective kernel of truth", and an "objective basis"? If so, would not such an "objective basis" run counter to Science? Or is the reference to Science in this context too narrow or irrelevant? And would this "intuitive but somehow objective knowledge" be *necessary* for the higher realization that is being taught? If there was no objective basis for it, how can meditation on something that has no objective basis produce knowledge of Divinity or knowledge of Reality (Brahman)?

Prāṇa-Vāyu and Āyurveda. Some of these questions may be examined more concretely in this case of Prāṇa-Vāyu. Vāyu (or *Vāta*, a Vedic word) operating in the body in the form of *prāṇa* is a major element of Āyurvedic medicine which is likely to go back to Upaniṣadic times or earlier.[128] If so, it is very likely connected with the correspondence Prāṇa-Vāyu in the later Brāhmaṇas, Āraṇyakas and Upaniṣads. So part of the objective basis for the correspondence Prāṇa-Vāyu is "intuitive but objective knowledge of the objective world" found in Āyurvedic medical theory and practice. This makes a more detailed discussion of the questions raised in the preceding paragraph possible.

According to Āyurveda, the body is a composition of the major elements (*bhūtas*), space (*ākāśa* or *antarikṣa*), wind or air (*vāyu*), fire (*tejas*), water (*ap*), and earth (*pṛthivī*), plus thought (*cetana*). These elements in turn form the seven differentiated substances of the organism, the so-called *dhātus*. As described by J. Filliozat in his *The Classical Doctrine of Indian Medicine*, the *dhātus* consist of

> the organic juice (*rasa*) which is the chyle, the blood (*rakta*) which is the chyle coloured in red, the flesh (*māṁsa*), fat (*medas*),

> bones (*asthi*), the marrow (*majjā*) and the sperm (*śukra*), all of which, starting from *rasa*, derive one from the other. The *rasa* is therefore the primordial substance of the organism and certain authors took it to be the essence of water which generates everything. Besides, in all things there is a *rasa*, a "taste", the liquid element which constitutes simultaneously the substratum and the sign of the properties, of the virtues of this thing.
>
> The substances contain a liquid principle of effulgence (*tejas*) which makes them alive and which is known as *ojas*, that is to say, "force". It is the material of vitality and it may be called "vital juice". It stays in the heart; the breath (*prāṇa*), which is going to be discussed shortly hereafter is based on it and it is distributed in the body, along with *prāṇa*, by the blood vessels.
>
> Such is the substances of the body. The interplay of the three chief elements, which enter into its composition, namely, wind, fire and water, gives it life and movement. But when they are excited or when on the contrary, their action stops, disease comes in. They are, therefore, simultaneously the three elements, *tri-dhātus*, and the three troubles, *tri-doṣas*, of the organism. The wind, *vāta* or *vāyu*, introduces itself into the body in its own form just as in nature, that of breath, *prāṇa*; the fire in the form of bile, *pitta*, and water in that of phlegm, *kapha* or *śleṣman*. Each of them has many special forms.
>
> The *prāṇa* is divided into *prāṇa* proper, "breath of the front," which stays in the mouth and ensures respiration and deglutition; *udāna*, "breath which goes upwards", which produces speech; *samāna*, "concentrated breath", which provides the necessary amount of air to the internal fire for cooking, that is to say, for the process of digestion of the aliments; *apāna*, "breath which goes downwards", ensuring the functions of excretion and delivery; finally *vyāna*, "diffused breath", which circulates in all the limbs and explains their movement. In effect, all the movements of the body are related to the action of the wind; this is by analogy with what passes in the Universe where the wind is the motor *par excellence*.[129]

These conceptions are already expounded in the oldest Āyurvedic texts, the *Suśruta Saṁhitā* and the *Caraka Saṁhita*, the beginnings of which must go back to the last few centuries BCE.[130] The view that the chief elements or rather principles and cosmic deities Wind, Fire and Water are connected with and responsible for the life and movement of the body is remarkable. Filliozat argues that some passages in the Vedic corpus suggest that this conception existed already in the Vedic and Upaniṣadic periods.[131] Elsewhere he argues that the development must have been continuous "for the seven or eight centuries preceding the Christian era", culminating in the appearance of the great classical texts.[132]

The Āyurvedic Prāṇa-Vāyu Connection as a Cultural Reality. In the context of the questions to be addressed in this section, the picture painted by Filliozat needs to be reoriented and sharpened. Filliozat discusses the Āyurvedic and Vedic material largely from the point of view of a scientific, purely physical understanding of the body as we have it in modern physiology and medicine. But a much more emic understanding with complete empathy with the Vedic world-view is desirable. R.P. Das has argued, for example, that as far as getting an understanding of ancient Āyurvedic medicine is concerned, the usual Western categories ("scientific", "rational", "religion", "magic") are not helpful and are in fact ethnocentric.[133] Rather, "we must look at the problem anew", trying to enter the "*magische Weltbild*" or "*magische Weltanschauung*" ("magical world-view") that is expressed in the texts.[134] (Das' use of "magical" here may be accepted because it is not pejorative or reductionist; he is using the term mostly evocatively, trying to say something new.) This "magical world-view" has a number of characteristics. First, "(a) there is no distinction between living and nonliving, concrete and abstract, corporeal and noncorporeal, i.e. everything (even thoughts, words and deeds) is living and corporeal, even though not always perceptible to us; the world exists only of what is termed 'powers' and 'substance', in different states and forms". Further, these "powers" and "substance" (b) "have no immutable form or state and can 'penetrate' or 'capture' (i.e. take control of) each other"; they (c) "may act of their own volition or may be forced to act"; and (d) they are all "in a state of mutual balance or order; any action—be it ever so small—must disturb this balance and cause a reaction . . ." And finally, "(e) Since all actions, voluntary or involuntary, cause reactions, it is necessary to know all about such activities and reactions or at least to know which actions to avoid . . ." In this connection, "(f) knowing something about some 'power' or 'substance' (especially something secret) gives one might over it".[135]

Some of Das' characteristics are specific to Vedic culture [e.g. (e)-(f)]; others fit many primitive cultures.[136] But his main point that Vedic texts in general (including the Brāhmaṇa and Upaniṣadic texts) should be understood intuitively directly along such lines[137] states a great ideal. Many of the classic studies of particular cultures in anthropology have permanent value precisely because they enter a magical *Weltbild* to such an extent as to make it believable to a modern Western reader.[138] When one truly enters the world of another culture, one will automatically grant that in terms of objective events, and in terms of concepts and values, that culture works and has validity much like one's own. One will not immediately try to reduce an Āyurvedic principle or cure to something that is reasonable from a rational, scientific western point of view,[139] or interpret a sacrifice in terms of motivations that are common in our own society today.[140] For "[both] modes of looking at the world [i. e., the rational Western and the magical *Weltbild* of the other culture] build the frameworks, and one can be as 'rational,' 'logical,' 'objective,' or 'scientific' within the one as within the other".[141] In our textual discussions here we have not achieved a complete *Einfühlung* into a magical *Weltbild*, but in a purely scholarly treatment this would be a goal. Note in particular that in all the texts so far (including those of chr. 3), the peculiar fluidity of the Powers of Sight, Hearing, Mind, and Prāṇa in being able to take on connotations of individual powers, abstract faculties, universal aspects and cosmic entities, is presumably connected with Das' characteristics (a) and (b) [and possibly (c)]. Similarly the constant device of a higher entity that pervades them or mounts them may be discussed in terms of (b) or considered as perhaps falling under (c).

Now recall that we are focussing on the "objective basis" of the correspondence *Prāṇa*-Vāyu. Let us assume that embryonic conceptions of the Brāhmaṇical Vāyu, Wind, operating in the body and giving it life and movement similar to those in the ancient Āyurvedic texts were already present in late Brāhmaṇa and early Upaniṣadic times.[142] And let us assume further that these conceptions were used by some practitioners in what could be called medical practice for purposes of healing. Then these conceptions, *qua* working elements of the whole system "functioning society (including medical practice) plus magical *Weltbild*", represent what we called above "intuitive but objective knowledge of the world", linking as they do wind and life processes and approved as they are by the society at large.

We will call this knowledge "the knowledge of the action of Vāyu in the body". Now, because this "knowledge" was constantly used in diagnoses and treatment (as a basis for action), it must have had a special depth. One connot learn how to diagnose and treat a range of illnesses in terms of Vāyu's action in the body overnight. Rather, such knowledge is developed over years of apprenticeship with a competent teacher, involving first hand experience with hundreds of concrete cases. For lack of a convenient term let us say that the knowledge of Vāyu in the body has "practitioner depth".[143] Then the problem of judging whether and to what extent the knowledge of Vāyu acting in the body has an objective basis involves making a judgement on cultural knowledge that has "practitioner depth". Since the "practitioner depth" of the knowledge of "the action of Vāyu in the body" presupposes a shared system that the Āyurvedic student can absorb and develop in himself, this knowledge is more likely to have an objective basis.[144]

How did this knowledge of Vāyu, and with it the correspondence *Prāṇa*-Vāyu, come to be established in the first place? Modern anthropology has tended to give two kinds of answers to such questions: Either (1) the knowledge is motivated by empirical observation (a naturalistic explanation—the action of Vāyu in the body is based on the seeing wind make objects move, or the like); or (2) it is determined historically largely by the type of language spoken in the society (as in G.P. Murdock's work on explanations of illness[145]). In the case of the Āyurvedic action of Vāyu in the body, however another kind of explanation is also possible, which I would argue for, viz. that it is based on higher yogic or spiritual experience in the heart. Recall that according to Āyurveda, the *prāṇas* are based on *ojas*, "lifeforce", which stays in the heart and is endowed with *tejas*, "effulgence". These Āyurvedic conceptions may well be connected with the facts that (1) in the Upaniṣads, the *prāṇas* are said to be contained in the heart;[146] that (2) there are a variety of teachings on *light* in the heart in the Vedic literature (cf. chr. 6); and that (3) much of the later yogic and tantric literature associates the heart with Vāyu.[147] In other words, the heart or heart center is experienced as expansion and as of the nature of air, Vāyu,[148] and this is connected with perception of the *prāṇas* being connected with Vāyu. Experience or knowledge of this kind in a person would have much higher force, and manifest much more powerfully in that person's convictions and concepts, than would insight in empirical matters. It is then easily conceivable that such experience/knowledge by a few individuals would lead to general belief and conceptualization in the society at large. True higher yogic and spiritual experience often comes out in the *Volksmund* as popular expressions and proverbs (cf. chr. 6.4). Thus it is not unusual to see something like the experience of Vāyu = "*prāṇa* in the heart" appear in some form in the society at large.

***Upāsanā* Based on Cultural Realities.** We are now ready to take up the question whether or to what extent the validity of an *upāsanā* depends on whether the cultural element on which it is based has some kind of "objective basis". From a philological-literary point of view, a correspondence like Speech-Agni or *Prāṇa*-Vāyu is simply a set of associations which is built up and traceable in various texts. The simplest way to understand it is as a complex of conceptions, intuitions, etc., and let that complex take its form and result in new emergents similar to the way one understands a poem. (This is basically the way the matter is handled in traditional Indology.) But we have seen that in the native culture, the correspondence also represents "intuitive but objective" knowledge which may have considerable depth in terms of being used in various concrete situations—even "practitioner depth". Is entering this knowledge to this depth a prerequisite for the partial or beginning knowledges of divinity that are associated with it? "*Prāṇa* is one foot of Brahman. With Vāyu as light it shines and glows. . ." says *ChāndUp* III.18. Does this mean that the *upāsanā* implied in the this text requires that we first get an accurate intuitive *Einfühlung* into Vāyu as source of movement and life in the body? Our answer must be: An accurate intuitive penetration is needed for an accurate complete understanding of how *ChāndUp* III.18 was originally understood. But it is not nearly that important for a realization of the knowledge of Divinity and of Reality (Brahman) that is referred to in the text. No matter how the world or one's mind is perceived, *serious* contemplation, meditation, *upāsanā* toward a higher aspect shining in it *always* leads to beginning knowledge of God. The "intuitive but objective" knowledge of Vāyu in the body, in the context of a magical *Weltbild,* is of course a very suitable channel or matrix for such contemplation, meditation, whatever. But it is not absolutely necessary for carrying out the *upāsanā* and attaining the fruit described. There is much less of a connection between the cultural matrix of a deeper spiritual practice or discipline and the Divine (or Transcendental, etc.) Aspect that appears in the course of such practice than often believed. (This is one of the truths that makes Universal Religion or Perennial Philosophy possible and a reality). Of course, both cultural matrix and the Divine (or Transcendental or higher) element realized form a unity and must be described as such if the aim is to accurately describe a total state. But the higher element will be much less affected.

***Upāsanā* Based on Cultural Realities, and Science.** But does this knowledge that has practitioner depth mesh with Science (here, biology and Western medicine), and if it doesn't, how can something that doesn't and is therefore ultimately only imagination lead to Knowledge of Divinity? *Upāsanā* using "intuitive but objective" knowledge implied in correspondences like *Prāṇa*-Vāyu and Speech-Agni undoubtedly leads to knowledge of Divinity which, if sufficiently described, would be universally acknowledged as such. But for knowledge of Divinity to arise, it is not necessary that the "intuitive but objective" knowledge involved in the *upāsanā* has some kind of validity from the point of view of Science, but that it has a degree of reality, or is acknowledged as valid knowledge, in the life and practice of the society. This is sufficient for the individual to use it for meditation, *upāsanā*, because then he/she can be free from doubts and give his/her heart to the *upāsanā*. The real issue here is the common assumption that unless the "intuitive but objective" knowledge can be given a scientific basis (ultimately a basis in "hard science", involving physical processes), it is somehow "not true", and must be "imagination". This assumption, however, is specific to the West (as Das notes it is ethnocentric) and suggests an unawareness of the extremely specialized, culture-dependent nature of Science. Not only are the nature and ideology of Science culture-bound and society-constructed, but so also is the nature of the very phenomena which Science describes, predicts, and wants to understand.[149]

But enough philosophy! We discussed the preceding issues in the context of *Prāṇa*-Vāyu, because there the possible connection with Āyurvedic medicine enables us to formulate these issues more specifically. Even if the Āyurvedic conception of Vāyu as *prāṇa* in the body is unrelated to the Brāhmaṇical correspondence *Prāṇa*-Vāyu, the issue of "intuitive but objective knowledge" and its relation to the realization of lower level forms of the Divine arises, and our responses to these issues would be the same.

9. *Ṣoḍaśa-Kala* or "Sixteen Parts" *Vidyā*: The First Three Quarters

From a textual point of view the most natural units of teaching in the Upaniṣads, apart from brief sayings (*ādeśas, nāmadheyas, upaniṣads*), are the larger teachings that outline a larger picture—how various *upāsanās* plus other *jñāna*-type knowledge are part of a direction of development or a whole path to Brahman. These larger units will be called *Brahma-vidyās* or simply *vidyās. Vidyās* represent a level of discourse at which, by inner intelligence, a whole path to Brahman is understood. The remainder of the book will be mostly concerned with a small number of *Brahma-vidyās* and their inner relationships, beginning, in this chapter, with the *Ṣoḍaśa-Kala* or Sixteen Parts *Vidyā, ChāndUp* IV.4-19, and the *Vaiśvānara Vidyā, ChāndUp* V.12-18.

The Sixteen Parts *Vidyā*[150] teaches that Brahman has four feet, each of which in turn has four parts; hence its name, *ṣoḍaśa-kala vidyā*, knowledge (*vidyā*) of Brahman in sixteen (*ṣoḍaśa*) parts (*kala*). The last foot consists of Prāṇa, Sight, Hearing, and Mind, i.e., four of the five Powers named in *ChāndUp* III.18. The text first narrates how the young Satyakāma Jābāla takes leave of his mother, the maid Jabālā, is accepted as a student by his teacher, Gautama, son of Haridrumata,[151] and is given the job of tending 400 lean and weak cows. He decides not to return until the herd has grown to 1000. Eventually, after a number of years, a Bull in the herd speaks to him. He says that they have reached one thousand and that he should take them back to the teacher's house.

Ṣoḍaśa-Kala or Sixteen Parts *Vidyā*: Text

IV.5.2. "Also let me tell to you one foot of Brahman." "Please tell me, revered Sir (*bhagavān*)." (The Bull) said to him: "The Eastern Quarter is one part (*kala*, literally, one sixteenth), the Western Quarter is one part, the Southern Quarter is one part, the Northern Quarter is one part. This verily, my dear one, is a foot of Brahman having four parts, named 'the Shining (*prakāśavat*)'.

5.3. He who, knowing this thus,[a] meditates on (or worships, regards, *upās*-) the four-part foot of Brahman (as, or in the manner of) 'the Shining [one]', becomes shining (*prakāśavat*) in this world; truly [after death] he wins the shining (*prakāśavat*) worlds."[b]

6.1. "[Your] fire (*agni*) will tell you a foot of Brahman." At dawn the next day he drove the cows on further. Towards evening, at the place where they settled down, he kindled the fire, penned the cows, laid on fuel and sat down west of the fire, facing east.

6.2. The Fire (Agni) addressed him, "Satyakāma!" "Yes, revered Sir," he responded.

6.3. "Let me tell you, dear one, one foot of Brahman." "Please tell me, revered Sir'. '(The Fire) said to him: "The earth is one part, the sky is one part, heaven is one part, and the ocean is one part. This indeed, dear boy, is one foot of Brahman, consisting of four parts, named 'the Endless (Infinite, *anantavat*).'

6.4. He who, knowing this thus, meditates on (*upās-*) the four-part foot of Brahman [as] "the Endless, *anantavat*", becomes endless (*anantavat*) in this world; truly, he wins the endless (*anantavat*) worlds."

7.1. "The Swan (*haṁsa*) will tell you of one foot of Brahman." At dawn the next day, he drove the cows on further. Towards evening, at the place where they settled down, he kindled the fire, penned the cows, laid on fuel and sat down west of the fire, facing east.

7.2. The Swan flew to him and addressed him, "Satyakāma!" "Yes, revered Sir," he responded.

7.3. "Dear boy, let me instruct you about one foot of Brahman." "Please instruct me, revered Sir." (The Swan) said to him: "Fire is one part, the Sun is one part, the Moon is one part, and Lightning is one part. This indeed, dear boy, is one foot of Brahman, consisting of four parts, named 'the Luminous (*jyotiṣmat*)'.

7.4. He who knowing this thus, meditates on (*upās-*) the four-part foot of Brahman [as] 'the Luminous, *jyotiṣmat'*, becomes luminous (*jyotiṣmat*) in this world; truly (after death) he wins the luminous (*jyotiṣmat*) regions."

8.1. "The Diver-bird (*madgu*) will tell you of one foot of Brahman." At dawn of the next day, he drove the cows on further. Towards evening at the place where they settled down, he kindled the fire, penned the cows, laid on fuel and sat down west of the fire, facing east.

8.2. The Madgu bird flew to him and addressed him, "Satyakāma!" "Yes, revered Sir," he responded.

8.3. "Dear boy, let me instruct you about one foot of Brahman." "Please instruct me, revered Sir." (The Madgu bird) said to him: "Prāṇa is one part, Sight (*Cakṣus*) is one part,

Hearing (*Śrotra*) is one part, and Mind (*Manas*) is one part. This indeed, dear boy, is one foot of Brahman, consisting of four parts, named 'that Having an Abode (or seat, *āyatanavat*)'.

8.4. He who knowing this thus, meditates on (*upās-*) the four-part foot of Brahman [as] '[that] which has an abode (or seat), *āyatanavat*,' becomes one having an abode (*āyatanavat*), truly he wins the worlds that are endowed with an abode (*āyatanavat*)."

9.1. Then he (*Satyakāma*) reached the residence of the teacher (*ācārya*). The teacher addressed him: "Satyakāma!" "[Yes,] revered Sir," verily he responded.

9.2. "Truly you shine (*bhā-*) like a knower of Brahman (*brahma-vid*). Who is it that has instructed you?" "[Ones] other than men," he answered, "but I wish that your lordship himself would declare [the same teaching] to me.

9.3. For I have heard indeed from [men] similar to your reverence that knowledge (*vidyā*) learnt [directly] from [one's] teacher is one whose path is the straightest." Then he (= the teacher) taught him this very same [thing]. In that (what he taught him), nothing deviated [from what Satyakāma had been taught before].[152]

The whole narration represents a stylized version of what was originally an account of a historical individual's (Satyakāma's) spiritual path and experience.[153] At the center stand the four successive inner revelations or realizations which are given to Satyakāma by a bull, his night fire, a swan and a diver bird respectively. Interpreters disagree on the question why Satyakāma was instructed by precisely these particular four and whether his teacher, when he returned, merely told him the very same things or instructed him more deeply.[154] As in *ChāndUp* III.18 the student is asked to contemplate a series of major features of the external world and experience as Brahman. But now there is more detail, there are additional terms. The first foot of Brahman for instance is the *prakāśavat*. This is traditionally translated as "the Radiant", "the Shining", corresponding to the most common meaning of the noun *prakāśa*, "light".[155] Similarly the second foot is the *anantavat*, the Endless, Infinite. Obviously, such "indicator-terms" must have some reference to experience in meditation or other spiritual experience/knowledge. Basically, they are names for particular divine or transcendental elements. But they are also often used to teach essential elements of the *upāsanā*, or to indicate signs or symptoms of the realization of the divine or transcendental aspect in question, or indicate a state after death. This is their role here. "He who, knowing this thus (i.e. we who, knowing this teaching), meditates on (regards, *upās-*) the four-part foot of Brahman [as, or in the manner of] 'the Shining (*prakāśavat*)' becomes shining (*prakāśavat*) in this world" and so on.[156] The general schema is "he who . . . meditates (*upās-*) on X as, or in the manner of, 'Y'. " X (each of the four Quarters as a foot of Brahman) is, *qua* direct object and object of meditation, in the accusative case. But "Y", *prakāśavat*, that what the object (the Quarters) is to be regarded as, namely a foot of Brahman named *prakāśavat,* is in quotes (final *iti*) and in the nominative case. This peculiar format, which is also found in other "*upāsanās* with formulas "(cf. Table 4.2), suggests that Y is to be experienced directly (because of the quoting in the nominative). And it also accommodates the fact that Y ("the foot of Brahman which is *prakāśavat*") will at first be merely an ordinary idea or intent, but that as the *upāsanā* progresses and the higher element which Y represents is more clearly glimpsed or realized, it takes on a new meaning. (This change in meaning is allowed by the device of quoting). Accordingly, we have to take our exemplary sentence as saying "he who, knowing this thus (or who, knowing this teaching), meditates (*upās-*) on the Quarters as being a foot of Brahman and meditates on them in such a way that he realizes them as an aspect of Brahman which he would readily agree to call 'he shining', *prakāśavat,*—such a person will [himself] be shining, *prakāśavat*, in this world". That does justice to the general features of the "meditate on X as 'Y'" schema, as well as to the intent of the statements about the fruits of the meditation. A study of different occurrences of the "meditate on X as 'Y'"—schema suggests that it should not be mechanically interpreted in the same way in every case. Its exact import has to be determined separately in each case.

So contemplating on a Quarter,[157] facing it mentally, feeling that this great glorious Existent has been given to one as part of one's life experience, as a companion and presence in one's mind throughout one's life, thinking from one's heart that it and all four Quarters are (a foot of) Brahman, and making one's mind one or flow at one with such thought and feeling, there comes from within formless feeling, perception, whatever, a Shining, an Existent. This Existent is sacred, tranquillizing, subtilizing the mind. In the course of time it seeps into the mind, into the self-mind unity. Just as the knowledge of the Quarters accompanies one or is a subconscious or subliminal presence in one's consciousness when one is outside the house and during many other periods, so this Shining may become a subconscious or subliminal presence. This is accompanied by subtle changes of behavior. The eye of one's heart may be on this Shining for some times during the day; one may look differently at one's environment; there may be in the mind something metaphysical, divine, whatever, that subtly imbues the body also; and so on.

There is a progression in the meditations and spiritual life corresponding to each of the four feet (or quarters), but it defies any simple formula. The second foot is made up of Earth, the "Space Between Heaven and Earth" (often rendered the "mid-region" or "atmosphere"), Heaven, and Ocean (*Pṛthivī, Antarikṣa, Dyaus*, and *Samudra*). To a student in Upaniṣadic times the first three at least would be great and sacred manifestations and Divinities.[158] Even to us each is a metaphysical entity different in nature than the four Directions. One cannot naturally with one's whole being "face" Earth, or Mid-region, for example, as one can face the East. It is a different kind of meaning-content, somehow less connected with the body (one's bodily self can be forgotten more easily when one is facing and contemplating the Earth or Mid-region, etc., than when facing East). And it is somehow more mental: even when one is looking into the Mid-region while contemplating it, one feels a more mental experience. Similar comments apply to Earth and Heaven. Contemplating then these great aspects which exist with unending beauty, nobility, etc., which have been given us to be our constant companions and subliminal constituents of our consciousness as far back as we can remember; trusting that they somehow are directly an aspect of Brahman and keeping the mind on that Infinite aspect, there comes knowledge, perception, whatever, of a higher order, viz. an Endless, Infinite, *anantavat* (from *ananta,* "endless, infinite"). Now such an "Endless" is an image or reflection of God. One feels that this is how God has put his stamp on the world. Just as Earth, Intermediate space, Sky are everywhere, or ever present, so also that image of God is everywhere, ever present. This in turn again puts its stamp on the seeker, on the one who lives contemplating like this, subordinating himself to this teaching. The Endless is a reality in him, he has it in his consciousness or self, many times during the day or all the time; he sees the world as Endless; his vision in daily affairs is not toppled by the small and petty; his consciousness is fixed in the Endless. In this way, then, and in others, the *vidyā* brings glimpses of Divinity. Then "he wins (or conquers) the Endless regions". Whatsoever in inner experience or understanding relates to Endless, that opens to him; that knowledge or condition blooms for him; he is Endless in life and after death. This Endless is a foot of Brahman, Brahman is in the direction of this Endless.

Fire, Sun, Moon and Lightning (*Agni, Sūrya, Candra, Vidyut*) make up the third foot of Brahman; the corresponding *upāsanās* lead to Divine Light, Spiritual Light—the "full of Light" (*jyotiṣmat*, from *jyotiṣ*, "light"). A Brahmin in Upaniṣadic times would have deep and extensive understandings of these aspects, particularly the first two. Agni for example is not just Fire. He (or It) is the divine presence in the sacrificial fire in the ritual; He is a general metaphysical principle pervading the material creation; He is identified with the rising sun as a universal principle of life or energy, and so on. About 200 of the roughly 1,000 Hymns in the *Ṛg Veda* are in praise of Him. Comparably extensive spiritual understandings are associated with the Sun.[159] Still, the text does not intend simply ordinary meditation of the sacrificial Fire or the Sun as Divinity. Rather it enjoins meditation on them in such a way that the Light of Divinity associated with these Deities becomes perceived as a still higher element, as Brahman.[160] The initial goal is perception of the quality of Light that imbues them as Brahman. When meditating on Agni, Sūrya and so on there may be of course experience of other metaphysical or divine qualities, but ultimately the Divine or transcendental element must be seen as light, *jyotiṣ*. After some time the more specific meditations corresponding to the specific aspects like Sacrificial Fire, Sun etc. may merge or generalize into a single level of "Light", and then there is mostly only meditation on Brahman in that direction of "Light". Analogous statements hold also for the other feet of Brahman. There are only indicator terms for the feet as a whole, and these express a common quality of the parts.

When one becomes serious about Reality, about That which is the Source of all meaning and value, of Existence and Cognition itself, then the first, simplest, and most natural thing to do is to bow down to It and worship It in everything which one sees around oneself. This is the essential motivation in the first three Feet in this *vidyā*. For all the things around one are the Image of God, and by contemplating them right, the soul gets ideals and glimpses that are appropriate to her stage. "Behold! In the Creation of the Heavens and Earth, in the alternation of Night and Day, in the sailing of the ships through the ocean for the profit of mankind, in the rain . . ., in the beasts of all kinds, in the change of the winds . . .,—here indeed are signs for a people that are wise," says the Quran (II.164). Here indeed are the Imprints of God, which help the soul to beginning glimpses of divine qualities and more comprehensive Divinity.

10. The Fourth Quarter

But the *vidyā* does not stop here, and goes on to the fourth Foot or Quarter of Brahman, consisting of Breath, Sight, Hearing and Mind (*Prāṇa, Cakṣus, Śrotra, Manas*). These are four of the five "Powers" that are taught to be meditated on as Brahman in *ChandUp* III.18 (only Speech is missing). So perhaps we should interpret the *upāsanās* connected with this Quarter to be similar to those there. But *ChāndUp* III.18.3-6 brings in pairings, which are not suggested here, and besides we have a new, additional clue. The fourth foot of Brahman is the *āyatanavat*.

The noun *āyatana* means "place of support, resting place, seat,..., home", "the place where something belongs or from which it can achieve special successes".[161] The adjective *āyatanavat* then means "having, or being endowed with, a (place of) support, home, etc." Śaṁkara in his commentary on the *vidyā* suggests therefore that it refers to the mind, because "the experiences presented through all other organs converge—in this factor".[162] But an examination of other occurrences of *āyatana* in the early Upaniṣads suggests an experiential of "having an abode, a home". We saw in chr. 3.5 that in *AitUp* I.2 the deities of Agni, Vāyu, Āditya, Diśas and Candramas (Moon) asked the Ātman to find them an abode (*āyatana*) where they could eat food. Thereafter the Ātman gave them a man (*puruṣa*) and they entered the man's mouth, nostrils, eyes, ears and heart, becoming the individual's Powers of Speech, Breath, Sight, Hearing, and Mind. In other words, Agni, Vāyu, and so on have as their *āyatanas* the mouth, the nostrils, etc., and manifest there as the individual's powers of Speech, Breath, etc. Similarly in *BṛhUp* III.9.10-18, Earth, Desire, Forms, Space (mental) Darkness, Forms again, Waters and Semen (*Pṛthivī, Kāma, Rūpāṇi, Ākāśa, Tamas, Rūpāṇi, Āpaḥ*, and *Retas*) are each said to be the *āyatana* or seat of a metaphysical entity or Divine element (*puruṣa*). In both passages, *āyatana* is a locus or seat in which a deity or metaphysical entity (*puruṣa*) is present, something residing in which and functioning in which that deity or metaphysical entity reveals or manifests itself. In both cases there is a suggestion that the deity or metaphysical entity is directly known, "experienced".[163] (In *BṛhUp* III.9.10 ff. this is clear from the text—the Brahmin Śākalya brings the various "persons" up as entities which he *knows*; in *AitUp* I.2 it is suggested by the experiential overtones elsewhere in the text.) So when the *Sixteen Parts Vidyā* says that Breath, Sight, Hearing and Mind are a foot of Brahman called "having an abode, *āyatanavat*", an experiential element of "having a home, an abode" seems to be implied.

To understand this experiential aspect of *āyatanavat* better, we consider the fruits of the *upāsanā*. When a person meditates and knows the Powers as a foot of, or as the manifestation of, Brahman, says the *vidyā*, he or she becomes one who is *āyatanavat*, "possessed of an abode or seat"—then his or herself or consciousness will have a seat. This may give a clue. Ordinarily one looks at one's Prāṇa, Sight, and so on as different from oneself. But when one knows them all as Brahman, then they become one's home and abode, for then they are not separate from self. Then one's self and consciousness are more correctly established, then they truly "have a seat" or "a home". Thus when there is knowledge that the Powers of Life and Mind are Brahman, then oneself becomes *āyatanavat*, one with an abode, a home, namely Brahman. So the *vidyā* enjoins *upāsanā* on the Powers of Life and Mind as the (foot of) Brahman *āyatanavat*, or as the "having an abode"—Brahman.

11. Beyond the Four Quarters: Meaning of the *Vidyā*

So far we have taken the four feet of Brahman of the *vidyā* (the Shining, the Endless, the Full of Light, and that which has the Powers as its Seat) as corresponding to and being the object of four separate *upāsanās*, because they are treated as such in the text. They were revealed to Satyakāma separately on four different nights by four different deities, and they also have different fruits which are connected with the nature of each foot. The student becomes Shining, he becomes Endless, and so on. Thus at least in the initial stages, four separate *upāsanās* must be carried out. But the *vidyā* clearly teaches a single Brahman, and implies that it is one and the same Brahman that is seen and known in these four Feet—it is the One Brahman that is seen and known in these four "Perceptions" or Knowledges. This implies that there are more phases to this *vidyā*. When Satyakāma returns to teacher, the latter says "Truly, my dear, you shine (*bhāsi*, from *bhā*) like a knower of Brahman . . ." (9.2). He doesn't tell him he is *prakāśavat* or *jyotiṣmat*. Rather he uses bhā, which in the Upaniṣads describes the shining of Ātman/Brahman, and he calls him *Brahman-vid*, "Brahman-knower." The fruit of the *vidyā* as a whole is deeper than the fruits of the four individual *upāsanās*.

So the student must go beyond the knowledges of the four feet that he thinks he has, starting from and going further than the knowledge-state of the fourth foot. Brahman shines as all the four sets of aspects, as all the sixteen parts, and must be sought as *That*. The student realizes that his whole approach had been wrong. In the first three feet he had "meditated on (worshipped, etc. *upās-*) another deity, [in the manner] 'that [deity] is one and I am something else'" (*BṛhUp* I.4.10) without noticing that that way, "he didn't know". He begins to see that he has to drop all conceptions of Deities and Powers and give himself without assumptions and reservations to that which he has glimpsed as his Powers and as the Divine that pervades Nature. By including the fourth foot on a par with the other three, the *vidyā* is intending something beyond the beginning knowledge of Reality represented by the state of *āyatanavat*. He becomes sober, dispassionate, unified, still, and he devotes himself to Brahman only.

The *vidyā* does not discuss these further stages. Perhaps language at that time did not go any further. Perhaps there was only simply walking the path and no thought of description or instruction. Perhaps a student would at this point be able to continue with the teacher's subtle guidance without further verbal instruction. However this may be, there can be no doubt that the *vidyā* involves still unmentioned further inner evolution:

> Brahman is described as *ekam eva advitīyam*, one only without a second; all this visible world is denoted as *Tat-svarūpa* or the Form of Brahman; it can be realized by *saguṇopāsana*, or worship of the limited qualified Divinity, just as Saytakāma and others did. The path of *Brahmopāsana* [= *upāsana* on Brahman] is called the *suṣumnā mārga* also. The Omnipresent Brahman can be enclosed and discovered in the firmament of the heart! . . .[164]

Ṣai Baba is calling the *upāsanās* in this chapter *saguṇa upāsanās*, or *upāsanās* to realize [Universal] Divinity as it is manifested by Qualities (*guaṇas*). The aspects Mind, Speech, Earth, etc. are "forms" of Brahman, they are *tat-svarūpa*, the own-form (*sva-rūpa*) of That (*tat*), of the formless Absolute. So the *Brahma-upāsanā* of Satyakāma, i.e. the *upāsanā* of the *Sixteen Parts Vidyā*, is one path to this Knowledge of *Tat* and the *Tat-svarūpa*. So also are some of the other *saguṇa vidyās* in *ChāndUp* III-V. According to Sai Baba, the stages of *Brahma-upāsanā* may be described in two broad ways. One is the language of tantrism, specifically the central channel of spiritual force (*suṣumnā*) and the *cakras* (in tantra, the heart is generally identified with the *suṣumnā* or the heart-*cakra*). The other is the language of the *Dahara Vidyā* (chr. 6), which deals with the "subtle firmament", *dahara ākāśa*, of the heart. So both the earlier and the further stages in the *Sixteen Parts Vidyā* may be described in terms of unfolding of the student's heart. This will be the subject-matter of the *vidyās* in the next two chapters.

12. Relation to Puruṣa: *Saguṇa* and *Nirguṇa* Brahman

The preceding completes our substantive discussion of the *Sixteen Parts Vidyā*. Before going on to our third major teaching of this chapter, the *Vaiśvānara Vidyā*, we pause to consider two more general, historical or *geistesgeschichtliche* questions. The first is the problem of the *vidyā's* relationship to the Puruṣa Hymn. The second is concerned with exactly how the thought of the *vidyā* differs from Brahmaṇa- and Āraṇyaka-type thought. The two questions are related, and the first leads naturally to the second.

***AitĀr* II.1.7.** Is the *Sixteen Parts Vidyā* an outgrowth of the Puruṣa Hymn?[165] In chr. 3 we saw that *Aitareya Upaniṣad* represented a straightforward elaboration of the creation account of that hymn. Another example such an elaboration is *AitĀr* II.1.7, a teaching on "the powers of the Puruṣa". The text describes how from the Puruṣa's Speech, Breath and so on were created Earth and Agni, Midregion and Wind, and other deities. The first verse, *AitĀr* II.1.7.1 sets the pattern:

II.1.7.1. By His Speech (*Vāc*) are created Earth (*Pṛthivī*) and Fire

(*Agni*). On the Earth plants grow; Fire ripens them. "Take this, take this", thus saying to these two, Earth and Fire, serve their parent, Speech. And as far as the Earth extends, as far as Fire extends, so far extends this world, and as long as the world of Earth and Fire decays not, so long does his world decay not who knows thus the power of Speech.

2. By [his] Prāṇa the Heaven (*dyauḥ*) and Air (*Vāyu*) are created. . .[166]

The complete scheme has 15 terms (Table 4.4) and is obviously based the account in the Puruṣa Hymn (cf. Table 3.2). Now it is interesting that after going through all the Deities, the text simply stops—there is no higher-level climax, unless the teaching is thought to be completed by the immediately following *AitĀr* II.1.8. The latter suggests that *AitĀr* II.1.7 is indeed intended as a path to Divinity or Reality.

8. Was it Water? Was it Water? This world was Water. This was the root, that the shoot. This the father, those the sons. Whatever there is of the son's, that is the father's; whatever of the father's, that is the son's. So it is said. Mahidāsa Aitareya who knew this said, 'I know myself as reaching to the gods, and the gods as reaching to me.' For hence [i.e., by man] are they gifted [in the sacrifices], hence are they supported.[167]

Mahidāsa Aitareya's saying is meant to be testimony validating the principle or vision that "this was the root, that the shoot; this the father, these the sons". Mahidāsa "knew" this, *vid*, and this knowledge implied knowledge that he himself was contiguous with the gods through the sacrificial ritual and that he was Divine.[168] The same principle, however, is taught by the "Powers of the Puruṣa". The Puruṣa is the root, the father, and the Powers and the Deities in the world are the shoots, the sons of the Puruṣa, and thus Divine. (Note the singular vs. plural in "the father" vs. "the sons".) Hence it is reasonable to regard *AitĀr* II.1.8. as a kind of continuation or further amplification of the immediately preceding "Powers of the Puruṣa" and to assume that the "Powers of the Puruṣa" text teaches knowledge that oneself is Divine.

From a Schema based on the Puruṣa Hymn to a Schema based on Common Quality. If we lay out the *Sixteen Parts Vdyā* in the same way (Table 4.5), we find that it works with 13 terms,[169] 11 of which (all but "ocean" and "lightning") occur also in the "Powers of the Puruṣa." This does not necessarily mean that the *vidyā* is elaborating a "Powers of the Puruṣa" idea. True, it contains some general reflexes to the Puruṣa Hymn. The fact that Brahman has four feet, with three corresponding to the external world and one to the self, is reminiscent of the fact that the Puruṣa has four quarters, one down here below and three in heaven (the ratio is reversed).[170] More generally the four feet of Brahman symbolize the totalness of the reality and realization taught, just as they do in the Puruṣa Hymn.[171] Again, the sixteen parts bring to mind the Brāhmaṇa teaching that Prajāpati, the principle of Creation, has sixteen parts[172] and that, more generally, "the number sixteen is characteristic of the Totality".[173] Presumably all these connotations are intended to figure in the text and underscore its total, cosmos and all experience encompassing approach. But the conception that Powers of Puruṣa-Prajāpati like Speech and Sight give rise to the deities is a specialty of *Aitareya* and *Śāṅkhāyana Āraṇyaka* and the Puruṣa Hymn, and is not an element of the *Sixteen Parts Vidyā* (although it may be presupposed in the *vidyā* as background). The overall conception in Tables 3.2 and 4.4 is clearly a *cosmogonic*-metaphysical one. The Puruṣa is a unitary, cosmic and cosmogonic entity, and Tables 3.2 and 4.4 explicate how some of the major elements and meanings of the world are related to this one Entity. In contrast to this, the scheme of Table 4.5 still carries some cosmic overtones, but the explicit unitary *cosmogonic* aspect is absent. Instead, each of the four feet corresponds to a specific Divine Quality or element. So a comparison of Tables 3.2, 4.4 and 4.5 suggests that the explicit unitary cosmic-cosmogonic standpoint of the Puruṣa approach is replaced by a scheme organized according to "common divine quality, common divine element". A unitary cosmic standpoint is still present and reflected in the completeness of the coverage. The Four Directions; Earth, Mid-region, and Heaven; and Prāṇa, the Senses and Mind—all these are axes of the older cosmic-cosmogonic approach. But the presence of "common quality" as new organizing element is unmistakable.

TABLE 4.4
Powers of the Puruṣa
(Scheme of *AitĀr* II.1.7)

Verse	From the Puruṣa's	came	and came
1.	Speech *(Vāc)*	Earth *(Pṛthivī)*	Agni (Fire)
2.	Breath *(Prāṇa)*	Mid-region *(Antarikṣa)*	Vāyu (Air, Wind)
3.	Sight *(Cakṣus)*	Heaven *(Dyauḥ)*	Āditya (Sun)
4.	Hearing *(Śrotra)*	Quarters *(Diśaḥ)*	Candra (Moon)
5.	Mind *(Manas)*	Waters *(Āpaḥ)*	Varuṇa

TABLE 4.5
Ṣoḍaśa-Kala Vidyā
(Scheme of *ChāndUp* IV.5-8)

1st Foot	2nd Foot	3rd Foot	4th Foot
prakāśavat	*anantavat*	*jyotiṣmat*	*āyatanavat*
Directions	Earth	Fire	Prāṇa
	Mid-region	Sun	Sight
	Heaven	Moon	Hearing
	Ocean	Lightning	Mind

A basic impulse in the shift from a "arises from the Puruṣa" model to an approach working with "common Divine Qualities" must have been a clear perception of these "Divine Qualities" (*prakāśavat*, etc.), including an understanding of how the old deities fitted into them. The *vidyā* was not necessarily teaching a new knowledge/experience of Divinity. At least in the initial stages, the experience of the first three Qualities (the *prakāśavat, anatavat* and *jyotiṣmat*) were very likely part of the mainstream of knowledge/experience of Divinity taught in the Brāhmaṇas and Āraṇyakas (often in connection with the deities mentioned in this *vidyā*). But now this knowledge/experience is brought into relief as a framework organized by "quality of experience", and presented as a stage on the path to Brahman (or rather Ātman/Brahman) as the Supreme Reality and Goal. This approach is characteristic of many Upaniṣadic *vidyās*. Ātman/Brahman effectively supersedes all the Vedic Deities. The latter are not necessarily denied—although sometimes they are.[174] Rather the knowledge of Divinity inherent in them is used in a natural way as a stepping stone toward the new Goal. "Mind is Brahman. . . Speech is one foot. It shines and glows by Agni as light. . ."—there is no more natural way to teach approach to Brahman and make use of existing experience/knowledge of *Vāc*, Agni, etc., than this. Similarly, the fusion of various already existing lower level perceptions of Divinity into more universal "Divine Qualities" as in the case of the first three feet of Brahman in the *Sixteen Parts Vidyā*, represents a more sophisticated way of using the traditional experience of Divinity constructively.

The *Saguṇa* Approach. At this point, however, a problem presents itself. The "Nature *vidyās*" like *ChāndUp* III.18 and the *Sixteen Parts Vidyā* are intended to lead the student from the "quality-ful Divines" to the formless Reality,—either the Self or Brahman. How is it possible to go from a Divine that still has a nature of "Divine Quality" to the formless and (compared with these Qualities) qualityless Infinite Reality? This is the problem of *saguṇa* versus *nirguṇa* Brahman, Brahman which is "Itself (*sa-*) intrinsically endowed with qualities (*guṇas*)," versus Brahman which is "away from (*nis-*, *nir-*) qualities," or without qualities, which has a long history in Indian Tradition.[175] Sai Baba in sec. 11 above calls the visible world the *svarūpa* of *Tat*, the "characteristic form of the Formless Brahman." There is indeed an intrinsic connection between Brahman and the phenomenal world of name and form, and teachings involving *upāsana* on Powers and Deities can and do indicate paths to the formless Brahman. But the nature of this intrinsic connection dawns in the self only in some higher stages of Knowledge. As a result, there is often the question whether a given *saguṇa* teaching actually leads to Brahman. In the case of *ChāndUp* III.18, we decided this on the basis of the affinity of the knowledge taught with *asti, bhāti, priya*. But for the *Sixteen Parts Vidyā,* with its non-cosmogonic but still cosmic approach involving the new element of "Qualities" (*prakāśavat* . . .), the situation is more complicated. The *Sixteen Parts Vidyā* does not occur in the canonical lists of thirty-two *vidyās* mentioned in sec. 1, but Śaṁkara mentions it as a *brahma-vidyā* in *BraSūBh* III.2.23.[176] Presumably he regards it as a *saguṇa vidyā*,[177] i.e., a *vidyā* using *upāsanās* working with features of the world and experience and leading to knowledge of *saguṇa* Brahman. Śaṁkara admits that such *vidyās* may "lead on ultimately to high results, approximate to liberation" (sec. 2 above, [B]). Nevertheless, he distinguishes knowledge of *saguṇa* Brahman sharply from knowledge of Brahman which is *nirguṇa*, "without qualities" (see sec. 2 above).

The early Upaniṣads have no dichotomy of *saguṇa* and *nirguṇa* Brahman. On the contrary, they speak uniformly only of knowing (*vid*) Brahman or Ātman (or of attaining them, *āp*, etc.), without any further division. Considering the diversity of texts, this is striking and impressive. Some passages teach Brahman by denying qualities (and thus implicitly as being in some way *nirguṇa*), and most of the *vidyās* describe Brahman positively using specific qualities etc., but the same language and types of discourse are used in both cases. *Nirguṇa* Brahman is never specially distinguished or declared to be a higher or truer realization of Brahman than other types of realization of Brahman. One gets the feeling that the early Upaniṣads are dominated and pervaded by an experiential of Ātman/Brahman which is very definite, but which at the same time is somehow above, or unresponsive to, the *saguṇa-nirguṇa* distinction, and which allows for a large variety of individual manifestations.[178] *ŚvetUp* VI.11, the Upaniṣadic passage in which the term *nirguṇa* occurs for the first time, sees nothing wrong with describing the same entity, on the basis of its own vision and realization, as both "all-pervading" or "the ordainer of deeds", and as *nirguṇa*: "The one God (*deva*) hidden in all beings, all-pervading, the self within all beings, the ordainer of deeds, the dweller in all beings, the witness, the thinker (*cetā*), the only one (*Kevala*) and without qualities (*nirguṇa*) . . ." This is completely in the spirit of the old Upaniṣads. *Saguṇa* as opposed to *nirguṇa* is first attested only in Draviḍācārya (400 CE?).

13. *Vaiśvānara Vidyā: Śatapatha Brāhmaṇa* Text

While *ChāndUp* III.18 and the *Sixteen Parts Vidyā* teach Brahman using meditations on the Powers and Deities, the *Vaiśvānara Vidyā*, *ChāndUp* V.11-18,[179] works directly with the aspirant's self to seek in it the *Vaiśvānara*, the "One in the Many," or the *Vaiśvānara Ātman*.

Vaiśvānara is actually originally an aspect of Agni in the *Ṛg Veda*. For in the parallel text *ŚatBr* X.6.1, which is no doubt the more original version of the *vidyā, Agni Vaiśvānara* appears in place of *Vaiśvānara Ātman*. So in the *Śatapatha Brāhmaṇa* text, the goal is to realize the Divine (Agni) in its highest Universal (*Vaiśvānara*) Aspect, while in the Upaniṣadic *vidyā*, the aim is to realize the *Vaiśvānara Ātman*, the Self which is "the One in the Many". As mentioned in sec. 1, our approach will be to first get an understanding of the *Śatapatha Brāhmaṇa* version, and then use it to help elucidate the Upaniṣadic text.

In the *Śatapatha Brāhmaṇa* version, five prominent Brahmins deeply immersed in Vedic learning meet at the house of Aruṇa Aupaveśi to discuss "Vaiśvānara". Unable to come to any agreement, they go together with Aruṇa to Aśvapati Kaikeya, king of Benares. The king treats them with greatest respect, but hesitates when they ask him for instruction, because it was not proper for kṣatriyas (noblemen-warriors) like him to instruct Brahmins. Then, however, he admits that he "thoroughly knows" (*samprati vid-*) Vaiśvānara and teaches them.

4. He then said to Aruṇa Aupaveśi: "O Gautama, as whom (or as what) do you know Vaiśvānara?" (Or: "What Vaiśvānara do you know?") "[The Vaiśvānara] Earth (Pṛthivī) indeed, O king," he replied. "Yes," he said, "that indeed is the Vaiśvānara 'Foundation' (*pratiṣṭhā Vaiśvānara*); and because you know the Vaiśvānara 'Foundation', you are 'firmly established' (*pratiṣṭhita*, a wordplay) with offspring and cattle; and, verily, he who knows that Vaiśvānara 'Foundation', wards off repeated death and attains all life. But, in truth, this is only the feet of Vaiśvānara, and your feet would have withered away, if you had not come here." (Or: ". . . the feet [of the true Vaiśvānara] would be unknown to you, if you had not come hither.")

The next five verses follow verbatim the same pattern. The second Brahmin, Satyayajña Pauluṣi, knows [the Vaiśvānara] Water, *ap* (sing). This, the king says, is the Vaiśvānara "Wealth", *rayir Vaiśvānara*. Because Satyayajña knows this Vaiśvānara "Wealth", he is "endowed with wealth," *rayimat*, and with prosperity, *puṣṭimat*, but really this Vaiśvānara is only the bladder of (the real) Vaiśvānara. The third Brahmin is Mahāśāla Jābāla. He knows Vaiśvānara as *ākāśa*, "Space".

This, the king acknowledges, is the Vaiśvānara "Plenteous", *bahula Vaiśvānara*. Because Mahāśāla knows this Vaiśvānara "Plenteous", he is plentiful (*bahu*) in offspring and cattle, but in truth this Vaiśvānara is only the trunk (body, *ātman*) of Vaiśvānara. The fourth, Buḍila Āśvatarāśvi, knows Vaiśvānara as the Wind-Divine, Vāyu. This is the Vaiśvānara "Diversely Behaving", *pṛthag-vartmāna Vaiśvānara*, because of which diverse rows of cars (*ratha*) follow Buḍila. But really it is only the breath, *prāṇa*, of Vaiśvānara. The fifth, Indradyumna Bhāllaveya, knows Vaiśvānara as the Sun-Divine, Āditya. This is the Vaiśvānara "of Soma splendour", *suta-tejā Vaiśvānara* (*suta*, lit. "pressed out", refers to the Soma juice pressed out of the Soma plant). Because of this knowledge of his, the same-day Soma juice preparations are established in Indradyumna's house, but in truth the Vaiśvānara he knows is only the eye (*cakṣuḥ*) of Vaiśvānara. And finally the sixth, Jana Śārkarākṣya, knows Vaiśvānara as Heaven, *dyauḥ*. This is the Vaiśvānara "standing out beyond", *ati-ṣṭhā vaiśvānara*, because of which Jana is now standing out beyond his equals. But in truth, this Vaiśvānara is only the head, *mūrdhā*, of Vaiśvānara.

10. He said to them: "You then, knowing diverse Vaiśvānaras, have been eating diverse food. But verily, of the measure of a span [from thumb to tip of index finger] (*prādeśa-mātra*), as it were (*iva*), have the well-known gods (*devas*—Earth, etc.) become [in what I will teach you now], and I will tell them so that I shall cause [them] to become [in my account] of the measure of span (*prādeśa-mātra*) (or: . . . that I shall cause [you] to attain [them as] of the measure of a span)."[a]

11. He said, pointing at the head, "This, indeed, is the Vaiśvārara 'Standing out'." Pointing at the eyes he said, "This, indeed, is the Vaiśvānara 'of Soma's Splendour';" Pointing at the nostrils he said, "This, indeed, is the Vaiśvānara 'Diversely Behaving';" Pointing at the space in the mouth he siad, "This, indeed, in the Vaiśvānara 'Plenteous;'" Pointing at the water in the mouth he said, "This, indeed, is the Vaiśvānara 'Wealth'; " Pointing at the chin he said, 'This, indeed, is the Vaiśvānara 'Foundation.' He [is] this Agni Vaiśvānara who [is] the Puruṣa. And, verily, whosoever thus knows that Agni Vaiśvānara as of the form of man (*puruṣa-vidha*), as established within man (*puruṣa*),

> he wards off repeated death, attains all life, and, verily, Vaiśvānara does no harm to him that speaks of him."[180]

14. *Vaiśvānara* = "the One in the Many": *ŚatBr* IX.3.1.3-6

An unusual element in both versions of the *vidyā* is the fact that the realization taught is presented as the culmination of truly understanding the meaning of *Vaiśvānara*. In other words, the higher knowledge taught is represented as the realization or knowledge (*vid*) of a concept which by then had already had a long history in Vedic and Brāhmaṇa religion. So the first question which arises is, what was this concept of *Vaiśvānara* that the Brahmins were trying to understand, what was their shared, general idea of *Vaiśvānara*? And why did they meditate on Vaiśvānara the way they did? These questions are largely answered by *ŚatBr* IX.3.1.3-6, a text which is clearly related to the *Śatapatha Brāhmaṇa* version of the *vidyā*. The passage describes Agni Vaiśvānara as "the One Factor that is operating in all the visible diversity everywhere", and we will argue that this is the general meaning of the adjective *Vaiśvānara* in the Brahmins' minds. It also explains the choice of the six objects of meditation (Heaven, etc.). But this is not the only text which stands behind this *vidyā*. There is in the Vedas and Brāhmaṇas a whole tradition which exalts Agni Vaiśvānara as a Universal Divine Aspect in both the human heart and the world, and thus something which is in various ways "the same in the Many". This tradition will be sketched briefly in the next section as an appendix.

***SátBr* IX.3.1.3-6** aims to explain the inner meaning of a certain offering (a cake on twelve potsherds) to [Agni] Vaiśvānara near the end of the *agnicayana*. The offering is made immediately after the altar has been completed and the fire has been lit at the top, and is therefore the first sacrifice offered to that fire.[181] It is thus one of the most important offerings in the whole *agnicayana*. The fact that this offering is made to [Agni] *Vaiśvānara* suggests that *Vaiśvānara* is the most important aspect of Agni. Since the altar (which, it may be recalled, is called Agni) has just been completed, Agni Vaiśvānara may also be associated with completeness in a highest and most encompassing sense:

> 3. Now, that Vaiśvānara is all these worlds (*ime lokāḥ*): this Earth (*pṛthivī*) is the All (*viśva*), and Agni is its Man (*nara*);

the Air (Midspace, *antarikṣa*) is the All, and Vāyu (Wind) is its Man (ruler); the Sky (*dyauḥ*) is the All, and Āditya (Sun) is its Man.

4. And these worlds are the same as this head—this (lower part of the head) is the earth, the plants (being) the hair of its beard: this is the All, and Agni is speech, he is the Man. That (speech) is at the top thereof, for Agni is on the top of this (earth).
5. This (central part of the face) is the air, whence it is hairless, for hairless, as it were, is the air; it is this All, and Vāyu (Wind) is the breath, he is the Man; he is the middle thereof, for the wind is in the middle of the air.
6. The sky is the (upper part of the) head, and the stars are the hair; it is the All, and Āditya (Sun) is the eye, He is the Man: it is in the lower part of the (upper) head, for the sun is below the sky. Vaiśvānara is the head thereof and this built-up Agni (the altar) is the body: thus, having completed his body, he restores the head thereto.[182]

Analysis of the Text. "Vaiśvānara is all these worlds," namely earth, mid-region (between earth and sky) and sky (*pṛthivī, antarikṣa* and *dyauḥ*). In addition each of the worlds is analyzed into a diversity, its *viśva* or "All" aspect, and an inner unitary aspect, an ensouling and ruling entity, its *nara* or "man" (v. 3). For example the *viśva* or all aspect of the earth is just the earth, as it is normally experienced, but its unitary principle, or *nara*, is Agni as an everywhere active metaphysical principle. (In the Brāhmaṇas, Agni is often the Earth.) The *viśva* aspect of the mid-region is just the mid-region, but its *nara* is Vāyu, the Divine seen in wind, which pervades the mid-region. And similarly, the *nara* of the sky is Āditya, the Sun-Divine, which rules the sky. The essential quality of Vaiśvānara therefore is being the *nara* or ensouling factor or principle that operates in the *viśva*, the diversity or the All—in other words, *Vaiśvānara* is *viśva-nara*.

Remarkably, however, each world is then made to correspond to a part of the head (vs. 4-6), and the *viśva-nara* analysis in v. 3 is thereby correlated with a second analysis, which represents Vaiśvānara as a human face or head. The entire structure, then, makes analogies between features of the three worlds and parts of a human face or head, with relations between these two levels staying constant or systematically varying across worlds. This is shown in Fig. 4.1. The top horizontal in each world is the correspondence which defines the

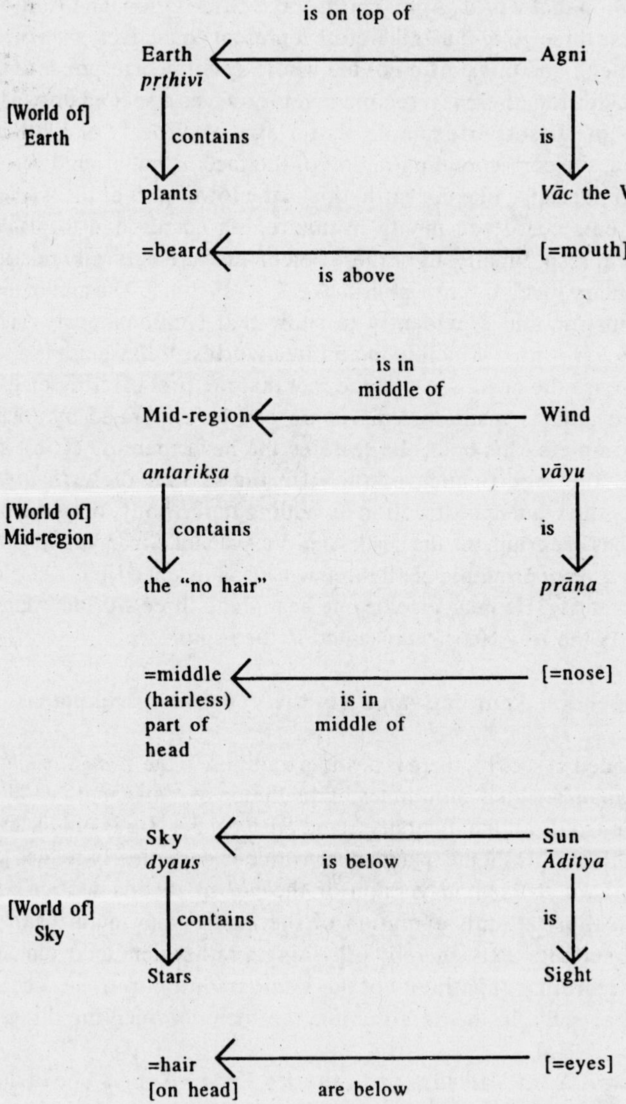

Fig. 4.1. Scheme of *ŚatBr* X.3.1.3-6. *Viśva* aspect is on the left, *nara* aspect on the right.

viśva-nara in that world (Agni-Earth, Vāyu-Mid-region, and Āditya-Sky). These three *viśva-naras* therefore represent collectively the *viśva-nara* element, and this portion of the whole system corresponds to v. 3. But in addition, there is a second level shown as a second horizontal below the first. For example, as far as the "World" of Earth is concerned, the corresponding region of the face is that around beard and mouth, because like the earth, this is the lower part of the whole. The elements beard and mouth in this region correspond to plants and speech, resp. Finally all of these "elements" are naturally related to the primary level divinities Earth-Agni, cf. Fig. 4.1. The aim of the whole construction is evidently to show that simultaneously with being the *viśva-nara* principle in all three worlds, Vaiśvānara is also in some sense the head—so that the fact that the first offering on the completed altar is made to Vaiśvānara can be explained by "thus having completed his body, he restores the head thereto" (v. 6). In that way, the significance of the offering is that the *adhvaryu* completes the whole construction by adding to the body, the Agni or altar that has been built up, the head, Agni Vaiśvānara. Since *Vaiśvānara* is the *viśva-nara* principle in all three worlds, and since He is a single Aspect or entity, He must also be one head in all three worlds, which is precisely the way He is represented in the Figure.

15. Appendix: Agni Vaiśvānara in the Vedas and Brāhmaṇas

As mentioned in sec. 13, there is a whole tradition in the *Veda Saṁhitās* and Brāhmaṇas which culminates in the theme of Vaiśvānara as "the One that ensouls all the diversity", and *ŚatBr* X.3.1.3-6 is only a text that articulates this theme in a manner which is very clearly related to the *Śatapatha Brāhmaṇa* version of the *vidyā*. In this section we digress to illustrate this evolution of the Agni Vaiśvānara idea by means of suitable texts, thereby providing a rather detailed example of the extraordinary continuity of the Vedic tradition from the Vedas to the Upaniṣads. In the next section, we then continue the discussion of the *vidyā*.

Agni and Agni Vaiśvānara in the *Ṛg Veda*. Agni is one of the three or four chief Divinities in the *Ṛg Veda*. At one level He is Fire, "or better: the phenomenon [of fire] seen as divine power",[183] and the hymns describe his innumerable forms of appearance and metaphysical and divine effects. He is the life-giving power in the waters, etc. But at another level, the meaning of Agni is based on the fact that He is the sacrificial fire. Because of this, He becomes the intelligent spirit and the protecting and leading force in the ritual. He is the mediating link between man (sacrificer and priest) and the gods; he inspires Divine Poetry in the priests and promotes good, God-directed thoughts. Here also He is the Lord, protector, and benefactor of the sacrifice, the household, and the communities that lead a harmonious ritual life. It is in this sphere, then, that Agni is the personally related-to Divine *par excellence*. In the *Gṛhya Sūtras* one prays to Him, the sacrificial Domestic Fire, in connection with virtually all important family affairs, and "already in the *Ṛg Veda*, the horses and cows come home to 'the great Lord of the house who never travelled away'. In short, there exists between Agni and His worshippers a sphere of intimacy which is missing in the cult of others gods".[184] Because of this personal relationship, and because as the Ritual Fire he carries the essence of the soul's striving toward the Divine, Agni becomes the primary ground of devotion in the soul, the immortal element of nectar that is experienced in the mind, and hence a primary locus or channel for experience of Divinity.

Now within this "ground of devotion" represented by Agni, Agni Vaiśvānara is a specific direction of conception and experience of Divinity that combines both cosmic or universal and self dimensions. This is illustrated by some of the common themes associated with Agni Vaiśvānara in the *Ṛg Vedic* hymns. The most prominent of these is Vaiśvānara as the Rising Sun. In the *Ṛg Veda* generally, Agni is often compared to the Sun, and in some passages, the Sun is explicitly dependent on Him in its functioning. But in the morning ritual, Agni Vaiśvānara, the Ritual Fire, becomes united with the Sun, no: He becomes the Sun.

***Ṛg Veda* I.98**

1. May we be in the favor of Vaiśvānara,
for he is indeed the king, the overlord of creatures.
Born from here (the earth), he beholds all of this,
Vaiśvānara joins with Sūrya (the Sun).
2. Sought in heaven, sought on earth (is) Agni;
sought, he has entered all the plants.
Agni Vaiśvānara is sought with power.
Let him protect us day and night from harm . . .[185]

V. 1, an important verse which is often quoted later,[186] shows Agni in the ritual (i.e., at the level of personal devotedness and inner experience that comes in devoted ritual practice, with Agni the Ritual Fire as focus for the meditation) and at the same time with a cosmic aspect, viz., the rising Sun bringing light and warmth and blessings to the world. These two aspects are experienced as one: Agni, "born from here (on earth)" as sacrificial fire and the object of devotion of the sacrificer, at the same time "beholds all this [world]" as the Sun. This unitary experience then resonates in other hymns like *Ṛg Veda* III.2 and IV.7. And it is this that ultimately finds an echo in our *Śatapatha Brāhmaṇa* text. King Aśvapati identifies all the cosmic-level Vaiśvānaras realized by his guests with part-realizations of one's self (v. 11).

Another theme in the *Ṛg Vedic* hymns is that Agni, being the numinous inner principle of devoted ritual life in the individual, is also a force at the levels of community, kingdom, and mankind. This higher level social and in this sense also cosmic manifestation of Agni is also Vaiśvānara. A key hymn here is *Ṛg Veda* I.59.

***Ṛg Veda* I.59**

1. The other fires are only branches from you, Agni! In you all immortals delight.
   Vaiśvānara! you are the navel of the settlements; like a pillar, a prop, you hold fast the peoples.
2. Agni is the head of heaven, the navel of earth, and he became the ministrant of both worlds.
   As such, the gods gave birth to you, the god, as light for the Aryan. Vaiśvānara!...
5. Over the lofty heaven, Jātavedas, Vaiśvānara, your greatness stretches out.
   You are the king of folk descended from Manu; through battle, you made freedom for the gods.
6. Now I proclaim the greatness of the bull, whom the Purus obey as the slayer of Vṛtra.
   When Agni Vaiśvānara had slain the Dasyu, he shook up the courseways (and) smashed down Śambara . . .[187]

V. 1, "You are the navel of the settlements . . .": "you are the Divine inner strength which manifests in living this ritual life centered on you as the Sacrificial Fire. This inner strength is the center of stability of the Aryan settlements and the pillar that holds up the Aryan peoples." Next, by of the juxtaposition of v. 1 against v. 2, this aspect of Divinity in the body of society is presented fused with a cosmic aspect, Agni as the Sun. "Agni, you are the One Divine that stands at the head of heaven and pervades it, not different from the Sun; looking at the Sun standing high in the heavens, I see you and your transcendence and your pervading. You are the navel, the one center of strength of all this earth, this creation: it is you who are the supreme center of stability and support for everything. In these functions I see you as the harmonious conductor of the whole world, heaven and earth." "As such, the gods gave birth to you as light for the Aryan:" "Manifesting your Divinity in this way, in the splendour of the Sun that we see and the Strength of the Earth that we feel, you have become our light".[188] The same kind of fusion of the cosmic level Divine (Agni as Sun) with manifestation at the level of society is found again in vs. 5-6. Agni Vaiśvānara, "stretching out . . . over the lofty heaven", "through battle made freedom for the gods" and "slew the Dasyus", the enemies of the Aryans. In other words, the Divine inner strength, fused with the cosmic functions, which the practice of Vedic religion is both at the level of the individual and at the level of the Aryan community, triumphed over the outside enemies.

Ṛg Veda VI.9 contains much of the experience of the two hymns just discussed, but at a higher level.

Ṛg Veda VI.9

1. Night and day (lit. black day and bright day) are revolving with purpose.
   Agni Vaiśvānara, just born, like a king overcame the darkness. . . .
4. He (Agni) is the First Hotṛ (offering priest). Behold Him, He is the Immortal Light among the mortals.
   He was born, immovably He possesses His seat, the Immortal one, growing in body.
5. He is the Light that is constantly planted for Seeing, the thought that is swiftest among things that fly.
   All gods meet unanimously, with one voice, correctly in the one thought (of Him, Agni).
6. My ears fly open, my eyes open, this Light arises that is set in the heart.

> My thought drifts away, meditating. What shall I see, what shall I think further [about Him]?[189]

This is a powerful Vision of Divinity/Reality. Agni Vaiśvānara is "the [Great] Light, both . . . the Light of the World (v. 1) and . . . the inner Light which illuminates the Seer and Poet" (Geldner).[190] There are echoes of both cosmic dimensions and dimensions of inner self, foreshadowing the Upaniṣadic teachings on the Self as Light in the space within the heart (cf. chr. 6).

From this, finally, it is only a small step to *Ṛg Veda* X.88, where Agni Vaiśvānara is glorified as All-god, the all-pervading source of all light, power and life for the world, and ultimately identified with "the One (*ekam*) which has unfolded itself into (or as) this whole world". This is similar to the Puruṣa Hymn and to king Aśvapati's teaching: "He is this Agni Vaiśvānara [which I have just explained by pointing etc.] [who is] what is the Puruṣa", i.e., this Agni Vaiśvānara is identical with the Puruṣa of the Puruṣa Hymn.

***Ṛg Veda* X.88**

13. The seers (*kavi*) worthy of sacrifices, the gods, gave birth to Vaiśvānara, Agni, the imagining,
[to] the heavenly body (*nakṣatra*), the ancient, unalterable, coursing, superintending the *yakṣa* (the secret, primeval power or being which becomes this creation).
14. We call with mantras on Vaiśvānara, the ever shining, Agni, the Seer.
[He is] the God who with Glory (*mahimnā*) encompasses the two wide ones [earth and sky] from below as well as above.
15. [There are] two paths, so I heard from the fathers,[a] for gods and mortals.
On these two all this [what is] living comes together, what is between Father and Mother (Heaven and Earth).
16. These two (Heaven and Earth), agreeing [with each other] (*samīcī*), carry the wanderer [who is] born from [their head], touched distinctly[b] by the mind.
He stands, directed towards all worlds, not separated [from them], energetic, shedding effulgence.[191]

The bulk of the hymn, up to v. 16, is dominated by the image of the Sun, Sūrya, coursing through the heavens. The seer sees in it the one Divine, Agni Vaiśvānara, who leads all (v. 13b), who encompasses the whole world (v. 14b), and who faces and is directly in touch with all worlds giving them life, light, glory (v. 14b, 16b). This image, touched on or recurring as it does in verse after verse, is the seer's secret inner source to which he comes back again and again. It is his meditation, the channel by which he attained immersion in Divinity. It becomes the force which forges the vision of the two paths in v. 15[192] and flowers into the vision of the comprehensiveness and all-sustaining, all-pervading quality of the Divine in v. 16. But after v. 16 the tone changes:

> 18. "How many fires (*agnis*) [are there], how many suns (*sūryas!*), how many red morning dawns (*uṣas*), how many waters [are there] really?" . . .

In the remaining mantras, the question is not answered, but the answer is apparently preserved in a disconnected verse in *Vālakhilya Hymn* 10.2:[193]

> 2. [There is] only one fire indeed [which is] often kindled, one Sun [only is] lord over all (*viśvam*, the whole world). One red dawn indeed [only] shines (*bhāti*) on all. One (*ekam*), verily, has become all this [world] here.

Even without this verse, the trend of *Ṛg Veda* X.88 is clear. Agni Vaiśvānara, the great Divine, the spiritual Reality "touched by the mind" (v. 16) when the seer meditates on it as the Sun, is "the One, *Ekam*, that has become all this [world]". It is this Great Divine, then, or the One-in-the-Many of Creation which this Divine thinly veils, that is the Vaiśvānara that the six Brahmins are seeking. For this Divine foreshadows the *viśva-nara* or One-in-the-Many of *ŚatBr* IX.3.1.3-6.

Agni Vaiśvānara in the Brāhmaṇas. Cursory examination of Brāhmaṇa texts mentioning Agni Vaiśvānara shows some common motifs like "Vaiśvānara is the year," or "Vaiśvānara is all the fires (*arka*)." But there are also some more extended passages which give a sense of a more specific meaning relevant to the *Śatapatha Brāhmaṇa Vaiśvānara Vidyā*. These include *JaimBr* I.45, *JaimBr* III.8, *TaittSaṁh*

V.6.6.2-3 and, most closely related to the *Śatapatha Brāhmaṇa* text, *ŚatBr* IX.3.1.3-6. The last of these was discussed in sec. 14 above, and here we consider only the others, labelling them for convenience [A]-[C].

JaimBr I.45 glorifies Agni Vaiśvānara as a single Divine both at cosmic levels and at the level of human life experience, using the image of a burning fire:

> [A] 45. The one that shines here (the Sun), that is Agni Vaiśvānara. Its fuel is the night, its flame the day, its smoke the rays of the sun, its sparks the stars, its coals the moon. In this same Agni Vaiśvānara the gods day by day offer immortality, the (heavenly) waters. From this oblation, when it has been offered, King Soma comes into existence.
>
> The thunder is Agni Vaiśvānara. Its fuel is heaven, its flame the lightning, its smoke the clouds, its sparks the hailstones, its coals the thunderbolt. In this same Agni Vaiśvānara the gods day by day offer King Soma. From this oblation, when it has been offered, rain comes into existence.
>
> The earth is Agni Vaiśvānara. Its fuel is the atmosphere, its flame the fire, its smoke the wind, its sparks the shining motes in the air, its coals the quarters. In this same Agni Vaiśvānara the gods day by day offer rain. From this oblation, when it has been offered, food comes into existence.
>
> Man is Agni Vaiśvānara. Its fuel is speech, its flame sight, its smoke breath, its sparks mind, its coals hearing. In this same Agni Vaiśvānara the gods day by day offer food. From this oblation, when it has been offered, seed comes into existence.
>
> Woman is Agni Vaiśvānara. Its fuel is the vagina, its flame the vulva, its smoke desire(?), its sparks the feelings of enjoyment, its coals the coitus. In this same Agni Vaiśvānara the gods day by day offer seed. From this oblation, when it has been offered, man comes into existence.
>
> Thus in this fifth creation man is born from the gods. At the fifth creation the divine waters speak with a human voice. And when he goes to yonder world—

46. —His (funeral) fire is Agni Vaiśvānara. Its fuel is the herbs and trees, its flame is just the flame (of the fire), its smoke just the smoke, its sparks just the sparks, its coals just the coals. In this same Agni Vaiśvānara the gods day by day offer man. From this oblation when it has been offered man comes into existence (and goes) to yonder world. That is for him the world in which he resurges.[194]

A single Divine shines both in the cosmic aspects of the Sun, Thunder, and Earth, and in the powerful dimensions of human existence, Man, Woman, and Death. When shining in the Sun, Its activity or shining is all-comprehensive, encompassing the whole world we see: Its fuel is the night, its flame is the day, etc. When shining in or as Thunder, Its activity or shining is all-comprehensive, permeating the world in which we live: Its fuel is heaven, its flame is lightning, etc. When shining in or as Earth, Its activity or shining is all-comprehensive, all-pervasive: Its fuel is the atmosphere, its coals are the quarters. When shining in or as Man, Agni Vaiśvānara shines as Speech, Sight, Breath, Mind, and Hearing—the same aspects which were named in the *upāsanā* of Mind and Ether and the *Sixteen Parts Vidyā*, and which are also aspects important to man from the point of view of his role in the community. Similarly, Agni Vaiśvānara shines in the aspect of woman. The systematic elaboration of a single common Divine that is seen in many different contexts (Sun, Thunder, Earth, Man, and Woman), giving the impression of a single, universal principle, is new. Expressing this principle using a fixed image (a fire) with a fixed set of component aspects (fuel, smoke, etc. as well as oblation into this fire), however, is a common Brāhmaṇa device.[195]

The other *Jaiminīya Brāhmaṇa* passage (III.8) is mostly an "etymology", not a great mythic and evocative poetic production like [A].

[B] Verily, Prajāpati created the creatures by the *Daśāha* [form of the Soma] sacrifice. They, created of him, were scattered everywhere.

He [then] saw those two *atirātras* of Vaiśvānara (two 24-hour long ritual sequences in the Soma sacrifice). With them (= the *atirātras*) he seized them (= the creatures) from both sides, with this one [from] here, with that one from above. With these two indeed he held them captive (*vāraya*-). He held captive (*vāraya)* what had become the All (*viśvam*)—that is the Vaiśvānara-hood of the [two] Vaiśvānaras (= the two Vaiśvānara *atirātras*).[196]

The text uses an "etymology" to explain the inner meaning of the two Vaiśvānara *atirātras* or overnight sessions of the twelve day Soma ritual (on this inner meaning the Sāman priests are to fix their mind during the *atirātras*). Vaiśvānara is derived from *viśva* (all) + *vāraya*-, a derived stem meaning "holding captive, holding back, covering, concealing". This becomes by a natural process (called *vṛddhi*, "strengthening") *vaiśva* + *vāraya*, and then, by the principle that "consonants count for nothing" and contraction, Vaiśvānara.[197] But what exactly is this etymology trying to say? The text refers to a form of Soma sacrifice that takes twelve days (called *dvādaśāha*), in which a ten-day sequence called *dāśa-rātra* ("ten nights") is flanked by two intensive day-and-overnight sacrifices called *atirātras* as opening and closing days (*atirātras* = those sacrifices which have "a night, *rātra*, over and above, *ati*, [the ten regular nights]"). "Prajāpati (the creative power) created the creatures (*prajā*) by the *daśāha*," i.e., by the ten-day portion of the twelve-day sacrifice. The creatures were scattered everywhere, and thus the creation by the *daśāha* presents the vision of diversity. But then Prajāpati "saw those two *atirātras* of Vaiśvānara," which preceded and followed the ten-day portion, as the means of bringing about a oneness. So, just as he had earlier implemented the diversity, he now goes and implements a unification leading to oneness: By means of the two *atirātras* he holds the creatures, who had become all (*viśva*), captive (*vāraya*). This *viśva-vāraya* or "holding all captive", then, is the Vaiśvānara-hood of the two Vaiśvānara *atirātras*. In other words this *viśva-vāraya* or "holding all captive" is the essential element for which the two *atirātras* are called Vaiśvānara *atirātras*. So the essence or inner meaning of the adjective *vaiśvānara* is the unifying and oneness-producing *viśva-vāraya* or "holding all captive".

Our third passage is *TaittSaṁh* V.6.6.2-3, one of a series of otherwise unrelated comments on the piling up of the fire altar in the *agnicayana*.

[C] (The fire) to be piled is the body of Agni, Vaiśvānara is the self; in that he offers to Vaiśvānara after the piling, he prepares its body and mounts it; the sacrificer thus pre-

> pares his body, in that he piles the fire; in that he offers to Vaiśvāṇara after the piling, verily having prepared his body he mounts it with the self; therefore they do not cut off from it; verily living he goes to the gods.[198]

The new element here is "Vaiśvānara is the self [of Agni]." The offering to Vaiśvānara mentioned is the same one as in sec. 14 (a cake on twelve potsherds, the first sacrifice to the Fire on the completed altar). [C] thus explains that the first sacrifice on the completed altar is to Vaiśvānara because "Vaiśvānara is the self [of Agni]." The self is the essential, most important aspect of an individual, and so Vaiśvānara, being the self of Agni, is the essential, most important aspect of Agni and is sacrificed to first. Thereafter [C] goes on to suggest that the dichotomy "[Agni's] body—[Agni's] self" has analogies in "piling the fire-offering the sacrifice into it" and in "[the sacrificer's] preparing his [own] body—[the sacrificer] mounting it [the body, the whole *agnicayana*] with his own self".

Comparing [C] with *ŚatBr* IX.3.1.3-6, we might say that while the *Taittirīya Saṁhitā*, which belongs to the black Yajur Veda, explains the importance of Agni Vaiśvānara in the ritual by saying that "Vaiśvānara is the self of Agni," the *Śatapatha Brāhmaṇa*, which is the Brāhmaṇa of the white Yajur Veda Saṁhitā, explains the very same fact by saying that "Vaiśvānara is the One [that is] in all [*viśva*] these worlds," using as a generating configuration the analysis Vaiśvānara = *viśva nara*, "the man (=active principle) of all". Vaiśvānara is compared to a head in much the same way that he was compared to the self in [C]: the built up Agni, i.e., the fire-altar, is the body of Agni, and Vaiśvānara is the head to that body (in [C] he is the self of that body). In both cases the whole of Agni (body and self, body and head) includes Agni Vaiśvānara as most important, leading part. Thus the two texts, although from different branches of Yajur Vedic tradition, are to a large extent aiming at the same thing.

This concludes our discussion of [A]-[C]. But before turning to the implications of all this for the *vidyā* in *Śatapatha Brāhmaṇa*, we have to consider an additional point. The *Śatapatha Brāhmaṇa Vidyā* ends with ". . .and verily, Vaiśvānara does no harm to him who speaks of him." Now "Vaiśvānara doing harm" sounds rather strange. But this also has Vedic and Brāhmaṇa resonances which provide further insight into Vaiśvānara. We saw in *Ṛg Veda* I.59 that Agni Vaiśvānara was praised as the power that enabled the Vedic Aryans defeat their enemies, the Dasyus. In *Atharva Veda* III.21.3 Agni is praised as an all-pervading Divine, and as Vaiśvānara, is called on as the destructive power of war:

> 3. He who, a god, goes in the same chariot with Indra (leader in war), he that "belongs to all men" (= Vaiśvānara) and is of all conflagrations,[a] whom, very powerful in fights, I call on loudly—to those fires be this oblation made.[199]

In *Atharva Veda* IV.36, a hymn described by Whitney as "against demons and other enemies", he is invoked as destructive power, period:

> 1. Then let him of real force burn forth—Agni Vaiśvānara, the bull, [-burn them] who so shall abuse and harm us, likewise who so shall play the niggard to us.[200]

A remarkable story in *Śatapatha Brāhmaṇa* illustrates that this destructive "burning power" was thought of and experienced very concretely:

> 10. Now Videha, the descendant of Madhu, carried Agni Vaiśvānara in his mouth. The Ṛṣi Gotama Rahūgaṇa was his family priest. When addressed (by the latter), he made no answer to him, fearing lest Agni might fall from his mouth.
> 11. He (the priest) began to invoke the latter with verses of the Ṛg Veda, 'We kindle thee at the sacrifice, O wise Agni, thee the radiant, the mighty caller to the sacrificial feast (*Ṛg Veda* V.26.3)!—O Videha!'
> 12. He (Videha) did not answer. (The priest went on) 'Upwards, O Agni, dart thy brilliant, shining rays, thy flames, thy beams (*Ṛg Veda* VIII.44.16)!—O Videha-a-a!'
> 13. Still he did not answer. (The priest continued), "Thee, O butter-sprinkled one, we invoke! (*Ṛg Veda* V.26.2);" so much he uttered, when at the very mentioning of butter (the sacrificial offering, actually ghee), Agni Vaiśvānara flashed forth from the mouth: he (Videha) was unable to hold him back; he issued from his mouth, and fell down on this earth.
> 14. Videha the descendant of Madhu was at that time at the

(river) Sarasvatī. He (Agni) thence went burning along this earth towards the east; and Gotama Rahūgaṇa and Videha followed after him as he was burning along. He burnt over (dried up) all these rivers. Now that (river), which is called 'Sandanira,' flows from the northern (Himalayas) mountain: that one he did not burn over. That one the Brahmins did not cross in former times, thinking, 'it has not been burnt over by Agni Vaiśvānara'.

16. Even in late summer that (river), as it were, rages along: so cold is it, not having been burnt over by Agni Vaiśvānara...[201]

The text is often cited because it seems to refer to the historical spread of Brāhmaṇism to the east. But the spiritual representations are of equal interest. Perhaps Videha was figuratively said to be holding Agni Vaiśvānara in his mouth because he was a great commander and champion of Brāhmaṇism. But he also must have held Agni Vaiśvānara in his mouth in a more literal sense, and the latter must then have literally flashed forth—in other words, the text must be describing some kind of powerful spiritual experience that Videha and his priest had at a sacrifice. Most important, however, is the fact that both of these things are at the same time regarded as part of the manifestation of Agni Vaiśvānara on a cosmic scale. The transition form the individual to the cosmic (end of v. 13 and v. 14) is completely natural and has archetypal force.

In view of these and related facts,[202] then, we may say that in the *vidyā* in *Śatapatha Brāhmaṇa,* Vaiśvānara means not only the *nara* of the *viśva*, the one ensouling the diversity, but also a concrete cosmic and otherwise universal power that operates in the world. This is also the traditional position. According to Sāyaṇa's commentary on *Śatapatha Brāhmaṇa*, the knowledge of Vaiśvānara is knowledge of *Parameśvara*, the Supreme (*parama*) Almighty Lord (*īśvara*), who is the sole power of creation, maintenance, and destruction of the world.[203] In this connection it is significant that the *Vaiśvānara Vidyā* is taught by a king who knows (Skt. root *vid*) Agni Vaiśvānara "thoroughly". (Similarly in *ŚatBr* I.1.4, Agni Vaiśvānara is manifested through Videha, a *kṣatriya* leader and later founder of the kingdom of Videha.) It is only natural that exemplary, devout and powerful kings and leaders have experience of Agni in His Universal and Cosmic aspects, since they are already naturally engaged in a more universal type of thinking and since they already naturally exercise power on a large scale.

16. Structure of the *Śatapatha Brāhmaṇa* Text

Starting Point of the *Vidyā*. The considerations in secs. 13 and 14 give us a basic insight into what must be the starting point of the *Śatapatha Brāhmaṇa Vaiśvānara Vidyā*. There can be little question that the specific *Vaiśvānaras* which the six Brahmins know correspond to the six aspects of Divinity in *SātBr* X.3.1.3-6 (sec. 14 above), except that their grouping into three pairs (which is central in the latter) is disregarded. Four of the aspects are the same. Only the mid-region, *antarikṣa*, has been replaced by space, *ākāśa*, and Agni by Water, *ap*. The change from Agni to *ap* is perhaps motivated in part by the fact that Agni is an All-Deity. Cosmologically, the All-ground

TABLE 4.5
Deities in *ŚatBr* X.6.1

Earth, Pṛthivī	(Agni), water, ap,
Space, *ākāśa*	Wind, Vāyu
Heaven, *dyauḥ*	Sun, Āditya

is the Waters. In addition, already from the *Ṛg Veda* on, Agni pervades the waters and is the power that impregnates them with life. At any rate, accepting the substitution, the *Vaiśvānaras* of the six Brahmins are basically the members of the three *viśva-nara* pairs in *ŚatBr* X.3.1.3-6 which, as said before, elaborate the scheme of the three worlds and form a subset of the "Powers of the Puruṣa". This in turn

TABLE 4.6
Scheme of *Vaiśvānara Vidyā* Superimposed on the "Powers of the Puruṣa" (Table 3.5)

1.	Speech, *Vāc*	Earth, *Pṛthivī* (1)[6]	Agni
2.	Breath, *prāṇa*	*antarikṣa* = *ākāśa*, (3)[4]	Wind, Vāyu (3)[3]
3.	Sight, *cakṣuḥ*	Heaven, *dyauḥ* (6)[1]	Sun, Āditya (5)[2]
5.	Mind	Waters (2)[5]	Moon

Key: Numbers in parentheses give order of occurrence in the *Śatapatha Brāhmaṇa* version, numbers in brackets, in the Upaniṣadic version.

suggests that in the *vidyā* in *Śatapatha Brāhmaṇa*, the *viśva-nara* pairing of *ŚatBr* X.3.1.3-6 is neglected, and the essence of Vaiśvānara which the six Brahmins are after is precisely the One-in-the-Many that is represented there by the principle of *viśva-nara*. (That same principle is represented in other ways in sec. 15 [C], [A] and [B]). The starting point of the *vidyā* is therefore that each of the six had a different knowledge (*vid-*) and realization of the nature of this Universal One-in-the-Many, developed in his own spiritual and meditative life, in combination with scriptural study, over many years.

"Partial" Knowledges of Vaiśvānara. The level and nature of these "knowledges" are reminiscent of those in the first three feet of the *Sixteen Parts Vidyā*.[204] We can imagine that Aruṇa Aupaveśi had meditated on and regarded the Divine that can be seen in the Earth as "the *Vaiśvānara*". The Earth's inner strength, its stability and firmness, the selfless support which it gives to living beings,[205] all these sublime qualities lead a worshipper to perception of something Divine. But Aruṇa had come to regard and at some level know this Divine as the *Vaiśvānara,* the One Unitary factor in everything. The king immediately tells him that he had essentially realized the Vaiśvānara *pratiṣṭhā,* the Vaiśvánara (or One Principle of) "Foundation" or "Fundamental Basis of the Many". Because of this realization, of this dawning of a great Divine or this partial dawning of Reality in his mind and being, says the king, Aruṇa is now established or firmly founded in sons and cattle, the two most important indices of a fulfilled life in the community. But, says the king, this realization of Vaiśvānara is incomplete: this Divine or partial glimpse of Reality is only the feet of Vaiśvānara.

On the one hand Aśvapati acknowledges that Aruṇa has some understanding of Vaiśvānara, some knowledge of the One-in-the-Many. He even gives it a name, he introduces an "indicator term", *pratiṣṭhā,* the knowledge of "Foundation". Because the knowledge of "Foundation" must be tinged with the quality of "being a foundation", this is another sign that we are here dealing with types of knowledge or realization of the Divine similar to that in the initial stages of the first three Quarters in the *Sixteen Parts Vidyā.* But then the statement that "this is only the feet (also *pratiṣṭhā*) of Vaiśvānara" comes as something of a shock. If one mistakes the feet (and later the bladder and so on) of Vaiśvānara for Vaiśvānara itself, then one must be still fairly removed from a real knowledge of Vaiśvānara. A serious difficulty for the reader here is that the king is giving the impression that the real knowledge of Vaiśvānara has parts. He seems to be drawing an image of Vaiśvānara as having for its feet a Divine Element "Foundation", *pratiṣṭhā,* as having for its bladder a Divine Element "Wealth", *rayi*, and so on. But on this have to suspend judgement for the moment. By talking this way the King is certainly unifying his six students. He is reassuring them that their existing understanding has indeed some relation to the Vaiśvānara which they are seeking, and that their different knowledges and understandings are all more or less equally justified (they are all body-parts of the real Vaiśvānara). At the same time he makes it clear that in their quest they have all had basically the same problem, or had all made the same mistake. And finally he points out the difficulty. "You, then, knowing different Vaiśvānaras, have been eating different [kinds of] food." You six have been absorbing and feeding on different qualities in which Supreme Divinity, Brahman, manifests itself. These qualities correspond to your respective *upāsanās*, to your particular objects and paths of meditation, worship, and living your vision. Because of this you now have different realizations of what is in reality only One Supreme Divinity, one Reality, and you cannot come to any agreement.

The King's Main Teaching. And then the King starts on his real teaching. "But verily, of the measure of a span as it were have the well-known gods become." Sāyaṇa seems to read this as "but the gods, knowing well that (essential element) which is merely of the space of a span (*prādeśa-mātra*)", have attained, i.e., "have become successful".[206] Eggeling points out, however, that "the gods" here may very well refer to Earth, Water, and so on,[207] i.e., to the Brahmins' vehicles of meditation, and thus to the Vaiśvānaras which the Brahmins had realized. If so, the sentence must mean something like "but verily, these deities (vehicles of meditation, and thus the Vaiśvānaras) have become (in me, in my realization) of the measure of a span," i.e., they have become me, my self—with "of the measure of a span" interpreted as referring to the dimensions of the features which the king points out on his head in the immediately following v. 11, which amounts to a reference to the self. For the only meaning which pointing out the different individual Vaiśvānaras as different parts of the head can have is that they are all oneself, aspects of oneself, or self. In the next sentence, "I will so tell them unto you . . .," Sāyaṇa too agrees that the "them" refers to the vehicles of meditation, and that the king is referring to how he is about to resolve the problem in v. 10.

The whole device of pointing to different parts of the head is completely different from the language of Vaiśvānara being something with person-parts, *puruṣa-vidha*, which the king had been using in vs. 4-9. The parts of the head he points to are different from the parts of the body which he earlier connected with the individual Vaiśvānaras, because the latter cover the whole body. The Vaiśvānara "standing out", *atiṣṭhā*, which was earlier said to be the head of Vaiśvānara, is still identified with the head. The Vaiśvānara "of Soma's Splendour", realized by meditation on Āditya (the Sun-Divine) as Vaiśvānara, is still the eyes. But the "Diversely Coursing", arising from meditation on Vāyu, Wind, which was earlier the *prāṇa* of Vaiśvānara, is now pointed to as the nostrils. And thereafter the differences become larger. The Vaiśvānara "Plenteous", earlier the trunk (*ātman*), is now the space in the mouth. The Vaiśvānara "Wealth", before the bladder, is now the water in the mouth. And the *pratiṣṭhā*, which was the feet, is now the chin. So the king has here a completely different intent than he did in vs. 4-9. There he provided an overall framework for describing where the students stood in relation to their goal. Now he is simply saying that all the Vaiśvānaras of which they had developed knowledge, were oneself, one's self.

But that cannot be the whole or only point the king is making. For in the Upaniṣadic version of the *vidyā*, the Brahmins meditated on Earth and so on as the Self, *ātman*, and they realized "the Vaiśvānara Self [called] *pratiṣṭhā* (*pratiṣṭhā ātmā Vaiśvānara*)" and so on. That is, their meditation was probably *ahaṁgraha*, of the form "This Earth-Divine is my very self," etc. and they did not need to be told that the various Vaiśvānaras that they had realized were simply their self. (In fact, in the Upaniṣadic version the king does not point to different parts of the head at all.[208]) But still there was a problem—they "knew this Universal Self as if it were diverse, *pṛthag* . . ." This is similar to "you, then, knowing diverse (*pṛthag*) Vaiśvānaras, have been eating diverse (*pṛthag*) food" here in the *Śatapatha Brāhmaṇa* text. So in both versions of the *vidyā* there is an additional aspect the king is stressing. *All* the Vaiśvānaras which the Brahmins knew were (aspects of the true) Vaiśvānara, and *all* of them are pointed to as different parts of the head, i.e. they are all identified as part of one's self. But actually the true Vaiśvānara the king was indicating, oneself or the Self in the oneself, was of a different order than all these parts. It was a One-in-the-Many of a different order than the various Ones-in-the-Many which the Brahmins had realized. The latter were Ones-in-the-Many based on essence of quality like Earth. This point is similar to the transition in the *Sixteen Parts Vidyā* from the four feet of Brahman individually to Brahman being one but having four feet (secs. 7-8, vs. sec. 9, above). The knowledge of the One-in-the-Many as the Divine quality of Foundation (*pratiṣṭhā* Vaiśvānara), or as the Divine quality of Wealth (*rayir* Vaiśvānara), represents a valid but limited realization of the true One-in-the-Many, the true *viśva-nara* = Vaiśvānara. The true Vaiśvānara is the same as the Puruṣa of the Puruṣa Hymn. The Puruṣa is the great One, the One-in-All and the All, from the beginning, before there was Earth etc. It produces the deities Earth, Sun, etc., but It itself is higher than them and cannot be gotten at by staying with the qualities associated with Earth etc.

So by pointing to different parts of the head, the king is saying that the One that is in the Many, the *nara* (man) of the *viśva* (all), should be sought in one's self, or in oneself, and not in the specific Nature of a cosmic-level Divinity (Earth, Water, etc.), in the Quality of Divinity embodied in these. There is a higher level transcendental to the six Divine *nara*-qualities, which is the *viśva-nara* from the very beginning, beyond any thought of time or deities or *viśva*. This is the Puruṣa that produced/became all this, this is the changeless Entity from the very beginning, beyond any consideration of time or diversity. *This* is to be sought in one's self. It is *this* knowledge, and thus preoccupation with this fact, that makes man immortal (by it one wards off repeated death).

The Agni Vaiśvānara Taught is the Puruṣa. Finally the king adds some concluding comments (end of v. 11). "He is this Agni Vaiśvānara who is the Puruṣa." The Puruṣa in question is no doubt the Puruṣa of the Puruṣa Hymn. Hence *puruṣa-vidha* may be interpreted as "of the shape of the Puruṣa [of the Puruṣa Hymn]", because the Earth is the feet (=*pratiṣṭhā*) of this Vaiśvānara, etc. so that the whole Cosmos is Vaiśvānara. But *puruṣa-vidha* may also have the sense of "of the shape of a man (or person)", or "with person parts", and thus may refer to the person as such or his/her self, because the king just demonstrated how the Vaiśvānara "standing out" is a person's (one's own) head, etc. On this reading, the king is saying: "Whoever knows that Agni Vaiśvānara as being oneself, in the form of a person in the way I have just explained him, viz. with his aspect *atiṣṭhā*, 'standing out', which is the *mūrdhā*, the head of Vaiśvānara, being really part of self [indicated by pointing to the head], and similarly with the other aspects—whoever knows like this, wards off repeated death . . ." If this interpretation is adopted, the next phrase, "established within the *puruṣa,*" *puruṣe'ntaḥ pratiṣṭhitam*, would then continue to elaborate this and we should read "Whoever knows that Agni Vaiśvānara as being with person parts (*puruṣa-vidha*) (i.e., as the person him/herself), established within a person . . .," i.e. "established as a person's self, as his/her soul . . .' Overall, this appears to be a very natural reading.[209]

Vedānta, however, reads "established within a person" as "established in a person [as the fire of digestion]", not "established in a person [as his/her self or soul]."[210] For beginning with *BṛhUp* V.9, the idea becomes established that Agni Vaiśvānara is the fire of digestion, and from then on Agni Vaiśvānara has primarily this meaning.[211] However, the idea that Agni Vaiśvānara is the gastric fire is not found directly in the preceding Brāhmaṇa and Saṁhita literature.[212] *ŚatBr* X.6.1.11 would be the only occurrence. The fact that Agni Vaiśvānara may be the gastric fire in the Upaniṣads does not mean that it is so here. Accordingly we read "established within a person" as "established within [the self or soul of] a person".

17. Meaning of the *Śatapatha Brāhmaṇa Vidyā*

The heart is expanded and breathes the Divinity associated with Earth and Sky, Agni and Āditya, the Quarters, and so on! This is the state from which the *vidyās* in this chapter start! In the *Vaiśvānara Vidyā*, however, there is an additional starting element: the idea of Vaiśvānara, the luminous One that is the *nara*, the single "ruling" entity, in the *viśva*, in all the things there are. This idea is held out as an ideal and goal by the Scriptures, and each of the six Brahmins is seeking to realize this goal in the Divine that is breathing in his heart. Each one feels that he has glimpsed it there—Vaiśvānara is in the direction of the Earth-Divine, or in the direction of the Wind-Divine, etc. But, says the king, these realizations are not really realizations of Vaiśvānara. They are at best partial realizations, and indeed misleading. Vaiśvānara is the self—the awareness of the Earth-Divine or the Wind-Divine as the One in everything must become the awareness of self being in, or being the *nara* of, all there is. This "Vaiśvānara-self", *because* it is *self,* is beyond and different from things seen in Divine Aspects like Earth and Vāyu, which are still in a sphere of "quality" (even though that sphere is a sphere of "Divine Quality"). This "Vaiśvānara-self" is the Vaiśvānara which the Brahmins are seeking; it is the Puruṣa of the Vedas and Brāhmaṇas (and later the Ātman of the Upaniṣads).

Beyond this re-orientation, however, the king's teaching also presents a stark juxtaposition. On the one hand, there is an implication that Vaiśvānara, the One-in-the-Many, is indeed a reality at a cosmic, cosmos-pervading, cosmos-encompassing level. On the other hand, Vaiśvānara is the (or is to be sought in the or as the) individual self.

Thus the self (or Self), although the knower and thus different from the known, is indeed somehow intrinsically connected with the cosmos, the totality of all visible manifestations, the known. In particular, since the pointing to the various features of the head in v. 11 had the function of indicating that the six Vaiśvānara already realized by the Brahmins were really "parts of oneself (or self)," the correspondence of these Vaiśvānara with the specific parts of the head in that verse has no further deeper meaning. But the identification of the Vaiśvānara realized by the individual Brahmins with the feet, the bladder etc. of the true Vaiśvānara must have some significance. It affirms an intrinsic inseparableness of the true One-in-the-Many and the Many. This is an aspect that goes beyond what is taught in the *Sixteen Parts Vidyā*, and it is significant that it is precisely this aspect that is highlighted in the version in *Chāndogya Upaniṣad*. Later, in *Māṇḍūkya Upaniṣad*, this same aspect becomes part of the supreme analysis of waking state consciousness.

18. *Vaiśvānara Vidyā:* Upaniṣadic Text and *Vaiśvānara* Ātman

In this section and the next, finally, we discuss the Upaniṣadic version of the *Vaiśvānara Vidyā, ChāndUp* V.11-18. Our approach will be to focus on differences *vis-à-vis* the *Śatapatha Brāhmaṇa* version to highlight the Upaniṣad's contribution to the common *vidyā* involved in both texts.[213]

Upaniṣadic Text. As in *Śatapatha Brāhmaṇa*, there is first the story of the six Brahmins going to see King Aśvapati of Benares. But there are some notable differences. For example, the same five Brahmins as in *Śatapatha Brāhmaṇa* first question Uddālaka, the son of Aruṇa, not Aruṇa. Uddālaka does not feel he can answer them adequately and advises that they all go to king Aśvapati. So he goes to see the king, not his father. More important, the Brahmins are enquiring about the Vaiśvānara Ātman (V.11.2), not (Agni) Vaiśvānara. Their questions are "Who is our Ātman? What is Brahman?" (V.11.1). This difference becomes more developed as the king talks to them individually, this time beginning with Prācīnaśāla Aupamanyava:

V.12.1. "Aupamanyava, what Ātman do you meditate on (*upās-*)?" "[Just] Heaven (*dyauḥ*), revered Sir, oh King." [The king] said: "The Ātman[a] on which you meditate is verily the brightly shining Vaiśvānara Ātman (*sutejā Ātmā Vaiśvānaraḥ*).

For that reason the *suta, pra-suta*, and *ā-suta* [Soma pressings] are [cultivated] in your family.

2. You eat food; you see what is pleasing. [Similarly] he eats food, he sees what is pleasing, [and] there is Brahman vitality in his family who meditates on (*upās-*) the Vaiśvānara Ātman thus. That, however, is only the head of the Ātman,[b]" he said. "Your head would have fallen off, if you had not come unto me."[214]

Instead of "what Vaiśvānara do you know (*vid-*)", the Upaniṣad has "what Ātman do you meditate on (worship, etc., *upās-*)". While in *Śatapatha Brāhmaṇa*, Jana Śārkarākṣya meditated on Heaven, here in the Upaniṣad Prācīnaśāla does. And instead of getting as fruit of the meditation the knowedge of the Vaiśvānara *ati-ṣṭhā*, "standing forth", here the meditator has realized the Vaiśvānara Ātman [which is] "of Good (*su-*) Splendour (*tejas*)", *Sutejā Ātmā Vaiśvānaraḥ*. This is similar to but not identical with the *Suta-tejā Vaiśvānara* which in *Śatapatha Brāhmaṇa* was associated with Āditya, the Sun Divine. More important, in the *Śatapatha Brāhmaṇa* version *upāsanā* is not mentioned—we are only told about knowing (*vid-*) the Vaiśvānara in question. Here in the Upaniṣad it is explicit (*upās-* in both 12.1 and 12.2). Lastly, as in *Śatapatha Brāhmaṇa* in the case of the *Suta-tejā Vaiśvānara*, the king notes that one side-effect of the *upāsanā* is that the office of soma-pressing preparations runs in the Brahmin's family. But he adds that the *upāsanā* has also another, more general side effect, viz. that Prācīnaśāla Aupamanyava was always provided for with food, that he saw many pleasing things in his life, and that there was the vitality of Brahman (*Brahmavarcas*, the vitality that goes with knowledge of Brahman) running in his family line. These things, says the King, come to anyone who meditates on Heaven as the Vaiśvānara Self.

The accounts for the other Brahmins use the identical wording. Apart from Aruṇa, who as said before is replaced by his son Uddālaka, the other Brahmins are unchanged, as are the vehicles of meditation (*devas*, deities, like Earth). Besides the change from *Atiṣṭhā* to *Sutejas*, the *Śatapatha Brāhmaṇa* Vaiśvānara "of Soma's Splendour", *Suta-tejā Vaiśvānara*, embodied in the Sun Divine (Āditya), is now *Viśva-rūpa Ātmā Vaiśvānara*, the Vaiśvānara Ātman "of All Forms" (the Sun-Divine, which is the inner principle of vision, discloses "all forms").

Finally comes the Full Teaching:

V.18.1. Then he said to them: 'Verily, indeed, you here eat food, knowing this Vaiśvānara Ātman in different ways (*pṛthag*, "manifold"), as it were. He, however, who regards (worships, *upās-*) this Vaiśvānara Ātman as of the measure of the span (*prādeśa-mātra*)—thus (the king demonstrates), [as] to be measured by thinking of oneself (*abhivimāna*)—he eats food in all worlds, in all beings, in all selves.

2. The "Bright-Shining" (*Su-tejā*) is indeed the head of that Vaiśvānara Ātman. The "of all Forms" (*Viśva-rūpa*) is his eye (or sight). The "Diversely Coursing" (*Pṛthag-vartmā*) is his breath. The "Plenteous" (*Bahula*) is his body (*sandeha*). The "Wealth" (*rayi*) is indeed his bladder. The Earth (*pṛthivī*) is indeed his feet. The Sacrificial Area (in the sacrifice, *vedi*) is indeed his breast. The Kuṣa grass (in the sacrificial area) is his hair. The Gārhapatya fire is his heart. The Anvāhāryapacana fire is his mind. The Āhavanīya fire is his mouth.

There are several new points. In 18.1, the king describes the Vaiśvānara Ātman not only as *prādeśa-mātra*, as in *Śatapatha Brāhmaṇa*, but also as *abhivimāna*, to be discussed below. Then he gives an *upāsanā* (in *Śatapatha Brāhmaṇa* he merely tells how he is going to explain things), with a fruit never mentioned before: "He who worships (meditates on, *upās-*) the Vaiśvānara Ātman as *prādeśa-mātra* and *abhi-vimāna*, he eats food in all the worlds . . ." (The usual quotation marks or *iti* after *abhivimāna* are missing). The largest changes, however, come in V.18.2. As already mentioned there is no pointing to parts of the head, only a summation: "Of that very Vaiśvānara Ātman, the *Su-tejas* is the head, the *Viśva-rūpa* is the eye (or Sight), . . ." This is remarkable. In the *Śatapatha Brāhmaṇa* version, the fact that the different Vaiśvānaras of the Brahmins are all "body-parts" of what is really Vaiśvānara, the One-in-the-Many, is to some extent a device for leading the Brahmins to the central point, viz. that the individual Vaiśvānaras are all the self (indicated by pointing to the head etc.). But here in *Chāndogya Upaniṣad*, this same fact is explicitly picked out and assembled from all that has been said before and is dramatically set forth as *the* characterization of the Vaiśvānara Ātman. There is no mention of Puruṣa or any fruit. Instead, the statement is meant to simply stand on its own, as the supreme statement on the Vaiśvānara

Ātman. Indeed, in the movement of V.18.1-2, it is presented as the highest wisdom, the final statement, exceeding even the *upāsanā* in V.18.1.

Discussion of the Text. The new emphasis on the Vaiśvānara Ātman having the partial Vaiśvāṇaras as parts is connected with the fact that in the Upaniṣad, the focus is from the very beginning on the aspect of Ātman, of "Self". In the *Śatapatha Brāhmaṇa* text, the object was Vaiśvānara, the One-in-the-Many, the Self of Agni, etc., as an initially external, highest Divine, highest reality. It was the One Divine that is immanent in and the active principle of everything. In the Upaniṣad on the other hand, the goal is from the beginning framed as finding that same One Immanent in one's own self. The six Brahmins are asking "who (what) is our Ātman", their *upāsanās* are *ātman-upāsanās*, they meditate on (worship, regard, *upās-*) Heaven, etc. as (the Self in) their self, and the final statement is one about the Self. In particular, the previous *upāsanās* of the six Brahmins, and the resulting initial knowledges with which they came to the king, are described differently and have a different character than the corresponding *upāsanās* and initial knowledges in *Śatapatha Brāhmaṇa.* By meditating (*upās-*) on Heaven etc. as one's self, there arises a particular plane of Divinity and Universality in one's being. "The infinite and world-of-light quality that shines in Heaven is part of my being, my nature and consciousness, and I am this quality, everywhere"; "the universal, nourishing-all, serving-all and yielding-to-all quality that shines in Water is part of my being, and I am this everywhere", etc. And the perception or awareness of self at that point will be a reflection of the Vaiśvānara Ātman in oneself. For that reason the King calls this reflection the *Sutejā Ātmā Vaiśvānara.* But there is still a problem. The Brahmins know the Vaiśvānara Ātman "manifold, as it were", *pṛthag iva.* Their perception/awareness of the One Self in the Many (the Vaiśvānara Ātman) is so fused with the Divine qualities of their vehicles and paths of meditation that they themselves had not really realized this Ātman's real nature, and each one defended his perception against the others.

The *Upāsanā* in V.18.1. So the king, following up on the "you eat food" in vs. 12.2, 13.2, etc., first teaches an *upāsanā* of his own. "[He] who thus worshipfully meditates on (*upās-*) this Vaiśvārana Ātman—[viz.] as of the measure of a span, *prādeśa-mātra*, and as *abhivimāna*—he eats food in all worlds, in all beings, in all selves." Here several questions arise: (1) the meaning of *prādeśa-mātra* and *abhivimāna*; (2) the question whether the *upāsanā* involves the conception of Agni Vaiśvānara as the fire of digestion; (3) the problem of the nature of the fruit that "he eats food in all the worlds, all beings, all selves"; and (4) the question of whether the *upāsanā,* in addition to "eating food in all the worlds," might not also lead to the knowledge declared in 18.2. We begin with (1). *Prādeśa-mātra* was discussed earlier in the context of the *Śatapatha Brāhmaṇa* version, where we accepted the translation "of the measure of a span [from chin to forehead]". Śaṁkara in his commentary on *ChāndUp* 18.1 rejects this "literal sense" because it does not relate to the main teaching (18.2). Instead he gives four other meanings, beginning with "as a whole, composed of parts",[215] his own preference. But there is really no strong reason to think that the method of *upāsanā* in 18.1 should agree with the final supreme description of the Vaiśvānara Ātman in 18.2. So we stay with "of the measure of a span". Indeed the *Brahma Sūtra* implies that some well-known teachers took "of the measure of a span" figuratively while others adopted some of the other meanings mentioned by Śaṁkara.[216] (The Sūtra does not clearly take sides and seems to regard all the views as valid possibilities.) In the *Śatapatha Brāhmaṇa* text, "of the measure of a span" referred perhaps to the dimensions of features of the head, and in any case figuratively to the individual self. In the Upaniṣad, where there is no pointing to the head, the reference is probably to the heart. The heart or chest is of the measure of a span,[217] and the *evam*, "thus", suggests that the king may have shown this with a gesture. The fact that Self and the Universe are in the heart, or are the Heart, is a cardinal teaching of the early Upaniṣads (see chr. 6)

Regarding *abhivimāna* there are two main lines of interpretation. The traditional one is "one who is to be understood as the inner I", from *man-*, "to know".[218] But T.V. Kapali Sastri points out that "the word *vimāna*, wherever it occurs in the *Ṛg Veda*, is used in the sense of a word derived from *mā*, 'to measure.'"[219] He notes that Sāyaṇa takes it always either as "'measure', 'limit', and 'make definite', or [as] 'construct and create.'"[220] On this view, to worship and meditate on (*upās-*) the Vaiśvānara Self as *abhivimāna* is to focus on its role as constructing the world (bringing it into existence) or making it definite. For "whether the word *vimāna* is taken to mean 'measure with distinction,' *viśeṣeṇa māna*, or 'to build or create', *nirmāṇa māna*, it does not make any essential difference. For whatever is created is measured; measure itself is 'setting a limit to and making definite what is to be created.'"[221]

The Agnihotra into the Prāṇas (*ChāndUp* V.19-24). The next two questions, viz. whether the *upāsanā* in 18.1 involves the notion of Agni Vaiśvānara as the gastric fire and what it means to "eat food in all the worlds, all beings, all selves", leads to a consideration of *ChāndUp* V.19-24, immediately following the *Vaiśvānara Vidyā*.[222] This text deals with the practice, at mealtimes, of mentally offering portions of one's food to the five *prāṇas* or breaths. This so-called *prāṇāhuti*, or "offering (lit. pouring) into the *prāṇas*", is presumably intended to be combined with the *upāsanā* in 18.1. Equally important, the text explains the inner meaning of "he eats food in all the worlds. . ." First, offering the food into the *prāṇas* has a cosmic-universal effect: The whole cosmos is satiated and satisfied (root *tṛp*).

> V.19.1. Therefore the first portion which one may come to, that should be offered. The first oblation (*āhuti*) which he would pour, that he should pour with "to the *prāṇa* breath (the first of the five breaths or vital airs), hail".[a] Then the *prāṇa* breath is satisfied (*tṛpyati*).
>
> 19.2. With the *prāṇa* breath being satisfied, Sight is satisfied. With Sight being satisfied, the Sun-Divine (Āditya) is satisfied. With Āditya being satisfied, Heaven (*dyauḥ*) is satisfied. With Heaven being satisfied, whatever Heaven and Āditya stand over (= are lord over), that is satisfied. Along with (or: in accordance with) the satisfaction of that, he (the sacrificer) is satisfied with offspring, cattle, food, splendour (*tejas*), and Brahma vigour.[223]

Similar offerings are then made to the *vyāna, apāna, samāna* and *udāna* breaths respectively, in this order. "The general concept is that by eating one satisfies the *prāṇas* (vital powers), which in their turn satisfy the corresponding deities and parts of the cosmos. On account of micro-macro-cosmic identifications the *prāṇāhuti* is interpreted as a *tarpaṇam* [or satiating, from *tṛp*] of the whole cosmos."[224] At the end the text relates the knowledge of the inner effect of the *prāṇāhuti* to similar cosmic-level effectiveness of one's *agnihotra*, the daily milk offering into the sacred fire (V.24.2):

> 24.1. He who, not knowing this, offers the *agnihotra* (daily milk offering),—as if, having removed the live coals, he poured it in [dead] ashes, so would that be.
>
> 2. But who offers the *agnihotra* knowing this thus - his offering takes place[a] in all worlds, in all beings, in all selves.
>
> 3. As the fibre of the *iṣikā* reed, when laid on fire, is burnt up, just so are burnt up the sins of the one who offers the *agnihotra* knowing this thus.
>
> 4. Therefore, if one who knowing this thus offers the remnant of his food to a *caṇḍāla* (lowest caste person), that food would be offered in his (the *caṇḍāla's*) Vaiśvānara Ātman. As to this there is this verse:
>
> 5. As here hungry children sit [expectantly]
> around (*pari-upās-*) their mother,
> so all beings sit around (*upās-*!) the
> *agnihotra* (daily milk offering).[225]

V.19.2 and the corresponding verses on the offerings to the other *prāṇas* strongly suggest that the devoted student can have direct knowledge ("experience") of the cosmic-level satisfactions (*tarpaṇas*) described.[226] And similarly, the text speaks as if the knowledge of the *agnihotra* taking place in, and thereby benefitting, "all the worlds, all beings, all selves" was equally direct cosmic-level or universal knowledge (V.24.2). This in turn, together with the numerous other textual links,[227] suggests that we interpret "he eats food in all worlds in all beings, in all selves" in V.18.1 in a similar way. He who reverentially meditates on the Vaiśvānara Ātman as being *prādeśa-mātra* and *abhivimāna* will attain a state in which there is direct knowledge, "experience", that he is "eating food in all the worlds . . ." This "eating food in all the worlds . . ." will be at the same time a sacrificing in, and a being of benefit to," all the worlds . . ."

The preceding interpretation is not only suggested by the Upaniṣadic text (V.19-24). As Swami Krishnananda notes, "eating food in all the worlds, . . ." also recalls

> the famous story of Śrī Kṛṣṇa taking a particle of food from the hands of Draupadī, in the Kāmyaka forest, when she called to

> Him for help, and with this little grain that He partook of, the whole universe was filled, and all people were satisfied, because Kṛṣṇa stood there tuned up with the Universal Virāṭ.[228]

The similarity is so strong that the simplest way to explain it is to assume that we are dealing with a specific, direct (supersensuous) spiritual knowledge that is common to both the Upaniṣad and the *Mahābhārata* episode, in other words with a common specific experiential (described in the *Mahābhārata* as exemplified in Kṛṣṇa).

The *Upāsanā* in V.18.1 and the Main Teaching V.18.2. There are no strong reasons to think that this experiential was already intended in the *Śatapatha Brāhmaṇa* version of the *vidyā*. In fact according to our reading in sec. 14, the text there mentioned food only metaphorically. In contrast the Upaniṣadic version has it several times: "You eat food, you see what is pleasing . . ." in the king's discussions with the Brahmins individually (12.2, 13.2, . . ., 17.2); then in 18.1, in "... You here eat food knowing the Vaiśvānara Ātman in different ways," like *Śatapatha Brāhmaṇa*, and then as fruit of the *upāsanā*; and finally in the teaching on the offering a portion of one's food to the *prāṇas* at mealtime, vs. 19-24. Because of the strong connection between V. 24.2 and V.18.1 in terms of knowledge/experience of "all the worlds, in all beings, in all selves", it is simplest to consider the main teaching of the *vidyā* to be V.18.2, and to regard the *upāsanā* in V.18.1 and the Agnihotra into the *Prāṇas* (vs. 19-24) as an addition to this main teaching.[229]

19. Meaning of the Upaniṣadic *Vidyā*

We have half argued and half assumed that the *upāsanā* V.18.1 is to some extent separate from the main teaching, "Of that Vaiśvānara Self, the Bright-Shining (*Sutejas*) is indeed the head . . ." (18.2). The latter is the real highpoint of the *vidyā*; it is the real continuation of the Brāhmaṇa teaching and gives that teaching a new, sharper form. Let us now consider V.18.2 by itself.

Verse 18.2 as a Unified Statement which Expresses the Highest Vision of the *Vidyā*. A striking feature of 18.2 is that while the enumeration of the different parts of the Vaiśvānara Ātman starts off with the Vaiśvānaras individually realized by the six Brahmins, there is a change after the fifth. When he comes to the sixth, the feet of the Vaiśvānara Ātman (here realized by Uddālaka Āruṇi), the king does not say "the 'Foundation' is its feet," but "the Earth is its feet", the Earth being Uddālaka's vehicle for meditation. And then he continues things that fit naturally with "Earth": the Sacrificial Area (*vedi*) is its chest, the sacred Kuśa grass that is spread in that area is its (chest-) hair, and the three sacred fires around which to much of the sacrifice revolves are its heart, mind and mouth, resp. Śaṁkara comments:

> Why is it so? Because of this same Vaiśvānara Self—[which is] indeed the subject-matter of the section—the *Sutejas* is in fact the head and the *Viśvarūpa* is the eye, the "Diversely Behaving" Self is the vital air, the "Plenteous" is the trunk, the "Wealth" is the bladder, [and] the Earth is the feet. Or this [passage] may be taken as an injunction [viz.] "meditate in this manner". The text proceeds to show how, in the case of the Vaiśvānara knower, the act of eating is an Agnihotra. Of this Vaiśvānara—of the eater—the sacrificial area is the chest, . . .[230]

It seems that Śaṁkara sees here two distinct phases. The first six body parts—from head down to feet—describe the Vaiśvānara Ātman the way it actually is (the way it was taught before in vs. 12-17), and this portion of the text can thus be used for *upāsanā*. The remainder of the text, on the other hand, describes how for a knower of the Vaiśvānara Self, the act of eating constitutes the Agnihotra offering.[231] No such division is suggested in the Upaniṣadic text, however. For after the first six aspects of the Vaiśvānara Ātman, the *vidyā* simply continues to enumerate additonal aspects of the Vaiśvānara Self in exactly the same manner as before, without any change. In fact, one gets the distinct impression that *the whole of 18.2* was intended as single unified description of the Vaiśvanara Ātman. This description deliberately combines both the Vaiśvānaras of the individual Brahmins, the corresponding aspects of the cosmos (Earth), and central elements of the sacrifice like the sacrificial area and the fires into one continuous sequence, suggesting that all of them are equally aspects of the Vaiśvānara Ātman. (The Vaiśvānara "Foundation" may have been changed to "Earth" because "Earth" is ideally suited to be the transition from the higher realizations *Sutejas*, etc., to the physical entities *vedi*, Kuśa grass, and the three fires. The *vedi* is simply a rectangular area, and the other things are likewise all on the earth.) Hence we take *ChāndUp* V.18.2 as giving a unified description of the Vaiśvānara Ātman which is independently motivated and does not necessarily refer to the Agnihotra. In this description, king Aśvapati's teaching in *Śatapatha Brāhmaṇa* that the Vaiśvānaras of the Brahmins are parts of the real Vaiśvānara is upheld as the highest description of the Vaiśvānara Ātman. But it is also elevated and expanded. First, it is squarely in the language and experiential level of "Self". And second, although beyond the Universal Divine Self-Qualities realized by the six Brahmins and formless, this Self is articulated both in the major features of the cosmos, in the types of Universal Divine realized by the Brahmins, and in the sacrifice. This is the climax and the highest vision in the *vidyā*. And this is also precisely the way the text is interpreted by Śaṁkara in his commentary on *Māṇḍūkya Upaniṣad*.[232]

This vision is extremely mystical. It implies that there is an inherent inner connection between, on the one hand, the One Self (the Vaiśvānara Self), and on the other hand, major aspects of the Cosmos (Heaven, Sun-Divine, Wind-Divine, etc.), corresponding to perceptions of Universal Divine aspects of self such as those developed by the six Brahmins, and the elements of the sacrifice. While on the one hand the One Ātman cannot have the Universal Divine qualities which the Brahmins meditated on and found in their self—it must be beyond these—on the other hand there is an identity of that Formless Ātman with the Cosmos and the Divine, half individual—half universal selves, as well as with the sacrifice. *Māṇḍūkya Upaniṣad* does not change this picture. It merely notes that it applies only to the Ātman as it is seen in the field of the waking state. It turns out that such an inner connection between the formless Ātman which is beyond all form, and the "form-ful" Divine Qualities, Deities, Worlds and Elements of Sacrifice which is declared in this *vidyā* is also echoed in other great texts such as the *Dahara, Bhūmā*, and *Gāyatrī Vidyās*.

Appendix: Swami Krishnananda's Meditation. To illustrate how the *Vaiśvānara Vidyā* is taught today, and how V.18.2 might be practiced as meditation, we look briefly at the treatment of the *Vidyā* by Swami Krishnananda of the Divine Life Society. Referring to V.18.2, the Swami says:

> Now the Upaniṣad introduces us to an immediate consequence that follows from such meditation. The meditator cannot stand outside this Great Object of meditation. This is very clear. Be-

> cause of the comprehensiveness of the Object, the Universality of the Vaiśvānara Ātman, the meditator has already undergone a transmutation of personality, entered into the bosom of Reality. And, *whatever one does, then, becomes an action of the Vaiśvānara Ātman*. This is a very serious consequence that follows from an intense meditation in this manner. *Whatever I think becomes the Thought of the Vaiśvānara Ātman. Whatever I speak becomes an Expression of the Vaiśvānara Ātman, and whatever I do becomes Its Action. And, then my actions become a Cosmic Sacrifice*, just as the gods thought Creation as a Universal Sacrifice, as we have it in the *Puruṣa Sūkta*.[233] (Italics added)

In other words, living according to the *Vaiśvānara Vidyā* gradually results in a consciousness and self in which there is no sense of "I am the doer" in, and no attachment to, any action I am performing. "Whatever I think becomes the thought of the *Vaiśvānara Ātman*" (it is not my thought); "Whatever I do becomes Its action" (it is not something that I am doing for my own purposes). Such a way of being would be intrinsically free from self-centeredness, self-interest, ego, and beyond the constantly on-one's-self-centered perspective and way of operating that characterize the normal mind.

A little later, Swami Krishnananda expands on the *upāsanā*.

> In this meditation, one contemplates the Cosmos as one's Body. Just as, for example, when one contemplates one's individual body, one simultaneously becomes conscious of the right eye, the left eye, the right hand, the left hand, the right leg, the left leg, the head, the heart, the stomach, and all the limbs of the body at one and the same time, and one does not regard the different limbs of the body as distinguished from one another in any manner, all limbs being only apparently different, but really connected to a single personality, so, in this meditation, the consciousness is to be transferred to the Universal Being. Instead of one contemplating oneself as the individual body, one contemplates oneself as the Universal Body. Instead of the right eye, there is the sun. Instead of the left eye, there is the moon. Instead of the feet there is the earth. Instead of the head, there is the heaven, and so on. The limbs of the Cosmic Person are identified with the cosmic elements, and *vice versa*, so that

> there is nothing in the Cosmos which does not form an organic part of the Body of the Virāṭ, or Vaiśvānara. When you see the vast world before you, you behold a part of your own Body. When you look at the sun, you behold your own eye... When you see all the people moving about, you behold the various parts of your own personality. The vast wind is your breath. All your actions are cosmic movements. Anything that moves, does so on account of your movement. Your breath is the Cosmic Vital Force. Your intelligence is the Cosmic Intelligence. Your existence is Cosmic Existence. Your happiness is Cosmic Bliss.
>
> . . . We may be sitting in our rooms, and the first things that attract our attention may be the objects spread out in the rooms. When we identify these objects with our Body, we will find that there are also objects outside these rooms. And, likewise, we can slowly expand our consciousness to the whole earth, and, then, beyond the earh, to the solar and stellar regions, so that we reach as far as our minds can reach. Whatever our mind can think, becomes an object for the mind; and that object, again, should become a part of the meditator's Body, cosmically. And, the moment the object that is conceived by the mind is identified with the Cosmic Body, *the object ceases to agitate the mind* any more, because that object is not any more outside; it becomes a part of the Body of the meditator. When an object becomes a part of our own body, *it no more annoys us because it is not an object at all.* It is *a subject.* The object has become the Cosmic Subject, in the Vaiśvānara meditation. (Italics added)[234]

This meditation, worship and way of thinking is basically an adaptation of V.18.2 taken as *upāsanā*. The spiritual effects which are mentioned are implicit in the Upaniṣadic text. Although this meditation uses specific thoughts and elements, the new consciousness or way of being that emerges and becomes dominant is completely independent of them.

20. Epilogue: The Emergence of the Upaniṣdic Teachings

The three or four main texts in this chapter (if we count the two versions of the *Vaiśvānara Vidyā* separate) all illustrate the emergence of the Upaniṣadic Wisdom as an independent, distinctive new thrust out of the earlier Brāhmaṇa literature. What can we say about this new thrust on the basis of these few examples, what factors are involved in its emergence? And is the knowledge taught really new and comparable to that of the great teachings in chr. 2 and the infinite *vidyās* in the following chapters? Of course the conclusions must be limited, because the texts were chosen within very narrow limits. But even in this very limited sphere, some reflection about the emergence of the Upaniṣadic teaching is worthwhile.

Considered as a group, all four of the texts are strikingly similar and take a very similar approach. Apart from *ŚatBr* X.6.1, they all teach Ātman/Brahman as a new goal which transcends and supersedes to some extent the conceptions and experience of the Vedic-Brāhmaṇical deities Agni, Vāyu, etc. Next, all four texts accept the knowledge and experience of Divinity represented by the Powers and Deities as a first step, and proceed basically by providing some reorientation and additional steps. And finally, the additional steps always involve two similar types of ingredients. First, the initial, presupposed knowledge of Divinity is always (apparently completely consciously) radically universalized, or made absolutely omni-directional, so that a completely new, much more powerfully transcendental and formless direction appears (viz., precisely the direction of Ātman/Brahman). And second, this expansion from initial knowledges of Divinity and Divine qualities to levels of absolute, absolutely universal immanence and transcendence often involves *upāsanā*-cum-analysis of one's own knowledge processes and consciousness.

The fact that all four texts seem to be aiming at a common, new level of knowledge, realization, being, whatever—viz. the level of Ātman/Brahman—leads naturally to the next question: Is this new knowledge of Ātman/Brahman really something completely new and beyond the compass of Brāhmaṇical and Vedic religion? Or is it more a re-crystallization of the highest knowledge in these traditions, a recrystallization which has made that earlier highest knowledge much more directly and universally accessible? Obviously our own as well as the traditional attitude to this has been the latter.[235] Knowledge of Ātman/Brahman is present already in some forms in the Brāhmaṇas and Vedas. But in the Brāhmaṇas it forms an indivisible whole with the whole Brāhmaṇa way of life and spiritual life. And in the Vedas it is inseparable from the state of the Vedic seers. It is sometimes thought that the Upaniṣads declare a new wisdom, higher than or different from the knowledge of Divinity of the Brāhmaṇas or Vedas.[236] Of course it is true that knowledge of Ātman/Brahman is different from many other knowledges, and that it is *sui generis*. But even in the

Upaniṣads we find some great *vidyās* dealing with highest knowledge (such as the *Madhu* and *Gāyatrī Vidyās*) in which knowedge of Brahman appears as the core of what is basically traditional (Brāhmaṇa) wisdom, and is not opposed as a separate category to traditional knowledge of the Divine. The situation is analogous in the case of the *Vaiśvānara Vidyā*. The *Śatapatha Brāhmaṇa* version of the *vidyā* is well within the range of deeper Brāhmaṇa and Āraṇyaka teaching. The nature of Agni Vaiśvānara is a theme that is not far from the center of the mysticism of the *agnicayana*, itself one of the greatest and deepest Brāhmaṇa mystical developments. And the main points, that Agni *Vaiśvānara* is the Puruṣa and the self, are implicit in earlier Brāhmaṇa teachings and on a par with the *Tad-eva* and other developments of the Puruṣa Hymn. The Upaniṣadic version of the *vidyā* does not negate these things. On the contrary, it honors them by highlighting (in V.18.2) something that is implicit in the earlier version but not fully brought out there, thereby showing that that version had a more profound significance. A student in immediate post-Upaniṣadic times may perhaps have studied and tried to follow both versions at the same time.

If the Upaniṣadic *vidyās* represent re-distillations and re-crystallizations of the deepest knowledge of the Vedic and Brāhmaṇa tradition, the problem becomes one of showing in detail how that knowledge was re-shaped to arrive at the soon universally shared level of Ātman/Brahman. As a very simple start we can arrange the three Upaniṣadic texts in various series. All of them use the terms Brahman or Ātman. All of them deal to some degree with walking the path to and attaining Brahman or Ātman, and rely for that purpose partly on *upās-*, "meditating on, worshipping, regarding as". But there are differences in the complexity and level of expression in the area of the "indicator terms". *ChāndUp* III.18 had no indicator terms, only "Brahman", if one wants to count that. The *Sixteen Parts Vidyā* had four of them (*prakāśavat* etc.), all doing double and triple duty; the *Vaiśvānara Vidyā*, six (*Sutejas* etc.), to which must be added *Vaiśvānara*. There were also differences in the way the basic paradigms for Ātman/Brahman were drawn. According to *ChāndUp* III.18, Brahman has four feet or quarters, *pādas*, corresponding to pairs of powers and deities, and all equally expressing the shining and glowing-creating of Brahman. In the *Sixteen Parts Vidyā* Brahman has also four *pādas*, but now identified by special indicator terms (*prakāśavat* etc.); the first three correspond to Divine Qualities and the fourth marking an initial level of realization. And the *Vaiśvānara Vidyā* says that the *Sutejas* is the Head of the Vaiśvānara Self, and so forth. This relates perceptions of higher, Divine self-qualities (*Sutejas* etc.) directly to a still higher knowledge of Ātman.

But there are also other, more sophisticated developments. For example *ChāndUp* III gets along with the standard Brāhmaṇa devices of an *adhyātmam—adhidaivatam* pairing, pairings of Powers and Deities, and a fourfold pattern, and relies only on a refrain of *bhāti, tapati,* and *jyotiṣā* and the four feet of Brahman to lead the student to the Truth. The *Sixteen Parts Vidyā* uses a conceptually more developed scheme of spiritual evolution based on "common (metaphysical or divine) quality", going so far as to make the fourth foot a "quality", *āyatanavat,* treated formally on a par with the three other Divine qualities. The Upaniṣadic *Vaiśvānara Vidyā* finally is even more "advanced" and takes as its starting-point metaphysical or divine *self*-qualities, i.e. qualities of self (or Self) realized by meditating on Earth etc. as the Self. Again, all three Upaniṣadic teachings use the device of describing Brahman as having a certain structure (It is four-footed, *catuṣ-pād,* or has four quarters; or It has a head etc.). This is already a sophisticated procedure, because after all, this structure involves *upāsanā* which operates for many years at many levels in the aspirant's spiritual life.[237] (In the Puruṣa Hymn, which is a hymn of praise and expresses a single transcendental understanding, the question of inner development to attain fuller understanding is not addressed). Here the *Vaiśvānara Vidyā* is likewise noticeably different from the other two by discussing what is intrinsically a One using the language of parts (earth, bladder, etc.). The most impressive and sophisticated difference in the three texts however, lies in the three "stances of mind" or "existential stances" adopted (which are automatically adopted and lived by the student when he follows these teachings). As noted earlier, in the *Sixteen Parts Vidyā* one thinks "Mind is Brahman," "the four-directions are (a foot of) Brahman, called 'the radiant'" and so on, i.e. one adopts a mental stance in which Brahman is treated as something external (to some extent even in the fourth foot) and lets the inner realizations unfold that way. The *Vaiśvānara Vidyā* (V.18.2) works with an *ahaṁgraha* ("I am") stance. But *ChāndUp* III.18 is very interesting because it works with both Powers and Deities simultaneously in a fashion which tends to move it away from both a strictly external and a strictly *ahaṁgraha* approach.

All these things illustrate the development of new language and new conceptual power to express and promote inner awareness that had not been expressed before, and as well as increasing intellectual sophistication. They also illustrate thought that is becoming or has become independent of standard Brāhmaṇa features such as the conception of Puruṣa, the cosmological (cosmogonic) standpoint, and ritual as a mode of knowledge and path to Brahman. There is really no evidence that the Brāhmaṇa knowledge was fundamentally different or less than the Upaniṣadic Knowledge. On the contrary, one gets the impression that the same knowledge, which is present but hidden in the Brāhmaṇa way of life (including spiritual life), is responsible for these new channels of language and paradigmatic expressions. For in the Brāhmaṇas, there was little need for systematic use of special higher "indicator terms" in the context of an unfolding of Higher Knowledge. The usual terms for the Deities, supplemented with suitable identifications with ritual objects or aspects of life or the universe were sufficient. For ultimately, the Higher Wisdom was obtained from these teachings naturally, by imbibing the total idea from the teacher, by living it in the ritual, by living it as life within the ritual and social order, and so on. Knowledge arose as part of the whole Brāhmaṇa way of spiritual life.

NOTES

1. Buddha's phrase in the *Majjhima Nikāya*, quite similar to *neti, neti* and related texts (cf. chr. 5).
2. It occurs at *ChāndUp* VII.6, *ŚvetUp* I.3 and I.6, and *MaitrUp* IV.18, always in the sense of "meditation". And at *ChāndUp* I.3.12, *PraśnaUp* V.1 and *MuṇḍUp* II.2.6 the verb *dhyai* is used in the sense of "meditating". But at *BṛhUp* IV.4.21, *AitUp* I.3.8, and *KaṭhaUp* I.28 it means "thinking".
3. MW Dictionary. The *St. Petersburg Dictionary* (v. 1, cols. 732-734) gives 14 meanings; see especially the citations for "to regard something as" under meaning 13.
4. Sharma, *Concept of Ātman*, pp. 1-2 and notes, and H. Falk, Vedisch Upaniṣad. *ZDMG*, v. 136 (1986), pp. 80-97, pp. 80-81 and notes, survey past scholarship on the subject. At the VIIIth International Sanskrit Congress in Vienna, A. Bharati defined *upāsanā* informally simply as "observance".
5. H. Oldenberg, Vedische Untersuchungen. 6. Upaniṣad. *ZDMG*, v. 50 (1896), pp. 457-462; Vedische Untersuchungen. 9. Upaniṣad. *ZDMG*, v. 54 (1900), pp. 70-78. Repr. in Oldenberg, *Kleine Schriften*, v. 1, pp. 35-40 and 62-71 resp.

6. Oldenberg, *op. cit.*, p. 460 (resp. p. 38), for "the natural position of the one who meditates is sitting", etc., *ibid.*, p. 460 (resp. p. 38).
7. *Ibid.*, p. 461 (resp. p. 39).
8. S. Schayer, Über die Bedeutung des Wortes Upaniṣad. *Rocznik Orjentalnistyczny,* v. 3 (1925, pub. 1927), pp. 57-67. Schayer sees in *upās-* an "active and aggressive moment . . . One steps up to the deity and presses on it (puts pressure on it) with wishes [which one wants to be fulfilled]", (*ibid.*, p. 59).
9. One of Schayer's expamples, *ibid.*, p. 61.
10. *Ibid.*, p. 61.
11. *Ibid.*, p. 59, the concluding statement of the section on *upās-*. Schayer's views on Brāhmaṇa ritual and religion may be found in Die Weltanschauung der Brāhmaṇa-Texte, *Rocznik Orjentalistyczny,* v. 2 (1919-24, pub. 1925), pp. 26-32, and in his book *Die Struktur der magischen Weltanschauung nach dem Atharvaveda und den Brāhmaṇas*, Munich: 1925, which *n.v.*
12. L. Renou, 'Connexion' en Vedique, 'Cause' en Buddhique. In *Kunhan Rao Presentation Volume*, Madras, 1945, pp. 55-60; P. Thieme, ādeśa. *Melanges d'Indianisme a la Memoire de Louis Renou.* Paris: 1968, pp. 715-723; repr. Thieme, *Kleine Schriften*, pp. 259-267. Same author, *Upanischaden*, p. 83.
13. Sri Sathya Sai Baba, *UpVahini*. Ind. ed., p. 51.
14. On Śaṁkara's view of meditation, see H. Nakamura, Śaṁkara on Meditation. *Journal of Religious Studies* (Punjabi University, Patiala), v. 7 (1979), pp. 1-18; and Bader, *Meditation*, chapter 2.
15. Commentary on *TaittUp* I.3.2-4, transl. Gambhīrānanda, *Eight Ups. Comm.*, v. 1, p. 247. Similarly in the introduction to his commentary on *ChāndUp* I.1.
16. Transl. Mādhavānanda, *BṛhUp Comm.*, p. 65.
17. The classical definition of *dhyāna* is as a deeper stage following *dhāraṇā*, itself defined as "fixation of the mind (*citta*) on a particular region [such as the heart, or a visualized divine effulgence]" (*YoSū* III.1). Namely, "there (i.e. in *dhāraṇā*, or in that region) the continuous flow of the same knowledge is called *dhyāna,* meditation" (*YoSū* III.2, cf. Hariharananda Aranya, *Yoga Phil.*, p. 279; literally the aphorism says "the [state or condition of] having one thought only is *dhyāna*"). But as Bader notes (*op. cit.*, p. 40), *dhyāna* "does not necessarily entail a devotional attitude". It is more a phase in a larger enterprise of controlling the mind in order to produce supernormal powers, transcendence or liberation.
18. If Nakamura's view that the *Brahma Sūtra* represents the efforts of many centuries by parts of the Brahmin community to systematize and articulate general principles regarding the teachings of the Upaniṣads is accepted, one would expect the Sūtra to preserve the general idea of *upasānā*.
19. "Fruits" here and elsewhere are taken in the most general sense, including by-products of the *upāsanā* as well as realization of the principle on which one is meditating.
20. Cf. Thibaut, *BraSū Rāmānuja Comm.*, pp. 14 ff.; R.D. Karmarkar (ed. and transl.), *Śrī-Bhāṣya of Rāmānuja*, Part I. *Catuḥsūtrī* [=commentary on the first four aphorisms]. Poona: Univ. of Poona Sanskrit and Prakrit Series, v. 1, 1959, paragraphs [13]-[15]. Brahmānandin is author of a gloss (or according to others, a *sūtra*-like text), *Vākya*, on *Chāndogya*

Upaniṣad and is often referred to as the *Vākya-kāra*. Rāmānuja and Viśiṣṭādvaitic tradition after him call him Ṭaṅka. The identity of Brahmānandin and Ṭaṅka is sometimes questioned because these teachers belong to different traditions (e.g., S.L. Pandey, *Pre-Śaṁkara Advaita Philosophy*. Allahabad: Darshan Peeth, 1983, 1st ed. 1974, pp. 203, 208), but is here accepted following J.A.B. Van Buitenen, *Rāmānuja's Vedārtha-saṁgraha*. Poona: Deccan College Postgraduate and Research Institute, 1956 (Deccan College Monograph Series No. 16), pp. 24-29. Van Buitenen also gives the extant fragments pp. 303-307. The dating (550 CE) follows Potter's *Bibliography*.

21. See van Buitenen, *op cit.*, pp. 305-306 (fragment X). Like van Buitenen I take the whole to be single statement without a gap. (a) *darśanāt*.
22. Assuming Ṭaṅka = Brahmānandin, cf. note 20.
23. K. Pratap, *Śravaṇa, Manana and Nididhyāsana as Triple Means to Mokṣa*. Tirupati, 1983, discusses the different meanings of *śravaṇa* . . .in the systems of the different Vedāntic *ācāryas*.
24. In Christianity, constant remembrance is represented by praying the Lord's prayer several thousand times a day (in the medieval Dominican sister houses, see P.H. Wilms, *Das Beten der Mystikerinnen*. Leipzig: Otto Harassowitz, 1916. Quellen und Forschungen zur Geschichte des Dominikanerordens in Deutschland, P. v. Loë and B.M. Reichert, eds., v. 11), by "practice of the presence of God" (Brother Lawrence), by the Jesus Prayer in Eastern Christianity, and others.
25. Cf. Lester, N.C., *Rāmānuja on the Yoga*. Adyar, Madras: Adyar Library and Research Centre, 1976, pp. 17-34, 49-62, and 100 ff. For example "[The text] 'the higher [Knowledge] is that by which the Indestructible is apprehended' (*PraśnaUp*) refers to *upāsanā*, which is knowledge which has reached the form of *bhakti* and is characterized by direct perception of Brahman," *Śrī-Bhāṣya* I.2.23.
26. In *BṛhUp* I.4.9, *ChāndUp* VIII.1.2, 1.4, 2.1, 8.1, and in *MuṇḍUp* I.1.1, 1.2, 1.13, III.1.10; also in *Maitrāyaṇīya Upaniṣad*.
27. This important element of the Sūtra's treatment has not received much attention in the West.
28. The only general historical discussion on the topic on *vidyās* I know are V. Raghavan's comments in his Introduction to K. Narayanaswami Aiyar, *The Thirty-two Vidyās*. Adyar (Madras): Adyar Library and Research Center, 2nd ed., 1962, pp. v-xxiii.
29. "Again it is recognized that in all the Upaniṣads the two words 'know' (*vidi*) and 'meditate' [or 'worship'] (*upāsti*) are used without distinction." Śaṁkara, *BrSūBh* IV.1.1, cited in Nakamura, Meditation in Śaṁkara (note 14 above), p. 3; and "[In the Upaniṣads] 'knowing' [as in 'knowing Brahman,' etc.], [which is] intended as means of salvation, is understood as *upāsanā* (worship), the roots *vid* (to know) and *upās* (to worship) being seen used without any distinction." Rāmānuja, *Śrī Bhāṣya*, Commentary on *BraSū* I.1.1; R.D. Karmarkar, *op. cit.*, paragraph [13].
30. According to V. Raghavan, "the earliest publication to give a list of these *vidyās* is the Telugu edition of the *Śrī Bhāṣya* of Rāmānuja. Alkondavilli Govindacharya then gave a list of thirty-two *vidyās* in his English translation of Rāmānuja's *Gītā Bhāṣya*, chr. III" (V. Raghavan, *op. cit.*, p. xvii). Govindacharya's book appeared in 1898, and his list was used by

Narayanaswami Aiyar in the first edition of *The Thirty-two Vidyās* in 1916.

31. Nos. 1-32 are from S. Reddiar, *Religion and Philosophy of Nalayiram.* Tirupati: Sri Venkateshwara University, 1977, Appendix I, pp. 879-881 (I have ommited the references to aphorisms in the *Brahma Sūtra* which are taken to allude to the *vidyās*.) Reddiar's list in turn is said to be based on a Tamil commentary on a work of Vedānta Deśika's (1268-1369 CE), a famous *Viśiṣṭādvaita* preceptor (Vedānta Deśika, *Hastigiri Māhātmyam,* with Tamil commentary by M.M. Cetlur Narasimhacarya. Triplicane, Madras: Nigama Parimala Office, 1993, *n.v.*).

32. The question of how much of the surrounding text should be taken as part of the *vidyā* is often intimately related to the interpretation of the *vidyā.* Deussen in *Sixty Ups.* is very aware of this problem.

33. In a remarkable series of editorial covering different spiritual disciplines, including prayer, worship, and meditation, in vols. 85-87 (1980-82), with a follow up in vol. 91 (1986). The main sections on Upaniṣadic *upāsanā* are Types of Meditation I and II, *Prabuddha Bhārata,* v. 86 (1981), pp. 202-207 and 242-248; Higher Harmony through Meditation, *ibid.*, v. 87 (1982), pp. 5-10; and Jñāna-mārga: Its Meditation Techniques, *ibid.*, v. 91 (1986), pp. 326-337. The treatment is similar to Swami Gambhīrānanda, Upaniṣadic Meditation, in S. Radhakrishnan (chief editor), *The Cultural Heritage of India,* v. 1, The Early Phases. 2nd ed. 1958, Calcutta: Ramakrishna Mission Institute of Culture (first ed., 1937), pp. 375-385.

34. Swami Ananyananda, Types of Meditation I (Editorial), *Prabudha Bhārata,* v. 86 (1981), pp. 200-207; p. 206.

35. Deussen, *Geschichte*, v. 2, pp. 91-114; *Phil. Ups.*, pp. 99-125. Deussen discusses the "symbolic representations" (*Vorstellungen*) of Brahman as *prāṇa, vāyu, ākāśa* (space, ether), mind, Āditya (Sun), the fire of digestion, and as Om. Since Deussen, sensitivity to the use of symbols in the Upaniṣads has grown enormously, so that this point could be greatly expanded. Thus D. Frawley, *The Creative Vision of the Early Upanishads. Udgītha Ādityasya, the Exalted Song of the Sun.* Madras: publ. by author, 1982, pp. 56-129 (esp. pp. 65-74) has many insightful general observations (e.g. "A symbolic language deals with neither concrete fact nor abstract idea. It merges both . . . into the symbol, wherein they reveal each other simultaneously in the spiritual apprehension of the world," *ibid.*, p. 66). S.P. Singh, *Upaniṣadic Symbolism.* New Delhi: Meharchand Lachhmandas, 1981, emphasizes the Upaniṣads' use of symbols for Brahman etc. for spiritual evolution. "The capability of the human psyche not only to visualize the Transcendent but also to realize it . . . is [according to the Upaniṣads] possible . . . through the commitment of the latter as a whole by means of symbolic *sādhanā* [systematic spiritual practice]. The Upaniṣads convincingly bring out the capability of symbols to make one reach the Reality and show how the latter is not to be confused with the symbol itself" (*loc. cit.*, Preface, p. vi). P.E. Muller-Ortega briefly notes some well-known Western approaches to the role of symbols in religion (including M. Eliade, S. Langer, C. Geertz, and P. Ricoeur), of which that of P. Ricoeur seems the most relevant (P.E. Muller-Ortega, *The Triadic Heart of Śiva.* Albany: SUNY Press, 1989, pp. 9-13).

36. V. Raghavan, *op. cit.*, pp. vii-viii.
37. *Ibid.*, p. xix.
38. *Ibid.*, pp. xix-xx.
39. Swami Ananyananda, *ibid.*, p. 209. The author goes on to discuss the causes for the subsequent neglect of the *vidyās* in Vedānta and in the next editorial describes how the Vedic *upāsanās* were merged with or superseded by Yogic and Tantric techniques.
40. The key formulation in an *upāsanā* or *vidyā* is in fact a *logos* in Socrates' sense of a higher rule to be lived in one's life (at *Phaedo* 99E ff.). Socrates' *logoi* all had a higher element in them.
41. Sri Sathya Sai Baba, *UpVahini*, Am. ed., p. 53, Ind. ed., p. 57. Similarly "*Upāsanā* helps to focus the attention on the Universal and the Absolute. Then, *jñāna* emerges." Sri Sathya Sai Baba, *Voice of the Avatar*. Prasanthi Nilayam: Sri Sathya Sai Books and Publications, Am. ed. (2 vols. in one), 1980, v. 1, p. 128.
42. Transl. Müller, *Upanishads*, v. 1 (*SBE*, v. 1), pp. 200-201.
43. Cf. also Sri Ramana Maharshi: "Until the mind becomes established in itself, some kind of *bhāvanā* (contemplation of a personified god or goddess with deep emotion and religious feeling) is essential . . . Without spending all the time in practicing *bhāvanās* like 'I am Śiva' or 'I am Brahman,' which are regarded as *nirguṇa upāsanā* (contemplation of attributeless Brahman), the method of enquiry into oneself [=*ātma-vicāra*] should be practiced as soon as the mental strength which is the result of such *upāsanā* is attained." *Spiritual Instruction* 16. Similarly: "The means that make one qualified for enquiry [*atma-vicāra*] are meditation, Yoga, etc. One should gain proficiency in these through graded practice, and thus receive a stream of mental modes that is natural and helpful . . ." *Self Enquiry* 20. Ramana Maharshi, *Collected Works*, Indian ed., pp. 61, 71.
44. Sri Sathya Sai Baba, *UpVahini*, Ind. ed., p. 57, while distinguishing the great *vidyās* in *ChāndUp* VI-VIII from the *upāsanās* and *vidyās* in *ChāndUp* I-V. This alludes to Śaṁkara's *pramāṇas*, "correct means of (or toward) knowledge".
45. *Aitareya Upaniṣad* is exceptional in having only one occurrence. Presumably this reflects its predominantly mythic mode. Outside the old Upaniṣads, only *Kena* and *Maitrāyaṇīya Upaniṣad* have more than two occurrences each (5 and 12, resp.). The three middle group Upaniṣads have only one occurrence each.
46. The Sūtra's conception of *upāsanā* is an unjustly neglected topic, important both for understanding the nature of this text (what it is trying to do) and for Śaṁkara's and Rāmānuja's positions in their commentaries. The main points of this section, that the character of the *Brahma Sūtra's* conception of *upāsanā* as unitary, "generic activity" is reflected in its notion of *samanvaya* and *upasaṁhāra* and is ultimately tied up with the overwhelming and singular dominance of Brahman in the Sūtra's vision, are treated rather differently by F.X. Clooney, Binding the Text, in J. R. Timm, ed., *Texts in Contexts*. Albany: SUNY Press, 1992, pp. 47 - 68; secs. II and III.
47. *ānandādayaḥ pradhānasya*. See Radhakrishnan, *Brahma Sūtra*, p. 473.
48. *ānanda-rūpatva, vijñāna-ghanatva, sarva-gatatva, sarvātmatva.*
49. Cf. Radhakrishnan, *Brahma Sūtra, ibid.*, p. 473. (a) lit., "increase and

decrease, *upacayāpacayau*, [obtain only] in the case of difference, *bheda* [and not in Brahman, which is non-dual]".

50. Radhakrishnan's description of the topic of *adhikaraṇa* III.3.11-13 (*ibid.*, p. 473).

51. Cf. Radhakrishnan, *Brahma Sūtra*, pp. 235-251. The traditional treatments account for the ablatives in *BraSū* I.1.3 and 4 in different ways. E.g. Śaṁkara gives as one interpretation of I.1.3 "[Brahman is omniscient] because of Its being the womb of Scripture."

52. A rephrase of Radhakrishnan's summary of the purport of *BraSū* I.1.4, *tat tu samanvayāt* (*ibid.*, p. 246). Clooney notes the prominent role which *samanvaya* plays in *BraSū* I.1 and says that a "significant effect of the demonstration of *samanvaya* was the regularization of the Upaniṣads, the homogenization of . . . [their discourse] into an informative 'metadiscourse' about *brahman* ..." (*op. cit.*, p. 51).

53. This philosophy is actually a rather fundamental component of *Brahma Sūtra* philosophy and practice. Its corner stone, the principle of *upasaṁhāra* of "coordination" of different attributes in meditation has been discussed by F.X. Clooney in Binding the Text, *op. cit.* (note 46), sec. III, and in his book *Theology after Vedānta: An Experiment in Comparative Theology*. Albany: SUNY Press, 1993. Clooney treats the practice of *upasaṁhāra* as "designed to safeguard the ongoing act of reading, remembering, and combining texts selectively in acts of meditation" (p. 67). This is part of the art of engaging in the "primarily textual process" which he considers "learning [and living!] Advaita" to be (*ibid.*, pp. 70-75). (I am grateful to Clooney for advance copies of his work).

54. The *adhikaraṇas* represent the basic grouping of the individual aphorisms into small groups corresponding to specific issues. In particular, they function as "practical units of debate". See Clooney, *op. cit.*, p. 45 ff., who also discusses the standard structure of *adhikaraṇas* and principles which govern the organization of a sequence of *adhikaraṇas*.

55. *ātmā iti tu upagachanti grāhayanti ca*. Cf. Radhakrishnan, *Brahma Sūtra*, p. 525.

56. *Ibid.*, p. 526

57. *Ibid.*, p. 526.

58. Some hold that *BraSū* IV.1.3 implies that Brahman should not be approached with *pratīka upāsanās*.

59. Comprehensive discussions of Śaṁkara's views on *upāsanā* and his own teachings on developing knowledge of Brahman include Bader, *Meditation*, chrs. 3-5; A. Rambachan, *Accomplishing the Accomplished. The Vedas as a Source of Valid Knowledge in Śaṁkara*. Honolulu: Univ. of Hawaii Press, 1991 (Monographs of the Society for Asian and comparative Philosophy, No. 10), chrs. 3-6 and conclusion; and A.J. Alstons's presentations of excerpts in his *A Śaṁkara Sourcebook*, v. 6. *Śaṁkara on Enlightenment*. London: Shanti Sadan, 1989, chrs. XIV, The Indirect Path, and XV, The Direct Path. Bader also cites a Ph.D. thesis by Barbara Doherty (Fordham University, New York, 1979) which *n. v.* (Bader, *Meditation*, pp. 45, 48-49).

60. See A.J. Alston, *A Śaṁkara Sourcebook*, v. 1. *Śaṁkara on the Absolute*. London: Shanti Sadan, 1980 (repr. 1981, 1987), p. 26. Alston notes that this principle is found in Mādhyamika philosophy (Candrakīrti), and is

developed by Draviḍācārya, the pre-Śaṁkara commentator of Brahmānandin's *Vākya*. According to Ānandagiri's Ṭīkā on Śaṁkara's commentary on *Gītā* II.32, "Draviḍa taught that the Veda was able to fulfil its office of communicating the transcendent through the process of negating later what had first been proposed provisionally." In fact, "Draviḍa taught that the content of all other texts had ultimately to be negated in favor of the supreme text 'That thou art' " (Alston, *op. cit.*, p. 31).

61. Nakamura considers this to be Śaṁkara's own teaching with little precedent in the preceding tradition. Cf. Nakamura, Meditation in Śaṁkara (note 14 above), p. 6.
62. Alston points to "two surviving pre-Śaṁkara Vaiṣṇava works which in certain passages dismiss the world as an illusion" (Alston, *ibid.*, p. 36), namely the *Paramārthasāra* (before 600 CE) and the *Viṣṇu Purāṇa* (ca. 400 CE?).
63. *BraSūBh* I.1.4, transl. Alston, *Śaṁkara on Enlightenment: A Śaṁkara Sourcebook*, v. 6. London: Shanti Sadan, 1989, pp. 4-5.
64. *BraSūBh* I.1.11, transl. Alston, *ibid.*, pp. 5-6. The first text is untraced; the second is from the *Śāṇḍilya Vidyā, ChāndUp* III.14.1.
65. *Comm. on ChāndUp* I.1.1 (Introduction), transl. Alston, *ibid.*, pp. 7-8.
66. "Even if Brahman be different from oneself, there can be no acquisition, for Brahman being all pervasive like space, It remains ever attained by everybody" (*BraSūBh* I.1.4, transl. Rambachan, *op. cit.*, p. 59).
67. This and some of the following points are beautifully developed in Rambachan, *op. cit.*, chrs. 2-3.
68. Cf. Śaṁkara, *Upadeśa-sāhasrī* I.18.178-181, transl. S. Mayeda, *A Thousand Teachings*. Tokyo: Univ. of Tokyo Press, 1979, pp. 190-191; Sureśvara, *Naiṣkarmya-siddhi* II.8, 9, and III.31.
69. Cf. Mayeda's analysis of the method in Mayeda, *op. cit.*, pp. 52-53; Bader, *Meditation*, pp. 40-71; and G. Cardona, On Reasoning from Anvaya and Vyatireka in Early Advaita, in D. Malvania and N.J. Shah, *Studies in Indian Philosophy* (Pandit Shuklaji Sanghvi Memorial Volume). Ahmedabad: LD Institute of Indology (LD Series, No. 84).
70. Śaṁkara, *Upadeśa-sāhasrī* I.18.179-181.
71. *Ibid.* I.18.181.
72. Alston, *op. cit.* (note 67), pp. 136-137 regards *abhyāsa* (together with *dhyāna*, meditation) as a specific type of approach within what Śaṁkara sees as a "direct path" to realization of Ātman/Brahman. The texts which he presents as to be repeated and affirmed are sections from the *Upadeśa-sāhasrī* (Alston, *ibid.*, pp. 142-145). Perhaps the most powerful form of *abhyāsa* is the *parisaṁkhyāna* or "recapitulating consideration" that concludes the *Upadeśa-sāhasrī* (*Upadeśa-sāhasrī*, Prose Part, chr. 3, transl. Mayeda, *op. cit.*, pp. 251-254).
73. Cf. for example Swami Satchidanandendra Saraswati: "*Nididhyāsana* no doubt is mental too, and it is also a kind of steady flow of thought enjoined by the *Śruti* (Scripture) just as any other *upāsanā* is. But the former is a mental process of focusing one's closest attention in order to realize the nature of its object. 'Come, sit down, I shall explain it to you. You had better try to assimilate it by close attention (*nididhyāsasva*)' (*BṛhUp* II.4.4). In this passage Yājñavalkya in using the word *nididhyāsasva* evidently exhorts Maitreyī to concentrate her mind upon what he says so

that she might understand the thing without any doubt or difficulty" (Swami Satchidanandendra Saraswati, *Salient Features of Śaṁkara's Vedānta.* Holenarsipur: Adhyatma Prakasha Kavyalaya, 1967; p. 49). Rambachan argues that for Śaṁkara, *nididhyāsana* is "continuous fixing of attention on knowledge [of Brahman] already gained" (A. Rambachan, *op. cit.*, note 59 above, p. 112), not, as is often held, the last stage of the process of *śravaṇa, manana, nididhyāsana* which leads to knowledge of Brahman. But in practice, "gaining Knowledge" and "fixing attention on Knowledge already gained" constantly interact and equilibrate each other.

74. The Power of the Divine word can be felt, and is thus an "experiential", but not many scholars seem to agree.
75. Śaṁkara, Comm. on *KaṭhaUp.* I.3.12; Alston, *ibid.*, p. 86.
76. Śaṁkara discusses *adhyātmayoga* in his commentary on *Kaṭha Upaniṣad* (cf. Gambhīrānanda, *Eight Ups. Comm.*, pp. 171-172; Alston, *ibid.*, excerpt XV.1.2 pp. 84-85), and at the end of *BraSūBh* I.4.1 (transl. Alston, *ibid.*, excerpt XV.1.3, pp. 85-86).
77. See C.A. Cole, *Asparśa Yoga.* Delhi: Motilal Banarsidass, 1982, pp. 103-124, who tries to reconstruct this yoga by using as background *Gītā* V.21-22 and VI.23 and going more deeply into the flow of *Kārikās* III.29-48; and R. King, Asparśa Yoga: Meditation and Epistemology in the Gauḍapādīya Kārikā. *JIP*, v. 20 (1992), pp. 89-131, who discusses *asparśayoga* more generally in the context of a larger range of concepts and issues. Śaṁkara mentions *asparśayoga* in his commentary on *Kārikās* III.38 ff. (up to III.46). See Alston, *ibid.*, excerpt XV.1.7 (pp. 90-92).
78. Cf. *Kārikās* III.38 (immediately before *asparśayoga* is mentioned in III.39), IV.26-28, "consciousness [*citta*] has no contact with (*na saṁspṛśati*) objects . . .," III.26, and others.
79. The main modern translations are Böhtlingk, *ChāndUp* (see Abbreviations and Conventions); Morgenrot, D. (ed. and transl.), *Chāndogya Upaniṣad.* Unpub. Dissertation Jena, 1958 (*n.v.*) (both in German); and Senart, E., *Chāndogya Upaniṣad.* Paris: 1930 (in French) (*n.v.*).
80. A brief survey of the Kauthuma Vedic corpus is given in Caland, W. (transl.), *Pañcaviṁśa Brāhmaṇa.* Calcutta: Asiatic Society, 1982 (repr. of 1st. ed. 1913) (Bibliotheka Indica No. 255), pp. i-viii.
81. Available in German translations, cf. Caland, *op. cit.*, p. iv.
82. Cf. the parallels II-VI given in H. Örtel, Extracts from the Jaiminīya Brāhmaṇa and Upaniṣad-Brāhmaṇa parallel to passages of the Śatapatha-Brāhmaṇa and Chāndogya-Upaniṣad, *JAOS*, v. 15 (1883), pp. 232-251.
83. Cf. A. Parpola, *The Literature and Study of the Jaiminīya Sāmaveda in Retrospect and Prospect.* Helsinki, 1973 (*Studia Orientalia* XLIII: 6).
84. Like the *Śāṇḍilya* and *Vaiśvānara Vidyās.*
85. Cf. L. Renou, Remarques sur la Chāndogya-Upaniṣad. In L. Renou, *Etudes Vediques et Pāṇiniennes*, v. 1. Paris: E. de Boccard, 1955, pp. 91-102 (Publications de l'Institut de Civilization Indienne); pp. 96-100.
86. Cf. Eggeling, *ŚatBr* v. 1, pp. xxix-xxxv and pp. xlv ff.
87. Cf. the tabulations in S.M. Bhatkhande, *The Chhandogya Upanishad and the Brahmasutras of Badarayana.* Bombay: Univ. of Bombay, 1982, pp. 172-248, esp. p. 247.
88. Gonda, p. 431.
89. There seems to be no detailed modern treatment of the text. Lüders

comments on it in his discussion of the *Ṣodaśa-kala Vidyā* (cf. note 150 below). An earlier version of the treatment here was presented at the VIIIth International Sanskrit Congress, Vienna, 1990, and published as *Chāndogya Upaniṣad* III.18 in the Light of Two Other Texts, *WZKSA*, 1992, Supplement, pp. 323-333.

90. (a) *mano brahmetyupāsīteti.*
91. Recall that Śaṁkara cites this very text "The Mind is Brahman" as one in which Mind is used as a symbol (*pratīka*) for Brahman. By *BraSū* IV.1.4, one should not regard Mind in this text as the Self. Instead, says Śaṁkara, we are dealing here with an example of *upāsanā* involving superimposition, *adhyāsa*, in the sense that while the idea of the symbol persists, the idea of Brahman is superimposed on it. In other words, mind is to be regarded as Brahman. This is consistent with the literal interpretation given here. One's mind and mental-physical processes, Speech, Sight, etc., are different from self; one meditates "my mind is Brahman", "my seeing is Brahman," and so on only for the sake of directness, because my mind, my seeing is the only mind, the only seeing that I am directly familiar with.
92. In the Brāhmaṇas it is often treated as a sixth *prāṇa*, on a par with Sight, Speech etc.
93. For a convenient survey of the Āraṇyaka, see Müller, *Upanishads*, v. 1, p. xcv. The standard scholarly translation is Keith, *AitĀr* (see both under Abbreviations and Conventions). Classical commentaries include Śaṁkara's (on *AitĀr* II and III), Ānandatīrtha's (or Abhinavanārāyaṇendra Sarasvatī's) (a subcommentary on Śaṁkara's commentary, and a separate commentary giving a Vaiṣṇava interpretation), Sadguruśiṣya (11th cent. CE), and Sāyaṇa (13th cent. CE) (cf. Keith, *AitĀr*, pp. 11-15).
94. Keith, *AitĀr*, p. 43.
95. There seems to be no modern treatment of this text.
96. Cf. Müller, *op. cit.*, pp. 208-209; and Keith, *AitĀr*, pp. 206-207. (a) *prahitām* is "very difficult", Keith, *ibid.*, note 3; see the discussion below. (b) *natasyeśe yanmahyam na dadyur iti*, a difficult sentence. The translation follows Sāyaṇa; differently Keith, cf. his discussion *ibid.*, note 5. (c) also problematic.
97. "*Vorwärts schaffen*," Grassmann, *Wörterbuch*.
98. K. Raghavan Pillai, ed., *Aitareya Āraṇyaka, with Mokṣapradavṛtti of Sadguruśiṣya*. Trivandrum: Univ. of Kerala Oriental Research Institute and Manuscript Library, 1968 (Trivandrum Sanskrit Series, No. 221).
99. From *prahit*, an "agent-noun", also from *pra + root hi*, with zero suffix. Proposed by Keith, *ibid.*, p. 208; cf. M.C. Patyal, A note on the word *prahitām* in the Aitareya Āraṇyaka 2.1.5. *Vishveshvaranand Indological Journal*, v. 10 (1972), pp. 11-13; p. 13.
100. From *pra* + root *dhā* (*prahitām* short for *prahitānām*); *pra*, related to Latin *prae*, carries a connotation of motion.
101. MW Dictionary. The primary meaning is "to shine", cf. Mayrhofer, *Etym. Wörterbuch*, v. 2 (1963).
102. E.g. *ŚatBr* X.5.2.18-19, "'Concealed in food, he, the immortal, shines (*bhāti*) at the flowing together of vital saps;—yonder shining orb (the Sun) is food, and the man in that orb is the eater: being concealed in that food, he shines" etc. (transl. Eggeling). Cf. also *BṛhUp* I.3.16: "When

that [mind] was realised beyond death it became the moon (*candramas*). That very moon (*candra*), crossing over beyond death, shines (*bhāti*)."

103. Grassmann, *Wörterbuch*, under *vi-bhā*, meaning 5, refers to *Ṛg Veda* II.23.15, "[that] which shines distinctly (i.e. appears as, *vi-bhāti*) bright, powerful among men, the treasure . . .," *yad . . . dyumad vibhāti kratumaj janeṣu* . . . For many later examples with *vi-* from the *Mahābhārata*, see *St. Petersburg Dictionary*, v. 5 (1865-68), cols. 231-233.

104. In the *Śāṇḍilya Vidyā*, *ChāndUp* III.14.2, the Ātman is *bhā-rūpa*, "of the form of effulgence"; in the *Vidyā* of the Five Fires, at *ChāndUp* IV.15.4, Ātman/Brahman is said to be called "Light-bringer, " *bhā-maṇīḥ*, "for it shines (*bhā*) in all the worlds". The stanza "The sun does not shine there, nor the moon and stars. . . After Him, as He shines (*bhāti*), does everything shine, the whole world is illumined by His light," occurs unchanged in *KaṭhaUp* II.2.15, *ŚveUp*. VI.14, and *MuṇḍUp* II.2.10.

105. Śaṁkara doesn't use it in his *BrSūBh*, but it occurs in works like *Ātmabodha*, *Aparokṣānubhūti*, etc.

106. Swami Nikhilananda, ed. and transl., *Dṛg-Dṛśya-Viveka*. Mysore: Ramakrishna Ashrama, 6th ed., 1976; Raphael, transl. and commentary, *Self and Non-Self. The Drigdriśyaviveka Attributed to Śaṁkara*. London: Kegan Paul International, 1990 (or. Italian ed., *Dṛgdṛśyaviveka*, 1977).

107. Bhāratī Tīrtha was head of the Sriṅgeri Math (one of the four or five great monastic centers founded by Śaṁkara) from 1328 to 1380 CE, and is mentioned in an inscription detailing a land grant to the Math dated 1340 CE. It is widely believed that he also wrote the last several chapters of the *Pañcadaśī*. Cf. Swami Nikhilananda, *op. cit.*, Introduction, p. vi.

108. E.g., the definitions of six kinds of *samādhi* (vs. 22-29).

109. (a) *aṁśa-pañcakam*, lit. "the [having a] portion-fivefold," i.e., "the fivefold 'sharing in'" (b) *Brahma-rūpam*, "of the form of Brahman" (c) *jagad-rūpam*, "of the form of the world".

110. Cf. already *Sandeha Nivarini*, 1985, pp. 71-73, and *Geetha Vahini*, 4th ed., 1980, p. 130 (these are collections of articles originally published in the 1960's in the monthly *Sanathana Sarathi*); and *Sathya Sai Speaks*, v. 4, 4th ed., 1981, p. 236 (Discourse given 1-13-65); all Prasanthi Nilayam: Sri Sathya Sai Books and Publications, Sri Sathya Sai Central Trust.

111. Discourse given Oct. 27, 1982. *Glimpses of Divinity* (Toronto, Canada), No. 25 (April 1983), p. 5.

112. Discourse given May 29, 1990 at Brindavan; *Sanathana Sarathi*, v. 33 (1990), p. 236.

113. Cf. D.M. Knipe, *In the Image of Fire: Vedic Experiences of Heat*. Delhi: Motilal Banarsidass, 1975, pp. 107 ff, and the references and reviews there. Knipe argues that "ancient Indian religious experience did not have to wait until the seeing of the [cosmogonic hymns in *Ṛg Veda* X] to appreciate the cosmogonic significance of heat [= *tapas*]," as suggested by Renou and others. Instead, a cosmogonic force of *tapas* may be found already in the "earliest Vedic expressions and even beneath them [in] the Indo-Iranian epoch" (*op. cit.*, p. 111).

114. Knipe, *op. cit.*, pp. 117 ff.

115. *ya eṣa tapati*, e.g. *ŚatBr* I.4.6.18, II.2.4.6, *AitĀr* II.2.1, etc. *Atharva Veda* X.8.19, "by truth he [= Āditya] burns aloft"; XIII.3.13, "he [Agni], having become Indra, burns through the midst of the sky [as the Sun]";

XIX.53.6, "Time created the earth, in time burns the sun, in time are all existences, in time the eye looks abroad" (transls. Whitney, *Atharva Veda*).

116. E.g. *ŚatBr* II.23.4.6, II.4.2.15; *Atharva Veda* XIII.3.13 above.
117. E.g. *AitĀr* II.2.1.
118. *AitĀr* II.2.4.4, transl. Keith, *AitĀr*, p. 215.
119. "One of the oldest forms of Brahminical monism" (Keith, *ibid.*, p. 215, note 9).
120. Cf. Schayer, *op. cit.* (note 8 above), p. 61.
121. Cf. note 12 above.
122. Thieme, Ādeśa (*op. cit.*, note 12 above), pp. 718 ff. (resp. 262 ff.).
123. Keith, *Phil. of Veda*, pp. 486, 558-559. More specifically in this direction Gonda: "[The Brāhmaṇas aimed] to explain the meaning and the raison d'etre of the ritual acts as well as . . . their connexions with the phenomenal reality on the one hand and the person of the sacrificer on the other. This purpose entailed elaborating a theory of ritual-macrocosmic-microcosmic relations in order to explain, as far as man's interests are concerned, the world and the powers operating in it. . . ." (J. Gonda, *Triads in the Veda*. Amsterdam: North Holland, 1976; VKNAWAL, NR No. 91, p. 50).
124. Thus Frawley has an insightful discussion of the *adhyātmam— adhidaivatam* correspondences as "the ultimate rock of analogical thinking". (Frawley, *op. cit.*, note 35 above, p. 70). "Analogical thinking" here includes both correspondences of two series of things from different realms, and numerical correspondence, the meaningfulness of series of n things, say, simply because of the connotations of the number n. Analogical thinking is "a way of organizing our world experience in an orderly way . . ." By this device, the mind intuitively "apprehends an inner dimension to things in which phenomena of even diverse levels can be integrated according to a common perspective" (*ibid.*, p. 69). Frawley speculates that the prominence of "analogical thinking" in the Brāhmaṇas derives in part from the Vedic notion of *ṛta*, the divine world order. "This intuitive understanding [obtained from correspondences etc.] is the result of a cosmic rather than socially conditioned orientation of mind. For the laws of right thinking . . .should parallel the laws of the cosmos, by which day, night, the seasons, life and death, joy and sorrow all come in their respective time according to a comprehensive yet immutable law" (viz. *ṛta*) (*ibid.*, pp. 69-70). In a related vein, W.A. Borman says that the correspondences establish "a cumulative sense of the identity of all phenomena" and create "an intuitive sense of the metaphorical character of the entirety of phenomenal existence" (W.A. Borman, *The Other Side of Death: Upaniṣadic Eschatology*. Delhi: Sadguru Pubs., 1990, p. 8).
125. Coomaraswamy renders *adhidaivatam* several times as *in divinis* and *adhyātmam* as "within you" (Coomaraswamy, *Papers*, v. 2, p. 114, 363); also "spiritual and literal" (*ibid.*, p. 217 note 18); ". . .transcendent and . . . immanent" (p. 393).
126. In later tantric literature.
127. In the Vedic case, "the fact of this microcosm-macrocosm identity is explained by the original self-bifurcation of the nondual Brahman and subsequent parallel evolution . . . [of the two realms]" (Borman, *op. cit.*, p. 8). But it may also reflect other things, such as the nature of ritual, or

of *Vāc*, the Word.

128. "The evidence indicates that Āyurvedic medicine is at least as old as the sacred brahminical tradition [i.e. the Brāhmaṇa literature] and that systematic compilations of medical knowledge were prevalent before the time of Gautama the Buddha" (A.J. Larson, Āyurveda and the Hindu philosophical systems, *Philosophy East and West*, v. 37 (1987), pp. 245-259; p. 246). This, together with the fact that almost all important secular knowledge at that time was related to the Veda, is sufficient to suggest that there were substantive connections between some of the Brāhmaṇical correspondences and Āyurvedic conceptions and practice, and that both involved a mixture of physiological etc. observation and esoteric and spiritual experience. But K. Zysk draws a different picture of the evolution of Indian medicine [K. Zysk *Asceticism and Healing in Ancient India: Medicine in the Buddhist Monastery*. Oxford: Oxford Univ. Press, 1991; and The Science of Respiration and the Doctrine of the Bodily Winds in Ancient India. *JAOS*, v. 113 (1993), pp. 198-213].

129. J. Filliozat, *The Classical Doctrine of Indian Medicine. Its Origins and its Greek Parallels*. Delhi: Munshiram Manoharlal, 1964 (or. French ed., 1949), pp. 27-28; passages in the *Caraka, Bhela* and *Suśruta Saṁhitās* on which this account is based are translated *ibid.*, pp. 196-218. For an exposition of this framework by a contemporary Āyurvedic physician, see P.M. Datye, *A Glance at Ayurveda*. Belgaum: P.M. Datye, 1971, pp. 1-29.

130. Filliozat, *op. cit.*, p. 15 argues that the *Suśruta Saṁhitā* was composed in the last centuries BCE (one stylistic argument gives 300 BCE) and assumed its present form in the first centuries CE. The *Caraka Saṁhitā* "can be anterior to the Christian era but not by a long period of time" (*ibid.*, p. 22). Both works are now available or being published in multivolume English translations using Western medical and contemporary Āyurvedic concepts.

131. Filliozat, *op. cit.*, pp. 54-79. Indeed, Filliozat thinks that it may not be even specifically Vedic but date back to the Indo-Iranian period, which precedes the Vedic. "Right from the Indo-Iranian period, several general notions concerning the cosmic role of the natural elements, such as the Waters, Fire, the Wind, had come into being. At the same time an idea of the correspondence between these elements and the constituent principles of the body had been developed and this must have prepared the latter day development of the two parallel [medical] physiologies and cosmologies" (*ibid.*, p. 79).

132. *Ibid.*, p. 194.

133. R.P. Das, Review of A.U. Thite, *Medicine. Its Magico-Religious Aspects according to the Vedic and Later Literature* (Poona, 1982), *IIJ*, v. 27 (1984), pp. 232-244.

134. *Ibid.*, p. 234.

135. *Ibid.*, pp. 234-235.

136. Some of Das' characterization could no doubt be further developed and refined.

137. Das feels that Thite's book does just this and that this is what makes it important. "[Thite's monograph] is actually a study of the Indian system of medicine within the framework of the magical *Weltbild*. This makes the monograph important, as *this way of looking at Indian medicine*

seems to be the best way of doing so, at least the further back we go in time" (*ibid.*, p. 235, italics added).

138. For example, Reichel-Dolmatoff's *Amazonian Cosmos*.

139. A common feature of western descriptions of nonstandard systems of medicine, even anthropological ones. In India, where Āyurveda competes with Western medicine, there seems to be a movement to cooperation and mutual respect. "Top Āyurvedic physicians and modern medical men are cooperating and giving their full support to each other in a large number of research centres in India today." Pt. Shiv Sharma, An Introduction to Āyurveda. In Shiv Sharma, ed., *Realms of Āyurveda*. New Delhi: Arnold Heinemann, 1979, pp. 11-21; p. 21.

140. A common problem in Indology in the early part of the century.

141. Das, *op cit.*, p. 234. An important contribution to the problem of overcoming the bias of the actually extremely specialized science-inspired view of rationality and the "scientific world-view" which dominates the West today may be found in a paper by the anthropologist R.A. Shweder, Divergent Rationalities. In Fishke, P.W., and Shweder, R.A. (eds.), *Metatheory in Social Science*, Chicago: Univ. of Chicago Press, 1986, pp. 163-196 (I am grateful to J. Donlon for calling my attention to this). "We seem to have carved out for ourselves a rather unfortunate set of choices. One is to argue, along with Murdock, Schneider, and Spiro, that the things to which ghosts, souls, witches, and demons refer do not exist, that ghosts and souls exist solely as elements in psychic reality, and that the idea of a ghost or a soul is totally subjective. The problem is that to argue this way is to transform religious concepts into either 'symbols' (Schneider) or 'delusions' (Spiro), despite the fact that the native does not use his idea of a witch or demon as though it were arbitrary, conventional, or a marker of something else; nor does he apply his ideas irrationally. The only alternative seems to be to argue that religious concepts are objective. But to argue that way is to risk to be branded an enemy of reason . . . I want to argue that ghosts, spirits, demons, witches, souls, and other so-called religious or supernatural concepts are, in some important sense, real and objective, and that if we understood the meaning of those concepts properly and learned how to apply them to experience, we would see that there exist things to which ghosts, demons, witches, and souls refer, things that can be interpreted using those concepts . . ." (Shweder, *op. cit.*, pp. 171-172). Here the "things to which ghosts, demons, witches and souls refer" and which "can be interpreted using these concepts" are precisely the subject-matter of what we have been calling "intuitive but objective knowledge" above (they are objective because they refer to things that "exist," Shweder, last sentence). The older approach to this whole problem was largely history and philosophy of science based (J. Kuhn's "paradigms", Feyerabend, and many others). Shweder argues that recent progress in the understanding of "human subjectivity" requires a broader view of rationality, and in this context introduces his idea of "divergent rationalities".

142. Cf. note 128 above.

143. So does the expert knowledge of ghosts, souls, witches and demons of appropriate cultural practitioners (Shweder, note 141 above).

144. In Shweder's terms, the knowledge of Vāyu acting in the body is not

totally subjective precisely *because* it has practitioner depth. On the other hand, the knowledge of "Agni being present in, or being a divine factor in, Speech," since it does not involve any "real world practitioner depth", is less tied to an objective basis.

145. Cf. Shweder, *op. cit.*, pp. 170-171.

146. In the *Gāyatrī Vidyā, ChāndUp* III.12.4. Cf. also *ŚatBr* XIV.3.2.1, commenting on *VājSaṁ* XXXIX.1: "'Hail to the vital airs with their overlord'—the overlord of the vital airs, doubtless is the mind (soul), for in the mind all the vital airs are established" (transl. Eggeling).

147. Dr. H. Ladanyi pointed out to me that according to Haṭha Yoga, Prāṇa moves in the heart, and that in fact the whole concept of "*prāṇayoga*" is based on this "*prāṇa* in the heart". He refers to B.K.S. Iyengar, *Light on Yoga*, revised ed., New York: Schocken Books, 1977 (1st. ed., 1966), p. 45, where the author outlines the approach of the Yoga Upaniṣads to *prāṇa* under the heading of *Prāṇa Vāyu*. For tantric Yoga, cf. the description of the *Anāhata Cakra* in *Ṣaṭ-Cakra-Nirūpaṇa*, vs. 22-27, in A. Avalon (Sir John Woodroffe), *The Serpent Power*. Madras: Ganesh & Co. (1964) (repr. Dover Pubs., 1974), pp. 371-383.

148. Cf. Sri Sathya Sai Baba, *Summer Showers*, 1977, pp. 231-232.

149. The literature on this is very large and presents a welter of approaches, many showing large and deep presuppositions of the same order of magnitude as those implicit in the ideas of "rationality" and "epistemology", and in the identification of "rationality" and "epistemology in practice" with Western-type Science. At the most fundamental levels of philosophical motivation, all such frameworks must be questioned.

150. Modern scholarship: H. Lüders, *Zu den Upaniṣads*. II. Die Ṣoḍaśakalavidyā. Repr. in H. Lüders, *Philologica Indica*, Göttingen: Vandenhoeck and Ruprecht, 1940, pp. 509-525. H. Lommel, Jugendliche Gotteserkenntnis. Aus einer Upanischad. *Paideuma*, v. 2 (1941-43), pp. 109-123; repr. K. Janert, ed., *Herman Lommel, Kleine Schriften*. Wiesbaden: Franz Steiner, 1978 (Glasenapp Stiffung, v. 16), pp. 174-188. S.P. Singh, *Upaniṣadic Symbolism* (*op. cit.*, note 35 above), pp. 227-231. Lommel takes the text as built around a natural experience of the Divine (*es überkommt ihn die Ahnung eines Unendlichen*, "he is overcome by the premonition of something Infinite", p. 113, resp. 178; *das Erlebnis selbst ist Gefühle des Unendlichen*, "the experience itself is feeling the Infinite," p. 122, resp. 187).

151. Western-type scholarship reads the text as implying that Satyakāma was born out of wedlock and was not a Brahmin. Cf. Lüders.

152. (a) Another grammatically possible reading is "He who, knowing this four-part foot of Brahman thus, meditates [on it as] 'the Shining [One]'..." (similarly at 6.4, 7.4 and 8.4). (b) The text here goes on and repeats "who, knowing this [foot] thus, meditates on the four-part foot of Brahman [as] 'the Shining [One]'" for emphasis and to indicate the conclusion of this important teaching. (Similarly at 6.4, 7.4 and 8.4). (c) Following Lüders, *op. cit.*, p. 511. (d) Following Lüders, *op. cit.*, pp. 519-521.

153. So also essentially Lommel, who pictures an actual experience ["*ein wirkliches Erlebnis*", Lommel *op. cit.*, p. 118 (resp. 183)]. Satyakāma Jābāla is mentioned as a teacher in *BṛhUp* VI.3.19 (M) [= VI.3.12 (K)]. In

ChāndUp V.2.1-3 he teaches the *Prāṇa Vidyā* (also in *ŚatBr* XIII.5.3.1), and in *ChāndUp* IV.10-15 the *Akṣi Puruṣa* or *Upakosala Vidyā*.

154. Lüders (*op. cit.*, pp. 513-515) argues that the four beings, bull etc. are also mentioned in *MaitrUp* VI.34,which he restores and translates as "the goldenhued bird, which dwells in the heart and in the Sun, the diverbird (*madgu*), the goose (*haṁsa*), the glow (*tejas*, for *agni*), the bull (*vṛṣa*), he is in this fire here. We worship him (*yaj-*)". Lüders argues that this mantra cannot be older than the Laws of Manu and that the author used the four entities from the Sixteen Parts Vidyā as "representatives of Brahman" (*ibid.*, p. 514). Lommel thinks that the bull, *madgu* bird and swan are mythic-symbolic representatives of the realms of earth, water and air, similar to other such triplets in Grimm's fairytales and the *Avesta* (Lommel, *ibid.*, pp. 118-120, resp. 183-185). Śaṁkara interprets the four teachers as the deities Vāyu, Agni, Āditya, and Prāṇa, resp. and connects them with the teachings which they give.

155. Lüders argues strongly for Deussen's translation "of (the nature of) wide expanse", *weitenhaft* (Lüders, *op. cit*, note 135, p. 516). But "shining" is what arises in the meditation.

156. *sa ya etaṁ evam vidvāṁś catuṣkalam pādam brahmanaḥ prakāśavān ity upāste, prakāśavān asmiṁl loke bhavati.* The pattern is common; the classical examples are "he who meditates on name [as] 'Brahman' . . ." in *ChāndUp* VII.1.5, VII.2.2, VII.3.3, etc. Under the alternative reading mentioned in note 153 a, X would have to be supplied.

157. In the Vedic literature the different Quarters East, South, etc. have different feelings associated with them, so that in the initial stages, meditation on the first Quarter of Brahman might have involved a merger of the individual divine qualities associated with the four directions into a larger divine. Today the Quarters should be taken generically.

158. Less so *samudra*, e.g. *JaimUpBr* I.25.

159. There are many Brāhmaṇa and Upaniṣadic teachings on the Sun, Sūrya or Āditya, which lead to some level of perception of the Divine. Mystical teaching on *vidyut: JaimUpBr* I.27.

160. Śaṁkara, Commentary on *ChāndUp* IV.7, calls the teaching of the swan "the philosophy which has light as [its] subject", thus explicitly naming the common quality.

161. MW Dictionary, quoting Roth and Oldenberg. J. Gondas paper *āyatana*, *ALB*, v. 23 (1969), pp. 1-79 (repr. in J. Gonda, *Selected Studies*, v. 2, *Sanskrit Word Studies*, Leiden: E.J. Brill, 1975, pp. 178-256), gives a feeling for the meaning of this important word.

162. Transl. Jha, *ChāndUp Commentary*, p. 197.

163. Lüders rejects *AitUp* I.1 as a parallel in the grounds that there the *āyatanas* are the physical organs, not the powers, and suggests instead *BṛhUp* IV.1.1, which I consider as later. However in *BṛhUp* III.9.10-18, which Lüders accepts as related, there are even more serious changes of category.

164. Sri Sathya Sai Baba, *UpVahini*, Am. ed., p. 60.

165. Cf. Lüders, *op. cit.*, pp. 521-524. S.P. Singh, *Upaniṣadic Symbolism* (*op. cit.*, note 35 above), pp. 225-231 compares the *vidyā* with *ChāndUp* III.18 and sees the Puruṣa as the "antecedent symbol" for both texts.

166. Transl. with notes by Keith, *AitĀr*, pp. 208 ff.

167. Transl. Keith, *ibid.*, p. 210.
168. Even Keith notes (*ibid.*, p. 210, note 3) that "[Mahidāsa's] saying here may no doubt be regarded as one of his *upaniṣads* in the sense of secret teachings."
169. Lüders, *op. cit.*, pp. 521-522.
170. Gonda, *Triads in the Veda, op. cit.*, pp. 115 ff., 121 f.
171. Lüders, *op. cit.*, pp. 522-524.
172. Cf. J. Gonda, The Number Sixteen. In *Change and Continuity in Indian Religion*. The Hague: Mouton and Co., 1965, pp. 115-130; pp. 121 ff. Gonda traces the idea to *VājSaṁh* VIII.36 and gives many examples.
173. Gonda, *ibid.*, p. 121. For that reason, *kala* in the Sixteen Parts *Vidyā* is both "a small part of the whole", and "especially used for a one sixteenth", St. Peterburg Dictionary. On *kala*, see Gonda, *ibid.*, pp. 119-120.
174. E.g. in *BṛhUp* I.5.14. For related texts in the Brāhmaṇas see Lüders, *ibid.*, p. 523.
175. Related dichotomies are between Brahman as "endowed with form" or "form-ful", *rūpa-vat*, and as "not endowed with form" or "non-formful", *a-rūpavat*. P.M. Modi in several of his publications argues that according to the *Brahma Sūtra* and the whole Vedic tradition up to the Upaniṣads, Reality is both, with the *rūpavat* aspect being called *puruṣa* or *puruṣa-vidha*.
176. Noted by V. Raghavan, *op. cit.*, p. xxi, who therefore classes it as a *vidyā*.
177. Śaṁkara uses the term several times in the *BraSūBh*. *Saguṇa* is used as opposite of *nirguṇa* already by Dravidācārya. See S. L. Pandey, *Pre-Śaṁkara Advaita Philosophy*. 2nd ed. Allahabad: Darshan Deeth, 1983 (1st ed., 1974), p. 205 and *ibid.*, notes 7 and 8.
178. This is also more or less the attitude of the *Brahma Sūtra*.
179. The oldest comments on the *Vidyā* are *BraSū* I.2.24-32 and III.3.57. A scholarly Indian treatment is T.V. Kapali Sastry, Lights on the Upanishads. In M.P. Pandit, ed., *Collected Works of T.V. Kapali Sastry*, v. 1. *The Book of Lights*-1; Pondicherry: Dipti Pubs., 1977, pp. 209-222. (*Lights on the Upanishads* first pub. 1974) (the author was a devotee of Sri Aurobindo's and Ramana Maharshi's). Also S.P. Singh, *op. cit.* (note 35 above), pp. 112-124.
180. (a) *prādeśamātram iva ha vai devāḥ suviditā abhisampannās tathā tu vā enān vakṣyāmi yathā prādeśamātram eva abhisampādayiṣyāmīti.*
181. *ŚatBr* XI.3.31 explains that at that point, "that Agni has now been completely restored; he now is that deity, (Agni) Vaiśvānara (belonging to all men): to him he offers this oblation, and by the oblation he makes him a deity, for whatever deity an oblation is prepared that is a deity, but not one for whom no (oblation) is prepared. It is one of twelve potsherds: twelve months are a year, and Vaiśvānara is the year". (Transl. Eggeling, *ŚatBr*, v. 4, p. 207).
182. Cf. Eggeling, *ŚatBr*, *ibid.*, p. 208. The implications of this and passages [A]-[C] in sec. 15 for the meaning of *Vaiśvānara* were discussed in a talk "The *Vaiśvānara Vidyā* in the Light of the Brāhmaṇas" given at the International Congress of Vedānta at Miami University, Oxford, Ohio, April, 1990.
183. J. Gonda, *Religionen Indiens*, p. 67.

184. Gonda, *ibid.*, p. 70.
185. Transl. E.B. Findly, The meaning of Vedic Vaiśvānara, *WZKSA*, v. 86, 1982, pp. 5-22; p. 8.
186. Findly, *ibid.*, p. 8.
187. Transl. Findly, *ibid.*, pp. 16-17. For vs. 1b-2ab see also L. DeVries, vaiśvānara-, *Zeitschrift für vergleichende Sprachforschung*, v. 93, 1979, pp. 8-24; p. 9 and note 5.
188. The spirit of the text is caught by Swami Dayananda's free translation, Dharma Deva Vidya Martanda, transl., *The Rig Veda with Maharishi Dayananda Saraswati's Commentary*, v. 1. New Delhi: International Aryan League, 1974.
189. Transl. after Geldner, *ibid.*, pp. 101-102.
190. Geldner, *Ṛg Veda*, v. 2, p. 101.
191. (a) So Geldner. Alternatively, "there are two paths, I heard, for the [deceased] fathers, gods, and mortals". For detailed discussion see Geldner, *Ṛg Veda*, v. 3, p. 283. (b) *vimṛṣṭa*, from *vi* + *mṛṣ*, to touch.
192. The two paths are described in the Brāhmaṇas and Upaniṣads in many ways.
193. = *Ṛg Veda* X.58.2 in Geldner, *Rig Veda*, v. 2, p. 379; Aufrecht, *Hymnen*, v. 2, p. 160. According to Geldner, the Vālakhilya hymns consist of genuine *Ṛg Vedic* verses which were, however, considered apocryphal (*khila*) and transmitted separately.
194. Transl. H.W. Bodewitz, *JaimBr*, v. 1, pp. 114-115.
195. The *Jaiminīya* passage [A] has fairly close parallels in *ChāndUp* V.4 ff., and *BṛhUp* VI.2.9 ff. (K) [almost = *BṛhUp* VI.1.9 ff. (M)], which are known as the *Pañcāgni Vidyā* of the five (*pañca*) fires (*agnis*). In *Jaiminīya Brāhmaṇa* this passage is followed by various descriptions of the soul's path after death. In the Upaniṣadic versions, the paths become the major focus, and the *pañcāgni* text is treated as general wisdom about death. At the same time, Agni Vaiśvānara is replaced by simply Agni. See Bodewitz, *JaimBr*, v. 1, pp. 110-123, and L. Schmithausen, Zur Textgeschichte der *Pañcāgnividyā*. *WZKSA*, v. 38 (1994), pp. 43-60.
196. Skt. in Raghu Vira and Lokesh Chandra, eds., *Jaiminīya Brāhmaṇa of the Sāmaveda*. 2nd ed., Nagpur: Lokesh Chandra, 1954 (Saraswati Vihara Series, No. 31), p. 348.
197. This derivation contrasts with that from *viśva* + *nara* in *ŚatBr* IX.3.1.3-6 (above). Modern philology derives *Vaiśvānara* from Indo-Iranian **Hnara*, "vital strength", in the sense of "relating to Him who possesses the total amount of Vital Strength" (cf. E.B. Findly, *op. cit.*, pp. 5-6, and L. DeVries, *op. cit.*, pp. 11-12, resp.). All these meanings play a role in the *Ṛg Vedic* and Brāhmaṇa notions of Agni Vaiśvānara.
198. Transl. Keith, *TaittSaṁh*, v. 1, p. 4.
199. Transl. Whitney, *Atharva Veda*, v. 1, p. 124. (a) *viśvadavyas*. Whitney follows the Paippalāda reading *viśvadevyas*, "he that belongs to all gods".
200. Transl. Whitney, *Atharva Veda*, v. 1, p. 209. There are similar invocations of Agni, but without Vaiśvānara, in *Atharva Veda* II.6.3-4, II.19.1-3.
201. Transl. Eggeling, *ŚatBr*, v. 1, pp. 104-106, with small modifications following R. Hauschild, Uber die frühesten Arier im Alten Orient, *Berichte der sächsischen Akademie der Wissenschaften Leipzig, Phil.-hist. Klasse*,

v. 106, No. 6, pp. 55-58, and R. Hiersche, Die Sage von der Weiterwanderung der Arier, *Zeitschrift für vergleichende Sprachforschung*, v. 90, 1976, pp. 48-49.

202. Large scale or cosmic-level powers were thought to be embodied in a king's *purohita* or personal priest. In the Vedas, the divine *purohita* is Agni, but in the Brāhmaṇas, he is Agni Vaiśvānara. See e.g. J. Gonda, Purohita, *Studia Indologica. Festschrift für Willibald Kirfel*. Bonn: 1955, pp. 107-124; repr. *Studies*, v. 2, pp. 320-337, esp. pp. 118 ff. (resp. 331 ff.).

203. Eggeling, *ŚatBr*, v. 4, p. 393, note 3.

204. They are still more similar to the teaching of Dhīra Śātaparṇeya to Mahāśāla Jābāla in *ŚatBr* X.3.3 that Agni is Speech, etc. The exchanges between Dhīra and Mahāśāla are almost identical: "What Vaiśvānara do you know?" Earth, indeed, oh King" vs. "What Agni do you know?" "Speech," etc. (*kam tvam vaiśvānaram vettheti? pṛthivīm eva, rājanniti* vs. *kam agnim vettheti? vācamiti*, etc.).

205. Some of these connotations are found in *Śatapatha Brāhmaṇa*.

206. Eggeling, *ŚatBr*, v. 4, p. 397, note 1.

207. *Ibid*., same note.

208. Deussen thinks that in the Upaniṣad, the pointing to the parts of the head is implied because of the *Śatapatha Brāhmaṇa* text.

209. So apparently Eggeling, who simply translates "established within the Puruṣa" and does not mention the fire of digestion.

210. This interpretation is already found in *BraSū* I.2.26. The Sūtra rejects the position that ". . . [Vaiśvānara] is not [Brahman] because of the word [Vaiśvānara, which means gastric fire] etc. and on account of [Vaiśvānara's] being established inside (*antaḥpratiṣṭhānāt*)" (the same words as in *ŚatBr* X.6.1.11). Instead, it says, Vaiśvānara (in both *Śatapatha Brāhmaṇa* and the Upaniṣadic version) is the fire of digestion which is enjoined (taught, *upadeś-*) to be regarded (or seen, *dṛś-*) as Brahman. Śaṁkara comments that by saying "he knows Him as being inside man", *puruṣe antaḥ, ŚatBr* X.6.1.11 says something "about [Vaiśvānara] having a locus internally (in the body)", and "this is possible only in the case of the gastric fire." "... the instruction [in the *vidyā*] is about looking upon Vaiśvānara as the Highest Lord, without giving up the looking upon Vaiśvānara as the gastric fire. The instruction here is to look upon the gastric fire as the Highest Lord, just as in the passage . . . 'The Mind is Brahman' [*ChāndUp* III.18, sec. 4 above]" (Śaṁkara, *BraSūBh*, transl. V.M. Apte, *Brahma-Sūtra-Śaṁkara-Bhāṣya*. Bombay: Popular Book Depot, 1960, p. 135).

211. *BṛhUp* V. 9 says: "Vaiśvānara is this fire (*agni*) which is (or: This Agni Vaiśvānara is what is this) within man (*antaḥ puruṣe*), by means of which the food that is eaten is cooked (= digested). The sound of that is what one hears when one has covered the ears thus. He who is about to depart (= die) does not hear that sound." *MaitrUp* II.6 elaborates on this in terms of a creation story involving Prajāpati and the five vital breaths that has esoteric and perhaps also Āyurvedic overtones.

212. Filliozat (*op. cit*., pp. 57-58) suggests that *Atharva Veda* VI.71.3 might allude to a relationship between digestion and the Vaiśvānara Fire, and in a footnote (*ibid*., p. 57, note 4) discusses *Ṛg Veda* X.5.1 in which Bergaigne saw "a reference to the internal fire". Narayana Aiyangar, *Ancient Hindu*

Mythology. Repr. New Delhi: Deep and Deep Pubs., 1983 (1st ed., ca. 1870), an important book for the interpretation of Vedic and Brāhmaṇa myths, thinks that Agni Vaiśvānara was "probably" the gastric fire in the *haṁsa* mantra, *Ṛg Veda* IV.40.5, and in the Brāhmaṇas (*op. cit.*, p. 332 and pp. 477 ff.).

213. According to the traditional interpretation of *BraSū* III.3.19, the two *vidyās* are the same because they come from the same tradition.

214. (a) literally "which Ātman" (b) *sic* (no Vaiśvānara).

215. "He is *prādeśa-mātra* which means that (a) he is one who is known in the physical form through his compound parts, such as the Heaven as his head, ending with the Earth as his feet; or (b) it may mean that he is inferred as the 'Eater', in regard to the organs; or (c) that he extends from heaven down to the Earth; or (d) '*Prādeśa*' may be taken as standing for the Heavenly and other regions, in the sense that they are flatteringly described in the scriptures, and the Vaiśvānara is of the same size as all these—(e) In another Vedic text [*ŚatBr* X.6.3] this Self has been described as *prādeśa-mātra* in its literal sense—namely of the same size as the distance (between the head and the chin); but this is not the sense intended here; as is clear from the summing up contained in the next text." Transl. Jha, *ChāndUp Commentary*, pp. 283-284. Śaṁkara gets (a) perhaps from *pra-ādeśa*, "command" or "instruction" (viz. the instruction given in 19.2), or from *pra-diś-*, "to point out, give out, command" (see T.V. Kapali Sastry, *op. cit.*, p. 219, footnote). Or he may be thinking of the standard derivation, *prādeśa* from *pra-deśa*, "(specific) region, area", so *prādeśa* = "pertaining to, or involving, (specific) regions or areas." The latter may be the basis of (a), (c), and (d).

216. In *BraSū* I.2.24-32. According to Śaṁkara, *BraSū* I.2.29 implies that Āśmarathya took *prādeśa mātra* to mean "extending from heaven down to earth", while I.2.30-32 imply that Bādari, Jaimini and the Jābālas read the phrase figuratively as "of the measure of a span".

217. According to *BraSū* I.2.30, this was Bādari's interpretation of the text.

218. T.V. Kapali Sastry, *op. cit.*, p. 212. Cf. *Pratyag-ātmatayā'bhivimīyate'ham iti jñāyata iti,* "he [i.e., the Vaiśvānara Ātman] is cognized as the individual self in the notion of 'I'", Śaṁkara on *ChāndUp* V.18.1, transl. Jha, *ChāndUp Commentary*, p. 272. So also Sri Sathya Sai Baba: "[Vaiśvānara] is the Divine in every being, who identifies himself as 'I'. . . Vaiśvānara is the entity that makes every being use the term I to distinguish oneself." Discourse given at Brindavan (Bangalore), May 31, 1991; *Sanathana Sarathi*, v. 34 (1991), p. 267. The MW Dictionary glosses *abhivimāna* "endowed with the faculty called *abhi-māna* ('Self-reference')".

219. Kapali Sastry, *ibid.*, p. 217.

220. *Ibid.*, pp. 217 ff. and p. 218, note 4.

221. *Ibid.*, p. 218. D. Frawley's translation "the full measure of all things" (D. Frawley, *op. cit.*, pp. 94, 95) is related, with *prādeśa-mātra* correspondingly meaning "[being] the indicative measure" (*ibid.*, p. 94).

222. The most thorough discussion of the text is by Bodewitz, *JaimBr* v. 1, pp. 265-269 and elsewhere in the same volume. Bodewitz regards the text as one of the earliest examples of a *prāṇa-agnihotra*, an "*agnihotra* into the *prāṇas*", "a *bhojanam* [= meal] ceremony in which food is offered as an oblation to the [vital] breaths [i.e., the *prāṇas*] . . . representing the sacred

fires [of the Brahmin household]. This *prāṇā-huti* [offering into the *prāṇas*], the central element of the *prāṇa-agnihotra* ritual, forms the regular introduction to the Hindu meal". (Bodewitz, *op. cit.*, p. 318). (The *agnihotra*, from which the *prāṇa-agnihotra* is derived, is the daily oblation of milk into the fire obligatory for Brahmins). Parallels to *ChāndUp* V.19-24 are the *antara agnihotras* or "inner *agnihotras*", *ŚāṅkhĀr* 10 and *Gopatha Brāhmaṇa* I.3.14.

223. (a) *prāṇāya svāhā. Svāhā*, "hail", is a common exclamation accompanying offerings.
224. Bodewitz, *ibid.*, p. 265.
225. (a) *hutam bhavati.*
226. Bodewitz traces the element of *tarpaṇam* or satisfaction (the satisfaction of the universal vital powers on a cosmic scale or at a cosmic level) to *Gopatha Brāhmaṇa* I.3.14 (*ibid.*, p. 269).
227. The phrase "in all worlds, in all beings, in all selves" in 24.2 is the same as in 18.1, and the constructions are parallel ("eats food", *annam atti*, parallel to "is offered", *hutam bhavati*). Further, 24.2 makes a parallel to 18.1. Just as in the higher stages of the *upāsanā* 18.1 one eats foods in all the worlds etc., so in the higher stages of the practice of offering food to the *prāṇas* 19-24, one offers the *agnihotra,* i.e., one makes the inner offering of food, in all worlds, etc. Verse 24.4 makes the point that if a Brahmin "knowing thus" (i.e., knowing and practicing 19-23 at this level) offers the remnants of his food to a *caṇḍāla*, he is still making an offering to the sacrificial fire (Agni = Agni Vaiśvānara, presumably = the fire of digestion in the *caṇḍāla*). Normally only a Brahmin would be considered fit or worthy to receive such an offering, never a *caṇḍāla* (cf. Bodewitz, *ibid.* p. 267). This is another allusion to 18.1: Agni Vaiśvānara eats food also in the *caṇḍāla*.
228. Swami Krishnananda, *Vaishvanara Vidya (with Panchagni Vidya)*. Shivanandanagar, Rishikesh: Divine Life Society, 1982, p. 41.
229. So also Bodewitz: "Apparently this *prāṇāgnihotra* passage was later [after *ŚatBr* X.6.1] combined with the Agni Vaiśvānara discussion . . ." (Bodewitz, *op. cit.*, p. 293).
230. Cf. Jha's translation, *ChāndUp Commentary*, p. 285.
231. In his commentary on *Māṇḍūkya Upaniṣad*, where he cites this passage, Śaṁkara also distinguishes between the partial Vaiśvānaras of the Brahmins and the additional sacrificial aspects. *MāṇḍUp* 3 says that the Self consists of four quarters of which the first is called *Vaiśvānara* and "has for its field the waking state". (The other three correspond to dream, deep sleep, and the all pervading *Turīya* or Fourth State.) Further, it says, this Vaiśvānara Self is "seven limbed". Commenting on this, Śaṁkara cites *ChāndUp* V.18.2 up to "the Earth is his feet" (cf. Shastri, *UpBhāṣyam*, v. 1, p. 219) and then adds that the Āhavanīya fire has been described as the mouth of Vaiśvānara "in order to complete the imagery of the Agnihotra sacrifice".
232. Cf. Śaṁkara: "(Objection:) How is it that heaven and the rest are presented as the head etc. [of the Self]? (Answer:) That is nothing incongruous, inasmuch as the intention is to show that *the entire phenomenal universe and the world of gods, together with this (gross cosmic) Self, contribute to the constitution of the four parts* [of the Self taught in

Māṇḍūkya Upaniṣad]. If the presentation is made in this way, non-duality stands established on the removal of the entire phenomenal world, and the Self existing in all beings is realized as one, and all beings are seen as existing in the Self." Śaṁkara, Commentary on *MāṇḍUp* 4, transl. Gambhīrānanda, *Eight Ups.*, v. 2, p. 183 (italics added).

233. Swami Krishnananda, *op. cit.*, p. 34.
234. *Ibid.*, pp. 39-40. These passages also appear in the frontispiece to Swami Krishnananda, *The Māṇḍūkya Upaniṣad. An Exposition.* Shivanandanagar: Divine Life Society, 1977.
235. Cf. Sharma, *Concept of Ātman*, who discusses intuitions and realizations in the Vedic Saṁhitās related to the Ātman, pp. 29-94.
236. E.g., Deussen, *Phil. Ups*, pp. 16 ff. argued that the higher philosophy of the Upaniṣads was really due to the Kṣatriyas or noblemen-warriors, not the Brahmin priests. See Keith, *Phil. of Veda*, v. 2, pp. 492-497. There is still sometimes a tendency to see the extreme forms of monism and the emphasis on renunciation in the Upaniṣads as due to the *śramaṇa* tradition, the traditions of the wandering ascetics known from the early Buddhist and Jain literatures. See G.C. Pandey, *Śramaṇa Tradition*. Ahmedabad: L.D. Institute of Indology, 1978 (L.D. Series No. 66).
237. The device is already common in the Brāhmaṇas.

CHAPTER 5

Five Sheaths and *Antar-jyotir Vidyās*

1. Major Avenues to Ātman/Brahman in the Great *Vidyās*: Outline of Chapter

In the Upaniṣads, the Highest Wisdom is communicated most fully and completely in only a dozen or so very great *vidyās*, and the fullest description of the Infinite Reality is obtained by pooling these texts. In this chapter, then, we begin this description with the aspects of *vijñāna*, "beginning or higher knowledge and awareness of Ātman/ Brahman", *ānanda*, "bliss", and "beyond *ānanda*" or "merger into Brahman", which are described in the so-called *Vāruṇī* of Five Sheaths *Vidyā, TaittUp* II.[1] *Vijñāna, ānanda*, and "beyond *ānanda*" are essentially phases or levels of spiritual awareness or being ("phases of the human being",[2] stages of the self in spiritual development) which are found in spiritual development along Upaniṣadic lines generally. They form a dimension that touches most of the higher aspects described in the other great *vidyās*, and thus cuts across the entire realm of higher knowledge and being dealt with in the Upaniṣads. As such, the Five Sheaths *Vidyā* is one of the most important *vidyās* in the Upaniṣads, and will be our first deep penetration into the Upaniṣadic Supreme Wisdom.

The Five Sheaths *Vidyā*. The Five Sheaths *Vidyā* teaches that there are five selves (*ātmans*, or *puruṣas*, persons) which exist in oneself and which one can feel oneself to be, and that the spiritual path consists of discriminating these selves and fostering their unfolding in one's spiritual life and ultimately going beyond them and merging in Brahman. The first self is oneself as a physical person, and then each succeeding self lies within, and animates, the preceding one. Thus within (1) the physical person that one is (the *anna-rasa-maya puruṣa* or "person consisting of the essence of food") is (2) oneself felt as vital, emotional, and subtle (psychic) energy (the *ātmā prāṇa-maya* or "self consisting of *prāṇa*"). Within the latter is (3) oneself felt as mind (the *ātmā mano-maya* or "self-consisting or mind"); within that is (4) the self that is inner spiritual awareness or knowledge, *vijñāna* (the *vijñāna-maya* self), and within that, (5) the self which is bliss, *ānanda* (the *ānanda-maya* self). *Vijñāna, ānanda*, and "beyond *ānanda*" are thus spiritual realities that pertain to the *vijñāna-maya* and the *ānanda-maya* level or self, and they come into view and become part of the aspirant's knowledge and experience when the corresponding spiritual levels or stages are entered. The whole *vidyā* is named *Vāruṇī Vidyā* after the great Vedic god Varuṇa, who in the very next chapter of the Upaniṣad (*TaittUp* III.1-7) teaches his son, the mythical sage Bhṛgu, to realize the same five levels (food, *prāṇa*, mind, *vijñāna*, and *ānanda*) as Brahman.[3] In later Vedānta the five selves are called the "five sheaths" (*kośas*, "vessels") in which the One Self is encased, and the whole *vidyā* is more commonly known as the *Pañca-kośa* or "Five Sheaths" *Vidyā*.

The Five Sheaths *Vidyā* is not really a *vidyā* in the sense that it defines a specific path to Brahman, although it may and is often taken to do so.[4] Rather it describes certain relatively specific, fundamental qualitative aspects of inner experience and inner state that characterise spiritual evolution along Upaniṣadic lines. Of the five selves, the fourth or *vijñāna-maya* self represents the first really higher level of spiritual development. The fifth or *ānanda-maya* self forms a further stage. In addition, the *vidyā* says that when certain high levels of *vijñāna* and *ānanda* have been reached, then one should go beyond all consideration of *vijñāna* and *ānanda* and find fearlessness as a foundation in one's *vijñāna-ānanda* state (*TaittUp* II.8). This may be regarded as spiritual instruction for "merger in Brahman". So the *vidyā* is teaching a very general progression in spiritual life of *vijñāna, ānanda*, and "beyond *ānanda*". In these terms, Brahman begins to be known at the *ānanda-maya* stages of inner evolution, and is merged into while going beyond an *ānanda-maya* framework.

Vijñāna may be described as an element of inner consciousness and knowledge that is pervasive through an individual's personality and consciousness, a relatively permanent and pervasive transcendental component of normal awareness. It can range from emergent *jñāna* or embryonic Ātmic or Brahmic consciousness to (varieties of) fuller knowledge of Ātman/Brahman. *Ānanda* or bliss is more fundamental than *vijñāna*. It arises when a person is established in beginning levels of *vijñāna* and then occurs in conjunction with *vijñāna*. Both *vijñāna* and *ānanda* are kinds of consciousness, i.e. properly speaking, there is no "*vijñāna of*" anything, there are only types and levels of *vijñāna*.

Various kinds of *Vijñāna*. The terms *vijñāna-maya, vijñāna*, and to a lesser extent also *ānanda-maya* and *ānanda* occur also in other Upaniṣadic teachings. It is possible by detailed textual analysis to relate many of these occurrences to the *vijñāna-maya* and *ānanda-maya* levels of the Five Sheaths *Vidyā*. In fact, the Five Sheath *Vidyā's* understanding of *vijñāna* seems to be shared by a whole layer of old Upaniṣadic teachings, and is then further developed in the Middle Upaniṣads and *Maitrāyaṇīya Upaniṣad*. We will argue that the old Upaniṣads more or less imply that *the knowledge taught in several texts are all higher forms of vijñāna in the sense of TaittUp II*. These texts are usually taken to independent *vidyās* in their own right and include the *Satya Brahma Vidyā, BṛhUp* V.4-5, which teaches a state "before" or "at the beginning of" creation or any manifestation; the *Antar-jyotir Vidyā, BṛhUp* IV.3.1-33 (K), which deals with experience of one's self as a *vijñāna-maya puruṣa*, an entity made of *vijñāna*, "higher knowing", and as "light within the heart"; and the *Dahara Vidyā*, which says that in the heart there is a "subtle space", *dahara ākāśa*, which contains all things and which is the immortal Ātman. Thus *vijñāna*, and the *vijñāna, ānanda*, and "beyond *ānanda*" scheme generally, is associated with a whole broad avenue of approach to Ātman/Brahman that is articulated in these "*vijñāna vidyās*" and includes various additional spiritual aspects and concepts besides *vijñana*. Since the relevant *vidyās* involve in varying degrees what may be called "*vijñāna* in the heart", this approach may be called "the path of *vijñāna* in the heart".

Different Avenues of Approach to Ātman/Brahman in the Upaniṣads. The "*vijñāna* in the heart" approach contrasts with the "Puruṣa and Powers and Deities" approach to Ātman/Brahman in chrs. 3 and 4. The latter is steeped in Vedic and Brāhmaṇa religion, in the deities, cosmology and view of the human faculties found in Vedic and Brāhmaṇa thought, and in the sacrificial ritual. It takes these earlier strands and makes them part of a single fabric which, however, as a totality of religious culture and knowledge or awareness, has as its center Ātman/Brahman (not the sacrificial ritual). The "*vijñāna* in the heart" approach on the other hand is powerfully articulated in the Yājñavalkya teachings, *BṛhUp* II.1 and III-IV, long considered by Western-type scholarship to represent a newer layer of "Upaniṣadic speculation".[5] Another source of it seems to be in *Chāndogya Upaniṣad*. Both approaches lead to the same Reality. Even though "Puruṣa" and "Brahman as *satyam, jñānam, anantam* (Truth or Being, Knowledge, and Infinite)," the motto of the Five Sheaths *Vidyā*, appear different, and the approaches to them even more so, they all points to the same thing. "When we talk of the Veda or use the word Brahman or the word Puruṣa, these are only different names given to the same aspect and to propagate the same idea that is contained in all these words. The words are different but they describe the same idea." (Sai Baba, above, chr. 3.11). It is interesting that Sai Baba here also names "Veda" as synonymous with Brahman. "Veda" stands for the Vedas and thus for *Vāc*, "Speech," similar to the Christian "The Word" or Logos. This *Vāc* or Logos represents another stream of approach in the Upaniṣads.

From Only Waking to Waking, Dream and Deep Sleep. Besides defining the axis of *vijñāna, ānanda*, and "beyond *ānanda*" to chart the regions of the high and highest states, some of the "*vijñāna* in the heart" *vidyās* also illustrate another phenomenon which ultimately becomes an approach to Ātman/Brahman in its own right. This is the extension of the arena of spiritual awareness and activity from waking consciousness to include also dream and deep sleep consciousness. The "Powers and Deities" approach in chrs. 3 and 4 has the characteristic that it works mostly with the consciousness and capabilities of the waking state. The Sixteen Parts and *Vaiśvānara Vidyās* represent paths in which initially mostly waking state consciousness unfolds and becomes transformed. With "*vijñāna* in the heart", however, we come to a set of *vidyās* which deal in the initial and middle stages with a much larger spectrum of consciousness, including dream, perhaps meditative states with effects reminiscent of out of body and other psychic experience, and deep sleep. Thus *BṛhUp* IV.3, *BṛhUp* II.1, *BṛhUp* IV.2 and the *Dahara Vidyā*, which are all textually closely tied to the "*vijñāna* in the heart", also involve an unfolding of the inner consciousness at levels related not only to the waking but also to dream, meditative and psychic states, and deep sleep consciousness. Or, to use a different metaphor, they involve not only the waking but also a dream and a deep sleep self (see below) both in meditation and in normal every day living (in the waking state). It is interesting, however, that the *Satya Brahma Vidyā* (*BṛhUp* V.4-5), which is textually also closely tied to the *vijñāna* of the Five Sheaths *Vidyā*, seems to work at least in its beginning stages entirely with inner consciousness related to the waking state, just like the Sixteen Parts and *Vaiśvānara Vidyās*. In other words the Five Sheaths *Vidyā's* sense of "higher spiritual knowledge/awareness", *vijñāna*, includes both the older forms of knowledge of Ātman/Brahman, typified by the *Satya-Brahma Vidyā*, as well as the knowledge of the Ātman taught by the new *vidyās* working with a wider range of (inner) consciousness.

In the old Upaniṣads, this new focus on a wider range of consciousness is relatively unsystematic. The vast potentialities that are opened up by it only start to take form in *PraśnaUp* V and culminate in the twelve mantras of *Māṇḍūkya Upaniṣad* (ca. 300 BCE-0 CE). According to this Upaniṣad, the Self has four quarters or feet (*pādas*), the first three appearing in the states of waking, dream, and deep sleep, and the fourth being a completely pure and transcendental form called *turīya*, "the Fourth". In mature Vedānta, the old Upaniṣadic "*vijñāna* in the heart" *vidyās* and this *Māṇḍūkya* teaching are then elaborated further. Thus there are three types of consciousness (*adhiṣṭhāna-caitanyas*), corresponding to the waking, dream, and deep sleep state levels, to which correspond ". . . three forms in which the transcendental Brahma-*tattva* (lit. "Brahman Suchness," Brahman-Substance) manifests Itself. The three forms are: Virāṭ [= Virāj]; Hiraṇyagarbha; and Avyākṛta. These three forms are related to the gross, the subtle, and the causal (forms of the human body [= human being])."[6] Other names of Virāṭ are Vaiśvānara and Vairāj; Hiraṇyagarbha is also called Sūtrātman and Prāṇa; and Avyākṛta is equivalent to Antar-ātman and Īśvaratva.[7] In other words, later Vedāntic Tradition develops and systematizes the various terms and passages in the Upaniṣads into its own array of higher meanings, each emphasizing one or another aspect of Ātman/Brahman and corresponding to one or another type or level of inner experiential and realization of Ātman/Brahman. These later Vedāntic meanings are related to Upaniṣadic meanings, and are useful in sensitizing one to various possibilities. But one has to be careful not to read into the Upaniṣads later interpretations. In this chapter we will discuss the unfolding of *vijñāna* as intimated in the *Antar-jyotir* and *Dahara Vidyās* using "subtle inner consciousness" (a favourite of Sri Satya Sai Baba's) and "subtle inner consciousness with qualities of the self in dream" etc.

Outline of the Chapter: Overall Plan. The overall plan of the chapter is to take up the five selves or levels of the Five Sheaths *Vidyā* one after another. Sec. 2 introduces *Taittirīya Upaniṣad* and gives a complete translation of the *Vidyā*. The next three sections discuss the first three selves which are common experience: the *anna-rasa-maya* person or person consisting of (*-maya*) the essence (*rasa*) of food (*anna*); the *prāṇa*-self; and the mind-self (secs. 3, 4, and 5, resp.). Thereafter secs. 6-17 deal with *vijñāna*, secs. 18-22 with *ānanda*, and sec. 23 with the fact that the overall center and goal of the *vidyā* are "beyond *ānanda*". To get a more specific idea of at least some forms of *vijñāna*, the discussion of *vijñāna* is expanded to include the beginning stages of the *vijñāna* taught in the *Antar-jyotir Vidyā* and in Ajātaśatru's teaching to Bālāki (or *Bālāki Vidyā*) (secs. 13-16 and 17 resp.). Similarly the discussion of *ānanda* in the Five Sheaths *Vidyā* (secs. 18-20) is amplified by a treatment of the *ānanda* stages of the *Antar-jyotir Vidyā* (sec. 21). This is the overall organization.

Vijñāna. As can be seen, most of the effort is devoted to trying to understand *vijñāna*. The starting point is the meaning of the *vijñāna-maya* self or self identified with *vijñāna*, as defined by the Five Sheaths *Vidyā* (sec. 6). This *vijñāna*, which corresponds to initial stages of *vijñāna* in a person's inner development, is "beginning awareness of the Infinite-base of self", and this is then related to other, both lower and higher forms of *vijñāna* taught elsewhere in the Upaniṣads (sec. 7). But it is also deeply related to ordinary understanding and intelligence, which are also called *vijñāna* in the Upaniṣads (sec. 8). Next, we argue that Knowledge of "the Invisible, Center-less, Undefined, Non-based" mentioned in the second part of the Five Sheaths *Vidyā* represents a higher form of *vijñāna* which is one, and probably even the main, higher form of *vijñāna* envisaged by the *vidyā* (secs. 9 and 10). It is probably very similar to the *vijñāna* associated with those Yājñavalkya teachings which describe Brahman in negative terms, in other words the "Invisible, Center-less . . ." represents a higher stage of realization of Ātman/Brahman along the lines of *neti, neti*, and articulates one of the basic characteristics of states close to "merger into Brahman".

The text of the *vidyā* as a whole, by its very flow of discourse, however, suggest that there are other forms of *vijñāna* taught elsewhere in the Upaniṣads which would be, or are, considered by it to be *vijñāna* in the sense of the fourth sheath. Examination by simple textual indicators produces three major *vidyās* which teach such forms of *vijñāna* (sec. 11): The *Antar-jyotir* or "Inner Light" *Vidyā, BṛhUp* IV.3.1-3.34 (K); the combined *Satya-Brahma* and Heart *Vidyās, BṛhUp* V.1-6; and the *Dahara Vidyā, ChāndUp* VIII.1-6. These three *vidyās*, then, describe what the Five Sheaths *Vidyā* would consider different but still related "forms of *vijñāna*". In order to get a more specific understanding of *vijñāna*, therefore, we discuss the beginning stages of the *vijñāna* taught in the *Antar-jyotir Vidyā* (secs. 12-16) and in the *Bālāki Vidyā* (sec. 17) as examples.

Ānanda. But the aspect or level of *vijñāna* is only one deeper spiritual level taught by the Five Sheaths *Vidyā*. At the core of it, and actually inseparable from it lies a still more fundamental aspect, level of being, or whatever, namely *ānanda* or bliss. Again we first try to get a glimpse of the nature of *ānanda* and the whole *vijñāna-ānanda*-beyond *ānanda* progression (secs. 18-20) and then amplify and develop this further by pooling other relevant texts. The parallels in question are the *Antar-jyotir Vidyā* as a whole, sec. 21, and a poem of Yājñavalkya's on the meaning of man, sec. 22. Because it teaches a continuous series of forms of *vijñāna*, from awareness of a *vijñāna-maya* self which is inner light in the heart to highest *ānanda* and merger in Brahman, the *Antar-jyotir Vidyā* is the only major *vidyā* that illustrates the full progression of *vijñāna, ānanda,* and "beyond *ānanda*" of the Five Sheaths *Vidyā*. (The *Dahara Vidyā*, which also ends with merger into Brahman, does not stress *ānanda.*) The treatment of the *Antar-jyotir Vidyā* in this chapter, however, is incomplete, because an essential stage involving "deep sleep consciousness" [*BṛhUp* IV.3.19-20 (K)] is only clarified in chr. 6 below, in secs. 18, 19, and 21.

Merger into Brahman. Sec. 23 finally deals with the question whether the *vidyā* treats Brahman as lying beyond the *ānanda-maya* stage or whether it treats the *ānanda-maya* stage itself as representing (a " state of") Brahman. Since the highest state is a state of *neti, neti*, etc., we assume that the *vidyā* should be seen as avoiding a closed position like Brahman = the *ānanda-maya* self. Rather, the Vidyā appears to be pointing to inner evolution "beyond the *ānanda-maya*" which with later tradition may be called "merger into Brahman".

Other Issues. In contrast to the two previous chapters, few attempts are made to relate the *vidyās* in this chapter to possible Brāhmaṇa and Vedic Saṁhitā antecedents. There exist some very interesting speculations on the origins of the Five Sheaths *Vidyā* by J.A.B. van

Buitenen and L. Renou.[8] But if the understanding of the *Vidyā* developed in this chapter is accepted, these ideas raise many more problems than they solve. In the previous chapters we were always able to see specific inner, spiritual connections between a given Upaniṣadic text and its proposed antecedent. And it was always possible to understand the specific contribution made by the Upaniṣadic teaching. But in the case of the Five Sheaths *Vidyā*, we are for the first time dealing with a very clear and detailed exposition of Highest Knowledge. To connect this Knowledge with the texts discussed by van Buitenen and Renou would require a much deeper understanding of the Brāhmaṇa wisdom than I have at this point.

On the other hand, the analysis of *vijñāna* in secs. 6-17 does have some important byproducts. It appears, for example, that there is considerable justification for Sri Aurobindo's elaboration of *vijñāna* into the Supermind and Truth-Consciousness levels of his own system. According to Aurobindo, the latter mediate between what we usually call mind on the one hand and Absolute Brahman on the other, and are a culmination of "inner yoga" (our term). The *Taittirīya Upaniṣad vijñāna-maya* level performs the same function and overlaps significantly with the Supermind and Truth-Consciousness levels described by Aurobindo. Similarly the various apparently *ad hoc* or contradictory meanings given to *vijñāna* by great classical Vedāntic teachers and by divine personalities of modern times like Sri Ramakrishna and Sri Ramana Maharshi appear quite natural. It seems that *vijñāna* is *sui generis* and an essential element in beginning to approach Ātman/Brahman. It may be that *vijñāna* cannot be completely reduced to perception of the Divine or Transcendence of Desire. It is also not clear whether there is something analogous to *vijñāna* in other higher spiritual traditions.

2. *Taittirīya Upaniṣad*; Text of Five Sheaths *Vidyā*

Taittirīya Upaniṣad belongs to the Taittirīya school of the black Yajur Veda,[9] making up chapters 7-9 of *Taittirīya Āraṇyaka*. Its three chapters are called *vallīs*, "vines". The first is a mixture of rather different sections and modern scholarship regards it as a composite. M. Witzel, working from Kashmiri collections of Vedic quotations by medieval commentators, has reconstructed a *Kaṭha-Śikṣā-Upaniṣad* (an Upaniṣad of the Kaṭhas, a Vedic school like the Taittirīyas) which corresponds closely to *TaittUp* I.1. 4. 11 and 12.[10] The hypothesized text consists mostly of mantras for a Vedic student or his teacher (*TaittUp* I.1, 4, 12), and instructions on *dharma*, "inner attitudes having as ideal right conduct", which are given to the student when he has finished his studies and is ready to start his life as head of a household (*TaittUp* I.11). Another component of *TaittUp* I is I.5-6, a yogic text. But while *TaittUp* I is thus probably a composition incorporating originally different texts, the unity of *TaittUp* II, what we are calling the *Vāruṇī* or Five Sheaths *Vidyā*, has never been seriously questioned.[11] The chapter is called the *ānandavallī* or "vine dealing with bliss", after a famous consideration of bliss, *ānanda*, in *TaittUp* II.9. *TaittUp* III finally describes how the primeval Sage Bhṛgu under the guidance of his father Varuṇa successively realized food, *prāṇa*, mind, *vijñāna* and *ānanda* (bliss) as Brahman—the same stages as in *TaittUp* II. Vallīs II and III are traditionally considered as complementary and dealing with the same teaching.[12]

Structure of the Text. The text of the Five Sheaths *Vidyā* has a dense, complex structure. First there is an opening statement, and a stanza which says that Brahman is *satya, jñāna, ananta*. These are something like mottoes prefixed to the *Vidyā* as a whole. Next comes what looks like a brief cosmological preamble. Then follows the teaching on the five selves or sheaths (II.1-7), which we may call Part I. And finally there is a very substantial remainder which is less clearly organized and which we will call Part II. In this section we give a translation of the entire text. For convenience of reference, the conventional subunits of the chapter (the *anuvākas* II.1, II.2, etc.) are subdivided further, introducing a second level of subdivision (II.1.1, II.1.2, II.1.3 and so on).

Text of *Vidyā*, Part I. First the opening statement and stanza:

1.1. Om! The Brahman-knower attains the highest! As to that, this has been declared:

1.2. He who knows Brahman as the real (*satya*), as knowledge (*jñāna*), infinite (*ananta*),[a]
Set down in the secret place [of the heart] (*guhā*), in the highest heaven (*parame vyoman*),
He obtains all desires,
Together with the ecstatic-knowing (*vipaścit*)[b] Brahman[c].

Then comes the preamble, which actually sets up the whole teaching of the five selves:

1.3. From this Ātman, verily, Space (Ākaśa) came into existence; from Space, Wind (or Air, Vāyu); from Wind, Fire (Agni); from Fire, Water (Ap); from Water the Earth (Pṛthivī); from the Earth, Herbs; from Herbs, Food (*Anna*); from Food, [Semen; from Semen,][d] the [human] Person (*Puruṣa*).[13]

And then comes Part I, the teaching on the five persons or selves, beginning with "the person that consists of the essence of food":

1.4. This [last named person] verily, is this person [here] consisting of the essence of food (*anna-rasa-maya puruṣa*[a]). Of him this [head here] is the head, this [here] the left side (literally "wing," *pakṣa*), this [here] the right side, this [here] the trunk (central part, *ātman*), this the tail [-piece, to lean on for support], the foundation.

1.5. On this there is also this verse:

2.1. (1)[b] From food, truly, are all beings born,
Whoever are dwelling on earth.
Then, by food do they live.
Then, they enter into that at the end.

(2) For Food is the oldest of beings,
therefore it is called "All-herbs" ("Cure-all").
All Food, truly, obtain they
who regard (*upās-*) Food as Brahman.
For Food is the oldest of beings,
therefore it is called "All-herbs".

(3) From Food are beings born.
The ones that are born grow by Food.
It is eaten and it eats the beings,
Hence that is called Food.[14]

Next the self that consists of *prāṇa* (*ātmā prāṇa-maya*):

2.2. Verily, other than and within that one that consists of the essence of food is the self that consists of *prāṇa*. By that this is filled. This (*ātmā prāṇa-maya*), verily, has the form of a person. According to the person-form scheme of that [physical person] is this one of the form of a person. The inbreath (*prāṇa*) is its head; the diffused breath (*vyāna*), the right wing (side); the out-breath (*apāna*), the left wing;

space (*ākāśa*), the trunk (*ātman*); the earth (*pṛthivī*), the tailpiece, the foundation.

2.3. On this there is also this verse[a]:

3.1.[b] (1) The gods breathe along with Breath,
also men and animals.
For Breath (*Prāṇa*) is the life (*āyus*) of beings,
therefore it is called All-life.

(2) They indeed go to All-life,
who regard (*upās-*) Prāṇa as Brahman.
For Prāṇa is the life of beings,
therefore it is called All-life.

3.2. Of that [self consisting of *prāṇa*, just described], this [body] is the bodily self, as [it is] of the previous [-ly described self, the self consisting of the essence of food] (i.e. both this and the previous self have the same *śarīra ātman* or bodily self)[c].

The teachings regarding the other three selves follow the same format:

3.3. Verily, other than and within that one that consists of *prāṇa* is the self that consists of mind (*ātmā mano-maya*). By that this is filled. This, verily, has the form of a person. According to the person-form scheme of that (physical person) is this one of the form of a person. The *Yajur-Veda* is its head; the *Ṛg-Veda*, the right side; the *Sāma-Veda*, the left side; instruction (*ādeśa*), the trunk (*ātman*); the Hymns of the Atharvans and Aṅgirases (the *Atharva Veda*), the lower part, the foundation.

3.4. As to that there is also this verse:

4.1.[d] Wherefrom words turn back,
Together with the mind, not having attained,
The bliss of Brahma he who knows,
Fears not at any time at all.

4.2. Of that [self consisting of mind, just described], this [body] is the bodily self, as [it is also] of the previous [-ly described self, i.e., the *prāṇa-maya* self].

4.3. Other than and within that one that consists of mind is the self that consists of *vijñāna* (*ātmā vijñāna-maya*). By that this is filled. This, verily, has the form of a person. According to the person-form scheme of that (physical person) is this one of the form of a person. Faith (*śraddhā*) is its head; eternal right (*ṛta*), the right wing; the true (*satya*), the left wing; *yoga*, the body; *mahas*, the tailpiece, the foundation.

4.4. As to this there is also this verse.

5.1.[e] (1) *Vijñāna* spreads out the sacrifice,
and it also spreads out the deeds.
All the gods worship (*upās-*)
the oldest Brahman as *vijñāna*.

(2) If one knows Brahman as *vijñāna*.
and if one does not swerve from this,
Having left the sins in the body,
then he attains all desires.

5.2. Of that (self consisting of *vijñāna*), this [body] is the bodily self, as [it is] of the previous [-ly described *mano-maya* self].

5.3. Verily, other than and within that one which consists of *vijñāna* is the self that consists of bliss (*ātmā ānanda maya*). By that this is filled. This, verily, has the form of a person. According to the person-form-hood of that (physical person) is this one of the form of a person. Being dear (*priya*) is its head; delight (*moda*), the right wing; great delight (*pra-moda*), the left wing; bliss (*ānanda*), the body; Brahman, the tailpiece, the foundation.

5.4. On that there is also this verse.

6.1.[f] A non-being one (*a-sat*), indeed, does he become
if he knows Brahman [in the manners of] "*asat*" ("Non-Being").
If he knows Brahman [in the manner of] "*asti*" ("it is"),
such a one [people] know as a being one (*sat*).

6.2. Of that [self consisting of *ānanda*], this [body] is the bodily self as [it is] of the previous[-ly described *vijñāna-maya* self].[15]

This teaching on the *ānanda-maya* self completes the systematic part of the *vidyā*, what we called Part I above. Part II, below, strikes one at first as a jumble of different things. But one can distinguish five main segments, labelled for convenience [A]-[E], of which [B]-[E] follow a coherent plan.

[A]

6.3. Now then, questions (or: Next, the follow-up questions): Does anyone [who is] a non-knower, after dying, go to that world yonder? Or does anyone [who is] a knower, after dying, attain that world?

This segment is something of a puzzle. The word "Now, then", *athātaḥ*, indicates the start of a new topic. Śaṁkara interprets the world yonder as Brahman. But the questions are apparently never answered.[16] Our only choice appears to be to assume with Rau[17] that there is a break after [A]. As far as interpretation of [A]-[E] is concerned, [A] will be simply ignored. The remaining portion, [B]-[E], is unified in terms of content and will therefore be taken as the primary unit of analysis.

[B]

6.4. He desired: "May I be many! May I be born!" He heated (*tap*) heat (*tapas*). He, having heated heat, created all this, whatever there is at all (in this world). Having created that, he indeed entered into that. Having entered into that, he became the *sat* and the *tyat*, the uttered (*niruktam*) and the un-uttered (*a-niruktam*), the based (*nilayanam*) and the non-based (*a-nilayanam*), knowledge (*vijñānam*) and non-knowledge (*a-vijñānam*), the true (*satyam*) and the false (*anṛtam*). He became the *Satyam*. [All] this [here] whatever there is, that they call "the *Satya*" ("the True").

6.5. As to this there is also this verse (*śloka*):

7.1.[a] Nonbeing (*a-sat*), verily, was this [world] in the beginning.
From that, verily, Being (*sat*) was born.
That made its own self (*svayam akuruta*), the Self (Ātman).
Therefore it is called the well-done (*su-kṛta*).

[C]

7.2. Verily, what that well-done is—that, verily, is flavour (Sai Baba: "Sweet-Nectar," "Pure Emotion [= Feeling]"), *rasa*. For truly, on getting the *rasa*, one becomes blissful. For who indeed could here breathe in, who could breathe out, if there were not this "space-bliss", *ākāśa-ānanda*! For truly, this (*rasa*) makes blissful. For as soon as he indeed finds in this Invisible, Bodiless, Undefind, Non-based fearlessness as foundation (*pratiṣṭhā*) [for himself], then he becomes one [who is permanently] gone to fearlessness. But when indeed he makes in this (Invisible, etc., or in this standing in fearlessness) even a tiny difference (or gap), then fear becomes his (i.e. he becomes fearful). But that indeed is the fear of one who thinks of himself [to be] a knower.

7.3. As to that there is also this verse:

8.1.[b] Through fear of Him the Wind (Vāyu) blows.
Through fear of Him the Sun (Sūrya) rises.
Through fear of Him both Agni (Fire) and Indra
And Death (Mṛtyu) as fifth hurry along.

Immediately after this comes a famous 'inquiry into bliss" (*ānanda-mīmāṁsā*)

[D]

8.2. This is a consideration (*mīmāṁsā*) of bliss.

Let there be a youth, a good (*sādhu*) youth, well-read, very quick, very firm, very strong. Let this whole earth be full of wealth for him. That is one human bliss.

A hundred human blisses are one bliss of the human Gandharvas (lower level celestial beings)—[as] also of a man who is versed in the scripture (*śrotriya*) and who is not hit by desire.

A hundred blisses of the human Gandharvas are one bliss of the divine Gandharvas—[as] also of a man who is versed in the scriptures and who is not hit by desire. . .

The text continues in this way, proceeding to higher and higher levels of being(s) and bliss, until on the 10th step, it reaches Brahman and the bliss of Brahman. At each step, the bliss (or unit of bliss) of the new level is 100 times that of the old, and the bliss at this level is also that of a man who knows and understands the words of the scriptures and is not hit, marred, by desire. Many years ago, when I read this for the first time, this passage gave me, in one stroke, faith in the reality of the Infinite, of Enlightenment, whatever, and confirmed for me the transcendental nature of desirelessness as it appears in the Early Buddhist *Majjhima Nikāya* (the only Enlightenment scripture I had studied at that time).

...A hundred blisses of Prajāpati are one bliss of Brahman[c] —[as] also of a man who is versed in the scriptures and who is not hit by desire.

[E]

9.1. Both he who is here in a person and he who is yonder in the Sun—he is one.

9.2. He who knows this, on departing from this world, proceeds on to that self which consists of food, proceeds on to that self which consists of breath, proceeds on to that self which consists of mind, proceeds on to that self which consists of *vijñāna*, proceeds on to that self which consists of bliss.

9.3. As to that there is also this verse:

9.4. Wherefrom words turn back,
    Together with the mind, not having attained—
The bliss of Brahma he who knows,
    Fears not from anything at all.

9.5. Such a one, verily, the thought does not torment: 'Why have I not done the good (*sādhu*)? Why have I done the evil (*pāpa*)?' He who knows this, delivers (*spṛṇute*) himself (*ātmānam*) from these two [thoughts]. For truly, from both of these the delivers himself—he who knows this!

9.6. Such is the teaching (*upaniṣad*)![18]

3. The First Level or Self (the Physical Person)

The first self that is being taught is "the person that consists of the essence of food," the *anna-rasa-maya puruṣa*. It is described schematically as having the form of a person or bird, and the same schema is used for the other more interior selves later. Its head is simply the head that one has ("this head here"), its left side (or left wing) is simply the left side of one's body ("this left here"), and so on. Thus the *anna-rasa-maya* person is clearly the physical individual which one thinks oneself to be. But the model or schema to which this physical person is assimilated is not just the (physical) human form, because of the use of the words "wing" and "tail" (*pakṣa* and *puccha*). Rather it is a form of alternatively a human person and a bird. This combined representation comes from the *agnicayana*, in which the fire altar, thought of as both Agni and the self of the sacrificer, is laid out in the form of a bird. "In such descriptions (of Agni = the fire altar) the representations of bird and man are oddly mixed. To the bird apply the wings (*pakṣa*) and tail (*puccha*), but they are equally applied to the man: Then *pakṣa* is reinterpreted (or we might better say: translated by us) as though it meant 'side', while *puccha* is qualified by an added *pratiṣṭhā* (foundation, feet.".[19] As understood by Vedānta,[20] the *anna-rasa-maya* person is introduced in the *vidyā* in part as a familiar baseline and starting point against which the other persons or selves will be defined. For that reason he is commonly just called the *anna-maya* person—the physical individual "consisting of food", *anna-maya*.

The *anna-rasa-maya* as Something to be Realized. But there is more to the *anna-rasa-maya* person than that. This is suggested by some aspects of *TaittUp* III which, as mentioned before, is traditionally considered as being complementary to *TaittUp* II and as teaching the same thing. *TaittUp* III begins with Bhṛgu asking his father Varuṇa to teach him Brahman:

III.1.2. To him (Bhṛgu) he (Varuṇa) recited[a] the following: Food, Prāṇa, Sight, Hearing, Mind, Speech—this [is Brahman].

1.3. To him he (Varuṇa) said: "That, verily, from which these beings are born, [that] by which, [when] born, they live, [that] into which, [when] dying, they all together enter—that seek to know (*vi-jñā-*) [for yourself], that is Brahman."

1.4. He [= Bhṛgu] heated [his] heat (=performed austerity). Having done so,

2.1. He knew (*vi-jñā-*) "Brahman is Food. For truly, these beings here are born from food, (when) born, they live by food, (when) dying, they [all] together enter into food."

2.2. Having realized (*vi-jñā-*) this, he again approached his Father Varuṇa. "Teach me Brahman, revered Sir."

2.3. To him, he (Varuṇa) said: "Seek to know Brahman by austerity (*tapas*). Austerity is Brahman."

2.4. He [= Bhṛgu] performed austerity (as in 1.4)...[21]

Thereafter Bhṛgu realized successively and always in the same way that Brahman was Prāṇa, Brahman was Mind, Brahman was *Vijnāna*, and Brahman was *Ānanda*—the same sequence as the sequence of five selves in *TaittUp* II.

Now let us consider this. By practicing austerity, *tapas*, by using III.1.3 as his criterion (cf. III. 2.1), and by taking a hint from his father (III.1.2, "food"), Bhṛgu first realized that "Brahman is Food," *annam brahma*. Since in II.2.1 (2) the text talks about "meditating (worshipping, etc., *upās-*) that "Brahman is 'Food,' *annam brahma*," this means that Bhṛgu realized the knowledge which is the aim of that *upāsanā*.[22] Thus, "knowing that 'Brahman is Food. For truly, these beings here are born from Food, . . .' " [II.1.2 (1) = III.2.1] represents a level of deeper knowledge or insight. But this is not all. II.2.1(3) says that Food is not only eaten by the living beings, it also eats them. Because they constantly have to procure it and are dependent on it, beings are the slaves to Food: Food is something greater than them. *ŚatBr* XII.9.1.1 says that "whatever food a man consumes in this world, that (food), in return, consumes him in yonder world".[23] So Food is a higher force. By regarding it (*upās-*) as a higher force, as Brahman, according to Varuṇa's criterion in III.1.3, one is lifted to a level where one has a more universal outlook and less self interest, and where one gets some kind of knowledge, represented by III.2.1, which, because of the universality of outlook, contains a touch of knowledge of Brahman.[24]

So II.1.4 does not merely set up the *anna-rasa-maya* self as a familiar reference point against which the subsequent selves are distinguished. For then there would be no need to bring in *upāsana* on and realization of "Brahman is Food". What then is the purpose of bringing these in? We will see that in the case of some of the other selves there are also similar elements which go beyond a simple scheme of "five selves, each one to be discriminated within the preceding one one". We have to wait until we look at these also.

4. The Second Level or Self (*Prāṇa*)

Within the person that is made of the essence of food, and different from him, is the person or self that is *prāṇa-maya*, "of energy (*prāṇa*) consisting," says the *vidyā*. This is the self that one thinks one is when one feels at one with one's vital power, one's various mental and emotional dynamics, and one's subtle energy (in psychic, yogic, and spiritual experience).[25] Instead of "energy" we can also say "breath" for in general, experience of energy is intimately connected with breath. One's vital energies and emotional state are closely mirrored in one's breathing, and from the point of view of yoga, stilling the breath leads to stilling the mind. Experience of subtle energy is also intimately connected with breathing. In other words, breath is an alternative way of conceiving and experiencing vital powers, mental dynamics *and* subtle energy. So the *prāṇa-maya* self is "the (individual) self feeling that he/she is energy or breath".

The *prāṇa-maya* and Subtle Energy in the Vedic Literature. An important question is to what extent full comprehension of the *prāṇa-maya* self as an independent self, "within and other than" one's normal self as a physical person, implies perception of subtle energy and the feeling and belief that one is a subtle energy being. For it may be argued that unless there is extensive development of subtle perception, one is not likely to get the idea that one is something that consists of energy etc., which exists "within" the physical person which one is, is different from that "physical person self", and fills that self. In addition, the fact that the *prāṇa-maya* self is said to have *prāṇa* as head, *vyāna* as left wing and so on may be regarded as further evidence that this self involves identification of oneself with subtle energy. The *prāṇa, apāna* and *vyāna* breaths in 2.2[26] are the first three of the system of five *prāṇas* that occurs several times in the old Upaniṣads[27] and that is elaborated in many forms in later yogic and Āyurvedic literature.[28] The three by themselves form a still older system which is found commonly in *Vājasaneyī Saṁhitā* and *Atharva Veda*.[29] Because this system is so ancient, these *prāṇas* are likely to be (from a western point of view) complex unities of aspects of the functioning of body and the psyche and subtle (psychic) and spiritual elements.[30] The latter become prominent in the later literature. Thus in the (*Yoga-*) *Darśana Upaniṣad*, a late (400-1000 CE?) Yoga Upaniṣad presupposing the Patañjali *Yoga Sūtra*,[31] *prāṇa* is described as omnipresent but residing permanently in throat, nose, navel and heart. *Apāna* inhabits the anus, thighs, knees, and the lower part of the body generally up to the navel, while the *vyāna* is in the head, ears, eyes, neck down to the level of the shoulders.[32] As they stand, these definitions are likely to be based on subtle perception as well as somatosensory observation and conceptions of physiological and subtle body functioning.[33] Later in the text their primarily subtle nature becomes unmistakable. They are conceived to circulate in certain subtle channels or *nāḍīs*[34], and to be accessible to and subject to conscious control and modification by *prāṇāyāma* or yogic breathing. Typically the breath must be guided inside the body in specific ways, in a specific direction or into a specific area—belly, heart, feet, eyes—

along specific channels, always in conjunction with specific mental attitudes and in a certain sequence of steps.[35] "Clearly this can only be understood with reference to the subtle body [*sūkṣmaśarīra*], since the Hindus know just as well as we do that 'material' air penetrates no further than the lungs."[36] So here in the *Yoga Upaniṣads* we have a very clear description of an *ātmā prāṇa-maya*, a self that feels itself as operating purely with and as a vital-energies-and-breath-system. This system, or the self identified with the functioning of this system, is the so-called *sūkṣma śarīra* or "subtle body" (partly spatialized in terms of one's subjective body frame of reference and partly with *sui generis* experiential, non-spatial dimensions).[37] It is felt to be virtually independent of and "truer" than the physical body or the physical self.

In *TaittUp* II—more than a thousand years earlier than the *Yoga Upaniṣads*—a highly developed conception of a subtle body cannot necessarily be assumed. But several factors suggest that experience of "subtle (and spiritual) energy" is at this time widespread in the Brāhmaṇical culture. First, the idea in the Brāhmaṇas of the two-sided nature of *prāṇa* as both vital force and breath facilitates conception and experience of subtle *prāṇas* and eventually leads to perception/conception of a "subtle body"; then, the connection of *prāṇa* with Vāyu and of individual *prāṇas* with deities and metaphysical aspects is likely to involve experience at subtle levels because knowledge/experience of deities generally does; and finally, meditative type concentration such as is found in ritual, *upāsanā* and spiritual life generally likewise favors development of subtle experience and perception. In view of all this, there is a good possibility that subtle perception plays a major role in the knowledge/experience of the *prāṇa-maya* self.

Finally the last two components of the *prāṇa-maya* self are said to be *Ākāśa*, Space, and *Pṛthivī*, Earth. The classical commentaries explain the first as referring to the equalizing or circular *prāṇa*, the *samāna*, centered in the middle of the body around the navel.[38] But *ākāśa* in the sense of space as the metaphysical generative ground of all physical manifestation seems also reasonable. Indeed, the cosmological preamble *TaittUp* II.1.3 says explicitly that from *Ākāśa* arose Vāyu, which is the Divine element in *prāṇa* gross *and* subtle. *Pṛthivī* (Earth or the Earth Divine) as stabilizing foundation of the *prāṇa-maya* self could also be interpreted directly in terms of subtle/spiritual experience.[39]

The *prāṇa-maya* and Subtle Energy Today. Outside very orthodox kinds of Vedānta, the *prāṇa-maya* sheath is usually assumed to refer to subtle energy.[40] If preoccupation with the subtle body is properly channelled by integrating it with the inner pursuit of higher spiritual principles, gradually deepening knowledge of the *prāṇa-maya* can signal genuine spiritual progress.

> To progress with the Brahmic outlook, that you are Brahman and not the body etc., the *prāṇa-maya* is the first instrument. It is subtle and separate and different from the body. It is activated by Vāyu and is saturated with it. It pervades and subsumes the entire *anna-maya kośa*. You can say that the *prāṇa-maya* is the soul of the *anna-maya*, for it makes it function from head to foot. By contemplating that the *prāṇa-maya* is the *ātmā*[*] of the *anna-maya*, the notion that the body is the Self will disappear. You rise from the gross to the subtle. *Prāṇa* is like the molten metal in the crucible. By effort, the *prāṇa-maya kośa* can be experienced.[41]

By describing the *prāṇa-maya* self as other than and within the *anna-rasa-maya* self, the Upaniṣad itself practically suggests that one should regard the former as the self of the latter, and Sai Baba then explains what happens (or what ideally should happen) when this is done. By more and more cultivation (over years) of the *prāṇa-maya* as a distinct realm of I-experience, distinct from and imbuing the physical person that one is, the hold of the idea that one is the physical individual will be lessened. It is a fact that in ordinary life as well as in the yogic, psychic and spiritual fields, experiences of a subtle nature are felt to be more powerful than ordinary experience based on the senses, and one attributes to them greater significance. So the *ātmā prāṇa-maya*, as a separate functional entity, may naturally become an object of absorbing interest. Ideally the consequences of this would be that "the notion that the body is the Self will disappear" and "one rises from the gross to the subtle".

The *Upāsana* of *Prāṇa* as Brahman. As in the case of the physical self, the stanzas following the description of the *prāṇa-maya* self mention *upāsanā*, in this case, *upāsana* on *prāṇa* as Brahman. Since *prāṇa* is here treated also as a universal aspect, not just as a sensory, vital and subtle phenomenon, the *upāsanā* would no doubt make one develop a more universal outlook. It would give one some kind of realization of Universal Divinity (just like the meditations of the six Brahmins in the *Vaiśvānara Vidyā* gave them some knowledge of Universal Divinity). But again the role of this *upāsanā* in the scheme of the *vidyā* as a whole is still unclear.

5. Third Level or Self (Mind)

According to Śaṁkara, in the *mano-maya* or "of-mind-consisting" self, the term *manas*, "mind", refers to the *antaḥ-karaṇa*, the "inner organ,"[42] the inner agency that perceives and feels, directs the attention, and whose movements are the movements of one's mind. So the *mano-maya* or "of-mind-consisting" self is the self that one believes oneself to be when one is identified with one's mental impulses and decision making, one's current personality, perception of things, and mentation generally. It is a self *within* the *prāṇa-maya* self in the sense that it is ultimately behind all the detailed *prāṇa-maya* level phenomena.

Meaning of the *mano-maya* Self. But that is not yet the whole story. Like the other selves, the *mano-maya* self has a structure, on the model of the physical person or bird. Somewhat surprisingly, this structure is specified in terms of the different types of Vedic mantras —"the *Yajur Vedic* mantras are its head," and so on. Śaṁkara explains that the "*Yajur Vedic* mantras" stand for the various mental states involved in uttering the mantras (and similarly for the *Ṛg* and *Sāma Vedic* mantras and chants).[43] This line of thought is supported by *AitĀr* III.2.3.1-6,[44] with focus on v. 5:

1. "[There are] four persons (*puruṣa*)" [says] Bādhva,
2. "the person of the body (*śarīra*), the person of the meters, the person of the Veda, [and] the great person."[a]
3. Whom we called "the person of the body", he is the bodily self (*daihika ātmā*, from *deha*, body). Of him he is the essence (*rasa*) who is this bodiless conscious self (*a-śarīra prajñātmā*).
4. Whom we called "the person of the (Vedic) meters," he is the collection of letters (*akṣara*). Of him [that is] the essence which is the latter[a].
5. What we called "the person of the Veda" is [that] by which one knows (*vid*) the Vedas—the *Ṛg Veda*, the *Yajur Veda*, the *Sāma Veda*. Of that the essence [is] Brahman (masc.).[b]

6. Therefore one should choose [for the sacrifice] a Brahman priest who is full of Brahman (= Brahmic power) and can discern flaws in the sacrifice. . .[45]

Bādhva says that there are four major metaphysical (Divine, transcendental, whatever) entities that he knows. He calls these "persons," *puruṣas*, and gives for each of them both an external description and its essence, *rasa*, which is the metaphysical or Divine or transcendental element in question. The one of interest here is "the person of the Veda" (singular—so both "the three Vedas" and "knowledge"). This person, described as "[that] by which one knows (*veda*) the Vedas" (a word play on *veda*) is not further named, but all commentators agree that it is the mind, *manas* (e. g. on the basis of *ChāndUp* VII.3.1, "For when one through mind has in mind 'the mantras are to be learned', then one learns them"). Bādhva says that the essence of this person is Brahmā (masc.). The commentators explain this as Hiraṇyagarbha, the Divine Universal Mind. Thus the essence of the person of the Veda is the Divine Universal Mind, God (or an aspect of God), that is operating in the world, and that has through the Vedas shaped society into a meaningful whole in which the individual can lead a meaningful life. For the person which Bādhva is describing is the mind's effort and capability to know and live by the Vedas, and thus lead a meaningful life both personally, as a member of society, and as a part of Nature.

Bādhva's "person of the Veda" is the same as the *mano-maya* self of the Taittirīya text. That is to say, the *ātmā mano-maya* is that aspect of one's self and mind by which one is capable of knowing and comes to know the Vedas—memorizing the mantras, knowing their spirit, and living them in one's life in ritual and in spirit and faith. In more general terms this means worshipping and interacting with the Divine, and subordinating oneself to It in spirit, by accepting and bowing to the word of Scripture and the moral, social and cosmic order in which one finds oneself placed. (Subordinating oneself in spirit and accepting is the first step to knowing.) This is a spiritual element found in all mankind, and is the traditional aspect presented by religion everywhere. The importance of this aspect, and thus the rationale for focussing on the *mano-maya* self (which corresponds to it) is noted by Sai Baba: "The sound of Yajus produces modifications which are auspicious. That is the reason for the significance attached to the other Vedas also. Thus, all mantras become the causes of mental modifications."[46] When one lives a religious life, then one's mind becomes more and more shaped by the principles and moral and divine ideals which are enshrined and intangibly present in the words of the Scripture that one follows and practices. In this process the words or sounds that enunciate the principles and ideals play an essential role. In this way the mantras "produce auspicious modifications" and "all mantras become the causes of mental modifications" in the individual, and the same will be true at the level of the society. Then indeed the *ātman*, the trunk or soul of this *mano-maya* self that one is, will be the *ādeśa*, the scriptural command or teaching inscribed in one's inner conviction.

So the *mano-maya* self is indeed oneself when one is thinking, feeling, making decision, i.e. oneself felt as and assumed to be an independent mental being. But this state is viewed exclusively from the point of view of living a religiously directed life: the only thing of interest is knowing and living the word of Scripture. Further, a knowledge of the *mano-maya* self is clearly more than an intellectual recognition of one's mental being as a semi-independent level or phenomenon of one's experience. Rather, it implies a clear apprehension of the nature of the words of Scripture (in this case the Vedic mantras) as a metaphysical or other higher element in oneself, and a clear awareness of their role and importance in shaping one's ideals, conduct, and character. In terms of Bādhva's teaching, the *mano-maya* self is the "person of the Veda," but knowledge of the *mano-maya* self is knowledge of the essence or *rasa* of the person of the Veda, i.e. (in the commentators' terms) some knowledge of Hiraṇyagarbha, a metapghysical or Divine aspect. It is *this* knowledge that Śaṁkara describes in terms of the Eternality of the Vedic mantras and the fact that they are part of the self in the mind. "Hence the mantras called *yajus* are (in the last analysis) nothing but consciousness of the self—that is identical with the beginningless and endless Self—lodged in and conditioned by the mental functions that act as Its limiting adjuncts."[47]

Finally, instead of concluding with verses glorifying mind as an instrument for pursuing religious life, as might be expected, the *mano-maya* teaching ends instead with an enigmatic *śloka*. This contrasts the nature of mind as a necessary and fundamental instrument for a traditional religious life, the matrix in which the path of Brahman is pursued, with its inability, in principle, to reach Brahman. The same mind that is needed to memorize and accept scripture as true, live accordingly, and in this way get steadiness, faith, maturity and beginning wisdom—that same mind, all its words and conceptual understanding, turn back from Brahman, in principle unable to touch it. But the verse also mentions what a state of knowledge of Brahman is really like. It involves, it says, feeling the bliss of Brahman and fearlessness. These are beyond the *mano-maya* self and the level of awareness and knowledge represented by it.

Overall Trend of the Teaching of the Five Selves So Far. At this point, therefore, the overall trend of the teaching is becoming clear. An individual may be said to have a series of selves, corresponding to different points in spiritual unfoldment, beginning with oneself as a physical being and ending with oneself consisting of bliss. Each of these selves pervades the preceding ones and "Brahman is the inmost of all [these] selves."[48] The *vidyā* teaches to develop knowledge of these selves by contemplation, meditation, etc. and by carrying that into one's daily life. A basic factor in the whole scheme is that of inner discrimination (*viveka*). The development of knowledge of each self (or sheath) involves discriminating the level of principle of living and experience involved in the given self from that of the preceding one, and thereby transcending the knowledge of the preceding one. This gives the *vidyā* an "analytical" and "*jñāna*" aspect which is lacking in the *vidyās* in chr. 4. At the same time each level is approached with wisdom, and knowledge of the nature of that level is presented as a wisdom, involving a widening, deepening and subtilizing of one's capacities of inner balance and inner perception. Each substantive level—Food, Prāṇa, Mind, and so on—is treated as sacred and as being a Divine or otherwise higher aspect. Indeed, each of them, and the wisdom of being able to feel and understand each of them, can be described in a general way as being more subtle than the preceding one, involving subtler powers and objects of apprehension, subtler awareness:

> This body is also called the food sheath. It is a gross form. In this gross form a subtle entity is present and that is the life sheath. There is an even more subtle entity than this life sheath and that is the mind sheath. Underlying this mind principle is an even more subtle entity and that is the principle of intellection. The basis on which the intellect rests is an even more subtle entity and that is the Rapture [Bliss, *ānanda*] sheath or embodiment of delight. This Rapture is absorbed in the Spirit

> [Ātman/Brahman]. The gross body, the life sheath, the mind sheath, the intellection sheath are not immersed in the Spirit to the degree that the Rapture sheath is. It is because of the Rapture being so close to the Spirit that man has been called the one who aspires for Rapture.[49]

This is in Vedāntic language, using "is *based* on a more *subtle entity* that is *within it*" as conceptual organizing device. But it must be noted that the entities in question are very different kinds of things, and that the type of subtleness involved in *prāṇa-maya* perception is qualitatively and metaphysically different from that involved in perception of the *mano-maya* entity.[50] (The kinds of subtleness characteristic of the *vijñāna-maya* level and the *ānanda-maya* level are different still.) In any case, in addition to a strong element of inner discrimination and "self-enquiry", the *vidyā* also involves a positive element of unfoldment in new directions of awareness and experience.

6. *Vijñāna-maya* Level: The Nature of *Vijñāna*, Based on *TaittUp* II.4.3

We said that *vijñāna*, "higher spiritual knowing/awareness", and the *vijñāna-maya* self or sheath represent the first really higher aspect taught by the *vidyā*. Everyone is naturally endowed with perception and consciousness at the level of *vijñāna*. But such awareness may be fleeting, infrequent, and thus almost unknown to the individual. On the other hand, "knowing Brahman as *vijñāna*" (i.e. as *vijñāna*-consciousness) is presented as a higher spiritual level, because by 5.1(2), if one does know this *vijñāna* as Brahman and does not deviate from it, then one leaves all sins in the body (after death or possibly already while living). So the *vidyā* teaches that one develop and foster *vijñāna* and the *vijnǎna-maya* level as an aspect of oneself, that one encourage the arising of perception and consciousness at this *vijñāna-maya* level and that one live the *vijñāna* that arises in one also in one's life. Indeed, we will see that inner development at the *vijñāna-maya* level leads to full *Ātma-jñāna* or Ātma consciousness as the highest *vijñāna*.

The Nature of *Vijñāna*, Based on *TaittUp* II.4.3. But what is *vijñāna*? Etymologically it is "distinct knowledge, knowing" (*vi* + *jñā* + *ana*) and thus (here) a "state of knowledge, knowing". The *vijñāna-maya* self is described as having *śraddhā, ṛta, satya*, and *yoga* as aspects.

Śraddhā is trust, faith, with a connotation that religious actions are not only accomplished with but also undertaken on the urging of *Śraddhā*.[51] An important text on *Śraddhā* relevant here is *JaimUpBr* IV.11.4.1-2 = IV.25.1-2.

> Being (or the manifested, *Sat*) and Non-Being (*A-sat*), and Non-Being and Being, and Speech (*Vāc*) and Mind (*Manas*), and Mind and Speech, and Sight and Hearing (*Cakṣus* and *Śrotra*), and Hearing and Sight, and *Śraddhā* and austerity (*Tapas*), and austerity and *Śraddhā*—these sixteen are the Brahman with sixteen parts (*Ṣoḍaśa-kala* Brahman).

Here *śraddhā* is paired with *tapas*, "the fire (heat) of austerity" (recall chr. 4.5), in either order, suggesting a constant coupled-ness and mutual interaction. In addition, this combined aspect is seen directly as a part of Brahman, as a foot or quarter of Brahman, on a par with the three other pairs, *sat-asat* etc. That is, it is one of the fundamental categories of existence.[52] This is the level at which we have to take *śraddhā* here also. Next, *ṛta* is the cosmic order, so here (as part of the *vijñāna-maya* self) "oneself being in harmony with the cosmic order". Similarly, *satya* = "(oneself) following truth". *Yoga* is literally "yoked[ness]" (of the mind), from the root *yuj*, "bind, yoke". So as aspect of the self, it has the sense of "practicing sense control, curbing oneself appropriately, inner discipline, keeping oneself yoked to the path".[53] Now all these aspects suggest that *vijñāna* must be something in the direction of "inner higher knowledge and awareness". If the aspects of faith, harmony with the cosmic order, truth, and curbedness are demonstrated in one's behavior consistently and at the highest level, then there must be in one's mind a corresponding deep-seated awareness and knowledge, for otherwise one would swerve from this. There must be something permanent in one's soul or being, an awareness present much of the time, in all one's behavior. There must be some kind of knowing by the inner consciousness that keeps the mind content and still and that manifests in *śraddhā*, having faith, in walking in accordance with *ṛta*, the inherent order of the universe, and in producing the *satyam*, "the true". There must be a knowledge or consciousness at the bottom of the mind that gives inner peace and sureness of one's path. This deep-seated awareness is *vijñāna*, and this is what we take as the starting point for our own understanding of *vijñāna*. This *vijñāna* has all four aspects named in the *vidyā* (*śraddhā*, etc.) as symptoms. It is different from *mano-maya* level knowledge where the words of Scripture and their spirit provide the principles and ideals to which one subordinates oneself and aspires. At the *mano-maya* level, although the Divine Word or text is experienced in many different ways, that Word tends to have always a quality of irreducibility and finality. Although one may feel its power and divine character keenly and try to live according to it, the sum-total of one's perception and awareness do not go beyond a feeling of the power, rightness and validity of the Scriptural Word. *Vijñāna*, on the other hand, has qualities associated with true wisdom. It pervades the self, enabling it to transcend and abide unperturbed among the innumerable influences that impinge on it from within and without.

Characterization of *Vijñāna* by Sri Sathya Sai Baba. The preceding characterization is supported by Sri Sathya Sai Baba, when he calls *vijñāna* "the superknowledge that confers perfect equanimity and purity":

> [A] *Cit* in *sat-cit-ānanda* means *vijñāna*, the superknowledge that confers perfect equanimity and purity, in fact, the *ātma-jñāna* which can be experiencd by one and all. In common parlance *vijñāna* is used to indicate the sciences, but really it means the Higher Wisdom. In that *sva-rūpa* ["own-form," or "own-form of the self"] there is no room for "impressions from karma" nor for wishes that prompt karma. Wishes vitiate the mind. Wishes lead to action, action leaves a scar, a *vāsanā* on the mind [a latent tendency that leads to further desire action]. Be alone with yourself and, then the mind can be negated. . .[54]

This describes the essence of one aspect of *vijñāna* in the sense used by the *vidyā*. When there is *vijñāna*, then impressions from karma and desires are not operating. For that reason, *vijñāna* will grow naturally into *Ātma-jñāna*, knowledge of the Self. *TaittUp* II.5.1(2) merely says that knowing Brahman as *vijñāna*, knowing Brahman as or in the direction of the *vijñāna* which pervades one, makes one leave one's evils in the body (i.e., they are thereafter not anymore supported by oneself). [A] takes this further and says that when true *vijñāna* becomes prominent in one, then "impressions from karma" and new wishes that prompt action will not arise. If they do, they do so in a defused form, i.e., one does not "hook in" with attachment and self-interest and acts on them on that basis. When that condition starts taking hold, then in the course of time there arises *Ātma-jñāna,* knowledge of the Ātman. Finally Sai Baba also ties *vijñāna* to the aspect of *cit*, "pure consciousness," in the standard Vedāntic description of Brahman as *sat-cit-ānanda*. In the course of spiritual unfolding, the *vijñāna* one feels and is becomes *cit*.

It may take many years of religious or spiritual life before one is able to identify *vijñāna* unmistakably in one's experience. Or *vijñāna* may be in one's inner experience already from childhood on. In any case it is the first really deeper stage, or set of stages, on the road to becoming Brahman, and a prerequisite for still further stages. Realization of the Truth comes only after there is *vijñāna*, and involves entering and passing through the *ānanda-maya kośa,* which is deeper than the *vijñāna-maya-kośa*:

> [B] In order to attain this *vijñāna* [viz. that "one *is* God"], man has to transcend three sheaths out of the five in which he is encased—the *anna-maya* or gross, with its equipment of the senses; the *prāṇa-maya* or subtle, with its instrumentality of vital airs and the nervous system; (and) the *mano-maya*, the causal, with its patterns of desires, resolutions, wishes, both positive and negative, which form the complex called mind. Deeper than these is the *vijñāna-maya kośa*, the Sheath of Intuition, which is laid over the *ānanda-maya kośa*, the Sheath of Bliss. But man is now caught up in the tangles of the first three, and he does not venture any deeper, so that he is denied a glimpse of the truth whose door lies at the *vijñāna* state only, and passes beyond the *ānanda-maya kośa* itself.
>
> Embodiments of the Divine Ātmā! It is only through the cultivation of love that the heart can be enlarged to receive these eternal absolute experiences; it is only through the practice of truth that the great truth can be experienced . . .[55]

This describes the general role of *vijñāna* in spiritual evolution. The "*vijñāna* state" is the door to the "glimpse of the truth," but the majority of mankind is caught in the pulls of the perceptions, desires, and activities at the first three levels, which are beginning to be overcome at the *vijñāna* level (see [A]). The *Ātma-bodha*, "knowledge of Ātman," a short (68 verses) Vedāntic tract,[56] says:

> 17. [Although] being always in all, the Self does not shine (*bhā*) everywhere. It shines only in the inner intelligence (*buddhi*), as a reflection shines in clear media (like in a mirror or water).

Here *buddhi* is not just intelligence but *vijñāna*: In the course of spiritual evolution, *buddhi* may be said to flower into *vijñāna*.[57] Thus the verse says that the Ātman is only really perceived shining in the *vijñāna-maya* self (of the perceiver). This is consistent with [A] and [B] and makes the *vijñāna-maya* self of highest importance in spiritual development. These same and other authoritative statements[58] also support the status of the *vijñāna-maya* self as an independent level of manifestation of the self (different from the "self as the mind living according to the Word of the Scriptures").

Characterization of *Vijñāna* by Śaṁkara. Śaṁkara and the commentators bring out another essential aspect of *vijñāna* and the *vijñāna-maya* self, which complements and rounds out the descriptions so far. *Vijñāna* comes by faith and in turn establishes faith and trust. Hence "faith is the head" of the *vijñāna-maya* self. As *śraddhā* develops more, one becomes fixed in *ṛta*, one comes to "oneness with the divine order," and becomes fixed in *satya*: One adheres to the true without reservations, and one's self is permeated with the changeless. There comes to be certainty in one's spiritual understanding and less and less contradiction between this understanding and one's actions. Śaṁkara writes:

> [C] The self consisting of mind has been said to be the Veda-self[a] (the self consisting of the Vedic mantras). *Vijñāna* is the [deeper inner] knowledge (*buddhi*), relating to the import of the Veda, [which is] of the nature of determination (or ascertainment, *niścaya*).[b] And that [*vijñāna*], at the plane of mental effort,[c] is the nature (*dharma*) of the inner organ (*antaḥ-karaṇa*). The *vijñāna-maya* self [is] that [self] made of [such] certain *vijñāna* (spiritual consciousness which is certain of the import of Vedic mantras) [which has] become of the form of [correct] means of knowledge (*pramāṇa*).[d] For sacrifices etc. are undertaken when accompanied by *pramāṇa-vijñāna*. And the next

> verse [*TaittUp* II.5.1(1)] will declare that it is the origin of sacrifices . . .[59]

Evidently Śaṁkara regards *vijñāna* as growing naturally out of the preceding mind-influenced-by-mantras or *mano-maya* level. *Vijñāna*, he says, is not just belief in the mantras. It is the inner knowledge faculty (*buddhi*) relating to the import of the mantras, which has the nature or quality of coming to a complete ascertainment of determination (*niścayātmikā*) of that import. This characterization is at the inner level of *TaittUp* II.4.3 and is consistent with our understanding of *vijñāna* above (cf. the comments immediately preceding [C]). When one engages in mental effort, Śaṁkara adds, *vijñāna* manifests itself at the level of the *antaḥ-karaṇa*, the inner organ that decides on action good or bad. It is the *dharma*, the nature, of the inner organ. The *vijñāna-maya* self finally is the self that is aware of itself as made of such *vijñāna* and that is in its functioning and expression the embodiment (*sva-rūpa*, own-form) of true (or valid) means of knowledge, *pramāṇa*, which will take it to the highest goal. "For," Śaṁkara goes on, "sacrifice etc. are undertaken when accompanied by *pramāṇa-vijñāna* . . ." In other words, when one has to decide on performing a sacrifice, at the point when one's self or inner organ is at the level of mental decision making effort (*adhyavasāya lakṣaṇam*), the decision to perform the right sacrifice at the proper time and the correct execution of the sacrifice are indeed done with *pramāṇa-vijñāna*. As may be seen, this does not conflict with the "inner" characterization of *vijñāna* earlier, because Śaṁkara has moved away from "inner-experienced" *vijñāna* itself to the way *vijñāna* manifests at the plane of mental effort, or at the level of the *antaḥ-karaṇa*, as exemplified in properly performed sacrifice.[60]

The fact that Śaṁkara here uses the term *pramāṇa-vijñāna*, "*vijñāna* of the nature of *pramāṇa* or 'right means of knowledge'," is significant. *Vijñāna*, being of the nature of "true wisdom" (above, right before [A]), must have a *pramāṇa* element in it because it is "knowledge in the direction of true knowledge of Ātman". So by prefixing *pramāṇa* to *vijñāna*, Śaṁkara is emphasizing the charater of *vijñāna* to be in the direction of true Ātmā consciousness. It is for that very reason that *vijñāna* "spreads out" the sacrifice and also one's other actions [*TaittUp* II.5.1(1)]. The word "spreads out," *tanute*, is from the Vedic root *tan*, "to extend, spread, be diffused (as light) over, . . ., extend towards, . . . , to stretch (a cord), extend or bend (a bow), spread out, weave (from *Ṛg Veda* onwards)".[61] The expression "he (or it) spreads out the sacrifice," *yajñam tanute*, is very common in *Śatapatha Brāhmaṇa*. Typically a person who does a particular ritual action in a certain way, knowing that such and such is the inner reason for this, "spreads out the sacrifice".[62] This may have a meaning like "if he does the action this way, knowing that this is the inner reason for it, then he really spreads out the sacrifice—all its component elements—like a weave on a loom".[63] But in view of the fact that the other, non-sacrificial uses of *tan* involve only very general and continuous meanings like "extending over," "spreading" "stretching," "continuing," "increasing" and "endowing someone with something,"[64] "spreads out the sacrifice" is likely to have also an inner significance. This might be along the lines "when he does it in this way knowing such and such, the sacrifice becomes effective and, as a subtle, spreads out through the universe, has connection with the Universal Divine, promotes the world order, and produces the results desired by the sacrificer".[65] The Upaniṣad would then in effect be saying: "*Vijñāna* (in our sense and the sense of [A] and [B] above) is what *really* 'spreads out the sacrifice,' and it 'spreads out' one's (ordinary) actions in the same way. A man who does a sacrifice or any action for that matter with *vijñāna*, in other words, a man of 'true wisdom,' will automatically, by his being of the nature of true wisdom or *vijñāna*, promote his own well-being and the well-being of the world." This would be completely consistent with both our and Śaṁkara's understanding of *vijñāna* above.

According to our reading, therefore, Śaṁkara's view of *vijñāna* [C] is completely compatible with our characterization of *vijñāna* earlier. While before we emphasized the inner qualities and the resulting equanimity, Śaṁkara focuses on the certainty and trueness of the knowledge and on the way in which that expresses at the level of action. We can therefore summarize the general meaning of *vijñāna* as it has emerged so far as follows. *Vijñāna* in general is higher (i.e. spiritual) awareness or consciousness. In its beginning stages it involves deep-seated inner awareness (much of the time during the day) of higher or transcendental qualities. This leads to a transmutation of the inner consciousness, as well as gradual imperturbability and transcendence of desire (when one dies one leaves one's sins in the body, *TaittUp* II.5.1(2), also [A] above and *KaṭhaUp* I.3.3-9, to be discussed shortly). Since it includes the awareness of having in oneself (and indeed of somehow *being*) the Transcendental or Eternal, it gives inner certitude regarding the meaning of Scripture and that one is walking the path correctly. It gives correct attitude, knowledge and reasoning if necessary with the actions which one undertakes. (For these points see Śaṁkara [C].) Finally *vijñāna* exists naturally (though perhaps only little developed or buried) in everyone. But even more than in the case of the *prāṇa-maya* and *mano-maya* levels, there are many levels and types of actual *vijñāna*, which collectively form the *vijñāna-maya* level of development. They are differentiated by increased *vijñāna* as indicated by increased spiritual insight and manifestation and experience of *vijñāna* states during the day, and by modes and degrees of permanent realization of oneself as *vijñāna-maya*, or consisting of *vijñāna*.

The conception of *vijñāna* just sketched emphasizes the role of *vijñāna* as a beginning stage of the arising of higher knowledge (*jñāna*) (although higher forms including aspects of *Ātma-* or *Brahma-jñāna* are not excluded, see below). This conception fits in about half a dozen of the 26 odd other occurrences of *vijñāna* in the Vedic Upaniṣads.[66] These include "This [that I have told you, Maitreyī,] is enough for *vijñāna,*" *BṛhUp* II.4.13 (K) (in the Kāṇva recension of the Yājñavalkya-Maitreyī Dialogue, and in *BṛhUp* II.4 only); "Brahman is [in the direction of] *vijñāna, ānanda*" [Yājñavalkya at *BṛhUp* III.28.1 (K)]; and an important passage in *Kaṭha Upaniṣad* (I.3.3-9). The latter gives perhaps the clearest Upaniṣadic statement of the nature of *vijñāna* and needs to be considered more fully.

***Vijñāna* in *KaṭhUp* I.3.3-9.** *KaṭhaUp* I.3.3-4 compares man to a chariot that is moving over the land. The Self, Ātman, is the Lord of the chariot who stands behind the charioteer, and the body (*śarīra*) is the chariot itself. The inner intelligence (*buddhi*) is the driver; the mind is the reins; the senses are the horses; and the sense objects are the paths over which the horses range. Then the text goes on:

I.3.5. He who is (*bhavati*) without *vijñāna* (*a-vijñāna-vān*),
with mind always unrestrained,
of him the senses [are] [out of control]
like difficult horses for the charioteer.
6. He however who is endowed with *vijñāna* (*vijñāna-vān*),
with mind always restrained,
of him the senses [are]
like good horses for the charioteer.
7. He who is without *vijñāna* (*a-vijñāna-vān*),

mindless, always impure,
He does not reach that station (*padam*)
and comes back to *saṁsāra* (the round of birth and death)
8. [But] he who is endowed with *vijñāna* (*vijñāna-vān*),
mindful, always pure,
he attains that station
from which he is not born again.
9. [He who] has *vijñāna* as charioteer,
the man who has the mind as reigns,
He reaches the end of the journey,
that highest station of Vishnu (or of the All-pervading, *Viṣṇu*).[67]

The text contrasts the person that is endowed with *vijñāna* (*vijñāna-vat*), and has mind and senses disciplined and under control, with one that is without *vijñāna* (who is *a-vijñāna-vat*), and is at the mercy of the vagaries of his mind and the demands of his senses. This illustrates perfectly the nature of *vijñāna* in its initial stages as described in *TaittUp* II.4.3. It is *vijñāna* or deep-seated inner awareness of something of the Infinite, deep-seated inner Infinite-consciousness, which leads and enables the individual to live his life with senses, mind and passions held in control (v. 6); without this, senses and mind will become a plaything of the forces that one is subjected to in life (v. 5). And it is such *vijñāna* or deep-seated higher awareness, different from the perceptions of Divinity in the initial phases of the *vidyās* in the last chapter, that ultimately enables the individual to transcend rebirth (vs. 8-9). These points lead naturally to the overall characterization of *vijñāna* in [A].

7. Higher Levels of *Vijñāna:* Forms of *Vijñāna*

A Broad Range of *Vijñāna*. *KaṭhaUp* I.3.8-9 as well as Sai Baba's comments [A] in sec. 6 suggest that *vijñāna*, beginning with stages such as described above, evolves naturally and in a continuous fashion into highest levels and states of knowledge or realization of Ātman/ Brahman. This is precisely what is found in the middle and later Upaniṣads. Thus *MuṇḍUp* I.2.12 says that the Uncreated, *a-kṛta*, can not be gotten by doing something (by deed, *kṛta*); "(hence) for the sake of that *vijñāna* (i.e. of that 'uncreated-*vijñāna*')" one should approach a teacher (*guru*). And *Maitrāyaṇīya Upaniṣad* speaks of *vijñāna* that has the character of non-duality (*advaitī-bhūta vijñāna*, "*vijñāna* that has become [a] non-dual [seer]," *MaitrUp* VI.7), and of difference-less *vijñāna* (*a-viśeṣa vijñāna, MaitrUp* VI.24). Since these passages are likely to be considerably later than *Taittirīya* and *Bṛhadāraṇyaka Upaniṣads* and their authors may be assumed to be quite familiar with the latter, they may be regarded as representing the way in which the *Taittirīya* and *Bṛhadāraṇyaka Upaniṣads' vijñāna* was interpreted in the last phases of the Vedic Upaniṣadic Tradition. This does not necessarily represent the original meaning of *vijñāna* in the sense of *Taittirīya* and *Bṛhadāraṇyaka Upaniṣads*, but it is reasonable to assume it does. It might be noted that similar high-level uses of *vijñāna* are also found later in some of the great classical Advaitic teachers and modern spiritual figures. Thus we have "Although [there is] appearance of having an origin, appearance of movement, appearance of being an object, [yet] there is [only] non-dual (*advaya*), quiescent *vijñāna*, unoriginated, not moving, not having the quality of an object," *Gauḍapādīya Kārikās* IV.45.[68] Or again, "*Vijñāna* is that tranquil state of existence-consciousness which is experienced by the aspirant and which is like the waveless ocean or the motionless ether," Sri Ramana Maharshi.[69] Such examples could be multiplied.[70] We find therefore that, in harmony with sec. 6 [A], there is in the Upaniṣads and later tradition a consistent pattern of using *vijñāna* as covering a wide range of *jñāna*-consciousness, from beginning level "deep-seated inner awareness" (our characterization of the *vijñāna* in *TaittUp* II.4.3 in sec. 6) to (varieties of) near-highest Ātman- or Brahman-consciousness.[71] On the one hand Yājñavalkya is telling Maitreyī "this much (i.e. what I have said) is enough for *vijñāna*," and on the other hand we have [*akṛta*]—*vijñāna, MuṇḍUp* I.2.12 etc. Such a broad yet unitary understanding of *vijñāna* is deeply impressive.

***Vijñāna* a State of Consciousness or Knowledge**. But that is not all. *Vijñāna* in this fundamental sense is also almost always treated as a form of consciousness or as a knowledge state, not as consciousness or knowledge "of" something. Looking over the usage of *vijñāna* in the sense of "higher spiritual knowledge" elsewhere in the Upaniṣads, one is impressed by the fact that one finds almost no "*vijñāna* of" (like "knowledge of" something, with a genitive).[72] *Vijñāna* is not infrequently specialized, qualified, restricted to a specific form, but not by relating it to any kind of "knowledge content". Thus we have e.g. "non-dual *vijñāna*" (*advaitī-bhūta vijñāna*) and "non-difference *vijñāna*" (*a-viśeṣa-vijñāna*) (in *MaitrUp* VI.7 and VI.24, resp.), and *vedānta-vijñāna*, "the *vijñāna* described and realized in Vedānta" (*MuṇḍUp* III.2.6). In all these cases the accompanying adjectives or nouns function to qualify, restrict, or specialize—they do not add a knowledge object. Thus, *vijñāna* is treated as a type of state of consciousness, or a spiritual level or stage (a "level of consciousness"), not as a state of knowledge "of" something, or a state of knowing something, where the "something" is a knowledge-object or content. In this connection also, *MuṇḍUp* I.2.12, which was mentioned earlier, is instructive. The text says that "the Uncreated, *a-kṛta*, is not [obtained] by action (*kṛta*)"; hence, "for the sake of that *vijñāna*," one should approach a teacher (*guru*), and so on. It does not say "for the sake of *vijñāna of* that (Uncreated)," but instead treats the Uncreated itself as a type of consciousness or being. That consciousness is the *vijñāna* for the sake of which one approaches a *guru*. This powerful way of speaking is intensified by the terse "the uncreated is not (*na asti*) by action" (rather than "is not obtained by action", "is not attained by action" etc.).

So after *TaittUp* II, *vijñāna* in the higher sense is virtually always treated as a state (or type or stage) of consciousness, or of being, not qualified by reference to some content of consciousness or object of knowledge. *MuṇḍUp* III.2.6 also illustrates that this "state" is not distinguished from the higher reality that is being taught. "*Vijñāna* [of the Uncreated]" is the "state" when the Uncreated "is" (*asti*). Naturally that is not attained by action, but by approaching and being blessed by a teacher (*guru*). Again it is reasonable to assume that these kinds of understandings are already implicit in the *vijñāna* of *TaittUp* II.4 also. So for practical purposes we may and will speak of "*vijñāna of* something" for convenience. But we must always remember that *vijñāna* is a state (or a species or a stage) of consciousness, or may even be the Reality itself. It is not further analysable in terms of relationships to some content of consciousness or object of knowledge.

What Makes *Vijñāna Vijñāna*. Finally, as in the case of transcendence of desire, it is the fact of *vijñāna, vijñāna* itself, which tells the devotee of Ātman/Brahman that so many different levels and forms of *vijñāna* are all *vijñāna*. *Vijñāna* has a nature which makes it able to be present in any personality, mind, and constellation of circumstances. Although it has perhaps few distinctive objective qualities, it has a flavor, an essence—a *rasa*—which enables it to be recognized in every person, form, and situation. This flavor, this *rasa*, is deeper, fuller, than the flavor of transcendence of desire which was discussed in similar terms in chr. 2.3. Indeed, *vijñāna* in some sense includes transcendence of desire. The flavor of "beyond desire" is a symptom, a sign of *vijñāna*.

8. *Vijñāna* and Ordinary Knowledge and Understanding

Before we turn to the topic of how *vijñāna*, although always *vijñāna*, nevertheless assumes various more specific forms which could be called "*vijñāna* of" something, we have to discuss an important point that has major implications later. This is the fact that there is an inner connection between *vijñāna* in the general sense of the two preceding sections and ordinary knowledge and understanding. In the Saints of all religions, great Spiritual Wisdom typically occurs combined with unusual insight and knowledge relating to the world. The latter might include an immediate and effortless intuitive grasp of the essence of people's personality and character or of social situations, or great scholarly acumen, or even various forms of omniscience. (A few of the greatest Upaniṣadic *vidyās* teach levels of realization that include as possible by-products, perhaps limited-forms of omniscience, see chr. 6.14). Philosophically this raises the question that both *vijñāna* in the sense of secs. 6-7 and ordinary knowledge and understanding, such as is found in ordinary life and the sciences, have a common substrate or source. In this section our aim is primarily to identify some of the pieces of this whole problem complex; further discussion will then be found in chr. 6.14.

***Vijñāna* Both as Ordinary Understanding and Higher Spiritual Awareness.** A good starting point is the fact noted earlier that in a number of cases in the old Upaniṣads, *vijñāna* refers to knowledge or understanding in the ordinary sense.[73] In two of these, "ordinary *vijñāna*" is found side by side with *vijñāna* in the sense of *TaittUp* II. The first is *BṛhUp* II.1.17. There king Ajātaśatru of Benares, referring to a man whom he has just woken up from sleep, says: "When this one (this man) was asleep thus, then this person who consists of *vijñāna*, having by his *vijñāna* taken to himself (*ādāya*) the *vijñāna* of these senses, rests in [that place] which is this space within the heart (*antarhṛdaya ākāśa*) . . ." Here the "*vijñāna* of the senses" refers to the intelligence and knowledge-consciousness inherent in the senses when they function in the normal way as instruments of knowledge in the waking state. In other words, the *vijñāna* of the senses is ordinary "conscious knowing"—seeing a tree and knowing that it is a tree, etc. But in addition to this "ordinary" *vijñāna*, the passage also mentions another kind of *vijñāna*: viz. the *vijñāna* by means of which in deep sleep a person takes the sense-consciousness *vijñāna* to him/herself and rests in the space of the heart. Since the *vijñāna-maya puruṣa* in *BṛhUp* II.1.17 is likely to mean the same as the *ātmā vijñāna-maya* in *TaittUp* II.4.3, the "self when it appears as *vijñāna*," the higher *vijñāna* referred to in *BṛhUp* II.1.17 is the same as the *vijñāna* in *TaittUp* II.4.3.

The second example where ordinary and "higher" *vijñāna* occur in one and the same text is found in the *Bhūma Vidyā, ChāndUp* VII. In *ChāndUp* VII.7.1 ff., *vijñāna* occurs as the seventh member of a long series of things each greater than the one before, and each enjoined to be worshipped etc. (*upās-*) as Brahman. It is greater than "deep thought," *dhyāna*. By *vijñāna* one understands the Vedas, all the worldly arts and sciences such as grammar, logic, ethics and politics, and snake charming, "as well as heaven, earth, wind, space, the waters, *tejas* (brilliance), gods, men, animals, and birds, grass, trees, animals and [what is] worms, flies and ants, *dharma* (conduct according to one's duty) and non-*dharma*, the true and the false, the good and the not-good, [that which] gladdens the heart and [that which does] not, food and taste and this world and the next. [All this] one knows (*vi + jñā-*) by *vijñāna*. Worship (*upās-*) *vijñāna* [as Brahman]" (*ChāndUp* VII.7.1). Here *vijñāna* means "understanding" in the usual sense, including "understanding of things," "knowledge how," and also some spiritual understanding. But then this *vijñāna* is superseded by something greater, Strength (*bala*), which is the eighth member of the series. "For one man endowed with strength causes a hundred men endowed with *vijñāna* (*vijñānavat*) to tremble. . ." (*ChāndUp* VII.8.1). The series goes on in this way up to the 15th entity, *Prāṇa*, "Life". Thereafter, it continues with successively still more fundamental aspects: *satya*, truth (16th), *vijñāna* (17th), *mati*, "deep thinking" (18th) *śraddhā*, faith (19th), and so on, until the pinnacle is reached with *Bhūman*, "the Vast" as 23rd. There is no question that the second *vijñāna* in the 17th position denotes something much deeper, or higher level, than that in position 7. Indeed, the mention of *satya* and *śraddhā* in 16th and 19th position suggests that we may well be in the general area of *TaittUp* II.4.3, which names *satya* and *śraddhā* as the wings/arms of the *vijñāna-maya* self. *ChāndUp* VII as a whole, therefore, clearly countenances two kinds of *vijñāna: vijñāna* as ordinary understanding (in a very comprehensive sense), and *vijñāna* as a state of higher spiritual awareness and knowlege.

Inner Connection Between Ordinary and Higher *Vijñāna*. Clearly there must be an inner connection between ordinary and higher *vijñāna* which led to the use of *vijñāna* for the latter in the first place. By the time of *Maitrāyaṇīya Upaniṣad*, this connection becomes explicit:

> VI.7. ... "Now [there] where knowledge *(vijñāna)* is of a dual character (*dvaitī-bhūta*), there indeed one hears, sees, smells, tastes and touches even. [In these cases] the Self knows (*jñā*) [these things]." [But there] where knowledge (*vijñāna*) is of a non-dual character (*advaitī-bhūta*), devoid of effort, cause, [and] action, unspeakable, incomparable, indescribable—what [is that]? That is beyond speech.
>
> VI.24. ... Meditative awareness (*dhyāna*) rests in the highest aspect
> (*pare tattve*) within and in the objects [outside].
> Hence the differences-less knowledge (*aviśeṣavijñāna*)
> becomes [knowledge characterized by] difference
> (*viśeṣa*).

In VI.7, the starting-point is ordinary knowledge, ordinary consciousness: "In knowledge (or consciousness) where there is separation between the knower and the known, it is really the Ātmā that knows." But then the text goes on to describe a higher state or condition—"*vijñāna* of a non-dual character"—which presumably is something close to "feeling being Ātman/Brahman". As a by-product, *vijñāna* emerges as a fundamental term common to both. In VI.24 on the other hand, non-dual consciousness is primary and forms the starting-point. It becomes (*bhavati*) ordinary consciousness characterized by "consciousness of differences". Again *vijñāna* is the fundamental term common to both states. But here there is a second fundamental term: *dhyāna*, here perhaps "thought" or "meditative awareness". Both passages imply that "really" there is only one kind of *vijñāna*, and that what makes the *vijñāna* of *Taittirīya Upaniṣad* appear as a different, higher phenomenon is only the fallen condition of man.[74] In any case, as the hold of ego in one gets gradually lessened, there arise not only levels of *vijñāna* (deep-seated inner awareness in the direction of the Infinite Self as in sec. 6, developing into *Ātma-jñāna*), but at the same time one's objective knowledge becomes clearer, deeper, surer, and one intuitively hits the mark better. Sai Baba explains that these are both manifestations of the functioning of the *vijñāna-maya kośa*:

> [A] The *vijñāna-maya kośa* has the function of enabling man to get the discriminatory power by which he distinguishes between good and bad. [It] enables us to learn the nature of matter and how matter functions. We shall here give an example by which we will understand the inner meaning. This is a table and is made of wood. I am making an attempt to hit on this hard matter. When I describe this act of mine, I say that I have hit the table with my hand. This is not a full description. The table has also hit my hand equally strongly. The quality in you, which enables you to recognize the conduct of the table in this act, is the *vijñāna-maya kośa*. This *vijñāna-maya kośa* enables us to recognize whatever reactions and resounds exist in all the material world. We can take another example for this. When we open our eyes and look at the external view, we see so many people and so many heads [in this hall]. We ask if it is the eye which enables us to see all this or whether it is the light in the eyes that enables us to see all the heads? If we regard that the external light is important, by closing our eyes we cannot see the matter. If we regard that the light in our eyes is important, if we extinguish the external light, we cannot see the matter. It is only when both are present that we can see the form of man. In this manner, the inner vision and the outer vision are together responsible for our vision. This is the function of the *vijñāna-maya kośa*. Truly, if we are perceiving all the creation with our eyes, this creation is being seen because of our eyes. There is no creation separate from our eyes. What we see in the world are all reflections of the forms that are formed inside by our own inner vision. If an artist is painting a picture, he is not painting the picture straightaway on the canvas. He first forms this picture in his mind and then he puts in on the canvas with paint. If a director of a cinema directs various actors to do this and to do that, he takes the preliminary steps by which he thinks of this picture in his own mind and then brings

> the actors into the picture. Similarly, every writer thinks of the theme in his own mind before he writes and then begins to write out the play. So, these thoughts and ideas, which emanate from within oneself, have been called *vijñāna*.[75]

These are unusually specific and profound statements. In the example of the hand hitting the table, the insight that the table is hitting the hand equally strongly is celebrated in the West as Newton's third law of motion, and is a corner stone of physical theory. The generalization, "the *vijñāna-maya* sheath enables us to recognize whatever reactions and resounds exist in all the material world," suggests insight into any type of interaction involving energy; this may even include the repercussions and implications which an action has at the karmic level. In the second example, it is the irreducible element that includes both what comes in through the eyes and the meaning which we give it, the understanding we have, in an indivisible oneness, that indicates *vijñāna*. This irreducible element is actually an aspect of *Cit* (which, as an aspect of Brahman, similarly is a single element that underlies the internal, subjective and the external, objective worlds). It can be to some extent felt as an aspect of self because *I* have this taken-for-granted understanding of what I see. *I* am the meaning of what I see and of what I am seeing both.

9. The "Invisible, Center-less, Un-defined, Non-based"

Vijñāna in the sense of higher awareness or consciousness or knowledge, or emerging or fully established *jñāna* consciousness, as in secs. 6-7, only describes *vijñāna* in general as a general quality or level, and only helps getting a general idea of what it might mean to know one's self as *vijñāna-maya*, as being made of *vijñāna* or being *vijñāna*. For so far the *vidyā* has not given any specific example of what *it* would consider higher level *vijñāna*. In this section we focus on the "Invisible, Self-less (or Center-less), Undefined, Non-based" mentioned in *TaittUp* II.7.2, which, as a state or level of consciousness or being, is "space-bliss". This state or level of being is *vijñāna* in our sense in secs. 6-7, and our aim in the rest of this section is to get an idea of this *vijñāna* and its relation to the rest of the *vidyā*. In sec. 10 we then argue that probably this state or level of being is also *vijñāna* in the sense the *vidyā* (i.e. in the sense of *TaittUp* II.4.3).

The "Invisible, Center-less, Un-defined, Non-based". "For indeed as soon as he finds in this In-visible (*a-dṛśya*), Self-less (or Centerless, *an-ātmya*), Un-defined (*a-nirukta*), Non-based (*a-nilayana*) Fearlessness as his foundation . . ." says the text. Obviously this speaks from direct knowledge. If a person speaks like this, he/she is often feeling, or aware of, what he/she is talking about (the Invisible, and having Fearlessness as a foundation in it); or perhaps he/she is very familiar with the topic (the Invisible), and not feeling it strongly at the moment, but he/she is bringing it up in order to make a point (the point about fearlessness). For the statements on fearlessness are direct spiritual instruction. In addition, in such a situation (i.e. when giving spiritual instruction) the teacher is also assuming that the students can identify some of the things he is talking about in their own experience, and that they can benefit from what he says. He is therefore automatically (if not feeling, at least:) engaged in the meaning of what he is saying—in a realistic situation he would be ready for questions, etc.

So when the teacher begins to speak about "this Invisible, Centerless . . .," he is speaking from direct knowledge. But we can go a little further. The term *adṛśya*, "not visible, not seen, unobserved" occurs here for the first time.[76] So does *an-ātmya*, "having no specific intrinsic nature,"[77] and *a-nilayana*, "without [an own] dwelling-place, home, resting place".[78] Only *a-nirukta*, "not explicitly of distinctly expressed or indicated," occurs in the Brāhmaṇas, where it "plays a most important part in the thought inspiring these texts".[79] "The very term points to something which may be found only beyond *ukta* [*nirukta* = beyond, *nir*, what can be expressed, uttered, *ukta*], beyond those narrow boundaries which are those of intelligible speech, of the exact representation circumscribed by the word."[80] To find a combination of three completely new negatives and a traditional term that broadly points to what is inexpressible, altogether describing what is ostensibly a spiritual state, is most unusual in this literature. The sentence looks very much like a deliberate effort by a teacher to describe some qualitatively specific things that he wants his students to identify in their own experience. Can we identify these things more precisely? Indeed, "the Invisible, Centerless, . . ." does appear to refer to something that gradually arises when one tries to live according to highest *jñāna* principles such as not identifying with anything as relating to self (which is very definitely but only "secretly" taught in Part I with the teaching of the five selves), and more generally *neti, neti*, "'[this is] not [self],' '[this is] not [self]'". In other words, "the Invisible, Centerless . . ." refers to a rather specific kind of higher "Experiential" or "knowledge/Being" that arises when one lives according to *jñāna* principles of this type. More generally our thesis will be that the *vidyā* has the "Invisible, Centerless, . . ." as its main focus. In fact this "Invisible," which is "space-bliss" or "bliss everywhere," is the near-culmination of the path of "developing knowledge of and at the same time transcending all the five selves" in Part I. The *vidyā's* highest instruction is not to make a gap in this (yoga of the) Invisible, and find Fearlessness in it as foundation.

For why are these five selves described in the first place? In our study of the text so far, we saw that *every* self or level was treated in a positive manner, from a larger perspective. Beginning with the *prāṇa-maya* level, awareness of a given level as a semi-independent level of self, development of perception at that level, and proper attitudes and *upāsanā* at that level were all presented as each in some way beneficial and leading to spiritual progress. For all these activities help to some degree to transcend the narrow identification of oneself as a physical individual, to expand, to develop a broader, more universal outlook and become less self-centered. So in setting forth these levels, the *vidyā* brings out various inner potentialities that are in any human being. But apart from this, one cannot help but sense a still further element also. This is that the five selves are presented so as to engender in one a realization that actually, one has to turn away from any kind of conception of what oneself is. Although one must abide in inner discipline (*yoga, TaittUp* II.4.3), one must cease to try to attain a particular kind of self (or Self). Within each level or self there is a another deeper, more fundamental one, but each one, except the *ānanda-maya* one, has to be abandoned. And even the *ānanda-maya* self is not the end. When one apprehends the Invisible, Centerless which is "bliss everywhere," no doubt *ānanda-maya* stages have been reached. But even then there is the instruction: "Don't make a gap, an interval in the (yoga of the state of) 'the Invisible' etc. with its 'bliss everywhere'. Only if there is no such gap, can true gone-to-fearlessness arise. Normally one always makes such gaps, one is still subject to fear, and one's knowledge at this stage is still largely delusory. One thinks that one has glimpses, one thinks one has *vijñāna* and *ānanda*, but these are not the real thing." So while the *vidyā* is teaching to develop various higher potentialities in oneself, it is also subtly suggesting that ultimately, all that has to be turned away from, or let go of. One has to go beyond any conception of what oneself or the Self is and simply inhere in the state of "the Invisible" which is "space-bliss". This state is the highest state, and Brahman is only truly fully attained by "finding fearlessness as foundation" in that state. The *vidyā's* highest teaching is to inhere in that state of 'space-bliss' cum 'Invisible, Centerless, Non-based," not to make gaps in it, and to find in it fearlessness as a foundation.

The "Invisible . . ." and *Neti, Neti*. Now textual considerations suggest that this "Invisible" which is "space-bliss" is associated with *neti, neti* (chr. 2.5) and that it thus corresponds to a stage that arises on the path of *neti, neti*. For "the Invisible" represents a description of Brahman in negative terms, and may therefore be compared with other descriptions of this kind. When this is done (Table 5.1), inspection shows that of the five basic passages, four (all except the first) are associated with *neti, neti*. (And even the first occurs in the same dialogue as the second, and might therefore have to be read in the light of that.) All four *neti, neti* passages are followed by the same formula "[The Self] is ungraspable, . . ., it is not injured." (Thus really there are altogether only three descriptions of Brahman in negative

TABLE 5.1
Negatively Described Brahman

BṛhUp III.8.8-9 (also *MuṇḍUp* I.1.6-7)	That . . ., Gārgi, they call the Imperishable (*Akṣara*). It is	
	a-sthūla,	not gross,
	an-aṇu,	not fine,
	a-hrasva,	not short,
	a-dhīrga,	not long,
	a-saṅga,	not attached,
	a-rasa,	without taste,
	a-gandha,	without smell,
	a-manas,	without mind,
	a-mātra,	without measure,
	an-antara,	without inside,
	a-bāhya,	without outside.
	At the command of that Imperishable, Gārgi, Sun and Moon [the two] stand in their positions,. . . Heaven and Earth stand in position . . .	

BṛhUp III.9.26 (K)	This Self is "not," "not" (*neti, neti*). It is *a-gṛhya*, un-graspable, *a-śīrya*, in-destructible, *a-saṅga*, un-attached, *a-sita*, un-fettered, it does not suffer, it is not injured. These are the eight abodes, the eight worlds, the eight gods, the eight persons (taught earlier). He who, having taken apart and put together these persons, rises beyond, Him I ask you about [as] the Upaniṣadic puruṣa. . .
BṛhUp IV.2.4 (K)	This Self is "not, not" (*neti, neti*). It is ungraspable... (as in *BṛhUp* III.9.26, up to ". . . it is not injured"). Verily, Janaka, you have attained fearlessness ...
BṛhUp IV.4.22 (K)	They (=the ancient sages), having risen above the desire for sons and the desire for wealth and the desire for worlds, walk the path of mendicancy . . . This Self [is] "not, not". It is ungraspable . . . (as in *BṛhUp* III.9.26, up to ". . . it is not injured"). Him [who knows this] these two [feelings] do not overcome: "Now, I have done evil," "Now, I have done the auspicious." Truly he overcomes both of these. Something done and something not done does not burn (affect) him.
BṛhUp IV.5.15 (K)	But where everything has become his (= one's) self, then by what should one see what? Then by what should one smell what? . . . Then by what should one know (*vijñā-*) what? By whom all this is known, by what should one know him? This Self [is] "not," "not". It is ungraspable) as in *BṛhUp* III.9.26, up to ". . . it is not injured"). Indeed by what should one know (*vijñā-*) the [one] knower (*vijñātṛ*)?

terms, viz. *BṛhUp* III.8.8-9, the four *neti, neti* passages, and *TaittUp* II.7.2.) And second, even more astonishing, three of the five passages in Table 5.1 contain elements that have clear analogues in *TaittUp* II:

- in *BṛhUp* III.8.8-9, "at the command of that Imperishable, . . ., Sun and Moon stand in their positions," vs. "Through fear of him the Wind blows," *TaittUp* II.8.1;
- in *BṛhUp* IV.2.4 (K), "Janaka, you have attained fearlessness," vs. "fearlessness" in *TaittUp* II.7.2;
- in *BṛhUp* IV.4.22 (K), "him these two [feelings] do not overcome: 'Now, I have done evil,'" vs. "him the thought does not torment: 'Why have I not done the good? Why have I done evil? "' in *TaittUp* 9.2.

In view of all this, it is at least not unreasonable to think that "the Invisible . . ." in *TaittUp* II.7.2 is similar to the Self which is *neti, neti* and "not graspable," etc. (the last four passages in the Table) and that it also describes the Imperishable that is "not gross," etc. (the first passage). And since the latter states or states of knowledge would normally arise only in the course of some kind of inner practice or spiritual life involving turning away from all conceptions of the Reality (as in the first passage), or saying no to anything that might be Self (*neti, neti*), similar inner practice may be implicit in the state of the "Invisible . . ." Note finally that the "Invisible . . ." is described in "experiential" terms. The lists "not gross, . . ." and "ungraspable, . . ." in Table 5.1, on the other hand, are constructed in part with other literary or philosophical aims in mind (although experiential nuances are present also).

The Nature of the Invisible, Center-less, Un-defined, Non-based. We have argued that the "Invisible, Center-less, Un-defined, Non-based" with its *ānanda* corresponds to a near final stage that comes under the heading of the *ānanda-maya* level in the sequence of five levels taught in Part I. To get an idea of how the all-pervasive Infinite is "centerless" and "non-based," we draw on some comments by Sri Sathya Sai Baba. Sai Baba is discussing knowledge of *asti, bhāti, priya*, here taken as equivalent to realization of Brahman. At a certain point, he becomes extraordinarily expansive. He refers to the "one and the same thing" denoted by *asti, bhāti, priya* (cf. chr. 3.11) as the "Full," the "Essence of the Absolute," and finally simply as "Divinity". This Divinity, he implies, may be described as being "non-based," "un-defined".

> In this world all that we see is characterized by different names and forms. These could be changing. But the underlying truth in them, the characteristics of the spirit do not change. These three, "Being, Awareness, Delight" [*asti, bhāti, priya*, "Divine Attributes that can be found in everything"] are changeless, and due to them we must recognize the changeless in the changing. But then, how can this (= all this that we see around us) be full (*pūrṇam*)? . . . You go to a store and purchase one kilogram of molasses. This quantity tastes sweet. We now take a small piece and stir it into a cup of coffee. That small piece is also sweet. The remaining portion is also sweet. Its sweetness has not changed.

So is the true nature of that which does not change, that which is full. The yardstick by which you may judge or measure, or the name and form, may undergo change. You could talk of a kilogram or of a tonne, but its inherent characteristics are the same. That nature which is full at all times, which does not suffer any shortcoming or shortage is a full entity. You cannot possibly come across any period of time when there will be a shortage of this full entity. The entire creation is replete with the essence of the Absolute. To say that this is full of Essence of the Absolute and that is not, is not possible. You cannot say that this is Truth and that is not, it is not possible. You cannot say that this is Truth and that is untruth. Neither can you say that this changes while that is changeless. It is not possible for anyone to detail these matters. You could possibly base your judgments on your external senses and perception, but you cannot stand judgment on that which is Divinity Itself. So, we must try to understand what is truly Divine and what is His [the Ātmā's] nature. We cannot say: 'these are the attributes of Divinity, these behaviors or attributes are those of Divinity'. All names and forms are Divinity. Nobody has the right to talk of Divinity while differentiating. If you make an attempt to understand and unravel Divinity, it is foolish. All that pervades in the form of diverse forms of life, all that exists in all the inert materials is Divinity and nothing but Divinity.[81]

This passage is moving and gives a glimpse. Sai Baba says that in the context of an enterprise like Science, which has empirical and sensory-level aims, one might be able to "base" one's judgment on "one's external senses and perceptions," but "you cannot stand judgment on (i.e. make judgments on the basis of or about) that which is Divinity itself." Divinity cannot be defined by saying "these are the attributes or behavior of Divinity". In the realm of Divinity, or better, in Divinity, one cannot define by characteristics and differentiate. Thus Sai Baba is describing what he is here calling "Divinity" as non-based, un-defined, not explicitly indicateable, *a-nilayanam, a-niruktam*. The passage gives not only a glimpse of the *an-ātmyam, a-niruktam, a-nilayanam* of *TaittUp* II.7.2, it also describes the general character of Universal Divinity.

10. "*Vijñāna* of" the "Invisible . . ." The Essence of the *Vidyā* as a Whole

In the last section we focussed on the "state" of "the Invisible . . ." with its "space-bliss". We argued that this state was the state taught by the *vidyā* and that it represented knowledge of Ātman/Brahman which arises in the path of rejecting any conceptions of Brahman or of self, on the path of *neti, neti*. We now look at the *vidyā* as a whole and argue that the dynamics of the flow of discourse in Part II implies that "the Invisible, Centerless, . . ." represents a form of *vijñāna in the sense of the vidyā,* i.e. in the sense of *TaittUp* II.4.3. In fact it is the highest *vijñāna* which in the view of the *vidyā* should emerge from the traditional wisdom which the teacher summarises immediately before (in *TaittUp* II.6.4).

By the end of Part I, the teacher has explained the five selves. He has described their nature as semi-independent selves and the type of awareness and perception that is associated with them. He has shown how each fits into a larger spiritual context, how it arises, how it is nourished, and what its value is. But he has not said anything about the role or function of this set of five selves as a whole. Thus there is somewhat of an expectation that the important thing, the real meaning of all this, the really big wisdom, is still to come. What is more natural, therefore, than to assume that at this point, when the teaching of the five selves is finished, the teacher freely and expansively begins to speak from the high levels which he has outlined—that he starts to speak from the (levels of) *vijñāna* and *ānanda* which he has just described? By doing so he would be illustrating the nature of these selves in front of the students' eyes (here we have to imagine how an enlightened teacher might teach). And what would be more natural for him in this kind of informal but yet not purposeless discourse than to take the opportunity and point out what he sees as the crucial element in the whole enterprise? Precisely this is what happens when he talks about "the Invisible. . ." in *TaittUp* II.7.2, and similar motivations may be seen also in other sub-units of Part II.

The teacher begins by mentioning a number of traditional wisdom-teachings and bringing them all under one heading. "He, Prajāpati/Brahman/Ātman, created, entered and became all there is" (II 6.4). This creation account is reminiscent of *AitUp* I, so "He" = Ātman/Brahman. But the examples that follow (*sat* and *tyad*, etc.) all have different character and status. The very fact that they represent a diversity of dimensions (polarities) suggests that they are not intended to elaborate a single dichotomy or theme, but are meant to call to mind and circumscribe the entire landscape of traditional wisdom.[82] In particular the final *satyam* is not just "the True, the Real". It is "a word symbol summing up the entire universe, created and uncreated,"[83] or physical-mental and spiritual-transcendental.

The following verse II.7.1 plays a transitional role. It expands the grand synthesis of II.6.4 and at the same time serves as a lead-in to II.7.2. Recalling *AirUp* I 2.3 (*sukṛta*), it sets up a sequence *asat* ⟶ *sat* ⟶ *akuruta* (or *asat* ⟶ *akuruta*) ⟶ *ātman* = *sukṛta* (resonates with *svayam akuruta*) which then = *rasa* in II.7.2. But the intended meaning is uncertain; there are at least half a dozen different readings and interpretations.[84] The immediately following II.7.2, however, is very clear. As suggested above, the teacher lets himself speak freely from high level *vijñāna* and *ānanda*. The fact that the relatively dry summary of traditional widom in II.6.4 is followed by such extraordinary high-level and inspired statements suggests that II.7.2 is meant to express the climax of this traditional wisdom—its essence or highest state. This is the state of the "Invisible, Centerless . . .," which represents a level of knowledge of Ātman/Brahman. "Finding fearlessness" there as the foundation is then the same as "merging into Brahman". So in II.7.2 the *vidyā* goes beyond the *vijñāna-ānanda* scheme, and thus beyond the whole teaching of the five selves in Part I, and points to something "beyond (*vijñāna* and) *ānanda*".

The instruction given for this "beyond *ānanda*" level, "finding fearlessness as a foundation" in the Invisible and "not making any gap [in the true state of Brahman]," is the highest instruction and automatically puts the five selves in proper perspective. Trying to become one particular kind of self, to develop that view of self, that level of consciousness and being, all these are limited things compared to finding, in the Brahman which one is feeling, fearlessness as the foundation. It is the latter, and thus absolute given-ness or commitment to the Infinite Supreme Divine, which is the central element of the whole enterprise, and not any kind of self-development. The *vidyā* no doubt teaches an unfolding of two higher selves or levels of being, and a firm understanding of the natures and roles of all five of them from a larger perspective, but ultimately, the five selves or levels have to be let go of and turned away from, so that Truth may become permanently one's true state. No wonder that the instruction to fearlessness in the "Invisible" is textually related to *neti,*

neti and the theme of the One Seer (cf. above, Table 5.1 ff.). The central inner teaching of the *vidyā* is that of a path of non-identification with anything, non-holding to anything, a path of negation. On that path, when it is walked correctly and with absolute givenness and commitment, there comes knowledge of Brahman (awareness of the all-pervasive, Centerless and Non-based) and ultimately merger into Brahman ("fearlessness"). But that path should be walked in the context of the wisdom and the higher and highest teachings of the tradition. The teaching of the five selves is given both as showing various forms of wisdom and as a rough perspective and yardstick on the whole realm of spiritual experience one encounters in the process.

In the same spirit we also have to understand the following statement on bliss, *ānanda*, [D]. Although presented in a controlled, "objective" fashion (Western students have called the passage a "calculus of bliss"), its very tone and format suggest absolute imperturbability and highest realization. There is no suggestion that the levels of bliss mentioned "should" be attained, or form regular stages in a path. But there is the clear statement that bliss of various kinds will arise if the path is walked correctly, and that "bliss of Brahman" will be "experienced" when the goal is reached.

11. Different *Vijñāna Vidyās* that Teach Different Kinds of *Vijñāna*

Different *Vijñāna Vidyās*. The fact that we can speak of "*vijñāna* of the 'Invisible, Center-less, Un-defined, Non-based'" suggests the possibility that other "higher knowledges" taught in the old Upaniṣads might also have been regarded by the Upaniṣadic seers and redactors as *vijñāna*, or as exemplifying the *vijñāna-maya* level. This appears to be the case. There are a number of texts in *Bṛhadāraṇyaka Upaniṣad* and *Chāndogya Upaniṣad* which are tied to *vijñāna*, or to the *vijñāna-maya* self, either directly (the teaching talks about *vijñāna*, or the *vijñāna-maya puruṣa*), or circumstantially (see Table 5.2). All of these are independent teachings that can stand on their own. But because of textual relationships and for other reasons, they appear to be almost consciously using the *Taittirīya's* understanding of *vijñāna* and the *vijñāna-maya* self. As a result, it looks very much as if there is in the old Upaniṣads a shared understanding of *vijñāna* and of perception of and being at the *vijñāna-maya* level. In terms of "content," these "*vijñāna vidyās*" cover a considerable range: knowledge or awareness (*vijñāna*) of the *vijñāna-maya* self within the heart being the light of knowing or awareness, of the self in the heart being smaller than a mustard seed and larger than space, and of the "space within the heart" which contains all things and is the Self; knowledge of the spiritual heart, and of that being all there is; knowledge that all objective manifestations, or *sat-yam* (esoterically "the true") is *Prāṇa,* and that the Self is "the Truth of that True;" and others. These "knowledges" may therefore be said to form different manifestations and types of *vijñāna* (different "*vijñāna* of" -s, sec. 7), or to exemplify different forms of *vijñāna* in the *vijñāna-maya* self. Note that several of these *vijñānas* are at cosmic levels, implying knowledge of Creation, awareness of omniscience, or forms of omniscience.

TABLE 5.2
Important Texts Associated with *TaittUp* II.4.3, *Vijñāna*

1. *BṛhUp* V.1-6 (K), including Heart and *Satya Brahman Vidyās*
2. *Dahara Vidyā, ChāndUp* VIII.1-6
3. *BṛhUp* IV.2
4. *ŚatBr* X.4.1 (ŚatBr version of *Śāṇḍilya Vidyā*)
5. *Śāṇḍilya Vidyā, ChāndUp* VIII.14
6. *BṛhUp* VI.3.1-34 (K)
7. *BṛhUp* II.1.16-20 (K) (Ajātaśatru-Bālāki dialogue)
8. *KauṣUp* IV.19-20 (Ajātaśatru-Bālāki dialogue)
9. *BṛhUp* II.3 (K)
10. *ŚatBr* X.3.5
11. *Atharva Veda* X.7.8

Textual Indicators. The textual elements which suggest that the texts in Table 5.2 all teach different forms of *vijñāna* are summarized in Table 5.3. Typically there will be two or three specific phrases, or the same sequencing of similar elements, which suggests that two given texts are related. Thus, three of the texts in Table 5.2 use the phrase *vijñāna-maya puruṣa*, "the entity made of *vijñāna*," or *ātmā vijñāna-maya*, the *vijñāna* self. Two of them say that the *vijñāna-maya* entity or self is in the space within the heart, the third, that it is the light within the heart. It is reasonable to suppose that the self-knowledge in all three cases is an example of knowledge of the *vijñāna-maya* self of *TaittUp* II.4, and that it represents specific *vijñāna* and specific developments at the *vijñāna-maya* level of spiritual unfoldment in the sense of *TaittUp* II. Accordingly, use of the phrase *vijñāna-*

TABLE 5.3
Textual Indicators in Teachings in Table 5.2

Text	(1) *vijñā-na-maya*	(2) *ant. hṛd-āk.*	(3) in *hṛd. guhā*	(4) *satya* etym.	(5) *satyam Brahma* etc.	(6) *satya-sya sat.*	(7) *svap-na*	(8) *nāḍīs, hitā,* death	(9) *naḍīs hitā,* sleep	(10) colors, fine as hair	(11) Person in Sun	(12) Person in Eye
1. *BṛhUp* V.1-6			X	X	X						X	X
BṛhUp V.4-5				X	X						X	X
BṛhUp V.1-3			X									
2. *ChāndUp* VIII.1-6		X	X	X	X		X	X	X	X		
ChāndUp VIII.1-3.3		X	X									
3. *BṛhUp* IV.2			X					X		X		X
4. *ŚatBr* X.4.1			X		X							
5. *ChāndUp* III.14			X									
6. *BṛhUP* IV.3.1-34	X		X				X		X	X		
7. *BṛhUp* II.1.16-20	X	X	X			X			X			
8. *KauṣUp* IV.19-20							X		X	X		
9. *BṛhUp* II.3			X			X					X	X
10. *TaittUp* II	X		X	(X)	(X)						X	(X)

maya puruṣa (or *ātmā*) and *the space within the heart, antar-hṛdaya ākāśa*, and more generally teachings that something is *within the heart*, are important textual indicators, presence or absence of which are indicated in Table 5.3 in columns (1), (2), and (3), resp. Another common element in many of the teachings in Table 5.2 is that they contain "etymologies" of *satya* (*m*), "(the) true, (the) real," or "word-plays" to bring out a certain inner meaning and experience associated with the term. They analyze *satya* into *sat* and some thing else, e.g. *satyam* = *sat* + *tyam* or *satyam* = *sat* + *ti* + *yam*, sometimes with an allusion to the *Nāsadīya* Hymn. These etymologies differ in their specific intents, but they have a common denominator in that they all distinguish something more real, permanent and that is one (the *sat*) from variable or transitory multiplicity which we see, and that they use *satyam* as a symbol for the whole.

Closely associated with the *satya* etymologies are three particular *ādeśas* or *upaniṣads*, code phrases that point to specific types of knowledge or realization:

1. *Satyam Brahma*, "Brahman is the *Satyam*;"
2. "The name of this Brahman [that is being taught] is *Satyam*;"
3. *Satyasya Satyam*, "the True of the True," "the Real of the Real."

Typically the knowledge or realization taught in a given text is said to be the knowledge "of" one of these sayings.[85] Accordingly, columns (4), (5) and (6) of Table 5.3 indicate whether or not the text represents itself as teaching the real meaning of saying 1 or 2 or 3, resp. The remaining columns in the Table code other textual elements which will be noted later. Note that Table 5.3 is only an aid to keep track of whether or not the texts in Table 5.2 show these elements or not. A judgment whether two teachings are related, or whether what is taught exemplifies *vijñāna* or *vijñāna-maya* type spiritual knowledge in the sense of *TaittUp* II, must always be based on a more detailed comparison of the texts involved and on a consideration of the spiritual import of the teachings.

The most important texts in Table 5.2 are *BṛhUp* V.1-6, the Heart and *Satya Brahma Vidyās; ChāndUp* VIII.1-6, the *Dahara Vidyā*, dealing with the "space within the heart;" and *BṛhUp* IV.3.1 ff., the *Antar-jyotir Vidyā* dealing with the Self as the light in the heart. These *vidyās* describe what we might call the most important "types of higher *vijñāna*" in the old Upaniṣads. The discussion of *vijñāna* so far gives no hint of the wealth and diversity of *vijñāna*; to get an idea, one has to try to follow these *vidyās* in one's life and inner spiritual life. To get an orientation, we briefly summarize them and then take up the *Antar-jyotir Vidyā* for more detailed consideration.

Heart and *Satya Brahma Vidyā*. *BṛhUp* V.1-6 first teaches that "the Heart is the same as Prajāpati (Lord of Creation), it is Brahman, it is All" (*BṛhUp* V.1-3). This may be called the *Heart Vidyā* (it is a *vidyā* in the sense used here although it is not one of the canonical *vidyās* in Table 3.1). In this *vidyā*, the Heart is specifically associated with the inner disciplines of self control, giving, and compassion, which in this context must be regarded as disciplines of the Heart. (Needless to say, the inner discipline of giving involves physically etc. giving, but physically giving without giving from the heart is not enough.) Then the text goes on and ties this to the *Satya Brahma Vidyā*, V.4-5 (or V.4-6), regarding the knowledge taught in the latter as equivalent to the knowledge of this Heart. The *Satya Brahma Vidyā* begins: "That [Heart] verily is That. This, indeed, was That (*tad*), indeed [it was] the Real (or True, *satyam*).[86] He who knows this Great (*mahat*) Divine Being (*yakṣa*) as the firstborn,—[in the manner of] 'Brahman is the Real (*Satyam Brahma*)'—overcomes these worlds." The "great *yakṣa*" is a mythic-archetypal representation of the total of existence—self, One Self and Universe—in a primeval state. Next the *vidyā* specifies *upāsanās* on the close relationship between the "person in the Sun" and the "person in the right eye," as well as transcendence of these two persons and rising to a single higher level, represented by the three "hidden utterances" *bhūr, bhuvaḥ, svāḥ*. To realize the person in the Sun there is the *upaniṣad* (secret formula) "day," and to realize the person in the right eye, one uses the *upaniṣad* "I." According to my understanding, the *Satya Brahma Vidyā* is based on older, Brāhmaṇa- and Vedic-type thought. The combined text *BṛhUp* V.1-5 may be regarded as a new, fuller *vidyā* which takes the old knowledge of the *satyam* and of *Satya* Brahman and presents it in terms of a new, more universal language, the language of the Heart. The Heart is Brahman, it is All.

***Dahara Vidyā* and Associated Texts.** The central teaching of the *Dahara Vidyā* is that of a "subtle (or small, *dahara*) space within the heart," in which are contained all things and all desires and indeed the whole universe. In the course of spiritual unfoldment, this "space" ultimately becomes Ātman/Brahman. The *Dahara Vidyā* is vast and infinitely profound, and resonances to it are found throughout *Bṛhadāraṇyaka* and *Chāndogya Upaniṣads*. The most important related text is the *Śāṇḍilya Vidyā*, named after one of the chief architects of the deeper spiritual aspects of the *agnicayana*. Basically the *Śāṇḍilya Vidyā* gives a powerful meditation on the self "in one's heart," *antar hṛdaye*. "[He] who consists of mind (*mano-maya*!), whose body is Life-Spirit (*prāṇa-śarīra*), whose form is effulgent shining (*bhā-rūpa*), . . . this is my self within the heart, smaller than a grain of rice, . . . , greater than the Earth . . ." The phrases and flow of meaning in this meditation are reminiscent of the initial teaching on the space or ether in the heart in the *Dahara Vidyā*, and we will argue that the *Śāṇḍilya Vidyā* can be regarded as a more popular, less esoteric version of the latter. The *Śāṇḍilya Vidyā* has a well-known parallel version in *ŚatBr* X.4.1, which has almost the same meditation. It is also briefly echoed in *BṛhUp* V.6. In addition the *Dahara Vidyā* overlaps somewhat the Heart *Vidyā*. While the *Satya Brahma Vidyā* seems to largely grow out of ancient traditions of meditation on the Sun, the *Dahara Vidyā* draws mostly on the perception/experience of the heart in the *Ṛg Veda*. But both the teaching on *Satya* Brahman and on the Ātman in the Heart are basically already found in *Atharva Veda* X.7 and X.8, two awesome and sprawling mystical hymns on *skambha*, the "pillar" that supports the entire Creation.

Antar-jyotir Vidyā. The *Antar-jyotir* or "Light Within" *Vidyā*, *BṛhUp* IV.3.1-34 (K), begins with King Janaka asking Yājñavalkya "what is (*bhavati*, exists [as]) the light for man?" The latter responds "the Sun". But what if the Sun has set? Then the light of man is the Moon. And so on. Finally Yājñavalkya says the light of man is the Self, Ātman (v. 6). It is He "who is made of *vijñāna* (is *vijñāna-maya*), in the heart (*hṛdi*), the entity [who is] the inner light (*antar-jyotiḥ puruṣa*)". The *vidyā* teaches that this entity or Self is to be realized by contemplating dream and other states and by inner development in these states, and eventually rises to great heights: "The [One] seer becomes the ocean . . . This is [the aspirant's] highest world (*loka*), this is his highest bliss."

12. *Antar-Jyotir Vidyā, BṛhUp* IV.3.1-34 (K): Text

Outline. Recall that we are actually still in the middle of the discussion of the Five Sheaths *Vidyā*, trying to get a deeper understanding of *vijñāna* as it is understood in the old Upaniṣads. In sec. 10 we argued that the Five Sheaths *Vidyā* itself in its Part II focussed on "perception of" the "Invisible . . ." as a high-level form of *vijñāna*, and in sec. 11 we suggested that on textual grounds, it appeared that the old Upaniṣads acknowledged other forms of higher awareness as other forms of *vijñāna*. Now the importance of the notion and phenomenon of *vijñāna* lies in the fact that *vijñāna* can guide the aspirant or devotee of Reality at beginning and intermediate levels of the spiritual path. Hence it is important to get an idea of *vijñāna* at a more beginning level than that represented by the "Invisible, . . .," which represents rather high-level *vijñāna*. Accordingly, we interrupt our treatment of the Five Sheaths *Vidyā* to discuss (in secs. 12-16) the beginning stages of the direction of *vijñāna* represented by the *Antar-jyotir Vidyā*.[87] Apart from providing an introduction to one broad avenue of *vijñāna* in the Upaniṣads, this *vidyā* is important because it is the only major *vidyā* in the old Upaniṣads that provides clear analogues of all three of the phases *vijñāna, ānanda*, and "beyond *ānanda*", in a specific line or direction of inner development (viz. development along the line of oneself as the "light of knowing in the heart"). In the present section, therefore, we give the text of the entire *vidyā*, and in secs. 13-14 we focus on the initial segment *BṛhUp* IV.3.1-20, which describes the initial stages of knowledge of the *vijñāna-maya puruṣa* as "light within, in the heart." Secs. 15-16 then explore further aspects of this "light within" *vijñāna* and sec. 17 deals with a parallel text which gives a related teaching. Secs 18-20 return to the Five Sheaths *Vidyā* and discuss the *ānanda-maya* level of that *vidyā*, while sec. 21 considers the *ānanda* and 'beyond *ānanda*' phases of the *Antar-jyotir Vidyā* as an example of the general *ānanda* level of the Five Sheaths *Vidyā*. But as noted in sec. 1, the treatment of the *Antar-jyotir Vidyā* in this chapter is not complete and a crucial missing link is discussed in chr. 6.17.

The Term *Svapna*. In the *Antar-jyotir Vidyā*, the term *svapna* presents some problems. The usual meaning of *svapna* is "sleep," and more specifically "sleep with dreams, dream".[88] In the old Upaniṣads the expression "he (they etc.) sees [something in] a dream" (*svapnam paśyati*, etc.) becomes common,[89] suggesting that an ingredient of "experiencing visual elements" starts being emphasized, but *svapna* may still be simply "dream-sleep". The problem is, however, that some segments of the *Antar-jyotiḥ* text do not seem to fit a meaning of "dream-sleep" and appear to allude to spiritual states with effects reminiscent of out of body experiences and clairvoyance. In the translation, therefore, we sometimes use the term *svapna* state, and discuss the intended meaning later in sec. 13.

Text of the *Vidyā*. (For convenience of reference, some verses have been subdivided, e.g. IV.3.7a and IV.3.7b):

IV.3.6. When the sun has set, when the moon has set, when the fire has gone out, when speech has been stilled, what light [does] this person [have]?" "The Self (Ātmā) indeed is his light. For with the Self [as] light he sits, moves about, does work, returns."

3.7a. "Which [one] is the Self?" "[The Self is He] who is *vijñāna-maya*, in the midst of the senses (*prāṇas*), the person who is the light within the heart (*hṛdi antar-jyotiḥ*)[a]. He, being [ever] the same, walks alongside both [of the two] worlds,[b] as if thinking (*dhyāyatīva*), as if moving to and fro (*lelāyatīva*; "as if trembling, quivering, shaking, moving to and fro"[c]).

3.7b. Verily (*hi*), he, having become [one in] *svapna*, steps beyond this world, [beyond] the forms of death.

3.8. He verily, this person, being born, acquiring a body, is enmeshed with evils. He, going up, dying, leaves the evils behind.

3.9a. Verily, of this very person there are two states (stations, *sthānas*): this [state] and the other-world state (after death). The *svapna* state is a third, a juncture-state (intermediate or twilight, *saṁdhya*, state). Standing in the intermediate state, he sees both states, this [state] and the other-world state. Now of whatever nature this approaching to the other world state is, by having attained that approaching, he sees both the evils and the joys.

3.9b. Where he is in [the] *svapna* [state] (here = dream), having taken to himself (*apādāya*) a degree (measure, *mātrā*) of this all-sustaining world (*loka*), himself tearing [things] apart, himself building [things] up- [there] he is by his own effulgence, by his own light in the *svapna* [state]. There (in that state), this person becomes himself light (or "becomes, on his own, light," *svayaṁjyotir bhavati*).

3.10. There are no chariots there, no [animals] yoked to chariots, no roads, but he creates (*sṛj-*) chariots, [animals] harnessed to chariots, roads. There are no joys, delights, great delights, but he creates joys, delights, great delights. There are no water reservoirs, lotus pools, rivers, but he creates water tanks, lotus pools, rivers. For he is the (or a) doer (*kartṛ*).

3.11. As to this there are these verses (*ślokas*):[d]
Having struck down what pertains to the body in the *svapna* state,
sleepless (*a-supta*), he keeps looking down on the sleeping ones (= the senses).
Having taken to himself light (*śūkram ādāya*), he goes again to [his] state (*sthāna*),
the golden person, the single (or solitary) swan (*ekahaṁsa*).

3.12. Guarding the low nest (= the body) with *prāṇa*,
the immortal one, having gone outside the nest,
Goes as is his desire, the golden person, the single swan.

3.13. In the sleep-like end condition (*svapna-anta*), going up and down,
the god makes (*kṛ*) many forms for (or of) himself,
now as it were enjoying with women, laughing,
now as it were also seeing fearful things.

3.14a. They [i.e., others] see his rest (*ārāma*),
no one sees him.

3.14b. "[Therefore] one should not wake that one abruptly," they say. [For] a difficult cure is there for him (= for someone) to whom he (= the *puruṣa* in 3.12-3.14a) does not return.

3.14c. Now further, (some) say "That (*eṣa*) is just his waking world, for what [things] he sees when awake, those [he sees] when asleep (*supta*)." [But his is not so, for] there the person is himself light (*svayaṁjyotiḥ*).

3.14d. [King Janaka:] "Sir, I give [you] a thousand [cows]. Speak what is higher [than this] for [the purpose of] release."

3.15. He, having had enjoyment (or: become quiet) in this complete bliss (*saṁprasāde*), having roamed about and seen good and evil, hastens again back according to his departure, to his origin (= to where he came from), indeed to *svapna*. Whatever he sees there (in *svapna*?), he is not followed by that. For this person (*puruṣa*, refers to the Ātman which the text is teaching) [is] not attached (literally "is one having no bond")." [Janaka said:] "Just so,

Yājñavalkya. I give [you], revered Sir, a thousand [cows]. Speak [what is] higher than this for [the purpose of] liberation (*mokṣa*)." (This verse has no analogue in the Mādhyandina recension).

3.16. Having had enjoyment in this *svapna* state, having wandered about, having seen, indeed, good and evil (*puṇya*, meritorious, and *pāpa*), he hastens again back according to where he came from, indeed to the waking end-condition (*buddha-anta*). Whatever he sees there (in the *svapna* state), he is not followed by that, for this person is not attached (lit. "one having no bond"). [Janaka said:] "Just so, Yājñavalkya, Revered Sir, I give [you] a thousand (= many cows). Speak [what is] higher [than this] for [the sake of] release (*mokṣa*)."

3.17. Having had enjoyment in this waking end-state (*buddha-anta*), having wandered about, having seen indeed good and evil, he hastens back according to where he came from, to the *svapna* end-condition (*svapna-anta*). (This verse has no analogue in the Mādhyandina recension).

3.18. As to this, as a great fish moves along the [two] banks [of a river], the closer one and the further one, so indeed this person moves along both *antas* (end-conditions), the *svapna-anta* and the waking *anta*.

3.19. Just as in this [physical] space a hawk or [other] bird, having flown all over, exhausted, having folded its wings, is indeed borne down to its nest, even so runs this person to that *anta* where he doesn't desire any desire and where he does not see any dream (*svapna*).

3.20. These indeed are his vessels (*nāḍī*) named *hitā* ("placed [for something], good for [something]"). Just as a hair divided a thousand fold, with so much fineness they stand (i.e. so fine they are), filled with white, blue, yellow, green, red [fluid?]. Now when they kill him, as it were, (when) they overpower [him], as it were, (when) an elephant deprives him of shadow, as it were, (when) he falls into a well as it were,—what fear(-ful thing) he sees awake, that he thinks here (in *svapna*) through non-knowledge (*a-vidyā*). And likewise when like a god, [or] like a king, he thinks "I am this world, I am all," this is his [in this state] highest world.

3.21. This (following), verily is his form beyond desire, free from evils, fearless. As [a man] completely embraced by his dear wife doesn't know any (particular) thing outside or inside, just so indeed does this person (*puruṣa*), [when] completely embraced by the *prajñā*-Self, not know any (particular) thing outside or inside. That indeed is his form [in which] desire [is] fulfilled, [in which] self [only is] desired (or: [in which] self is the desire), without desire—[his form which is] other than sorrow.

3.22. There a father is (or becomes) a non-father, a mother a non-mother, (there) the worlds (are, or become) non-worlds, the gods non-gods, the Vedas non-Vedas. There a thief is (becomes) a non-thief, a murderer a non-murderer, a *cāṇḍāla* (outcast) a non-*cāṇḍāla*, a *paulkasa*(?) a non-*paulkasa*, a mendicant renunciant a non-mendicant renunciant, an ascetic a non-ascetic. [That form is] unaffected by good deed, unaffected by evil deed. For he is [one] crossed over all sorrows of the heart.

3.23. When he then does not see there, verily, Seeing he does not see [i.e., while he does not see anything, there is still Seeing in some sense]. For (*hi*) no destruction of the Seeing of a Seer is found there, because of imperishability. For (*tu*) there is no second, different from him and separated, which he could see.

In 3.24-3.30, this statement is verbatim repeated with see (and seer, seeing) replaced successively by smell (smeller, smelling, etc., root *ghrā*), taste (*ras*), speak (*vad*), hear (*śru*), think (*man*), touch (*spṛś*), and know (*vi-jñā-*):

3.31. Verily, where there is, as it were (*iva*), another [thing], there one might see the other [thing], one might smell the other, one might taste the other, one might speak the other, one might think the other, one might know the other. (This verse is missing in the Mādhyandina version.)

3.32. The Seer becomes an Ocean (*salila*), one, without second. He (or this) is the world (*loka*) of Brahman, oh great king, thus (said) Yājñavalkya to him and continued. "This is his highest path, this is his highest treasure, this is his highest world (*parama loka*), this is his highest bliss (*ānanda*). On a particle of that bliss indeed do other beings live."

3.33. Now, he among men who (or: that [life] of men which) is perfect of body, prosperous, lord over others, most completely endowed with all human enjoyments—he (or: that) is the highest [unit of] bliss among men. Next, a hundred blisses (= units of bliss) of men—that is one (unit of) gandharva world bliss. Next, a hundred gandharva world blisses, that is one (unit of) bliss of the gods-by-action, who obtain divinity by action. Next one hundred gods-by-action blisses, —that is one (unit of) bliss of the gods-by-birth, as well as [the bliss of one] who is a knower of the *śruti* (scripture), guileless, [and] not affected by desire. Next, one hundred blisses of the gods-by-birth—that is one (unit of) bliss of the Prajāpati-world, as well as [the bliss] of one versed in the *śruti*, guileless, [and] not affected by desire. Next, one hundred Prajāpati-world blisses—that is one (unit of) bliss of the Brahman world, as well as [the bliss of one] who is versed in the *śruti*, guileless, [and] not affected by desire. Now this indeed is the highest bliss. This is the Brahman world, oh great king, said Yājñavalkya. (Janaka said:) "I, revered Sir, give you a thousand [cows]. From now speak [what is] for liberation (*vimokṣa*) indeed." Then Yājñavalkya was afraid: "The wise king would drive me to the ends of [my] (discursive) thought."

3.34. This very one, having had enjoyment in this *svapna* state, having wandered about, having indeed seen good and evil, hastens back according to where he came from, to the waking end-condition (*buddha-anta*).[90]

13. *Antar-Jyotir Vidyā*, Beginning [*BṛhUp* IV.3.1-20 (K)]

The text is difficult, and particularly modern interpretations differ widely. In this section, we first describe the general intent of 3.1-3.20, and then go through the text in some detail. Then in sec. 14, we discuss the teaching as a whole.

The Basic Idea Behind 3.1-3.20: Traditional View. Assume for the moment that *svapna* throughout means dream (which is the traditional view). Then the basic idea behind 3.1-3.20 is that in dream, the senses are not operating, and one's self is nearer to its true nature, to what one really is. In deep sleep, both the senses and the mind are not functioning, so then the self is closer to its true nature still. Then it "rests in its own nature, in the deepest core of its own being. . ."[91] Then it has the possibility of becoming aware of what it is, that it is the basis of all seeing and all manifestation. So in a general way, 3.1-3.20 teach that by correct understanding of dream and deep sleep experience, *and* by correct inner development in the dream and deep sleep states, one can come to an initial understanding of the Self.

The idea that in deep sleep, the self is united with its own being is explicitly taught in the *Sad Vidyā*, at *ChāndUp* VI.8.1:

> Uddālaka Āruṇi said to his son Śvetaketu: [Learn to] know from me the nature of sleep (*svapna-anta*). When a man is asleep (or goes to sleep, *svapiti*), so-called, then he is (or becomes) united with Being (or the Real, *Sat*)[a] and one who has attained himself.[b] For that reason people say "he is asleep (*svapiti*)"—for he has become one who has attained himself (*svaṁ hy apīto bhavati*, a wordplay).[92]

The same idea is echoed by Sai Baba:

> Become aware of your reality and lose the sense of identification with your body. . . This is quite easy, [i.e.] understanding that you are not the body. . . Everyday when you sleep, where are you? Who are you? Your senses are inoperative, your intelligence is in abeyance: Your mind creates a world of its own, and after playing in it for sometime, it lapses into inactivity. That is sleep, the nearest you reach in your journey to *samādhi* [absorption in the Ātman]. Live in the *Ātma-tattva* [the Ātman reality; *tattva* = "that-ness] . . . If you experience that *Ātma-tattva*, you become Bhagavān [= God and the Reality] Himself.[93]

The implication is that the Ātman can be appraoched and attained by contemplating and making deeper use of the dream and deep sleep states. Dream and deep sleep play a special role because the senses are not operating during dream, and the whole mind is shut down during deep sleep; this enables the infinite basis, the *Ātma-tattva* to emerge and become part of awareness (*vijñāna*). This general idea is found in a number of Upaniṣadic teachings such as the *Bālāki Vidyā*.[94]

Basic Idea of 3.1-3.20: Expanded View. In the traditional interpretation of *BṛhUp* IV.3.1-20 just described, *svapna* in 3.7b-3.18 refers to dream. We will, however, take a somewhat expanded view and assume with Coomaraswamy[95] that *svapna* in 3.7-3.18 is used to refer not only to dream, but also to other states besides dream. Thus in 3.9b-3.10 it may refer only to dream, but in 3.7b and 3.9a it seems to refer to meditation states with effects reminiscent of clairvoyance, and in 3.11-3.14a to meditation with effects reminiscent of Out of Body Experiences (OBEs). In all these states the senses are dormant, and one is therefore, as in the case of *svapna* as dream, closer to a truer, "higher" self that one really is. This truer, higher self is said to be *vijñāna-maya*, in one's heart, the constant light of all experiences and existence, and is to be realized as such by contemplating and making deeper and correct use of these *svapna* states. Knowledge of the self in deep sleep (3.19-3.20) represents a further, deeper stage of this whole process. Thus with the expanded interpretation of *svapna* described, the basic idea of 3.1-3.20 is simply a correspondingly expanded version of the traditional interpretation of the text.

Vs. 3.1-3.7a. In vs. 3.1-3.6, Yājñavalkya declares that ultimately the Self or Ātman is the light of man: "With the Ātman [as his] light he sits, moves about, does his work, returns" (v. 3.6). When the king then enquires more closely "which [one of various possibilities] is the Self," Yājñavalkya responds: "[The Ātman is He] who is made of *vijñāna* (is *vijñāna-maya*), in the heart (*hṛdi*), the person [who is] the inner light (*antarjyotiḥ puruṣa*)." The Sanskrit is somewhat ambiguous—the individual terms may be associated in different ways, although all of them refer to the Self that the king is asking about. One thing seems clear, however: the aspects "consisting of *vijñāna*," "in the heart," "light" (or "light within") highlighted in 3.7, as well as the overall "the Ātman is the light of man" in 3.6, are set up as a general theme which is then amplified and explained in the specific developments in 3.7b-3.34. This may be argued on the basis of the numerous textual resonances to these aspects in the remainder of the *vidyā*.

Vs. 3.7b-3.9a. "He," the person who is *vijñāna-maya*, "being [always] the same (*samāna sat*), walks alongside both worlds, seeming to think, seeming to move about:" One thing that can be said about the *vijñāna-maya* person is that he now walks in this world and now in the next. In other words, for the *vijñāna-maya* person this life is not the whole story,—it is only a small part of a much larger continuum of now life and now "the next world". While in life one believes that one is thinking, that one is moving about, this is only the way things look: one *seems* to think, one *seems* to move about. The whole perspective of "[life in] this world" vs. "[the state in] the other world, after death" is maintained into v. 3.8 and even 3.9a. Here, in this world, one is enmeshed with evils, but after death, the evils are left behind (3.8). Both these worlds are seen in the *svapna* state (3.9a). As a result, *svapna* in v. 3.7b, "Verily (*hi*), he, having become [one absorbed in] *svapna* (noun), goes beyond this world, [beyond] the forms of death," is not likely to mean dream, or only dream. Wedged in between passages that talk about life and death ('he walks alongside both worlds, . . .," 3.7a, and 3.8, which described man's basic condition across life and death), the term more likely refers to meditative states in which the senses are dormant and which are at a level of "seeing both life and death," although dream may be included as one possiblility.

V.3.9 returns to the *svapna* in 3.7b and explains its nature in more detail. To this end it introduces two new terms, *sthāna*, "station," and *ā-kram-*, "to step close to, approach". "Verily, this *puruṣa,* "person, entity," has two stations, *sthānas*," with the second station now explicitly named "other world station," *para-loka-sthānam. Svapna* is a third, intermediate *sthāna* from which "the person sees both *sthānas*, the this-world *sthana* and the other-world *sthāna*". The text does not say "the person sees this world and the other world," rather, "the person sees the two stations"—suggesting that the seeing involves spiritual perspective or understanding in addition to simply "seeing" as in dream or in, say, a clairvoyant or out of body state. "Now of whatever nature his approach (or "essential ingredient," *ā-krama*, a noun) to the other-world state [is], using that approach (*ākramam ākramya*, a wordplay), he sees both the evils and blisses (*ānandas*)."[96] That again makes it unlikely that *svapna* is simply "dream" (because dream would not be descibed as allowing different appoaches),[97] but that it refers to a state or states with some of the qualities of dream.

Vs. 3.9b-3.10. This segment may describe only dream; I don't know whether "being the doer, creator" in 3.10 rules out the kind of meditation states described in 3.11-3.14a (see below). The connection between 3.9a and 3.9b seems to be that in both cases one sees evils and joys.

Vs. 3.11-3.14a. We first discuss these verses—a set of inspired stanzas quoted as known—as a separate text in its own right,[98] and then consider their implications for 3.7-3.9a and for the *vidyā* as a whole. In "*Having struck down* in *svapna* what pertains to the body, sleepless, *he keeps looking down, abhicakṣati*, on the sleeping [senses]," and "*guarding* the low nest (the body) *with prāṇa*, the immortal one, *having gone outside the nest* (the body), . . ." the phrases in italics suggest what in Western psychical research and parapsychology is called "Out of Body Experience," OBE or OOBE, or "travelling clairvoyance."[99] For "having struck down what pertains to the body" and "looking at the sleeping [senses]" implies that there is no waking state sense or body awareness, and "looking down on" and "having gone outside the nest" both suggest out-of-body travel or consciousness outside the body. In addition, "guarding the low nest with *prāṇa*" might refer to the special breath and energy states that accompany OBEs. (For purpose of discussion, the term OBE is used here to suggest "consciousness outside the body"[100] while clairvoyance is used to refer to "vision of things distant in time or space". In laboratory research the two have so far not been clearly separated.[101] OBE as a phenomenon overlaps with experience in the "astral body" of theosophy and the "dream body" of other Western occultisms and Indian texts.)[102]

But, other things in 3.11-3.12 suggest meditation, spiritual path, higher (transcendental) knowledge, etc., and these elements are clearly dominant over OBE. To be begin with, the *vijñāna-maya* person who is (or is endowed with) inner light in the heart is called "golden person" and "single (or solitary) swan". The "golden person" has deep meanings in the *agnicayana*, the ritual of the piling of the fire place. There it refers to a golden figure, which ultimately represents the golden, deified and thus immortal body of the sacrificer which is created by the ritual and which the sacrificer will take on after death.[103] In the *Śāṇḍilya Vidyā* in the *Śatapatha Brāhmaṇa*, this teaching is developed further and given a more universal form. The *Vidyā* says that an immortal Divine body doesn't have to be constructed by the *agnicayana*: the One Immortal Self exists already in one's heart. It is the "golden person within the self, as indeed a smokeless light, greater than space, greater than this earth, greater than all things," and one should make it one's *kratu* or "will, purpose" to realize it.[104] Apart from the *agnicayana*, there is also a whole tradition of the "golden person in the Sun," and beginning in *Śatapatha Brāhmaṇa* and culminating in the Upaniṣads, there is the teaching that the "person in the eye" and the "golden person in the Sun" are the same.[105] In general, therefore, the golden person stands for the Divine element in the human being, and ultimately for the Supreme Divine, and the *ślokas* 3.11-3.14a must be intended as indicating a level of higher spiritual realization. The swan or *haṁsa* in v. 3.11 also has higher or divine connotations, beginning already in the *Ṛg Veda*. Gonda, in a discussion of the *haṁsa* and other birds in Vedic thought,[106] documents its association with higher knowledge, its use as a form of appearance of a deity, and its role as a higher or the highest Divine.[107] Besides the appellations "golden person" and "the one swan," other allusions in 3.11-12 also point to an "experiential" context that is purely spiritual. For example, although the individaul is in *svapna*, he is said to be sleepless, *a-supta*: He is conscious as a soul engaged in a spiritual enterprise. Again, "Having gone outside the nest, he goes as is his desire" may merely describe the freedom of movement in OBEs. But it may (like the "sleepless") also suggest more deeply self-directed consciousness as in meditation. Finally "having taken to himself light, he goes again to his state" suggests that the single swan is returning to a state that is more natural for him than the normal body-bound waking consciousness—the soul is finding its true state.[108]

Since the dominant point of view in 3.11-12 is thus one of the soul (or self) on the path to, and interpreting his/her experiences in regard to, higher spiritual knowledge, we will regard these verses as alluding to experience in meditation which includes effects phenomenologically similar to effects in OBE(s).[109] The text presupposes that such meditative experience is a vehicle for the rise of certain higher knowledge or realization, and teaches that it should be used to develop knowledge and realization such as are discussed in 3.6-3.10 (knowledge that one's self is the light in all states, and that one is in fact immortal). Of course, experience of this type is merely the garb in which such knowledge should be embodied as an integrated conviction—it does not "prove" the knowledge. For the knowledge is at the level of the soul; forms, when taken as "experience," are an almost unrelated outer garb. It might be noted that in the West, accidental vivid and veridical OBEs (or dream body experiences etc.) can have a profound spiritual impact and can lead to similar knowledge.[110]

Appendix: Vs. 3.7b-3.9a Revisited. If *svapna* in vs. 3.11-3.13 refers to experience and realization through meditation which includes effects reminiscent of OBEs, it is conceivable that vs. 3.7b-3.9a refer to states in which there is perception of the other, after death world. Seeing the joys and evils of the other world and seeing the other world state may mean seeing spirits of the deceased and having other after death intuitions.[111] In Western psychical research, experience of this type comes under the heading of "clairvoyance" (recall that from the point of view of Western Psychical Research, clairvoyance and OBE are closely related). Again, however, spiritual aspects are dominant. As discussed earlier, "he, being ever the same, walks along both worlds" is a fundamental insight which is conducive to dispassion and wisdom. "He, having become [immersed in] *svapna*, steps beyond this world, [beyond] the forms of death" may mean "he rises above both worlds". Even if the "forms of death" refer to the forms of this world, there is still a connotation of "rising above them," and thus a spiritual element. Similar comments hold for "seeing both the evils and the joys" in 3.9. Accordingly, 3.7-3.9a may be interpreted as saying that meditation states containing effects reminiscent of spirit clairvoyance and after death aspects should be used as a vehicle for developing knowledge that one's self is *vijñāna-maya* and light in the heart, always the same in all states (3.7).

Vs. 3.15-3.18 and 3.19-3.20. Finally, if the themes in the preceding segments are the self *vis-à-vis* this world and the next, the self freely moving and constructing worlds with the body asleep, and meditative experience with overtones of clairvoyance and OBE, then the theme of 3.15-3.18 is the impermanency of all these forms of experience. By emphasizing the alternation between states, the text is suggesting an ultimate deficiency in the sum total of these levels of experience, and thus a deficiency in the whole level of realization of the *vijñāna-maya* self taught so far (i.e. in 3.1-3.14a). Accordingly it moves to a deeper level of analysis/instruction, viz. instruction regarding "deep sleep" (3.19-3.20). Only after the knowledge suggested in 3.1-3.14a is extended to include deep sleep, where there is no more perception of form (although the state is not identical with deep sleep), can a truly Infinite stage be reached (3.21ff.).

14. The *Antar-jyotiḥ* Teaching

Now let us try to get an idea of the essence of the *Antar-jyotiḥ* teaching in *BṛhUp* IV.3.1-20 as a whole. In each of the blocks of verses discussed in the last section, the text is elaborating the self described in 3.7a, the entity (*puruṣa*) which is *vijñāna-maya prāṇeṣu*, "made of *vijñāna*, in (or behind) the senses," and *hṛdi antar-jyotiḥ*, "in the heart (*hṛdi*) the interior light (*antar-jyotiḥ*)". The first phrase is presumably to be understood in the same way as the *vijñāna-maya* person in Ajātaśatru's teaching in *BṛhUp* IV.2.17 cited earlier, and the *prajñā-ātman* in *KauṣUp* III. The idea is that when a person is in dream-sleep or in certain meditation states without body-consciousness, then an infinite (Śaṁkara) higher self or level of being comes into play. This self is made of higher *vijñāna* (as in Ajātaśatru's "having *by his vijñāna* taken to himself . . ."), or *prajñā*, Wisdom. It holds and stills the body,[112] and has (at the level of knowledge and meditation in question) still something like the knowledge capabilities of the senses, having taken on their light or absorbed them.[113] This self, says the *vidyā*, (1) is in the heart (3.7a, as theme for the whole remainder 3.7b-3.20 and beyond); (2) is essentially immortal and unconnected with good and evil (3.8, 3.9a, and suggested in 3.11-3.14a); (3) is the light of all one's seeing and experiencing (suggested in 3.7a as general fact and then spelled out for dream, 3.9b-3.10, and for meditation-OBE in 3.11-3.14a); and (4) is even the maker of the experiences (at least in dream and other *svapna* states). This self is to be realized. The experiences in the different *svapna* states are not important—what is important is realization and knowledge that oneself is this kind of a higher order immortal reality and that formful experiences in these states are ultimately all only activities of that reality and don't affect it. It seems clear that this self is essentially the same as that described in *BṛhUp* II.1.17 and *KauṣUp* III.3, and is very likely an example of what *TaittUp* II.4.3 has in mind with its *vijñāna-maya* self. In other words, the knowledge taught in 3.1-3.18 is an example of beginning *vijñāna* and of knowledge at the *vijñāna-maya* level. But up to 3.18 the *vidyā* teaches only one level of intuitional understanding of oneself as *vijñāna-maya*, so to speak. For a second, deeper level is indicated in vs. 3.19-20, and a further level, a first clear realization of the One Ātman, is then described in vs. 3.21 ff. So while the teaching in vs. 3.1-18 represent beginning phrases of *vijñāna*, the following verses 3.19-20 and 3.21 ff. describe further stages (3.21 ff. corresponds to realization of the One Self).

Light in the Heart. An important indication for the aspirant/devotee who is trying to follow the *vidyā* in his/her life is the phrase "in the heart." In dream and deep sleep, as well as in the other types of meditative states mentioned, says the *vidyā*, the aspect of being immortal and *vijñāna-maya* is present in one's heart. Initially this may be understood as "[felt] localized in the area of the chest, in the center of one's deeper being". But more fundamentally it means that it is found when one "rests in one's true nature, in the Self that is unaffected by all the experiences in all the states". The constant movement from a more normal (waking or dream) state to another *svapna* state or back simply emphasizes that the higher reality which one is (here the *vijñāna-maya* self) is in fact in the direction of one's true nature, one's true Self. What one really is is always unaffected in all *svapna* states, it is immortal. The other basic point is the fact that this higher self or reality which one is is "(the) light (in the heart)". It is the light in all states, as brought out already in 3.1-6. At first sight the light by which one sees, hears, acts, etc., or the light of the Self "by which one sits, moves about, does work, returns," might be taken as merely a metaphor (merely a verbal figure), or as "symbolic". But the whole subsequent development 3.7-3.18 makes it clear that that "light", or the light of the Self, is something transcendental to be realized. As a matter of fact, the realization of the *vijñāna-maya* self in 3.7-3.18 and in 3.19-3.20 are merely the first steps toward its realization.

Here a question arises to what extent the realization of the *vijñāna-maya* self in 3.7-3.18 involves experience of light. The wording in 3.9, "Where he is in the . . . *svapna* state . . ., there he is by his own effulgence, by his own light, in that state. There, this person is himself light" suggests a strong realization of self as the source and the process of seeing or apperception in that state. But the language of light and luminosity does not necessarily imply "photic experience" of light.[114] It may be suggestive of a Divine quality or modality to be realized. Or it may involve a figurative, still experiential but non-"photic" "higher" "light of knowing". The latter seems to be the situation in Ajātaśatru's teaching at *BṛhUp* II.1.17 and *KauṣUp* III.3, which talk about the *vijñāna-maya* or *prajñā-ātman* taking on the *vijñāna* of the senses, or absorbing the senses, but do not mention light.[115] In addition, "the Ātman is the light of (for) man" (it is that "by which" he sees, etc.) unfolds as much in the description of the one Seer in vs. 3.23-3.31, for example, or in 3.32, as it does in 3.1-3.18. So knowledge that the Ātman is the light by which man sees can be at various levels, and one would not necessarily expect the same type of "experiential" at every level. On the other hand, the "interior light in the heart" in 3.7 suggests something like experience of light, because that is something that is perceived in the heart. But that light is a higher modality, different from ordinary perception or mental images of light.

The *Antarjyotir Vidyā* is important because in spite of the difficulties of putting in words some of the beginning stages (attitudes and convictions one should have, and correct realizations) in the path it describes, we get for the first time an idea of how large the task of developing directly something of the knowledge of the texts in chr. 2 in oneself is. For the *vidyā* implies that after there is knowledge of the *vijñāna-maya puruṣa* as "light within, in the heart," a major further qualitative deepening has to occur (represented by the discussion of deep sleep, 3.19-3.20) before the Self is clearly realized (3.21 ff.). From this point of view, the *vidyā* represents an extraordinary elucidation of the nature and direction of the great transcendental teachings in chr. 2.

15. The Light of Knowledge or Awareness in the Heart, and Dream

We have argued that the whole of *BṛhUp* IV.3.1-18 (or IV.3.1-20) is a seminal text intended to indicate directions of inner experience in which the student can develop one form of *vijñāna,* viz. knowledge of the self as *vijñāna-maya*, the light of knowledge, immortal and beyond life and death. (More precisely, the *vidyā* shows the student the spirit in which to do that.) In later tradition, this teaching was developed further. These developments are important partly because they contain hints regarding possible experiential elements in the original *vidyā*, and partly because they represent more modern inner experience and practice related to the *vidyā.*

In this section we discuss as one such development the traditional Vedāntic teaching that a basic milestone on the spiritual path is realization of one's individual self as self-luminous and as light in the heart, and that that luminosity and being light is intrinsically connected with dream. For example Swami Ananyananda writes:

> [A] The first genuine spiritual experience that comes to the aspirant is the direct perception of the light of his own true Self in the chamber of his heart. The experience of the interior light is not like seeing the external light. When you see the light of the sun or an electric lamp, you know it as an object different from you and never identify it with your own self. The experience of Ātman's light is not objective [i.e. the light of the Ātman is not experienced as

> an object external to oneself]; it is not different from you; rather, you feel that you *are* that light. You immediately know that it is the light of your own self, that you are self-luminous. Along with this photic experience comes the knowledge that you are the spirit separate from the body and also from the mind.[116]

The author then goes on to discuss the corresponding experience/realization in Patañjali's Yoga Sūtra, in the *Bhakti* schools, in Christian mysticism and in the Hindu Tantras. His comments on *bhakti* are of particular interest:

> [B] The experience of the inner Ātman in the chamber of the heart is the first milestone on the path of spiritual realization. Every aspirant must pass through the chamber of the heart, for the only door to the divine lies hidden there. However, some aspirants who follow the path of devotion may not recognize or understand the inner Light (*pratyag-jyoti*) as the experience of the Ātman. When during meditation the image of the Chosen Deity appears vivid and luminous, they understand it to be the light of God rather than the light of their own higher self.[117]

In other words, the Chosen Deity is experienced as Luminous and as Light, and this Light is taken to be the Light of God. The experience of the Light of Self is thus interpreted as experience of the Light of Divinity. Meditation on an image of the "chosen deity" as described in [B] is of course a later (medieval and modern) practice. But meditation in one's heart on Śiva, with the conception of Śiva clearly involving visual elements, is taught already in *Kaivalya Upaniṣad,* which dates from the early centuries CE. (Already the *Ṛg Vedic* seer often mentions or asks for the vision of the deity in his heart.) Swami Ananyananda's comments also apply to meditation on the Sun, as in the *Satya Brahman Vidyā.*

Swami Ananyananda relates this self that experiences itself as self-luminous to dream, and at this point his connections to *BṛhUp* IV.3.7 ff. become more specific. Essentially, he takes *svapna* as dream, as is traditional, and explains the unusual elements in 3.7-9 and 3.11-12 in terms of an "awakened dream-self":

[C] This [self when it knows itself as self-luminous] is the self which sees dreams. What meditation does is to wake up this dream-self from its sleep and make it conscious of its intrinsic luminous nature. Owing to the lack of self-awareness, the waking state is not much different from the dream state—for the majority of the people. Just as in the waking state the self can be trained to detach itself from sense objects and to remain alert as their witness, so also the ... dream-self can be trained to remain alert as a witness without identifying itself with dream objects. This is what meditation actually does; it inhibits the dreaming process itself. Then the [dreamself] ceases to be the dream-self. Its light can then be focussed on the subtle inner worlds and made to reveal the presence of gods and goddesses: this is how one gets visions and spiritual experiences. Or this awakened dream-self can be trained to awaken its next higher dimension known as *prajñā* which then experiences its oneness with Infinite Consciousness.[118]

In other words, one's self in dream can be in a state where it is not identified with the objects which it experiences in dream in the way it typically is in normal dream experience. Then it may be called the "awakened dream-self" and it is in this condition that it can become aware of its own luminosity and other things. It may then also have many other powers besides. This overall conception is basically consistent with the analysis in the last section, and represents an alternative way of expounding the text (the "photic" in [A] is suggestive only and corresponds to what we called "Divine quality [of light]," not to imagery of light). Instead of a "dream-self" as in [C], one could also discuss this "path of *svapna*" [*BṛhUp* IV3.1-18 (K)] in terms of "dream-consciousness," or a generalized version of the latter which accommodates clairvoyance and meditation phenomena reminiscent of OBEs. Another possible way of talking is in terms of the "subtle inner consciousness" (so Sri Sathya Sai Baba). In this area one may expect different teachers to have quite different ways of talking about what is going on.

16. The Light of Knowledge as Awareness of One's Own Mental Phenomena

If realization of one's self as a Divine Luminous is the heart represents one focus of Vedāntic experiential interpretation of *BṛhUp* IV.3.1-18, another is the position that "experientially," the "light by which man sees" is to be sought at that level or in that substrate of mind or experience where one is intuitively aware "of" the phenomena in one's mind—aware of one's perceptions and memories as well as of one's dreams. This leads to another, also authentic and viable direct approach to *BṛhUp* IV.3.1-18 (K) which was expounded by Swami Satchidanandendra Saraswati (1880-1975) on the basis of Śaṁkara's commentaries.[119] The Swami entitles this approach "The genuine Intuition of the Ātman," and makes it the central chapter of a small book called "Intuition of Reality".[120] "Intuition" here is *vijñāna,* and Swami Satchidanandendra notes that among the several variants which Śaṁkara uses for *vijñāna*, the most appropriate one is *anubhava,* "intuition," "immediate apprehension".[121] This *anubhava* or intuition-*vijñāna* is, according to Swami Satchidanandendra, found in all perceptual and mental activity as well as in all higher knowledge.

> It is well-known how we intuit color with the help of the organ of sight and how we intuit joy or sorrow, fear or curiosity without any assistance of reason. All such intuitions, however, are events in time, and so they are all born and cease to exist in time. But how are we aware of the senses or of these sensations themselves? How do we come to know the mind or its intuitions themselves? And how do we come to know the presence or absence of the mind itself together with its various modifications? The senses cannot objectify and know themselves; nor can the mind know itself, and much less is it possible for the mind to become aware of its own absence. Nevertheless, it is common knowledge that we do know when the mind or the senses function, or when they cease to function, in such states, for instance, as deep sleep. Now this faculty which enables us to have this direct insight, is what is called *anubhava* in Vedānta. This is what has been rendered by the term 'intuition' here.[122]

Similarly, when one recollects events or feelings that one experienced, "what is it that enables us to be aware of these [past] temporal happenings without undergoing any change in itself? This is what is called *anubhava* in Vedānta".[123] Swami Satchidanandendra's main thesis is that this intuition or *anubhava* is the "light of knowledge" of *BṛhUp* IV.3.1-18:

> . . . "It is by the light of the Ātman alone that this puruṣa [person] sits, goes out, does any work, and returns" (*BṛhUp* IV.3.6). This inner Light of Ātman, is the Intuition which constitutes the inherent nature of man or any other individual creature. That light or intuition can directly apprehend and serves as the eternal guide for all procedure for the assemblage of body and senses called man in ordinary life.[124]

In our terms, this identifies the level of inner experience where beginning level *vijñāna* of the Ātman should be sought. Swami Satchidanandendra is saying: "When you look into yourself then you find that there is something like an awareness or intuition of when the senses or the mind are functioning, or an awareness that a memory is only a memory etc. This awareness or this intuition is a direct manifestation of or glimmer (*Ahnung*) of Ātman. This is embryonic or beginning *vijñāna* of Ātman."

The crucial element of Swami Satchidanandendra's notion of "intuition" is that it is changeless and always there. This is the import of "eternal" when he says that this "light" or "intuition" "serves as the eternal guide for all procedures," i.e., all our activities (above), and is the theme of the section in which the excerpt appears: "2. How sensuous and mental intuitions [i.e. direct mental apprehensions] presuppose a *changeless* intuition" (italics added).[125] In the following sections Swami Satchidanandendra then proceeds to show that the kind of awareness he calls "intuition" or *anubhvava* operates not only in moments when one is aware of the senses or sensations, but is always present, using an argument consisting of a sequence of steps very similar to the stages in the *Antar-jyotir Vidyā*. The section headings are "3. Intuition unaffected by waking and dream . . .," "4. The Intuition of Deep Sleep . . .," and "5. Intuition which is constant throughout all states" (i.e., waking, dream, and deep sleep).[126] Under "3. Intuition unaffected by waking and dream," the author quotes *BṛhUp* IV.3.9 (K), "When he dreams, having taken to himself or measure of this all-sustaining world, . . ." and amplifies:

> . . .What is the light which aids him to see this replica of waking [i.e., the dream world]? . . . There can be neither consciousness of the waking mind, nor the sensations of the waking state. Nevertheless, he objectifies all the dream-phenomena with the help of his own consciousness. Now this *constant* conscious-

> ness is the Intuition which is identical with Ātman. The Ātman does not make use of any light. . . . Ātman is His [or Its] own light when He objectifies dream as a whole just as He is, when he is conscious of waking as a whole.[127]

Similarly regarding "The Intuition of deep sleep," the author cites *BṛhUp* IV.3.21, which he regards as describing "intuition" also.

The preceding suggests that Swami Satchidanandendra is using "intuition" to teach an inner path which represents a reading of the *vidyā*. This reading is consonant with the spirit of the text and at the same time very close to Śaṁkara's whole incredible approach to Ātman/Brahman. Swami Satchidanandendra's approach is as much contained in the *vidyā* as is, say, a path of reflection on one's self as being *vijñāna-maya* and realization of it as self-luminous in the heart. In general we find that all the geat *vidyās* in the Upaniṣads allow unfoldment at different levels of the inner consciousness in various ways. Swami Satchidanandendra's path may, however, present a problem to some modern aspirants because it goes against some very deep presuppositions of mainstream Western psychology. For in cognitive psychology and brain process modelling, the kind of meta-effects and meta-levels which Swami Satchidanandendra focuses on ("awareness of" sensation etc.) are not regarded as leading beyond mind to something higher than cognition, something which at the same time underlies and is involved in what is ordinarily called "cognition". On the contrary, they would be merely regarded as another level of mind, or of "cognitive organization," "on top of" the more basic organization of sense-perception, motor behavior, etc. And they would be "modelled" in simple ways "on top of" this organization by introducing suitable higher order nodes, or modified configurations of the original functions, or by analogue effects like reflections. Again, we cannot discuss these things critically here.[128] Before rejecting Swami Satchidanandendra's approach, however, the reader is encouraged to examine more deeply the epistemological foundations of Western psychology, including the whole fact of his/her existence, consciousness and experience.

17. Ajātaśatru's Teaching to Bālāki

For completeness we briefly consider in this section the teaching which king Ajātaśatru of Benares gives to the Brahmin Bālāki at the end of the Ajātaśatru-Bālāki Dialogue.[129] This text, *BṛhUp* II.1.16-20 (K), already mentioned several times, is a useful parallel to the initial segment of the *Antarjyotir Vidyā*.

Ajātaśatru's Teaching to Bālāki. Actually, the teaching begins already in *BṛhUp* II.1.15, where Ajātaśatru takes Bālāki to a man who is asleep. He first talks to the man without getting a response, then wakes the man up, and then turns to Bālāki.

II.1.16. Ajātaśatru said: "When this one (the man) was asleep thus, where then was he who is this person consisting of *vijñāna* (*vijñāna-maya puruṣa*)? From where did he thus come back?" And this also Gārgya (Bālāki) did not think of.

17. Ajātaśatru said: "When this one (the man) fell asleep thus, then this person who consists of *vijñāna*, having by his *vijñāna* taken to himself the *vijñāna* of these senses (*prāṇas*), lies (or rests) in [that place] which is the space within the heart. When he restrains these [senses], that person is said to be asleep. Then indeed Breath is restrained, Speech is restrained, Sight is restrained, Hearing is restrained, the Mind is restrained.

18. He, when he moves about in that dream, these are his worlds: Then he becomes (or is) a great king, as it were, a great Brahmin, as it were, he enters as it were, high and low [conditions]. Like a great king, having taken the people, moves about in his country as he desires, so indeed that one, having taken his *prāṇas,* moves about in his own body (*śarīra*) as he desires.

19. Then, when he is in deep sleep, when he does not know anything of anything, the 72,000 vessels (*nāḍīs*) called *hitā* draw from the heart to the pericardium. He, having crept (down) towards [it], rests on the pericardium. As a boy or a great king or a great Brahmin would rest having reached the summit of bliss (*ānanda*), just so indeed does that one rest.

20. As a spider might come out with its thread, as small sparks come out in different directions (*vyuccaranti*) from the fire, even so from this Ātman come forth all vital energies (*prāṇas*), all worlds, all gods, all beings. The mystic meaning (*upaniṣad*) therefore is 'the Real of the real' (*satyasya satyam*). Vital energies (*prāṇas*), verily, are the real. He (It, the Ātman) is their Real.

At the simplest level, the king poses a question (v. 16): Where was the person who consists of *vijñāna* (i.e., where was his self) when that man fell asleep, and from where did that self come back when he woke up? Then the question is answered. The basic idea is stated first (v. 17): "When he (the man) fell asleep thus, [then] this person consisting of *vijñāna*, having taken [to himself] by his *vijñāna* the *vijñāna* of the *prāṇas*, lies in that what is the space in the heart." The answer to the king's first question, "where" the *vijñāna-maya* person had gone when he was asleep, is "[he has gone to rest] in that which is the space in the heart". The *prāṇas* appear in the waking state to have their own intelligence, knowledge and consciousness: the eye sees forms, etc. But in sleep, that *vijñāna-maya* person has taken (*ā+dā*, has given himself from, or has taken out of, the *prāṇas*), in accordance with the higher level intelligence and consciousness (*vijñāna*) which he is, their knowledge-consciousness capabilities (their *vijñāna*). Thus it is this higher *vijñāna* person or self which sees forms in dream *svapna* (v. 18), and he does so resting "in that which is the space in the heart". As noted in sec. 14, "rest in the space of the heart" also means "rests in his own true nature". In deep sleep, the *vijñāna-maya* person lies in bliss in the area around the heart, just like a king or great Brahmin might when he has reached the summit of bliss (v. 19). Here, the self is resting in its own nature in a deeper way than in dream.

Evidently, the whole episode of going to the sleeping man and waking him was merely staged by the king so he could ask "where the person was when asleep"—it was only a device to "cause [Bālāki] to know [Brahman] clearly". The "person" who is somewhere else when the man is asleep cannot be the ordinary physical person who looks at one and speaks to one, but is instead the *vijñāna-maya* person, the first approximate version of Ātman/Brahman which the king uses to "cause [Bālāki] to know [Brahman] clearly". The second question, "from where did he thus come back?," is no less a set up. The king doesn't say the *vijñāna-maya* person came back from the pericardium; instead, he gives two key images for how all emerges from the Self. "Just as (*yathā*) a spider comes out with the thread, [or] just as small sparks go up-and-apart from a fire, in the same way from this Self (Ātman) go up-and-apart all *prāṇas*, all worlds (*lokas*), all gods, all beings." (v. 20) "This Ātman" suggests that the king continues the topic of the *vijñāna-maya puruṣa* which he has been teaching throughout vs. 16-19. But now the latter appears as the all-embracing One Self. So the *vijñāna-maya* self is actually the One Self.

Finally, the king says that he has been expounding the formula (*upaniṣad*) "*satyasya satyam*," "the True of the True" or "the Real of the Real". The *prāṇas*, the breaths and senses are the *satya* and the Self is the *satya* of *that*. The phrase *satyasya satyam* occurs already as mantra glorifying the essence of the ritual in *TaittSaṁh* I.6.1.1,[131] and as a refrain in two mystical stanzas in *AitĀr* II.3.8:[132]

> (1) [That] Undying which the fivefold enters,
> [which] the harnessed steeds (the senses) draw around,
> Where there is yoked the True of the True,
> there all the gods exist as a One.
> (2) [That] yoked Undying which comes from the Undying,
> [which] the harnessed steeds draw around, . . . [as in (1)]

The Undying in v. 1, *akṣaram*, is the Universal Prāṇa into which the individual senses (the fivefold) enter on death, and *satyasya satyam* in line 3 refers to Brahman. With this reading the stanza becomes consistent with Ajātaśatru's teaching.[133] Similarly, the yoked Undying in v. 2 is Prāṇa which comes from the Undying Brahman. Thus Ajātaśatru is making the point that deepest Āraṇyaka wisdom is teaching the same Truth.

BṛhUp II.1.1.16-20	vs. 16-18	v. 19	v. 20
	vijñāna-maya *puruṣa* *ādāya* exp. in *svapna* *antar-hṛdaya* *ākāśa*	in deep sleep: *nāḍīs* called *hitā*, exp. in *svapna*	(The Self)
BṛhUp IV.3.7-32	vs. 3.7-11	vs. 3.19-20	vs. 3.21 ff.
	vijñāna-maya *hṛdi antar-jyotiḥ* *puruṣa* *ādāya* exp. in *svapna*	in deep sleep: *nāḍīs* called *hitā*, exp. in *svapna*	(The Self)

Fig. 5.1. Comparison between *Antar-jyotir Vidyā* and *Bālāki Vidyā*.

Comparison with *Antar-jyotir Vidyā*. If we compare Ajātaśatru's teaching with *BṛhUp* IV.3.7 ff., there is an obvious close correspondence in the two beginning stages (Fig. 5.1). The major differences come in the third stage which deals with realization of the One Self. While *BṛhUp* IV.3.21 ff. gives very detailed descriptions of states which recognizably continue the stages "*vijñāna-maya* self in *svapna*" and "*vijñāna-maya* self in deep sleep," Ajātaśatru gives only the images of the spider and the sparks as a kind of springboard and inspiration for the inner mind.

18. *Ānanda-maya* Level and Beyond

Recall that we left off *TaittUp* II, Part I, the teaching of the five selves, in sec. 11 to get a broader and deeper understanding of *vijñāna* and the *vijñāna-maya* self. We now return to that text and consider the fifth and last self, the *ānanda-maya* self or self made of bliss (*TaittUp* II.5.2-4).

The first and most important point about the *ānanda* that the *vidyā* is talking about is that it is *ānanda* or bliss which arises when there is *vijñāna* and some knowledge of oneself as *vijñāna-maya*. "Other than and with in . . . [the *vijñāna-maya* self] is the *ānanda-maya* self. By this [latter] that [former] is filled . . ." This means that the *ānanda-maya* self is to be realized *after* there is some *vijñāna* and knowledge that one is *vijñāna-maya*, and that is to be realized as more fundamental than these. This suggests that the kind of *ānanda* in question is intrinsically connected with *vijñāna* and spiritual unfoldment at the *vijñāna-maya* level.

These points are also borne out by II.7.2, the passage where the *vidyā* is speaking directly from high-level *vijñāna*, and which is the *vidyā's* experientially most immediate statement on bliss. The Self, which is also the principle of self, is *sukṛta*, "well done [deed]" (II.7.1). "Verily, what that *sukṛta* is—that, verily, is *rasa* (bliss-taste) (*raso vai saḥ*). For having obtained this very *rasa*, one becomes [a] blissful [one], *ānandī*." The basic meaning of *rasa* is "the sap or juice of plants, . . ., the finest or prime part of any thing, flavor, taste". Śaṁkara glosses it as "cause for satisfaction (*tṛpti*), producing joy (*ānanda*)". So feeling—or being—the self/Self (the *su-kṛta*) in a purer way (or having *vijñāna*), one feels *rasa*, which produces *ānanda*. The *ānanda* or bliss which emerges from *vijñāna* or Ātman-consciousness is something like "higher bliss". As noted earlier, the author at this point becomes visibly inspired, an *ānandī* himself: "For who could here breathe in, who could breathe out if there was not this *ākāśa*-bliss, 'space-bliss'?" The space of his heart, the firmament of his heart, is at the same time the space all around, and is all bliss, and the author is giving vent to his feeling.[134] Sri Sathya Sai Baba paraphrases:

> In the *Taittirīya Upaniṣad* it has been proclaimed thus: "The Paramātmā is the source of contentment, for He is the embodiment of the purest *rasa*, of the Purest Emotion. Attaining Him, the *jīva* [=living being] can be immersed in joy [=bliss]. If the Paramātmā is not shining in the firmament of the Heart, who is to taste, who is to live? He feeds all, with Ānanda."[135]

So in II.7.2, the *vidyā* exemplifies not only (a state of) higher *vijñāna*, as argued in sec. 9, but a combined state of higher *vijñāna* and *ānanda*, illustrating also the *ānanda-maya* level of *TaittUp* II.5.

Next, higher *ānanda* and *ānanda-maya* type awareness are not confined to meditation or times when one is alone, but may be felt in all one's states in daily life. This is implicit in *TaittUp* II.7.2, but is also already suggested in the description of the *ānanda-maya* self as having *priya*, "dear" for its head and *moda* and *pramoda* for its wings (*TaittUp* II.5.3). Śaṁkara explains the terms as "joy—from seeing beloved objects like a son," "enjoyment—the joy that follows the acquisition of an object of desire," and "[the state] when that enjoyment reaches its acme," respectively.[136] These are normal kinds of joy that one experiences in daily life. In view of the fact that the teaching of the *ānanda-maya* self in *TaittUp* II.5.3 undoubtedly refers to higher *ānanda* and to awareness of oneself being highest *ānanda*, this can only mean that the normal situations of joy normally referred to by *priya, moda,* and *pra-moda* provide the vehicles for higher *ānanda*. This interpretation is supported by some comments of Sri Sathya Sai Baba's:

> In experiencing the fulfilment of our desires we invariably pass through three stages. They are *priyam*, *modam*, and *pramodam* . . . [Gives as an example going to buy mangoes at the market, here *priyam* = the joy from seeing the fruit on sale, *modam* = the joy when buying it, and *pramodam* = the joy of eating it].[a]

> But even this '*pramodam*' is not a lasting experience so long as the object desired is a worldly object. Man gets real and everlasting happiness only if he desires for God and treads the Godward-path. When the mind is steadfastly centered on the Lord, '*priyam*,' '*modam*' and '*pramodam*' *acquire a Divine character and confer the Bliss of Immortality on man.*[137] (italics added).

In other words, when the human being "treads the Godward-path," the normal experiences of *priya, moda* and *pra-moda* are Divinized. It is in this way that we have to also understand the consideration of bliss, *TaittUp* II.8. "From the lowest joy to the highest *Brahmānandam* [bliss of Brahman], each step in an increase in the feeling . . . [all are] only stages of *ānandam*. As a matter of fact, all types of *ānandam* are derived from the basic source of *Brahmānandam*."[138]

19. The World Born out of the *Ānanda-maya*

We have seen that the *ānanda* of the *ānanda-maya* level is "higher *ānanda*" which is associated with *vijñāna*, and that it manifests in one's daily experience, not only in meditaion. An analogous statement holds for consciousness that one is *ānanda-maya*. There is however another aspect which is crucial to *ānanda* and *ānanda-maya,* and which in a way is the most important of all. This is the fact that all the other levels of being and experience, from *anna-rasa-maya* to *vijñāna-maya*, are mere evolutes out of the *ānanda-maya*. They are merely phonemena arising from and then dissolving again into the *ānanda-maya*, they are a mere play on the surface of the *ānanda-maya*. We first argue that this extraordinary understanding is already implicit in *TaittUp* II.8, and then consider an authoritative modern explanation.

Hints in *TaittUp* II.8. *TaittUp* II.8 begins with the state of a human being who is in the prime of his life, of sound body and mind, and placed in the most favorable circumstances, and takes this to be "one bliss". Thereafter, the bliss goes up in steps, with an increasse by a factor of 100 at each step. Clearly, the text does not mean for the higher levels to represent just longer periods of bliss. Nor is it only talking about increases in the "degree of bliss", so that the various levels would represent different "degrees" and "qualitatively different types" of bliss as they are "typically experienced" by men, human gandharvas, divine gandharvas, etc. No doubt differences in quality are implied. But this is not the whole story. The texts *takes the "levels"* of man, human gandharva, divine gandharva etc. *as wholes* because these levels represent forms-cum-levels of mind, self, cognition, existence, whatever, as well as of bliss. Expressed differently, they represent specific, "quantitatively" and "qualitatively" different "world-and-experienced-bliss wholes (or totalities)". At each level up to Prajāpati, the world as it is experienced at that level functions indissociably unified with bliss-experience at that level. And it is the combination of the two as a unified whole that the Upaniṣad takes as a unit of bliss. So as one goes up these levels, all three: degree and quality of bliss, manner of experience of world (including body), and their manner of integration, change. But "Bliss" increases, while "World" decreases. It becomes more and more an epiphenomenon or marginal effect, until at the level of Brahman, it is virtually gone, or, the diversity is replaced by only oneness. "Bliss," on the other hand, is still there. Thus "Bliss" is associated with Brahman in a different way than "World" ("Bliss" goes up, "World" goes down). Because the context is clearly cosmic and objective, the implication is that Bliss is in some sense the foundation of the world and all experience.[139]

Bliss or Ānanda is therefore something much more fundamental than *vijñāna. Vijñāna* is initially tied up with experience of oneself in the world, a finite aspect that is gradually transcended in further inner evolution. Bliss becomes more and more prominent and independent from the world.

A Statement by Sri Sathya Sai Baba. To get further insight, we draw again on Sri Sathya Sai Baba:

> [A] People, who truly want to understand yoga, should detach themselves from all ordinary worldly actions. Yoga connotes having a confluence with Divinity and the sacred aspects of Ātmā. Like the river, when once it enters the ocean, loses its name, its form and its taste, so also a human being; once he joins the Ātmic spirit, he will have nothing to do with the world. If we send a doll of salt into the ocean, can it come back again to us? This doll of salt, though it has come out of the ocean originally [because salt is a product of the ocean], once it goes back to the ocean, it will merge into it and become identical with

> ocean. In the same manner, for people who understand completely the meaning of yoga, there will be no further opportunity to have anything to do with the worldly *bhoga*, enjoyment.
>
> ·Here all the four *kośas*, the *anna-maya*, the *prāṇa-maya*, the *mano-maya* and the *vijñāna-maya*, are born out of the *ānandamaya kośa*. The primary objective of the *ānanda-maya kośa* is *icchā* or *saṁkalpa* [the deepest will or determination in oneself]. This *icchā* or *saṁkalpa* is merged with the [individual] *ātmā* and is contained inside as *ātmā*. Therefore, *saṁkalpa* loses all its manifestation once it merges with the inner self or the *ātmā*. The entire world is only a projection or an image of this *saṁkalpa*. It is not possible for the *saṁkalpa* to get into an illusion by looking at its own image in the material world. . .[140]

The crucial word at the beginning of the second paragraph is "here". "Here", in true inner yoga, when one has "detached oneself from all ordinary worldly actions" and when there is "confluence with Divinity and with the sacred aspects of the Ātmā," here one sees, knows, that the first four sheaths are all "born out of the *ānanda-maya* sheath". This being born is due to the individual's *icchā* or *saṁkalpa*, his/her inmost inner self-will and determination which is his/her life and which his/her course through many lives bring to realization and fulfillment. "This *icchā* or *saṁkalpa* is merged with the *ātmā*" or the individual self. The *ānanda* of the *ānanda-maya* sheath is connected with how at any time this inmost *icchā* and *saṁkalpa* are being realized, or brought closer to fulfillment. We might say that the *icchā* or *saṁkalpa* is a sacred aspect of the Ātman which represents the reason for the individual's existence. It has to do with the meaning of the individual's life, and with the contribution of the individual's existence (perhaps over many lifetimes) to creation, to the world-total. The *icchā* and *saṁkalpa* of the individual can be said to be contained in a universal *icchā* and *saṁkalpa* of the Ātman for the Universe. Then *ānanda* and the *ānanda-maya* self has to do with the feeling of this *icchā* becoming realized. Here one can see the unfathomable depth of this *vidyā*. For on the one hand, when there is the state of this *ānanda* where one's innermost purpose-desire, the seed of one's existence, is coming to fulfillment, then one sees that all the other sheaths, and the whole of existence, are born out of *ānanda*. "Here (in the stage of inmost *yoga*) all the four *kośas* . . . are born out of the *ānanda-maya kośa.*" And on the other hand, "here," when this *icchā* or *saṁkalpa* is being fulfilled, one *is being dissolved* by the fulfillment. Here one is the salt-doll that is being dissolved again in the Ocean from whence one came. From this we get a clue regarding Part II of this *Vidyā*. Basically, this whole Part revolves only around this dissolution, this fulfillment. The merger of the individual self into Brahman is the final fulfillment of individual self. It is becoming one with the Universal and the Total of world and existence as we know it, and with the source of that Universal and Total, Ātman/Brahman.

When there is complete yoga, then "all the four sheaths . . .are born out of the *ānanda-maya* sheath". Today in science and any more rigorous type of thought, there is a tendency to start with the physical level as the most reliable and real and then "proceed inwards" toward mind and Spirit, defining them by their outer manifestations in individuals etc. This is the "objective approach," as in the essentially matter-based "scientific method".[141] This kind of approach typically assumes that truth and certainty of truth ultimately need to be validated by agreement and that the latter can ultimately only be obtained by perceptual inspection of physical situations etc.[142] As a result there are widely shared extreme positions to the effect that mind or consciousness and the self are mere epiphenomena on a physical substrate, the brain, and that metaphysical experience or experience of the Divine or Transccendental is of the nature of subjective, psychological illusions, similar to hallucinations, which may be experienced but have no validity. [A] represents a totally different cognition. *All* the four other sheaths—and this means all the levels of *vijñāna*, mind, *prāṇa*, and food, as realms and universals, not as aspects of the individual—are born out of the *ānanda* sheath. Obviously in an aspirant on the spiritual path, this cognition would represent beginning merger with Ātman/Brahman, which is the goal. For when the first four sheaths are truly known to be born out of the *ānanda-maya*, then the hold of the whole physical-mental complex is permanently broken or transcended. Then indeed body and world (which are the same as the four other sheaths) are an outgrowth of ("born of") *ānanda.*

20. *Ānanda-maya* from the Point of View of the Aspirant—Devotee

Higher *ānanda* and stages of higher *ānanda* may take innumerable forms. As with *vijñāna*, it is the Infinite or the Reality that makes *ānanda* what it is. It is the fact of *ānanda*, or of various *ānandas*, the actual flavor, that is the crucial ingredient; knowing that actual flavor, one would recognize it in innumerable forms. Still, to get an idea, a more detailed statement by Shree Shree Anandamayee Ma will be cited (actually a summary of statements of Shree Ananadamayee Ma's by a close devotee). Shree Anandamayee Ma's general line of teaching may be summarized as "He alone is" ("He is formless yet all are his forms," etc.),[143] and may thus be regarded as amplifying one aspect of Upaniṣadic teaching (with He = Ātman/Brahman = God). But the Upaniṣadic element, although central, is in her an integral part of a larger whole whose leading aspects are absolute devotion (givenness) combined with complete authority and an extraordinary simplicity:

When Mother [Shree Anandamayee Ma] was approached with a prayer to let us know the various stages of *sādhanā* [effort on the spiritual path], she indicated four levels:

(i) **Concentration of the intellect on a focal point.** It is like setting fire to dry fuel. When wet wood has been dried by the heat of fire, the flames blaze up brightly. Similarly when by the force of contemplation of the Divine, our mind is released from the mist and moisture of desires and passions (*kāmanā, vāsanā*), it becomes light. It is a condition of mental purity which induces in certain cases a state of silent merging into a particular mood, or into an excess of emotion and agitation beyond one's power of control. All these moods emanate from one supreme existence in special directions.

(ii) **Concentration of one's emotional powers.** It induces a state of bodily inertness, of absorption in one holy sentiment arising out of one, indivisible supramental state. At that level the body may be likened to a burnt charcoal with the fire apparently gone out. In this state the devotee passes hours together in a condition of outer inertness; but in the core of his heart surges up an unceasing current of sublime emotion. When this state matures, the sentiment draws mighty powers from the All-Soul [the Ātman], and just as a vessel overflows when too much water is poured into it, it spreads out over the wide world in a mighty sweep under the intense pressure of expansiveness.

(iii) **Fusion of the inner and outer life.** This state is just like that of a burning coal. Fire pervades every atom of the inner and outer sheaths—all are aglow with one divine Light. The devotee lives, moves and has his being in one blissful ocean of Light.

(iv) **Full-concentration,** in which the devotee loses all consciousness of duality—of the functioning of the three *guṇas*. It is like the state of coal burnt to ashes. There is no distinction between the inner and the outer, between here and there; it is a state of absorption in the Supreme, of All-Oneness. Vibrations of thought, feeling or willing vanish altogether. It resembles the perfect tranquillity of a sleeping lake under a blue sky.[144] (Boldface added)

This illustrates the Supreme Upaniṣadic Wisdom in one of its garbs today. Note that *ānanda* occurs completely naturally in all the higher stages described. Although the *vijñāna-ānanda*-beyond *ānanda* scheme of *Taittirīya Upaniṣad* is not mentioned, it is fully exemplified. (i) refers to beginning awareness of *ānanda* in spiritual life, at a beginning level of *vijñāna* ("when by the force of contemplation of the Divine, the mind is released from . . . desires and passions . . ."). It describes *ānanda* as taking the form of "state[s] of silent merging onto a particular mood" or of a sudden "blazing" up of "excess of emotion" (the latter reminiscent of Henry Suso's or Jan van Ruusbroec's *jubilatio*). (ii)-(iv) then describe further phases of *ānanda* and of merger into Brahman. (ii) is clearly related to further levels of *vijñāna* (cf. "in the core of his heart . . ." and the implied awareness, whatever, of the "All-soul," the Ātman or Paramātman), and in (iii) lower level *vijñāna* is being transcended.

21. *BṛhUp* IV.3.1-34 (K)

So far we focussed on *ānanda* and the *ānanda-maya* level, trying to determine the major parameters of these aspects as described in *TaittUp* II and using some authoritative modern descriptions. Now we turn to the question whether the higher teaching of *vijñāna-ānanda*-beyond *ānanda* is also found elsewhere in the Upaniṣads. Two texts are relevant here, the full *Antar-jyotir Vidyā, BṛhUp* IV.3.1-34 (K), and *BṛhUp* III.9.27-8. In this section we discuss the fact that broadly speaking, *BṛhUp* IV.3.1-3.34 (K) as a whole decomposes into three or four phases or states which clearly illustrate a *vijñāna-ānanda*-beyond *ānanda* progression.

Four Phases Represented in *BṛhUp* IV.3. -3.34 (K):

(1) 3.1-3.18, discussed in secs. 13-15 above. According to our analysis there, this segment of the text teaches something like realization of oneself as light in the heart, and as immortal, unaffected and the same in waking, dream, and meditative states, the last possibly accompanied by psychic experience.

(2) 3.19-3.20, dealing with the Self in deep sleep. A similar statement occurs in an analogous position in the Ajātaśatru-Bālāki Dialogue (sec. 17 above). In both cases we interpreted this generally as a phase in which knowledge of the *vijñāna-maya* self in the heart in dream and other meditative states is deepened by extension to deep sleep. We will pursue this further in secs. 6.17 ff. below.

(3) 3.21-3.30. We will argue that this represents a further stage and deeper state(s) than (1) and (2), in which the dominant component is the One Self, with little awareness of any sense-based form (i.e. primarily formlessness). This stage appears to represent beginning but clear perception and full realization (knowledge, *vijñāna*) of the One Self.

(4) 3.32-33, an apparently still further stage involving merger with and perhaps the possibility of permanent dissolution into the Supreme. This stage is referred to in 3.32, with 3.33 (an enquiry into bliss similar to *TaittUp* II.8) a kind of comment on or glorification of it.

As noted, levels (1) and (2) have been discussed in secs. 13-16 and 17 and we consider only (3) and (4). Vs. 3.21-3.34 have a unity and they all seem to refer to the same state. The latter is first introduced in 3.21 as the form (*rūpa*) of the Self which is beyond desire, free from evil, free from fear, and then characterized as "that form of his [which is] desire-attained, having as desire [only] the self, without desire," "beyond sorrow" (*āpta-kāma, ātma-kāma, a-kāma, and śokāntara*). This may be associated with vs. 19-20 and regarded as a description of a state when the knowledge of the Self in deep sleep is sufficiently developed. 3.21 is then unfolded further in 3.22 and 3.23-3.31, "there a father is a non-father . . .," and "when he then does not see there, ... [then there is still seeing in some sense]" etc. The latter presumably continues the theme of the Ātman being the light of man at the beginning of the discourse (v. 3.1-3.6), but now at a level of the first true knowledge or perception of the Ātman. In the Upaniṣads there are a few very great texts which describe Ātman/Brahman as the Highest Light:

> III.13.7. Now [that] which shines as light (*jyotir dīpyate*) above this heaven, above the backs of all, above the backs of everything, in the highest worlds above which there is no higher, truly this light (here) is what this light within the person is (*ChāndUp* III.13.7).

> II.2.15. The Sun does not shine (*bhā*) there, nor moon and star,
> these flashes do not shine, where then is the fire?
> All shines (*bhā*) after the shining of Him;
> By His light (*bhā*) He illumines (*vi-bhā*) all this [world].
> (*KaṭhaUp* II.2.15 = *MuṇḍUp* II.2.1 = *ŚvetUp* VI.14)

These verses are at a cosmic or infinite level. Vs. IV.3.21-3.30, by comparison, are still at a level of individual seeing. But the trend seems clear. For 3.32 brings a still further phase, an Infinite Expansion of Self, a Becoming Infinite: "The Seer becomes the Ocean, one, without a second . . ." Ocean is *salila*, the *Ṛg Vedic* word for the Waters out of which all creations is fashioned. But the emphasis is no doubt on the oneness, the non-duality of this "state," and particularly its unlimitedness. "*Es wogt der ẹine Seher*" is Böthlingk's inspired translation.[145] Already in 3.21-3.31 there is no more concern with any "content" of *vijñāna*, or with any "cognitive content". The states and levels of 3.7b-3.9a and 3.11-14a are left behind. Instead the entire effort centers on describing the nature of "being the Seer" (including in this all the faculties mentioned in 3.23 ff. —seeing, smelling, thinking, knowing), or the nature of "being the Subject" (as Vedānta has it), a "state" which has no cessation (3.21-30) and is one without a second (3.21-3.30, and differently, 3.31). Still, these verses may originally have been intended to help with inner practice and may allude to experience as seen at the level of practice. This is suggested by the appeal to reasoning, "*for* there is found no destruction of the Seeing of a Seer, on account of imperishability," etc., as if these phrases were intended to be used in contemplation (*manana*) and inner repetition. In 3.32, however, there is no more inner practice, there is only the Infinite. "This is the realm of Brahman (*Brahmaloka*), oh great king." This is the highest realization of Brahman, Brahman itself. "This is his highest course, . . . this is his highest bliss." The Seer becoming the ocean is this person's highest course, *gati*, his/her highest going. It is this person's highest perfection or completion, *saṁpad* (Śaṁkara: "glory"). It is his/her highest world, *parama loka*, it is his/her highest bliss, *parama ānanda*. It doesn't matter whether we call it his highest course or perfection or *ānanda*, these terms are all equally applicable (or inapplicable).

22. "Brahman is *Vijñāna* and *Ānanda*"

In the last section we saw that *BṛhUp* IV.1-34, the first half of Yājñavalkya's greatest discourse in *Bṛhadāraṇyaka Upaniṣad*, contains essentially a specific elaboration of the *Taittirīya vijñāna-ānanda*-beyond *ānanda* scheme. Now there is also another passage in *Bṛhadāraṇyaka Upaniṣad* where Yājñavalkya refers both to *vijñāna* and *ānanda*. At the end of *BṛhUp* III, after having been challenged on spiritual matters by about a dozen interlocuters and come out victorious every time, the great sage poses to them in a beautiful poem a question about the nature of man of his own.[146] He asks "From what root does man spring forth when he is cut off by death," and answers in the last verse "[Brahman, and this] Brahman is *vijñāna* and *ānanda*." While it does not provide much additional detail about *vijñāna* and *ānanda*, the next does convey the centrality of *vijñāna-ānanda* in Yājñavalkya's whole teaching.

III.9.28. Then he questioned them with the following verses (*ślokas*):

(1) As a tree, lord of the forest,
so indeed is man.
His hairs are the leaves,
his skin is the outer bark.
(2) From his skin, indeed,
blood flows forth—[as] from
the bark-skin.
From him when he is wounded

it comes forth, just as sap
from the tree when it is cut.
(3) His parts of flesh are the parts of wood.
His tough sinew is the fibre.
The bones are the wood parts within.
The marrow is made like marrow (= pith).
(4) As a tree, when it is felled,
grows again newer from the root,
When a mortal is felled by death,
from what root, pray, does he rise up?
(5) Do not say "From semen."
That is produced from a living [person].
The tree likewise springs up from seed.
Having died, (?)
(6) What[ever] tree is pulled up by the root
does not come to be again.
When a mortal is felled by death,
from what root, pray, does he rise up?
(7) [Once] born (or: [although] born), he is not born [*aja*].
For who should bring him forth again?
Brahman is *vijñāna* and *ānanda*,
the final goal (refuge) of the generous giver (in sacrifices)
[(8)] [and of him] who is of steady mind, knowing it.

When a man is cut down by death, he rises up again from an invisible root [III.9.28.(4)]; death is not the end. What is the root from which he arises again? [(4)b] Yājñavalkya says that he is not talking about seed or bodily roots, and repeats the question [(6)b = (4)b]. And then in (7)b he makes a veiled comment on the true state of affairs. The root is Brahman, absolutely universal. One might have thoughts of *karma* causing man to arise again, or the subtle body or the causal body. But in truth, man arises from Brahman—that is the real source. This Brahman is *vijñāna* and *ānanda*; this Brahman is the goal and refuge for the devout and the knowers of Brahman.

23. Merger into Brahman

Throughout this chapter we have taken the view that the Five Sheaths *Vidyā* is essentially teaching Merger into Brahman as the final goal.

We assumed that the *vidyā* treated the *ānanda-maya* as simply a fifth stage or level beyond the *vijñāna-maya*, and that both the *vijñāna* and *ānanda* stages were preliminary and subordinate to Merging into Brahman. Implicit in this is an acknowledgement that the *vijñāna* and *ānanda* states are not the end and that Brahman is beyond them. We saw for example that the "Invisible, Centerless . . ." in *TaittUp* II.7.2 very likely refers to knowledge arising on the path of turning away from all things as being not Self. When walking such a path, one would not be likely to identify Brahman with something like the *ānanda-maya* self. And on such a path, the language of merger into Brahman would fit the "experiential" realities better than the language of *ānanda-maya* self or of "Brahman is *ānanda*". (Of course what "merger" might mean from an "objective point of view" is another question. The concepts of subjective and objective start becoming inapplicable even before the highest levels of *vijñāna* and *ānanda*.) Thus in our treatment the *ānanda-maya* stage is only a general phase before and during the "process of merging".

In Indian Philosophy, the question whether the *ānanda-maya* stage represents "being Brahman," or whether Brahman is beyond this stage, has a long history. Already the *Brahma Sūtra* deals with the question whether the *ānanda-maya* self or stage is Brahman (*BraSū* I.12-19). An independent reading of these aphorisms suggests indeed that "Bādarāyaṇa holds that Brahman consists of bliss [i.e., is *ānanda-maya*], is the fifth and final sheath, and is reached by the path described in the five steps which comprise this text [*TaittUp* II.1-6.1]."[147] But such impressions may be deceptive. Śaṁkara in his commentary and elsewhere argues that *ānanda-maya* does not indicate Brahman, and that Brahman is not the sheath of bliss, but lies within that sheath.[148] At the same time, he maintains that the highest bliss is Brahman.[149] With Rāmānuja the pendulum swings the other way: The *ānanda-maya* is Brahman.[150]

One fact often cited as evidence that the *vidyā* means to identify Brahman with the *ānanda-maya* self stage is *TaittUp* II.5, "He who knows this, on passing on from this world, proceeds on to that self which consists of Prāṇa" and so on. For that text simply stops with "proceeds on to that self which consists of *ānanda*". Similarly, the account of *Bhṛgu* in *TaittUp* III likewise stops with the latter's realization of Brahman as *ānanda*. In II.9.2 the difficulty is to interpret the word "proceeds on to," *upa-saṁ-kram-*, which contains both connotations of the process ("proceeds on to," *upa+kram-*), and of attaining a final result ("arrives at,"[151] "assimilates"[152] the level in question "to itself"). Since the term is used in a similar way in eschatological contexts in the Brāhmaṇas also,[153] something like "assimilates to himself (or attains) (after death) the essence of food, the essence of Prāṇa," etc. may well be right. But even so the fact that the Upaniṣad stops with "attains the essence of *ānanda*" does not necessarily mean there is no further merging into Brahman.[154] Sri Sathya Sai Baba explicitly regards not only Brahman but also Love as *within* and different from the *ānanda-maya* sheath.[155]

NOTES

1. Modern scholarly treatments of the *vidyā* as a whole: Deussen, *Sixty Ups.*, pp. 232-35; and Gispert-Sauch, *Bliss*, pp. 21-103, who summarizes much Western-type scholarship. J.A.B. van Buitenen's contributions, scattered over several publications, are partially summarized in his Ānanda or all Desires Fulfilled. *History of Religions*, v. 19 (1979), pp. 27-36 (repr. *Studies*, pp. 323-32); pp. 33-35 (resp. pp. 328-30) (cf. also Gispert-Sauch). Recent Indian treatments: Mukhopadhyaya, *Studies*, pp. 233-49; K. Krishnaswami, The *Taittirīya Upaniṣad*. A Study. *Vedānta Keshari*, v. 61 (1974/75), pp. 109-112, and 146-49. There are also some penetrating spiritual comments on the *vidyā* by Sri Gopinath Kaviraj, culled from his writings, in K. Bhattacharya (*Gopinath Kaviraj's Thought—Toward a Systematic Study*. Calcutta: Univ. of Calcutta, 1982, pp. 173-74 [nos. (44) and (45)], but I have not been able to trace their original source(s). A commentary on *Taittirīya Upaniṣad* by Lahiri Mahāśaya, which is to be published Swami Satyeshvaranand in his *Commentaries* series, would be of considerable interest also. There are three major Advaitic commentaries or subcommentaries on the Upaniṣad, by Śaṁkara, Sureśvara, and Sāyaṇa, respectively.
2. K. Krishnaswami, *op. cit.*, p. 110.
3. The *Kāṇḍānukrama*, a summary of the contents of the texts of the Ātreyī school of the Black *Yajur Veda*, calls *TaittUp* II-III *Vāruṇī Upaniṣad* [see Keith, *TaittSaṁh*, p. xxviii; Skt. text: A. Weber, *Indische Studien* v. 12 (1872), p. 352]. So does Sāyaṇa, in the introduction to his commentary on *TaittĀr* VII-X.
4. Standard mature Vedāntic exposition like *Vivekacūḍāmaṇi* 151-216 and *Pañcadaśī* III treat it as one of several elements in a whole arsenal of *jñāna* techniques. From their point of view the *vidyā* involves primarily "distinguishing self from non-self" (cf. chr. 2.5), and a positive element, "realization of subtler and subtler aspects of existence and consciousness".
5. So already E. Frauwallner in his Untersuchungen zum Mokṣadharma. Die saṁkhyistischen Texte. *Wiener Zeitschrift zur Kunde des Morgenlandes*, v. 32, 1925, pp. 179-206; p. 196 (repr. *Kleine Schriften*, pp. 55-82; p.

72); and Untersuchungen zu den älteren Upanischaden, *Zeitschrift für Indien und Iran*, v. 4 (1926), pp. 1-45; pp. 33-34 (repr. *Kleine Schriften*, pp. 95-139; pp. 127-128).

6. Sri Sathya Sai Baba, Discourse given May 31, 1991 in Brindavan. *Sanathana Sarathi*, v. 34 (1991), pp. 266-267.

7. Sri Sathya Baba, *ibid.*, pp. 7 ff. See below.

8. van Buitenen compares the *Taittirīya* teaching of the first three sheaths with *MaitrUp* VI.33, a meditation on the three domestic fires inspired by the *agnicayana* (van Buitenen, *MaitrUp*, pp. 29-33; *MaitrUp* VI.33 is translated *ibid.*, p. 148). The fires are each said to have a head, two wings (sides), a back and a tail and to be of the shape of a man, *pruruṣa-vidha*, and are equated with the earth/year, *prāṇa*, and Āditya (Sun)/Indra/Vedas, resp. Van Buitenen argues that these cosmically defined levels are equivalent to the *Taittirīya's* levels of food, *prāṇa* and mind, resp. (*ibid.*, pp. 31-32). Although much of *Maitrāyaṇīya Upaniṣad* is very late (much later than *Taittirīya Upaniṣad*), this portion of the Upaniṣad should be older because "it occupies a middle position between the notions already voiced in the Brāhmaṇas and the more advanced views quoted in *Taittirīya Upaniṣad*" (*ibid.*, p. 31). According to van Buitenen, the original three-layer scheme illustrated in *Maitrāyaṇīya Upaniṣad* was expanded to a fivefold one in *ŚatBr* X.4.5.3 and finally streamlined by *TaittUp* II into the form there. (In the *Śatapatha Brāhmaṇa* passage, Celaka Śāṇḍilyāyana teaches that the fourth layer of the fire-altar in the *agnicayana* is the sacrificer, and the fifth, all objects of desire. "And let him know that having built up these worlds [in the first three layers of the altar], he [builds up] both his self and all desires.") L. Renou has suggested that the view of Brahman as *vijñāna* and *ānanda* as in *BṛhUp* III.9.29 (sec. 20 below) may have an antecedent in *ŚatBr* X.3.5, a long mystical section on the *Yajur Vedic* mantras (see Gispert-Sauch, *Bliss*, pp. 218-220).

9. Modern translation: W. Rau, Versuch einer deutschen Übersetzung der *Taittirīya Upaniṣad. Festschrift der Wissenschaftlichen Gesellschaft der J.W. Göthe Universität Fankfurt am Main.* Wiesbaden: Steiner, 1981, pp. 349-379. I have not seen the French edition and translation by E. Lesimple in the *les Upanishad* series (cf. chr. 2, note) and the Italian translation by C. della Casa, Taittirīya Upaniṣad. In *Classici delle Religioni. Le religioni. orientali: Upaniṣad*, a cura di C. della Casa. Torissa, 1976, pp. 281-302. For general background on the Taittirīya tradition, see Gispert-Sauch, *Bliss*, pp. 21 ff.

10. M. Witzel, An Unknown Upaniṣad of the *Kṛṣṇa Yajurveda:* The *Kaṭha-Śikṣā-Upaniṣad. Journal of the Nepal Research Centre* 1 (1977), pp. 139-53 (1-10) (*n. v.*); the same author, Die *Kaṭha-Śikṣā-Upaniṣad* und ihr Verhältnis zur Śikṣāvallī der *Taittirīya-Upaniṣad, WZKSA*, v. 23 (1979), pp. 5-28; v. 24 (1980), pp. 21-82. In the last paper Witzel argues (note 2, p. 77) that both the *Taittirīya* and *Kaṭha* versions of the text go back to a common original which would have been part of an "Ur"—*Yajur Veda.*

11. However, in the *Oupnek'hat* and the Colebrooke Collection (the second of which represents a compilation of Upaniṣads which was widely desseminated and almost regarded canonical in the 17th century or so), *TaittUp* II and III appear as separate texts while *TaittUp* I is missing altogether. See Deussen, *Sixty Ups.*, pp. 559-661.

12. M. Falk, *Nāma Rūpa*, pp. 35-36, considers *TaittUp* II to be teaching a "microcosmic penetration through the [five] concentric *kośas* or bodies" (i.e., *ātman* = "body" rather than "self"), which is "equivalent to the macrocosmical ascension through the successive spheres of the cosmic Brahman-reality" taught in *TaittUp* III.
13. (a) Gispert-Sauch (*Bliss*, p. 38) points out that *ananta* is an adjective, hence possibly also "as infinite knowledge". Rau has an interesting reconstruction of a possible original form of the verse (Rau, *op. cit.*, p. 367). (b) From *vipa*, "trembling, excited, inspired." (c) Alternatively, "he together with Brahman obtains all desires". E.F. Beall, Syntactical ambiguity at *Taittirīya Upaniṣad* 2.1, *IIJ*, v. 29 (1980), pp. 97-102, argues that the ambiguity is deliberate. (d) Only in some versions.
14. (a) On the suffix *mayaṭ* see Gispert-Sauch, *Bliss*, pp. 50-52. (b) Vs. 2.1 (1)-(3) are *ślokas* and are discussed in Horsch, *Gāthā Literature*, pp. 183-86.
15. (a) *Śloka*, singular. (b) Cf. Horsch, *op. cit.*, pp. 186-87. (c) A very short phrase, occurring also in the descriptions of the remaining selves, whose meaning is problematic. The translation is based on arguments that *śarīra ātmā* = "the bodily self," as in Gispert-Sauch, *Bliss*, pp. 59-62; so also Rau, *op. cit.* (note 1 above), p. 358. But Śaṁkara takes it differently. (d) Horsch, *ibid.*, p. 187; (e) *Ibid.*, pp. 187-88; (f) *Ibid.*, pp. 188-89.
16. Deussen, however, feels that they are, and he elaborates a somewhat complex solution based on the following *TaittUp* II.7.1-7.2 which may conceivably be right (*Sixty Ups.*, v. 1, p. 234).
17. Rau, *op, cit.*, pp. 360, 371.
18. (a) For this *śloka*, see Horsch, *Gāthā Literature*, p. 189; (b) *Ibid.*, p. 190; (c) The sequence of beings is man, man-Gandharvas, *deva*-Gandharvas, Manes, *ājāna*-gods, *karma*-gods, gods, Indra, Bṛhaspati, Prajāpati, Brahman.
19. J.A.B. van Buitenen, *MaitrUp*, p. 30, citing *MaitrSaṁh* III.4.13 (8) and *ŚatBr* (K) X.4.5.2.
20. In the *Taittirīya* text the *rasa* is required because of II.2.1: beings spring from and are maintained by food in the sense that their bodies are the essence, *rasa*, of food.
21. (a) *pra-uvāca*.
22. Śaṁkara and Sureśvara, taking their clue from "the oldest of beings" and "obtaining all food" in II.2.1(2) as well as from *TaittUp* III.2.1, discuss this *upāsanā* in terms of Virāj, "the manifested God" [Mahadeva Sastry, *The Taittirīya Upaniṣad with the Commentaries of Śrī Śaṅkarācārya, Śrī Sureśvarācārya, Śrī Vidyāraṇya.* Madras: Samata Books, 1980 (1st ed. Mysore: Printing Works, 1903), p. 392], or in other words God as seen in Creation. "The God who has the Directions as organs, who wears the body of Five Elements, who shines with the notion 'I am all'—the Virāj was thus born" (Sureśvara, *Taittirīyopaniṣad Bhāṣyavārttika* II.158; Mahadeva Sastry, *ibid.*, p. 392; cf. J.M. van Boetzelaer, *Sureśvara's Taittirīyopaniṣad Bhāṣyavārttikam*, Leiden: E.J. Brill, 1971 [*ORT*, No. 12], p. 80). Food in II.2.1(2) (or more accurately, Brahman as Food) is identified with the Virāj (Sureśvara, *op. cit.*, II.253; v. Boetzelaer, *ibid.*, p. 97) and realization of "Brahman is Food" with becoming one with the Virāj (hence "obtains all Food") (Sureśvara, *op. cit.*, II.261-262; v. Boetzelaer, *ibid.*,

p. 99). This Virāj is the Vedāntic version of the Virāj of the Puruṣa Hymn, which is also "the oldest of beings". V. Boetzelaer gives a summary of Śaṁkara's and later Vedānta's notion of Virāj *(ibid.*, p. 81).

23. Transl. Eggeling, *ŚatBr*, v. 5, p. 260.
24. This is presumably as far as *TaittUp* II.1.4-2.1 intends to go. But *TaittUp* III.10.5, a song of a liberated or close to liberated being, uses only the language of food and says ia. "I, [being] food, eat the food-eater." This, as well as other occurrences of higher "food mysticism" in the Upaniṣads, make one wonder.
25. All these categories come in the early Upaniṣads at one time or another under the heading of *Prāṇa*. In the much later *Yoga Upaniṣads*, breathing discipline or *prāṇāyāma* gives access to a vast area of inner knowledge whose object is the subtle body, *sūkṣma śarīra* (see below).
26. I am assuming the series intended by the text is *prāṇa, apāna, vyāna*, the switch of *apāna* and *vyāna* being caused by the necessity of naming the right wing first. This order is much more common, and more likely to be intended here, than *prāṇa, vyāna, apāna*.
27. The series *prāṇa, apāna, vyāna, udāna* and *samāna* occurs already once in *Vājasaneyī Saṁhitā*, twice in *Śatapatha Brāhmaṇa* (at VIII.1.3.6-7 and XI.8.3.6), and nine times in *Taittirīya Āraṇyaka*. See A.H. Ewing, The Hindu Conception of the Functions of Breath.—A Study in Early Hindu Psycho-physics. *JAOS*, v. 22 (1901), pp. 249-308; p. 259. In the old Upaniṣads it is found at *BṛhUp* III.9.26. *ChāndUp* III.13 and V.19 (the adjunct to the *Vaiśvānara Vidyā* discussed in chr. 4.15) use the same five terms but in the order *prāṇa, vyāna, apāna, samāna, udāna*. The meaning of the individual breaths and the conception of the system as a whole seems to have changed as time went on. See the excellent paper by H.W. Bodewitz, Prāṇa, Apāna, and the othere Prāṇas in Vedic Literature. *ALB*, v. 50 (1986), pp. 326-348.
28. E.g. in (*Yoga-*) *DarśanaUp* IV.23 ff., transl. and dicussed in J. Varenne, *Yoga and the Hindu Tradition*. Chicago: Univ. of Chicago Press, 1976 (or. French ed., *Le Yoga et la Tradition Hindoue*. Paris: Culture, Art, Loisirs, 1973); pp. 208 ff., 158-59, and elsewhere; and in *Triśikhi BrāhmaṇaUp* 77-87, transl. and Skt. original in A. Danielou, *Yoga, The Method of Re-Integration*. New York: University Books; pp. 126-127.
29. In *Vājasaneyī Saṁhitā, prāṇa, apāna, vyāna* is by far the most common of all series of *prāṇas*, (9 occurrences, vs. three or less for each of the others), and in the *Atharva Veda* it is the only common series of three or more *prāṇas* (11 occurrences, vs. two or one for each of the others); cf. Ewing, *op cit.*, pp. 257-58. (For Brāhmaṇa comments on the occurrences in *Vājasaneyī Saṁhitā*, see *ŚatBr* VIII.7.1.22, VIII.7.3.19, and IX.2.1.17, all in the context of the *agnicayana*).
30. The *prāṇas* are the same as "vital power" or "life", *āyus*, see *ŚatBr* VIII.7.3.30.
31. Cf. Varenne's introduction to his translation of the Upaniṣad, Varenne, *op. cit.*, pp. 197-199.
32. *DarśanaUp* IV.26-28; Varenne, *ibid.*, p. 209. Cf. also *Triśikhi BrāhmaṇaUp* 79 ff.; Danielou, *op. cit.*, p. 127. Similar descriptions are found in the Āyurvedic literature.
33. Cf. Danielou (regarding the ten vital energies named in the *Yoga Upaniṣads*, which begin with the same five named in the Old Upaniṣads): "The vital

energies, however, are subtle energies . . ." (*ibid.*, p. 127). But the examples he gives are not clearly related to texts.

34. *DarśanaUp* IV.39 ff.; Varenne, *op. cit.*, pp. 210 ff.
35. E.g. *DarśanaUp* V.7 ff.; Varenne, *ibid.*, p. 213.
36. Varenne, *ibid.*, p. 158.
37. Described in experiential terms in various ways, such as "a sort of invisible maṇḍala—formed by a combination of symbolic (but also very real) geometric figures," "a structure of reference, and image, a *yantra*," Varenne, *ibid.*, pp. 153, 154 resp. The *sūkṣma śarīra* of the Yoga Upaniṣads must be distinguished from the *sūkṣma śarīra* of Vedānta, which is the second of the series of three bodies, the physical, the subtle, and the causal.
38. Because the *samāna* is like the atmosphere in its pervasiveness (so Śaṁkara and Sureśvara, cf. v. Boetzelaer, *op. cit.*, p. 101), and because it is "in the middle" of the *prāṇas* (Śaṁkara) or of the body (Sāyaṇa). According to *BṛhUp* III.9.26, all the *prāṇas* are ultimately based on the *samāna*.
39. A general connection between Earth and *prāṇa* and other subtle energies is assumed in various occult systems. E.g. A. Bailey teaches that the etheric bodies of healer and patient, which receive the *prāṇic* and other energies, are "integral, intrinsic parts" of the etheric body of the earth which is "whole, unbroken, and continuous" (A. Bailey, *A Treatise on the Seven Rays*, v. 4, *Esoteric Healing*, New York: Lucis Publishing Co., 1953, p. 645).
40. E.g. in yoga, in occult varieties of Vedānta, as well as in popular books. For example, in a popular combined psychic-spiritual book, Thiruvarul Thavayogi says that "all Hindu literatures teach us that human souls are given five layers or bodies called *kośas*," with the *prāṇamaya kośa* equivalent to "spiritual body, astral body, ethereal body, ghost in English, *sūkṣma śarīra, svapna śarīra, yātanā śarīra* in Sanskrit, *aavi, ulludal, nunnudal,* and *puhaludal* in Tamil" (*Hindu Yogi's Astounding Discoveries*, Madurai: Thiruvarul Thavaneri Aadheenam, 1978, pp. 163-164). In Theosophy, the *prāṇamaya kośa* is taken to consist of *Prāṇa*, "Life," and of the "vehicle of *Prāṇa*," the "astral body". See H.P. Blavatsky, *The Secret Doctrine*, v. 1 of *Collected Writings*. Adyar: Philosophical Publishing House, 1978 (1st ed., 1888); p. 157, who bases herself on a paper by T. Subba Row [Rao?—*n.v.*]. Row explains that the astral body is not mentioned separately in the Vedāntic classification "as it is merely the vehicle of *Prāṇa*" (and thus included in *prāṇa*) (*ibid.*, p. 158).
41. Sri Sathya Sai Baba, *UpVahini*, Indian ed., p. 75.
42. "*Manaḥ* means the internal organ comprising volition etc." Śaṁkara, commentary on *TaittUp* II.3, transl. Gambhīrānanda, *Eight Ups. Comm.*, p. 331.
43. Then he goes into the question of how it is possible that a Vedic mantra can be repeated if it is an ever existing eternal entity (*ibid.*, pp. 332-33).
44. Cf. Keith, *AitĀr*, p. 249.
45. (a) *śarīra-puruṣa chhandaḥ-puruṣa, veda-puruṣa, mahā-puruṣa.* (b) *tasyaitasya brahma rasa.* Keith takes *brahma* to refer to the Brahman priest.
46. Sri Sathya Sai Baba, *UpVahini*, Am. ed., p. 80.
47. Commentary on *TaittUp* II.3, transl. Gambhīrānanda, *Eight Ups. Comm.*, v. 1, p. 329. Śaṁkara cites *TaittĀr* III.2.1, "Where all the Vedas get united

is the Self in the Mind" as "declaring the identity of the *Ṛg Vedic* etc. mantras with the eternal Self" (*ibid.*, p. 333).

48. Śaṁkara, Commentary on *TaittUp* II.2.1, transl. Gambhīrānanda, *Eight Ups. Comm.*, p. 322.

49. Sri Sathya Sai Baba, Discourse given April 21, 1983. *Glimpses of Divinity,* No. 38 (May 1984), p. 7. The view that each sheath is more subtle than the preceding one is common among Vedāntins.

50. The language of "levels of increasing subtleness" suggests to a Western reader that the various changes from less to more subtle involve a single unidimensional continuum, like "of decreasing size" or "of increasing 'rate of vibration'". This is not the intent.

51. P. Hacker, *śraddhā. WZKSA,* v. 7 (1963), pp. 151-189 (repr. *Kleine Schriften*, pp. 437-475), discusses a number of passages that contain *śraddhā* (pp. 163-175, resp. 449-461), with often stringent interpretations. Gispert-Sauch, affected by v. Buitenen's conjectures about the origin of the *vidyā* in the earlier Āraṇyaka and Brāhmaṇa literature (note 8 above), argues that all five terms, *śraddhā*, etc. should be taken as referring to the ritual. In particular, "*śraddhā* is the absolutely necessary trust in the sacrifice," *yoga* should be "the 'application' or 'conjunction' of all the elements of the sacrifice," and *mahas* "the sacrificial invocation" ("in later times the most important of the sacrificial invocations"); Gispert-Sauch, *Bliss*, pp. 57-58. Hacker in his discussion of the passage (Hacker, *op. cit.*, pp. 172-173 resp. 458-459) also takes a ritualistic approach but comes out with different interpretations. See also M. Hara, *bhakti* and *śraddhā*, *IIJ*, v. 7 (1963), pp. 124-195; pp. 136-142.

52. Similarly Hacker, *ibid.*, p. 458.

53. Basically the meaning which *yoga* has in the *Gītā*, and which is perhaps the first general meaning of *yoga*, before the classical six and eight limbed yogas.

54. Sathya Sai Baba, *UpVahini*, Indian ed., p. 80.

55. Sathya Sai Baba, discourse given in Panjim, Goa, December 18, 1970; in N. Kasturi, ed., *Sathya Sai Speaks,* v. 7. 2nd Indian ed., Prasanthi Nilayam: Sri Sathya Sai Books and Pubs., 1982, chr. 66; pp. 405-06. Swami Ananyananda sees the five *kośas* as corresponding in a general way to levels of consciousness related to the seven Tantric *cakras*. "While the Tantras describe the different levels of consciousness as *cakras*, wheels or circles, the Upaniṣads describe them a *kośas* or sheaths. Consciousness limited by the five sheaths appears as five different selves . . ." "The three lower *cakras* stand for the levels of the unconscious, whereas the three higher centers for levels of the superconscious. The heart-center situated in between is the seat of true consciousness, the source of self-awareness. That is why in the Upaniṣads the heart is regarded as the *vijñāna-maya kośa,* the sheath of intelligence or self awareness." Seeking God through Meditation: The Golden Threshold. *Prabuddha Bhārata*, v. 87 (1982), pp. 446-453; p. 451. This agrees substantially with [A], [B].

56. The work is sometimes ascribed to Śaṁkara, but was perhaps written later. Potter's Bibliography (1983) lists about 50 editions and translations, including more than a dozen into English (nos. 2382-2435, pp. 131-133). The most popular ones are T.M.P. Mahadevan, *Self Knowledge (Ātma-Bodha) of Śaṅkarācārya*. Madras: Akhila Bharata Sankara

Seva Samiti, 1964; and Swami Nikhilananda, *Self-Knowledge of Śrī Saṅkarācāya.* Mylapore, Madras: Sri Ramakrishna Math, 2nd ed., 1962 (1st ed., 1947).

57. Cf. Gopinath Kaviraj's analysis: ". . .[*manomaya-kośa* is the] mind as the psychologist understands it . . . This *mano-maya kośa* has several layers. *Buddhi* (intellect) has its play at the farthest, innermost layer of this mind, where, from some distance as it were, the mind perceives the *sāttvika bhāvas* [morally pure feeling states]. At this stage it turns into *vijñāna-maya kośa* which is called 'overmind': it means that what here perceives the entire *bhāva* (*śuddha* [pure]) region (with its details) is the *mind* = *I*. The whole standpoint here is still that of mind. . ." Quoted in K. Bhattacharya, *op. cit.* (note 1 above), p. 173. The fact that *buddhi* and (lower levels of) *vijñāna* would be taken by modern psychology as mind is correct but with the caveat that modern psychology is unaware of or does not deal (in a non-reductionist fashion) with higher moral and ethical qualities (purity etc.) and with the implementation of higher moral-ethical principles in action, all things which are specifically associated with *buddhi*. (I don't know the specific provenance of Sri Kaviraj's other terms here).

58. E.g. Sri Ramana Maharshi: "The Self which is self luminous and the witness of everything manifests itself as residing in the *vijñāna kośa*" (i.e., in the *ātmā vijñāna-maya*). *Self Enquiry* 32; see *Collected Works*, Ind. ed., p. 30).

59. Cf. Gambhīrānanda, *Eight Ups. Comm.*, p. 101. (a) *vedātmā.* (b) *vedārthaviṣayā buddhir niścayātmikā.* (c) *adhyavasāyalakṣaṇam.* (d) *tanmayo niścayavijñānaiḥ pramāṇa-svarūpair nirvartita ātmā vijñānamayaḥ.*

60. Sāyaṇa in his commentary develops this into the view that *vijñāna* has to do with the power of action, *kriyā-śakti*, which was at first confusing to me.

61. MW Dictionary. The St. Petersburg Dictionary cites several dozen examples under seven different headings (v. 3, cols. 214-16).

62. E.g., *ŚatBr* I.9.2.16. Eggeling usually translates "he completes the sacrifice".

63. So the St. Petersburg Dictionary: "6. [When] transferred to ritual and prayer, whose structure and sequential order (*Gefüge und Aufeinanderfolge*) is compared with a weave, [*tan* means] to execute" (v. 3, col. 215).

64. *I.e.*, in terms of the St. Petersburg Dictionary (cf. the preceding note), very few of the dozens of examples under meanings 1-5 and 7 make one think of a structure, or of a particular order, of *discrete elements*.

65. This kind of interpretation is suggested by the Brāhmaṇa notion of *bandhu*, the divine element in or the divine effect associated with a sacrifice, which makes the sacrifice have efficacy. Cf. J. Gonda, *Bandhu* in the Brāhmaṇas. *ALB*, v. 29 (1965), pp. 1-29; repr. *Studies*, pp. 402-428.

66. Following Jacob's *Concordance*, up to but not counting the two occurrences of *Mahā-Nārāyaṇa Upaniṣad*. In addition to *vijñāna*, which is used here, a study of uses of the verb *vi-jñā-*, "know" and of *vijñātṛ*, "knower," would be of interest.

67. Cf. Edgerton, *Beginnings*, p. 186; F. Weller, *Versuch einer Kritik der Kaṭhopaniṣad*. Berlin: 1953; W. Rau, Versuch einer deutschen Übersetzung der *Kāṭhaka Upaniṣad*. *Asiatische Studien*, v. 25 (1976), pp. 158-174; p. 167.

68. This is the most natural translation (so also R.D. Karmarkar, *Gauḍapāda-Kārikā*. Poona: Bhandarkar Oriental Research Institute, 1973 (repr. of 1st ed., 1953) (Government Oriental Series, Class B, No. 9), p. 43 and notes pp. 125-26), and is consistent with the spirit of the text and the fact that Gauḍapāda elsewhere even cites *Bṛhadāraṇyaka Upaniṣad*. V. Bhattacharya, *The Āgamaśāstra of Gauḍapāda*. Delhi: Motilal Banarsidass, 1989 (1st, ed., 1943), p. 153, however, takes *vijñāna* in the Buddhist sense, as equivalent to *citta* and *manas*, mind, as in the *Laṅkāvatāra Sūtra*.

69. Sri Ramana Maharshi, *Spiritual Instruction*.

70. E.g. Maṇḍana Miśra, *Brahmasiddhi* I.1.2 says "Bliss, One Immortal, Unborn *Vijñāna*, Syllable, Not-All, All, Fearless—I bow down to Prajāpati," *ānandam ekam amṛtam ajam vijñānam akṣaram a-sarvam sarvam a-bhayam—namasyāmaḥ prajāpatim*. For Prakāśātman, "the Advaita authority par excellence," *vijñāna* is "consciousness which consists of pure knowledge, which has the capability to illumine everything, and which like the light of the Sun etc. does not presuppose the limiting adjuncts which are constituted by the objects" [quoted from Prakāśātman's main work, the *Pañcapādikā-vivaraṇa*, in K. Cammann, *Das System des Advaita nach der Lehre Prakāśātmans*. Wiesbaden: Otto Harassowitz, 1965 (Münchner Indologische Studien, ed. H.H. Holtmann, No. 4), p. 118]. Among modern teachers, compare Swami Shivananda: "Knowledge of the Supreme Self is *vijñāna*. It is direct intuitive perception of the Self through *nirvikalpa samādhi*" (Swami Shivananda, *Gyana Yoga*. Delhi: Motilal Banarsidass, 1973 (1st ed., Rishikesh, 1944), p. 107). For Shri Ramakrishna, *vijñāna* is higher than *jñāna* and represents fullest God Knowledge—knowledge of Brahman as well as Bhagavān, God with personal attributes and form. (Cf. Swami Nikhilananda, transl., *The Gospel of Sri Ramakrishna*. New York: Ramakrishna-Vivekananda Center, 1977 (1st ed., 1942; or Bengali ed., 5 vols., 1897-1932), p. 104, and see index under *vijñāna* and *vijñānī*. Also *Sayings of Sri Ramakrishna*. Madras: Sri Ramakrishna Math, 12th Impression, 1975; see index under *vijñāna*).

71. The major *vijñāna vidyās* like the *Antar-jyotir* and *Dahara Vidyā* may be regarded as sketching "stages" in the evolution of *vijñāna* that span this wide range, but in the context of a specific path. Sri Satya Sai Baba's recent elaboration of the higher functioning of the Mind into "Super Mind, Higher Mind, Illuminated Mind, and Over-Mind" describes general stages of *vijñāna* which (like the notion of *vijñāna* itself) cut across the various spiritual phenomena of the *vijñāna vidyās*. (See Sri Sathya Sai Baba, Discourses given May 20 and 21, 1993 at Brindavan, *Sanathana Sarathi*, v. 36 (1993), pp. 151 ff., 183 ff. etc.) (I do not know whether this teaching has precedents in earlier tradition).

72. The only exception is Yājñavalkya instructing Maitreyī: "Verily by the seeing of the Ātman, by the hearing [of it], by the thinking [of it], by *vijñāna* [of it], all this (world here) is known" [*BṛhUp* II.4.5 (M) *ātmano vā . . . vijñānena*; here *Ātmano*, "of the Ātman," to be supplied to *vijñānenaiva*, "by *vijñāna*," is in the genetive case]. Presumably, this is an artifact of the fact the *vijñāna* is treated in parallel with "seeing," "hearing," and "thinking," all of which have the Ātman as object.

73. E.g. at *AitUp* III.1.

74. This is even clearer in Ramana Maharshi's exposition, which is com-

pletely parallel to the *Maitrāyaṇīya* texts: "The Self is Wisdom. It functions in two ways. When associated with the ego, the knowledge is objective and called *vijñāna*. When divested of the ego and the Universal Self is realized, it is also called *vijñāna*. The word raises a mental concept [i.e., implies action by the mind] . . ." Ramana Maharshi, *Talks*, p. 203 (under 18th June, 1936).

75. Sri Sathya Sai Baba, *Summer Showers* 1977, p. 233.
76. Cf. the occurrences under A i and A ii in the Poona Dictionary.
77. The St. Petersburg Dictionary gives "nonpersonal, nonbodily," but the ususal meaning of *ātmya* is "having a specific intrinsic nature" (*ibid.*).
78. Poona Dictionary.
79. L. Silburn, in an important study with L. Renou, *Nirukta* and *Anirukta* in Vedic, in J.N. Agrawal and Bhim Dev Shastri, eds., *Sarūpa Bhāratī*. (Lakshman Sarup Memorial Volume). Hoshiarpur: Vishveshvarananda Institute Publications, 1954 (Vishveshvaranand Institute Series, Vishva Bandhu, ed., No. 6), pp. 68-79; p. 78.
80. Silburn, *ibid.*, p. 76. According to Renou, "the deep intention of *aniruktatva* [= *anirukta*-ness, "hiddenness, inexpressibility"] lies in the effort to specify beyond well-known things, beyond definite forms, a hidden zone where the things and forms take on an inorganic [=non-material] aspect . . . *Anirukta* sums up in the manner of the Brāhmaṇas the ancient conceptions of the hidden *pāda*, the mysterious "double" [which] so many notions possess in the [Vedic] Hymns" (*ibid.*, p. 76).
81. Discourse given Oct. 27, 1982. *Glimpses of Divinty*, No. 25 (April 1983), pp. 5-6.
82. Thus *sat* and *tyad* evoke teachings associated with the *Nāsadīya* Hymn, and the formula "Brahman is the *Satya*." Cf. van Buitenen, *Vācārambhaṇam* Reconsiderd. *IIJ*, v. 2 (1958), pp. 295-305 (correction, v. 4, 1960, p. 67); repr. *Studies*, pp. 121-134; pp. 301-02 resp. 125-26; and The Speculations on the Name "*Satyam*" in the Upaniṣads. *Studies in Indian Linguistics* (*M.B. Emenau Volume*), 1968, pp. 54-61; repr. *Studies*, pp. 263-272.) *Niruktam* and *a-niruktam* were discussed earlier; *nilayanam* and *a-nilayanam* are presumably only elaborations chosen with an eye on the *a-nilayanam* in II.7.2. *Vijñāna* and *a-vijñānam* are ambiguous, while *satyam* and *anṛtam*, "the true and the false," mark an ethical and transcendental dimension.
83. van Buitenen, The Speculations on the Name "*Satyam*" . .. (*op. cit.*, preceding note), p. 55 (p. 264, resp.).
84. In line 3 in II.7.1, "that made . . . the Ātman," the "that" is syntactically more likely to refer to the *sat* than to initial *asat* (Śaṁkara's reading). Rau, *op. cit.*, p. 360, referring to *TaittUp* II.1 and *AitUp* I, translates "it (*sat*) created itself a body," viz., the visible world. Then the fact that *sukṛta* = *rasa* = higher *ānanda* (II.7.2) would say that this visible world is Bliss, which is possible. The verse may be corrupt (incorrectly copied, etc.) because in almost every line the meter is defective (cf. Rau, *op. cit.*, p. 371, and Horsch, *Gāthā Literature*, p. 189).
85. Different texts all purporting to teach the knowledge of a particular saying may not necessarily teach exactly the same knowledge or state. Teachers in Upaniṣadic times may be assumed to have taken liberties in interpreting well-known sayings just as teachers today do. But also, such liberties

are within certain limits or taken deliberately for certain reasons.

86. van Buitenen reads the beginning differently (The Speculations on the Name "Satyam" . . ., *op. cit.*, p. 56 (p. 265 resp.).
87. Modern translations: Böhtlingk, *BṛhUp*, pp. 60-67 (in German); Edgerton, *Beginnings*, pp. 153-159 (both of the Mādhyandina version).
88. St. Petersburg Dictionary.
89. According to Jacob's *Concordance*, 6 times in the Upaniṣads up to *Maitrāyaṇīya Upaniṣad*. The expression is also found in the Sūtras, at *Katyāyana Śrauta Sūtra* XXXV.11.20 and *Aśvalāyana Gṛhya Sūtra* III.6.5.
90. (a) *yo'yam vijñāna-maya prāṇeṣu hṛdy antarjyotiḥ*. One can also read "[He] who is this person consisting of *vijñāna* [and who is, or is endowed with] the inner light in the heart." (b) *ubhau lokau*. (c) Perhaps, "seeming to move about," parallel to "seeming to think," so Radhakrishnan, *Principal Ups.*, p. 256. Śaṁkara takes it as describing the movement of the intellect and other internal organs and the *prāṇas*. (d) On these *ślokas*, see Horsch, *Gāthā Literature*, pp. 160-162.
91. So Mukhopadyaya, *Studies*, p. 229.
92. (a) *sampanno bhavati*; (b) *svam apīto bhavati*.
93. Sri Sathya Sai Baba, *Voice of the Avatar*. 2 vols. in one. Sri Sathya Sai Baba Book Center of America, 1987 (repr. of 1st Indian ed.), v. 1, p. 41.
94. This idea is also (but in a different way) found in *Māṇḍūkya Upaniṣad*.
95. Coomaraswaṁy translates *svapna* in *PraśnaUp* IV.5 as "clairvoyant sleep" and comments: "*Svapna* here as elsewhere is not ordinary sleep or dreaming, but a state of contemplation (*dhyāna*)" (Coomaraswamy, Recollection Indian and Platonic. In *Papers*, p. 51). In support he cites the present text and *BṛhUp* II.1.18-19 and gives analogues from other literatures (*Joel* 2.21; *Corpus Hermeticum*, book 1.1; *Piers the Plowman*, Prologue) (*ibid.*, p. 51, note 9, and continuation of the same note p. 52).
96. The translation assumes that "attaining the approach to the other-world-state" refers to attaning the *svapna-sthāna*, because from there one sees the other world state. Böhtlingk's translation of the Mādhyandina version, *BṛhUp*, p. 61, "Da es einen Aufstieg zum Standort in der jenseitign Stätte gibt, so betritt er diesen Aufstieg und sieht beides . . .," seems to take this the same way.
97. I am basing myself on the literal translation given. Śaṁkara interprets the joys and evils as impressions of experiences in previous lives and as glimpses of what is in store in future lives. For "*ā-krama* is that by means of which one proceeds, i.e. support or outfit," i.e. it is a person's *karma*. (Transl. Mādhavānanda, *BṛhUp Comm.*, p. 632).
98. Deussen (*Sixty Ups.*, p. 483) considers the verses inserted and thus presumably representing a separate, independent text. He thinks that they assume that "the soul leaves the body in the dreamstate in order to roam about in the world according to its pleasure" (*ibid.*, p. 483). Other modern interpreters also regard these verses as describing dream, including J. Gonda, *The Function and Significance of Gold in the Veda*. Leiden: Brill, 1991 (*Orientalia Rheno-Traiectina*, J. Gonda, ed., No. 37), pp. 191-92.
99. OBEs have a large literature and form a major area of research in Psychical Research and Parapsychology. For a brief survey with the standard reading list, see the entry "Out of Body Travel" in L.A. Shepard, *Encyclopedia of Occultism and Parapsychology*. 2nd ed., 3 vols. vol. 3. Detroit:

Gale Research Co., p. 990-92. For "traveling clairvoyance" see under "Clairvoyance," *ibid.*, v. 1, p. 23. The attitudes and assumptions implicit in the style of this work are here taken to represent those of Psychical Research and Parapsychology generally.

100. Shepard, *ibid.*, v. 3, p. 1600.
101. "Many laboratory experimenters regard OOB experiences as a form of traveling clairvoyance . . ." etc., *ibid.*, p. 992.
102. For brief orientations, see Shepard, *op. cit.*, under "Astral Body" and "Dream Body". To an outside observer, the astral body sometimes appears as the person's "double". In Western Psychical research and parapsychology there has been a large amount of research on such doubles. See Shepard, *ibid.*, under the entry "Double".
103. See J. Gonda, *The Function and Significance of Gold*, pp. 103-205.
104. *ŚatBr* X.4.1, see chr. 6.16.
105. *ChāndUp* I.6.6-8, 7.5-6; *MaitrUp* VI.1.
106. Gonda, *The Function and Significance of Gold* . . ., pp. 184-190.
107. Gonda, *ibid.*, pp. 184-187.
108. Śaṁkara and modern translators read "returns again to the [waking] state".
109. Vs. 3.11-3.14a do not really refer to OBE as understood in the West. A state of meditation implies a motivational matrix to the effect that (1) the individual, by the meditation activity, is aspiring to a higher or purer spiritual level; that (2) the higher Divine or Transcendental etc. element in the individual is to some extent consciously involved in directing his meditaion practice and manifesting in it; and that (3) progress in meditation is tied up with attenuation and gradual transcendence of desire. In the Western OBE literature, OBEs are typically either described as spontaneous experience (with emphasis on the phenomena, their veridicality and their meaning for the individual), or they form an area of experience which the individual wants to develop and explore for its own sake (for secular reasons). In the latter case, the individual typically develops and cultivates specific techniques to get into OBE. But her/his states would not likely fit a description of "the soul or self on the spiritual path coming to (or trying to come to) have higher knowledge" (above), which is the situation in 3.11-13. And they would not contain a motivational situation such as is presupposed in a state of meditation and is likely to have obtained in whatever meditation stands behind 3.11-13. Thus, with the whole set of motivational and spiritual condition of the individual so completely different, surface similarities do not necessarily permit the conclusion that the same kind of phenomenon is going on in both cases. Even if common mental-physical mechanisms could be shown to be operating in the both contexts, so that the OBE similarities would have a common basis, there would still be a critical difference in ethical-spiritual state.
110. In the Western literature there are many accounts that an individual has a vivid OBE, and that this experience then has a powerful spiritual impact on her/him. E.g. she/he may have the conviction that she/he is not connected with the body and will survive death, and turn very seriously to spiritual matters.
111. In India today, as well as among the medieval Catholic Saints and mod-

ern-day psychics, it is completely normal to say "in meditation, he saw the form of the deceased such and such". This is consistent with *svapna* being "a state of meditation" a la Coomaraswamy.

112. Cf. in our text, "Having in *svapna* struck down what pertains to the body . . .," 3.11; Ajātaśatru: "When that person takes ahold of (or restrains, *gṛhṇāti*) these [senses], he is said to be asleep. Then, when Breath is restrained, Speech [is] restrained, Sight [is] restrained, Hearing [is] restrained, Mind [is] restrained . . .").

113. Cf. in our text, "taking to himself, *apādāya*, a measure, *mātrā*, of this all sustaining world, *lokasya sarvavātaḥ*;" 3.9, and "having taken to himself light, *śukram ādāya*"; Ajātaśatru, "having by his *vijñāna* taken to himself, *ādāya*, the *vijñāna* of the senses . . ."; *KauṣUp* III.3, "then speech together with all names goes into it [i.e., into the *prāṇa* = *prajñā-ātman*]").

114. "Photic" is used here for descriptive purposes only, to suggest something like "experience of light". It does not imply the operation of mechanisms such as occur in after-images, or in eidetic imagery.

115. Another text in which a non-"photic" "light of knowing" is primary is *ChāndUp* III.13.7, the climax to a teaching on the five openings of the heart.

116. Swami Ananyananda, Seeking God through Meditation: The Golden Threshold (Editorial). *Prabuddha Bhārata*, v. 87 (1982), pp. 446-453; p. 449.

117. *Ibid.*, p. 449.

118. *Ibid.*, p. 448.

119. Swami Satchidanandendra (= Saccidānandendra) is an important modern Advaitin who has published in Sanskrit and English. Cf. J.W. De Jong's review of *The Method of the Vedānta. A Critical Account of the Advaita Tradition* (a translation, by A.J. Alston, of Swami Satchidanandendra's *Vedānta-prakriyā-pratyabhijñā*, 1964), London: Kegan Paul International, 1989, in *IIJ*, v. 35 (1992), pp. 66-69. A bibliography of this author's work may be found in the *Method of the Vedānta*, p. 974, and also in A.J. Alston, *A Śaṁkara Source Book*, v. 1, *Śaṁkara on the Absolute*. London: Shanti Sadan, 1980, p. 250 (under *Sac*).

120. Holenarsipur: Adhyatma Prakasha Karyalaya, 1973 (serial No. 161). "The genuine Intuition of the Ātman" is chr. 4 on pp. 39-51.

121. "*Avagati* (ascertainment), *adhyavasāya* (final understanding or determination), and *anubhava* (intuition) are some of . . . [the equivalents for *vijñāna*] that are used by Śaṁkara. We shall employ the English word 'intuition' uniformly while translating them all." Swami Satchidanandendra, *op. cit.*, p. 39.

122. *Ibid.*, p. 40.

123. *Ibid.*, p. 41.

124. *Ibid.*, p. 42.

125. *Ibid.*, p. 41.

126. *Ibid.*, pp. 43, 44, and 45.

127. *Ibid.*, p. 43.

128. Neural modelling approaches to this problem are likely to be more persuasive than "symbolic" approaches, which are more obviously programming techniques, but from an epistemological point of view, any attempt at understanding the nature of consciousness by "models" is wrongheaded.

129. An excellent modern treatment is Mukhopadhyaya, *Studies*, pp. 223-233. The dialogue in *Bṛhadāraṇyaka Upaniṣad* (*BṛhUp* II.1) differs considerably from the account in *KauṣUp* IV, both in the initial exchanges (*BṛhUp* II.1.1-14= *KauṣUp* IV.1-19a) and in Ajātaśatru's teaching at the end (*BṛhUp* II.1.15-20 = *KauṣUp* IV.19b-20). The initial segments are compared by E. Frauwallner, Untersuchungen zu den älteren Upaniṣaden, *Zeitschrift für Indien und Iran*, v. 4 (1926), pp. 1-45 (repr. G. Oberhammer and E. Steinkellner, eds., *Erich Frauwallner, Kleine Schriften*. Wiesbaden: Franz Steiner, 1982, pp. 95-139); pp. 10-11 (resp. 104-105). In *Bṛhadāraṇyaka Upaniṣad*, Ajātaśatru's aim is plainly to teach the *vijñana-maya puruṣa* and the fact that it is really the Ātman. *Kauṣītaki Upaniṣad* doesn't mention the *vijñāna-maya*, but has instead the *prajñā-ātman* with the same framework and sequence as in *KauṣUp* III.
130. Also Mukhopadhyaya, *Studies*, p. 229.
131. Uttered by the sacrificer while looking at the sacrificial butter in the New and Full Moon sacrifices, cf. Keith, *TaittSaṁh*, v. 1, pp. 83-84, note 9. On this and other occurrences of *satyasya satyam* in the Vedic literature and on the "intensification" which it illustrates, see H. Oertel, Zum altindischen Ausdruckverstärkungstypus *satyasya satyam . . . Sitzungsberichte der Bayerischen Akademie der Wissenschaften, Phil.-hist. Abt.*, 1847, No. 3, pp. 28-29.
132. Cf. Müller, *Upanishads*, v. 1, p. 233; Keith, *AitĀr*, p. 224 (Skt. p. 117).
133. Cf. Keith's notes, *ibid.*, pp. 223 ff.
134. According to Śaṁkara, the *ākāśa* here refers to the space within the heart, and the text says: "If this Bliss should not be there in the *ākāśa*—that is lodged in the cavity of the heart . . ." (Śaṁkara on *TaittUp* II.7, transl. Swami Gambhīrānanda, *Eight Ups Comm*, p. 360).
135. Sri Sathya Sai Baba, *Dharma Vahini*, revised ed. 1985. Prasanthi Nilayam: Sri Sathya Sai Books and Publications, p. 74.
136. Śaṁkara on *TaittUp* II.5. Swami Gambhīrānanda, *ibid.*, p. 337.
137. (a) Shri Ramana Maharshi gives the same example (*Talks*, 3rd Indian ed., pp. 636-37).
138. *UpVahini*, Ind. ed., p. 40.
139. A third suggestion that all the other sheaths are born from the *ānanda-maya* sheath is implicit in *TaittUp* III. Recall that there, Bhṛgu realized that Brahman was food, *prāṇa*, mind, *vijñāna*. And *ānanda*, and that these were aspects from which all beings are born, by which they are sustained, and into which they merge. Now in the case of Food, *prāṇa*, Mind, and *vijñāna*, Bhṛgu always returned to his father for further instruction. He was not completely satisfied, he was still subject to suffering, or the human condition. But on realization of Brahman as this *ānanda*, he did not return. There was complete satisfaction; suffering or the human condition had been transcended. The fact that this higher *ānanda*, realized as the substrate and basis from which beings are born and into which they are absorbed via death, includes true and permanent transcendence of the human condition suggests that indeed in some metaphysical or ontological sense the world *is* born out of (and ever merges into) "higher *ānanda*".
140. Sri Sathya Sai Baba, *Summer Showers*, 1977, p. 230. Cf. also "Next comes the Sheath of Bliss. It is the base for the entire Cosmos." Sri Sathya Sai

Baba, Discourse given May 20, 1993, Brindavan; *Sanathana Sarathi*, v. 36 (1993), pp. 150-154; p. 150.

141. There is little appreciation in philosophy of Science that scientific and mathematical rigour consists of cognitive structures that originally dealt with the organization and manipulation of physical objects, in other words, has from a psychological point of view a completely materialistic basis. It is no accident that the first version of Western Logic, viz. Syllogistic Logic, and scientific type sorting and classifying both originated from the same person, Aristotle.

142. In Philosophy of Science there seems to be surprisingly little work in this area.

143. Cf. for example Atmananda, compiler and ed., *Words of Sri Anandamayi Ma*. 2nd ed., Varanasi: Shree Shree Anandamayee Sangha, 1971 (1st ed., 1961?).

144. Bhaiji (Sri Jyotish Chandra Ray), *Mother as Revealed to Me*. Fourth ed., Varanasi: Shree Shree Anandamayee Sangha, 1972 (or. Bengali ed., 1973), pp. 64-65. "Bhaiji" or Sri Jyotish Chandra Ray was one of Shree Anandamayee Ma's early close devotees, and the excerpt is thus probably mostly but not entirely in her own words. It is the opening of a chapter called "State of Samādhi," in which the author recounts some of his experiences of Shree Anandamayee Ma's spiritual states.

145. Böhtlingk, *BṛhUp*, p. 65.

146. There seems to be no modern dicussion of this text.

147. F.X. Clooney, *Theology after Vedānta*. Albany: SUNY Press, 1993, p. 50. Clooney simplifies the individual aphorisms to show the reasoning which leads the Sūtra to this position.

148. Śaṁkara of *BraSū* I.1.19, transl. Thibaut, *Śaṁkara BraSū Comm.*, pp. 71 ff. Śaṁkara's arguments are sometimes seen as a deliberate bending of the Sūtra's text to conform to his own Advaitic bias, to give them the authority of tradition. But Clooney in his *Theology after Vedānta* regards the process of replacing a previously established "final, proved" position (*siddhānta*) by a new one as a normal feature of early Vedānta "Text" (Sūtra + commentary + subcommentary etc.). It is part of the normal way for the student to acquire the Vedāntic wisdom by "participating in the 'Text'".

149. This tension is brought out by A.O. Fort, Beyond Pleasure: Śaṁkara on Bliss. *JIP*, v. 16 (1988), pp. 177-89: pp. 183 ff.

150. Rāmānuja on *BraSū* I.1.12-19.

151. Cf. Gispert-Sauch, *Bliss*, pp. 84-85, and the comments of B. Heinemann cited there.

152. So Gispert-Sauch: "The *upasaṁkramaṇa*, the approach to these stages, should . . . [be regarded] as expressing an approach to these realities by their "assimilation" . . . and by integrating them into the experience of totality of being." (Gispert-Sauch, *ibid.*, p. 84).

153. E.g. *ŚatBr* IV.3.4.8, XII.3.4.11.

154. Gispert-Sauch argues that *TaittUp* II.9.3, "From where words turn back...," "leaves no doubt that the Ṛṣi (seer of the Upaniṣad) considered the *ānanda-maya* . . . as the very state of final liberation . . .," because "the bliss of Brahman" in the third line is a genitive of identity and the phrase means "*ānanda* which is Brahman" (Gispert-Sauch, *Bliss*, pp. 85-86).

155. E.g. "The Upaniṣads say that man is spark of Divine Love, encased in five sheaths, . . .[enumerates]. It is the fragrance of that Love that emanates from him as love towards things, beings and ideas. That Love is ever urging and surging for expression, enlargement, and enclasping. But the tangles of fear, greed, egoism, and aggrandizement do not allow the spark to grow and illumine the sheaths and the world around." Discourse given Oct. 29, 1970, in N. Kasturi, ed., *Sathya Sai Speaks*, v. 7, 2nd ed., Prasanthi Nilayam: Sri Sathya Sai Books and Pubs., 1982, chr. 60; p. 345. Srinivasa Prakhya (personal communication, 1995) sees Sai Baba's teaching here as similar to that of Jnaneshwar, a great Marathi Saint, who, although an Advaitin, "considered Prema/Bhakti to be the goal rather than a path".

CHAPTER 6

Dahara Vidyā

1. Introduction and Summary

A glance at column (3) of Table 5.3 shows that most of the texts which teach *vijñāna* in the sense of the Five Sheaths *Vidyā* are dealing with "knowledge of the Self in the heart". The most extensive, comprehensive and detailed teaching on "knowledge of the Self in the heart" is without question the *Dahara Vidyā, ChāndUp* VIII.1-6.[1] It complements and particularises the Five Sheaths *Vidyā*, and is comparable to it in scope, depth, and quantity of inner spiritual phenomena disclosed. Together the two *vidyās* form a unified complex of high level teachings which represents one of the major directions of thrust of the Upaniṣadic Wisdom as a whole.

The *Dahara Vidyā*. The importance of the *Dahara Vidyā* lies in part in its teaching of the *dahara ākāśa*, the "subtle (*dahara*) space (*ākāśa*)" (in the heart), also called the *antarhṛdaya ākāśa,* the "space within (*antar*) the heart (*hṛdaya*)". Instead of "space" the word "ether" is sometimes used (so "ether within the heart"), because of the "quality" sometimes felt with this "space". In the course of inner spiritual evolution, says the *vidyā*, the subtle space within the heart becomes the Ātman which contains all things and all desires, and is "with sins destroyed, divorced from old age, death, sorrow, hunger, and thirst, and of true desire and true resolve".

The conception of *dahara ākāśa* is a seminal one. Awareness of (forms of) *dahara ākāśa* in one's inner experience (in meditation or in one's being) often signals initial stages of *vijñāna*. Consciousness, being and knowledge at the level of the "space in the heart" are not only a kind of (beginning or intermediate) *vijñāna*, but represent quintessential *vijñāna*; the nature of the *vijñāna* of the "space (or ether) in the heart" may be at the root of why *vijñāna* represents a coherent level of spiritual evolution to begin with. The *vijñāna-maya kośa* has been called the *dahara ākāśa*.[2] At a more general level, the *dahara ākāśa* seems to be one if not the key element in the unfolding of the (spiritual) heart. In particular it seems to be involved in what enables one to see unity at simultaneously inner and universal levels, in areas like the unity of life, the unity of culture, or the unity of existence.

Dahara ākāśa seems to be also the main arena of much of the inner experience in "nature *vidyās*" like the Sixteen Parts and *Vaiśvānara Vidyās*. "Experientially", the development of perception or realization of, and thereafter the internalization of, pervasive Divine Qualities in the beginning and intermediate stages in these *vidyās* seem to be stages and forms of development of "*dahara ākāśa* consciousness". From this perspective, these "nature *vidyās*" represent, not a transition from a Puruṣa approach to an approach working with Divine Qualities (as in chr. 4.20), but the gradual becoming aware of a broad but unified level of spirituality epitomized by the term *dahara ākāśa*. Historically the Puruṣa approach had the function of being the road to crystallization and elaboration of Ātman/Brahman. But thereafter it was gradually superseded in the Upaniṣads by the approach of *vijñāna* and *dahara ākāśa*. "The *Dahara Vidyā* must have been widely practiced in Vedic [= Upaniṣadic] times. It serves as the prototype of most of the meditation techniques still practiced in modern times."[3] The teaching on the *dahara ākāśa* has numerous parallels in the Upaniṣads, some of them discussed earlier. *BṛhUp* IV.3.1-20, on the *vijñāna* of the light of the self within the heart, is a very important one. Others are "This Heart (*hṛdayam*) is the same as Prajāpati. It is Brahman. It is All" (the "Heart *Vidyā*," *BṛhUp* V.2-3), and *BṛhUp* IV.4.22 (K) = IV.4.25 (M), "In the ether within the heart is the Controller of all, the Lord of all, the Ruler of all," which was part of our first Upaniṣadic text in chr. 2.2. Unmistakable allusions to Ātman/Brahman being in the heart and containing all things are already found in *Taittirīya Brāhmaṇa* and *Taittirīya Āraṇyaka* and probably already in the *Atharva Vedic skambha* hymns mentioned in chr. 5. After the old Upaniṣads, essentially the same Knowledge is elaborated further in *Muṇḍaka* and *Maitrāyaṇīya Upaniṣads*, in *Mahā-Nārāyaṇa Upaniṣad* (twice), and in *Kaivalya* and *Subālā Upaniṣads* (the last two are generally classed among the later, non-classical Upaniṣads as "old Vedānta Upaniṣads"). Thus "the conception of

Brahman as transcendent but still dwelling in the centre of the individual may even be claimed to be a fundamental doctrine of Upaniṣads. One will not be far wrong if one recognizes the *Dahara Vidyā* as a focal text in the entire bulk of Upaniṣadic literature".[4] However, in spite of all these textual resonances, there is a question regarding the exact nature of the "subtle space within the heart," and what kind of path the *Dahara Vidyā* originally intended. In any case, *dahara ākāśa* was already in late Upaniṣadic times, and is certainly today, a broad type of spiritual unfoldment that can occur in both *jñāna* and *bhakti* paths.

So far we have focussed only on the *Dahara Vidyā's* teaching of *dahara ākāśa*, particularly as it pertains to beginning stages of deeper spiritual development. But the *vidyā* is also important for its statements on further stages of the path to Brahman through the heart, corresponding to the *ānanda-maya* and beyond *ānanda-maya* stages of the Five Sheaths *Vidyā*. The text of the entire *vidyā* divides naturally into two parts, very similar to the Five Sheaths *Vidyā*. Part I, *ChāndUp* VIII.1.1-3.2, develops the teaching of the *dahara ākāśa.* Part II (VIII.3.3-6.6), just like Part II of Five Sheaths *Vidyā*, is more advanced, disjointed and obscure. In our treatment we concentrate mostly on the last section of the *vidyā* (*ChāndUp* VIII.6), on the channels of the heart, and argue that this section gives a partly yogic path for passing from the stage of *dahara ākāśa* to full knowledge of Ātman.

Outline of the Argument of the Chapter. After giving a complete translation of the *vidyā* in sec. 2, we first clarify the structure of Part I of the *vidyā* and describe the general intent of the teaching on the *dahara ākāśa*. At the most general level the text says that the Ātman is in the heart. "The heart" here means something like one's spiritual center, something in or from which arise higher feelings and knowledge, and which is conceived to exist, more or less concretely localized, in the chest or in the region of one's physical heart. It is partly a structure of beliefs about oneself and about self, and partly experience (including experience of the center of one's self or of one's awareness being in the region of the chest). So the basic teaching is that the Ātman is in the inner center of oneself, in one's heart. More specifically, there is in one's self or heart a subtle (or small) space, which by appropriate inner evolution can be realized to be the immortal Ātman which contains all things and all desires.

The conception that the center of one's self (or of one's being and higher essence) is "the heart" is found in the Upaniṣads generally and goes back to the *Ṛg Veda* (sec. 4). It is similar to the conception of the heart in the West and in fact exemplifies a fairly universal phenomenon, what in comparative religion is called "the symbol of the Heart". In many religions, philosophies and literatures all over the world, the Heart is the seat or locus of manifestation of the Divine or is itself the Divine (hence it is "a symbol of" the Divine). So the *Dahara* teaching, *ChāndUp* VIII.1.1-1.5, can be regarded as an exposition of how the Supreme Divine can be realized by a path of unfolding the awareness of the Heart. As such it is actually an important ingredient of the *philosophia perennis*.

Now from the text of the *vidyā* it is not completely clear what precisely the *dahara ākāśa* refers to in inner experience, and the same holds for the process of passing from a stage of *dahara ākāśa* to realization of the Ātman. In subsequent tradition, these questions are answered in different ways. On the one hand there is a traditional approach found in the *Brahma Sūtra* and *KaivalyaUp* 6-7 (secs. 5-7), in which one meditates on the Self as "sinless, divorced from old age, divorced from death . . ." (the words in *ChāndUp* VIII.1.5). In addition, this meditation involves centering one's mind in the area of the heart or the chest, in accordance with the *vidyā's* teaching that the *dahara ākāśa* and the Ātman are "in one's heart". But there is also a second approach in which the *dahara ākāśa* is something like the proverbial "firmament of the heart," or an "inner consciousness". This kind of interpretation of *dahara ākāśa* fits well with parallel texts like *Mahā-NārUp* XII.16-17 and *MaitrUp* VI.28, both of which use meditation with Om (secs. 8-10). It also seems to be continued in the teaching of the five spaces or *akāśas* in Vedānta (*ghaṭa ākāśa, jala ākāśa, dahara ākāśa, cit-ākāśa*, and *mahat-ākāśa*), each of which denotes a spiritual level or type of consciousness (secs. 11-12). Although these two approaches initially involve completely different kinds of meditation and different types of spiritual life, in the course of time, when *vijñāna* arises and begins to infiltrate and become part of the individual's consciousness, being and knowledge, the differences tend to become less prominent, and the *vijñāna* or knowledge more and more the same. Actually this phenomenon is found in several other *vidyās* also, and seems to be characteristic of the Upaniṣadic *sādhanā* in general. Regardless which approach is taken, in the course of spiritual life the *dahara ākāśa vijñāna* tends to become the normal inner consciousness and being of the aspirant/devotee.

So far the focus has been on the awareness of *dahara ākāśa* in the earlier stages of inner evolution, as a basic orientation and aid for the student to proceed further on the path (as in *ChāndUp* VIII.1.1). But there are also two other areas that need discussion. The first is the *vidyā's* statements that the space within the heart (or Ātman/Brahman) contains all things (or the whole Universe), and that the Ātman is *satya-kāma*, "of true desire (which is always fulfilled)," and *satya-saṁkalpa* "of true resolve (which is always realized)". The first of these implies that the human soul is in some sense "omniscient," and suggests the possibility that something like "specific forms of omniscience" may manifest in individuals. This violates some deep-seated attitudes and assumptions in Science and Western Psychology, but has some resonances with Plato's *anamnesis* and the *ālayavijñāna* of Buddhism (sec. 14). Similarly the *vidyā's* teaching that the Ātman is *satya-kāma*, "of true desire (which is always fulfilled)," is very unusual (sec. 15). The *Dahara Vidyā* does not stand alone in teachings of this kind. Some forms of "omniscience," and beyond that some kinds of direct "participation in the All at cosmic or universal levels," are also implied by the *Bhūma Vidyā*, the *Gāyatrī Vidyā*, and other *vidyās*. These teachings, which are foreshadowed in some of the mystical cosmic-cosmological hymns of the *Atharva Veda*, are in some sense the culmination of the whole cosmic orientation of the Vedas and Brāhmaṇas. At the same time I would say that they represent perennial philosophy which is also echoed in some of the Mahāyāna Sūtras and elsewhere. The second aspect of the *Dahara* teaching *ChāndUp* VIII.1.1-1.5 that needs further discussion is the way in which according to the *vidyā* the Ātman should be realized by a path of *dahara ākāśa* (*ChāndUp* VIII.1.3-5). This problem is taken up later in secs. 18-21.

With the intital exposition of the *Dahara* teaching is completed, section 16 is devoted to the *Śāṇḍilya Vidyā*, an independent text with a somewhat similar spirit as *ChāndUp* VIII.1.1-5. Then discussion turns to the Full *Dahara Vidyā, ChāndUp* VIII.1.1-6.6. From surface indications it appears that VIII.1-5 form a single unified text (sec. 17). But the role and intent of VIII.6 on the channels (*nāḍīs*) in the heart are unclear. This text is analyzed using Śaṁkara's commentary on a parallel text, *BṛhUp* IV.2.2-4. There Śaṁkara discusses the deeper penetration into the space in the heart in terms of "subtle *prāṇas*" in the heart. His account uses the terminology of *Māṇḍūkya Upaniṣad* (which is considerably later than *Bṛhadāraṇyaka* and

Chāndogya Upaniṣads) and distinguishes two stages of knowledge/ awareness within the heart: one corresponding to the "self at one in the heart" or *dahara ākāśa*; and a second, deeper stage, where the self is aware of and identifies itself with the "subtle *prāṇas*" in the heart. In addition Śaṁkara mentions a third step or sage, which is also found in *BṛhUp* IV.2.4, where the student identifies him/herself at this "subtle *prāṇa* in the heart" level with the directions of space and their deities, and thus with the All. When this identification is effective, true knowledge of the One Ātman arises (sec. 18). Because of Śaṁkara's use of the *Māṇḍūkya* scheme, this whole approach via a "subtle *prāṇa* All-Self" looks like a later technique. But the Yājñavalkya-Śākalya dialogue in *Bṛhadāraṇyaka Upaniṣad*, where the Brahmin Śākalya asks Yājñavalkya "what deity are you in the East" etc., suggests that something like this approach was already well-known among teachers in the old Upaniṣads (sec. 19). This makes the "path of the subtle *prāṇa* All-self" the first Upaniṣadic path to the Ātman that we find spelled out completely in some detail. As far as the *Dahara Vidyā* is concerned, it looks as if *ChāndUp* VIII.6 on the *nāḍīs* or vessels in the heart may be aiming at a similar teaching, connecting the subtle *prāṇas* in the heart with the Sun through the Sun's rays. Because the rays pervade and encompass the whole cosmos, this conception provides a channel to an infinitization of the self which is equivalent to the method of identifying the subtle *prāṇas* in the heart with the four directions. This teaching may thus have been added to the rest of the *vidyā* (*ChāndUp* VIII.1.1-5.4) to provide some hints on the path through the heart taught in the initial *Dahara* section (VIII.1.1-5) (sec. 20).

Śaṁkara's "path of the subtle *prāṇa* All-self" also sheds some light on the meaning of the deep sleep passages in *BṛhUp* IV.3.1-34 and in the Ajātaśatru-Bālāki dialogue that we left unresolved in chr. 5. These texts seem to imply something like Śaṁkara's stage 2—becoming aware of and identifying oneself with the subtle *prāṇas* in the heart —because that stage is equivalent to knowledge of the self in deep sleep. Śaṁkara's scheme of two "in the heart" stages (*dahara ākāśa* and subtle *prāṇa* in the heart) together with a last step leading to a true infinitization of the self seems to represent therefore a general pattern among the *vijñāna* of the heart *vidyās* in the old Upaniṣads, and defines one avenue of approach to the Ātman through meditation in the heart (end of sec. 20, and sec. 21).

This relatively yogic path, however, contrasts with a second general type of approach, meditation using repetition of Om and with the bow and arrow simile as a general guide (or *vidyā*!), as in *MuṇḍUp* II.2.3-4 (sec. 22). While Śaṁkara's "path of the Subtle *Prāṇa* All-self" seems to be correlated with more traditional *Dahara upāsanā,* the *Muṇḍaka* approach with meditation using Om may underlie or lead more to a knowledge of *dahara ākāśa* as "firmament of the heart" or "sky of (subtle or inner) consciousness". A still third way of approaching the full *Dahara Vidyā* is represented by *Mahā-NārUp* XIII.6-12, a strictly yogic text (sec. 23).

The final section summarises some of the conclusions of the last several sections and reflects briefly on the "Infinitization" of the individual self to the Supreme Self or Paramātman, which was identified as a distinct step or stage in most of the texts in this chapter. The significance of the old Upaniṣads consists in the fact that they for the first time elaborate this "Infinitization" in a concrete and most direct form; through the Upaniṣads it then became part of the essence of Indian culture and the Indian mind. In turn, one significance of the vast sea of Indian spiritual literatures for mankind today is that the Infinite Divine or Reality which this Infinitization leads to shines in them in innumerable forms.

2. *Dahara Vidyā:* Text

VIII.1.1. Now what subtle (or small) lotus-like abode there is, here, in this city of Brahman (the body), within (or: interior to) that is a subtle (or small) space (*dahara ākāśa*). What is within (or interior to) that should be searched out. That surely is what one should desire to understand (literally, make clearly known [to oneself]).

1.2. If they should say to him: "[As to] what subtle lotus abode there is here in this city of Brahman (the body), within that is a subtle space, what now [is it that] exists here, which is to be sought out?,"

1.3. He should say: "As far extending, truly, as this space here (= this physical space) is, so far extending is this space inside the heart (*antarhṛdaya ākāśa*). In this both Heaven and Earth are [wholly] placed within (*antar eva samāhite*), both Fire and Wind, both Sun and Moon, Lightning and the stars, both what there is of his (= what belongs to him or is part of his life) here and what is not, everything here is placed (*samāhita*) in it."

1.4. If they say to him: "If within this city of Brahman all this [world] here is contained, all beings and all desires, [then], when that reaches old age or [when] it perishes, what remains over of it?,"

1.5. (Then) he should say: "That [part] of him (or it) does not age, nor is it killed by killing him. That is the real city of Brahman. In it desires are contained. That is the Ātman, free from evil, ageless, deathless, sorrowless, hungerless, thirstless, whose desire is True, *satya-kāma*, whose conception is True, *satya-saṁkalpa.*" For, just as here on earth human beings follow [along] according to command, so, of whatever object they are desirous, whether a nation (to rule over) or a part of a field, that they live on.

1.6. As here [on earth] the world [which is] won by work (action)[a] becomes destroyed, even so there [after death] the world which is won by merit[b] becomes destroyed.

Now those who move around here [in this world] without having found the Self and their true desires,[c] for them in all the worlds there is no freedom. But those who move around here [in this world] having found the Self and their true desires, for them in all the worlds there is freedom (lit: [there is] "going according to [their] desire").

2.1. If he becomes desirous of the world of fathers, out of his determination (or desire to do, *saṁkalpa*), indeed, fathers arise. Possessed of that world of fathers, he is happy.

In 2.2-9 this is repeated, with "fathers" and "world of fathers" replaced successively by "mothers" and "world of mothers," and similarly by "brothers," "sisters," "friends," "perfume and garlands," "food and drink," "song and music," and "women". Finally 2.10 sums up the whole sequence:

2.10. Of whatever end he becomes desirous, whatever end-goal he should be desiring, out of his determination, indeed, it arises. Possessed of it he is happy.

3.1. These here are the true desires covered by un-truth. Of these, while [really] being true, [there is] a covering [that is] untruth. [Now] surely (*hi*), whoever of one's [relatives or friends] departs from here, one does not get him [back] here to see.

3.2. But those of one's [relatives or friends] who are alive here and those who have departed, and whatever else one is desiring but does not get—all this one finds having gone here (i.e., in the interior of the ether in the heart). For here, truly, are those true desires of his [which are] covered by untruth.

So, just as those who do not know a field, walking around on top of a hidden treasure of gold again and again, would not find it, even so all creatures here go day by day to that Brahman-world (*brahma-loka*) but do not find it; for truly they are carried astray by untruth.

3.3. Verily, this Ātman is in the heart. The etymological explanation (*nirukta*) of it is this: "This one [is] in the heart (*hṛdy-ayam*)"; therefore it is [called] the heart (*hṛdayam*). Day by day, verily, he who knows thus goes to the heavenly world (*svargaloka*).

3.4. Now, that serene one (*samprasāda*) who, rising up out of this body, having reached the highest light, enters into with (or becomes) his own form—that is the Self (Ātman)," said he [i.e. the teacher]. "That is the immortal, the fearless. That is Brahman." Of that very Brahman, the name is *Satyam*.

3.5. Verily, these are these three syllables (of *Satyam*): *sat-ti-yam*. That which is the *Sat*—that is the immortal. [That] which is the *ti*, that is the mortal. That which is the *yam*, by that one upholds (root *yam*) the two (mortal and immortal). (Because) by that one upholds both, therefore [it is] *yam*. Day by day, truly, [he who] knows thus goes to the heavenly world.

4.1. Now, the Self (Ātman) is the dam (or bridge, *setu*), the separation for keeping these worlds apart. Over that dam there crosses neither day nor night, neither old age nor death nor sorrow, neither the well-done, nor ill-done. All evils turn away from it, for this Brahman-world is freed from evil.

4.2. Therefore, verily, upon crossing that dam, if one is blind, he becomes no longer blind; if one is wounded, he becomes not wounded; if one is sick, he becomes not anymore sick. Therefore, verily, upon crossing that dam, night appears even as day, for the Brahman-world is illumined once and for all.

4.3. But only they who find that Brahman-world through the chaste life of a student of sacred knowledge (*brahmacarya*)—only theirs is that Brahman-world. For them there is unlimited freedom in all worlds.

5.1. Now, [that] which is called the "(Vedic) sacrifice" (*yajña*), that is indeed the chaste life of a student of sacred knowledge, *brahmacarya*. For by *brahmacarya*, indeed, does [he] who is a knower get that (Brahman-) world. And [that] which is called the "sacrificial worship (of the Divine)," *iṣṭa*, that is indeed *brahmacarya*. For, by sacrificial worship with *brahmacarya* does one attain the Self.

5.2. And [that] which is called a *sattrāyaṇa* (a long sequence of Soma sacrifices), that is indeed *brahmacarya*. For by *brahmacarya* indeed does one find the [saving] protection of the real self (*sata ātmanas trāṇam*, a wordplay; additional word plays up to 5.4, see notes). And [that] which is called a "(vow of) silence,"[d] that is indeed *brahmacarya*. For having discovered the Self by *brahmacarya* indeed, does one reflect.[d]

5.3. And what is called a "course of fasting,"[e] that is indeed *brahmacarya*. For the Self which one gets to by *brahmacarya* does not perish.[e] And what is called "forest (hermit) life,"[f] that is indeed *brahmacarya*. For truly, *ara* as well as *ṇya*[f] (an allusion to *KauṣUp* I, see chr. 4) are the two seas in the Brahman-world in the third heaven from here.

5.4. [They] indeed who discover the two seas *ara* and *ṇya* in the Brahman-world through *brahmacarya*, the Brahman-world is indeed theirs. Theirs is unlimited freedom in all the worlds.

6.1. Now, as for these channels (*nāḍīs*) of the heart—they "arise from the finest essence, [which is] reddish brown, white, blue, yellow, and red". Verily, yonder Sun is reddish brown; it is white; it is blue; it is yellow; it is red.

6.2. Now, as a great highway, extending, goes to two villages, this one and the one yonder, even so these rays of the Sun go to two worlds, this one and the one yonder. They extend from yonder sun, and creep into these channels. They extend from these channels, and creep into yonder sun.

6,3. Now, when one is thus sound asleep, composed, serene (*saṁprasanna*), he knows no dream; then he has crept into these channesls; so no evil touches him, for then he has reached the Bright Power (*tejas*).

6.4. Now, when one thus becomes reduced to weakness, those sitting around say: 'Do you know me?' 'Do you know me?' As long as he has not departed from this body, he knows them.

6.5. But when he thus departs from this body, then he ascends upward with these very rays (of the Sun). With "*Om*" as vehicle he reaches the gate.[g] As quickly as one could direct his mind to it, he comes to the Sun. That, verily, indeed, is the world gate, an entrance for knowers, a stopping for non-knowers.

6.6. As to this there is the following verse (*śloka*):
There are a hundred and one channels of the heart.
  One of these passes up to the crown of the head.
Going up by it, one goes to immortality.
  The others are for departing in various directions.[5]

3. The *Dahara* Teaching, *ChāndUp* VIII.1.1-1.5

The central teaching of Part I of the *vidyā* is on the space or ether within the heart, which contains all and which is the Ātman, "sinless, ageless . . ." The basic satements here are 1.1-1.5, and these are further expanded in 1.6-3.2. Verse 1.5 says that the Ātman is *satya-kāma* and *satya-saṁkalpa*, "of true desire" and "of true determination". The second half of 1.6 and 3.1-3.2 explain "of true desire" by introducing the idea of "true desires," and 2.1-10 explains "of true determination". So the initial teaching on the *dahara ākāśa* occupies 1.1-3.2, the central teaching being 1.1-1.5.

The *Dahara* Teaching. In the "city of Brahman," i.e. in the human being, in his or her body and mind, is a subtle or small (*dahara*) lotus-like abode (house, mansion, *veśma*). This lotus-like abode is the heart or *hṛdaya*. Now interior to or within (*antar*) this abode or the heart, says the text, there is a subtle (or small) space, *dahara ākāśa*. *Ākāśa* originally means "an opening to see into or through," "a free or open space", then also "ether, sky, atmosphere" and "space". *Dahara* means "small, fine, thin," and so here, "small" or "subtle". So *dahara ākāśa* is "a small, or subtle, space". And finally, "what is within that [*dahara ākāśa*], that should be desired to be understood" (*vi-jñā-*, so "of that one should desire to have *vijñāna*"). Thus V.1.1 apparently sets up in one sweep a framework of three levels each next one within (*antar*) the preceding one:

(1) the heart, *hṛdaya*, as it is generally understood, viz. the center of the whole psyche of the whole individual;
(2) the *dahara ākāśa* or subtle (small) ether within the heart; and
(3) that what is within the *dahara ākāśa*, that should be sought out, that one should desire to realize clearly.

However, the exchanges in 1.2-1.3 and 1.4-1.5 indicate that (3) is related to (2) in a certain way. In 1.2, the disciples are asking not so much about the *dahara ākāśa* of V.1.1 but about what it is within it that should be sought and known. It seems they think they already know the former a little, they are willing to accept their idea or knowledge of it as adequate for the moment, and they are going ahead and asking about the mystery inside it that they should seek out and realize, or attain. The teacher's response is most instructive. He does not immediately answer their question. Instead, he first introduces a new term, "the space within the heart," *antarhṛdaya ākāśa*, for what was called *dahara ākāśa* in V.1.1 and says that "this space in the heart" is as large as this world and that all things are placed in it. The "this," *eṣa*, has the force of referring to something mentioned earlier and thus "this space in the heart" refers to the *dahara ākāśa* in the subtle lotus flower abode, i.e., in the heart, in V.1.1. But the teacher gives it a larger meaning. Within *this* space in the heart that *he* is talking about, there is placed the whole world, as well as all desires (V.1.5). Further (V.1.5), "that"—that knowledge, that condition of vision, that ether in the heart, there is grammatically no clear referent—that "does not age . . ., that is the Self". The overall thrust is clear. The teacher is saying: "You are asking what it is that should be realized in the *dahara ākāśa*, the subtle (or small) space in the heart which I just mentioned (V.1.1). You already have some inkling of this subtle (or small) space. But if this subtle (or small) space is truly known, one sees that it is as extensive as this world and that all things, all beings and all desires are placed within it. And then one also sees that is unaging, . . .". Hence instead of a having a three level scheme as in (1), (2), (3) above, there are really only two levels, the heart (1), and the *dahara ākāśa* = *antar-hṛdaya ākāśa* which is actually the same as the Ātman ((2) and (3) are ultimately one). The Ātman may appear as something new and as a separate level, but really the *dahara ākāśa* should be realized to be Ātman/Brahman. This is more or less how we have to read 1.3 if we are to understand the realities of the teaching, as opposed to inappropriately reifying things. And this will also help explain different ways of understanding the space in the heart in later tradition.

Next, "as far as this space here (*ayam ākāśa*) extends, so far extends the space within the heart, *antar-hṛdaya ākāśa*". The phrasing suggests more than a certain parallelism; it almost alludes to an interpenetration or containment of the world of ordinary experience by the space in the heart. In addition, it suggests a certain "expansive" quality. These are all "experiential" aspects. At the same time the space in the heart has a certain timeless aspect (also an "experiential"), simultaneously including and transcending all detail and forms. Next, "Within it are placed together (*sam-ā-hita*) both Heaven and Earth, both Fire and Wind, both Sun and Moon . . ." "Whatever there is of him (or "of this [world] here") and what is not, all that is deposited within it." That is, whatever is part of one's world, or belongs to one's concerns, and everything else too, past and future—all that is contained in this space. "That does not grow old with this one's old age; it is not slain with this one's (this person's) murder." In other words, that reality that is there, or that one is, when one is aware of all things being contained in the space in the heart—that reality is always, beyond one's physical existence and beyond the transmigrating self, that reality is the One Self. Time and the experienced physical existence are changing temporary forms, but that is ever independent of them. "That is the real city of Brahman." That timeless entity is what should be called the abode of Brahman, not the transient body and mind. "In it are placed (*sam-ā-hita*) the desires," i.e., the "true desires"—here the teacher is acknowledging the disciples' point in 1.4 that the "fortress of Brahman" contains all desires. "That is the Ātman." And then comes a famous series of eight attributes traditionally accepted as describing the Ātman:

apahata-pāpman	with sins destroyed
vi-jara	without old age
vi-mṛtyu	without death
vi-śoka	without sorrow
vi-jighatsa	without hunger
a-pipāsa	without thirst

satya-kāma "of true desire"
satya-saṁkalpa "of true resolve"[6]

This is for the time being the high point of the teaching, and the highpoint of Part I. For the remainder of Part I, 1.5 and 1.6 as well as 2.1-210 and 3.1-3.2, all deal in various ways with *satya-kāma* and *satya-saṁkalpa*, the two positive attributes of the eight attributes named. Over all, therefore, we may say that the basic teaching (until 3.2) is 1.1-1.5. Here, the disciples are instructed to penetrate more deeply into the *dahara ākāśa* or space in the heart and in this fashion realize the Ātman.

Precursors of the *Dahara* Teaching. The teaching 1.1-1.5 is surely very ancient. It is probably present already in *Atharva Veda* X.8.43-44:

43. The lotus-like [body] with nine gates, covered with three strands (*guṇas*)—what *Yakṣa* [Supernal Being] abides in it as self, that verily the Brahman-knowers know.
44. Without desire, stable, eternal, self-existent, content with the essence, not lacking in any respect[a],—knowing Him indeed one has no fear of death,—[Him,] the Ātman, the stable, ageless, young[b] one.[7]

Another equally important precursor is *TaittBr* II.8.8. [8]-[9] (= II.8.8.(y)-(z) in Dumont's text). The second verse, (z), occurs already in *TaittSaṁh* V.7.8.2(b).

(y) In (*antar*) this [Brahman] are these worlds (*ime lokāḥ*), within [it] is all this [world here]. Brahman is indeed the best (or eldest, *jyeṣṭham*) of beings. Who might vie with it?

(z) In Brahman (locative) are the thirty-three gods. In Brahman are Indra, Prajāpati. In Brahman verily are all beings, placed within [it] (*antaḥ samāhita*) like in a boat.[8]

The important element here is "in Brahman, verily, are all beings, *viśvabhūtāni*, placed within, *antaḥ samāhita*, like in a boat". Correspondingly, *ChāndUp* VIII.1.4 has "[in this city of Brahman] are contained, *samāhita*, all beings, *sarvāṇi bhūtāni*, and all desires". The agreement is so specific (see sec. 13 below) that the two texts must be dealing with the same knowledge. Both describe an inner knowledge as clear as perception (not necessarily visual, of course) that all beings (and all things) "[are placed within it] like in a boat". In *Taittirīya Brāhmaṇa*, they are contained (or placed within) Brahman, while in *Chāndogya Upaniṣad* they are contained in the *dahara ākāśa*, which ultimately is the Ātman.

While *TaittBr* II.8.8 [8]-[9] thus confirms the presence in 1.1-1.5 of a strong "experiential" element, viz. "like in a boat," *Atharva Veda* X.8.43 suggests that in 1.1, the city of Brahman, *Brahma-pura*, is the body.[9] The "nine gates" may refer to the nine openings of the body. Alternatively, the Brāhmaṇa explains that "[just] as the city of a king contains his subjects and attendants who carry out his behests, similarly the body is the city of Brahman containing the several senses, the mind and the intellect, all serving the purposes of the master," and Śaṁkara repeats this simile.[10] The small (or subtle), lotus-like abode in the body on the other hand is the heart, both the physical heart and the heart in a figurative sense thought of as localized in and represented by the physical heart or chest. In *Atharva Veda* X.8.43 above, the same term "lotus flower" is used for the body, but the body is not distinguished from the mind. So the use of "lotus-flower" in *Dahara Vidyā* 1.1 to describe the heart may well be simply a transference.

4. The Heart in the Upaniṣads: Vedic Roots and Universal Significance

The Heart in the Upaniṣads. To get an idea of the nature and importance of the *Dahara* teaching, a good starting point is the observation by G. Mukhopadhyaya[11] that in the old Upaniṣads great human attributes, inner stability, and deep, true feelings and realization are generally referred to as having their seat in the heart. This is also true today in the West. Thus we have in English "I knew (felt, realized) it in my heart . . ."; "In my heart I decided then and there . . ." (note the typical past tense); "he has a large heart" and so on,[12] and there are similar expressions in German[13] and other Indo-European languages.[14] Indeed we are dealing here with an element of Universal Religion/Perennial Philosophy, which manifests itself in the secular and sacred literatures of many civilizations: The heart is the seat of the True, of higher qualities and aspirations, and of the Divine (cf. below). The *Dahara Vidyā* at one stroke gives a deep explanation of this primacy of the heart. The heart, it says, contains the *ākāśa* in the heart, the *ākāśa* which when truly known is the Ātman, the One Reality. *Because* the Self or Brahman is in the heart, the heart is the seat of all higher knowledges and aspiration, in fact it is the source of the Universe and all manifestation ("it is Brahman, it is All," *BṛhUp* V.3.1).

It is interesting that in the early Upaniṣads this "modern" and more universal meaning of the term "heart" is evoked primarily by Yājñavalkya. "Of all *vidyās* (knowledges and ways of knowing) the uniting point is the heart," is one of his similes to Maitreyī, and he instructs Janaka to worship/regard the heart as the source of all stabilities (*BṛhUp* IV.1.7). In *BṛhUp* IV.4.9 (M) = IV.4.7 (K), he cites the verse (*śloka*):

> When all desires are expelled,
> which lurk within his heart,
> then a mortal becomes immortal,
> he attains Brahman here.[15]

But most remarkable of all is *BṛhUp* III.9.19-25 (K), where the great sage extols the heart as the near-ultimate foundation in some deeply interesting ways. The text is actually part of an important *vidyā*, *BṛhUp* III.9.19-26, the final segment of the Yājñavalkya-Śākalya dialogue, *BṛhUp* III.9.1-26. The *vidyā* falls into two parts. First, Yājñavalkya explains to the Brahmin Śākalya that he (Yājñavalkya) has been able to talk down the Brahmins of the Kurupañcālas because he knew "the quarters of heaven together with their deities and their bases (*pratiṣṭhā*)," and when Śākalya questions further, the basis turns out in every case to be the heart (*BṛhUp* III.9.20-25). This is Part I and is the segment of interest here. But then Śākalya asks still further on what he (Yājñavalkya) and his self are supported, and now the answer is, the Self. This is Part II. Here we only discuss Part I; for Part II and the *vidyā* as a whole, see sec. 19 below:

> III.9.20. (Śākalya:) "What deity (*devatā*) are you (sic!) in this Eastern Quarter?"[a]
> (Yājñavalkya:) "The Sun Deity (Āditya-*devatā*)."
> "That Sun, on what is it based?"
> "[On] the Eye."
> "And on what is the Eye based?"
> "On forms (*rūpa*), for one sees forms with the Eye."

"And on what are forms based?"
"On the heart (*hṛdaya*)," he said. "For through the heart one knows (root *jñā*) the forms. Truly, [only] based in the heart do the forms exist.[b]"
"Just so [it is], Yājñavalkya."

Thus all visible forms are based (*pratiṣṭhita*) on the heart, cf. *Dahara Vidyā* 1.3. In the following verses III.9.21-24, faith, semen, truth, and speech are all similarly said to be based on the heart.

21. (Śākalya:) What deity are you in this Southern Quarter?"
"The Deity of Death, *Yama-devatā*."
"That Yama Deity, on what is it based?"
"On the sacrifice, *yajña*."
"On what is the sacrifice based?"
"On the offerings to the priests."
"And on what are the offerings to the priests based?"
"On faith, *śraddhā*, indeed; for when he has faith, he gives offerings to the priests. Thus the offerings to the priests are based on faith."
"In what then is faith based?"
"In the heart," [Yājñavalkya} said. For by the heart he knows (root *jñā*) faith. "Verily, in the heart alone is faith based."
"Thus it is, Yājñavalkya."
22. (Śākalya:) "What Deity are you in this Western Quarter?"
"The Varuṇa Deity, *Varuṇa devatā*."
"That Varuṇa, on what is he based?"
"On Water (plural)."
"On what then is Water based?"
"On Semen, *retas*," [Yājñavalkya] said. Therefore also they say of a newborn who looks like his father, 'he is like one who slipped out of his [father's] heart, like one built out of his [father's] heart.' "In the heart indeed is semen based."
"Thus it is, Yājñavalkya."
23. (Śākalya:) "What Deity are you in this Northern Quarter?"
"The Soma Deity, *soma-devatā*."
"This Soma, on what is he supported?"
"On the initiation rite, *dīkṣā*."
"On what then is the initiation rite supported?"

"On truth, *satya*." Therefore also they say to the initiate, 'Speak the truth.' "Thus indeed the initiation rite is based on the truth."

"In what is truth based?"

"In the heart," [Yājñavalkya] said. For by the heart he knows the true. "Verily, truth is based in the heart alone."

"Thus it is, Yājñavalkya."

24. (Śākalya:) "What Deity are you in this Fixed Quarter (the zenith)?"

"The Fire Divine, *Agni-devatā*."

"On what is Agni based?"

"On speech, *Vāc*."

"In what then is Sppech based?"

"In the heart."

"In what then is the heart based?"

25. "Ghost," said Yājñavalkya, "if you would think [that] that would be somewhere else than in us. For if that were somewhere else than in us, the dogs might eat it or the birds tear it to pieces."[16]

We will see later (sec. 19) that this teaching is likely to have esoteric (yogic) undertones. But in view of the whole dramatic setting (a public wisdom contest) and the fact that Yājñavalkya's initial answers before he gets to the heart are familiar from earlier Brāhmaṇa and other Upaniṣadic literature, it is likely that when at the end of each verse he finally gets to the heart, his explanations likewise appealed to his audience's general understanding of the heart. His answers are not presented as new teachings about the heart, but rather as samples of insights which illustrate his spiritual understanding. To appreciate these, some general (popular) understanding of the heart along these lines was a prerequisite. Thus we can regard Yājñavalkya's statements about the heart not only as representing his own deeper insight and knowledge, but also as consonant with the general (popular) meaning of "heart" at the time.

The Heart as *Buddhi*, "Inner Intelligence". But the heart was not only understood as the foundation of higher qualities. It was also beginning to be regarded as the center of *buddhi*, "inner intelligence," a term first used in *Kaṭha Upaniṣad* and the *Gītā*.[17] *Buddhi* is (inner) intelligence in a very broad sense, including higher feelings (compassion etc.), inner perception of truth, knowledge of what is the right path to take etc. (all of which come into play when one tries to make decisions on the basis of one's conscience and when one contemplates how to lead one's life), but it also includes beginning *jñāna* consciousness. "Heart here refers to intelligence (*buddhi*) and mind taken together" says Śaṁkara on *BṛhUp* III.9.20 above.[18] The general significance of the heart as *buddhi* has been argued by G. Mukhopadhyaya.

> That the heart signifies the deepest center of *buddhi* is clear from the use of the term *guhā*, again and again, in the Upaniṣads, where the Ātman, we are told, remains concealed. . . The *guhā* or the cave and the heart are identical, as is evident from the use of such terms as *guhāgranthi* and *hṛdayagranthi* [= knots of the heart] in the same sense. The knots that bind the soul are all in the *buddhi*, for it is through the *buddhi* that the soul gets connected or entangled with the outer world in infinite ways... That the *hṛdaya* is identical with the *buddhi* is further made clear by such statements as "the desires are all deposited in the heart," or "one crosses beyond all the sorrows of the heart," where the term "*hṛdayam*" evidently signifies the "*buddhi*," which is the store of all desires and sorrows and other allied feelings.[19]

In the oldest Upaniṣads, the deepest general meaning of the term heart is found in the Yājñavalkya teachings discussed above, and this is the closest thing to a comprehensive notion of *buddhi*. References to loosening etc. the "knots of the heart," in which the heart is "the deepest center of *buddhi*" (Mukhopadhyaya above) occur mostly in the later Upaniṣads (*Kaṭha, Muṇḍaka*, etc.).[20] The same thing holds also for statements that Brahman is in the cave (of the heart).[21] This general distributional picture suggests that a fuller meaning of heart as the center of *buddhi* and *vijñāna*, combined with a then standard conception of its role as seat of the Ātman etc., developed from and in response to the *Dahara Vidyā* and the Heart *Vidyā*, *BṛhUp* V.2-3 (K). In other words, the distributional picture suggests a historical sequence:

general meaning of heart as seat of higher feelings, deeper knowledge (in old Ups.)	→	great *vidyās* (in old Ups.)	→	fuller image of heart, and of heart as containing the Supreme (in *KaṭhaUp* etc.)

According to this, the *Dahara* and Heart *Vidyās* take the general meaning of "heart" represented in the dialogue with Śākalya and give it an Infinite foundation. This in turn stimulates further deepening and widening of the popular meaning of "heart" in the subsequent literature (*Kaṭha Upaniṣad* etc.), with the heart being the center of *buddhi* and the latter being the seat of the Ātman.

The Heart in the *Ṛg Veda*. The powerful popular understanding of the heart as man's spiritual center and basis that is reflected in the Yājñavalkya texts may be traced to the *Ṛg Veda*. There the heart is the seer's basic organ of divine experience and process, the basic arena of his inner Divine life.[22] J. Gonda has sensitively brought together a number of passages which evoke an extraordinary picture of an inner world of Divine vision, light, and formless knowledge/experience combined with mantra making.[23] Thus for example *Ṛg Veda* I.105.15, "Varuṇa causes manifestation of Brahma to appear in material form; we turn to him who opens the ways (to success); he opens in the heart the 'thought' (*mati*); a new manifestation of *Ṛta* [the divine cosmic order] must appear,"[24] or *Ṛg Veda* I.64.4, "when they pronounced the sacred texts which were fashioned by the heart".[25] In this context, the Soma Sacrifice had a special significance; it was an occasion of highest mystical and spiritual experience. The Soma juices which the priests had drunk were in their hearts, and the process of purification and clarification of the priests' words in the heart was "similar to, or parallel or identical with"[26] the straining and clarification of the physical soma juice with three sieves. Thus *Ṛg Veda* IX.73.7, "the inspired poets (*kavi*) clarify their words in the sieve that has been extended and discharges a thousand streams".[27] "'Because he had, with three strainers, clarified the hymn of praise (*arka*), he, tracing with (or within) the heart the 'thought' (*mati*), the light (*jyotiḥ*), has made himself, according to his own nature, the highest gem; then he beheld heaven and earth' [*Ṛg Veda* III.26.8]. . . [The gist is:] By finding, with or in the heart, the light of higher insight and contact with the Transcendent, one becomes an all-seeing Ṛṣi."[28] This resonates with *Dahara Vidyā* 1.3 and 1.5. Gonda sees a "historical and fundamental connection" between this understanding of the heart in the *Ṛg Veda* and the great Upaniṣadic *vidyās* such as "'Which is the Ātman?' 'The person here who consists of knowledge among the senses, the light within the heart'"[29] (*BṛhUp* IV.3.7, chr. 5 above). The latter is in fact in some way parallel to the *Dahara Vidyā* (sec. 21 below).

While Gonda concentrates strictly on the inner experience expressed in the hymns, F.B.J. Kuiper has suggested that the *Ṛg Vedic* mystical understanding of the heart has a cosmological dimension: It is rooted in an ancient "Aryan mysticism" which is connected with Old Iranian (pre-*Ṛg Vedic*) cosmology.[30] According to Kuiper's reconstruction, Varuṇa, a major deity in the *Ṛg Veda* and even more so in Old Iranian religion,[31] is *inter alia* Lord of the nether world, under the earth. There he watches over the cosmic order, *ṛta*, and supports the sky and the earth by something like a cosmic axis (*skambha*), later identified with Mount Meru, or by holding the roots of the cosmic tree to which the axis is often equated. His dwelling is a dark stone house (*harmya*). Now in the evening, the Sun sets in Varuṇa's domain becomes Varuṇa, and so more generally does Agni (the Sun is a form of Agni). The Sun then becomes the "Sun in the rock, *svar yád áśman*," and Agni, "Agni in the Rock." Only great and mythical seers and gods could see the Sun in the rock: Vāsiṣṭha was granted this vision by Varuṇa and made a seer thereby (*Ṛg Veda* VII.88); Mitrā-Varuṇa were "sun-seers, " etc. Finally "during the night, this picture . . . alters fundamentally. Varuṇa's nether world then extends over the earth as the night-sky. The cosmic waters [on which lies, or which are contained in, the cosmic mountain] are at that time a celestial ocean (*samudra*). . ."[32] "Several details [then] show unequivocally that during the night the nether world [including cosmic mountain or tree and cosmic ocean] was thought of as hanging over the earth *in an inverted position*;"[33] so that "in the nocturnal aspect of the cosmos, the sky is the nether world . . . turned upside down".[34] Correspondingly, the cosmic tree whose roots Varuṇa is holding is inverted, with its branches hanging down.[35]

According to Kuiper, "Agni's birth, or the vision of the Sun in the darkness, was the central theme of what can be denoted by no other term than Aryan mysticism."[36] More specifically, the central elements were "the cosmological ideas about light in the darkness of the nether world, which was obviously considered a mystery," and "the presence of potential life in death [i.e., immortality]".[37] Kuiper cites as an example of a "correlate of this cosmological notion in the religious experience of individuals" the stanza *Ṛg Veda* VI.9.6, "My ears fly open, my eyes open, this light arises that is set in the heart..." on Agni Vaiśvānara (chr. 4.15 above). "One gets the impression that the seer, by meditating upon the sacrificial fire (stanza 5), attained a vision of the cosmic mystery, the 'Sun in the rock' (or, Agni in the nether world . . .)."[38] More generally, Kuiper suggests that "the later speculation of the Upaniṣads about the *ātman* 'placed in the cavity' is a direct continuation of the older mystical speculation of the Veda".[39]

> . . . the *Ṛg Vedic* seer gets his vision with or in his heart (*hṛdā́* or *hṛdi*). This heart is equated to the cosmic mountain and its subterranean ocean. Hence it is that the *Ṛg Veda* refers to the "ocean of the heart" (IV.58.5 *hṛ́dyāt samudrā́t*, cf. 11, *antáḥ samudré hṛdy antár*) and divine inspiration is looked upon as an "opening of the doors of the mind" that is parallel to the opening of the cosmic "enclosure" (*vrajá-*). Just as the *Ṛg Vedic* poet prays that Agni may open his "thought" like an aperture (*khá-*, viz. in the cosmic hill of the primeval world), so the *Mahānārāyaṇa Upaniṣad* says that Prajāpati, who is "hidden in the cavity" of the heart, pierces from within the *khāni* (of the mind) to "enjoy the objects". If it may be assumed that *guhāyām* in the Upaniṣads is a substitute of the later language for such *Ṛg Vedic* terms as *vrajé, ūrvé, áśman*, which all denote the nether world viewed as an enclosure, the parallelism between the revelation of "the Sun in the rock" and the Upaniṣadic vision of the *ātman* "placed in the cavity" is apparent.[40]

Kuiper's cosmological reconstruction explains many details in Vedic studies which have puzzled Vedic scholarship for a long time. But it is difficult to judge whether the conceptions he has sketched could form a viable, lived belief-system for a group of people, let alone a path of higher spiritual experience. To be sure, the cosmological ideas which he outlines very possibly play a role in *Ṛg Veda* VI.9.5-6. But the essential element in these stanzas is the vision of "this light that is set in the heart," which represents universal type of inner spiritual experience found in many higher spiritual traditions. This realization does not *substantively* derive from or depend on the cosmology. Rather, the latter functions as a vehicle or channel in which the necessary universality of vision, intensity of worship, and overall detachment leading to this knowledge or experience can arise and be expressed. Similar comments apply to "in the cave". The Divine, the Infinite, is the fundamental and the only real universal element. This Divine is at most only mediated by and expressed in terms of a particular cosmology ("the Sun in the rock"), or location ("in the heart"). Actually, the hymn exemplifies a universal way in which this Divine surfaces in the higher experience of mankind, viz., as Light in the heart, as the Divine in the heart.

The Heart and Perennial Philosophy. Indeed, the vision and experience of the *Ṛg Vedic* seers, and the supreme Wisdom developments of this experience later in the *Dahara* and Heart *Vidyās* are not an isolated phenomenon limited to the Vedic culture. For a general conception/experience and understanding that the seat of higher feelings and deeper, truer understanding in a human being is the heart, that the heart is the seat of the Divine, and that the Divine can be reached by a path through the heart is found in many cultures and societies.[41] And a few religious-philosophical traditions go on and indentify this heart with the Universe, the Reality, or the Supreme Divine.[42] For example,

> The Heart which goes not astray
>   in the way of Heaven and Earth,
> Knows neither Birth nor Death.
>
> Though Heaven and Earth were
>   thought to be extremely broad,
> They are indeed contained
>   within my heart.
>
> The Heart of Heaven and Earth
>   is none other than your own.
> Do not imagine the existence
>   of any Heart besides.
>
> Whether you call it God or Buddha,
>   the Living-Thing
> Which dwells within the Truth
>   of Heaven and Earth is meant.[43]

These are verses by Kurozumi Munetada (1780-1850), founder of the Kurozumi Sect of Shinto in Japan, who uses Taoist, Buddhist and Shinto Language.[44]

5. *Dahara Ākāśa* as a Small Space in the Heart

Traditional Exegesis of *Dahara Ākāśa*. We said that the *dahara ākāśa* is taught in the *Dahara Vidyā* as an intermediate stage in the unfolding of the individual's *Ātma-jñāna* or Ātma-consciousness. But what exactly is *dahara ākāśa*, how does one develop/recognise it in oneself, and how does one thereafter go to full *Ātma-jñāna*? In this and the next two sections we consider the traditional approach to the *vidyā* represented by the *Brahma Sūtra*, Śaṁkara, and other classical commentators. This approach involves a type of meditation which has its own validity and is widely practiced by aspirants and devotees today.

The traditional approach to the *vidyā* has the following characteristics:

(1) The heart is (a) understood as described in the preceding section, specifically as the center of *buddhi* or inner intelligence, and (b) thought to be experienced as somehow localized in the body, the chest.

(2) *Dahara* is taken to mean small, *alpa*, so that in 1.1, *daharam puṇḍarīkam veśma* means small lotus-like mansion, and *dahara ākāśa* indicates a (very) small space or spot.

(3) *Ākāśa* is regarded as a name for Brahman, and *dahara ākāśa* and *antar-hṛdaya ākāśa* as designations of Brahman.

(4) The meditation has the form of the thought that the Supreme is within one's heart, or oneself in one's heart is the Supreme, and that It is (or one's true Self in the heart is) "free from evil, ageless, deathless . . ." (the attributes in V. 1.5, and also additional attributes from related texts).

Dahara = "small". A prominent feature of this approach is (2): Both the *Brahma Sūtra* and Śaṁkara take *dahara* to mean "small," *alpa*,[45] and advocate meditation involving a strong focussing on or centering in the region of the physical heart or chest. Apart from the fact that *dahara* does in fact most commonly mean "small," this choice may also have been influenced by the fact that the self is often described as being in the heart of the size of a thumb or a point, or finer than the top of a hair. Such texts are found mostly in *Śvetāśvatara* and *Kaṭha Upaniṣads* and play an important role in the *Brahma Sūtra*.[46] It seems likely that they helped to establish the Sūtra's interpretation of the *dahara ākāśa* as a small (*dahara*) space = spot in the chest. In any case, they represent significant levels or phases of experience/

knowledge of Ātman in the heart, and thus may seem to be relevant to the *Dahara* teaching.

The Self of the Size of a Thumb and a Point. A particularly important text is *ŚvetUp* V.8-10,[47] because here several of these descriptions form part of a larger whole:

> 8. Of the size of a thumb (*aṅguṣṭha-mātra*), of Sun-like appearance,
> [is he] who is endowed with *saṁkalpa* (determination)
> and *ahaṁkāra* (I-organ).
> But another, endowed only with the attribute of *buddhi*
> (inner intelligence) and self (*ātman*),
> is seen of the size of the tip of a goad.
> 9. On the one hand to be known as a hundredth part of the
> top of a hair divided a hundred fold,
> is the *jīva* (the living one); and on the other it is of the
> nature of (lit. "suitable for"[a]) infiniteness.
> 10. It is neither male nor female
> nor is this indeed neuter.
> Whatever body it takes to itself,
> by that very same one it is held.[48]

First v. 8 describes two types of perceptions, in meditation, of the self (note the *dṛṣṭa*, "[is] seen"). Both of them are perceptions in one's heart (cf. *ŚvetUp* III.13, below). The first is something like a vision of the self as Divine, while the second is further along on the path to the pure Ātman. Here the self has only the nature of "inner intelligence" and of "[being] self". Next in v. 9 a certain ambiguity or two-sidedness of the self is described: on the one hand it is perceived as finite, finer and smaller than what can seen with the eye (this refers to "experience" or knowledge similar to that in v. 8b), but at the same time there is also an infinite aspect at play, viz. the Infinite Ātman.[49] The latter is reminiscent of the fundamental response of the teacher in *Dahara Vidyā* VIII.1.3, "As far extending as this space here is, so far extending is this space inside the heart." The perception of the self as the Self may in some sense, somehow, still be "in one's heart," conceived very vaguely as localized in or connected with the body. But at the same time it is beyond that whole framework: the self = Self is "of the nature of infiniteness," and is actually without any limitations, as described in the highest texts. And finally v. 10, still under the impact of this two-sided nature of the self in v. 9, continues to describe this total reality in a third, more objective manner.

Passages in the Upaniṣads like this, which describe perceptions or intuitions of the self or of the Divine in the heart, deserve a special study of their own. They present a wide range of experience or knowledge of self and Self in the heart, and often show a similar two-sided aspect as *ŚvetUp* V.8-10.[50] So *Dahara Vidyā* VIII.1.3, which conveys the beginnings of a perception of the double-sided nature of the Self (and that also in a very specific form), is in some way connected with this whole body of texts.[51] The *Brahma Sūtra*, faced with this polyphonous testimony, takes all the different expressions of knowledge/experience at face value (as operating at the same level) and tries to develop an overall conceptual framework that is consistent with all of them.[52]

***Dahara Ākāśa* is Brahman.** So far we have looked only at point (2) above, that the space within the heart is a small space in the area of the physical heart or the chest. The *Brahma Sūtra* also takes the view that the *dahara ākāśa* is Brahman, or in other words, point (3).[53] Such a straight forward identification seems to neglect the very definite role as an "aid" and "intermediate" which *dahara ākāśa* is apparently intended to play in the spiritual instruction given in the text. VIII.1.1 clearly implies, and the exchange VIII.1.1-1.3 suggests, that one should identify the *dahara* or *antar-hṛdaya ākāśa* in one's experience and then go further, further "into it". And this "going into it" is then further elaborated into different stages of perception in VIII.1.3. If knowledge of *dahara ākāśa* is regarded as identical with knowledge of Brahman, then the *dahara ākāśa* cannot play such a role in *sādhanā*. We will see, however, that Śaṁkara (and therefore probably also the Sūtra) has a very deep understanding of *dahara ākāśa* which does full justice to its role as an intermediate stage.[54] So point (3) seems to be merely somewhat awkward language and does not constitute a real problem.

6. Traditional *Dahara Upāsanā:* Meditation Involving Qualities of the Self

In view of the traditional exegesis (1)-(3) and the Upaniṣadic texts discussed in the preceding section, the traditional approach to following the *Dahara* teaching VIII.1.1-1.5 naturally involves centering in the core of one's heart, and feeling oneself (what one really is, one's being) as localized in a small (*dahara*) region in one's physical heart or chest. The *Brahma Sūtra* does not discuss this in any more detail, but Śaṁkara's commentary on *Dahara Vidyā* VIII.1.3 clarifies matters a little. In addition, the traditional *Dahara* meditation also involves meditating on the Ātman as having the qualities or *guṇas* enumerated in *Dahara Vidyā* VIII.1.5— "with sin destroyed, divorced from old age, . . . , having desire that is true (*satya-kāma*), having resolve that is true (*satya-saṁkalpa*)". No such meditation is enjoined in the *Dahara* text. But a similar meditation, along with thought of the form and attributes of Rudra-Śiva, is taught in *Kaivalya Upaniṣad,* one of the older Vedānta or Śiva Upaniṣads (before 500 CE). This, together with the Sūtra's general philosophy of pooling different versions of a *vidyā*, leads naturally to meditation on the Ātman as having these attributes. The *Kaivalya* meditation is also of independent interest because it links the traditional *Dahara* meditation with meditations involving visualization of a divine form such as are described in the Purāṇas.

Śaṁkara's Commentary on *Dahara Vidyā* VIII.1.3

[A] Listen, [disciples]! What you are saying [in 1.2], "based on the smallness (*alpatvāt*) of the space (*kha*) within the [heart-] lotus, that what is within it (*tatstham*) should be [still] smaller"—that is not right (*asat*). For I did not mean the space in the lotus mansion[a] was smaller than the lotus. "The *dahara ākāśa* within that [heart lotus]"—[that means:] "With the lotus being small, the inner organ (*antaḥkaraṇa*) being in that (*tatstham*), [and] conforming to that (lotus), is lotus-space-circumscribed.[a] In that [inner organ] of yogins, purified by the withholding of the organs of sense and speech (*karaṇas*), is perceived[b] Brahman, like a reflection of a real form is seen in clear water[c] or [other] pure [substance], clear,[d] appearing as the own-form of the light of consciousness,[e] and of the same extent [as the inner organ]."—[This is what] I meant [by] "the *dahara ākāśa* within that [heart lotus]".[54]

Assuming the voice of the teacher in the Upaniṣad, Śaṁkara is explaining what he meant by "the *dahara ākāśa* within that [heart-lotus]" in *Dahara Vidyā* 1.1, because he thinks the disciples have gotten the wrong idea. Evidently he is trying to take care of several things at the same time. One problem is how the small space, *dahara ākāśa*, within the heart-lotus can contain all things and be the Ātman —must that small space, since it is within the heart, not be smaller than the heart? His solution is to distinguish between the physical heart and a small space within it on the one hand and the inner organ "in that (small space)" which "conforms to that (small space)" on the other. One's self and mind, when centered in the small space in the heart, are *anu-vidhāyin*, literally "of a form, *vidhā*, which follows or conforms to, *anu*, [that condition]". They take on a special form in accordance with their being centered in the small region in the heart, which latter functions as an *upādhi*, a limiting adjunct. In other words, there is no contradiction, because awareness that all things are in the space in the heart, as well as perception/realization of Ātman/Brahman, is in the inner organ (locative, *tasmin*) and not in the small space.

Apart from dealing with the problem of small vs. infinitely large, Śaṁkara doesn't address himself further to the *dahara ākāśa*; in particular he doesn't deal with the *dahara ākāśa* as an intermediate stage of inner knowledge. Nevertheless, [A] makes two important additional points. One is that in order for perception of Brahman to arise, the inner organ has to be purified by the withdrawal, *saṁhṛta*, of the instruments, *karaṇas*, i.e. the senses and speech. This may refer to absence of sensory awareness (awareness of body and surroundings) during meditation. But the term *saṁhṛta*, from *saṁ-hṛ*, "to pull back, curb", is not specifically yogic and is used largely in narrative contexts.[55] Śaṁkara is thus not necessarily (or not just only) talking about *pratyāhāra* and *dhāraṇā*, "withdrawal of the senses" and "fixation of the mind substance on a particular locus" (here, the region of the heart) as they are used in the *Yoga Sūtra*.[56] Rather, "withdrawal of the instruments" may refer more generally to purification of the moral ethical nature by curbing the senses and speech (something that involves changing one's way of life). Or it may refer to pulling back the instruments as part of turning away (in one's heart) from things in the world, a different kind of purification of the mind.

The other important detail in [A] is the description of *how* Brahman is perceived in the heart. Brahman is perceived *in* the inner organ (locative), in the limited self, consistent with the fact (noted in chr. 5) that the Self is realized in the *vijñāna-maya* sheath. It appears "like a reflection of a form seen in clear water", and as the "own-form" of the light of consciousness, *vijñāna-jyotiḥ svarūpa*, i.e., as the light of consciousness itself "perceived in an essential manner, as an essence". And the "experience" is like seeing a reflection of a real thing (a form, *rūpa*) in water, although it is unlike perception or intuition in the normal sense because there is no separate perceiver. This is beautiful poetic language to hint at what is beyond words and mind.

Rationale for Meditation on the Eight Qualities. The need for meditation on the eight qualities of the Ātman enumerated in VIII.1.5 ("sinless . . .")—the second major ingredient of classical *Dahara upāsanā*—is discussed at length by Rāmānuja.[57] Rāmānuja takes *Dahara Vidyā* VIII.1.1, "what is within that [heart or *dahara ākāśa*], that should be searched out" as the basic instruction for meditation. "[The text] then refers to Brahman . . . as the small ether within the heart, meaning thereby that Brahman who for the benefit of the devotee is present within that palace (*veśma*) should be meditated on as minute in size, and finally—in the clause 'that is to be searched out' —enjoins as the object of meditation that which abides in that Brahman, i.e., on the one hand, its essential freedom from evil . . . [etc., in other words the eight qualities in VIII.1.5]. The 'that' (in 'that is to be searched out') enjoins as objects of search the small ether, i.e., Brahman itself, as well as the qualities abiding within it."[58] And as if this was not enough, he then goes through the whole text VIII.1.3-1.5, explaining the role of each phrase, and finds that this "connected consideration of the whole chapter" leads to the same conclusion.[59]

Śaṁkara also describes the *vidyā* as involving "meditating on (*upās-*) Brahman as abiding within the heart and as endowed with qualities . . ."[60] But he is critical of this approach as being *saguṇa* and characterizes the *vidyā* as intended for spiritually less mature aspirants. "Though [in *ChāndUp* VI and VII, the *Sad* and *Bhūma Vidyās*] . . . it has been learnt that 'Brahman is real (*sat*), one, without a second' and 'the Self is all this,' free from all diversities of space, place, time and all the rest—yet . . .," for the benefit of individuals of "dull intellect," who are too much enmeshed in space and time and the rest, "it is necessary to convey the teaching *indirectly*".[61] This is done, "in the first instance, by indicating the particular spot within the lotus of the heart [as the abode of the self, the Brahman]. Secondly . . . the person of dull intellect has his heart so fixed upon the Highest Being possessing the highest qualities, that it is found necessary to speak of such qualities *belonging to him* as *satyakāma*, 'being of unfailing wish,' and so forth. . . . Fourthly, though in the case of persons who have realized the unity of the Self, there can be no goer or going or place to go to, all of which involve diversity... yet there are many persons whose minds are still beset with such diversities as the goer, the going, and the place to go to and who are still given to meditating on Brahman as abiding within the heart and as endowed with qualities . . ."[62] Even "to enjoin such detailed means of accomplishing the end as *brahmacarya* and the like" is merely another compromise of the scripture to help less mature aspirants "divert the longing of sense-gratification that has grown through long continued indulgence extending over several births".[63]

Śaṁkara's reservations here are based in part on his own sharp distinction between *saguṇa* and *nirguṇa* Brahman and his emphasis on *jñāna* as the only path to *nirguṇa* Brahman. But they also suggest that "*upāsanā* of Brahman in one's heart as endowed with qualities" was at his time *the* generally established meditative practice associated with the *Dahara Vidyā*. As noted above, the *Dahara* text does not specifically enjoin such meditation. It only says that what is within the *dahara ākāśa* "should be searched out," and that "that is what one should desire to know".

S. Subrahmanya Shastri's Description of *Dahara Upāsanā*. In modern Vedāntic practice, other attributes are also used in meditation besides the eight in the *Dahara* text. This may be illustrated with a summary of traditional *Dahara upāsanā* by S. Subrahmanya Shastri.[64] Subrahmanya Shastri's remarks are addressed to Indian scholars who are practicing Advaitins, but they also appear to be intended as a guide or resource for *daśanāmī* monks (see below). We take the text in sections, commenting on specific aspects as we go along.

> And that [*vidyā*], on account of its occurrence in many *śākhās*, is indeed one [single] *vidyā*, by *BraSū* III.3.1, and it must be stated that [there should be] "combination [= pooling of attributes]" (*BraSū* III.3.5). Similarly in the *Dahara Vidyā Prakāśikā* composed by Parama-Śivendra Sarasvatī, disciple of Abhinava-nārāyaṇānandendra Sarasvatī [the same view is set forth].
>
> (1) **The eight attributes in *ChāndUp* VIII.1.5,** beginning with "with sin destroyed, ageless . . ." have been settled [as to be used in meditation] on account of their nature of [being attributes that are] worthy of being meditated on (*upāsyatayā nirdhāritāḥ*). *Upāsanā* on "heaven and earth [are contained in it . . .]" has the character of being a

> support [consisting of] saying in the heart the name and telling the true import of Om, this way and that, for the purpose of driving out doubt, but not on account of worthiness of being worshipped.[65] (Boldface added)

The author begins by referring to the *Brahma Sūtra's* principle of "combining [attributes of Ātman/Brahman in meditation]" (*upasaṁhāra*) which is the dominant feature of the Sūtra's philosophy of *upāsanā* (cf. sec. 4.3 above).[66] This principle underlies the exposition of *Dahara upāsanā* that follows and is also the guiding principle in a work on the *Dahara Vidyā* by Parama-Śivendra Sarasvatī (ca. 1700 CE), apparently the only work by a classical Vedāntic author ever devoted to an Upaniṣadic *vidyā*.[67] Next (1) the use of the eight attributes in *Dahara Vidyā* VIII.1.5, "with sin destroyed . . ." in *upāsanā* is distinguised from contemplation of the phrases "in it are contained heaven and earth . . ." (*Dahara Vidyā* VIII.1.3), which performs only a supportive, stabilizing function. It removes doubt, but does not *per se* bring one closer to Ātman. The exposition continues:

> (2) **In the *Bṛhadāraṇyaka* [*Upaniṣad, BṛhUp* IV.4.22 (K) = IV.4.26 (M)],** the trio of attributes (*guṇas*) "The Controller of All, the Lord of All, the Ruler of All" is given for the purpose of *upāsanā*. "He does not become greater by deed" and so on is the telling of the fruits for the knower. "He is the Lord of All, He is the Ruler of Creatures" and so forth is praise (*stuti*) of the Supreme Lord (*īśvara*). But "What this space within the heart is, in that lies . . ." is the statement of the place of *upāsanā*.

The attributes "He is the Controller of all . . ." are also to be used in meditation, in addition to the eight from *Dahara Vidyā* VIII.1.5. One is to think in one's heart "I am Brahman, without sin . . ., the Controller of All . . ."

Apart from *upasaṁhāra*,[68] another rationale for using attributes in meditation is *BraSū* III.3.1, "[The essence of meditation] described in all Vedānta [is the same] on account of the non-difference in injunction and so on."[69] In the Upaniṣads the *upāsanās* typically include injunctions to the effect that such and such should be regarded as, worshipped (*upās-*) as Brahman. The aphorism can thus be interpreted as saying that whatever one intuitively already correctly understands as Brahman when one sits down to meditate, that should function in the meditation as part of the meaning of Brahman. Whatever there is already in oneself that is inner determination toward and premonitions or vague intuition of Brahman, all that should be allowed and encouraged to participate in the meditation, so that the knowledge of Brahman may become clearer, truer. Ultimately it is Ātman/Brahman that is at the basis of a person's inner determination to reach the Supreme Divine, and of his or her premonitions of It. That is what one is in reality. The meditation only serves to enable that Aspect to emerge more purely and clearly, so that one is It more purely and clearly in one's consciousness. So the meditation uses as supports *guṇas*, attributes like "without Sin," "Controller of All," because these are the semantic garb in which the aspirant/devotee's premonitions and intuitions of Brahman are already flowing. They are therefore the natural channels for having Brahman-awareness emerge in him or her in purer form. For the same reason, all attributes should be used together because the basic principle is to allow the Inner Supreme Divine to flourish in their combined total. That is the real *upasaṁhāra*.

But this is not all. Only the first three attributes in *BṛhUp* IV.4.22 (K) are to be used in *upāsanā*. The others have different functions. We saw in chr. 4 that meditation or *upāsanā* on things like the Sun Divine or the Earth Divine (Āditya, Pṛthivī) as Brahman, or as the Vaiśvānara Ātman, leads to various lower level realizations of Divinity, but not necessarily to knowledge of Ātman/Brahman. The same is true for meditation on Ātman/Brahman in the heart as having certain *guṇas* or attributes. So point (2) is very careful to identify *guṇas* whose use in meditation will promote emergence of *Brahma-* and *Ātma-jñāna*, not only various types of knowledge of Divinity. Other *guṇas* which might be considered for *upāsanā* are eliminated because they are *stuti*, "praise," or "[descriptions of] the fruit" of the *upāsanā*.

> (3) **In *Kaivalya Upaniṣad*,** [the passage] beginning with "meditating on the heart-lotus" up to ". . . the sage reaches the origin of being" is the injunction for *upāsanā* together with the fruit.

Kaivalya Upaniṣad[70] is not one of the Vedic Upaniṣads, but it cannot be far removed from them in time. It is usually considered to be one of the older Vedānta or Śiva Upaniṣads but is not cited by Śaṁkara. Consisting of 25 verses, it contains at least 10 substantial quotations, mostly from *Śvetāśvatara* and *Kaṭha Upaniṣads*. The passage in context says:

> 5. In a solitary place and seated in an easy (yogic) posture, pure hearted, with head, neck and body straight
> established in the last (*saṁnyāsa*) order of life,[a] controlling all the senses, [and] bowing to the teacher with devotion (*bhakti*),
> 6. Having reflected on (*vi-cintya*) the heart lotus [which is, or as] divorced from passion,
> in the middle [of which is] the pure (*viśada*), the sorrowless (*vi-śoka*),
> unthinkable, unmanifest, of infinite form, supremely tranquil, immortal, the womb of Brahmā,[b]
> 7. He who is without beginning, middle, and end, [who is] one, everywhere present, who is *cit* and *ānanda*, without form, wondrous,
> who has Umā [= Śiva's consort] for companion, the Supreme Lord, the Ruler, endowed with three eyes, a dark throat and supremely peaceful,
> having meditated (*dhyātvā*) on Him, the sage (*muni*) reaches the womb of beings (*bhūta-yoni*), the witness of all, beyond darkness.
> 8. He is Brahmā (the Creator), He is Śiva, he is Indra, He is the Imperishable, the Supreme, the Self-Sovereign.
> He indeed is Viṣṇu, he is Prāṇa, He is Time (and) Agni, He is the Moon.
> 9. He indeed is all that was and will be, eternal.
> Knowing Him one goes beyond death. There is no other way to liberation (*vimukta*).[71]

Instructions for *upāsanā* begin at v. 6. First one should reflect on one's heart, to the effect that it has nothing to do with passion (it is *vi-rajas*, divorced from, *vi*, passion and activity, *rajas*), and that it is really completely pure, unstained by anger and other emotions that one may sometimes get involved in. This reflection is discursive (*vi-cint-*, "diversely thinking about"). The degree of localization of the heart (lotus) is left unspecified, suggesting that it may vary from "the lotus of my heart [thought localized in my chest]" to "the lotus of my inner intelligence, my inner soul". (In any case "lotus" is figurative.) Then comes reflection, meditation, identifying oneself with the attributes in v. 6 ff. and the conception and attributes of Śiva in v. 7 (up to "supremely peaceful"). The verb "having meditated on," *dhyātvā*, doesn't come until the second half of v. 7, suggesting that it functions as a more general term that may include different forms and stages of engagement with the attributes indicated. These latter fall into three groups: v. 6, the pure (*viśada*) and so on, to end of the verse; v. 7a, "without beginning, . . ." to "wondrous;" and v. 7b, "who has Umā for companion . . ." to "supremely peaceful," *praśānti*. The last group evokes images or figural conceptions of the deity which the student is assumed to have worshipped and meditated on before often from childhood on. The whole meditation is remarkable for the easy and natural way in which it integrates the different attitudes or orientations implied in these groups: the strong "my heart is the Infinite" focus in v. 6, the universal, all-encompassing, boundariless spirit in v. 7a, and the divine image or figural aspects of the deity and the personally conceived of and related to Divine in v. 7c. It represents an example of how the original *Dahara* teaching (VIII.1.1-1.5), in harmony with the philosophy of *upāsanā* that crystallized in the *Brahma Sūtra*, was adapted and fused with deep theism (here, worship of Rudra-Śiva as Supreme Divine).[72] S.S. Shastri's inclusion of this element in the ambit of the *vidyā* is thus not only motivated by the principle to pool meditations and attributes of different versions of a given *vidyā* in different *śākhās*,[73] but also by what is done in *Kaivalya Upaniṣad*.

(4) **In *Taittirīya Āraṇyaka* [i.e., *Mahā-Nārāyaṇa Upaniṣad*],** [the text] "small, sinless, . . ." [231-232 in Varenne's edition] is injunction for *upāsanā*; "That which is the [sound] *svara* . . ." [Varenne 233-234] is praise (*stuti*) by means of [the property of] being Om and being the Supreme Lord... [goes on to mention Varenne 234-246, a paean on Nārāyaṇa, and Varenne 247-259] . . . Then with the *Ṛg Vedic* mantra "*Ṛta, Satya*, the Supreme Brahman, . . .," the eight qualities for *upāsanā* are mentioned. Therefore the eight *upāsanā* qualities are to be meditated on having been made into one (*ekīkṛtyopāsyāḥ*).

This deals with certain sections of *Mahā-Nārāyaṇa Upaniṣad* (here cited according to Varenne's edition[74]). Var. 231-232 is close to *Dahara Vidyā* 1.1-1.3 and is discussed in the next section as illustrating a meaning of *dahara ākāśa* as something like "(subtle) sky of awareness [in daily life]". The mantra mentioned at the end runs in literal translation:

> The Right (*Ṛta*), the True (*Satyam*), the Supreme Brahman,
> of the quality of Puruṣa[a], of dark blue and reddish-brown hue,[b]
> above the semen [principle],[c] of unusual eyes,[d]
> to [him] of all forms, [to him] alone, obeisance, obeisance.[75]

This is in the form of worship of Lord Śiva, but identified with higher principles and essences at the level of creation and transcendent to creation (*Ṛtam, Satyam*, Supreme Brahman, and *ūrdhva-retam*, "what is higher than the semen [principle], *retas*").[76] Presumably the point is that the eight qualities in *Dahara Vidyā* 1.5 are all contained in one of these latter. For that reason also, they should be meditated on "having been made into one".

7. Stages in Traditional *Dahara Upāsanā*

In view of its rather catholic aproach, one cannot expect traditional *Dahara upāsanā* to show much of a progression of specific types of experience or the like. Swami Nikhilananda of the Ramakrishna Order writes:

> [A] For the beginner the heart is the physical organ, shaped like a lotus-bud. Inside there is a subtle, luminous space which is often described as the Brahmapura, the Abode of Brahman.[a] As he makes progress in meditation and becomes capable of subtle perceptions, he realizes that the heart denotes not really the physical organ but the *buddhi*. At this stage the meditation is raised from the physical to the psychic level. The devotee casts the Absolute, as it were, in the mould of his mind and fashions out of it a mental image of Brahman. Finally he transcends both the heart and the mind and realizes Brahman, the All-pervading Consciousness, in his inmost consciousness. The image in the heart and the reflection in the *buddhi* become one with Universal Consciousness.

> The Ideal may be associated with or conditioned by a sound-symbol or a form-symbol. In the meditation associated with a sound-symbol, the aspirant repeats a Vedic aphorism such as "I am Brahman" (*Aham Brahmāsmi*). While repeating the sacred formula he also reflects on its meaning . . . In this form of meditation, the sound is emphasized. The sound, as we shall see, ultimately leads to silence, as the form leads to the ineffable experience of formlessness.
>
> In the meditation associated with a form-symbol, the aspirant observes that there arise constantly in his mind such forms or ideas as desire, determination, doubt, belief, non-belief, fear and fearlessness. He meditates on the Consciousness which is the Witness of these forms . . .[78]

Occurring in a section called "meditation," and introduced as one of two major types of meditation in Advaita Vedānta, this presumably describes meditational development in traditional *Dahara upāsanā.* The statement envisages three stages (first paragraph): (1) an initial stage of concentration with consciousness of the ideal in the region of the physical heart; (2) a second stage where the state of concentration is perceived as the *buddhi*, as one's own mind, or consciousness; and (3) a third stage involving a true transcendence of heart and mind and one's own consciousness and a oneness with a true Infinite Aspect. Swami Nikhilananda's second stage is clearly related to, and seems to be a more general version of, Swami Ananyananda's description of the realization of one's self as the light of knowing in the heart (discussed in connection with the first phase of the *Antar-jyotir Vidyā* in chr. 5.15). The main difference is that Swami Ananyananda focusses on the realization of one's self as light of knowledge, understood of course as a level of realization of the Ātman, but that here the realization is of one's state in the heart as Brahman. As Swami Nikhilananda notes, this state, or this Brahman that is realized, is strictly speaking still only a mental image of Brahman. (The devotee, by the attitude of *upāsanā*, has "cast the Absolute, as it were, in he mould of his mind and fashions out of it a mental image of Brahman".) This stage is formally reminiscent of the realization of the fourth foot of Brahman in the Sixteen Parts *Vidyā*, and of the "knowledge of mind" or *mano-vijñāna* taught in *ChāndUp* III.18 (cf. chr. 4). These knowledges do not, it is true, involve a path of meditation on and in the heart. But they are *vijñāna* in the heart (the relevant *upāsanās* in these teachings are *upāsanās* in the heart).

According to my present understanding, experience/knowledge of *dahara ākāśa* may occur right before Swami Nikhilananda's stage 2, or in stage 2. The space in the heart is often described as luminous in later texts, and in accounts by saints, devotees, and Divine Manifestations.[79] But it seems possible that knowledge/realization of the type described for stage (2) may also arise without perception of a luminous space in the heart. If the *Dahara* meditation includes meditation on a Deity or divine form as in *Kaivalya Upaniṣad*, the whole perception of and attitude toward Divinity which the student has developed in connection with the Deity earlier in his life form a spiritual-attitudinal matrix which may lead to perception of the Light of Divinity, but the subsequent development may still be colored by the aspirant's chosen Deity.[80] In this connection, Love plays a large role—particularly if the path is mostly one of absolute dedication and Love to the Highest. The degree to which there is Love toward the Deity, or toward the Infinite Self, including Love toward the whole of Creation, is perhaps the single most powerful factor in the aspirant's spiritual life and will be strongly reflected in his/her meditation. Accordingly it seems best to regard the traditional *Dahara upāsanā* as a broad avenue of meditation in which inner development can take many forms. After an initial development of knowledge of God or the Self or Light in the heart, the only step that may be in common to all these possible forms seems to be the final transcendence to the third stage mentioned by Swami Nikhilananda at the end of the first paragraph.

Traditional *Dahara Upāsanā* Today. Traditional *Dahara upāsanā* is still important in Vedānta today. According to Swami Maheshanand Giri, "this meditation is very popular among the monks of the order of Śaṁkara even today, and it is a must for those who belong to the Tradition of Śrī Dakṣiṇāmūrti".[81] In addition to the Upaniṣadic passages above and Parama-Śivendra's work, Swami Maheshanand also cites the *Sūta Saṁhitā* (a section of the *Skanda Purāṇa*), and Vidyāraṇya's *Anubhūti-Prakāśa* as having relevant chapters on this topic.[82] It seems patent that the traditional meditation on the Supreme in the Heart has been elaborated in the Purāṇas[83] and elsewhere, but no systematic studies are available.

8. *Dahara Ākāśa* as a (Subtle) Sky of Awareness: *Mahā-NārUp* XII.16

Two elements dominate the traditional approach to the *Dahara* teaching. One is that *dahara* is taken to mean "small," so that in VIII.1.1 *dahara ākāśa* becomes a "small spot" in the region of the heart or the chest. This corresponds to a strong emphasis on a physical locus where the heart in the sense of the center of the person is located. The other is the use of the eight attributes of Ātman in *Dahara Vidyā* VIII.1.5 in meditation, *upāsanā*, in accordance with the general philosophy of *upāsanā* of the *Brahma Sūtra*. However, as noted before, the *Dahara Vidyā* itself does not mention *upāsanā*. Like several other great *vidyās* in the old Upaniṣads, it does not really indicate any particular meditative path. There is an implication that the path taught involves work in and inner transformation in the heart, i.e. in one's self, more or less thought of as localized in one's physical heart or chest. But beyond that, little else can be concluded.[84]

Now it turns out that there is in Vedānta another approach to the *vidyā* which does not have these characteristics and which may well be closer to the *vidyā's* original intent. According to this, the *dahara ākāśa* is something like the proverbial "firmament of the heart" or "sky of awareness," or perhaps a subtle aspect of this "sky of awareness". This would correspond to a meaning of *dahara* as "fine, subtle". In agreement with our analysis in sec. 3, this (subtle aspect of) "firmament" of the heart or "sky" of awareness called *dahara ākāśa* would in the course of spiritual evolution change to knowledge/awareness of the Infinite Brahman, and eventually to "being Brahman". The degree and manner of localization implicit in the conception of a person's heart as in sec. 4, however, would be left open. This whole general approach may be based on *Mahā-NārUp* XII.16,[85] which may be regarded as explicitly rephrasing the *Chāndogya* text using "subtle firmament [of the heart]," *dahra gagana*, in place of *dahara ākāśa*. It also fits well with certain other Upaniṣadic texts, and it is significant that all these texts mention meditation using Om. As already mentioned, however, the "firmament" or "sky" approach overlaps with the traditional approach described in secs. 5-7. In the course of spiritual life, the *dahara ākāśa* of traditional *Dahara upāsanā* very likely becomes similar to the *dahara ākāśa* as a subtle state of the heart (or a subtle aspect of the aspirant's awareness), both in meditation and in daily life.

***Mahā-NārUp* XII.16 (= Varenne 231-232).** *Mahā-Nārāyaṇa Upaniṣad* is actually the tenth and last chapter of *Taittirīya Āraṇyaka* (coming in that text immediately after *Taittirīya Upaniṣad*).[86] But judging from the language, most of it consists of additions made many centuries after Āraṇyaka times. Apart from a few great hymns and some powerful single verses, the work consists largely of passages used in various rituals.[87] The critical stanzas are:

227. Not by action, not by (their) offspring [and] wealth,
only by renunciation (*tyāga*) have [individuals]
obtained immortality.
228. Beyond heaven, placed in the cave [of the heart],[a]
shining [resplendent], that [is what] the hermits penetrate.
229. Ascetics with the goal of the Vedānta *vijñāna* ascertained,
purified by the yoga of renunciation (*saṁnyāsa*),
230. —into the world of Brahman are they at the moment of death[b]
all released, being [already] beyond death.
231. Small (*dahra*), sinless, become the abode of the Supeme,
what lotus [is] established in the midst of the citadel [of the body].
232. There (or in that) is also the subtle (*dahra*) firmament
(*gagana*), free from sorrow.
What is interior to that,—that should be worshipped
(*upās-*)!
233. [That] which [is] the sound (*svara*) that is uttered
at the beginning of Veda [recitation]
and is established in the Vedānta (i.e., the sound Om)—
234. He who is beyond the dissolution into Prakṛti of that [sound]—
He is the Supreme Lord (*maheśvara*).[88]

There is little question that 231-232 is familiar with and essentially means to restate *Dahara Vidyā* 1.1, not only because of the large number of common terms,[89] but also because the verses deliberately echo the structure of *Dahara Vidyā* 1.1. There are some important differences, however. In 231-232 the lotus of the heart for example is called sinless, *vi-pāpam*. In the *Dahara Vidyā,* this kind of characterization is only applied to the space in the heart (it is *apahata-pāpman*, with sin destroyed). Since the lotus is sinless and established in the midst of the body, it must be the heart in the figurative sense described in sec. 4. *Mahā-Nārāyaṇa Upanisad* is therefore saying that one's heart has a natural sinless aspect and that this sinless aspect must be blooming in order to clearly perceive the *dahara ākāśa* that is free from sorrow. When that iotus blooms, then there (or therein) is also, *tatra api*, the *dahram gaganam*, the subtle sky. *Ākāśa*, space, has been replaced by *gagana*, "sky, firmament".[90] Hence *dahram gaganam* may very well mean "(subtle) sky, firmament".[91] (Indeed although the heart lotus in 231 itself is figurative, *dahra* in 231 may well be "small" as a word play against "subtle" in 232.) In *Dahara Vidyā* 1.1, the *dahara ākāśa* was said to be almost spatially "within," *antar*, the lotus abode. In *Mahā-Nārāyaṇa Upaniṣad* the spatial element and the element of subordination are weaker: The subtle firmament is *tatra api*, "in that also" (in the lotus or figurative heart, or, less likely, in the citadel of the body, v. 231), or simply "there also" (where the heart is). In addition, the subtle firmament is free from sorrow, *vi-śoka*. In *Dahara Vidyā* 1.5, this attribute was used to describe the Ātman, beyond the *dahara ākāśa*. Finally, "within that (*tasmin*, supply "firmament"), [that] which is interior (*antaḥ*), that is worthy of being worshipped (*upās-*)." This again echoes *Dahara Vidyā* 1.1. So overall the text restates *Dahara Vidyā*. 1.1, but there is also some reformulation: the text describes an inner perception, the "sorrowless subtle [inner] sky," and hints at a supreme mystery very much interior to that.

The Sorrowless Sky or Firmament and Meditation using Om. In Varenne 234 Swami Vimalānanda, following the classical commentaries, interprets the dissolution of Om into Prakṛti (the primordial Unmanifest or Causal Principle) as the final stage of meditation using Om, and the Great Lord in the last line as that what is said to be within the subtle firmament of the heart in v. 232. According to this reading, vs. 231-232 and 233-234 form a larger unit, to the effect that the *upās-* mentioned in 232 includes meditation using Om, that the dissolution into Prakṛti in 234 refers to a near final phase in that meditation, and that the Supreme would be what emerges beyond that phase. At any rate, when there is a level of awareness of *dahara ākāśa* = *dahram gaganam*, further progress would be by means of meditation involving Om.

It is possible, however, although less likely, that the dissolution of Om into Prakṛti in 233-234 does not refer to meditation. The stanzas may simply be a transition to the great hymn of Nārāyaṇa that follows immediately thereafter (235 ff.) and which gives the Upaniṣad its name. This interpretation is in line with S.S. Shastri [sec. 5, (4)] who classifies 233-234 as praise, *stuti*, of the Supreme that is within the *dahara ākāśa*.

The New Language of the Firmament of the Heart. In any case, however, we can regard *Mahā-NārUp* XII.16 (=231-232 Varenne) as a deliberate reformulation of *Dahara Vidyā* 1.1-5 in a new language which is rather clearly suggestive of a different direction of experience and inner practice than centering oneself in a small spot in the region of one's heart or chest. The "lotus" is now squarely the heart in the sense of the center of one's being, one's soul and the higher forces of one's soul (cf. sec. 4). The *dahra gagana*, the subtle sky or firmament, which is an obvious replacement for the *dahara ākāśa*, the small space in *Dahara Vidyā* 1.1, is now part of this heart (or an aspect of this heart). The main characteristic of this subtle sky of the heart is that it is *vi-śoka*, free from sorrow (Varenne 232). In *Dahara Vidyā* 1.5 *viśoka* was an attribute of the Ātman, i.e. it described an aspect that was experienced when knowledge of Ātman or Ātma-consciousness was firmly established. Here it functions at a somewhat lower level, as a characteristic by which the student might recognize the subtle sky, *dahra gagana*, in his or her own experience. (The latter may be experienced in meditation, or a subtle awareness in the waking state, see below). The Ātman is, as in *Dahara Vidyā* 1.1, within (*antaḥ*) that subtle sky (Varenne 232). That should be meditated on (*upās-*). Note that we don't have here "meditate 'X is Brahman,'" as in the *upāsanās* in chr. 4, only "meditate on X". Details regarding the meditation are sparse, however. Even assuming that the meditation involves Om, it is not clear what this might involve at this point in the Upaniṣads' historical development. Of the major texts dealing with meditation using Om, the one closest in time to Varenne 231-234 is perhaps *PraśnaUp* V. We will see in the next section that the meditation in *PraśnaUp* V. appears to be indeed in the heart, and that it may thus be similar to the meditation implied in the *Mahā-Nārāyaṇa Upaniṣad* text here.

The new language in *Mahā-NārUp* XII.16 has an important feature: it applies as much to experience in meditation as *outside* it, in daily life. Textually this is suggested by the fact that in v. 231, the topic is the figurative heart (the "lotus established in the midst of the citadel [of the body]"), which is sinless and can be experienced throughout the day. For vs. 231-232 should continue at the general level of discourse of vs. 227-230, dealing with how one should live (namely in *tyāga* and *saṁnyāsa*, 227 and 229), and with references to highest level experience inserted now and then for inspiration. In other words the subtle firmament is "there also," along with the sinless heart and only slightly different from it, and thus it is a general fact of living during the day, just like the sinless heart. The reference to the Supreme Lord being beyond the dissolution of Om is then again mysterious and inspiring, just like 228 and 232b. If the *vidyā* involved mental repetition of Om and thinking about its meaning, such inner practice could be carried easily into many of the activities during the day. In such inner life, when there is at the same time sustained effort in the form of service of truth, sacrifice, concern for the welfare of beings, and meditation, one can expect awareness of the subtle sky or firmament in the heart to arise naturally on and off during the day. For "atmosphere, sky, firmament" is the natural character of one's self or heart when attachments and evils (like greed, anger, low opinions of others or of things) become attenuated. (For that reason the lotus of the heart is called "divorced from evil," *vi-pāpam*—in this kind of state, there is innocence and some beginning of being "apart from the evil.") Then, when there are not too many other thoughts, when there is a state of lightness and subtle being, or being at one with one's heart and at the same time of being like the sky, perhaps with a faint perception of subtle air or subtle space, then this may be beginning experience in the direction of *dahara ākāśa*. For then one's awareness is not only "subtle," or "awareness of something subtle," but that subtle is also experienced as *viśoka*, free from sorrow.

Sai Baba's "Firmament of the Heart". Sri Sathya Sai Baba in his discourses often talks about the sky of the heart or the (subtle) sky of awareness, and in his commentary on *Chāndogya Upaniṣad* he ties these directly to the *dahara ākāśa* of the *Chāndogya* text. For although he is undoubtedly discussing *Dahara Vidyā* 1.1-1.5, he uses "sky of the heart" instead of *dahara ākāśa* or "space within the heart".

> [A] The path of *Brahma-upāsanā* is called the *Suṣumnā Mārga* also. The Omnipresent Brahmam [= "Brahman-substance," see below] can be enclosed and discovered in the firmament of the heart! It is the capital of that *rājā* [king]. Since He is seated there, the heart is called *Brahma-veśma*, or the House of Brahmam. That firmament cannot, of course,

limit or set boundaries to the illimitable Brahmam!

Yogis who are turned away from the objective world can attain the Para-Brahmam [= Supreme Brahman], with Its splendour of Realised Knowledge, in the pure clear sky of their hearts. The worlds are fixed as the spokes of the wheel in the hub of Brahmam. Decline, decay and death do no affect it. Since that Supreme Entity can achieve whatever it decides on, It is called *satyakāma* and *satyasaṁkalpa*. Now, what exactly is the Para-Brahmam? We can know it by a single test. That which remains, after everything is negated as 'Not this,' 'Not that'—that is Brahmam.

This is the Truth that all aspirants seek. Attaining it, they get the status of emperors and can travel wherever they like. The *jñānī* who is established in the pure Reality sees all desires that dawn in his heart as expressions of that Truth only.

The Ātmā transcends all the worlds. It is uncontaminated. He who is aware of only the Ātmā is ever in Bliss. The *brahmacarya* stage is an important step for attaining Ātmic Wisdom. . .[92]

The "omnipresent Brahmam" (apparently a neuter adjectival form often used by Sri Sathya Sai Baba, presumably for its "experiential" overtones, so "the Brahman-like, the Brahman-substance") "can be enclosed and discovered" in the firmament of the heart. That is, one way to attain Brahman is to discover it in the firmament of the heart. This restates *Dahara Vidyā* 1.1 ("can be discovered in" echoes "should be searched out;" "enclosed" is used to create an effect against "omnipresent"). But "firmament of the heart" is used instead of *dahara ākāśa*, and this is reminiscent of *gagana*, "sky, firmament," in Varenne 232. There *gagana* is very distinctive because it may be the earliest occurrence of this term in the Vedic literature. "That firmament cannot . . . limit or set boundaries to the illimitable Brahman," i.e., Brahman is beyond the way it can be experienced in the firmament of the heart. The next sentence, "yogis can attain the Para-Brahmam in the pure clear sky of their hearts," echoes "what is interior to that [subtle firmament], that should be worshipped (known, *upās-*)" in both the *Dahara Vidyā* and *Mahā-Nārāyaṇa Upaniṣad*. But evidently, Sai

Baba is still expounding the *Dahara Vidyā*, because the continues with *satya-kāma* and *satya-saṁkalpa* (*Dahara Vidyā* 1.5 ff.). Similarly, "decline, decay and death do not affect It" echoes "free from old age, without death" (*ibid.*, 1.5), and the *Brahmacarya* stage is emphasized as an aid to attaining Ātman similar to *Dahara Vidyā* 5. So in this passage, Sai Baba is taking Varenne 231-232 as equivalent to a part of *Dahara Vidyā* 1.1 ff. and uses sky or firmament (of the heart), *gagana*, for space (of the heart), *ākāśa*. This is further borne out by his comments on the *dahara ākāśa* in sec. 10 below.

9. *PraśnaUp* V and *Mahā-NārUp* XII.16-17

We saw that the understanding of the *dahara ākāśa* as the subtle sky of consciousness or the firmament of the heart represented by *Mahā-NārUp* XII.16 = Varenne 231-232 is likely to have been associated with meditation using Om, and at any rate this is the way the Upaniṣadic text has been interpreted traditionally. But how would such a meditation using Om proceed? Of the texts dealing with meditation using Om the one closest to *Mahā-NārUp* XII.16-17, and thus the one most likely to be able to shed light on the meditation probably being referred to in *Mahā-NārUp* XII.17 = Varenne 233-234, is *PraśnaUp* V.2-7. There are some weak textual suggestions that the meditation in *PraśnaUp* V.5-7 represents indeed a deeper penetration into the (figurative) heart. *PraśnaUp* V and Varenne 231-234 may be also related in that *PraśnaUp* V.7 describes the Highest as Śāntam, "the Tranquil, Peaceful," while Varenne 234 describes the Supreme Lord as beyond the resolution of Om into the Primordial, which should be also Supremely Peaceful.

Prâsna Upaniṣad[93] is one of the late Vedic Upaniṣads (cf. Table 2.1). It is made up of six chapters, each of which consists of a set of questions (*praśnas*) put to the Sage Pippalāda by his disciples, together with Pippalāda's response. The text has the kind of unity that one feels in a text that gives different teachings by the same teacher.[94] In the fifth chapter, the so-called *Parama Puruṣa Vidyā* (see Table 4.1),[95] the question is what world a person wins who meditates on Om all life long. In reply, Pippalāda distinguishes several ways of meditating on Om of which the best one involves decomposing Om into three sounds or letters A, U, M, and contemplating their meaning. This leads to the realm of Brahman and the vision of the Puruṣa

(*PraśnaUp* V.5).

Decomposition of Om into A, U, M. Here we need some background. In Sanskrit, if in a sentence or phrase a word ending in *a* is followed by one that begins with *u*, the two words are pronounced as a single word with the *a-u* replaced by *o*. In this sense therefore, *a* + *u* = *o*. As a result, the sacred syllable Om may be analysed into A + U + M. Om occurs already in the *Yajur Vedic Saṁhitās*. But the decomposition of Om into A, U, M is first found in *AitBr* V.32,[96] a famous creation account the elements of which resonate in many later developments involving Om. The text says that Prajāpati first created the worlds, earth, midspace, and sky; from these he created the lights, Agni, Vāyu (Wind), and Āditya (Sun), resp.; from these, the three Vedas, *Ṛg*, *Yajur*, and *Sāma Veda*, resp.; from these three pure essences, viz. the mystical utterances *bhūr*, *bhuvaḥ*, and *svāḥ*, resp.; and from these, the three sounds or *varṇas*, viz. A, U, M. "That [last step] made 'Om.' Om is the heavenly world (*svarga*). Om is He that glows [= the Sun]." Thus Om appears here as the ultimate essence of the created world, and A, U, M have cosmic meanings, viz. the three worlds. At the same time Om is also the essence of the Vedas, which are the Logos, so to speak, and A, U, M are associated with the three different Vedas and the mystic utterances. The level of sound is explicitly given higher, metaphysical status; A, U, M are sounds, *varṇas*. And finally Om is identified with the Highest Reality, here symbolized by the Sun. *PraśnaUp* V echoes this account and makes use of most of these elements. But in addition, it brings in parts of the scheme of *Māṇḍūkya Upaniṣad*, where A, U, M represent the waking, dream, and deep sleep states (quarters) of the Self.

PraśnaUp V: Text

V. 2. That verily, O Satyakāma, which is the AUM-sound, is both the Higher and the Lower Brahman. Therefore, with this as [his] abode [in meditating, *abhidhyai-*], one who knows reaches one or the other.

3. If he meditates on a one-element [Om][a], he, made knowledgeable indeed by that, returns quickly to the world (for another human life). The *Ṛg*-mantras lead him to the world of man. There, endowed with self control, inner chastity (*brahmacarya*) and faith, he experiences glory.

4. If he is united in mind[b] with a two-letter [Om],[c] he is led by the *Yajur*-mantras to the intermediate space, the world

of Soma (the Moon) (or: with a two-letter [Om], he attains to Mind. He is led . . .). He, having experienced power (*vibhūti*) in the Soma-world, returns from there again to here.

5. Again, [he] who meditates (*abhi-dhyāyati*) "Om" in a three-element fashion,[d] indeed [who meditates] with this syllable on the Supreme Puruṣa (*param puruṣam*), he becomes one with the light [in] the Sun (*Sūrya*). As a snake is freed from its slough, in exactly the same way, verily, is he freed from sin. He is led by the Sāman-chants to the world of Brahman. From this mass of life,[e] he sees the Puruṣa that is Higher than the Highest (*parāt-param*) and dwells in the body. On this there are these two verses:

6[f]. The three elements are deathless when they are performed
joined one to another and not separate.
In external, internal, and intermediate, together-performed
actions, the knower does not waver.

7. With the *Ṛg*-mantras he [attains] this [world], with the
Yajur-mantras, the intermediate space, with the Sāmans
[he attains] that which the Poet-seers (*kavi*) cause [one]
to know.
With the Om-sound (*oṁkāra*) as his abode (*āyatana*), the
knower goes[g] to that which is peaceful, ageless, deathless, and Supreme.[97]

A and U. As may be seen, the individual elements A and U are associated with the states of waking and dream in an indirect manner. A is summarily stated to only lead to another life on earth—a life of glory, greatness, *mahimā*, in other words, a fulfilled waking life. Unlike meditation with U, there are no other fruits, he "quickly" returns to earth. With A and U, however, one attains the world of Soma, the world of the Moon, of the mental untouched by the physical. This corresponds to *Māṇḍūkya Upaniṣad's* dream state. There one experiences "power," but still one has to return. Pippalāda's language is revealing. Through meditation on only a one-element Om, a person will be "made wholly knowledgeable" (*saṁveditas*). If, however, he is "united in mind" whith the two-element [Om], or in the two-element manner (*dvi-mātreṇa,* instrumental), not just in meditation, but in his living and his being, in other words if he has reached that stage of transformedness of self, then he is led to the world of Soma etc. An alternative reading says that "by the two-element [Om] he succeeds (*sampadyate*) in mind," he attains it. Then, when he dies, he is led to the world of Soma.

The "Three-Element Way" of Meditating Using Om: Śaṁkara. Regarding the correct, "three-element way" of meditating "Om" in v. 5, we get some valuable hints in the *ślokas* 6 and 7. The translation follows Horsch.[98] Presumably v. 6, first half, says that in meditation, the sounds A, U, M are to be said mentally in sequence, slowly, while at the same time keeping in mind their meaning. In the second half, the intent of "in actions," *kriyāsu*, and the sense in which these actions are *samyak prayukta*, "properly performed" or "performed together," are moot. Śaṁkara explains these terms as referring to "yogic actions, associated with the waking, dream and deep sleep state person".[99] These yogic actions, he says, "are properly resorted to" in the meditation.

If Śaṁkara's comments represent what is intended in the text, the meditation discussed in vs. 6-7 would come in the general sphere of inner disciplines involved in the dream- and deep-sleep stages in the *Antarjyotir Vidyā* and the Bālāki instruction discussed in the last chapter. A textual clue that this may be the case are the terms the Peaceful, *śāntam*, the Ageless, *ajaram*, Deathless, *amṛtam*, and Fearless, *abhayam*, in v. 7. The last three terms occur in this order also in *BṛhUp* IV.4.25 (K): "This is that great unborn Self, unaging (*ajara*), undying (*amara*), immortal (*amṛta*), fearless (*abhaya*) . . ." In this sequence, the subsequence of *amṛta, abhaya* is distinctive. Apart from *BṛhUp* IV.4.25 (K), it occurs only in *Chāndogya Upaniṣad*.[101] In *ChāndUp* I.4.4 and I.4.5 it describes Om. In the other six occurrences it is always part of the same stock phrase, "this is the Self. This is the Immortal, the Fearless, this is Brahman." Five of these six are found *ChāndUp* VIII, the full *Dahara Vidyā* and its adjunct, the *Indra Virocana Vidyā*, and three of these are set in the context of the waking, dream and sleep states. In order to teach Indra and Virocana the Self, Prajāpati successively describes first one's reflection in a pan of water, then "[him] who moves about happy in dream," and lastly "where that man is asleep, composed, serene (*samprasanna*)," all as "that is the Self. That is the Immortal, Fearless, that is Brahman." In view of this distribution of *amṛtam, abhayam, PraśnaUp* V.7 may very well be continuing the tradition of *ChāndUp* I and VIII, and the meditation on Om in *PraśnaUp* V.5 and 6-7 is likely to be in the heart (five of the six non-Om occurrences of *abhayam, amṛtam* are in *ChāndUp* VIII). In addition the use of *amṛtam, abhayam* in the *Indra Virocana Vidyā* suggests that consistent with Śaṁkara, this meditation is not a new technique, but a heart path with stages similar to the dream and sleep stages in the *Antarjyotir* and Ajātaśatru *Vidyās* (cf. chrs. 5.13-14, 15 and 20). Thus in the case of the "dream-state person," Śaṁkara's "yogic actions"[100] could refer to the thoughts and disciplines by which one penetrates more deeply into the heart to the levels of *dahara ākāśa* or the dream stage (the first level in the *Antar-jyotir* and Ajātaśatru *Vidyās*). In the deep sleep phase (the second level in these *vidyās*), they could refer to disciplines involving the "subtle *prāṇas* in the heart," see sec. 17 below. So Pippalāda's meditation may have involved saying A, U, M mentally and in sequence in the heart, keeping in mind their meaning as waking world or waking state, mind (or dream), and deeper than mind (or deep sleep) resp., regarding them as the expressions of the Puruṣa = Brahman (cf. v. 5), and integrating these thoughts with the inner disciplines mentioned. But this is only one possible approach to the text.

But it is conceivable that the "external, internal, and intermediate, together-performed actions" in v. 6 refer to living Om throughout the day (repeating Om while doing one's normal work), and not to the inner disciplines involved in the dream- and deep-sleep stages in the *Antarjyotir Vidyā* and the Bālāki instruction. It seems quite possible for a teacher at the time of *Praśna Upaniṣad* to be familiar with a yogic-type path through the heart a la Śaṁkara but at the same time enjoin a broader approach of this kind which does not involve "(inner) yogic actions". In this connection it is significant that Sai Baba in a recent discourse, while accepting Śaṁkara's reading of Brahma-loka in *PraśnaUp* V.5 as Hiraṇyagarbha, nevertheless discusses the teaching in that verse solely in terms of the heart, similar to the Heart *Vidyā* and the related *Mahā-NārUp* XII.16.

10. The *Dahara Ākāśa* in *Maitrāyaṇīya Upaniṣad*

The line of understanding of *Dahara Vidyā* 1.1 ff. which takes the *dahara ākāśa* as a (subtle) sky of awareness or as the firmament of the heart is further developed in some texts in *Maitrāyaṇīya Upaniṣad.* The most important of these is *MaitrUp* VI.28,[102] because it explicitly treats the space within the heart as an arena of inner experience in its own right. It talks of crossing this space to the other shore with the boat of Om and then dispersing the first four sheaths. *MaitrUp* VI.28 has a parallel in *MaitrUp* VI.27, which is unfortunately obscure.

Maitrāyaṇīya Upaniṣad,[103] which was described as an aggregate text in sec. 2.1, has a complex history of composition. The passages around *MaitrUp* VI.28 in particular, although clearly related to one another, are semi-independent statements that cannot be assumed to fit completely together and form a single whole. Their position in *Maitrāyaṇīya Upaniṣad* as a whole is also unclear. In a detailed analysis of the common or vulgate version of the Upaniṣad (the version translated by Hume and Radhakrishnan), van Buitenen notes that there is a Southern recension of the Upaniṣad which is only about half the size of the vulgate text, omitting most of chrs. VI and VIII.[104] He argues that this "*Southern Maitrāyaṇīya*" *Upaniṣad (SM)* was not derived from the vulgate version and that in fact the vulgate was produced sometime early in the CE by combining the *SM* with an old (pre-*Taittirīya Upaniṣad*) Upaniṣad of the Maitrāyaṇīyas and then making further additions. According to his detailed further analysis, *MaitrUp* VI.27 and 28 would belong to the very latest layer of additions, and therefore date from the early centuries CE.[105] Some of van Buitenen's scheme has been questioned, however.[106]

***MaitrUp* VI.27-28**

VI.27. Now elsewhere it has also been said: "This verily is the glow (*tejas*) of brahman, of the supreme, immortal, bodiless, [namely that] which is the heat (*uṣṇya*) of the body. For that [Brahman], this [body heat] is the ghee (melted butter offered in the Vedic sacrifice). Now [while] being manifest [as heat], that [Brahman] verily is set in the sky (*nabhas*) [of the heart]. Thus with one pointed [mind] they disperse the space within the heart (*antarhṛdaya ākāśa*), which [mind or ether] appears (becomes) as the light (*jyoti*), as it were, of that (Brahman). Then one goes quickly to that condition (*bhāva*) (i.e. one quickly becomes that light of Brahman). Just as a lump of iron that is put in the earth quickly goes to [the condition of] earth-ness, [and] just as fire or a blacksmith cannot prevail over a lump of iron that has taken on a configuration like earth, just so the mind-substance (*citta*) perishes together with its substratum.[a]"

For thus one says:

The vessel (sheath, *kośa*) consisting of the space in the

heart (*hṛdyākāśa-maya*), bliss, the supreme dwelling (store, *ālaya*) [of all things]
itself—[that we pursue].[b] From that [arises] both our yoga and the glow (*tejas*) of Agni and Sun.

VI.28. Now elsewhere it has also been said: "Having transcended the elements, senses, and objects, then having grasped the bow whose cord is renunciation (*pravrajyā*, relinquishment) and whose wooden part is steadfastness,and having, with the arrow consisting of lack-of-self-conceit, struck down the first Brahman door boundary,—[him who has] confusion as crown, ambition and envy as earrings, [who is] carrying sloth as his stick, and sins, and, guided by self conceit, having grasped the bow whose cord is anger and whose wood is greed, kills these beings with the arrow that consists of self-will (*icchā*) —having slain him, having with the boat of Om crossed to the other shore of the ether within the heart (*antarhṛdaya ākāśa*), one should, in the inner space (*antarākāśe*) that becomes apparent, gradually enter the hall of Brahman as a miner in search of minerals enters a mine. Then one should disperse the fourfold net (snare?), the vessel (*kośa*) [enclosing] Brahman (= the first four sheaths), through the teaching[c] of [his] guru." Then the pure, purified, empty, tranquil, *prāṇa*-less, selfless, infinite, imperishable, stable, permanent, unborn, independent one [or the pure etc. entity—all adjectives are masculine] stands in his own greatness. Then, having seen [the one] abiding in his own greatness, one looks down on the wheel of transmigration like on a rolling wheel (of a chariot).

For thus one says:

Of the embodied [being] who, [though] eternally released, is bound in yoga six months,
there proceeds the infinite, supreme, mysterious complete yoga.
[But] of the embodied [being] who is penetrated by *rajas* and *tamas* (passion, activity, and delusion or darkness), highly inflamed,
bound to son, wife and household—no, never at all.[107]

In VI.28, "having crossed over ("forded," *tīrtvā*) to the other shore of the space within the heart, one should, in the inner space (*antarākāśe*) that becomes apparent, enter the hall of Brhaman . . ." suggests that the space in the heart represents a stage before perception of Brahman (before entering the hall of Brahman etc.). Further, at that stage, perception or awareness of the space within the heart is likely to be simply one's general way of being (in meditation and normally during the day). From the phrasing it is not completely clear whether the "inner space that becomes apparent" does so during or after the crossing over of the space within the heart—the usual sense of *tīrtvā*, "having crossed over," would imply the latter, but the former seems also possible. Still, the text gives a remarkable amount of detail. "Crossing the space of the heart" means proceeding in spiritual life generally at intermediate *vijñāna-maya* levels. The inner space that then "becomes apparent" (or "present"—*āvirbhūta*) as well as the dispersing of the first four sheaths (including the *vijñāna-maya*) must likewise (according to my understanding) refer to one's general state and not merely to meditation. (There is no problem with having an "inner space" present during the day.) At the same time the aspirant or devotee should enter the "hall of Brahman" like a miner desirous of minerals enters a mine, i.e., focussed on perception of Brahman. Finally after seeing the highest there is complete transcendence of desire ("one looks down on the wheel of transmigration . . .").

MaitrUp VI.27 is rather impenetrable to me. Like *MaitrUp* VI.28 it deals with how the stage of space within the heart (*antarhṛdaya ākāśa*) is gradually replaced by a higher state. (In the final verse the *hṛdyākāśa-maya kośa* or sheath consisting of the ether in the heart is presumably equivalent to the *vijñāna-maya* sheath). While *MaitrUp* V.28 speaks of an inner space which appears and is the hall of Brahman, *MaitUp* VI.27 says that the aspirant or devotee's state becomes like light. The rest is unclear. Perhaps *uṣṇya*, "heat-like," refers to a yoga of heat. The stanza and its connection with the preceding prose is also unclear.

The crossing over to the other shore in *MaitrUp* VI.28 and several other textual parallels suggest that the text is closely related to (and probably deliberately harks back to) *MuṇḍUp* II.2. This text will be disucssed in sec. 21 below.

11. *Dahara Ākāśa* as one of a Series of Five *Ākāśas* in Vedānta

In sections 8 and 10 we looked at Upaniṣadic texts in which the *dahara ākāśa* of *Dahara Vidyā* 1.1-1.5 seems to be something like an awareness or subtle consciousness (hence "the sky of the inner consciousness" in which normal thoughts occur, or "the firmament of the heart"). Now this kind of approach is also found in later Vedānta. One example is a teaching involving a series of five *ākāśas*, corresponding to different levels of spiritual development, in which *dahara ākāśa* is the third and *cit-ākāśa* (or *cidākāśa*) the fourth level. This series has been discussed by Sri Sathya Sai Baba.[108] The series of five *ākāśas* is related to an earlier series of three *ākāśa* in the *Yoga Vāsiṣṭha*, viz. *bhūta-ākāśa*, the physical space; *citta-ākāśas*, the space of mind; and *cit-ākāśa*, the space of *cit*, "pure consciousness".[109] Swami Ananyananda has given an exposition of *dahara ākāśa* based on this latter series, which will be discussed in the next section.

The Series of Five *Ākāśas* in Vedānta. As discussed by Sai Baba the series of five spaces includes:

1. *ghaṭa-ākāśa*, the "pot-space" or "space inside the pot, *ghaṭa*";
2. *jala-ākāśa*, "the sky reflected in water, *jala*";
3. *dahara ākāśa*, "the sky that is reflected in the heart" (= *hṛdaya-ākāśa* of the *Dahara Vidyā*);
4. *cit-ākāśa*, the sky of Pure Consciousness, *cit;*
5. *mahat-ākāśa*, "the Great Sky".[110]

Sri Sathya Sai Baba talks about these in the context of overcoming *jaḍatva*, "inertness". Inertness is what is opposite of self, (pure) consciousness, or in other words, inertness is what characterizes not-self. The five kinds of *ākāśa* are "phases or aspects of this inertness [*jaḍatva*]". "When we look at these five kinds of *ākāśa*, they are all inert or *jaḍa*."[111] *Ghaṭa-ākāśa* "is the state which says 'this [body] is I'."[112] Next,

> [A] Coming to '*jala-ākāśa*,' it is that state which is full of '*saṁkalpa*' or intention and may be described as the sky reflected in water. If in a little pond of water, the blue sky is reflected and the sky may also have the shining moon, we have the illusion that the sky and the moon reflected in the water seem to be mobile or moving. The sky and the moon do not move, but only the water moves when the breeze blows over it. The '*saṁkalpas*' and the '*vikalpas*' [intentions and imaginations] in us are the water.[113]

In this state, one makes some distinction between one's body and self, like "there is a pain in my stomach," but "the self remains chained to the subtle body,"[114] such as in the automatic reaction "I am hurting (in my stomach)."

[B] '*Dahara ākāśa*' is the state when one looks at '*saṁkalpas*' and '*vikalpas*,' but one is aware that he is looking at them. Let us take an example. We pour water into a tub and we look at it. We see our own face reflected in it and we say that it is a reflection. Even though that image reflected in the water is beaten, not even a single stroke is felt by the object, namely, the body. If the object and the image were one, any injury done to the image must be felt by the object also. Though your face is reflected in water, the goodness or the badness of the image does not affect you, the object. You may then ask, "Is it not my reflection?" Yes, it is yours. When the image is hurt and that injury is not registered by you, it is "not you". But when you are abused, you and the image become one. When the image is hurt physically by anybody, that injury is not felt by the object, but when the image is insulted and abused by anybody, then the object, whose reflection is found in the water, also feels the insult. You feel angry because you are there in the image also. In *śabda* or sound, there is unity, but in action or *kriyā* there is no unity. And the nature of *Śabda-brahma-tattva* is hidden there. In *jala-ākāśa*, we also find the nature of *Dahara ākāśa*.

Coming to *cit-ākāśa*, this refers to man remaining a mere spectator. *Cit-ākāśa* is the state when a man, without being upset, without being in anyway influenced by emotion, just observes and remains like an observer or a spectator. Whatever may happen to the body—it may be insulted and injured—the person is not affected by it; he is always engrossed in the higher consciousness and that is the state of *Cit-ākāśa*. The pot may be broken, the pond may run dry, the canvas may be torn to shreds, but that "*ākāśa*" stands there. The sky reflected in the pot, the sky painted on the canvas, only refer to the media, but not to the great sky itself. Though this is reflected in our body, mind and senses, this *tattva* is something which transcends all of them.

Only when the senses are brought under control and there is the state of *Nirvikalpa*, we reach the highest state of realization. It is possible for us to realize the nature of the *Mahat-ākāśa* or the great sky in the state known as *Nirvikalpa*. *Nirvikalpa* means arresting the activity of all the senses and assuming supreme control over them. Then the consciousness is not lost in the body or in any part of the body, but it is entirely devoted to that higher or transcendental state. The *Mahat-ākāśa* is called *ākāśa* because it has [still] an element of *jaḍa* or inertness in it.

We sometimes call a conglomeration of clouds by the name of sky. The sky has no separate entity or existence. It is not a shape which is concrete and made up of the five elements . . . The sky is known by several names such as '*ākāśa*', '*gagana*', '*śūnya*' or nothingness and so on. There is nothing there in the sky. When we sometimes refer to our heart and say, this is '*hṛdaya-ākāśa*', it is because there is no shape for the '*hṛdaya*' or heart in a spiritual sense. The '*ākāśa*' has to be cleared of all baser intentions and instincts, all '*saṁkalpas*' and '*vikalpas*'.[115]

Jala-ākāśa represents a stage where one has perhaps some indication and glimpses of the Divine (here, the moon) or the Infinite (the sky). But these are momentary and tend to be swamped, distorted, and submerged by the many intentions and imaginations one has at that stage with respect to worldly and also spiritual things. *Dahara ākāśa* represents a further stage where there is true realization that the state of one's body has nothing to do with one's self. At that stage there is a basic peacefulness to the effect that if the body is harmed, the self that one is will not be affected. This peacefulness or knowledge is comparable in strength and certainty to the knowledge that if one's reflection in the water is beaten or harmed, then one's body is not in the least affected. Being a permanent condition that the aspirant or devotee is in, it is experientially an *ākāśa*, a space or ether in the sense of a feeling of being, a subtle state or aspect on which all the thoughts that one has during the day are superimposed. As such, it can become a state of subtle engrossment. At the stage of *cit-ākāśa*, that basic awareness (that peacefulness, or way of being, the subtle engrossment) has become an "engrossment in the higher consciousness". *Cit-ākāśa* is a reality, a "thus-ness," *tattva*, which one is aware of, which one may ultimately feel oneself to be part of or to be, and which is unaffected even when body and mind fall apart. "The pot [of the body] may be broken, the pond [of mind, life] may run dry, but that '*ākāśa*' stands there." *Mahat-ākāśa* presumably represents a still further state of realization of *nirguṇa* Brahman involving cosmic (large-scale) and universal levels of manifestation, but at the same time also strong presence in the world.

The last paragraph of [B] addresses the question of why in all the five cases one speaks of an *ākāśa* or space, or sky in the first place. We talk about a sky of awareness etc., but such a sky, while looking like a phenomenal structure in which various contents are placed, has, *qua* structure or entity, no reality of its own. By *gagana*, "sky, firmament," Sai Baba no doubt alludes again to the firmament of the heart in *Mahā-NārUp* X.16 (sec. 8 above), because this is the only occurrence of *gagana* in Vedic *śruti* literature. *Śūnya*, the Empty, refers to the Buddhist emptiness, expounded for example in the "Lesser Discourse on emptiness" in the *Majjhima-Nikāya*.[116] In all these cases the sky as a separately perceived/conceived entity has no independent existence. In this sense also all the five *ākāśas*, even *mahat-ākāśa*, have an element of inertness, of non-self-ness, in them. But the sky has a reality as a part of self and in fact in the course of inner development becomes Brahman/Ātman, the One Reality.

As described in [B], *dahara ākāśa* is a form of (beginning and lower level) *vijñāna* in the sense of chr. 5.6. *Cit-ākāśa* is a form of higher level *vijñāna* which develops out of *dahara ākāśa*. Sai Baba regularly equates *cit-ākāśa* or *cit-ākāśa* consciousness with Ātman, and Indian tradition does likewise.[117] In general, only very few aspirants or devotees pass from the stage of *dahara ākāśa* to that *cit-ākāśa*.[118] One reason for the difficulty is pointed out in [B]. At the stage of *dahara ākāśa* there is knowledge that when the physical person (the image in the water) is injured etc., the self (the person looking in the water) is unaffected. But if the physical person (image) is insulted or abused, the self itself feels the abuse and gets angry or depressed. Sai Baba sees in the fact that one is "unified with the abuse" in this way the workings of the reality of *Śabda*-Brahman, the "Sound Brahman" from which arises "the Word" (*Vāc*, the Logos) and the whole world. When there is an understanding of *cit- ākāśa,* then the aspect of *Śabda*-Brahman is recognized as what it is; this is a hint on possible future experience in the approach to the stage of *cit-ākāśa*. Elsewhere Sai Baba gives another important hint that *cit-ākāśa* "corresponds to subtle experiences" where the self is a "witnessing consciousness".

> [C] . . . When you reach the state of *Dahara ākāśa*, you start enquiring about the nature and origin of "I," distinguishing it from the body, and ultimately apprehending that this "I" arises from your innermost being. This kind of enquiry can be compared to an enquiry that one makes about worldly matters in the state of wakefulness. During wakeful awareness all your organs like the eyes, and the limbs of the body and even your mind are active. You travel with your body, you see with your eyes, and you experience with your mind. Therefore *Dahara ākāśa* corresponds to wakeful experiences.
>
> *Cit-ākāśa* corresponds to subtle experiences, wherein the Self remains the witnessing consciousness. In that state you are above and apart from your body and your life. It can be compared to a dream state. In a dream you may feel that someone has come and cut off your head. You yourself are seeing the head being separated from the body. In that situation, you are quite apart from the body. Your life has not gone although your head has been separated. You are only witnessing the subtle drama. The same can be illustrated thus: if you cause a hurt with a knife to another person, it can be looked upon as an offense. But if you dream of having cut off the head of a judge, and even after waking up you confess it to the judge, he is not empowered to take any action. Therefore in the realm of dreams, you only remain an onlooker.[119]

So in a certain sense, "*dahara ākāśa* corresponds to wakeful experiences," while "*cit-ākāśa* corresponds to subtle experience wherein the self remains the witnessing consciousness". Broadly speaking, *dahara ākāśa* is *vijñāna* or spiritual consciousness that arises when there is full inner effort in lived spiritual life. Such effort is similar to a full effort which one makes in ordinary waking life, and *dahara ākāśa* as experiential is indirectly colored by this. (Because of this, also, full inner effort in lived spiritual life gradually leads to the stage and experience of *dahara ākāśa*.) But note that *dahara ākāśa* cannot be really be reduced to "waking state experience". It "*corresponds* to waking state experience," [C] (italics added.) It is a spiritual condition, a type of *vijñāna*, that arises in the course of true effort of the self toward the spiritual. As such it includes an experiential higher element. Similarly *cit-ākāśa* is *vijñāna* that is similar to the witnessing consciousness that is experienced in dream and other *svapna* states as discussed in connection with *BṛhUp* IV.3.1-18, but at an infinitely more fundamental level. This is suggested in [C] by the simile of the judge.

Obviously the distinctions between *dahara-*, *cit-*, and *mahat-ākāśa* are not found in the *Dahara* text or in the *Antar-jyotir Vidyā*. It can be argued, however, that much of the knowledge, experience, or awareness behind this series of states is contained in these *vidyās* in less differentiated form. The series of five *ākāśas* is simply a way in which later tradition brings out the scope of the original *Dahara* teaching on the basis of its own knowledge. The very existence of the Vedāntic teaching supports our attempts here to interpret the *dahara ākāśa* in *Dahara Vidyā* 1.1-1.5 as something that is recognizable in spiritual experience before the full realization taught in 1.5, and in terms of which deeper inner spiritual evolution toward that realization can be discussed.

12. Alternative Exposition in Terms of the Three Kinds of *Ākāśa* of *Yoga Vāsiṣṭha*

The series of five *ākāśas* in the last section harks back in part to a scheme of three *ākāśas* used in the *Yoga Vāsiṣṭha*, a vast *jñāna* Scripture perhaps dating from the 10th century CE.[120] Swami Ananyananda has recently used this scheme to give an exposition of *dahara ākāśa* which complements the approach in the preceding sections and clearly shows the basic common trend of all the discussions so far.

The Three *Ākāśas* in the *Yoga Vāsiṣṭha*. The *Yoga Vāsiṣṭha* system of three *ākāśas* or spaces consists of *bhūta-ākāśa*, "physical element-space," *citta-ākāśa*, "the space of Mind (*citta*)," and *cit-ākāśa*, "the space of Pure Awareness (*cit*)". The system is introduced in the story of Līlā, wife of King Padma, where it is used to explain how it was possible for Līlā to experience both a past and a future incarnation (or life) of here beloved Padma after he suddenly dies. (In this as well as other stories of the *Yoga Vāsiṣṭha*, the basic ordering of events, or rather, of existences or lives, is by "arises from desire from a prior existence or life," or "arises from the nature of *cit-ākāśa*"; no linear temporal order is assumed into which all these events could be fitted.)[121] When the schema is first introduced, Sarasvatī, the goddess of wisdom, explains:

> Of the three kinds of *ākāśa*, namely *cit-ākāśa, citta-ākāśa* and *bhūta-ākāśa, citta-ākāśa* is that intermediate state in which the mind is when it flits from one object to another in the elemental *ākāśa* of objects (= physical space). When the hosts of *saṁkalpas* in us (ideas of what we want to or need to do) perish, then the light of *cit*, which is quiescent and immaculate and manifests itself as the universe, will shine in us. If one becomes convinced of the unreality of visible objects, then, through that *jñāna*, he will attain *cit-ākāśa* at once. Mayest thou attain through my grace that *cit-ākāśa.*[122]

This defines *citta-ākāśa*, "Mind-space," and suggests the exact sense in which it is a space, an *ākāśa*: It is the mental space or arena in which exist the images and thoughts ("representations") of all the things that are seen or perceived in the world. *Cit-ākāśa* on the other hand is represented as something to be attained with *jñāna*. Later in the story it is described as "stainless and immaculate," as being "immeasurable, transparent and subtle," and as containing in it all the major features of the universe as well as innumerable gods. "Becoming convinced of the unreality of visible objects" indicates a way to transcendence of desire and *jñāna*, because one is then not subject to desires and fears *vis-à-vis* them.

The text gives the impression that just as *citta-ākāśa* or the mental space is the mental medium or environment in which one sees physical objects and beings, so *cit-ākāśa* is the normal environment or space of the enlightened one, of one with *jñāna*-vision—it is the state of *jñāna* itself.[123] This interpretation is supported by the fact that in the story of Līlā, *cit-ākāśa* is several times rendered *jñāna-ākāśa*. The only unusual feature is that although being the space or state of a person with *jñāna*-vision, it overlaps directly (or interpenetrates, or forms a natural combination) with what we would call "physical reality". Various concrete situations (a person living at a certain place, a place, or a certain event) are said to be in the *cit-ākāśa* just like a person or object may be said to be seen in the mental space of one's mind and in ordinary physical space and time. At the same time, however, *cit-ākāśa* has some universal characteristics, because it is after all both consciousness and being, existence. The fact that *cit-ākāśa* contains all beings, places, events, as well as gods, present, past, and future, is reminiscent of *Dahara Vidyā* 1.3-1.4, to the effect that the space within the heart, when seen as it is (i.e. as the Self), contains heaven and earth, all beings and things. But while the *Dahara* text is strictly at a level of inner knowledge or vision, in the *Yoga Vāsiṣṭha* this is concretely fused with "physical reality". In addition to knowledge or vision of things, participation in the things seen, past as well as future, is also possible. The *Yoga Vāsiṣṭha* is widely studied not only by advanced Vedāntins, but also by yogis and occultists for what are perceived to be its extraordinary yogic or occult teachings.[124]

The Three *Ākāśas* in *Yoga Vāsiṣṭha* and the Five *Ākāśas* in Vedānta. The *Yoga Vāsiṣṭha's* series of *bhūta-*, *citta-*, and *cit-ākāśa* may well have been one of the inspirations behind Sai Baba's series of five spaces above. For as levels of spiritual development, *bhūta-ākāśa* corresponds to *ghaṭa-ākāśa, citta-ākāśa* has been split in two, *jala-* and *dahara ākāśa,* and *cit-ākāśa* has likewise been split (or better, clarified) into *cit* and *mahat-ākāśa*. This is the correspondence obtained when the stage of *dahara ākāśa* in sec. 11 [B] is regarded as involving a change in the *citta*, the mental tissue, to an only mildly improved *citta*. But when *dahara ākāśa* is regarded as an initial level of perception of *cit-ākāśa*, the stage of *dahara ākāśa* may by taken as the first substage of the development of *cit-ākāśa*. This was our standpoint our treatment of the realization of the self as *svayamjyotiḥ*, self luminous, in chrs. 5.13-15, and is also the point of view of Swami Ananyananda in his exposition of "three kinds of space" in Vedānta.[125]

Swami Ananyananda's "Three Kinds of Space" in Vedānta

> Just as the mental space has two dimensions, the indivdual and the cosmic, so also the *cit-ākāśa* has two dimensions, the individual and the infinite. The individual *cit-ākāśa* is called *dahara-ākāśa* in the Upaniṣads. It is consciousness limited by the *buddhi,* the faculty of intelligence and intuition in man. It is identified with the cavity (*dahara*) of the heart, not the physical heart but the spiritual heart. It is in this space that the *jīvātman* or individual self dwells. In fact *daharākāśa* itself is the individual self.
>
> The infinite dimension of *cit-ākāśa* is known in the Upaniṣads

> as *parama-vyoman*; we may call it *paramākāśa*, the Supreme Space. It is not a mere extension of the heart-space, for it permeates and supports the heart-space as the *antaryāmin* or Inner Controller. It is the consciousness of Hiraṇyagarbha, the Cosmic Soul. It is here where the Yogi seeks to unite the individual spirit with the Supreme Spirit. . .
>
> Since the *paramākāśa* is self-luminous (for it is nothing but pure consciousness which is self-luminous) it is also called the Supreme Light, *param-jyoti* . . .[126]

These three kinds of space are similar to the three *ākāśas* of *Yoga Vāsiṣṭha*. Instead of *bhūta-ākāśa*, Swami Ananyananda has *sthūla-ākāśa* or *bāhya-ākāśa*, gross space or outside space, and the other two terms *citta-ākāśa* and *cit-ākāśa* are the same. At the level of mind, however, he distinguishes individual mind and universal (and cosmic) Mind, *Mahat*, and defines *citta-ākāśa* as "the space of the individual mind" and *mahat-ākāśa* as "[the space] of the universal mind". "[The two] are in dynamic contact with each other and together constitute the subtle space, *sūkṣma-ākāśa*."[127] In the *Yoga Vāsiṣṭha, citta* may include a universal dimension, and *citta-ākāśa* might thus correspond to Swami Ananyananda's *sūkṣma-ākāśa*. Finally, Swami Ananyananda's *cit-ākāśa* is "the pure consciousness of the ultimate reality" which supports, pervades and transcends *bhūta-ākāśa* and *citta-ākāśa*.[128] As a level of spiritual evolution, the *mahat-ākāśa* in Sai Baba's statement [B] seems to be, different from *cit-ākāśa* and the universal and cosmic mind.

13. The One Self in the Heart: *Atharva Veda* X.7.7-16

In the preceding sections we pursued the inner meaning of the *dahara* or *antar-hṛdaya ākāśa* in *Dahara Vidyā* 1.1-1.3. We first described the orthodox approach, in which *dahara ākāśa* is the inner space that develops in meditation on (or meditation involving "centering" in) a spot or region in the heart or chest, and then a second approach, in which *dahara ākāśa* is something like (a subtle aspect of) the sky of awareness, or the firmament of the heart. This represents a level of spiritual awareness or being that develops both in meditation and in normal consciousness during the day. My personal feeling is that the difference between the two approaches tends to diminish if not vanish as inner spiritual life develops further, with the first becoming absorbed into the second. But all this is concerned primarily only with the many forms of the initial dawning of *dahara ākāśa* in the individual, *Dahara Vidyā* VIII.1.1-3. We now continue further with the text, focussing on some of the other aspects of *Dahara Vidyā* 1.1-5.

***Dahara Vidyā* VIII.1.3-5.** The teacher says: "In it (the *dahara ākāśa* or space within the heart as it really is) are placed both heaven and earth . . . Whatever exists here that is his and that is not his, all that is placed in it" (v. 1.3). Further, "that does not age . . .that is the Ātman, free from evil . . ." (v. 1.5). So the text describes first of all (a) a perception or awareness that in the ether of the heart are contained all things and all desires. And second, (b) this perception or awareness is part of a much larger, more fundamental perception or awareness of something ageless, deathless, free from sorrow, etc., i.e., of the Ātman. According to my own understanding: (a) by itself here does not represent an independent level of inner evolution, it does so only in the context or as part of (b). Expressed differently, (a) and (b) form a single movement which refers to the process in which the *dahara ākāśa* consciousness transmutes into knowledge of Ātman, or the *vijñāna* of *dahara ākāśa* becomes *vijñāna* of Ātman. In this section we discuss the textual aspects that lead us to understand the text in this way. The next two sections then deal with more specific problems raised by this part of the teaching, viz. the possibility that (a) implies awareness that the self is in some sense omniscient and manifestations of omniscience (sec. 14), and what is meant by the Ātman being of true desire and of true resolve, *satya-kāma* and *satya-saṁkalpa* (sec. 15).

In v. VIII.1.3, "In this [infinitely extended *ākāśa*] both heaven and earth are wholly placed within," the language suggests perception of heaven and earth etc. placed in an infinite expanse or subtle space, this perception being at the same time "in the heart". The things enumerated are first the major Divinities and Divine features of the world—Sun or Āditya, Moon, Agni, and Vāyu or Wind, and finally "everything here" (end of 1.3), "all this [visible Universe here]" (1.4). As inner experience and inner knowledge, this is undoubtedly related to *TaittBr* II.8.8 mentioned in sec. 2, "within (*antar*) this [Brahman] are these worlds, . . . in Brahman verily are all beings, placed within [it] (*antaḥ samāhita*) like in a boat". The terms *antar*, "within, interior," and *samāhita*, "placed completely," are used conspicuously in both texts (in *Dahara Vidyā* VIII.1.1-5 a total of 8 times, in *Taittirīya Brāhmaṇa* 4 times). Note further "these worlds" similar to "heaven and earth" in the *Dahara* text; "all this [here]" in both texts; "all beings" in both texts (*viśvabhūtāni* vs. *sarvabhūtāni*); and "the thirty-three gods" similar to "Āditya and Moon, Agni and Vāyu" (the same kind of generalizing expansion in both texts). So in the *Dahara Vidyā* also, we may assume that the deities, the worlds, all beings, all this [universe] is placed in the infinite expanse of the *ākāśa* in the heart "like in a boat". This is a rather specific description. Still, since it is addressed to several students, the teacher may be expected to be giving only a typical picture, just enough to enable them to relate to it, to be sensitive to it and to identify it in their experience.

The Formless Perception of Ātman in *Atharva Veda* X.7 as a Precursor of *Dahara Vidyā* VIII.1.3-5. There is no doubt, however, that this perception (or knowledge amounting to perception) of all things placed in the heart is subordinate to, or part of, a much larger, more formless and powerful perception/knowledge, viz. of the Ātman, of something that does not age, is sinless, etc., in v. 1.5. This is clear from the parallel text *Atharva Veda* X.7.7-16[129] (in the *Dahara* text, the teacher is in v. 1.5 ostensibly responding to the new question raised by the disciples in v. 1.4, and so the role of 1.5 as the real level or framework for 1.3 is not so obvious). The Atharva Vedic mantras seem closely related to *TaittBr* II.8.8[8]-[9] and may well show the earliest more detailed formulation of the knowledge/perception (a) above. They are part of the extraordinary pair of hymns on and to the *skambha* or "(world-) pillar," which contains also the two verses on the Ātman in heart quoted in sec. 3.[130] The two hymns are closely related and one can make a good case that they contain a significant portion of the highest knowledge in the old Upaniṣads. This would include, besides the *Dahara Vidyā*, the *vijñāna* portion of the Five Sheaths *Vidyā*, the *Satya Brahman Vidyā*, the knowledge of Ātman as the sole seer, as well as some level of realization of *Vāc* and *Śabda*-Brahman.[131]

***Atharva Veda* X.7.7-16**

7. In [that] which, having established them [in it], Prajāpati supports all the worlds,
   That Skambha tell: which one in truth is that?
8. [That] which Prajāpati created as the highest, the lowest, the middle one, the manifold,
   By how much did Skambha enter (*pra-viś*) there! That which He did not enter, how much was that?

9. By how much did Skambha enter the Existent (*bhūtam;* creation)? How much of Him lies along what will exist [in the future]?
   Which Limb did he make [into] a thousand things, by how much did He enter there?
10. Where (i.e., within which) men know the worlds, the vessels (*kośas*), the waters, the *brahman* (the Divine word),
    In which are the non-existent and the existent (*a-sat* and *sat*),
    That Skambha tell: Which in truth is he?
11. Where austerity (*tapas*), having stridden forth, maintains the higher vow,
    Where both *ṛta* (the cosmic order) and *śraddhā* (faith), the primeval waters, [and] brahman (the Divine word) are placed (*sam-ā-hita*),
    That Skambha tell: Which in truth is that?
12. In which earth [and] intermediate space, in which sky is set (*adhi-ā-hita*),
    Where Agni, Moon, Sun (*Sūrya*), Wind (*Vāta*) stand fixed (*arpita*, or many Mss: *sam-ā-hitā*),
    That Skambha tell: Which in truth is that?
13. In [one] limb of whom the thirty-three gods are all set together (*sam-ā-hita*),
    That Skambha tell: Which in truth is that?
14. Where the first-born seers (*Ṛṣis*), the *Ṛg-mantras*, the *Sāmans*, the *Yajur-mantras*, in which the great one,
    the Sole Seer (*ṛṣiḥ*) is fixed (*arpita*), .
    That Skambha tell: Which in truth is that?
15. Where both immortality (*amṛta*) and death are set (*sam-ā-hita*) in a person (*puruṣa*),
    Of whom the ocean, the *nāḍīs* are set (*sam-ā-hita*) in man,
    That Skambha tell: Which in truth is that?
16. Of whom the four directions (*pradiśaḥ*) are (literally sit as, *ās*) the channels (*nāḍīs*), teeming,
    Where the sacrifice rose up,
    That Skambha tell: Which in truth is that?[132]

This is recognizably an awesome invocation and glorification of That which contains all things—in which all the worlds are established (v. 7), in which men lead their lives (v. 10), and in which both the existent and the non-existent and all things are placed (v. 10, 11, 12, 13, 14, 15, 16, 17). Clearly this passage must be tapping some of the same knowledge or experience as *Dahara Vidyā* 1.3-1.5 and *TaittBr* II.2.8. Like these it is dominated (in vs. 11-15) by *sam-ā-hita*, "wholly (or all together) placed [within *Skambha* = Brahman]," with *arpita*, "fixed [into place]," and *adhi-ā-hita* as additional descriptors or near-equivalent alternates (there are one or two occurrences of these terms in every verse). The world and all things are placed in, *sam-ā-hita*, the Skambha, in the "unaging, . . .," the immortal Ātman (*Dahara Vidyā* 1.3-15), in Brahman (*TaittBr* II.2.8). Verse 15 suggests that Skambha is experienced via a path that involves *prāṇa* yoga and thus probably goes through the heart.

The progression of these texts suggests that the specific contribution of the *Dahara Vidyā* consists of distinguishing in the originally undifferentiated knowledge/vision of the Supreme as Skambha or Brahman a preliminary stage of *dahara ākāśa* and a later stage where the *dahara ākāśa* is transmuted into full Ātman/Brahman, and of becoming aware that both stages may be/are associated with the heart. This fits naturally into our treatment of the *dahara ākāśa* as an intermediate stage on the path to Ātman/Brahman.

14. Relation to *Anamnesis*, Omniscience etc.

The very fact that there are texts going back from *Dahara Vidyā* 1.3-1.5 to considerably earlier Brāhmaṇa and Saṁhitā literature which say that all things are placed in an all-pervasive higher Aspect (the ether within the heart, *Dahara Vidyā* 1.3, or Brahman, *TaittBr* II.2.8, or Skambha) raises the possibility that "all things are placed in an all-pervasive higher Aspect" represents a more universal experience/knowledge which may be found in also outside of Vedic culture, religion and spirituality. Indeed this is suggested by Plato's "theory of recollection," *anamnesis*; by the Buddhist *ālayavijñāna* or "consciousness that includes awareness of a universal store (of content)"; and by teachings in various yogic and tantric literatures that at some stage the yogi becomes in some sense actually omniscient. For all these have in common intuition or knowledge that the human soul is inherently, by its nature, omniscient, which also seems to be implicit in the *Dahara* teaching. Here we give only a preliminary discussion of this whole problem complex, with focus on *anamnesis* and omniscience.[133]

***Anamnesis* in Plato.** At *Memo* 81a ff., Socrates suggests that man's soul can get knowledge and understanding about something by recollecting what it has been before. For "it is immortal and has been born many times". Although here Socrates is talking as if he meant a recollection of things learned in previous incarnations, later it becomes clear that he assumes that "man has been in a state of knowledge throughout all times".[134] This "theory of 'recollection' or *anamnesis*" has been interpreted in Platonic Studies in various ways, and indeed underwent considerable further evolution in Plato himself.[135] The form in which it appears in the *Meno* can be regarded as an early basic intuition or intuitive understanding of Plato's which thereafter plays an important part in the evolution of his conceptions of soul and the *ideas*.[136] Now such an intuition would be completely explained by "within that (space within the heart) indeed are placed heaven and earth . . . everything here is placed within it" (*Dahara Vidyā* 1.3). If at some point there is clear inner apperception or realization of the type "all things are placed in that . . .," then later the individual would feel that "in reality, the soul or self is always in a state of knowledge of everything". Conversely, in the spiritual field generally, a correct spiritual intuition or feeling is very often a darker (coarser, etc.) form of what later becomes direct apperception or realization (it must be remembered, of course, that the clarity and spiritual power of the latter is not derivable from any clarity of material form or from any structuring). Hence Plato's intuition of *anamnesis* can be regarded as a preliminary version of the *Dahara* knowledge 1.3-5. By the same argument, the *Dahara Vidyā* is relevant to any position that holds that the human being or his or her soul in some sense knows already everything—that all knowledge is already somehow in him/her or it. For it says that everything, all (ideas of) objects, principles (deities), desires are already in his heart.[137]

Omniscience. From the feeling that the human soul is in a state of knowledge "throughout all times," it is not a large step to the position that it can in some cases be omniscient or manifest (perhaps limited forms of) omniscience while in the world. In the traditional Western philosophies and religions, omniscience appears almost only as an attribute of God. But in many Indian religions and philosophies and also in Taoism, it is regarded as a capability latent or potential in the human being in general, and to have been manifested by a few great spiritual personalities in history.[138] It is really not clear whether and in what way there is an intrinsic direct connection between the teaching in *Dahara Vidyā* 1.3 and specific "forms of omniscience" in an individual. But if one accepts the possibility that a few individuals may be manifesting specific "forms of omniscience" with specific "experiential qualities," then a substantive connection is likely. Other Upaniṣadic *vidyās*, as well as certain other High Wisdom scriptures in Hinduism, Buddhism and Taoism, all suggest that higher and near highest stages of an individual's spiritual path may be accompanied in a natural way by specific, perhaps limited, "forms of omniscience". In the rest of this section we discuss this topic with an eye on what might be examples of qualitatively different specific "forms of omniscience".

Qualitatively Different "Forms of Omniscience" in Great Spiritual Personalities. "In India, there are not only as many as four distinct [traditional] systems of Philosophy that regard . . . [omniscience] . . . as integral to their thought, but even pre-systematic Vedic and Upaniṣadic thought has something to say about it." All four systems hold that the final goal is attained through knowledge and "their unstated argument is that saving knowledge would not be knowledge if it were not knowledge of all i.e., 'omniscience.'"[139] But there is also little question that in these great and vast traditions this deeply ingrained preoccupation with omniscience is to some extent based on experience with omniscience. A few individuals were experienced as omniscient by some of their immediate disciples and devotees. Buddha and Mahāvīra (the founder of the Jain religion) are well-known examples. The impact of these two men, and their extraordinary words and activities which are enshrined in the older layers of the Buddhist and Jaina canons, form an invaluable and still neglected resource for trying to get an intuitive idea of the qualitative forms of omniscience that seem to have been involved.[140] As an example, *Kalpa Sūtra* 120-121 describes how Mahāvīra

> [A] . . . in a squatting position with joined heels, exposing himself to the heat of the sun, after fasting two and a half days without drinking water, being engaged in deep meditation, reached the highest knowledge and intuition, called *Kevala*, which is infinite, supreme, unobstructed, unimpeded, complete and full. He had become a *Kevalin*, omniscient (*sabbaññū*) and comprehending all objects (*sabbabhāva-darisī*); he knew and saw (*jāṇamāṇe pāsamāṇe*) all conditions of the world, of gods, men and demons:

whence they come, whether they go, whether they are born as men or animals or become gods or hell beings, the ideas, the thoughts of their minds, the food, doings, desires, the open and secret deeds of all the living beings in the whole world; he the Arhat, for whom there is no secret, knew and saw all conditions of all living beings in the world.[141]

As it stands this seems definite enough. But the kind of omniscience which manifested in the historical Buddha is more difficult to pin down. In the "lesser Discourse to Sakuludāyin", the wanderer Udāyin tells Buddha that he met Mahāvīra who was "all-seeing, all-knowing, claiming all-embracing knowledge-and-vision, saying: 'Whether I am walking or standing still or asleep or awake, knowledge-and-vision is constantly and perpetually before me".'[142] Buddha responds [for convenience of reference we subdivide the text into segments (a)-(c)]:

[B] "Udāyin, [(a)] whoever could recollect a variety of former habitations [i.e. "past lives"], that is to say: one birth, and two births . . . [to] a hundred thousand births, and could recollect thus in all their mode and detail a variety of former habitations, either he could ask me a question concerning the past or I could ask him a question concerning the past; either he could turn his mind to answering my question concerning the past or I could turn my mind to answering his question concerning the past. Udāyin, whoever could with the purified *deva*-vision surpassing that of men [(b)] behold beings as they are passing hence and coming to be, mean, excellent, comely, ugly, well-going, ill-going, . . . could comprehend creatures according to the consequences of deeds, either he could ask me a question concerning the future [32] or I could ask him a question concerning the future; either he could turn his mind to answering my question concerning the future or I could turn my mind to answering his question concerning the future.

Wherefore, Udāyin, [(c)] let be the past, let be the future. I will teach you *dhamma*: If this is, that comes to be; from the arising of this, that arises; if this is not, that does not come to be; from the stopping of this, that is stopped. . ."[143]

The threefold schema (a)-(c) occurs at several places with much the same wording.[144] It illustrates several points. In (a) there is an emphasis on Buddha's ability to call to mind his "former abodes" (in "previous lives"), an ability which is elsewhere said to be "without suggestion of limit".[145] This plays a prominent role in accounts of Buddha's omniscience and seems to be special to Buddha. Part (b) deals with the future course of beings; a similar segment is also found in the description [A] of Mahāvīra's omniscience above ("he knew and saw, *jāṇamāṇe pāsamāṇe*, all conditions of the world, of gods, men and demons: whence they come, whither they go, whether they are born as men or animals or become gods or hell (beings"). Of interest here is a certain running together or fusion of the particular (objects, events, here: beings, persons) and the universal (the person's qualities, larger life contexts), together with an emphasis on seeing ethical or spiritual qualities or conditions. A similar emphasis on seeing ethical-spiritual conditions, and similarly unusual mixtures of the particular and universal, are found in the descriptions of the near-omniscience of some of the great saints, as well as some of the forms of omniscience described in yogic traditions. There is often a suggestion of forms of ordinary knowledge and perception deeply fused with perception of subtle spiritual (moral etc.) qualities, and perhaps preferred cognitive modes as far as type or level of generality is concerned. Thus there may be different forms of omniscience, depending on the exact form and fusion of these factors.

Segment (c), finally, illustrates the fact that omniscience is intrinsically tied up with transcendence of desire. This amplifies the point made in (b). Awareness of being omniscient as well as forms of actual omniscience arise when there is the perception, the taste, the reality, whatever, that comes with transcendence of desire. But (c) also clearly implies that the knowledge in (a) and (b), which together with other aspects could from a worldly point of view be regarded as making up a limited form of omniscience, are insignificant compared to knowledge of *dhamma—dhamma* being both the Teaching that takes one beyond desire to "the incomparable security from bonds," and Knowledge of Reality. *That*, says Buddha, is really what should be called omniscience. In fact, both in Theravada tradition and from the point of view of universal religion—*philosophia perennis*, the knowledge in (a) and some of that in (b) represents "mundane powers [that are in principle] unrelated to the path and hence accessible, in varying degrees, to adepts in yoga".[146] To focus on forms of omniscience as objects of interest, say to approach them as powers or states of consciousness from a "purely descriptive" or "scientific point of view" would be bizarre. Before doing so, the meaning and value of "knowing" and "understanding" the world of form and meanings in a mental way must be questioned. If becoming Ātman/Brahman implies a true transcendence of mind and space and time, one must take a much larger view where the very nature of cognition and of cognition as an existing phenomenon is to be illuminated. Indeed the Scriptures must be studied both in regard to omniscience as an aspect of "the Path" to the Infinite Reality, and in regard to what deeper attitude one should have toward it. On the other hand, knowledge of *dhamma* leads to things like "the ultimate beginnings I know, and more than that".[147] This is an example of knowledge of a completely different order than (a)-(b).

As another example, Gauḍapāda (ca. 600 CE), Śaṁkara's "Supreme Teacher," should be credited with at least "awareness of his soul's omniscience," if not omniscience manifested in concrete situations in his own subjective experience (showing him that he was omniscient), or as a phenomenon to the eyes of others. Virtually nothing is known about him personally.[148] But in his Kārikā ("Stanzas"), he describes the Ātman when it is realized in the *Turīya* state as "ever existent, ever all-seeing".[149] "All" here should in some sense be taken literally, and the stanza should be regarded as expressing at least full awareness of omniscience of the Self. For the spiritual power of the Kārikā is such that Gauḍapāda must have written them from high direct knowledge and realization.[150] Something like the knowledge described must have existed in the author.

Different from all the examples above, finally, is Sri Sathya Sai Baba, who is regarded as fully omniscient by most of his devotees.

> When some one asked him 'What is this power that you possess by which you are able to read us like a book [past, present, future]?" Baba replied, "This is no power which I have earned; this is no power which I use in specific instances. This is my very nature. I do not 'enter' into your mind, and 'discover' all that lies hidden there and 'reveal' them to you: I am ever there; I am the motivator of all minds. You cannot think or feel or act without My being aware of it."[151]

This is similar to Lord Kṛṣna in the *Gītā*:

> "I am the Self, Guḍākeśa (= Arjuna),
> [which is] established in the heart (literally, resting place) of all beings.
> I am both beginning and middle of beings,
> and indeed their end too."[152]

These are supreme Divine expressions. But "being indweller in all," *sarvāntaryāmin*, and "being all" are essential components of the combined decription of Ātman/Brahman given in the greatest Upaniṣadic *vidyās*, and must for that reason be at least considered capable of being glimpsed, if not fully represented, in a human being.

Finally we conclude this brief survey with noting that omniscience is not limited to the Indian religions. For example, Hadrat Abul Hasan al Kirqhani (10th century CE), a great Islamic Saint, "instructed his disciples thus:

> 12. By God's grace he [Abul Hasan] knew every creature's past, present and future at all times. Whosoever is not equipped with such knowledge cannot be a teacher. If even a thorn pricked anybody's foot anywhere in the world, he [Abul Hasan] would know that incident and experience it himself, and point out the person who thus suffered. This was because he had identified himself with the creation."[153]

This account is by Attar, himself a great Saint, so the testimony cannot be simply discounted.[154]

Omniscience in Yogic Scriptures and Texts. Apart from historical spiritual figures who embody some form of omniscience, many yogically oriented texts from a variety of traditions teach some kind of omniscience as arising in the penultimate or highest stages. A good example is *YoSū* III.49:

> To one established in the perception (*khyāti*) of the difference between *sattva* (= *buddhi*) and *puruṣa* (Pure Spirit, the Sāṁkhya analogue of Ātman) belongs supremacy over all states of existence and all-knowership.

Vyāsa's commentary says "the aspects (*guṇas*) which are the essence (the soul, *ātman*) of all things, which have both the determinations [i.e., the subjective ideas of things] and the objects-of-determinations [i.e., the corresponding objective physical objects etc.] as their essence, present themselves as being the essence (*ātman*) of the object-for-sight in its totality to their owner, the Soul (*kṣetrajña*) [the Ātman]".[155] "'All knowership' means knowledge [born from] discrimination and rising simultaneously [into awareness], of the *guṇas* which are essences (*ātmans*) of all things, quiescent or uprisen or undeterminable (i.e., past, present or future)."[156] The three *guṇas* (*sattva, rajas* and *tamas*) are spiritual qualities which, to enlightened vision, underlie and account for all the objects and phenomena of the experienced world. They are what *puruṣa* and the yogin at this stage see when they look at the world ("*puruṣa* is the witness onlooker of the *guṇas*," Vyāsa on *YoSū* II.20).[157] Attainment of this is "[the state of] *viśokā,* sorrowless-ness," presumably related to the *viśoka* quality of the Ātman in *Dahara Vidyā* 1.5. So like Buddha's omniscience, this is another form of omniscience involving spiritual qualities. Like the former, it is also based on transcendence of desire, more specifically, on being permanently established in the perception of *puruṣa*, or the true self, as distinct from *buddhi*, or the apparent self which says "I see, I think, I decide, . . ." According to the *Yoga Sūtra*, this kind of omniscience comes after a stage of higher psychic powers called *madhu-pratīkā,* "honeyed images," but before the highest state, *kaivalya* or "isolation" (of the Self from non-Self).[158]

The *Yoga Sūtra* is only one example of an authoritative, high-level text that teaches omniscience as part of the yogin's path. Other instances may be found in the *Yoga Upaniṣads*[159] and other Yoga texts,[160] and in high-level tantric traditions such as the non-dual Śaivism of Kashmir.[161] In Buddhism also, omniscience is taught as a stage in spiritual development or as characteristic of a certain spiritual level, always associated with Transcendence of Desire.[162]

Summary: Awareness of Omniscience, Omniscience, and the *Dahara Vidyā*. The preceding suggests that consciousness of one's self being omniscient is a fundamental spiritual phenomenon which reflects the nature of the human self and of Transcendence of Desire. In addition, manifestation of some form of omniscience may occur in individuals in very advanced stages of spiritual path, or naturally in Divine Manifestations.[163] *Dahara Vidyā* 1.3-1.5 seems significant in respect to both of these points. It describes perception/realization which can be taken as a form of "awareness of [one's self's] omniscience" (different from forms of "subjectively experienced omniscience"). The particular formulation "in it are wholly palced Heaven and Earth, Fire and Wind, . . ." also suggests specific levels of thinking (specific levels of generality at which omniscience is experienced), and thus a specific form of "omniscient awareness". At the same time, the *vidyā* does not seem to imply that knowledge of Ātman automatically implies some form of omniscience apparent to outsiders, or even only subjectively experienced omniscience.

15. *Satya-kāma* and *Satya-saṁkalpa*, "of True Desire" and "of True Resolve"

In trying to understand the descriptions of *Dahara Vidyā* 1.1-1.5 in more detail, we have focussed in the last section on "in this [space within the heart] heaven and earth are placed within, . . . all this [world here] is placed in it," which suggests a connection, at ieast in principle, with *anamnesis*, *ālayavijñāna*, and omniscience. But the fact that the Ātman is described in 1.5 as *satya-kāma*, "of true desire," and *satya-saṁkalpa*, "of true resolve," is equally unusual and fundamental. Both of these terms carry connotations that the desire that one sets one's heart on, or the object that one resolves on, is pure, not tained by self interest or attachment, and that it will be unfailingly fulfilled or realized. This may strike one as strange, because so far in this book, knowledge of the Ātman was described mostly in terms of consciousness (or knowledge), or of being the One Self, being the One Seer. There was little indication of effects at the level of action, like *satya-saṁkalpa*. But each *vidyā* makes its own specific and special contribution to illumining the Infinite Ātman/Brahman, and brings to light aspects that are not apparent in other *vidyās*.

***Satya-kāma*. The True Desires in the Heart.** In the *Dahara Vidyā*, the topic of *satya-kāma* and *satya-saṁkalpa* is broached even before these terms appear as part of the eight term description of the Ātman in 1.5. In 1.4 the disciples, in paraphrasing the teaching in 1.3 that the space in the heart contains all things, specifically add that that space (or rather, the Brahman city) contains "all desires". And in 1.5, the teacher, picking up on this, responds with a description of the "true city of Brahman" (namely "that does not age . . .") and then acknowledges, "In it (the true city of Brahman which I have just described) are placed the desires." All these references evoke the mystery of Desire and Resolve. The fact of Desire, the fact that it is a basic given for everyone, its universality in the world and in human life, is a mystery. In any larger perspective, e.g. as far as the meaning of life is concerned, or the meaning of Creation, desire and resolve are central, but their roles are a mystery. The fact that the One Self is *satya-kāma* is equally a mystery. But when there is experience and realization of the Self as *satya-kāma*, desire will have been left behind.

In *Dahara Vidyā* 1.5-6, the text is trying to express such a realization in worlds. The chief characteristic of desire is that one "lives dependent on it" (end of 1.5), or in terms of later language, that it binds the individual. (Here *kāma* has the element of attachment in it.) So instead, one has to find the Self and the "true desires" (*satyān kāmān*). Then there will be true freedom in this world and the next (1.5, 1.6), and one will not be bound by desire, one will not live dependent on it. But what are these "true desires"? Of course they are only truly seen as such when there is some knowledge of the Self (in 1.6, people must have "found the self and [the, or their] true desires"). But to give an idea, an answer is given anyway in 3.1-3.2. The desires one normally has, says the text there, may be compared to true desires which are "endowed with a covering of [what is] false," *anṛta-apidhāna* (*an-ṛta*— "un-true," "false"; *api-dhāna*— "cover, a covering cloth"). In other words, they may be compared to true desires that are tainted by (or are covered by) a selfish motive. And then comes an example: "For (*hi*) whoever of one's [kin] departs from here (i.e., dies), one does not get him [back] here for seeing." In other words: longing for a deceased loved one, wanting him back etc. involves something untrue, *an-ṛta*. One knows that one cannot get a dead person back, the relationship cannot continue forever, and one has no business in engaging in such longing. On the other hand, "Those of one's [kin] who are alive here and those who have departed and whatever else one, [although] desiring [it], does not get—all that one finds when one has gone there," i.e. into the space within the heart, "for (*hi*) here, truly, are those true desires of his covered by untruth". This is a deep truth. All of a person's desires (cf. *Dahara Vidyā* 2.10) are in his or her heart. However, normally these involve aspects which are untruth: sense-longing, dependence, indulging, feelings of self-importance, self-interest. But deeper in the heart, at the level of the *dahra gagana*, the subtle inner firmament which is *viśoka*, without sorrow, there are true things, "true desires," which underlie the tainted desires in the heart. The true love for a living or departed loved one, as well as the object of that love (the loved one), are something like a purer reality which is unaffected by whether the object of love is present or not or whether it has died. This purer reality is completely divorced from the aspects of untruth, which are ultimately only sorrow. And then the text gives another illustration. "Just as these who do not know a field," viz. their own heart, "walking around on top of a hidden treasure of gold," viz. the treasure of knowledge/awareness at the level of *dahara ākāśa* and of Ātman, which is buried in the heart ("underneath the field"), "but do not find it, even so all creatures [though] going day after day to that Brahma-world," i.e., in the same way all creatures go daily into their hearts, which should be the Brahma world (or *dahara ākāśa* = Ātman/Brahman), "but do not find it," they do not find the treasure of *dahara vijñāna* or Ātma-*vijñāna*. "For truly they are carried astray by untruth," they are dominated by the aspect of dependence on, wanting, wanting to indulge in, the loved one.

Śaṁkara takes the place where one finds the loved ones, and all the other things which one desires but cannot get, to be "the Brahman called the *ākāśa* in the heart". As a result, he regards the immediately following "going daily to the region of Brahman (Brahma-*loka*)" as referring to deep sleep.[164] This is the standard traditional interpretation. In our reading, the text refers to a reality at the level of of *dahara ākāśa* that can be felt in waking consciousness. There is a story about a devotee of Ramana Maharshi's who lost his wife with whom he had been happily married for twelve years and who could not overcome his grief for several months. Discussing his situation, Maharshi said to him: "True love is when there is the firm conviction that the object of love is eternal and is part of self."[165] When there is love of this kind, then the love and the object of love are partly higher, "eternal" aspects in the *dahara ākāśa* (or one's perception of these things is in the heart at the level of *dahara ākāśa*). And then the object of love is present in the space in the heart without there being any improper dependence, indulgence, attachment etc. The perception of all things as contained in the *dahara ākāśa*, which is really Ātman/Brahman would, by comparison, represent a still further stage.

True Desires, Being Part of a Purer Reality, Tend to Get Fulfilled. So far we have focussed on the nature of the "true desires," on what they are "experientially". But there is also *satya-saṁkalpa*, "of true resolve." At the level of the Ātman, says the text, true desires engender or take the form of resolves, *saṁkalpas*, which tend to ultimately get fulfilled (this is the connotation of the qualifier "true" in this context). This is more problematic. The fact that the Ātman is *satyakāma* is something that obtains at a cosmic level, because there is only one Self, and so all the true desires of all individuals must co-exist harmoniously in the One Self. And indeed Śaṁkara, explaining *satya-kāma* in 1.5, suddenly starts talking in terms of God: "'He (Ātman) is with true desires'—i.e. all His desires are infallible; the desires of worldly people are not true, they are not always fulfilled; but the desires of God are the contrary of that, they are infallible—similarly 'His volitions [*saṁkalpas*],' arising out of those desires, 'are also true'; in the case of God, both desires and volitions are due to the limitations of Pure *Sattva* (the attitude of Goodness) . . . "[166] This is theological language. To get an idea of the direction of inner development and experience implied, the following statement by Sri Sathya Sai Baba is fundamental:

> If we try to make our mind pure, then we shall be able to discover anything and everything. In our spiritual practice (*sādhanā*), the first thing we have to do is to deepen and steady our faith. God is all pervading and He knows everything, and so [when our faith is steady,] the essence of the Spirit that flows out of our mind will be very near to God. Because God comes out of our heart in the form of speech, we must try to make our speech as pure and as clean as possible. God is also in the form of Truth. So whatever we will be telling through our speech, God will say to it: "Let it be so!"—The world is part of a tree that fulfills all desires. If we think badly, bad happens to us and if we think in a good manner, good happens to us. So when our thoughts, when our contemplation and when our deeds are pure, the wish fulfilling tree of the world will be giving us the good things that we desire. Both good and bad will only come from our heart. They never come from outside. That is why, as a start, we have to make our heart as pure as possible.[167]

When one speaks to someone, whether it is in anger or lovingly or thoughtlessly or in anyway, the soul or essence that flows out with that speaking and feeling is the heart. Now the inmost essence of everyone is Ātman/Brahman (or in the terms here, God); this is the "basic substance of the Universe". This basic substance (Brahman, or Sai Baba would say, the Brahma-*tattva*, the Brahman-thatness) is completely stainless. Spiritual life is the endeavor to realize one's "oneness with this basic substance of the Universe, a substance that is attributeless yet is mistaken to have attributes like names and forms and functions," cf. the *mahā-vākyas* "You are that" and "I am Brahman". So in one's *sādhanā* or purposeful living toward that end, the inmost essence or soul that flows out of one when one engages in the innumerable interactions in daily life (or in other words the heart) must be purified so that there can be realization "I am Brahman." The essence that flows out of one in one's speaking should be pure in the sense that it should be unstained by self interest and attachment, it should come as part of noble or sweet sentiments, and be in accordance with *dharma* and truth. When there is such purity, then there is experience of *satya-kāma*. At that point, "whatever we will be telling through our speech, God will say to it let it be so," in other words, then there will be *satya-saṁkalpa* also. Obviously Sai Baba is using the language "God will say . . ." largely for convenience. The meaning is: When there is such purity, then the essence or soul of what is flowing out of one in one's speech will be very close to "the basic substance of the universe" which one really is, *and because of the nature of this substance*, what is said will come to pass or will be fulfilled. Because of the nature of that Infinite "substance," the Brahman-thatness, the words will come true and we have the aspect of *satya-saṁkalpa*. So in a way, *satyakāma* and *satyasaṁkalpa* may be said to be in the nature of Brahman (Ātman is *satya-kāma, satya-saṁkalpa, Dahara Vidyā* 1.5). But in terms of their real meaning, these terms refer to these kinds of realities of spiritual life. These realities, at first perhaps only more or lesss vaguely glimpsed and intuited, tend to become stronger, clearer as time goes on.

16. *Śāṇḍilya Vidyā*

The preceding completes our discussion of the teaching of the Self and the Universe in the Heart and some of its ramifications (*Dahara Vidyā* 1.1-3.2). Before taking up the larger text in which this teaching is embedded (the full *Dahara Vidyā* 1.1-6.6), however, we briefly consider the *Śāṇḍilya Vidyā, ChāndUp* III.14,[168] which is very similar in spirit to *Dahara Vidyā* 1.1-1.5. The main difference is that while the *Dahara* text is in yogic language, given by a teacher to his disciples, the *Śāṇḍilya Vidyā* gives a general resolution/meditation intended for everyone. The Upaniṣadic *Śāṇḍilya Vidyā* has a precursor in *ŚatBr* X.6.3. The latter begins with the words *satyam Brahma*,

"Brahman is the *Satya*," while the Upaniṣadic version starts with "Verily, all this [world here] is Brahman, *tajjalān*." But the subsequent teachings are almost verbatim the same. The *vidyā* is named after *Śāṇḍilya*, perhaps the greatest teacher of the *agnicayana*, the ritual of the fire altar. (In the *Śatapatha Brāhmaṇa*, the fire altar is several times called *śaṇḍilya; śāṇḍilya* literally means "(the one) of the *śaṇḍila*," or "descendant of Śaṇḍila".) Tradition ascribes to Śāṇḍilya the authorship of *ŚatBr* VI-X, including the *Agnirahasya* or secret teaching of Agni (i.e. of the fire altar), *ŚatBr* X, which contains the *Śāṇḍilya Vidyā*. The remaining books are attributed to Yājñavalkya. According to Western-type scholarship the Śāṇḍilya books are also somewhat later than the others, and were composed in the northeast, in present-day Punjab (which incidentally was also at one time Harappan territory).[169] The Yājñavalkya books are thought to have come from what is today Uttar Pradesh. The unification of the traditions of these two great teachers in the body of the *Śatapatha Brāhmaṇa* may account in part for the close relationship between *Bṛhadāraṇyaka* and *Chāndogya Upaniṣads*.

Upaniṣadic *Śāṇḍilya Vidyā*. The Upaniṣadic *Śāṇḍliya Vidyā* consists of four verses:

III.14.1. "Verily, all this [world] is Brahman, *tajjalān*,"[a] thus one should meditate (*upās-*) tranquilly. Now verily, man is made of purpose (or Brahmic power, *kratu*). As a person becomes purposed in this world, so does he become (or so is his state) in the next world. So let him make [this] purpose (or power, *kratu*):

2. Consisting of mind (*mano-maya*), having *prāṇa* for its body (*prāṇa-śarīra*), having effulgence for its form (*bhārūpa*), of true resolve (*satya-kāma*), of space-like essence (*ākāśa-ātma*), doing all actions, desiring all [desires], smelling all [smells], tasting all [tastes] (or: containing all actions, desires, smells, tastes), encompassing all this [world], unspeaking, unconcerned,

3. This myself (or: my self) within the heart is smaller than a grain of rice, a barley corn, a mustard seed, a grain of millet, a kernel of a grain of millet; this myself within the heart is greater[b] than the earth, greater than the intermediate space, greater than the heavens, greater than these worlds.

4. Doing all actions, desiring all [desires], smelling all [smells], tasting all [tastes], encompassing all this world, without speech, unconcerned, this [is] myself within the heart, this is Brahman. Into Him (or It) shall I enter after death.

   If one would have *this faith, he would* have no more doubt. Thus Śāṇḍilya used to say—yeah, Śāṇḍilya.[170]

The text breaks down into three segments: (1) the first sentence, an *upāsanā* which is almost a *vidyā* by itself;[171] (2) the remainder of III.14.1, a preamble to the "meditation" to follow; and (3) III.14.2-4, a powerful "meditation" on the Self in the heart no doubt based on experience and realization. The *Śatapatha Brāhmaṇa* version has the same structure.

Śatapatha Brāhmaṇa* Version of *Vidyā

X.6.3.1. "Brahman is the *Satya*,[a] [in this way] should one meditate (*upās-*). Now verily this individual (*puruṣa*) is made of [higher] purpose (Brahmic power, *kratu*). Whatever higher purpose having he passes on from this world, this purpose he becomes[b] [after] having passed on to the next world.

2. He should meditate (*upās-*) on the Ātman, [which is, or: as] made of mind, [which] has *prāṇa* for its body, effulgence for its form, *ākāśa* as its self, [which is or has] forms according to its desire (*kāma rūpiṇā*), [which is] swift as thought, of true resolve (*satya-saṁkalpa*), of true constancy (*satya-hṛti*); [smelling] all smell, [tasting] all flavor, [who has] become all the directions everywhere, pervading all this [world], without speech, indifferent.[c] As a grain of rice or a grain of barley or a grain of millet or a small granule of millet, so indeed is this golden person within the self, as indeed a smokeless light, greater than space, greater than this earth, greater than all things. This [inner] self of *prāṇa* is my Self. On passing away from this here I shall attain to (become) that Self.' [He] who [has this] faith, [for him] there is no uncertainty."

   Verily, [thus] Śāṇḍilya used to say. Thus it is.[172]

***Upāsanā* versus *kratu*.** The *upāsanā* at the beginning of the Brāhmaṇa version is equivalent to the initial *upāsanā* in the Upaniṣadic text.[173]

The two main "meditations" are also similar. But there are some differences. *Śatapatha Brāhmaṇa* has "the golden person" and "the self (essence) of *prāṇa* [itself]," terms which have familiar echoes in the Brāhmaṇa literature and are not represented in the *Chāndogya* text.[174] Thus *ŚatBr* X.6.3 may be older or more original. The largest difference, however, lies in the way the central "meditation" is presented. In *Śatapatha Brāhmaṇa* it is regarded as an *upāsanā* of the Ātman. This is very unusual for a Brāhmaṇa text, even for one in *ŚatBr* X. The comments on a person needing a *kratu*, "(higher) purpose, well, (divine) power" are equally unusual, and are presumably connected with the fact that the object of the *kratu* is the self. But at any rate, the *kratu* is implemented by the *upāsana* on the Self in heart (X.6.3.2). In *Chāndogya Upaniṣad*, however, the basic instruction is not that one should *upās-*, "worship, contemplate on, regard something as," but "he should make himself (or fashion himself, root *kṛ*) a purpose (*kratu*)". Instead of having recourse to the completely standard "he should meditate, regard, etc., *upās-*," which is still a norm at that time, the text boldly highlights the individual: "he *should make* himself a purpose (will, power, etc.)".

If the individual is enjoined to make himself a *kratu* regarding the Infinite nature of the Self, rather than to engage in an *upāsanā*, it is clear that the text is consciously dealing with the problem of doubt. Both versions of the *vidyā*, but particularly the Upaniṣadic one, address themselves to the problem of doubt (or at least, of the flagging of faith, cf. the conclusion in each case). There are bound to be moments where principles like "All this is Brahman," or "[the Self in one] encompasses all this world," seem impossible, where one's faith falters and one despairs over one's own confusion, inharmonious feelings, and incongruent actions. It is in this context that the text appeals to a basic fact of life. "As is a man's (*puruṣa*) *kratu* or "will," so is the deed he does; as is the deed he does, so is that which he attains to" (in this life and after death), says *BṛhUp*. IV.4.7 (chr. 2.3 above). "According to the purpose which a person has [set himself] in this world, thus does he become on departing hence," we have here. But what to accept as the purpose in my heart, that is up to me, that is something that comes out of my heart, my inmost self. All Scriptures teach that one be fully devoted to the Infinite, to God, to Ātman/Brahman, and that that is the purpose of life. All take for granted, there is never any question, that one can be thus devoted, and in this way realize and merge with the Infinite, the Reality. So an initial step is to actually resolve this, to actually have this desire or purpose in one's heart. "So let him form for himself [the following] purpose."

The Main Meditation in the *Śāṇḍilya Vidyā*, and Relation to Other *Vidyās*. Finally, both main meditations are strongly reminiscent of *Dahara Vidyā* 1.1-1.5, with overtones of the Five Sheaths and *Antarjyotir Vidyās*. The Self is in one's heart. It is "smaller than a grain of rice . . ., greater than (superior to; also more ancient than) the earth, . . .:" Compared to it the world, the universe and its contents pale into insignificance. The phrases evoke the same kind of simultaneous existence, or interpenetration of limited and infinite-spiritual, as in *Dahara Vidyā* 1.1-1.3. In spiritual life based on the *vidyā*, they may be expected to lead to the stage of *dahara ākāśa* and further. Most important, the real self is *satya-kāma* or *satya-saṁkalpa*, which in this meditation resonates powerfully with *kratu*, "will, purpose, (divine) power". But besides these resonances with the *Dahara Vidyā*, there are also clear contacts with the Five Sheaths *Vidyā* and the *vidyās* associated with it. Thus the Self is *mano-maya* (here perhaps only "incorporeal," but perhaps also like *mano-* and *vijñāna-maya* in the Five Sheaths *Vidyā*); it has *prāṇa* for its body (compare *prāṇa-maya* in the Five Sheaths text); and it is *bhā-rūpa* and "as indeed a smokeless light" (cf. the light within the heart, *BṛhUp* IV.3.7, etc.).

The close relationship of the *Śāṇḍilya Vidyā* and *Dahara Vidyā* 1.1-5 has some implications for our understanding of the *Dahara Vidyā*. The *Dahara* teaching doesn't really elaborate on how the Ātman "within" the space in the heart can be attained. But the *Śāṇḍilya Vidyā*, which has a similar spirit as the *Dahara* teaching and clearly deals with *dahara ākāśa* and with the process of realizing that *ākāśa* as the Self, enjoins a meditation which helps that process. The fact, therefore, that the *upāsanā* in the *Śatapatha Brāhmaṇa* version of the *Śāṇḍilya Vidyā* is in the Upaniṣad a *kratu* suggests that there may indeed have been considerable latitude (in terms of specific inner practice) in getting from beginning stages of *dahara ākāśa* to the universe in the heart and to the Ātman.

17. Full *Dahara Vidyā:* Overall Structure

The teaching on the space in the heart which contains all things and ultimately becomes, or is, the Ātman, is only the initial portion of a larger text, *ChāndUp* VIII.1.1-6.6, the full *Dahara Vidyā*. Turning now to this larger text, we first argue that it forms a connected whole and then suggest that it has a fundamentally similar trend of thought as *BṛhUp* IV.3-4 and *TaittUp* II, the most complete and profound texts considered so far.

Subunits of the Full *Dahara Vidyā*. On the basis of content, the full *Dahara* text may be divided into 6 subunits:

(1) 1.1-3.2, the teaching on the space in the heart;
(2) 3.3, "Verily, this Ātman is in the heart. . .;"
(3) 3.4-3.5, "That serene one . . .;"
(4) 4.1-4.3, the "bridge" that forms the "separation" for keeping these worlds apart., etc. V.4.3 then makes a transition between this and
(5) the teaching on *brahmacarya,* 5.1-4, which in 5.4 contains echoes of the *Paryaṅka Vidyā, KauṣUp* I;
(6) 6.1-6, a teaching on the channels of the heart and on the channel that goes up to the crown of the head.

Verse 3.3. First consider 3.3, "This Ātman is in the heart . . ." "This Ātman" must refer to the Ātman mentioned in 1.5 and described in 1.1-1.5. So by its structure and movement 3.3 is signalling that it is picking up the exposition where it was left off in 1.5: It summarizes 1.1-1.5 by "this Ātman is in the heart," and notes that this fact is supported by an etymology. So in effect it is a kind of conclusion to 1.1-3.2, making 1.1-3.3 a single, integrated unit.

Verses 3.4-3.5. At this point comes a new teaching (3.4, *sam-ud-sthāya,* first part = a): "That serene one (*sam-prasāda*) who, rising up (*sam-ud-sthāya*) out of this body (*śarīra*), having reached (*upa-sampadya*) the highest light (*paramjyotiḥ*), enters into it (= becomes it, *abhi-niṣ-padyate*) with his own form. This is the Self. . . ." This represents a new, higher level description of the Ātman than 1.5. For the phrases "having reached the *highest* light", "enters into (the light)" and "with *his own* form" all go beyond the straightforward description "free from evil, age-less, death-less, . . ." in 1.5 and suggest a climax, something like "merger in the 'supreme light', " further than which it is impossible to go. Evidently what is being described is a process (or state) of self merging more and more fully into the One Self. The initial segment, "this completely serene one, rising out of this body," looks as if it refers to a process in meditation. But *sam-ud-sthā*, "rising up [out of]," has also a figurative meaning, viz. utterly transcending the body and rising above it.[175] The remaining phrases are also used both literally, referring to meditation (or concentration), and to a person's spiritual state generally. It is in the latter sense that they describe "merger". There is however also another difference between 1.5 and 3.4 which contributes to the impression that they are at somewhat different levels. Although ostensibly "objective" and taking an external point of view ("that serene one, rising up out of . . ., having reached . . ., enters into . . ."), the description in 3.4 is expressed in the most direct form, as if it was directly present to the teacher, to his inner eye, at that moment. In 1.5, the situation is different. In 1.2 and 1.4 the disciples do not know the great teaching on the One Self that is to come in 1.5. And so the teacher assumes their standpoint to help them: "Not through that one's (the person's) aging does it age . . . It is free from sin. . . ," that is to say, "the thing you are asking about, the state described in 1.3, does not change when the body ages and dies . . ." In other words the teacher wants to help them understand the *dahara ākāśa* and identify the direction of the Ātman, and his description serves to identify it for them and fix the goal. It rounds out and completes the instruction begun in 1.1 and 1.3. In 3.4, the perception or knowledge indicated in 1.5 is assumed to be already to some extent present in the student, and the teacher describes and almost "demonstrates" some still further aspects of merger, "enters into the [supreme] light" "by his own form". (cf. the analysis of Five Sheaths *Vidyā* II.7.3 in chr. 5.)

Next this new teaching on direct, high level experience of Self and Brahman is immediately tied to the more traditional (Brāhmaṇa-based) teaching on *Satya* Brahman as represented in the *Satya Brahma Vidyā* and elsewhere (end of 3.4 and 3.5). This is done in the form of a comment on the earlier "That serene one . . ., that is Brahman." The comment is, "Of that [Brahman], now (that the teacher described), [it can be said that] 'the name of that Brahman is *satyam*,' " or alternatively, "in regard to that (*tasya*, that teaching), the name of that Brahman is '*satyam*'". In either case, the comment continues on in 3.5 with the etymology of *satya*. This further identifies the knowledge being currently taught as coming within the scope of the circle of traditional *Satya* Brahman teachings. Thus 3.4b-3.5, *qua* comment, form a unit. This unit is tied to 3.3 by the common refrain, "he who knows thus goes to the heavenly world". Hence 1.1-3.5 form a single unit.

Verses 4.1-3 and 5.1-4. The next major unit, 4.1-4.2, deals with the bridge (*setu*) or "separating boundary" (*vidhṛti*) "for keeping the worlds apart". This might be a continuation of 3.4, a kind of reflection on and description of the Self at roughly the level described there, but this is simply a guess; I have no clear intuition about what *setu* here might refer to. In any case 4.3 connects this unit explicitly with sec. 5, on *brahmacarya.* The sphere of Brahman described in 4.1-4.2 and thus the higher stages taught in the *vidyā* , says 5.1-4, can only be attained through *brahmacarya.* More than that, all kinds of other practices popular at the time, are all accomplished by *brahmacarya. Brahma-carya* is literally "Brahman walking," "walking the path of Brahman".[176] No doubt the term carries here the traditional connotations of being a Vedic student, Vedic study, and the state of inner and outer chastity and discipline that accompany these. But it also means following the teachings on Brahman, i.e. the Upaniṣadic *vidyās.* Whatever the exact meaning here, the text obviously places *brahmacarya* at a higher level than all the other methods mentioned. *Yajña* represents Vedic ritual in general; *iṣṭam* is grain or other vegetable offering that has been offered with a call of *vaṣaṭ*; and *sattrāyaṇa* is a sacrificial course arranged by Brahmins as part of their own *sādhanā* (without a sponsoring patron sacrificer). So these terms emphasize the reality of the ritual and the fact that it may be intensified by the sincere aspirant and used for higher spiritual development. The others—living in silence, undertaking a long-term regimen of fasting, and living the life of a hermit in the forest—are all common types of spiritual and ascetic discipline. All these methods, says the text, are just that—methods. The critical ingredient is *brahmacarya,* which involves complete and selfless dedication to Brahman.

The general conclusion therefore is that 3.4 continues the teaching of the Self in 1.5 to a further, cosmic-universal and more formless level. The comment 3.4b, that the name of that Brahman is *satyam,* and 3.5, as well as 4 and 5, are more general, objective elaborations on the knowledge in 3.4a. As a result, 1.1-5.4 form a single unified teaching which recognizes several phases of spiritual evolution: *dahara ākāśa* (1.1-1.3), some realization of the self along the lines of 1.3-1.5, and further phases of merging into Brahman described in 3.4a.

18. The Channels of the Heart: *BṛhUp* IV.2.2-4 and the "Path of the (Subtle) *Prāṇa* All-Self"

If *ChāndUp* VIII.1.1-5.4 forms a more or less unified, cumulative exposition, what about the remaining section, VIII.6, dealing with the "channels (*nāḍīs*) of the heart"? Is it part of the larger *Dahara Vidyā* also, and if so, what is its meaning?

Structure of *ChāndUp* VIII.6: Outline of Argument. Inspection of the text suggests that it decomposes into three blocks:

> 6.1-6.2, relation between the channels of the heart and the Sun;
> 6.3, the channels of the heart and deep sleep;
> 6.4-6.6, the channels of the heart and the process of dying.

The teaching 6.1-6.2 on the relationship of the channels of the heart with the Sun is probably intended as background for the following blocks. For in 6.3 the bright power, *tejas*, is presumably the Sun or the spiritual aspect represented by the Sun, and 6.5 talks about going to the Sun after death. V. 6.1 is a comment in the colors associated with the channels of the heart, connecting them with the equally esoteric colors of the Sun, and v. 6.2 amplifies the connection further in terms of the Sun's rays. The whole of 6.1-6 therefore seems to represent deeper spiritual wisdom relating to long-term yogic-type practice.

But 6.3 and 6.4-6 also have analogues elsewhere in the Upaniṣads, and 6.5-6 is an important teaching in its own right. In the remainder of this section we argue that *ChāndUp* 6.5-6 may be elucidated with the help of a parallel text, *BṛhUp* IV.2.2-4 and Śaṁkara's commentary on the latter. This commentary turns out to give a full description of a path to the Ātman which we will call the "path of the Subtle *prāṇa* All-self". The "path of the Subtle *prāṇa* All-self" is important because it involves the "space in the heart" as well as a deeper "deep sleep" stage (indicated by the "channels in the heart"), and gives hints on how it is possible to pass from this deeper stage to knowledge/realization of the Ātman. In addition, it represents a direction of inner discipline which may be involved in several of the Upaniṣadic dream and deep sleep teachings. For although described by Śaṁkara more than a millennium after the Upaniṣads, something like this path seems to be referred to already in *Bṛhadāraṇyaka Upaniṣad*, as having been practiced by Yājñavakya (sec. 19). Assuming therefore that the "path of the Subtle *prāṇa* All-self" is basically Upaniṣadic, the section in the *Dahara Vidyā* on the channels of the heart seems to be teaching an approach similar to the "path of the subtle *prāṇa* All-self," but involving instead of the latter an alternative "subtle *prāṇa*, Cosmos-encompassing, Sun-related self" (sec. 20). This suggests that the real purpose of the "channels of the heart" section may be to explain the passage from a stage of *dahara ākāśa* to realization of the Ātman in 1.1-1.5 by using this "path of a subtle *prāṇa*, Cosmos-encompassing, Sun-related self". So perhaps this section was later added to the *Dahara Vidyā* (end of sec. 20). In any case, the *Dahara Vidyā* and also other *vijñāna vidyās* we have been dicussing may be envisaging something like a "path of the subtle *prāṇa* All-self" to go from the stage of *dahara ākāśa* to true realization of Ātman (sec. 21).

***BṛhUp* IV.2.2-4:**[177] **Text.** This text is a continuation and climax of Yājñavalkya's teachings on *Vāc, Prāṇa*, and so on being Brahman (*BṛhUp* IV.1.1-7). King Janaka, after listening to Yājñavalkya's explanations, "descending from his cushion and approaching," asks for deeper instruction. Yājñavalkya responds with a question: "Whither, when released from here (i.e., when you die), will you go?" When the king admits that he does not know, the sage says:

IV.2.2. *Indha* (the Kindler) by name is this person here in the right eye. Him verily, who is that *indha* people cryptically call "Indra," for the gods are fond of the cryptic, as it were, and dislike the evident.

2.3. Now that which has the form of a person in the left eye is his wife, Virāj. Their meeting-place is the space in the heart. Their food is the red lump in the heart. Their covering is the net-like network in the heart. The path that they go is that channel which goes upward from the heart. Like a hair divided a thousandfold, so are the channels called *hitā*, which are established within the heart. Through these flows that which flows on [i.e. the subtle food—a wordplay]. Therefore that [soul which is composed of *Indha* and Virāj] is, as it were, an eater of finer food than is this bodily self.

2.4. The eastern breaths are his eastern quarter. The southern breaths are his southern quarter. The western breaths are his western quarter. The northern breaths are his northern quarter. The upper breaths are his upper quarter [i.e. the zenith]. The lower breaths are his lower quarter [i.e. the nadir]. All the breaths are all his quarters.

This Self (Ātman) is "not," "not" (*neti, neti*). It is unseizable, for it cannot be seized. It is indestructible, for it cannot be destroyed. It is unattached, for it does not attach itself. It is unbound. It does not tremble. It is not injured.

Indha, the kindler, is explained in *ŚatBr* IV.1.1.2 in the context of Creation as "the *prāṇa* in the midst", *madhye prāṇaḥ*, the fundamental energy *before* creation. "He [the fundamental energy], by his power (*indriya*), kindled those (other) vital airs from the midst; and inasmuch as he kindled (*indh-*), he is the kindler (*indha*): the kindler indeed, —him they call 'Indra' mystically (esoterically), for the gods love the mystic".[178] So it is this fundamental energy which is "this person here in the right eye", which is that which shines in a person's right eye when we look him or her in the eyes. Next, "what has the form of a person in the left eye is his wife, Virāj", the female, diversity-producing principle in the Puruṣa hymn. "There (Puruṣa's and Virāj's) union is the space in the heart, *antarhṛdaya ākāśa*." "Union" here is *saṁstava*, literally "(place of) praising together," in harmony and oneness. Since the context of discussion is what happens to the self at death (cf. IV.2.1; this is also confirmed in the next sentence, cf. below), this means that at the time of death there is a state or stage when the self (= Self) is in complete union or harmony with the material creation, the diversity of the world. This state is the space within the heart (intuitively this also makes sense because within the space of the heart is placed the entire universe, *Dahara Vidyā* 1.3). "Their path for going together (*saṁcaraṇī*) is that channel (*nāḍī*) which goes upward from the heart." This describes the path by which the Soul should leave the body (which is then left only a corpse). This interpretation is also supported by *ChāndUp* VIII.6.6 which is completely parallel: "One of these (101 *nāḍīs*) passes up to crown of the head. Going up by it, one goes to immortality (*amṛtatva*)." Both Yājñavalkya and the *Dahara Vidyā* are talking about many channels enveloping the heart one of which goes upward. Both are dealing with the case of a person bound for the Supreme (Yājñavalkya in v. 1 had extolled Janaka for how fully prepared he was for the journey, merger with the Supreme, and the description is intended for him, Janaka). And both are talking about what happens at death.

But at this point the teaching suddenly changes character.[178] The topic is suddenly not anymore death, but general facts of deeper inner experience. Through the extremely fine channels called *hitā*[179] flows something extremely subtle. This flowing subtle is like subtle food to the individual self (*Indha* and Virāj in the heart). Presumably this means that in the state when the individual self is in oneness in the space in the heart, there arises a still deeper state characterized by awareness of the subtle that is flowing in the channels called *hitā*.

That awareness is like an absorbedness, an absorbedness into something similar to taking in food.

Śaṁkara's Commentary. Śaṁkara's commentary on the text is remarkably esoteric. He interprets *Indha*, the union of *Indha* and Virāj in the space in the heart, and this last new state as the Self in the waking state, in the dream state, and in deep sleep, respectively. In addition, he regards the Self in the dream state as "the Self identified with mind", and the Self in the deep sleep state as "the Self identified with subtle *Prāṇa*", resp. To some extent these identifications represent a systematization which appears first in *Māṇḍūkya Upaniṣad*, much later than the Upaniṣadic text. The Self in the waking state is *Vaiśvānara*, the Self in the dream state is *Taijasa*, literally "(the one) endowed with light, *tejas*," and the Self in the deep sleep state, *Prājñā*. But at the same time Śaṁkara does appear to have a very specific understanding of the whole *vidyā*.

> He, this *Taijasa* [self] that is experienced as (*bhūta*, literally "become") the heart, is supported by the subtle-become *prāṇa* (*sūkṣma-bhūta prāṇa*), [he] becomes this *prāṇa* indeed. Of this sage, who attained *Taijasa* by proceeding from *Vaiśvānara*, who has reached the heart-self, and who has reached the *prāṇa*-self of the heart-self,[a] the *prāṇas* in front are the eastern quarter, the *prāṇas* on the right side are the southern quarter, . . ., all [his] *prāṇas* are all quarters. Knowing this, by the approach of (his) selfhood to the [subtle] *prāṇa* that has the nature of an all-self[b] (i.e. by the method of identification with the [subtle] *prāṇa* thought of as being everywhere), he becomes one gone to all-self-ness [a state of having all for his self]. Having withdrawn (or drawn together, collected, *upa-saṁ-hṛtya*) that all-self into the inner self (*pratyag-ātman*), he attains the state (*bhāva*) of Seer of what is seen, the Self [described by] "*neti neti*," the *turīya* [state].[c] [180]

With this, the outlines of the process described in *BṛhUp* IV.2.4 become reasonably clear. The state of the union of *Indha* and Virāj in the heart is re-interpreted as the *Taijasa* or dream self, which has thus "become" the heart. This *Taijasa* self becomes aware that it is supported by a still deeper level, the level of subtle *Prāṇa* in the heart, equated by Śaṁkara here with the "subtle" which according to the text is flowing in the channels *hitā*. The sage in the *Taijasa* condition thereupon identifies himsrlf with this (awareness at the level of) "subtle *Prāṇa*", or in Śaṁkara's terms he "becomes" this (subtle) *Prāṇa.* And finally, he identifies himself in this "subtle *Prāṇa*" state with the whole world. The eastern quarter (and its deity, cf. below) is the *subtle prāṇa* which he is aware of in front, the southern quarter (and its deity) is the subtle *prāṇa* which he is aware of on the right, and so on. The condition that results from this is that "all the quarters [of space, or of the world] are all the *prāṇas*," i.e., the entire external world has been assimilated to and become unified with the subtle *prāṇa* awareness. The resulting state may be called the "state of the (subtle) *prāṇa* All-self," a state where there is the conviction/knowledge that one's subtle *prāṇa*-self is All. At the very end, the sage collects or withdraws (*upa-saṁ-hṛ-*) this (subtle) All-self in his inner self, the *pratyag-ātman*. This, according to Śaṁkara, permanently dissolves the sage's self in the inner self and at the same time universalizes and infinitizes the inner self to the One Self which contains All, as in *Dahara Vidyā* 1.3-1.5. The *pratyag-ātman* is defined by *KaṭhaUp* II.1.1:

> . . . [normally] one looks outward (elsewhere), not inside oneself. [But] some sage, seeking immortality, saw the inner self (*pratyag-ātman*), with eyes turned inward.

Withdrawing the "subtle *prāṇa* All-self" into the inner self is likely to involve giving up paying attention to the external world *cum* subtle *Prāṇa* All-self, thereby waking up to a still more subtle level, viz. the level of Ātman.

The "Path of the (Subtle) *Prāṇa* All-Self". The preceding represents the first really detailed account of a path to realization of the Ātman. The path is partly yogic, in the sense that it involves several deeper stages that are normally presumably first reached in meditation (may be in *prāṇa-yoga* as in the *Yoga Upaniṣads*) and then become established in the personality in the waking state. These are

(1) A stage of union of the self (*Indha*) and *Virāj* in the space within the heart. This represents, according to the text, a state of one-ness or harmony in one's heart with the world. Śaṁkara calls the self when it is in this condition and identified with it, *taijasa,* i.e., "shining [as mind only]," or the self that has "become the heart," *hṛdaya-bhūta*, or

simply the heart-self, *hṛdaya-ātman*. This stage, therefore, corresponds to the (stage of) *dahara ākāśa*. Next, Śaṁkara distinguishes a still deeper stage that comes after the stage of *dahara ākāśa* has been reached.

(2) This is the stage where the "heart-self" has become aware of the "subtle *Prāṇa*" (*sūkṣma-bhūta Prāṇa*) by which it is "supported" (*vi-dhriyamāṇa*), and begins to identify itself with this "subtle *Prāṇa*". The fact that the state of the heart-self is supported by, and leads to perception of, still deeper "subtle *Prāṇa*" harks back to Upaniṣadic teachings to the effect that the heart is based on *Prāṇa* (*BṛhUp* III.9.26, cf. the next section), or that the *prāṇas* are in the heart (*Chāndogya Upaniṣad*). (These latter teachings are perhaps foreshadowed by *ŚatBr* XIV.3.2.3, which says that the "overlord of the *prāṇas*" in a certain mantra in *Vājasaneyī Saṁhitā* is the mind, "because in the mind are all the *prāṇas* established".) Next comes a third step or stage, viz.,

(3) identifying one's "subtle *prāṇa*" self in stage (2) with the Directions of space, or the Quarters. This appears to be also a yogic technique (as in the *prāṇa*-yoga of the *Yoga Upaniṣads*), or may conceivably be a yoga in the sense of the *Gītā*. This step or stage is then finally transcended by

(4) an attitude of *neti, neti*. For it is presumably just from such *neti, neti*, together with reliance of *pratyag-ātman* different from the "subtle *prāṇa* All-self," that the Infinite Ātman spontaneously appears. This Ātman will then naturally be *neti, neti* to a philosopher or "outside observer" who is trying to describe it or define it "objectively".

The path as a whole therefore involves, as far as meditation is concerned, both yogic type practice (meditation and concentration to the point of lack of body awareness, and operating at a level of "subtle *Prāṇa*"), and a *jñāna* element (discrimination between the "subtle *prāṇa* All-self" that one has become, and the formless *pratyag ātman*). It is not clear to me whether perception of superfine conduits *hitā* and something flowing in them is a necessary component of this process. The conduits called *hitā* are prominent in other Upaniṣadic texts, but for Śaṁkara they only signal a level of "being subtle *Prāṇa*," what he calls the "*Prāṇa*-self of the heart-self" (the heart-self being the self when it is unified with Virāj in the space within the heart). Thereafter, the *hitā* play no more role. It seems that one could go through the meditative levels involved without perception of the *hitā*, but I do not know. Similarly it is not clear whether these meditative levels require *prāṇāyāma*, breathing practice. In later literature *prāṇāyāma* and *pratyāhāra*, withdrawal of awareness from the senses, is the royal road to the subtle *Prāṇa* and the subtle geography in the body (cf. above). The subtle *Prāṇa* in the heart is the ultimate of this subtle geography. But it seems quite possible that Śaṁkara's "subtle *Prāṇa*-self" or "*Prāṇa*-self of the heart-self" also arises naturally in the course of meditation and spiritual life centered on *bhakti*, or on *jñāna*-paths like *neti, neti.* In that case it would not necessarily be thought of as subtle *Prāṇa,* however, but appear simply as a specific spiritual state. The subsequent identification of the subtle *Prāṇa*-self with the entire extension of the external world (a deliberate procedure strikingly similar to many other such procedures in the *Yoga Upaniṣads*) may also occur naturally in *bhakti* or *jñāna* paths as a result of attitudes such as "I am He (the Lord)" and "the Lord is All". In this context we may also note again that while the meditative-yogic component is no doubt important and perhaps even central, the identification of the "subtle *Prāṇa* self in the heart" with the Quarters of the physical world around one must also be lived, not only practiced in meditation. This is simply the nature of spiritual life. One somehow lives the levels one has reached in meditation in one's daily life.

19. *BṛhUp* III.9.19-26

As it stands, the particular, simultaneously yogic and *jñāna* path outlined by Śaṁkara in sec. 18 [A] above represents a later development. But it seems that versions of this path are implied in some of the *vijñāna*-of-the-heart *vidyās* in this and the previous chapter. In this section we argue that *BṛhUp* III.9.19-26, the end of the account of Yājñavalkya's and Śākalya's wisdom contest, suggests that something like the path [A] was already well-known in Upaniṣadic times. Then in sec. 20, we consider whether the path of the "subtle *prāṇa* All-self" is implicated in the passage from the space in the heart to the Ātman in *Dahara Vidyā* 1.1-1.5 and related texts.

***BṛhUp* III.9.19-26.** As noted in sec. 4, the final segment of he

Yājñavalkya-Śākalya dialogue[181] is a *vidyā* in its own right, and is divided into two parts. After Yājñavalkya has consistently handled Śākalya's questions, the latter finally asks him what Brahman it was the knowledge of which enabled him (Yājñavalkya) to talk beyond (*ati-vad*) all the learned Brahmins in the assembly (*BṛhUp* III.9.19). Yājñavalkya responds that he knows the quarters together with their gods and their bases, and then expounds this knowledge in *BṛhUp* III.9.20-25. This is Part I of the *Vidyā* and was translated in sec. 4 above. The element in this Part of interest here is the unusual phrasing "What deity *are you* in this eastern quarter" etc. (italics added) when Śākalya's asks Yājñavalkya which deities he knew associated with the different directions. Śaṁkara in his commentary suggests that Śākalya knew that Yājñavlkya through *upāsanā* was identified with the quarters, and thus with the whole Universe—as a result of *upāsanā*, he saw the whole Universe as his self.

> [B] *What deity are you identified with in the east*?—'what deity are you who are identified with the Quarters?' Yājñavalkya, realizing his own heart or mind—divided in five forms according to the Quarters and identified with the Quarters,—and through it the whole universe, as his own self, stood facing the East, with the conviction that he was the Quarters. We gather this from his claim that he knew the quarters with their supports [= bases]. Śākalya, according to Yājñavalkya's statement, asks, 'What deity are you identified with in this Quarter?' Everywhere in the Vedas it is stated that in this very life one becomes identified with and attains the god one meditates upon. It will be stated further on, "Being a god, he attains the gods" (IV.1.2). The idea is this: You are identified with the Quarters; who is your presiding deity in the East?—as the East, which deity are you united with?. . .[182]

So accoding to Śaṁkara, Śākalya is assuming that Yājñavalkya was by *upāsanā* identified with the Quarters. This by itself is sufficient to suggest that Yājñavalkya's *upāsanā* must have been similar to the process in *BṛhUp* IV.2.2-4 and sec. 18 [A] above, specifically to step (3). This conjecture is confirmed by *BṛhUp* III.9.26, or Part II of the final exchange in the Yājñavalkya-Śākalya dialogue. Recall that in sec. 4 we only looked at III.9.20-25 because we were only interested in the heart being the foundation of things. But there is one more last exchange between the sages, III.9.26, which is actually the climax of the whole dialogue and *vidyā*.

> III.9.26 (Śākalya:) "On what are you and [your] self based?"
> (Yājñavalkya:) "[On] *prāṇa*."
> "And on what is *prāṇa* based?"
> "[On] the *apāna* [breath]."
> "And on what is the *apāna* [breath] based?"
> "[On] the *vyāna* [breath]."
> "And on what is the *vyāna* [breath] based?"
> "[On] the *samāna* breath. That Self is *neti, neti*. It is ungraspable for it is not grasped . . . (as in Table 5.3, up to 'it is not injured'). These are the eight abodes, the eight worlds, the eight gods, the eight persons [taught earlier in III.9.10-17]. He who, having taken these persons apart and put them together again, goes beyond them, He is the Upaniṣadic Person about which I ask you. If you do not explain him to me, your head will fall off."
> Śākalya did not know Him, [and] verily his head fell off. Robbers took his bones away, thinking they were someone else's.

In III.9.20-24, Śākalya always stopped his questioning when Yājñavalkya got to the heart. But now, in a final effort, he tries to get to the root of Yājñavalkya's superior knowledge and asks on what he (Yājñavalkya) and his self are based. Yājñavalkya essentially tells him that when one looks for the basis of the heart, one finds that it is *Prāṇa*, and when one goes still deeper and looks for the basis of that, then one finds that that basis is the One Self, the Self which is described as *neti, neti*. So we have here the same stages as in *BṛhUp* IV.2.2-4 and sec. 18 [A] above, but in the terminology of "is based on". All powers of a person are based on the heart (corresponding to *dahara ākāśa* in *BṛhUp* IV.2.3). The heart, the person as a whole and his self, are based on the *prāṇas* (corresponding to Śaṁkara's subtle *prāṇa*-self in [A], and the *prāṇas* identified with the Quarters in *BṛhUp* IV.2.4). The *prāṇas* finally are based on the One Self, which is *neti neti* (described in the same terms in *BṛhUp* IV.2.4). In view of this correspondence and the fact that Yājñavalkya is the Quarters, it seems clear that *BṛhUp* III.19-26 presupposes the same kind of inner practice (yogic level meditation cum living in everyday life) as the "path of the 'subtle *prāṇa* All-self'. "[183]

20. A "Cosmos-Encompassing Sun-Related Self" Equivalent to the "Subtle *Prāṇa* All-Self"

We can summarize the argument in the preceding two sections by saying that there seems to be presupposed in the old Upaniṣads a certain (type of) inner path by which the Ātman is reached by meditation in the heart. This path, dubbed "the path of the subtle *prāṇa* All-Self," is indicated in *BṛhUp* IV.2.2-4 and explained in Śaṁkara's commentary on this text, and is also alluded to in the dialogue with Śākalya. Its most characteristic feature is the identification of oneself, at an extremely fundamental level (the level of the "subtle *prāṇas* in the heart"), with the (Deities of) the four Directions and thus with the Universe. But *BṛhUp* IV.2.2-4 was brought in as a parallel text to elucidate *ChāndUp* VIII.6. Is the same type of inner path presupposed there also?

Similarities Between *Dahara Vidyā* 6.5-6 and *BṛhUp* IV.2.3a. At the beginning of sec. 18 we noted the similarities between *Dahara Vidyā* 6.5-6 and *BṛhUp* IV.2.3 (first part = a) which led us to regard the latter as a parallel text. To these must added an additional point: In both texts knowledge of the soul's exit from the body at death is discussed in connection with knowledge of the channels *hitā* in yogic-meditative states. In *BṛhUp* IV.2.3-4 the switch from what happens at death to the semi-yogic process of realizing the Self which is *neti-neti* (v. 4) by going deeper and deeper into the heart is quite natural. For in *BṛhUp* IV.2.1, Janaka comes down from his high cushions and asks for real instruction as opposed to the preliminary teachings he had received up to then (*BṛhUp* IV.1.1-7). And at the end, in *BṛhUp* IV.2.4, he offers himself and his whole kingdom because he had reached the state of fearlessness, which is precisely associated with the realization of Ātman by *neti, neti* (cf. chr. 5). (So in fact, one might speculate, Janaka had the "subtle *prāṇa* in the heart"—state already in him because of his high spiritual level and all he needed was the last one or two steps, which came naturally as he was listening to Yājñavalkya). In *Dahara Vidyā* 6.1-6, we have the same juxtaposition of events at death and yogic knowledge, but the order of topics is different. First comes the general relationship between the channels *hitā* and the Sun; then (possibly application of this to) deep sleep (6.3); and then the period right before death (6.4) and death (6.5-6.6).

Some connection of this whole "channels in the heart" section with the preceding *Dahara Vidyā* 1.1-5.4 must of course be assumed. For the text which follows the "channels in the heart," the *Indra-Virocana Vidyā, ChāndUp* VIII.713, is a kind of adjunct to *ChāndUp* VIII.1.1-5.4, and if the channels of the heart section was entirely unrelated to the latter, it would be difficult to explain why it was placed between that text and its adjunct. Thus *ChāndUp* VIII.6 must be somehow related to the larger *Dahara* development *ChāndUp* VIII.1.1-5.4. The simplest assumption would be that it indeed alludes to the same type of the path of the *prāṇa* All-self, and that it was added to the main development *ChāndUp* 1.1-5.4 as a kind of semi-independent yogic statement in order to provide some perspective on the detailed passage from *dahara ākāśa* to Ātman in *Dahara Vidyā* 1.3-1.5.

***ChāndUp* VIII.6 as Path of a "Cosmos-Encompassing Sun-Related Self".** There is however also another possibility. The whole "channels of the heart" section can be regarded as drawing a grand picture of how a person is both life and soul connected to the Sun through the rays of the Sun. The rays of the Sun are connected with his essential life element, the channels *hitā*, and they are at the same time the conduits by which the self after death gets to the Sun (v. 6.5). So the section is drawing a grand picture of a single connectivity which unites the individual and the Sun, and which makes him akin to the Sun. Note especially the deliberately mystical allusion that the Sun is reddish brown, white, blue, yellow and red, just like finest essence, presumably the "subtle" *prāṇa*, from which the channels *hitā* arise, in 6.1. In other words, the message is: man's inmost essence is contiguous and of one piece with the Sun. Now the Sun's rays are all-pervading, in other words, the connectivity that unites man and the Sun pervades and encompasses the entire cosmos. Furthermore, that connectivity also involves the subtle *prāṇa* in the heart, because the rays are also channels of the heart into which the individual withdraws in deep sleep (*Dahara Vidyā* 6.3), and where he then contacts the "bright Power," *tejas*, the Sun. We may therefore speculate that instead of a method of identifying the subtle *prāṇas* with the Quarters or the Universe, the text is suggesting that one regard (*upās-*!) oneself, or rather oneself at the level of and experienced as the subtle *prāṇa* in the heart, as pervading the cosmos by this cosmos-encompassing connectivity with the Sun. This framework of thought would be different from but equivalent to a deliberate identification of oneself at the level of and experienced as the subtle *prāṇas* with the Directions and would give rise to a stage of "cosmos-pervading, Sun-related self". And we might speculate further that from this, the Ātman could be realized by a step like withdrawal of the cosmos-pervading Sun-related self into the inner self.

A cosmos-pervading, Sun-related self seems very old-Upaniṣadic. Something similar may already be taught in the *Satya Brahma Vidyā BṛhUp* V.5.2. But whether that represents a viable path to the Ātman of *Dahara Vidyā* 1.3-1.5, a la the "path of the subtle *prāṇa* All-self," is purely a guess. (The "path of the subtle *prāṇa* All-self" represents a path to the Ātman because Śaṁkara regards it as such.) If it was (and I am inclined to think so), it would explain both the content of the channels of the heart section and why it was added to the rest of the *Dahara Vidyā* (1.1-5.4). For the section teaches to develop a cosmos-pervading, Sun-related self at the level of the subtle *prāṇas* in the heart, and the teacher who added the section added it because he thought this instruction was needed for a passage from *dahara ākāśa* to the Ātman in *Dahara Vidyā* 1.1-1.5. Again, however, that is only a possibility. And in any case all this still does not answer the question whether the *Dahara* teaching 1.1-1.5 has a specific method of realizing the Ātman in mind. For the view that the passage from *dahara ākāśa* to Ātman involves the path of a subtle *prāṇa*, Sun-related, Cosmos-encompassing self may have only been the understanding of the teacher who added the section on the channels of the heart, and may not necessarily have been the intent of the *Dahara* teaching.

21. The Full *Dahara Vidyā* and *BṛhUp* IV.3-4

In this section we merely note that the Full *Dahara Vidyā* (including the postscript *ChāndUp* VIII.6) shows a similar trend of spiritual stages and discussion as *BṛhUp* IV.3.1-IV.4.6, the first third of the greatest Yājñavalkya-Janaka dialogue. This correspondence illustrates that old Upaniṣadic thought shows also some similar larger scale strands. It also raises the possibility that both *vidyās*, and more generally all the *vidyās* involving the "channels in the heart" and deep sleep, ultimately represent paths involving the subtle *prāṇas* in the heart (such as the path of the subtle *prāṇa* All-self).

We saw in chr. 5.21 that *BṛhUp* IV.3.1-34 (K) proceeded in four stages, corresponding to four stages of inner spiritual evolution. First there was an initial block (3.1-3.18) which dealt with realization of one-self as *vijñāna-maya* and light in the heart. Then came two verses on the self in deep sleep, whose import remained obscure (3.19-20); then a block of verses dealing with realization of the one Ātman (3.21-3.30); and finally another block dealing with a still further stage dubbed "merger into the Supreme" (3.32, "the Seer becomes the Ocean, One, Non-dual, . . .," and 3.33 on Bliss). There is a definite relationship between this scheme and the stages of text and inner development in *Dahara Vidyā* 1.1-5.4 which is shown in Fig. 6.1. The two beginning stages correspond exactly. As noted earlier, they represent beginning and intermediate levels of *vijñāna*. The correspondence between the texts may be extended further to include the common sequence of topics "events during coma before death" and "events at death". For after *BṛhUp* IV.3.34, Yājñavalkya turns to a discussion of death and dying (*BṛhUp* IV.3.35-4.6 (K)), which is similar and related to *Dahara Vidyā* 6.1-6 discussed in the last section.

The Same Process in all Three Deep Sleep *Vidyās*? The structure shown in Fig. 6.1 applies also to the Ajātaśatru teaching and *BṛhUp* IV. 2.2-4. In Ajātaśatru's teaching, *BṛhUp* IV. 2.2-4, and the *Antarjyotir Vidyā*, a stage of *dahara ākāśa* or "in the heart" is followed by a deeper stage involving the channels in the heart in the context of deep sleep (see Fig. 5.1), and this is in turn without further explanation followed by a description of (knowledge) of Ātman. The first two of these stages may thus correspond to stages (1) and (2) in our discussion of the "subtle *prāṇa* All-self" in sec. 18. For the dream and *svapna* levels in the Ajātaśatru and *Antarjyotir vidyās*, for example, both lead to knowledge of a *vijñāna-maya* self in the heart that stands behind the dream and *svapna* stages, which is just a different aspect of the stage of *dahara ākāśa*. And the deep sleep stages in these *vidyās*, which we earlier interpreted merely as "deeper in the heart states" (cf. chr. 5.16), may well refer to something like Śaṁkara's stage (2) in sec. 18. For Śaṁkara himself regards that stage as equivalent to knowledge of *Prajnā* or Ātman in the deep sleep condition in *Māṇḍūkya Upaniṣad*. Thus all the major "*vijñāna* in the heart" *vidyās* discussed so far may utilise some kind of technique involving the subtle *prāṇas* in the heart. But this is only a possibility.

	3.7-3.18	3.19-3.20	3.21 only	3.22-3.30	3.32-3.33
Bṛh-Up IV.3	self=*vijñānamaya*, light in heart, same in different states	*hitā*, colors,	*prajñā-ātman, āpta-kāma, śokāntara*	not a father, only one seer,	one seer ocean, *advaita*
	different *svapnas*	deep sleep	(same phase)		

	1.1-1.3	6.3	1.3-1.5	3.4
Full *Dahara Vidyā*	*dahara ākāśa*	*hitā*, colors, deep sleep	*satya-kāma viśoka* (8 qualities)	*param-jyotiḥ svarūpa*

Fig. 6.1. Correspondence of Stages in *BṛhUp* IV.3.1-34 (K) (top band) and Full *Dahara Vidyā* (lower band).

In later Vedānta, the dream and deep sleep phases are discussed in terms of the progression gross ⟶ subtle⟶ causal. I do not have a good understanding of the "spiritual life realities" involved in "causal" and how they might be connected to "subtle *prāṇa* in the heart".

22. *MuṇḍUp* II.2: The Path of Merger by Means of Om

We saw in the last several sections that some of the major "*vijñāna* in the heart"*vidyās* may involve a "subtle *prāṇas* in the heart" approach. But we also saw that the understanding of the *dahara ākāśa* as the subtle sky of consciousness or the firmament of the heart as in *Mahā-NārUp* XII.16 = Varenne 231-232 may well have been associated with meditation using Om. In this section we consider *MuṇḍUp* II.2,[184] a text which like *Mahā-NārUp* XII.16 teaches meditation in the heart to reach the Ātman, and where this meditation involves Om. It is conceivable that *Dahara Vidyā* 1.1-1.5 at least originally presupposed a path of Om similar to *MuṇḍUp* II.2. (It is also possible that *Dahara Vidyā* 1.1-1.5 involved no additional special inner practice, only letting the formulations of the text sink deeply into one's self and living in accordance with the inner states that develop.).

***MuṇḍUp* II.2:[184] Text.** *Muṇḍaka Upaniṣad*[185] is a carefully structured poetical composition of 66 stanzas in three parts (called *muṇḍakas*).

Each part is divided into two sections, with each section devoted to a single theme. In particular, II.1 deals with the Puruṣa, and II.2 with meditation on the Ātman in the heart using Om. Because *Muṇḍaka Upaniṣad* is one of the middle group Upaniṣads (see chr. 2.1), the text has a different character from the "*vijñāna* in the heart" *vidyās* in the old Upaniṣads and this must be taken into account.

***MuṇḍUp* II.2**

II.2.1. Manifest, well-fixed, known as moving in the secret [place, i.e. the heart], the great Support.
[In] here this is fixed—[all] that moves, breathes and winks.
What that is, that know as *sat* (being), as *asat* (non-being), as the supreme treasure—
[That know as that] which stands beyond the understanding of creatures.

2.2. [That] which is luminous (*arcimat*), and subtler than the subtle (*aṇu*),
and in which all the worlds and the dwellers in them are fixed (*nihita*),
That is that imperishable Brahman.
It is *Prāṇa*, as well as Speech and Mind.

2.3. Having taken as bow the great weapon of the Upaniṣads, one should put on it the arrow sharpened by *upāsanā*.
Having drawn [it] with the thought (*cetas*) gone to that [Brahman-] state,
penetrate, dear one, that Imperishable as the target indeed.

2.4. The bow is the *praṇava* (= the syllable Om), the self is the arrow, Brahman is called the target.
It is to be hit without distraction,
One should become absorbed in it (literally, of It consisting), like the arrow [-tip is absorbed into the target].

2.5. [He] in whom heaven, earth, and mid-space is sewn, and mind together with all *prāṇas*,
Him indeed know as the One Ātman.
Give up all other words.
That one is the bridge of (i.e., to) immortality.

2.6. Where the *nāḍīs* are brought together like the spokes in the hub of a wheel (i.e., in the heart),
within [that] this very [Self] moves on its own, becoming

many.

"Om," in this manner (*evam*) meditate (*dhyāyatha*) on the Self.

May there be success for you for [reaching] the other shore beyond the darkness [of mundane existence].

2.7. [He] who is all knowing (*sarva-jña*), all wise (*sarva-vid*), whose is this glory in the world (in creation),—

Indeed (*hi*) in the divine (or luminous, *divya*) Brahman-city, in the ether (*vyoman*) is this Self established.

2.8. Consisting of mind, [he is the] leader of *prāṇa* and body, established in food, controlling the heart.

By *vijñāna* the wise perceive fully

the bliss-nature, the immortal, which shines diversely (or appears diversely, *vi-bhāti*).

2.9. The knot of the heart is cut,

all doubts are dispelled,

and his deeds perish in the seeing [of Brahman],

the Higher and the Lower.

2.10. In the golden highest sheath (*kośa*)

is Brahman, stainless, without parts.

That is pure (*śubhra*), the light of lights (*jyotiṣāṁjyotiḥ*), that is what the knowers of the Self know.

2.11. There the Sun does not shine, nor moon and star, there these lightnings do not shine, where [then] this fire?

All shines [only] according to Him Shining (or: following His Shining).

By His Shine, all this shines.

2.12. The Immortal is indeed Brahman, Brahman is in front, Brahman is behind, to the right and to the left.

Below and above it extends. All this (world) is Brahman indeed. It is the greatest.

The Text as Poetic Evocation of a Whole Direction of Highest Wisdom. There is a great difference in style and spirit between this text and the old Upaniṣadic texts we have studied. In the latter, the student absorbs the highest wisdom for the life that he will lead as a Brahmin, as it is handed down in his own or another *śākhā* or Vedic school. This wisdom is the essence that underlies his activities for a livelihood as a priest, and of his personal religious, ritual metaphysical and wisdom life. It pervades his image of society and of the role of his caste in society, and it is for him as real and given and something that is to be worked with as a part of his body. Here in *Muṇḍaka Upaniṣad*, however, the situation is quite different. There is of course the Higher Wisdom and its exaltation. But the main aim is to communicate that Wisdom in a way that is inspired and inspiring. The Higher Knowledge is almost treated as something to be chosen by the listener, not something that by general consent is both the foundation and culmination of the society and of all one's activites and personal endeavors in life.

As a result, the *Muṇḍaka* text has a rather different character than that of the texts of the old Upaniṣads. In the old Upaniṣads and Āraṇyakas, a teaching is typically developed from its own inner resources in a single movement. Only now and then will there be a comment that the knowledge that has just been taught is the same as some other well-known knowledge. But here—and this is typical of the middle group Upaniṣads generally—many terms and metaphors are brought together, carrying essential connotations of well-known teachings from different layers of the Vedic tradition, and are used evocatively and with poetic effect to paint something like a broad canvas of a whole Area of Higher Knowledge. Here this is the Area of the Knowledge of, and the path to the Knowledge of, the Ātman in the heart. It is instructive to list some of the major terms. Thus in v. 1, "*samnihitam guhācaram*," "fully fixed (*nihitam*), moving (*car*) in the secret place (*guhā*, the heart)" is reminiscent of *TaittUp* II.1.2, "*nihitam guhāyām*. . .," "set down in the secret place". And *samarpitam* (same verse) recalls the *arpita* of *Atharva Veda* X.8 which we drew on in sec. 12 to get the correct perspective for *Dahara Vidyā* 1.3-1.5. In v. 2, "in which are set (*nihita*) the worlds and the dwellers in the worlds" is formed similar to "all that is placed (*samāhita*) within it [the space in the heart = Brahman]," *Dahara Vidyā* 1.3. Another echo comes in v. 5, "[He] in whom heaven, earth, and mid-space are woven (*otam*)." This recalls *BṛhUp* III.6, where Vācaknavī of the Garga lineage asks Yājñavalkya: "Since all this world is lengthwise and crosswise interwoven with (*otam* and *protam*, a standard expression) the waters, what then are the waters interwoven with?" When Yājñavalkya answers that the waters are interwoven etc. with the Wind, Vācaknavī repeats her question with "the Waters" replaced by "the Wind". The question-answer series then continues in the same pattern for a dozen or so exchanges, with always the same verbal frame (*otam* and *protam* in both question and answer), until it ends with "the worlds of Brahman". *Setu*, "bridge (of immortality)" in the same verse alludes to the bridge or dam (*setu*) in *Dahara Vidyā* 4.1 and 4.2 which, "having crossed, the blind one becomes no longer blind" etc. (4.2). (Besides these two places, the word occurs only at *BṛhUp* IV.4.24, also a parallel to the *Dahara* teaching). In v. 6 the *nāḍīs* or channels of the heart are familiar "within the space of the heart" language. The image of the spokes in the hub of a wheel is old but the application to the *nāḍīs* is new. The Self "moving within" harks back to v. 1. The divine or luminous "city of Brahman," *brahma-pura*, and the "ether," *vyoman*, in which the Ātman is established (v. 7) are again familiar from *Dahara Vidyā* 1.1 (in *Muṇḍaka Upaniṣad, brahmapura* denotes the heart, though) and *TaittUp* II.1.2, resp. *Mano-maya*, "consisting of mind," and *prāṇa-śarīra-netā*, "the leader who has *prāṇa* for his body," in the next verse echo the *Śāṇḍilya Vidyā* and the Five Sheaths *Vidyā*. Further allusions to the latter come with *anne . . . . samidhāya*, "seated in food," and "by *vijñāna* they see the immortal of the form of bliss" later in the verse. V. 10 finally makes the same transition from knowledge of the self in the heart to Infinite Supreme Knowledge which we found in the *Dahara* and *Antar-jyotir Vidyās*. For in "in the highest gloden sheath," *hiraṇmaya pare kośe*, the term *kośa*, "sheath," alludes to the (space within) the heart (cf. "the sheath consisting of the space within the heart, *hṛdi-ākāśa-mayakośa, MaitrUp* VI.27, above, sec. 9). But at the same time the reference of the verse as a whole is to highest knowledge only. This is clear formally from *para*, "highest," and *śubhra*, "pure," which is used in *Muṇḍaka Upaniṣad* only at this level. We already saw that "the light of lights," *jyotiṣām jyotiḥ*, and the following verse "By Its [Brahman's] Shine all this [world] here shines," are implied in the *Antarjyotir Vidyā*.

Use of Om. Nevertheless, besides this massive use of connotations and resonances of key terms from earlier literature, we also see the old Wisdom shining in a new garb. This new garb consists of new images and new emphases which dominate the text, and includes also a new method of meditation. The new images very likely correspond to specific experiential elements. They include (1) the image of the self "moving" (*car*, walking, showing behavior) in the cave of the heart (vs. 1, 6); (2) the recurring images of Brahman being set (*nihita*) in the heart and the world being fixed in Brahman; and (3) the image of meditation and spiritual life as shooting the arrow of the self with the bow of Om into the target Brahman. The last has the sub-image of (4) the self merging into Brahman just like the arrow becomes one with the target (vs. 3-4). Together with meditation using Om, these images define a new path to the knowledge declared in the *Dahara Vidyā.* In this path there is still an initial stage of *dahara ākāśa* (represented by *guhā*, v. 1). And there are also deeper stages within that, including perhaps perception of the *nāḍīs* around the heart, which before we took as indicating a stage of "subtle *prāṇa* in the heart". But the emphasis is clearly on merging the individual self into Brahman by meditating on it in the heart as Om (vs. 3-4). In v. 3, *cetas* means "thinking soul, heart, mind," and carries connotations of discursive thought in a state where one is at one with one's heart and more truly the self. Hence *tad-bhāvagatena cetasā* = "with the thought in the heart (*cetasā*) gone (*gatena*) to 'that-being,'" i.e., "being in a state where discursive thought coming from the heart has merged into a state of being that, or being Brahman". This "discursive thought from or in the heart" can only refer to thought of the meaning of Om, or of self as Om (v. 6).

As a unified teaching, therefore, *MuṇḍUp* II.2 seems to regard the various "*vijñāna* in the heart" *vidyās* in the old Upaniṣads as all more or less dealing with the same kind of thing. This "thing," this direction of realms of higher stages and experience, it says, can be penetrated, and the Supreme stage can be attained, by a path of meditation with Om based on the philosophy of the bow-arrow simile in vs. 3-4. Since *MuṇḍUp* II. 2 combines the image of the arrow becoming one with the target with repetition of Om, this path does not seem to involve any systematic working with the subtle *prāṇas* in the heart, and may therefore represent to some extent an alternative to paths of that type. But beyond that, little more can be said. It is not clear, for example, whether this meditation involved in the earlier stages a strong centering in one's heart or chest. It is quite possible that instead it emphasized centering in the center of one's being, leading more to an understanding of *dahara ākāśa* as the sky of the heart or consciousness. Whether the *MuṇḍUp* II.2 path was *the* meditative approach associated with *dahara ākāśa* = "subtle space of awareness" is also doubtful.

23. Appendix: *Mahā-NārUp* XIII.6-12

We mentioned in sec. 1 that besides traditional *Dahara upāsanā* and the two types of inner paths elaborated in secs. 18-22, there are also primarily yogic paths to Ātman/Brahman in the heart. In the Vedic

Upaniṣads, this approach is only represented by *Mahā-NārUp* XIII.6b-12 (= Varenne 247-259).[186]

Translation of the Text Given by Varenne

247. Appearing like a lotus chalice,
and also turned face down, the heart
248. is located below the neck (band),
nine inches above the navel.
249. It shines (*bhāti*), having a necklace of flames,
the great abode (*āyatana*) of all [things].
250. All enveloped by arteries (*śila*) it hangs,
yes, similar to a chalice.
251. At its end there is a small (or subtle, *sūkṣma*) cavity.
Within this all (the world) is founded (*pratiṣṭhita*).
252. In the middle of that there is a great Fire (*mahān agniḥ*),
an All-Flame facing in all directions.
253. It, standing there [is the Sun], the one first-enjoying the food
and portioning it out, the ageless seer,
254. horizontal and vertical, below and sideways,
its rays all spread out.
255. It (the Fire) causes the body which belongs to it to be heated all through,
from the sole of the foot to the crown.
256. In the middle of that [Fire] is a Blade of Flame (*vahniśikhā*),
fine (*aṇīya*), arranged pointing upward,
257. like a lightning-written [flash] leaving
from a dark cloud, resplendent;
258. having a thin middle like a wild rice parakeet (?),
it shines yellow, like an atom.
259. In the middle of that Blade abides the Paramātman.
He is Brahmā, He is Śiva, He is Hari, He is Indra,
He is the Imperishable, the Supreme Self-Sovereign.[187]

This text seems to be related to the perception of the Self in the heart in the middle Vedic Upaniṣads (cf. sec. 4 above), and also to various Upaniṣadic comments on the fire of Brahman in the body. But the details are unclear. It is sometimes accepted as an example of the *Dahara* Knowledge, and even used for *Dahara upāsanā*.[188] What makes the text so important, however, is its extraordinary clarity in describing higher spiritual realities in the language of form. Yoga in the sense of Patañjali or the *Yoga Upaniṣads* is sometimes taken as dealing mostly with physical and mental phenomena. But here it provides a language for some of the great mysteries of existence.

24. Epilogue: The Infinitization of the Self

The above completes the exposition of the *Dahara Yidyā* and we conclude with some reflections on the picture that has emerged in this and the last chapter.

"*Vijñāna* in the Heart" as a Unified Area a Higher Wisdom. The first general point that comes out of our various analyses is that the *vidyās* in Table 5.2 form indeed a single area of spiritual knowledge and approach, inter-connected and unified by inner qualities in various ways. They form a single area, a single Avenue of Higher Wisdom. In fact, we have argued that to some extent *MuṇḍUp* II.2 treats them as such. By building up a single picture, "the Self in the Heart," and of a path to that Self, and at the same time incorporating so many allusions to specific deeper realizations in the earlier texts, the message is inescapable that we are here dealing with a single Higher Wisdom, a single Area of Spirituality. It is interesting that such a broad, unified treatment is not only found in *MuṇḍUp* II.2 but also in other sections of this particular Upaniṣad. In each case, the Upaniṣad brings into relief and amplifies a whole general theme of old Upaniṣadic teaching and develops it further. One gets the impression that this represents a first digestion of the old Upaniṣadic teachings by sages of a later era, comparable to but completely different from the still later reflective digestion and systematization of the Upaniṣadic teachings that led to the Brahma Sūtra.[189] In our treatment, we accepted this digestion as still completely in touch with the original old-Upaniṣadic Knowledge.

The *Dahara Vidyā* as a Meta-*Vidyā*. The next point is concerned with the structure of the "*vijñāna* in the heart" Wisdom as a set of interrelated teachings. When we first surveyed the texts that define this area (Table 5.2, chr. 5.9), we regarded the Five Sheaths *Vidyā* as a kind of meta-*vidyā* which set up a general form or pattern, viz. the conceptions of *vijñāna*, (higher) *ānanda*, and the whole scheme of *vijñāna*—*ānanda*—beyond *ānanda*. Other *vidyās* were regarded as representing more specific exemplifications of this type or pattern, e.g. they taught specific forms of *vijñāna*. The study of the *Dahara*

Vidyā in this chapter suggests, however, that it, too, may be regarded as a kind of meta-*vidyā*. The conception of the Self and the Universe in the heart, in the context of the near-universal "symbol of the heart," has a profound force and may operate at beginning as well as at more advanced levels of inner evolution. This gives the *Dahara Vidyā* a scope comparable to the Five Sheaths *Vidyā*, where *vijñāna* and *ānanda* have similar inner power and depth.

The Infinitization of the Self. The last point is the most important. We have seen that all the "*vijñāna* in the heart" *vidyās* which exemplify the *Dahara* paradigm eventually lead to a point at which there is a kind of true "Infinitization of the individual self." This "Infinitization" takes place when the aspirant/devotee is at the level of the deep sleep stage and results in true and permanent Knowledge of the Self. There is no question that the texts speak from direct knowledge. Considering that they come from different teachers who were sometimes separated by several generations, the level of agreement regarding this "Infinitization" represents a powerful "objective" argument for the reality of the Supreme Knowledge taught. As said earlier, the significance of the Upaniṣads for mankind today consists in no small part in their testimony to the reality of this "Infinitization" and in their elaboration of it in concrete and direct forms. The "Infinitization of the individual self" is actually never described as an "event". Instead, the discourse simply switches suddenly from deep sleep to full knowledge of the Infinite Self. There is a suggestion, however, that a discrete step is involved (hence the conventional language in terms of "realization") and that a state of true Knowledge of the Self is discontinuous with the ordinary human state. In the *Dahara* teaching, *dahara ākāśa* functions as a preliminary level of perception and knowledge of the Self before realization of the Infinite Self, but that does not lessen the discontinuity.

Finally, two meditative paths were identified which address this "Infinitization" and by which it can be reached. These were the "path of the subtle *prāṇa* All-self" based on Śaṁkara's commentary on *BṛhUp* IV.2.2-4, with perhaps a "Cosmos-encompassing, Sun-related self" a la *ChāndUp* VIII.6 as an equivalent variant, and the "path of merger in Brahman by means of Om" as in *MuṇḍUp* II.2.3-4. The Yājñavalkya-Śākalya Dialogue suggests that the method of identifying the subtle *prāṇas* in the heart with the Quarters of Space and their Deities was already known among teachers in old Upaniṣadic times. Whether the path of Om also dates back to that period in some form is unclear. So actual use of these types of inner paths in the "*vijñāna* of the heart" *vidyās* in Upaniṣadic times is a good possibility but not certain. Nevertheless these paths are of great importance because I believe that both of them could, with true inner guidance, still be practiced by a modern aspirant or devotee today. In addition, all the "*vijñāna* in the heart" *vidyās* and both of the meditative paths mentioned also seem to involve some version of *neti, neti*. Of course, *neti, neti* is a very broad designation which probably covers various inner practices and principles at different levels. But in any case the *vidyās* discussed together with their various *upāsanās* and other inner (yogic, meditative and *jñāna*) disciplines represent ways in which, on the authority of the Upaniṣads and tradition, and with the Grace of the Supreme Divine or the Infinite Reality, true Infinitization of the self can come about. May that Infinite Divine, that Reality be gracious to us.

NOTES

1. Modern translations: Böhtlingk, *ChāndUp*, pp. 82-87. Modern treatments: Mukhopadhyaya, *Studies*, pp. 198-206; Ugaz Ortiz, A Hermeneutics of the Symbolism of the Interior Domain (*Guhā* and *Hṛd-Guhā*) in Abhinavagupta's Śaivism and in Vedānta. *Orientalia Lovanensia Periodica* v. 19 (1988), pp. 157-188; pp. 165-167.
2. Swami Ananyananda, Seeking God through Meditation: The Golden Threshold (Editorial), *Prabuddha Bhārata*, v. 87 (1982), pp. 446-453; p. 452, and elsewhere.
3. Swami Ananyananada, The Spiritual Centre Within (Editorial), *Prabuddha Bhārata*, v. 86 (1981), pp. 442-449; p. 448, and elsewhere.
4. Raghavacar, *Rāmānuja on Ups.*, p. 55. The author names the *Sad-Vidyā* (*ChāndUp* VI) and the *Antaryāmi Brāhmaṇa* (*BṛhUp* III.7) as of comparable importance.
5. (a) *karma-jita loka*; (b) *puṇya-jita loka*; (c) *satyāḥ kāmāḥ*; (d) *mauna—manute*; (e) *an-āśakāyana—na naśyati*; (f) *araṇyāyana*, "forest-life"—*araśca ha vai ṇyaśca*; (g) A famous problematic passage. The original has *sa om iti vā 'hodvā mīyate*, cf. W. Morgenroth, Glossen in der Chāndogya-Upaniṣad, *Indological Taurinensia*, vols. 8-9, 1980-1, pp. 283-291, who reviews classical commentators and modern proposed solutions (pp. 289-291). The translation follows Geldner, who amends *sa om iti vāho dvāram īyate*, "he, with [the thought] "Om" as vehicle, reaches the gate". Hillebrandt's restoration *sa om iti vāha, ūrdhvam īyate*, "It, 'Om,' is the vehicle, it (or he) goes up" is also possible (see Morgenroth, *op. cit.*, p. 290).
6. *vi*—means "distinct, divorced from," hence "without" etc. *a*—negates the word that follows, so *a-pipāsa* = "non-thirsty".

7. Compare Whitney, *Atharva Veda*, v. 2, p. 601 (a) *akāmo dhīro amṛtaḥ svayaṁbhū rasena tṛpto kutaścānonyaḥ*; (b) *dhīraṁ ajaraṁ yuvānam*.
8. Transl. Dumont, P.E., The Kāmya Sacrifices in the *Taittirīya-Brāhmaṇa*. *Proceedings of the American Philosophical Society*, v. 113 (1969), pp. 34-66; p. 63.
9. So Whitney, *op. cit*, p. 601.
10. Commentary on *ChāndUp* VIII.1.1, transl. Jha, *ChāndUp Comm.*, p. 415.
11. Mukhopadhyaya, *Studies*, p. 199.
12. See the examples given in the *Oxford English Dictionary*, 2nd. ed., v. 7. Oxford: Clarendon Press, 1989, under *Heart*, I and II, pp. 60 ff; also in S. M. Kuhn and J. Reidy, editors, *Middle English Dictionary*, v. H. Ann Arbor, Mich: University of Michigan Press, under *Heart*, pp. 707-716.
13. See the beautiful compilation in J. Grimm and W. Grimm, *Deutsches Wörterbuch*, v. 4 , Pt 1, Leipzig: S. Hirzel, 1877, under *Herz*, I (cols. 1207-1222).
14. E.g. A. Tobler and E. Lammatzch, *Altfranzösisches Wörterbuch*, v. 2. Berlin: Weidmannsche Buchhandlung, 1936, under *cuer*, cols. 1112-1120.
15. = *KaṭhaUp* II.3.14. Some regard the *śloka* as an interpolation from there.
16. (a) Yājñavalkya is in his heart identified with the quarters of space, see sec. 19 below. (b) *hṛdaye hyeva rūpāṇi pratiṣṭhitāni bhavanti;* the same wording also in vs. 21-23.
17. R.H. Robinson, Some Buddhist and Hindu Concepts of Intellect—Will, *Philosophy East and West*, v. 22 (1972), pp. 229-307, discusses the occurrences in *KaṭhaUp* I.3 and in the *Gītā* on pp. 300 and 302-303 resp. In *KaṭhaUp* I.3.8, *buddhi* is replaced by *vijñāna*, showing its connotations of higher spiritual intuition and *jñāna*-consciousness.
18. Mādhavānanda, *BṛhUp Comm.*, p. 548.
19. Mukhopadhyaya, *Studies*, pp. 201-202.
20. Already in *ChāndUp* VII.26.2, and then in *KaṭhaUp* II.3.15 and *MuṇḍUp* II.2.8 and III.2.9.
21. *KaṭhaUp* I.2.12, I.3.1, II.1.6: *MuṇḍUp* II.1.8, III.1.7; and *MaitrUp* VI.3.
22. Cf. F.B.J. Kuiper, "The *Ṛg-vedic* seer gets his vision with or in his heart (*hṛdā́* or *hṛdí*)," The Bliss of Aša, *IIJ*, v. 8 (1964-65), p. 125. For extensive examples see J. Gonda, next note.
23. J. Gonda, Some Notes on the Function of the "heart," = Chapter 12 of J. Gonda, *The Vision of the Vedic Poets*. The Hague: Mouton, 1963, pp. 276-288.
24. Gonda, *ibid*, pp. 277-78.
25. *Ibid.*, p. 278.
26. *Ibid.*, p. 278.
27. *Ibid.*, p. 279.
28. *Ibid.*, pp. 279-80.
29. *Ibid.*, p. 283.
30. F.B.J. Kuiper, The Bliss of Aša. *IIJ*, v. 8 (1964-65), pp. 96-129.
31. See the entry on Varuṇa by S. Bhattacharji in Eliade, *Encyclopedia of Religion*, v. 15.
32. Kuiper, *ibid.*, p. 114, and note 98, where the author quotes Lüders, who came to the same conclusion, and cites Middle Eastern parallels.
33. *Ibid.*, p. 116.

34. *Ibid.*, p. 118.
35. *Ibid.*, pp. 116-118.
36. *Ibid.*, p. 124.
37. *Ibid.*, p. 123.
38. *Ibid.*, p. 123.
39. *Ibid.*, p. 124.
40. *Ibid.*, p. 125.
41. It is the center of the person's psyche, and as such the natural locus of the action of, or the residence of, the Divine. This topic is sadly neglected in anthropology, historical linguistics, comparative literature, comparative religion, and perennial philosophy, although materials are abundant. In collecting material, one must distinguish between conceptions of the heart in the *Volksmund* (in the language and proverbs etc. of the common people), in "mythology", in literature (poetry, drama novels) and in didactic or edifying (moral, ethical and general wisdom) literature, and higher level teachings based on realization (although one can argue that the *Volksmund* often is similarly based on higher insight). (Some of these components might be missing or little developed.) An excellent starting point as far as the major Western religions are concerned are encyclopedias. See e.g. the entry *Kalb* by J.C. Vadet in the *Encyclopedia of Islam*, New Edition, Leiden: E.J. Brill, 1978; the entry *Heart* by T. Sorg in the *New International Dictionary of New Testament Theology*, C. Brown, ed., v. 2, Grand Rapids, MI: Zandervan, 1986 (transl. of *Theologisches Begriffslexikon zum Neuen Testament*, 1965) (more massive documentation may be found in the *Theological Dictionary of the New Testament*, Kittel and G. Friedrich, editors, Grand Rapids, MI: Erdmans Publishing Company, 1966-73, under *kardia* and *psyche*).
42. A similarly neglected topic in comparative religion and perennial philosophy; there are no book-length treatments of this subject. M. Meslin, in his admirable but all too brief entry *Heart* in the new *Encyclopedia of Relgion* (M. Eliade, Editor, McMillan, 1989), discusses the conception of the heart in ancient Egyptian religion, Greek Philosophy up to Plato, the Upaniṣads, the Bible, and the Koran, and in various mystical traditions of Christianity. But there are also extensive developments involving the heart in Judaism and the Kabbalah, in Sufism and in Taoism. If one believes that the human mind-body-spirit complex has a universal structure independent of culture, then this structure is assessed by yoga and rationales for the nearly universal elaboration of "the symbol of the heart" are provided by yoga. E.g., "The heart is the contact between the soul and the body. The part which is most sentient and has the most subtle feeling is the heart," Swami Hariharananda Aranya, *YogaPhil*, p. 338. Treatments of the heart in special religious and esoteric traditions: S. Murata, The Heart, in *The Tao of Islam: A Sourcebook on Gender Relationships in Islamic Thought*. Albany: SUNY Press, 1992, pp. 289-319 (a survey with many quotes); H. Corbin, *Creative Imagination in the Sufism of Ibn 'Arabi*. London: Routledge and Kegan Paul, 1969, pp. 221-245; and P.E. Muller-Ortega, *The Triadic Heart of Śiva*. Albany: SUNY Press, 1989 (a study of the inner dimensions of the Heart in Abhinavagupta, the great exponent of non-dual Kashmir Śaivism).
43. Transl. C.W. Hepner, *The Kurozumi Sect of Shinto*. Tokyo: Meiji Japan

Society, 1935, pp. 110, 111, 110 and 111-112. The verses are from the *Kurozumi-Kyo-Kyo-Sho*, vol. 1, p. 12, no. 27; p. 52, no. 1321; p. 10, no. 19; and p. 33, no. 86, resp. The *Kurozumi-Kyo-Sho* is the basic text of the Kurozumi Sect and has apparently not been translated it its entirety.

44. On Kurozumi Munetada see Hepner, *op. cit.*, chrs. 2 and 3.

45. See *BraSū* I.3.21.

46. E.g. as far as location and size of the individual Ātman are concerned.

47. Modern scholarship: R. Hauschild, Die Śvetāśvatara-Upaniṣad. *Abhandlungen für die Kunde des Morgenlandes*, v. 17, no. 3 (1927) (Kraus reprint, 1966); W. Rau, Versuch einer deutschen Übersetzung der Śvetāśvatara Upaniṣad. *Asiatische Studien*, v. 17 (1964), pp. 25-46; T. Oberlies, Die Śvetāśvatara-Upaniṣad. Eine Studie ihrer Gotteslehre. *WZKSA*, v. 32 (1988), pp. 35-62.

48. Cf. Hauschild, *op. cit.*, pp. 30-31. (a) following Rau, who reads *kalpate*.

49. The yogic description in *Mahā-NārUp* XIII.6 ff. = Varenne 247 ff. shows the same two aspects. The description of the self as point-like and extremely fine in *ŚvetUp* V.8-9 is analogous to the description of hyperfineness in Varenne 258, 259.

50. Compare, for example, *ŚvetUp* III.13.

A person of the size of the thumb, within the body,
is ever entered in the heart (*hṛdaya*) of the people.
By the heart, by thought, by the mind [He appears] adapted.
They who know thus become immortal,

(cf. Hauschild, *op. cit.*, pp. 18-19), with *ŚvetUp* IV.17:

This God, the All-Creator (*viśva-karman*), the great Self,
[is] ever entered in the heart of the creatures.
By the heart, by thought, by the mind he appears adapted.
They who know this become immortal,

(cf. Hauschild, *op. cit.*, p. 26). Although these verses share two halflines, III.17 refers mostly to the individual self, while IV.17 evokes universal overtones and an Infinite aspect. In *ŚvetUp* IV.12-13 on the other hand, the person of the measure of a thumb is the Universal Infinite Self:

12. A person of the measure of a thumb
stands in the midst of one's self (*ātman*),
Lord of what has been and of what is to be,
One, does not shrink away from Him.

13. A person of the measure of a thumb
like a light without smoke,
Lord of what has been and of what is to be,
He alone is, and tomorrow too.

51. Similar vacillations are found in descriptions of "experience of" the thumb-sized *puruṣa* by devotees and saints. Cf. for example Sri Babathakur: "One must concentrate on the heart. Not the physical one, but the spiritual heart-centre, for in the innermost heart-chamber resides the Divine Self; concentration of mind on that heart-centre interpenetrates all impurities, cells, obstructions etc. until it reaches the background (underlying) Essence of life. There It appears like a phallus—a Śiva-liṅga (symbol of Lord Śiva). It is represented first by an egg-size smooth stone but can be of various sizes, colors and may have different marks as three eyes, a moon, or some holy inscription. When one first experiences the vision of

a thumb-size stone, the light seen by the third eye is so bright, that the light of the sun seems dim. After that, the form of Lord appears . . . very sweet. At that moment individuality (or ego) dissolves. One who has experienced that, finds that there is no seed of action, desire, individuality, duality, relativity and so on, and that one has no more to take birth in a physical body by force.". . . Susmita Devi, compiler, *Nectar of Wisdom as revealed to Sri Sri Babathakur*. Delhi: Writers Workshop, p. 187.

52. As analysed by Nakamura, it holds that (a) the individual self is infinitesimal (*aṇu*), and that although it has sentiency in all parts of the body, it "resides in the heart, that is, in a special place within the body" (Nakamura, *History*, p. 510). But "(b) the highest Self also resides in the heart of man, and thus [(c)] the individual self and the Highest Self coexist in the heart" (*ibid.*, p. 510). This peculiar combination of doctrines is simply a direct reflection of the situation in the Upaniṣadic texts, where different texts express different perceptions and levels of knowledge.

53. The Sūtra says "The *dahara* [*ākāśa*] [is Brahman] on account of the following [statements in the *Dahara* text]" (cf. Radhakrishnan, *Brahma Sūtra*, p. 292). For justification both Śaṁkara and Rāmānuja point to *Dahara Vidyā* 1.3, "how widely extending as this [physical] space here is, so wide extending is the space within the heart. . .": This statement, they argue, implies that the *dahara ākāśa* cannot be anything but Brahman. Elsewhere, Śaṁkara glosses "*dahara ākāśa*" as "Brahman" and cites "*Ākāśa* is Its [= Braman's] Name," *ChāndUp* VIII.14.1 (Commentary on *Dahara Vidyā* 1.1: transl. Jha, *ChāndUp Comm.*, p. 415).

54. Cf. the transl. by Jha, *ChāndUp Comm.*, pp. 416-417. (a) *puṇḍarīka-ākāśa-paricchinnam*; (b) *upalabhate*; (c) *svaccha ivodake pratibimbarūpamādarśa iva*; (d) *svaccha*; (e) *vijñāna-jyotiḥ-svarūpāvabhāsam.*

55. Cf. the *St. Petersburg Dictionary*, v. 7, col. 1540, "3. to pull back in . . .(a drawn weapon, troops, a curtain etc.). . . . 4. prevent, make cease, suppress . . . 5. absorb, render naught . . . 7. pull, take to oneself."

56. *Pratyāhāra* (from *prati-ā-hṛ-*, "hold in") is defined as "imitation, as it were, by the senses of the own-form of mind (*citta*) by separating [themselves from] their objects (i.e. the things perceived)," which is more than just withdrawal of the senses. *Dhāraṇā* is "the binding of mind to [a particular] place," like the heart or navel (*YoSū* III.1). For attempts to understand *pratyāhāra* and *dhāraṇā* in terms of Western ideas see G. Feuerstein, *The Philosophy of Classical Yoga*. New York: St. Martin's Pres, 1980, pp. 81-84.

57. Rāmānuja, *Śrībhāṣya* on *BraSū* I.3.13 (= I.3.14 in Śaṁkara's count). transl. Thibaut, *Rāmānuja BraSū Comm.*, pp. 316-317.

58. *Ibid.*, p. 316.

59. "On the ground of this connected consideration of the whole chapter we are able to decide that the text enjoins as the object of search and enquiry both the highest Brahman and the whole body of auspicious qualities abiding with in it." *Ibid.*, p. 317.

60. Introduction to Comm. on *ChāndUp* VIII, transl. Jha, *ChāndUp Comm.*, p. 414.

61. *Ibid.*, p. 413.

62. *Ibid.*, pp. 413-14.

63. *Ibid.*, p. 413.
64. Shastri, *UpBhāṣyam*, v. 2, p. 344, footnote 1 (through p. 346).
65. I am grateful to Profs. H.H. Hock and R. Pandharipande for help with the translation.
66. "[There should be] combination (unification into a combined total, *upa-saṁ-hāra*) [of several attributes] on account of nondifference of [essential] import [of the different attributes], [as] in the common and subsidiary instructions [of different versions of the same sacrifice]" (*BraSū* III.3.5).
67. Cf. V. Raghavan, Introduction to K. Narayanaswami Ayar, *The Thirty-two Vidyās*. Adyar, Madras: Adyar Library and Research Centre, 2nd ed., 1962 (repr. 1975); p. xvii. Parama-Śivendra's work was published: Madras, Balamanorama Press, 1937, but was not available to me.
68. Traditionally, the aphorism on *upasaṁhāra* is regarded as referring to combining attributes occurring in parallel versions of the same *vidyā* in different *śākhās* or Vedic schools, and it is this form of the principle which Subrahmanya Shastri applies here. The *Dahara Vidyā* belongs to the Chāndogyas, a *Sāma Vedic śākhā*, while *Bṛhadāraṇyaka Upaniṣad* belongs to the Vājasaneyins of the White *Yajur Veda*.
69. *sarvavedāntapratyayaṁ codanādyaviśeṣāt*. Cf. Radhakrishnan, *Brahma Sūtra*, p. 468.
70. A standard modern treatment is H. Glasenapp, *Die Kaivalya Upaniṣad*, Königsberg: 1931, but *n.v.* Swami Chinmayananda, *Discourses on Kaivalyopaniṣad*. Madras: Chinmaya Pubs. Trust, 1978, gives spiritual commentary with explanations of terms.
71. (a) *saṁnyāsa āśrama*; (b) the Creator Deity.
72. Another example is *Pañca-Brahma Upaniṣad* 40-41, which says that *dahara ākāśa* in the middle of the (heart) lotus is Śiva, who is *Sat-Cit-Ānanda*. Cf. T.R. Sharma, *Studies in the Sectarian Upaniṣads*. Varanasi: Indological Book Hous, 1972, pp. 46-47.
73. Kaivalya Upaniṣad is regarded as belonging to the *Atharva Veda*, so that (3) continues the principle of *upasaṁhāra* in the sense of combining attributes contributed to the *vidyā* by different *śākhās*.
74. J. Varenne, *La Mahā-Nārāyaṇa Upaniṣad*, 2 vols, Paris: Editions Bocard, 1960 (PICI Fasc. 11 and 13), pp. 63 ff.
75. *Mahā-NārUp* XXIII in the Andhra version (Swami Vimalānanda, *Mahā-NārUp*, p. 188), and = *Māha-NārUp* XII.1 in the shorter version. (a) *Puruṣam*; (b) *kṛṣṇapiṅgalam*; (c) *ūrdhva-retam*, a simplified form; (d) *virūpākṣam*.
76. "Dark blue" and "unusual eyes"—Lord Śiva is represented blue with a third eye of *jñāna* in the middle of the forehead. On *retas* see Swami Vimalānanda, *op. cit.*, p. 190.
77. Swami Nikhilananda, *Self-Knowledge of Sri Sankaracharya*. Mylapore, Madras: Sri Ramakrishna Math, 2nd. ed., 1962 (1st ed., 1947), pp. 133-134. (a) This identification of the *dahara ākāśa* as the *Brahmapura* or city of Brahman appears unusual because we had taken *Brahmapura* in *Dahara Vidyā* 1.1 as the body. It may be a reference to *Dahara Vidyā* 1.5, "This [Ātman just described] is the true city of Brahman," or reflect the traditional equation *dahara ākāśa* = Brahman.
78. In Seeking God through Meditation (Editorial), *Prabuddha Bhārata*, v.

88 (1983), pp. 3-10, Swami Ananyananda is more explicit and gives four stages of meditation: (1) detaching the *cittākāśa* or mind-space from the external surroundings, thereby creating an inner space where we can "install our Chosen Deity or some other object of meditation" and be "without distraction"; (2) "the I-consciousness moves into the *dahara ākāśa* in the heart, and there shines in its own effulgence as the *Jīvātman*"; (3) "a stage where the soul becomes aware of a vaster state of existence and of its real nature as a part of the Paramātman"; and (4) 'the struggle of the Jīvātman [living individual self] to transcend its limitations and attain union with the Paramātman" (p. 9). This may likewise be correlated with Swami Nikhilananda's account.

79. E.g., "I stretch with great effort my mind toward the objects offered to me. This is because my *indriyas* (senses) remain drawn within the *hṛdayākāśa* which I see as extremely luminous. Just as the sky in the monsoon season is covered with innumerable clouds, my heart remains pervaded with great luminosity. Within this luminous light I see the image of God as extremely lustrous . . ." Svaminarayan, *Vacanāmṛtam* II.13, transl. H. Dave, *Vachanāmṛtam*. Bombay: Bharatiya Viday Bhavan, 1977, p. 380. Etymologically also, *ākāśa* means "shine" (see Mayrohfer, *Etym. Dictionary*, under *ākāśa*), and the term has this meaning in the *Yoga Upaniṣads*. Feuerstein in his *Encyclopedic Dictionary of Yoga* takes it as "radiance".

80. Visualization of a Divine form such as the form of Śiva or Kṛṣṇa leads to perception of the Light of Universal Divinity, and recall Swami Ananyananda's comment [B] in chr. 5.15.

81. Swami Maheshananda Giri, Introduction to S.S. Shastri, *UpBhāṣyam*, v. 2, p. 53. At their initiation *daśanāmī* monks are given a *mahāvākya* for meditation (cf. Ṣwami Prabhavanada, *Vedic Religion and Philosophy*. Mylapore, Madras: Sri Ramakrishna Math, 5th pr. 1968, p. 49 note 1). This meditation is to be in the heart (Prof. Klaus Klostermaier, personal communication). Dakṣiṇāmūrti is the auspicious Southern (*dakṣiṇa*) worship-form (*mūrti*) of Śiva, which shows him as supreme yogin and teacher of knowledge (*jñāna*), music, and the Vedas, the embodied Word. Worship of and devotion to Dakṣiṇāmūrti has a long and deep tradition in Tamil Nadu in South India, and use of the *Kaivalya* text by *daśanāmī* monks who are Dakṣiṇāmūrti devotees would be natural.

82. Swami Maheshananda, *ibid.*, p. 53. These works have not been translated.

83. Thus of the 18 meditations or *dhyānas* mentioned by G.V. Tagare in his translation of the *Bhāgavata Purāṇa*, two, namely II.2.8-13 and XI.14.32-46, are meditations on the form of the Lord in the heart. (Cf. G.V. Tagare, *The Bhāgavata Purāṇa*. 5 vols., Delhi: Motilal Banarsidass rev. ed., 1978 (Ancient Indian Tradition and Mythology vols. 7-11), in the index under *dhyāna*). The second of these gives instructions to move from the Form of the Lord to the Sky, and from there to the formless Brahman (*Bhāgavata Purāṇa* XI.14.44, transl. Tagare, *ibid.*, Part V, pp. 1995-96).

84. J. Ugaz Ortiz, in the paper cited in note 1, suggests a process of *dahara upāsanā* which, he says, is based on "the Vedāntic theory of perception". The "process of the *dahara-vidyā* consists in, first, entering in the *Brahmapura* through one of the 11 or nine gates of the city. These gates mean the senses. That is to say, in withdrawing the mind from the sense-objects,

catching hold of a sensory stimulation, or the breath, and following its course until the *buddhi* or 'heart', according to the Vedāntic theory of perception. In other words, the access to the mystic city is accomplished when the gross object is taken as a sign of, and a way leading to, its archetypal or subtle form, when it is dissolved in its basic constituents. Then, having penetrated into the 'inner abode of the heart' through one of the 'five heart-gates,' which are said to be the 'five petals of the heart-lotus' corresponding to the four quarters and the zenith and to the vital breath, until reaching the '*ākāśa* inside of the heart'. Finally, beyond the *ākāśa,* one reaches the center of being, the dweller (*BṛhUp* IV.4.20: *virajaḥ para ākāśāt*). It is on this imperishable being that *ākāśa* is supported (*ibid.*, III.7.12, III.8.11)." (Ugaz Ortiz, *op. cit.*, p. 167).

85. This is verses 231-232 in Varenne's edition, and is also the fourth text mentioned by Subrahmanya Shastri in sec. 6. I do not know of any independent discussions of this seminal text.
86. A traditional treatment in English in Swami Vimalānanda, *Mahā-NārUp*. Swami Vimalānanda follows the longer Andhra version in 80 sections and discusses the classical commentaries on each verse. The standard Western scholarly treatment is the edition and translation by Varenne (note 74 above).
87. Only two core sections, *Mahā-NārUp* I and XII-XIII, may be old.
88. (a) *nihitam guhāyām;* (b) *parāntakāle*, also "at the supreme [last] moment".
89. *dahra* (for *dahara*); *veśma*, house, abode; *puṇḍarīka*, (white) lotus; *pura*, city; *viśoka*, free from sorrow; *tasmin yad antaḥ*, what is within that.
90. *Luftraum, Himmelszelt*, St. Petersburg Dictionary.
91. This could be a poetic way of describing the "small space in the heart," as that may be experienced in traditional *Dahara upāsanā*, but then it would tend to refer to later stages of development in *upāsanā*.
92. Sri Sathya Sai Baba, *UpVahini*, pp. 60-61.
93. Philological transl. and notes: O. Böhtlingk, Drei kritisch gesichtete und übersetzte Upanishad mit erklärenden Anmerkungen. *Berichte über die Verhandlungen der köngl. sächsischen Gesellschaft der Wissenschaften Leipzig*, v. 42, pp. 127-197.
94. Deussen, *Sixty Ups*. v. 2, p. 589, sees no rhyme or reason in the choice of questions.
95. P.M. Modi, *Akṣara. A Forgotten Chapter in the History of Indian Philosophy*. Delhi: Satguru Pubs. 1985 (1st ed., Baroda, 1932), pp. 128-131 has a stimulating discussion of the text.
96. Transl. Keith, *Rig Vedic Brāhmaṇas*, p. 256.
97. Cf. Böhtlingk, *op. cit.*, pp. 192-194. (a) *eka-mātram*; (b) *manasi saṁpadyate;* (c) *dvimātreṇa*; (d) *tri-mātreṇa*; (e) *jīvaghana*; (f) vs. 6 and 7 are *ślokas* and are discussed by Horsch, *Gāthā Literature*, pp. 195-96; (g) *anu-eti*.
98. Horsch, *ibid.*, p. 195, reads *mātrā mṛtyumatyaḥ* as showing a double *saṁdhi* which, he says, is "so common in *ślokas*" and which gives the meaning "deathless" instead of "mortal". Śaṁkara and all modern translations before Horsch incl. Böhtlingk and Hume have "mortal".
99. *jāgratsvapnasuṣuptasthānapuruṣābhidhyānalakṣaṇāsu yogakriyāsu.* Commentary on *PraśnaUp* V.6.
100. Modern interpreters differ; e.g. Horsch suggests they are "grammatical

operations" (Horsch, *op. cit.*, p. 195).

101. For this and the following I used Col. Jacobs, *Concordance*, under *ajara* and *abhaya*.

102. There seems to be no modern substantive discussion of these two texts.

103. The most important modern treatment (edition, translation and discussion) is van Buitenen, *MaitrUp* (see Abbreviations and Conventions).

104. van Buitenen, *op. cit.*, chr. 1.

105. They are additions to a "nuclear text made up of these sections [cf. VI.1-17] which are not introduced with *athānyatrāpy uktam. . .*" (*ibid.*, p. 35). This nuclear text was added to SM and the original Upaniṣad of the Maitrāyaṇīyas. Cf. also the analysis of *MaitrUp* VI.1-32 on pp. 84-87.

106. The printed version of *Maitrāyaṇīya Upaniṣad* mentioned by P.T. Raju in his review of van Buitenen's work in *JAOS*, v. 85 (1965), p. 460, which contains material not taken into account by van Buitenen, as well as Raju's perspective on mixings with Buddhist and Jaina ideas (*ibid.*, p. 460) might affect the reconstruction. Bodewitz, *JaimBr*, v. 1, pp. 275 ff. clarifies some of van Buitenen's interpretations.

107. Cf. van Buitenen, *MaitrUp*, pp. 145-46 (original Skt. p. 114). (a) support, *āśraya*; (b) the first line has all accusatives; (c) *āgama*.

108. In *Summer Showers*,1972 and 1973. In spite of enquiries to well-known scholars, I have been unable to trace this exact series in the Advaitic literature. So it may be due to Sri Sathya Sai Baba.

109. Sai Baba's series of five *ākāśas* may also hark back to a rather sophisticated passage in the *Pañcadaśī* (VI.18 ff.) which compares the four aspects *Kūṭastha* ("the Immovable," "the Self as consciousness absolute," Swami Swahananda), Brahman, *jīva* (living being, embodied soul), and *Īśvara* (Lord), to *ghaṭa-ākāśa, mahākāśa, jala-ākāśa,* and *abhrakha,* "pot-*ākāśa*", "great *ākāśa*", "*ākāśa* reflected by water [in the pot]", and "*ākāśa* in a cloud," resp. [cf. Swami Swahananda, *Pañcadaśī*. Madras: Sri Ramakrishna Math, third ed. 1980 (1st ed., 1967), pp. 131 ff; also pp. 345 ff. on *Kūṭastha*].

110. *Summer Showers,* 1972, pp. 222 ff.

111. *Ibid.*, p. 222.

112. *Ibid.*, p. 222.

113. *Ibid.*, pp. 222-23.

114. Sri Sathya Sai Baba, *Summer Showers,* 1973, p. 245.

115. *Summer Showers,* 1972 pp. 223-225.

116. *Majjhima Nikāya*, Discourse no. 121 (*Culasuññatta sutta*), transl. I.B. Horner, *Middle-Length Sayings*, v. 3, pp. 147-152.

117. Svaminarayan, for instance, takes *cit-ākāśa* as synonymous with what he calls *akṣara* Brahman, which in terms of "experience" seems to be similar to the Brahman of many Upaniṣadic texts.

118. This step corresponds to passing from the second and third to the fourth stage of the conventional seven stages (*bhūmikās*) of the path of knowledge outlined in *Akṣi Upaniṣad* and the *Yoga Vāsiṣṭha*. The fourth stage is the stage of the *jñānī* or knower of the Self.

119. Sri Sathya Sai Baba, *Summer Showers,* 1973, pp. 245-246.

120. The work comes in two versions, the *Laghu* ("short") *Yogavāsiṣṭha* and a long version usually called the *Yogavāsiṣṭha Rāmāyaṇa*. There is a free translation of the former by K. Narayanaswami Aiyer, *Laghu Yogavāsiṣṭha*.

Adyar, Madras: Adyar Library and Research Centre, 1971 (1st, ed., 1896), but no satisfactory rendering of the long one. Modern scholarship: P. Thomi, The Yogavāsiṣṭha in its longer and shorter version. *JIP*, v. 11 (1983), pp. 107-116; and W. Slaje, A guide to the philosophical and religious terms in the (Laghu) Yogavāsiṣṭha. *WZKSA*, v. 34 (1990), pp. 147-179.

121. For a beautiful introduction, see the selection by Bhagavan Das, *Mystic Experiences. Tales of Yoga and Vedānta from the Yogavāsiṣṭha*. 3rd ed., Varanasi: Theosophical Bookshop, 1959.

122. K. Narayanaswami Aiyer, *op. cit.*, p. 68.

123. D.S. Subbaramaya, *Śrī Dakṣiṇāmūrtistotram*, Sringeri: Dakṣiṇamnaya Sri Sharada Peetham, v. 1 (1988), pp. 318 ff. discusses four Vedāntic *ākāśas* (*bhūta-*, *citta-*, *avyākṛta-*, and *cit-ākāśa*) from the general point of view of spaces in which objects are placed.

124. The *Yoga Vāsiṣṭha* is said to be for the *siddha avasthā*, the state when one has already attained considerable knowledge (Bhagavan Das, *op. cit.*, Preface).

125. Swami Ananyananda, Seeking God Through Meditation. *Prabuddha Bhārata*, v. 88 (1983), pp. 3-10.

126. *Ibid.*, pp. 6-7.

127. *Ibid.*, p. 4.

128. *Ibid.*, p. 6.

129. It is also suggested by *TaittBr* II.8.8 [8]-[9]. For if all things are placed in the "expanse" of Brahman "like in a boat," then the "expanse" in which they are seen thus placed is a much larger and more fundamental and dominant object than the things themselves.

130. Were these *Atharva Vedic* hymns known in *Taittirīya Brāhmaṇa?*

131. A relationship between *Atharva Veda* X.7 and 8 and the Upaniṣads is often acknowledged (Deussen, Edgerton, Sharma) but has not been carefully or deeply explored.

132. See Whitney, *Atharva Veda*, v. 2, pp. 590-591.

133. It is difficult to judge in which of the many texts that discuss *ālaya-vijñāna*, the *ālayavijñāna* is an "experiential" or is in some sense "direct knowledge". The only one I am completely sure about is the *Laṅkāvatāra Sūtra*. D.T. Suzuki discusses the *ālayavijñāna* in the *Laṅkā* in his *Studies in the Laṅkāvatāra Sūtra*. London: Routledge, 1930 (repr. 1957, 1968), pp. 171-189. He also translated the entire Sūtra (*The Laṅkāvatāra Sūtra*. London: Routledge and Son, 1933; repr. 1956, 1959).

134. Cf. R.S. Bluck, *Plato's Meno*. Cambridge: Cambridge Univ. Press, 1961, pp. 316-17. In *Meno* 86.a Socrates says "Well, if both in whatever time he is a human being and in whatever time he is not a human being there are going to be true opinions in him, which become knowledge when they have been awoken by questioning, won't his soul for the whole of time (*tón aeí chrónon*) be in a state of having learned (*memathekyta éstai*)?" Transl. R.W. Sharples, ed. and transl., *Plato: Meno*. Chicago: Bolchazy Carducci, 1985. "Clearly . . . Plato believed that this is in fact true. The slave, and of course all other men, have been in a state of knowledge (latent or actual) throughout all times," Bluck, *op. cit.*, p. 316. See Leisegang's critical discussion in Pauly-Wissowa, *Real-Encyclopädie der classischen Altertumswissenschaft*, v. 20, Pt. 2. Waldsee (Württ.): Alfred Druckenmüller,

1950, col. 2423.

135. See C.E. Huber, S.J., *Anamnesis bei Plato*. München: M. Hüber, 1964 (Pullacher Philosophische Forschungen, ed. W. Brugger, S.J. and J.B. Lotz, S.J., No. 6).

136. Hüber (*op. cit.*, pp. 582 ff.) discusses the roles which *anamnesis* plays in Plato under 4 headings. It is (a) "a specific [type of] participation of the human soul in the *idea*" (p. 582); (b) it indicates, *qua* memory content of the idea, "kinship of the soul with the idea" (p. 583); (c) it represents, *qua* process, a "transcendental process" or "method," by which man touches that which "exists by itself" (*das an-sich-seiende*) (pp. 589 ff); and (d) it represents the "reflected light" in Plato's amazing Sun-analogy of human vision and knowledge in Republic 506d-509d (pp. 591-610).

137. The principle that man's soul in some sense knows already everything is taken by Swami Vivekananda and others as a basic principle of philosophy of education. To connect this up with the *Dahara Vidyā* (or more generally with the whole teaching on Ātman/Brahman in the highest *vidyās*) requires of course additional assumptions. I am not aware of any systematic treatment of this problem.

138. This is another very much neglected topic in comparative religion and perennial philosophy. For example Eliade's *Encyclopedia of Religion*, which is unusually detailed as far as phenomena across different religions are concerned, deals with omniscience only under the heading of "Omniscience of Supreme Beings" (under "Supreme Beings").

139. K.K. Mittal, Buddhist View of Omniscience: Religious, Philosophical, Scientific, Or . . .? *Buddhist Studies (Journal of the Department of Buddhist Studies,* Univ. of Delhi*)*, No. 4 (1977), pp. 20-26, p. 22; the author goes on to give a spirited bird's eye-view of the conceptions of omniscience in the four systems, with some insightful characterizations. An unjustly neglected study of omniscience in the different Indian philosophical systems is G. Kaviraj, The Doctrine of Pratibhā in Indian Philosophy. In G. Kaviraj, *Aspects of Indian Thought*. Burdwan: Univ. of Burdwan, 1966, pp. 1-41. Kaviraj, one of the very great scholars of Indian philosophy and religion in this century, writes with a powerful spiritual grasp and insight. More detailed studies connecting his general picture with the relevant literatures would be desirable. See also E.A. Solomon, The Problem of Omniscience (*Sarvajñatva*), *ALB*, v. 24 (1962), pp. 36-77; and H. Bhattacharya, Omniscient Beings. *Jain Journal*, v. 11 (1976), pp. 64-69 and pp. 91-98.

140. Coomaraswamy, in Rebirth and Omniscience in Pāli Buddhism. *Indian Culture*, v. 3 (1936/37), pp. 19-34 (correction to this in the same vol., p. 760) and in Recollection, Indian and Platonic, in *Papers*, pp. 49-65, makes numerous comments which could be used as a startingpoint for a deeper portrait of the Buddha's omniscience. Another source is his Some Pāli Words, in *Papers*, pp. 264-329 (see e.g. *akāliko*, "intemporal," pp. 265-267; *Tathāgata*, which he connects with *yathā vādī, tathā karī*, p. 285; *sahājanetta*, "possessed of the innate eye," i.e. "possessing the power to respond spontaneously with higher insight," pp. 327-329; and note 44 on p. 290).

141. H. Jacobi, transl., *Jaina Sūtras*, Part I. Oxford: Clarendon Press (*SBE*, v. 22; repr. Dover Pubs.) p. 263. This and the following two excerpts are

cited by P.S. Jaini, On the *Sarva-jñatva* (Omniscience) of Mahāvīra and the Buddha, in L. Cousins, A. Kunst and K.R. Norman, ed., *Buddhist Studies in Honour of I.B. Horner*. Dordrecht, Holland: Reidel, 1974, pp. 71-90.

142. *Cūla-Sakuladāyisutta* (Discourse No. 79 in the *Majjhima Nikāya*), transl. I.B. Horner, *Middle Length Sayings*, v. 2, p. 298.

143. *Ibid.*, pp. 298 ff.

144. So in the Discourse on Fear and Dread, *Bhayabheravasutta*, the 4th Discourse in the *Majjhima Nikāya*, transl. Horner, *Middle Length Sayings*, v. 1, pp. 28-29, an account of the three knowledges which arose in Buddha the night he became enlightened.

145. *Saṁyutta Nikāya* II.212, cited by Coomaraswamy, Rebirth . . ., *op. cit.*, p. 23.

146. P.J. Jaini, *op. cit.* (note 141), p. 81.

147. *Dīgha Nikāya* III.28 (24.2.14), cited by Coomaraswamy, Rebirth . . ., *op. cit.*, p. 21.

148. The most detailed scholarly discussion of the problem of Gauḍapāda and the *Kārikā* is V. Bhattacharya, *The Āgamaśāstra of Gauḍapāda*, Repr. Delhi: Motilal Banarsidass, 1989 (1st ed., 1943), although few scholars subscribe to the author's extreme conclusions today.

149. *Sarva-sat, sarva-dṛk sadā, Kārikā* II.12.

150. Cf. C. Cole, *Asparśa Yoga, A Study of Gauḍapāda's Māṇḍūkya Kārikā*. Delhi: Motilal Banarsidass, 1982, p. 4, note 4. In the salutation at the end of his commentary, Śaṁkara bows to Gauḍapāda with his whole being for "destroying the darkness of delusion enveloping my mind" and for destroying "forever my (notions of) appearance and disappearance in this terrible ocean of innumerable births and deaths". Swami Nikhilananda, transl., *The Māṇḍūkyopaniṣad with Gauḍapāda's Kārikā and Śaṁkara's Commentary*. Mysore: Sri Ramakrishna Ashrama, 6th, ed., 1974 (1st ed., 1936), p. 310.

151. N. Kasturi, ed. and commentator, *Garland of 108 Precious Gems*, 5th Indian ed., 1984, p. 22 (under 14. *Oṁ Śrī Sarva Antaryāmine Namaḥ*, "Obeisance to the Indweller of All"). Cf. also the conversations with Sai Baba reported in J. Hyslop, *My Baba and I*, e.g. p. 195 (Dec. 9, 1980). Sri Sathya Sai Baba's omniscience deserves much deeper study than it has been accorded so far.

152. *Gītā* X.20. Cf. Sri Sathya Sai Baba: "I am present everywhere at all times; my will must prevail over every obstacle; I am aware of the past, present and future, of your innermost thought and your carefully guarded secrets. I am *sarvāntaryāmin*, indweller of all, *sarvaśakta*, endowed with all powers, and *sarvajña*, omniscient." N. Kasturi, ēd., *Sathya Sai Speaks*, v. 7, 2nd ed. Prashanti Nilayam: Sri Sathya Sai Education and Publication Foundation, 1982, p. 339.

153. Transl. B. Behari, *Selections from Fariduddin 'Attar's Tadkharatul-Auliya* [Memoirs of Saints]. Lahore: Sh. Muhammad Ashraf, 1961, p. 155. A.J. Arberry's translation of sections of this work does not include Abul Hasan. The sayings and traditions of Abul Hasan given by Behari are spiritually extraordnarily powerful; several others of them also deal with omniscience.

154. On Attar, see the *Encyclopedia of Islam*, 2nd. ed., v. 1, Leiden: E.J. Brill,

1960, under 'Aṭṭār, Farīd al-Dīn.

155. Vyāsa's commentary on *YoSū* III.49, transl. J.H. Woods, *The Yoga-System of Patañjali.* Cambridge: Harvard Univ. Press, 1914 (*HOS*, no. 17), p. 283. G. Kaviraj interprets: ". . . when the yogin succeeds in realizing himself as subject by means of the *grahītṛ-samāpatti* [= *sāsmitā-samāpatti*, a condition where "the consciousness is self-consciousness in its utmost purity," *ibid.*], the objective phenomena, infinite as they are, and their knowledge become simultaneously present to his cosmic consciousness . . . The Self-consciousness, which is All-consciousness, is *Pratibhā* (Supreme Intuition) in the light of which all things are simultaneously (*akramam*) and in all their aspects (*sarvathāviṣayam*) revealed. It constitutes the highest mystic acquisition of the yogin, next only to his Self-realization." (G. Kaviraj, *op. cit.*, note 139 above, p. 11).

156. Vyāsa's commentary on *YoSū* III.49; cf. Woods, *ibid.* Swami Aranya translates "Omniscience means simultaneous knowledge of the all pervading *guṇas* in their past, present and future states of existence" (*Yoga Sūtra*, p. 363).

157. The three *guṇas* are not just concepts, but refer to a specific spiritual (or yogic-spiritual) type or level of apperception.

158. Cf. Swami Ananyananda, Seeking God through meditation (Editorial). *Prabuddha Bhārata,* v. 88 (1983), pp. 3-10; p. 8. For a more detailed discussion, see the Shri Gopinath Kaviraj, Stages in Yoga. In G. Kaviraj, *Aspects of Indian Thought, op. cit.*, note 139 above, pp. 115-127.

159. In the *Yoga Śikhā Upaniṣad*, in the Telegu edition (III.25), omniscience is said to be the fruit of one's remembrance of the Absolute.

160. *Śiva Saṁhitā* V. 56-65 describes a meditation (or *dhāraṇā*) on the *mūlādhāra* region which results i.a. in the meditator becoming omniscient (*sarvajñatva*, V.65) (see Srisa Chandra Vasu, transl., *The Śiva Saṁhitā.* Delhi: Oriental Book Reprint, 1975 (1st ed., *SBH*, 1914-15), p. 64). Feuerstein in his *Dictionary of Yoga* places the *Śiva Saṁhitā* in the 17th or 18th century.

161. In all three of the major preceptorial lines of non-dual Kashmir Śaivism (Trika, Krama and Kaula), the highest state of the yogi is described as complete identity with Śiva, the Supreme, with full omniscience and omnipotence.

162. E.g. in the Large *Prajñāpāramitā Sūtra* (E. Conze, *The Large Sūtra on the Perfection of Wisdom.* Berkeley: Univ. of California Press, Chr. 17, on the stages of the Bodhisattva, beginning with the sixth stage, pp. 172-178).

163. Similarly G. Kaviraj: " 'What is known as the 'divine eye' is really the mind in its purified condition, as the *Chāndogya Upaniṣad* (VIII.12.5) expressly declares . . . . It is apparent, therefore, that every man, insofar as he is gifted with a mind, is gifted with the possibility of omniscience." The Doctrine of Pratibhā . . ., *op. cit.*, note 139 above, p. 41.

164. Commentary on *ChāndUp* VIII.3.2, transl. Jha, *ChāndUp Comm.*, p. 427.

165. Quoted from memory; I have not been able to trace this important quote.

166. Transl. Jha, *ChāndUp Comm.*, p. 421.

167. Sri Sathya Sai Baba, *Summer Showers,* 1972, pp. 154-155.

168. Modern scholarship: R. Morton Smith, Śāṇḍilya's Śāṇḍilya-Vidyā. *Proceedings* 27th *ICO* (1967), D. Siner *et al.*, ed., Wiesbaden: Otto Harassowitz, pp. 320-21.

169. Cf. the review of the problem in F. Staal, with C.V. Somayajipad and M. Itti Rasi Nambudiri, *Agni. The Vedic Ritual of the Fire-altar*, v. 1, Berkeley: Asian Humanities Press, 1983, pp. 90-91.
170. (a) *sarvam khalvidam brahma tajjalān iti*; (b) *jyāyān*, "of a higher order than"; Smith: "stronger than" (*op. cit.*, pp. 320, 321).
171. *Tajjalān* is explained by Śaṁkara as that from which all originates, into which it dissolves, and by which it is maintained, as in the instruction to Bhṛgu in *TaittUp* III.1 ff. van Buitenen has a different conjecture (Vācāraṁbhaṇam Reconsidered, *op. cit.*, p. 300; repr. *Studies*, p. 124).
172. (a) *Satyam Brahma*; (b) *abhisambhavati*; (c) *sarvam idam abhyāptam avāk kamanādaraṁ*; (d) *puruṣo hiraṇmayo yathā jyotir adhūmam evam.*
173. "*Satyam Brahma*" implies "Brahman is all this world here."
174. On the "golden Person," see J. Gonda, The Function and Significance of Gold in the Veda, *op. cit.*, pp. 191-201.
175. So Śaṁkara in his commentary on the verse, transl. Jha. *ChāndUp Comm.*, p. 429.
176. "Applying or devoting one self to Brahman, 'walking with Brahman,' 'cultivating Brahman,' faring in harmony with Brahman," J. Gonda, Brahmacarya, in *Change and Continuity in Indian Religion*, The Hague: Mouton, 1965, pp. 284-314; p. 284. *Brahmacarya* in Vedic times also means the state of being a Vedic student, and as such carries connotations of "state of continence, chastity," which meaning "has . . . always been central" (Gonda, *ibid.*, p. 284).
177. There seems to be to no independent modern treatment of this text.
178. The Mādhyandina recension starts here a new verse (= *BṛhUp* IV.2.4 (M)). While we take this merely as signaling a new turn in what is basically a completely unified text (= vs. 2-4), some modern interpreters see here a real discontinuity (Deussen, *Sixty Ups.*, and Sri Prajnan Yati).
179. There is a conspectus of the Classical Upaniṣadic passages mentioning the channels or *nāḍīs* named *hitā* by O. Haas in Hume's *Upanishads*.
180. Cf. Shastri, *UpBhāṣyam*, p. 296, and the translation in Mādhavānanda, *BṛhUp Comm.*, p. 591. (a) *hṛdayātmanaśca prāṇātmānam āpannasya* (b) *krameṇa sarvātmakaṁ prāṇam ātmatvena upāgato bhavati*, "by the approach by selfness to the *prāṇa* that is of the nature of self of all, he becomes one gone to [all-selfhood]." (c) *draṣṭurhi draṣṭṛbhāvaṁ neti neti iti ātmānaṁ turīyani pratipadyate.*
181. Swami Maheshananda Giri gives an exposition of it in his Introduction to Shastri, *Upbhāṣyam*, v. 3, pp. 42-47.
182. Transl. Mādhavānanda, *BṛhUp Comm.*, pp. 546-47.
183. Another possible allusion to the method of identifying one's self at the level of subtle *prāṇa* with the directions occurs at *ŚatBr* X.6.3.2, in the *Śāṇḍilya Vidyā*. Here the self is said to be affirmed in one's heart as "having become according to all the directions," *sarvā'anu diśaḥ prabhūtaḥ*.
184. A modern treatment is J.H.M. Whiteman, The Muṇḍaka Upaniṣad: Second Chapter. A new Translation and Commentary. *Studia Mystica*, v. 7 (1984), pp. 3-12.
185. Modern scholarship: W. Rau, Versuch einer deutschen Übersetzung der Muṇḍaka-Upaniṣad. *Asiatische Studien*, v. 18 (1965), pp. 216-26; Rau surveys earlier work on pp. 216-217. R.M. Smith, The Muṇḍaka Upaniṣad Reconsidered, *Vishveshvaranand Indological Journal*, v. 14 (1976), pp.

17-40, proposes numerous emendations.

186. The text has a parallel in *Mahā-Upaniṣad*, one of the *Saṁnyāsa Upaniṣads*. Besides Swami Vimalānanda's explanations in his notes (Vimalānanda, *Mahā-NārUp*, pp. 161-169), B.R. Sharma, *Concept of Ātman*, pp. 210-213, makes some comments on the text.

187. Cf. Varenne, *op. cit.*, pp. 64-67; I am grateful to Prof. R.S. Hart for helping me with Varenne's French.

188. Recall that the text is not included as part of *dahara upāsanā* by Subrahmanya Shastri. But it is accepted by Śrīkaṇṭha, a classical commentator dated a century or so before Rāmānuja (i.e., 10th century CE). Śrīkaṇṭha expounds a Vīra-Śaiva-Advaita path, and his commentary on the *Brahma Sūtra* is remarkable for its universal outlook. See R. Chauduri, transl., *Doctrine of Śrīkaṇṭha: Śrīkaṇṭha Bhāṣya*, or *Commentary of Śrīkaṇṭha on the Brahma-Sūtras*. Calcutta: Pracyavani, 1959 (Pracyavani Research Series No. 11). According to Appaya Dīkṣita (16th-17th cent. CE), Śrīkaṇṭha was devoted to the *Dahara Vidyā*. Śrīkaṇṭha himself argues several times that all the *dahara* meditations in the Upaniṣads are equivalent (e.g. in his commentary on *BraSū* III.3.1-4 and III.3.38, transl. R. Chaudhuri, *op. cit.*, pp. 300-305, 341-343).

189. Thus the Upaniṣad deals at length with the inadequacy of the path of ritual (I.2); integrates and distills the essence of the teachings on the Puruṣa as the origin and substance of the world to a new, highest level (II.1); similarly distills the *vijñāna* in the heart *vidyās* into a single Wisdom leading to the Highest Brahman (II.2); and develops in detail the conception of merger into Brahman (III.2) which in the old Upaniṣads is only suggested in a few places.

Index